WITHDRAWN FROM
MACALESTER COLLEGE
LIBRARY

D1376860

The SAGE Handbook of

Race and Ethnic Studies

The SAGE Handbook of

Race and Ethnic Studies

WITHDRAWN FROM
MACALESTER COLLEGE
LIBRARY

Edited by

Patricia Hill Collins
and John Solomos

Los Angeles | London | New Delhi
Singapore | Washington DC

Introductions, Conclusion and Editorial
    Arrangement © Patricia Hill Collins &
    John Solomos 2010
Chapter 2 © Caroline Knowles 2010
Chapter 3 © Joe R. Feagin and Eileen O'Brien 2010
Chapter 4 © Nancy A. Denton and Glenn D. Deane
    2010
Chapter 5 © Chetan Bhatt 2010
Chapter 6 © Satnam Virdee 2010
Chapter 7 © Margaret L. Andersen 2010
Chapter 8 © Joane Nagel 2010
Chapter 9 © Floya Anthias 2010
Chapter 10 © Peter Kivisto 2010

Chapter 11 © Athena D. Mutua 2010
Chapter 12 © Ralph Premdas 2010
Chapter 13 © Liza Schuster 2010
Chapter 14 © Maxine Baca Zinn 2010
Chapter 15 © James A. Banks and Caryn Park
    2010
Chapter 16 © Cheryl Townsend Gilkes 2010
Chapter 17 © Les Back 2010
Chapter 18 © Michael G. Hanchard and
    Mark Q. Sawyer 2010
Chapter 19 © Claire Alexander 2010
Chapter 20 © Patricia Hill Collins and
    John Solomos 2010

First published 2010

Apart from any fair dealing for the purposes of research or
private study, or criticism or review, as permitted under the
Copyright, Designs and Patents Act, 1988, this publication may
be reproduced, stored or transmitted in any form, or by any
means, only with the prior permission in writing of the publishers,
or in the case of reprographic reproduction, in accordance with the
terms of licences issued by the Copyright Licensing Agency.
Enquiries concerning reproduction outside those terms should be
sent to the publishers.

SAGE Publications Ltd
1 Oliver's Yard
55 City Road
London EC1Y 1SP

SAGE Publications Inc.
2455 Teller Road
Thousand Oaks, California 91320

SAGE Publications India Pvt Ltd
B 1/I 1 Mohan Cooperative Industrial Area
Mathura Road
New Delhi 110 044

SAGE Publications Asia-Pacific Pte Ltd
33 Pekin Street #02-01
Far East Square
Singapore 048763

Library of Congress Control Number: 2009932 886

British Library Cataloguing in Publication data

A catalogue record for this book is available from the British Library

ISBN 978-0-7619-4220-7

Typeset by Glyph International, Bangalore, India
Printed by MPG Books Group, Bodmin, Cornwall
Printed on paper from sustainable resources

Mixed Sources
Product group from well-managed
forests and other controlled sources
www.fsc.org Cert no. SA-COC-1565
© 1996 Forest Stewardship Council
FSC

Contents

Preface

A handbook such as this has a number of purposes. The first and most important of these is to provide a comprehensive and contemporary overview of major developments in the study of race and ethnicity. This in itself is a major task in this field which has undergone a series of shifts in approach over the past few decades as well as a major expansion within disciplines such as sociology, anthropology, politics, cultural studies and related disciplines. In many ways, the last two decades can be seen as ones that have helped to establish the study of race and ethnicity within both the social sciences and the humanities. This is evidenced in the wide range of books on almost every facet of this sub-field, as well as the establishment of a number of journals that are focused on the study of race and ethnicity viewed from a range of angles.

The second purpose of this handbook is to provide both general and specialist readers with a resource to explore the field of race and ethnic studies and all its different facets. The various chapters have been written in such a style that they provide an authoritative overview of the key research developments in their particular areas. In putting together our list of contributors, we impressed upon all of our authors the need for chapters that covered their specific areas in detail and from an analytically comprehensive angle. All of the chapters draw on a wide range of theoretical and empirical literatures and are carefully situated in relation to research that draws on examples from a broad range of national and geopolitical environments.

In our role as editors we have also sought, in the opening and concluding chapters, to provide overviews that highlight and bring to the fore some of the issues that run through the volume as a whole as well as some of the questions that we have not been able to cover fully.

In putting this handbook together, we have benefitted from the support and advice of colleagues at our institutions and beyond. First and foremost, we appreciate the support of our respective institutions – the production of volumes such as this is inevitably a long-term process and we are grateful to our institutions for providing us with the space to undertake such work. Both of us also benefitted from the support and guidance we have received from our publishers at Sage, in particular from Chris Rojek and Jai Seaman. They have put up with up with the delays in bringing this project to a conclusion with good grace and encouragement.

Patricia Hill Collins wishes to acknowledge the financial support provided by the Taft Program in the McMicken College of Arts and Sciences at the University of Cincinnati during the early stages of the project. Thanks also go out to Tamika Odum, the original editorial assistant for this project, and Julie Hilvers, for their contributions at the University of Cincinnati. At the University of Maryland, College Park, I would like to thank Tony Hatch, Zeynep Atalay and Chang Won Lee who each served as primary editorial assistants during different phases of the project. Valerie Chepp and Kendra Barber, research assistants who worked on various aspects of this project, were also invaluable to the completion of the handbook. Important editorial assistance was also provided by Heather Marsh and Kathryn Buford. Many of the ideas in this volume reflect my many conversations with our terrific sociology graduate students at the University of Maryland, both in my seminars in Critical Race Theory and outside of class. Special thanks go out to Emily Mann, Nazneen Kane, Carolina Martin, Michelle Corbin, Kimberly Bonner, Les Andrist, Michelle Beadle, Michelle Smirnova, Aleia Clark, Nihal Celik, Daniel Williams, Mehmet Ergun and Ying (Wendy) Wang. As always, special thanks to Roger and Valerie for supporting my professional endeavours.

John Solomos would like to acknowledge the support of the following during the period while he was working on the handbook: Les Back, Leah Bassel, Chetan Bhatt, Alice Bloch, Milena Chimienti, Michael Keith, Eugene McLaughlin, Karim Murji, Sarah Neal, Liza Schuster, Brett St Louis and Tony Woodiwiss. Thanks also to Adam and Sam for playing squash with me and taking me away from sitting down. Steve, Michael, Fran, Karim and others have been good company and sources of gossip in our gatherings to support the England football team. As ever Christine, Nikolas and Daniel saw me disappear to the office or the study too much and I thank them for their patience and understanding. My passion for the Baggies kept me going and listening to the sweet music of Prince Alla, Bob Marley, Fairouz, Horace Andy, Meri Linta, Maria Farantouri, Sotiria Bellou, Souad Massi and Gregory Isaacs helped me along the road and moved my soul.

Patricia Hill Collins
University of Maryland

John Solomos
City University London

Notes on Contributors

EDITORS

Patricia Hill Collins is Distinguished University Professor of Sociology at the University of Maryland, College Park and Charles Phelps Taft Emeritus Professor of Sociology within the Department of African American Studies at the University of Cincinnati. Her award-winning books include *Black Feminist Thought: Knowledge, Consciousness, and the Politics of Empowerment* (1990, 2000) which received the Jessie Bernard Award of the American Sociological Association (ASA), and the C. Wright Mills Award of the Society for the Study of Social Problems; and *Black Sexual Politics: African Americans, Gender, and the New Racism* (2004) which received ASA's 2007 Distinguished Publication Award. She is also author of *Fighting Words: Black Women and the Search for Justice* (1998); *From Black Power to Hip Hop: Racism, Nationalism, and Feminism* (2005); *Race, Class, and Gender: An Anthology 7th edition,* (2010) edited with Margaret Andersen, a reader widely used in classrooms in over 200 colleges and universities; and *Another Kind of Public Education: Race, Schools, the Media, and Democratic Possibilities* (2009). Professor Collins has taught at several institutions, held editorial positions with professional journals, lectured widely in the United States and internationally, served in many capacities in professional organisations, and has acted as consultant for a number of community organisations. In 2008, she became the 100th President of the American Sociological Association, the first African American woman elected to this position in the organisation's 104-year history.

John Solomos is professor of sociology in the Department of Sociology, City University, London. He is director of the Centre on Race, Ethnicity and Migration. Before that he was professor of sociology in the Faculty of Humanities and Social Science at South Bank University, London, and he has previously worked at the Centre for Research in Ethnic Relations, University of Warwick and Birkbeck College, University of London and the University of Southampton. He has published on various aspects of race and ethnic studies, including *The Changing Face of Football: Racism, Identity and Multiculture and the English Game* (co-author with Les Back and Tim Crabbe, 2001), and *Race and Racism in Britain 3rd ed.,* (2003). He has also edited *A Companion to Racial and Ethnic Studies* (co-editor with David Theo Goldberg, 2002), *Researching Race and Racism* (co-editor with Martin Bulmer, 2004) and *Racialization: Studies in Theory and*

Practice (co-editor with Karim Murji, 2005) among other edited books. He is editor of the international journal *Ethnic and Racial Studies*, published nine times a year by Routledge.

CONTRIBUTORS

Claire Alexander is reader in sociology at the London School of Economics. Her research interests are in the area of race, ethnicity, masculinity and youth identities, particularly in relation to ethnography. Her main publications include *The Art of Being Black* (OUP, 1996) and *The Asian Gang* (Berg, 2000). She is co-editor of *Beyond Difference* (*Ethnic and Racial Studies*, July 2002), and *Making Race Matter: Bodies, Space and Identity* (Palgrave, 2005) and editor of *Writing Race: Ethnography and Difference* (*Ethnic and Racial Studies*, May 2006). She is co-director, with Dr Joya Chatterji, of an AHRC-funded research project (2006–2009) on 'The Bengal Diaspora: Bengali Settlers in South Asia and Britain'.

Margaret L. Andersen is the Edward F. and Elizabeth Goodman Rosenberg professor of sociology at the University of Delaware. She is the author of *Thinking about Women: Sociological Perspectives on Sex and Gender; On Land and on Sea: A Century of Women in the Rosenfeld Collection; Living Art: The Life of Paul R. Jones, African American Art Collector; Sociology: The Essentials* (co-author, Howard F. Taylor), and two best selling-anthologies: *Race, Class, and Gender* (with Patricia Hill Collins; *Race and Ethnicity in Society: The Changing Landscape* (with Elizabeth Higginbotham); and, *Understanding Society* (with Kim Logio and Howard F. Taylor). She was elected vice president of the American Sociological Association (2007–2009) and is past president of the Eastern Sociological Society. She currently serves as chair of the National Advisory Board for Stanford University's Center for Comparative Studies on Race and Ethnicity.

Floya Anthias is professor of sociology and social justice at Roehampton University. Her primary research interests are in the areas of social divisions and identities, social exclusion and inequality and on migration, ethnicity, gender and multiculturalism. She has published extensively in these areas with a particular interest in the fields of ethnicity, class, gender, transborder movements, labour markets, identity, self-employment, intergenerational relations and Cypriots in Britain. Her publications include *Racialised Boundaries: Race, Nation, Colour, Class and the Anti Racist Struggle* (co-authored, Routledge, 1993), *Gender and Migration in Southern Europe: Women on the Move,* (co-edited, Berg, 2000) and *Rethinking Antiracisms: From Theory to Practice* (co-edited Routledge, 2002). She has also written numerous articles, particularly on theoretical issues around race and ethnicity, and on gender. These include recent contributions to debates on conceptualising ethnicity and racism, diaspora and hybridity, feminism and multiculturalism, narratives of identity, translocational belongings, social stratification and intersectionality and rethinking the concept of social capital.

Les Back is professor of sociology at Goldsmiths, University of London where he has been working since 1993. Before that he taught at the Department of Cultural Studies, University of Birmingham. His main focus over the years has been on race and racism, multiculturalism, urban life, popular culture and music and youth. In addition to the co-authored work with John Solomos his books include *The Art of Listening* (2007), *The Auditory Cultures Reader* (co-editor with Michael Bull) (2003), *Out of Whiteness: Color, Politics and Culture* (co-author with Vron Ware) (2002) and *New Ethnicities and Urban Culture: Racisms and Multiculture in Young Lives* (1996).

James A. Banks is the Kerry and Linda Killinger Professor of Diversity Studies and founding director of the Center for Multicultural Education at the University of Washington, Seattle (http://education.washington.edu/cme/). He is a past president of the American Educational Research Association and of the National Council for the Social Studies. Professor Banks is a specialist in social studies education and in multicultural education, and has written many articles and books in these fields. His books include *Cultural Diversity and Education: Foundations, Curriculum and Teaching; Teaching Strategies for the Social Studies*; and *Race, Culture, and Education: The Selected Works of James A. Banks*. Professor Banks is the editor of the *Handbook of Research on Multicultural Education* (Jossey-Bass), the 'Multicultural Education Series' of books published by Teachers College Press, Columbia University; and *The Routledge International Companion to Multicultural Education*. He is a member of the National Academy of Education and was a Spencer Fellow at the Center for Advanced Study in the Behavioral Sciences at Stanford during the 2005–2006 academic year.

Chetan Bhatt is professor of sociology and director of the centre for the study of Human Rights at the London School of Economics and Political Science. His research interests include religion, racism, nationalism, changing forms of civil conflict, social theory and the history of ideas, especially the development of romanticism in Europe. His publications include *Liberation and Purity: Race, New Religious Movements and the Ethics of Postmodernity* (Routledge, 1997), *Hindu Nationalism: Origins, Ideologies and Modern Myths* (Berg, 2001). He has written widely on violent movements of the religious Right, nationalism, racism and culture, and much of his recent work has focused on new transnational networks that are inspired by religious militias in south Asia.

Glenn D. Deane is associate professor of sociology at the University at Albany, State University of New York. His research activities include modelling the interrelationship between population and environment, multiple race identifications and intra-family dynamics.

Nancy A. Denton is professor of sociology at the State University of New York at Albany where she is the director of the Lewis Mumford Center for Comparative Urban and Regional Research and associate director of the Center for Social and Demographic Analysis. She received her MA and PhD in demography from the University of Pennsylvania and an MA in sociology from Fordham University, and is past president of the Eastern Sociological Society. Her major research interests are race and residential segregation and with Douglas S. Massey she is the author of *American Apartheid: Segregation and the Making of the Underclass*, winner of the 1995 American Sociological Association Distinguished Publication Award. Her current research projects include the neighbourhood contexts of children by race/ethnicity/immigrant generation and racial identity among Puerto Ricans.

Joe R. Feagin graduated from Baylor University in 1960 and acquired his PhD in social relations (sociology) at Harvard University in 1966. Over 44 years he has taught at the University of Massachusetts (Boston), University of California (Riverside), University of Texas, University of Florida, and Texas A&M University. He has done much research work on a variety of racism and sexism issues and has served as the Scholar-in-Residence at the US Commission on Civil Rights. He has written 58 books, one of which (Ghetto Revolts) was nominated for a Pulitzer Prize. Among his books, some co-authored, are Systemic Racism (2006); Racist America (2000 and 2010); The First R: How Children Learn Race and Racism (2001); Racial and Ethnic Relations (2008); The Many Costs of Racism (2003); White Men on Race (2003); Black in Blue: African-American Police Officers and Racism (2004); Two-Faced Racism (2007), and The White Racial Frame (2010). He is the 2006 recipient of a Harvard Alumni Association lifetime achievement award and was the 1999–2000 president of the American Sociological Association. He is currently Ella C. McFadden Professor at Texas A&M University.

Cheryl Townsend Gilkes is the John D. and Catherine T. MacArthur Professor of African American Studies and Sociology and director of the African American Studies Program at Colby College. She holds degrees in sociology from Northeastern University and has pursued graduate theological studies at Boston University's School of Theology. Some of her essays and articles are gathered in her book *If It Wasn't for the Women: Black Women's Experience and Womanist Culture in Church and Community* (Orbis Books, 2001). Several of her journal articles have been reprinted in anthologies, such as *African American Religious Thought: An Anthology*, edited by Cornel West and Eddie Glaude (Westminster John Knox Press, 2004) and *Women and Religion in the African Diaspora: Knowledge, Power, and Performance*, edited by R. Marie Griffith and Barbara

Dianne Savage (The Johns Hopkins Press, 2006). She is currently at work on several projects, one of which is tentatively titled *My Soul's Gotta Have Somewhere to Stay: The Black Church as a Cultural Production*.

Michael G. Hanchard is SOBA Presidential Professor in the political science department of The Johns Hopkins University, and co-director of the Racism, Immigration and Citizenship Program. He is the author of *Party/Politics: Horizons in Black Political Thought* (Oxford, 2006); *Racial Politics in Contemporary Brazil*, editor (Duke, 1999) and *Orpheus and Power: Afro-Brazilian Social Movements in Rio de Janeiro and Sao Paulo, Brazil, 1945–1988* (Princeton, 1994). His teaching and research interests include nationalism, racial politics, social and political theory.

Peter Kivisto is the Richard A. Swanson professor of social thought and chair of sociology at Augustana College. He received his BA from the University of Michigan and an MDiv from Yale. His MA and PhD were awarded by the New School for Social Research. Among his recent books are *Citizenship: Discourse, Theory and Transnational Prospects* (Blackwell, 2007, with Thomas Faist), *Intersecting Inequalities* (Pearson Prentice Hall, 2007, with Elizabeth Hartung), *Incorporating Diversity* (Paradigm, 2005) and *Multiculturalism in a Global Society* (Blackwell, 2002). He is currently the editor of *The Sociological Quarterly*. The Academy of Finland has recently appointed him a Finland Distinguished Professor. In 2009, he will begin a five-year affiliation with the University of Turku, working on a collaborative project on multiculturalism.

Caroline Knowles is professor of sociology and director of the Centre for Urban and Community Research at Goldsmiths, University of London. Her research interests are about the production of race and ethnicity, the circulation of people through migration and objects composing material culture. She has a long-term interest in biographical and visual research methods and has worked in collaboration with a number of photographers. Her current research investigates British migrants in Beijing. She is also working with artist Michael Tan on a project called 'Shoes and Social Fabrics: The Lifeworld and Journeys of a Pair of Flip-Flop Sandals' which investigates shoe production in Chinese factories and consumption in Addis Ababa. Her books include *Hong Kong: Migrant Lives, Journeys and Landscapes* (2009, University of Chicago Press) with Douglas Harper; *Making Race Matter* (2005, Palgrave) jointly edited with Claire Alexander; *Race and Social Analysis* (2003, Sage); *Picturing the Social Landscape* (2004, Routledge) jointly edited with Paul Sweetman and *Bedlam on the Streets* (2000, Routledge) with photographer Ludovic Dabert.

Athena Mutua is a professor of law at the State University of New York. She writes in the areas of critical race and feminist legal theory. Some of her recent work includes the edited collection entitled, Progressive Black Masculinities (Routledge, 2006); and articles titled, 'Restoring Justice to Civil Rights Movement

Activists?: New Historiography and the "Long Civil Rights Era'" (2010); 'The Rise, Development, and Future Directions of Critical Race Theory,' (Denver University Law Review, 2006); and 'Gender Equality and Women's Solidarity across Religious, Ethnic, and Class Difference in the Kenya Constitutional Review Process' (William and Mary Journal of Women and Law, 2006). The latter article involved activism and research for which she received the University at Buffalo's Exceptional Scholars Young Investigator's Award. One of her latest pieces explores issues of race and gender as they relate to class structures and introduces the concepts and boundaries of a project she helped to found called ClassCrits. It is entitled, "Introducing ClassCrits: From Class Blindness to a Critical Legal Analysis of Economic Inequality," (Buffalo Law Review, 2008).

Joane Nagel is University Distinguished Professor of Sociology at the University of Kansas. Her recent books include *American Indian Ethnic Renewal: Red Power and the Resurgence of Identity and Culture* (Oxford University Press, 1997) and *Race, Ethnicity, and Sexuality: Intimate Intersections, Forbidden Frontiers* (Oxford University Press, 2003). She is currently director of the US National Science Foundation IGERT program, C-CHANGE: Climate Change, Humans, and Nature in the Global Environment at the University of Kansas.

Eileen O'Brien was born and raised in Virginia. She earned a BA in sociology at the College of William and Mary in 1994, an MA in sociology at Ohio State University in 1996 and a PhD in sociology with a primary concentration in race relations at the University of Florida under the direction of Joe Feagin in 1999. After teaching at the State University of New York (Brockport), the College of William and Mary, and the University of Richmond, she has settled in her birth-place, Newport News, Virginia by joining the faculty at Christopher Newport University. Her dissertation on white antiracist activists became her first book *Whites Confront Racism* (2001). She also co-authored *White Men on Race* (2003) with Joe Feagin, and two editions of *Race, Ethnicity and Gender: Selected Readings* (2003 and 2007) with Joseph Healey. Her most recent book is *The Racial Middle: Latinos and Asian Americans Living beyond the Racial Divide* (2008). She resides in the town where she was raised, Williamsburg, Virginia, with her partner, Kendall James, and children, Kaya (2002) and Kaden (2007) O'Brien-James, her most challenging and most rewarding projects yet.

Caryn Park is a doctoral candidate in multicultural education at the University of Washington, Seattle. She has a background in early childhood education. Her research explores critical and interdisciplinary perspectives on race and ethnicity. She is also interested in how these constructions are reflected in the ways in which young children talk about and act upon their developing understandings.

Ralph R. Premdas is currently visiting professor in the Institute for the Study of Public Policy and Management (INPUMA) at the University of Malaya in Malaysia and is regularly Professor of Public Policy in the Sir Arthur Lewis

Institute of Social and Economic Studies (SALISES) at the University of the West Indies, St. Augustine Trinidad and Tobago. His research focus is on comparative ethnic politics; multi-culturalism, and migration. Among his most recent publications are *Trinidad and Tobago: Ethnic Conflict, Inequality, and Public Sector Governance* (Palgrave, 2008), *Homelessness and Street Children in the Caribbean* (2008), *Identity, Ethnicity and Culture in the Caribbean* (2000); *Ethnic Conflict and Development: The Case of Guyana* (1997); *Ethnic Conflict and Modes of Ethnic Conflict Management* (2000); *Comparative Secessionist Movements* (1994); and *Ethnic Conflict in Fiji* (1995).

Liza Schuster is a senior lecturer at City University, where she lectures on global migration, and historical and political sociology. Her research interests include asylum, migration and racism, and the relationship between all three. Most recently her research has focused on migrants in Morocco, Cyprus and in Paris. She is the author of *The Use and Abuse of Political Asylum in Britain and Germany* (2003, Frank Cass, London), and has published articles on aspects of European asylum and migration policy, as well the migration phenomenon more generally. Her *Beginners Guide to Migration* (OneWorld, Oxford) will appear in 2011.

Mark Q. Sawyer is an associate professor of African American studies and political science at UCLA and the director of the Center for the Study of Race, Ethnicity and Politics. He received his PhD in political science from the University of Chicago in December of 1999. His book entitled *Racial Politics in Post Revolutionary Cuba* (Cambridge University Press, 2006) received the Du Bois Award for the best book by the National Conference of Black Political Scientists and the Ralph Bunche Award from the American Political Science Association.

Satnam Virdee is professor of sociology at the University of Glasgow. His current research interests focus on mapping the relationship between racism and capitalist modernity; racism, class and labour markets, and the study of racist and antiracist collective action. His forthcoming book, *Racism, Resistance and Radicalism* will be published by Palgrave in 2011.

Maxine Baca Zinn is professor emeritus of sociology at Michigan State University. Her teaching and research areas are in the sociology of family, race, and gender. Her books include *Women of Color in U.S. Society* (with Bonnie Thornton Dill); *Diversity in Families; Social Problems; In Conflict and Order: Understanding Society; and Globalization: The Transformation of Social Worlds* (with D. Stanley Eitzen). She has served as president of the Western Social Science Association. In 2000, she received the American Sociological Association's Jessie Bernard Award in recognition of career achievements in the study of women and gender.

Introduction: Situating Race and Ethnic Studies

Patricia Hill Collins and John Solomos

In putting together this *Handbook of Race and Ethnic Studies* we have seen our editorial role as twofold. First, we aimed to bring together authors who could write chapters that map out the field of race and ethnicity as an evolving, dynamic and relevant field of scholarly debate and research. In doing we have made choices both about the chapters to include in the handbook, as well as the selection of specific authors to write those chapters and our editorial feedback and suggestions to them. We have always been conscious, however, of the need to allow for different voices and perspectives in the pages of this handbook, and this is no doubt reflected in the varied styles and analytical approaches of the different chapters. This diversity reflects a point reiterated by a number of authors in this volume that the very language and terminology used by researchers and scholars in this field remains a point of debate and contestation, much as it did during the 1980s and 1990s (see in particular Bhatt in Chapter 5 and Virdee in Chapter 6).

Second, we sought to provide an overview of the key debates in this field of scholarly study, the core changes that we have seen over the past few decades and at least a partial account of how the field is likely to develop and expand over the coming period. This is what we shall do in the course of this introductory chapter, in the short introductions to each part of the handbook and finally in the concluding chapter. This is not to say that there is simply one argument that runs through the volume. On the contrary, the substantive chapters that make up the handbook are written from a range of different theoretical paradigms and historical and empirical examples. It is this very diversity of perspectives that we have sought to give voice to in the context of this volume.

DEFINITIONAL AND CONCEPTUAL ISSUES

During the past three decades we have seen a proliferation of monographs, textbooks, journals and internet-sourced materials that explore in one way or another a range of theories about race and ethnic relations, racism and processes of racialisation and domination (Bonilla-Silva, 1997; Essed and Goldberg, 2002; Miles, 1993). This expansion of race and ethnic studies as a field of research has taken place both in sociology and related social science disciplines as well as in the humanities. Indeed, one of the most notable features of contemporary research has been the central role played by questions about culture and forms of cultural identity. This has resulted in a wide body of scholarship and research on the ways in which our social understandings of ethnicity and race need to be developed in such a way as to allow for an analysis of cultural forms and processes. We shall discuss key facets of this literature in the course of our introductory and concluding chapters. Before turning to these developments, however, we want to address some of the definitional issues that have resulted from these contemporary debates.

In addressing these points we shall focus on two key issues. First, we shall draw on some recent conceptual debates in order to clarify the meanings that have been attached to key concepts and notions. In doing so we shall focus specifically on some facets of debates that have emerged particularly in sociology over the past decade or so. Second, we shall attempt to delineate the political context within which the conceptual debates have taken place. This is an important issue to include in any analysis of theories of racism, since it is evident that questions about race and racism are inevitably part of political discourses as well as being embedded in academic and scholarly research (Lasch-Quinn, 2001; Singh, 2004).

Seeking to understand these phenomena means being clear about what is meant by concepts such as race, racism, race and ethnic relations and related social concepts. We need to be able to respond both theoretically and empirically to questions such as: How has the category of race come to play such an important role in the analysis of contemporary social relations? What is meant by the notion of race relations? What is racism? These are questions that are at the heart of contemporary debates about race and ethnic relations and yet there is surprisingly little agreement about what concepts such as race and racism actually mean, or indeed how they can be researched. This is even more evident in the debates about how to research questions about race from an empirical angle (see for example the discussion by Denton and Deane in Chapter 4).

Many of the questions raised amount to the following: Is race a suitable social category? What do we mean when we talk of racism as shaping the structure of particular societies? What roles have race and racism played in different historical contexts? Is it possible to speak of racism in the singular or racisms in the plural? These questions are at the heart of many contemporary theoretical and conceptual debates, and yet what is interesting about much of the literature about race and racism is the absence of commonly agreed conceptual tools or even agreement about the general parameters of race and racism as fields of study (Miles and Brown, 2003). Debates about these issues have raged over the past two decades and more and are reflected again in the pages of this handbook as well as in the wider social scientific literature (Essed and Goldberg, 2002; Gates Jr, 1986; Goldberg and Solomos, 2002; Miles, 1993).

In the context of the various contributions to this handbook, it is interesting to note that there are a range of definitional starting points in the usage of terms such as race and racism, reflecting both levels of agreement as well as the contested nature of these concepts. At one level, for example, in relation to the concept of racism there is some agreement that racism is an ideology of racial domination based on beliefs that a designated racial group is either biologically or culturally inferior and the use of such beliefs to rationalise or prescribe the racial group's treatment in society, as well as to explain its social position and accomplishment. This reflects the ways in which the historical as well as contemporary analysis of racism is linked to the sociological analysis of forms of discrimination, exclusion, domination and relations of power (Fredrickson, 2002; Mosse, 1985). This is a line of analysis that is explored on the basis of different historical as well as contemporary examples in a number of chapters in this volume.

From this perspective, racism as a concept is much more closely tied to the concept of race, and is a reminder that where members of society make distinctions between different racial groups, at least some members of that society are likely to behave in ways which give rise to racism as a behavioral and ideational consequence of making racial distinctions in the first place. Unfortunately, the opposite does not hold. A society which denied or did not formally acknowledge the existence of different racial groups would not necessarily rid itself of racism. Indeed, the recent literature on racial and ethnic classification in censuses, surveys and administrative records shows that the identification of members of a society in terms of the racial, ethnic or national origin may be a prerequisite to taking action to counteract racism (Goldberg, 2002; Nobles, 2000).

When it comes to the issue of the usage of categories such as race and ethnicity, however, it is also evident that there are noticeable divergences in the ways in which such categories are utilised. Although race and ethnicity are terms often used in conjunction, or in parallel, to refer to social groups which differ in terms of physical attributes accorded social significance in the case of race or in terms of language, culture, place of origin or common membership of a descent group without distinguishing physical characteristics in the case of ethnicity, there is no equivalent term to racism in relation to ethnicity (Brubaker, 2005; Cornell and Hartmann, 2007). As the account of Ralph Premdas in Chapter 12 argues, perhaps ethnic conflict is analogous, but this is more of a descriptive term used to describe certain consequences of the existence of different ethnic groups and the development of forms of conflict or tension between them.

The recent explosion of scholarship and research has not only highlighted a certain lack of consensus but has also led to intense debate about the very language that we use in talking about race and racism. Over the past two decades or so, the shifting boundaries of race and ethnicity as categories of social analysis have become ever more evident (Alexander and Knowles, 2005; Knowles, 2003). In particular, a plethora of studies have provided new perspectives on difference, identities, subjectivities and power relations (Alcoff and Mendieta, 2003; Cornell and Hartmann, 2007). In this environment, ideas about race, racism and ethnicity have become the subject of intense debate and controversy. The role of racial and ethnic categorisation in the construction of social and political identities has been highlighted in a number of recent conflicts in various parts of the globe (Brubaker, 2004; Calhoun, 2007). Yet, it is paradoxically the case that there is still much confusion about what it is that we mean by such notions, as evidenced by the range of terminological debates that have tended to dominate much discussion in recent years. A number of questions remain to be analysed: What factors explain the mobilising power of ideas about race and ethnicity in the contemporary environment? What counter values and ideas can be developed to undermine the appeal of racist ideas and movements? Is it possible for communities that are socially defined by differences of race, ethnicity, religion or other signifiers to live together in societies which are able to ensure equality, justice and civilised tolerance? All of these are questions that are addressed in one way or another in the course of this volume, although it is also evident that there is a need for more substantive scholarship in order to address them more fully.

HISTORY OF RACE AND ETHNIC STUDIES

An important facet of the literature on race and ethnic studies in recent years has been the attention given to the historical background and evolution of this field of scholarship. This interest in the history of this field is evident in the growing body of writing that retraces both the emergence of this scholarship in the disciplines of sociology and anthropology as well as in the specific experiences of countries such as the US, South Africa, Britain and other societies (Bulmer and Solomos, 2004; Holloway and Keppel, 2007; Stanfield, 1993).

This renewed interest in the history of the field is also evident in the growing body of research that is focused on the social and political impact of ideas about race in the context of the experiences of modernity and post-modernity, slavery and post-slavery, colonialism and racial and ethnic conflict. But if modern racism has its foundations in the period since the late eighteenth century, there is little doubt that it had a major impact on the course of historical development during the twentieth century and seems destined to continue to do so in this century.

It seems clear as we stand at the beginning of the twenty-first century that racist ideas and movements are continuing to have an impact on a range of contemporary societies in a variety of ways. What is more, we have seen the growth and genocidal impact of new forms of racial and ethnically based ideologies in many parts of the globe, including most notably in the 1990s and 2000s in both West and East Europe and parts of Africa. It is almost impossible to read a newspaper or watch television news coverage without seeing the contemporary expressions of racist ideas and practices, whether in terms of the rise of neo-fascist movements in some societies or the implementation of policies of genocide and what is euphemistically called 'ethnic cleansing'.

Such trends need to be situated both within the changing socio-economic environment of contemporary societies and within processes of cultural and social change. By this we mean that it is important not to lose sight of the complex social, political and cultural determinants that shape contemporary racist discourses and movements and other forms of racialised discourse and mobilisation. Indeed, accounts of the growth of new forms of cultural racism suggest that, within the language of contemporary racist movements, there is both a certain flexibility about what is meant by race as well as an attempt to reconstitute themselves as movements whose concern is with defending their nation rather than attacking others as such. It is perhaps not surprising in this context that within the contemporary languages of race one finds a combination of arguments in favour of cultural difference along with negative images of groups such as migrants and racial minorities as a threat and as representing an impure culture.

RACE AND ETHNIC IDENTITIES

Given the ways in which social theories have become increasingly focused on the changing forms of social and cultural identity in contemporary societies (Brubaker and Cooper, 2000; Calhoun, 1994), it is perhaps not surprising that the subject of identity has been central to much of the recent scholarship on race and ethnic studies. The question of identity is certainly one which has been at the heart of much of the literature in this field in the past three decades, both in terms of specific studies of racial and ethnic identity and conceptual debates about the role of identity in the construction of racial and ethnic boundaries.

The preoccupation with identity can be taken as one outcome of concerns about minorities in societies such as Britain, the United States and similarly advanced industrial societies. Yet, concerns about identity permeate relations among ethnic groups within and across all sorts of societies as well. At a basic level, identity is about belonging, about what we have in common with some people and what differentiates us from others. Identity gives one a sense of personal location, and provides a stable core of one's individuality; but it is also about one's social relationships, one's complex involvement with others, and in the modern world these issues have become even more complex and confusing.

As recent research has highlighted, each of us lives with a variety of potentially contradictory identities: as men or women, black or white, straight or gay, able-bodied or disabled. The list is potentially infinite, and so are therefore our possible belongings. Which of them we focus on, bring to the fore and identify with, depends on a host of factors. At the centre, however, are the values we share or wish to share with others.

In this context, it is interesting to note that much of the literature in the field of race and ethnic studies has emphasized that identity is not simply imposed but is also chosen and actively used, albeit within particular social contexts and constraints. Against dominant representations of others, there is resistance. Within structures of dominance, there is agency. Analysing resistance and agency re-politicises relations between collectivities and draws attention to the central constituting factor of power in social relations (Kibria, 1997; Song, 2003).

Yet, it is possible to overemphasise resistance; to validate others through validating the lives of the colonised and exploited. Valorising resistance may also have the unintended effect of belittling the enormous costs exacted in situations of unequal power, exclusion and discrimination. While political legitimacy, gaining access or a hearing, may depend on being able to call up a constituency and authorise representations through appeals to authenticity, it provides the basis for policing the boundaries of authenticity wherein some insiders may find themselves excluded because they are not authentic enough. For example, stressing race and ethnic differences can obscure the experiences and interests that women may share as women. We therefore need to ask: Who is constructing the categories and defining the boundaries? Who is resisting these constructions and definitions? What are the consequences being written into or out of particular categories? What happens when subordinate groups seek to mobilise along boundaries drawn for the purposes of domination? What happens to individuals whose multiple identities may be fragmented and segmented by category politics?

One of the problems with much of the contemporary discussion of identity politics is that the dilemmas and questions outlined above are not adequately addressed. This is largely because much discussion assumes that one's identity necessarily defines one's politics and that there can be no politics until the subject has excavated or laid claim to their identity. Inherent in such positions is the failure to understand the way in which identity grows out of, and is transformed by, action and struggle.

RACE, CULTURE AND ESSENTIALISM

The growth of identity politics can be seen to be challenging cultural homogeneity and providing spaces for marginal groups to assert the legacy and importance of their respective voices and experiences. From this perspective, the growth in forms of identity-based politics has allowed many formerly silenced and displaced groups to emerge from the margins of power and dominant culture to reassert and reclaim suppressed identities and experiences. This is certainly a feature of the politics of race and ethnicity in a wide range of societies today.

Stuart Hall's critique of what he defines in the British context as 'black essentialism' provides an important point of reference for the significance of identity politics to issues of race, culture and politics. Hall argues that essentialist forms of political and cultural discourse naturalise and dehistoricise difference, and therefore mistake what is historical and cultural for what is natural, biological and genetic. The moment, he argues, we tear the signifier black from its historical, cultural and political embedding and lodge it in a biologically constituted, essentialist racial category, we valorise, by inversion, the very ground of the racism we are trying to deconstruct (Hall, 1991, 1998). We fix the signifier outside history, outside of change, outside of political intervention. This is exemplified by the tendency to see the term 'black' as sufficient in itself to guarantee the progressive character of the politics articulated under that banner, when it is evident that we need to analyse precisely the content of these political strategies and how they construct specific racial meanings through politics. We have, Hall argues, arrived at an encounter, the end of innocence, or the end of the innocent notion of the essential black subject.

What is at issue here is the recognition of the extraordinary diversity of subject positions, social experiences and cultural identities that compose the category black and similar essentialist categories. This appreciation in turn reveals that black is essentially a politically and culturally constructed category, which cannot be grounded in a set of fixed transcultural or transcendental racial categories and which therefore has no guarantees. What this brings into play is the recognition of the immense diversity and differentiation of the historical and cultural experiences of what are seen as racial and/or ethnic communities across diverse societies.

While writers such as Hall have been attempting to question essentialist notions of black identity, it is interesting to note that new political discourses situated to the right, have become increasingly preoccupied with defending the importance of ever more fixed notions of culture and nation. They have sought to reconstruct primordial notions of ethnic exclusivity which celebrate national identity and patriotism in the face of criticism from multiculturalists and anti-racists. Central to such discourses is the attempt to fuse culture within a tidy formation that equates nation, citizenship and patriotism with a racially exclusive notion of difference (Ansell, 1997; Smith, 1994). It is also crucial to recognise that conservatives have given enormous prominence to waging a cultural struggle over the control and use of the popular media and other spheres of representation in order to articulate contemporary racial meanings and identities in new ways, to link race with more comprehensive political and cultural agendas, to interpret social structural phenomena (such as inequality or social policy) with regard to race. It has to be said that for the 'new right' the appeal is by and large no longer to racial supremacy but to cultural uniformity parading under the politics of nationalism and patriotism. The emphasis on heritage, the valorisation of an elitist view of self and social development, and the call to define civilisation as synonymous with selected aspects of Western tradition are being matched by a fervent attempt to reduce pedagogy to the old transmission model of teaching and learning now recoded around consecrated relics, shrines and tradition. In this case, difference is removed from the language of biologism and firmly established as a cultural construct only to be reworked within a language that concretises race and nation against the elimination of structural and cultural inequality.

GLOBALISATION AND DIFFERENCE

The preoccupation in much of the literature in this field with issues of identity and the assertion of the relevance and importance of understanding the role of new ethnicities has not resolved the fundamental question of how to balance the quest for ever more specific identities with the need to allow for broader and less fixed cultural identities. Indeed, if anything, this quest for a politics of identity has helped to highlight one of the key dilemmas of liberal political thought.

Yet, what is quite clear is that the quest for more specific, as opposed to universal, identities is becoming more pronounced in the present political environment. The search for national, ethnic and racial identities has become a pronounced, if not dominant, feature of political debate within both majority and minority communities across diverse societies of the early 21st century. One of the dilemmas we face in the present environment is that there is a clear possibility that new patterns of segregation could establish themselves and limit everyday interaction between racially defined groups.

The growing evidence of a crisis of race and of racialised class inequalities in the United States is a poignant reminder that the Civil Rights Movement and other movements since then have had, at best, a partial impact on established patterns of racial inequality and have not stopped the development of new patterns of exclusion and segregation. But it is also clear that there is evidence that within contemporary European societies there is the danger of institutionalising new forms of exclusion as a result of increased racial violence and racist mobilisations by the extreme right.

Given broad expressions of racial/ethnic conflict across quite diverse national political environments, who would argue with any real faith that we can ignore the significance of race and ethnicity to society overall? Can we be sure that the resurgence of racist nationalism does not pose a very real danger for the possibility of tolerant, equitable coexistence between groups defined as belonging to different racial, ethnic and national identities? One of the great ironies of the present situation is that transnational economic, social and political relations have helped to create a multiplicity of migrant networks and communities that transcend received national boundaries. Categories such as migrants and refugees are no longer an adequate way to describe the realities of movement and settlement in many parts of the globe. In many ways, the idea of diaspora as an unending sojourn across different lands better captures the reality of transnational networks and communities than the language of immigration and assimilation. Multiple, circular and return migrations, rather than a single great journey from one sedentary space to another, have helped to transform transnational spaces by creating new forms of cultural and political identity.

SOCIAL ORGANISATION OF RACE AND ETHNICITY

The question of what impact racism has on social relations has preoccupied many sociologists of race working within a variety of theoretical paradigms. The focus of much of the empirical research on contemporary racial relations has been on the analysis of specific aspects of inequality in areas such as housing or employment, or on the development and impact of anti-discrimination measures. Certainly the bulk of research in Britain, the United States and other advanced industrial societies has been on the changing face of racialised inequalities.

In Britain, for example, by now a panoply of studies have examined virtually all aspects of racial inequality from both a national and a local perspective. These have been supplemented by other studies which explore the complex ways in which various migrant communities experience inequality and disadvantage in their daily lives (Mason, 2000; Solomos, 2003). The United States has a similar tradition of studying racial discrimination (Brown et al., 2003).

However, what is interesting about this body of work is that there are a number of questions which need to be addressed in a fuller manner. For example: how does one account for the emergence and persistence of racialised inequalities in employment, housing, social welfare and education, as well as evident inequalities in other areas? What processes help to explain the structuring of inequalities along racial lines? What can liberal democratic societies do to ensure that racialised inequalities do not lead to the social and economic exclusion of minorities? These are some of the questions which have been raised in one way or another by researchers and politicians for at least the past three decades, and yet we do not seem to have moved much closer towards resolving them. Rather, we have seen deeply politicised public debates about both the origins and remedies for racial inequality.

The highly politicised nature of debates around racial inequality is partly the result of the fact that the interrelationship between racism and social inequalities has been and remains a deeply controversial question. It has given rise to quite divergent theoretical and political perspectives over the years. Part of the problem is that there is, in practice, very little agreement about how to conceptualise the interrelationship between racism and specific sets of racialised social relations. While some writers have used the notion of racism in a very broad social and political sense to cover both sets of ideas and institutional practices, this is by no means a position which is universally accepted. Indeed, some writers have questioned the way in which the general category of racism or the more specific notion of institutionalised racism has been used to describe forms of social relations and types of inequalities. Yet others have argued that the concept of racism should be delimited in such a way as to define it essentially as an ideological phenomenon. Over the past decade, the lack of a commonly accepted notion about what racism is has become even more apparent, particularly in the aftermath of the controversies about the development of Marxist and postmodernist perspectives to the study of race and racism.

This kind of debate and disagreement signals some of the real difficulties that exist with the ways in which the linkages between racist theories and practices have been conceptualised. There is a very real sense, for example, that terms such as institutional racism have become catch-all phrases which are used to describe quite diverse and complex patterns of exclusion. At the same time, such notions tend to be underpinned by instrumentalist notions of the relationship between racist ideas and specific types of inequality in a very undifferentiated sense. But such problems do not in themselves mean that we should not explore and understand the role of racism in structuring social relations. Rather, they point to the need to develop a more open and critical framework for analysing such processes.

Despite this, divergent perspectives about the interrelationship between racism and processes of racial discrimination persist. For example, an influential approach to this issue is the argument that racism can best be perceived as particular sets of ideological values, which propound either biological or cultural explanations of racial difference. From this perspective, racial discrimination is a practice which may or may not be the outcome of racist ideologies. Michael Banton articulates this argument clearly when he argues against the tendency to see racism and racial discrimination as interchangeable notions (Banton, 1992). For Banton and other researchers, there is a clear danger that the notion of racism can become a catch-all term that encompasses quite disparate forms of social, political and economic practices. Similar arguments have been made by Robert Miles, who warns of the dangers of 'conceptual inflation' in relation to the usages of the category of racism in the social sciences (Miles and Brown, 2003).

Yet it is also clear that in much contemporary political discourse and research, the concepts of racism and racial discrimination have become merged, so that they have little apparent difference. The concept of racism is used in practice to mean almost the same thing as racial discrimination. This is perhaps not surprising, in the sense that from a historical perspective the linkages between racist ideologies and social and economic relations have been an important feature of many societies over the past two centuries. But what is also clear is that the relationship between racist ideas and specific practices and institutional forms is by no means simple. From a historical perspective, it is quite clear that racism as an exclusionary practice can take various forms. The very complexity of the relationship between racism and forms of social exclusion makes it important that a distinction be maintained between racism and racial discrimination.

SITUATING THE PRESENT

One of the themes we have tried to explore in the course of this introduction is the development of new patterns of racial reasoning around key aspects of social relations in contemporary societies. This is not to say that what is at work is simply a process of linear evolution towards what is sometimes called 'new racism' or 'cultural racism'. For what is clear is that the framing of racialised discourses as 'new' does not necessarily help us to understand the complex variety of arguments and ideas that are to be found within contemporary racist discourses. Nor for that matter does it tell us much about what is new and what is old in the racial politics that confronts us in the present environment.

While it is important to be clear about the differences between contemporary and traditional forms of racism, it does seem that some of the arguments about this issue do not really add much analytical clarity to this complex issue. Henry Giroux, for example, argues for the emergence of a 'new racism' in the following terms: 'We are now witnessing in the United States (and Europe) the emergence of a new racism and politics of cultural difference both in the recognition of the relations between Otherness and difference, on the one hand, and meaning and the politics of representation on the other' (Giroux, 1993: 8). From rather different perspectives, other recent writings have talked of the emergence of 'meta-racism', new racism or more descriptively new cultural forms of racial discourse. While there is, as we have argued in the course of this book, something valuable and important about these arguments, it seems important to emphasise that what some writers have called new racism is not a uniform social entity as such. There is strong evidence that racial discourses are increasingly using a new cultural and social language to justify their arguments, but the search for a uniform definition of new racism has proved intractable, and has again emphasised the slippery nature of contemporary racisms. A key problem is that in a very real sense, what some writers today call *new racism* has in some sense always been with us. While it is true that in the nineteenth and early-twentieth centuries there was an emphasis in much racial thinking on the 'biological' superiority of some races over others, it is also the case that racial thinking has also always been about idealised and transcendent images of culture, landscape and national identity.

An important feature of racism over the years has been the various ways it has managed to combine different, and often contradictory, elements within specific social and political contexts. In this sense we would agree with Mosse that racism is not a coherent set of propositions that has remained the same since the eighteenth century, but can best be conceived as a scavenger ideology, which gains its power from its ability to pick out and utilise ideas and values from other sets of ideas and beliefs in specific socio-historical contexts (Mosse, 1985). There is, in other words, no essential notion of race that has remained unchanged by wider political, philosophical, economic and social transformations.

The characterisation of racism as a 'scavenger ideology' does not mean, however, that there are no continuities in racial thought across time and spatial boundaries. Indeed, it seems obvious that when one looks at the various elements of racial discourses in contemporary societies, there are strong continuities in the articulation of images of the 'other', as well as in the 'we-images' which are evident in the ways in which racist movements define the boundaries of 'race' and 'nation'. The evident use of images of the past and evocations of popular memory in the language of contemporary racist and nationalist movements points to the need to understand the complex ways in which these movements are embedded in specific images of landscape and territory.

CITIZENSHIP, MULTICULTURALISM AND ANTI-RACISM

As we look towards the next century, one of the main questions that we face is the issue of 'citizenship rights' in societies that are becoming increasingly multicultural. Within both popular and academic discourse, there is growing evidence of concern about how questions of citizenship need to be reconceptualised in the context of multicultural societies. Indeed, in contemporary European societies this can be seen as in some sense the main question which governments of various kinds are trying to come to terms with. Some important elements of this debate are the issue of the political rights of minorities, including the question of representation in both local and national politics, and the position of minority religious and cultural rights in societies which are becoming more diverse. Underlying all of these concerns is the much more thorny issue of what, if anything, can be done to protect the rights of minorities and develop extensive notions of citizenship and democracy that include those minorities that are excluded on racial and ethnic criteria (Castles, 2007; Castles and Miller, 2009).

There are clearly quite divergent perspectives in the present political environment about how best to deal with these concerns. There is, for example, a wealth of discussion about what kinds of measures are necessary to tackle the inequalities and exclusions which confront minority groups. At the same time, there is clear evidence that existing initiatives are severely limited in their impact. A number of commentators have pointed to the limitations of legislation and public policy interventions in bringing about a major improvement in the socio-political position of minorities.

This raises several questions. First, what kind of policies could tackle discrimination and inequality more effectively? Second, what links could be made between policies on immigration and policies on social and economic issues? What kind of positive social policy agenda can be developed to deal with the position of both established communities and new migrants? All of these questions are at the heart of contemporary debates and have given rise to quite divergent policy prescriptions. It is quite clear that in the present political environment, it is unlikely that any sort of agreement about how to develop new policy regimes in this field will be easy to achieve. On the contrary, it seems likely that this will remain an area full of controversy and conflict for some time to come.

But it is also the case that some key issues are coming to the fore in public debate. A case in point is the whole question of citizenship in relation to race and ethnicity. This is partly because there is a growing awareness of the gap between formal citizenship and the *de facto* restriction of the economic and social rights of minorities as a result of discrimination, economic restructuring and the decline of the welfare state.

MAPPING THE HANDBOOK

Before concluding this chapter, we want to provide a brief overview of the thematic structure of the four component parts of the handbook. More detailed overviews can be found at the beginning of each part, but here we want to map out core themes in order to guide readers about the preoccupations and aims of each part.

We have organised the handbook in four interlinked parts, each focused around a specific analytical frame or set of orienting concerns. For each part we asked the authors to provide an overview of their specific fields of research by using their own scholarship to outline key questions in their area. In this context, the chapters in each part are linked together by a common concern to situate the particular topic within a broader analytical frame. At the same time, each chapter can be read independently from other chapters in the volume. The broad array of approaches taken by the authors of the four parts of the handbook reflect this loose coupling of chapters.

Part I draws together four interlinked chapters that address the overarching question of outlining the history, development and contemporary preoccupations of race and ethnic studies as a field of scholarly research. The main concern of the chapters in this part is to outline and evaluate the origins and development of the field of race and ethnic studies and the articulation of the core theoretical and empirical approaches that have shaped research agendas. In this sense, they help to situate more fully the arguments that follow in the other three parts of the handbook.

In Part II of the handbook, the analytical focus shifts to the analysis of the intersections between race and ethnicity and other forms of social hierarchy. The four component chapters of this part are framed by a common concern to explore the ways in which race and ethnicity are shaped, and in turn shape, the experiences of class, gender, nation, sexuality and transnationalism. This is evidenced in the nuanced accounts to be found of the range of historical and contemporary social processes that have shaped these intersectionalities.

Part III of the handbook brings together four chapters that are focused on the organisation and construction of race and ethnicity in specific social and political environments. This is a facet of the contemporary literature that has expanded greatly in recent years and we have only been able to cover some sites of these processes in the context of this volume. Taken together they help to highlight the important role of key social and political institutions in structuring the experiences of race and ethnicity in contemporary societies.

Part IV is the final section of the handbook and the six chapters combine an overview of some key arenas of current debate with a forward look at issues that are likely to come to the fore in the coming period. In particular, we have selected chapters for this part that cover aspects of race and ethnic studies that are likely to grow further in importance over the coming period. In this sense, this is a part of the handbookthat is very much focused on the future as well as the past.

We conclude the handbook with an essay that provides an overview of some of the key themes raised within the eighteen substantive chapters. As a recurrent concern in the various chapters is the critical analysis of the changing terms of analysis in various sub-fields of race and ethnic studies as well as the emergence of new analytical perspectives and the articulation between academic and policy debates, we focus on these themes in this chapter. The concluding chapter also identifies some especially promising trends and developments that seem likely to shape the study of racial and ethnic relations in the coming decades. This forward-looking focus enables us to discuss emerging research questions and potential policy responses to the challenges that face a wide range of societies at the beginning of the twenty-first century.

CONCLUSION

We offer this handbook as an overview of this field of scholarly research on race and ethnic studies. It gives voice to the various perspectives that have shaped this field of research over the past few decades and it also highlights areas of innovation and change.

Perhaps the main point that we want to emphasise in conclusion is that there remains much to do if we are to develop an analytical framework that allows us to think through the various types of racial and ethnic processes, patterns of racialisation and related processes that are shaping the social and political environment of many societies across the globe.

Part of the dilemma we face at the present time is that there is a need for more detailed and historically grounded empirical research that focuses on the relationship between ideas about race, ethnicity and culture in specific social and cultural environments. This is partly because the preoccupation with developing ever more sophisticated theoretical narratives has led to a neglect of empirically focused research, whether at the local, national or transnational level. Yet, arguably, it is only through such research that we can begin to imagine what kinds of policies and political interventions may be able to challenge racism and the institutional processes of exclusion on which it is based.

REFERENCES

Alcoff, L.M. and Mendieta, E. (2003) *Identities: Race, Class, Gender, and Nationality*. Malden, MA: Blackwell.

Alexander, C.E. and Knowles, C. (2005) *Making Race Matter: Bodies, Space, and Identity*. Basingstoke: Palgrave Macmillan.

Ansell, A.E. (1997) *New Right, New Racism: Race and Reaction in the United States and Britain*. New York: New York University Press.

Banton, M. (1992) 'The Nature and Causes of Racism and Racial Discrimination', *International Sociology*, 7 (1): 69–84.

Bonilla-Silva, E. (1997) 'Rethinking Racism: Toward a Structural Interpretation', *American Sociological Review*, 62 (3): 465–80.

Brown, M.K., Carnoy, M., Currie, E., Duster, T., Oppenheimer, D.B., Shultz, M.M. and Wellman, D. (2003) *Whitewashing Race: The Myth of a Color-Blind Society*. Berkeley: University of California Press.

Brubaker, R. (2004) 'In the Name of the Nation: Reflections on Nationalism and Patrotism', *Citizenship Studies*, 8 (2): 115–27.

Brubaker, R. (2005) *Ethnicity Without Group*. Cambridge, MA: Harvard University Press.

Brubaker, R. and Cooper, F. (2000) 'Beyond Identity', *Theory and Society*, 29 (1): 1–47.

Bulmer, M. and Solomos, J. (eds) (2004) *Researching Race and Racism*. London: Routledge.

Calhoun, C.J. (ed.) (1994) *Social Theory and the Politics of Identity*. Oxford: Blackwell.

Calhoun, C.J. (2007) *Nations Matter: Culture, History, and the Cosmopolitan Dream*. London: Routledge.

Castles, S. (2007) 'Twenty-First-Century Migration as a Challenge to Sociology', *Journal of Ethnic and Migration Studies*, 33 (3): 351–371.

Castles, S. and Miller, M.J. (2009) *The Age of Migration: International Population Movements in the Modern World*. 4th edition. Basingstoke: Palgrave Macmillan.

Cornell, S. and Hartmann, D. (2007) *Ethnicity and Race: Making Identities in a Changing World*. 2nd edition. Thousand Oaks: Pine Forge Press.

Essed, P. and Goldberg, D.T. (eds) (2002) *Race Critical Theories: Text and Context*. Oxford: Blackwell.

Fredrickson, G.M. (2002) *Racism: A Short History*. Princeton: Princeton University Press.

Gates Jr, H.L. (ed.) (1986) *Race, Writing and Difference*. Chicago: University of Chicago Press.

Giroux, H.A. (1993) 'Living Dangerously: Identity Politics and the New Cultural Racism, Towards a Critical Pedagogy of Representation', *Cultural Studies*, 7 (1): 1–27.

Goldberg, D.T. (2002) *The Racial State*. Oxford: Blackwell.

Goldberg, D.T. and Solomos, J. (eds) (2002) *A Companion to Racial and Ethnic Studies*. Oxford: Blackwell.

Hall, S. (1991) 'Old and New Identities, Old and New Ethnicities', in A.D. King (ed.) *Culture, Globalization and the World System*. Basingstoke: Macmillan.

Hall, S. (1998) 'Aspiration and Attitude ... Reflections on Black Britain in the Nineties', *New Formations*, 33: 38–46.

Holloway, J.S. and Keppel, B. (eds) (2007) *Black Scholars on the Line: Race, Social Science, and American Thought in the Twentieth Century*. Notre Dame: University of Notre Dame Press.

Kibria, N. (1997) 'The Construction of "Asian American": Reflections on Intermarriage and Ethnic Identity among Second-Generation Chinese and Korean Americans', *Ethnic and Racial Studies*, 20 (3): 523–44.

Knowles, C. (2003) *Race and Social Analysis*. London: Sage.

Lasch-Quinn, E. (2001) *Race Experts: How Racial Etiquette, Sensitivity Training, and New Age Therapy Hijacked the Civil Rights Revolution.* New York: W.W. Norton.

Mason, D. (2000) *Race and Ethnicity in Modern Britain.* 2nd edition. Oxford: Oxford University Press.

Miles, R. (1993) *Racism after 'Race' Relations.* London: Routledge.

Miles, R. and Brown, M. (2003) *Racism.* 2nd edition. London: Routledge.

Mosse, G.L. (1985) *Toward the Final Solution: A History of European Racism.* Madison: University of Wisconsin Press.

Nobles, M. (2000) *Shades of Citizenship: Race and Census in Modern Politics.* Stanford: Stanford University Press.

Singh, N.P. (2004) *Black is a Country: Race and the Unfinished Struggle for Democracy.* Cambridge, MA: Harvard University Press.

Smith, A.M. (1994) *New Right Discourse on Race and Sexuality: 1968–1990.* Cambridge: Cambridge University Press.

Solomos, J. (2003) *Race and Racism in Britain.* 3rd edition. Basingstoke: Palgrave Macmillan.

Song, M. (2003) *Choosing Ethnic Identity.* Cambridge: Polity Press.

Stanfield, J.H. (ed.) (1993) *A History of Race Relations Research: First-Generation Recollections.* Newbury Park: Sage.

PART I

Locating the Field: Theoretical and Historical Foundations

Introduction

This introductory part of the handbook is structured around four overviews of key facets of the field of race and ethnic studies. The four chapters that compose this part of the volume are written by scholars and researchers who have been active through their research and scholarship in shaping the field of race and ethnicity studies through their empirical and theoretical contributions. Rather than limiting their field of vision to specific sub-fields, we intentionally asked our contributors to look first at the bigger picture. In other words, we wanted them to provide readers with overviews that help them to situate the broad contours of race and ethnic studies as an established field of scholarship and research. More specifically, we see this part of the book as providing an overview of key theoretical, historical and empirical research issues that will help to situate the substantive content of the chapters that follow.

The first chapter in Part I is by Caroline Knowles and it provides an overview of contemporary theorising on race and ethnicity that draws on a broad range of research and scholarship across a range of national settings. Knowles argues forcefully that theorising about race and ethnicity needs to move away from a formal abstractionism and engage fully with the empirical research agendas that we face today. In doing so, she also seeks to highlight the need to inject into our analytical categories in sociology and other disciplines, an awareness of the historical specificities in the ways in which race and ethnicity are constructed and given meaning. She acknowledges the important role of theorising in this field that has emerged over the past decades in both the US and Britain, and indeed the chapter covers key facets of these debates. At the same time, she suggests that there is a need to develop new theoretical perspectives that can speak to, and engage with, the complexities of contemporary multiracial, multiethnic and multicultural societies in various parts of the globe. The issue of how to inter-weave theoretical paradigms with historical and empirical research is a recurrent theme in the volume as a whole.

The next chapter by Joe Feagin and Eileen O'Brien shares some of the concerns highlighted by Knowles about the need to situate the study of race and ethnic relations within relations of power and social inequality. Feagin and O'Brien, nevertheless, look at the field of race and ethnic studies through a somewhat different lens. Taking their cue from Du Bois' famous statement about the central role of the 'colour line' in the twentieth century, they focus their account of theorising about race and ethnicity on the evolving and changing politics of race within American society. Feagin and O'Brien provide both a critical analysis of scholarship on race and ethnicity in the US and a historically focused account of the impact of racial and ethnic divisions, both on the wider society and on scholarly knowledge and research. This chapter thus provides an incisive and engaged account of the ways in which knowledge about racial and ethnic divisions is necessarily embedded in everyday social relations and political struggles.

The methodological challenges we face in developing empirical research in the field of race and ethnicity provide the analytical underpinnings of the chapter by Nancy Denton and Glenn Deane. Social scientific research on race and ethnic relations has been carried out for the past century using a range of both quantitative and qualitative research tools, ranging from social surveys, statistical analysis, ethnography, participant observation and cultural analysis. Yet, as Denton and Deane point out, there is often little agreement among social scientists about what it is that we study when we research social categories such as *race* and *ethnicity*. They suggest that an important starting point in any empirical research in this field is to clarify what it is that we are seeking to measure and the consequences of developing specific tools of measurement. Their analysis of how quantitative researchers have grappled with these issues is a clear and focused challenge that highlights both the need for greater conceptual clarity and more debate about how empirical research agendas can take up key methodological challenges.

The final chapter of this part of the handbook is by Chetan Bhatt and takes a broader look at the category of race and the ways it has been debated within philosophy and the social sciences. Bhatt's account helpfully situates the role that core metaphysical ideas about time, bodies and violence, and purity often play in shaping racist ideologies and practices in various societies and across historical time. His analysis of these issues starts with an exposition of the role of thinkers such as Immanuel Kant in shaping the use of racial and ethnic categories and moves on to deal with the debates that have influenced the study of race and racism in contemporary societies. His account ranges across a diverse set of issues and debates and highlights the importance of racial and ethnic questions in a variety of disciplines, geopolitical environments and policy debates. More importantly, he also seeks to question the notion that we can somehow dispense with the category of race as a research and policy issue in the contemporary world. His account suggests the need to think rigorously about the boundaries of what we study when we research racial and ethnic conflicts. This is evidenced in his suggestion that a silence in contemporary research on the 'ethnosupremacist' character of the Israeli state results from the conceptual limitations of debates about racism and anti-semitism.

Whatever the particular focus of each of the four chapters, we hope that they collectively situate the broad contours of the field of race and ethnic studies, and provide useful signposts for themes that will be addressed more fully in subsequent chapters.

Theorising Race and Ethnicity: Contemporary Paradigms and Perspectives

Caroline Knowles

INTRODUCTION

Contemporary theories of race and ethnicity[1] sustain a dissonance between conceptualisation and empirical research, and between both of these things and political activism. This stems from a failure to conceptualise race and ethnicity concretely, materially, in ways connected with their resonance in people's lives and the broader social and political circumstances in which they are set. In this chapter, I explore how this situation arose and what may be done to advance beyond it. I argue that the current situation needs new, materially grounded, approaches to race theory. We should focus on the *production* of race through human agency and routine social contexts of different scales. As well as grappling with micro-contexts, new approaches to race should engage with its global production in migration. Migration is a major issue in all nation states where a range of mobile populations from asylum seekers to economic migrants have become a focus for heightened localisms and political debates about access and entitlement. Centring on race production – *race-making* – reconnects race theory with empirical research agendas and race politics in a definitive move away from abstractionism.

Although race and ethnicity are concepts, constellations of ideas and speculative connections, a materialist approach can engage with these things in specific spatial and temporal contexts, with the ways in which they *matter* politically and *make matter* in the lives through which they reverberate. It is important to bear this in mind in the overarching attempt that follows to place contemporary debates, paradigms and perspectives in historical contexts that acknowledge the specificities of circumstances and micro-versions of place, on both sides of the Atlantic, as well as the dialogues, circulation of ideas and activists that bridge this gap. Theory does not always declare its location, and it is important to acknowledge the specifics. Britain and America (and Canada) have distinctive (racialised and ethnicised) immigration processes. Settler societies like Canada and America forged nation states out of the material of migrant ethnicities and retreating colonial powers (like Britain) which sustained and remade the fabric of the nation in ways that were all about race. These three countries, and I am aware that this focus ignores other places like Australia, New Zealand and South Africa, had different relationships to empire, to slavery, to first nations and to domestic – as opposed to colonial – racial segregation and social compacts with the settled descendants of slavery. With a past mired in the racial politics of colonial governance and the mid-twentieth century migration's contribution to the mongrel nation; Britain was in a different position than North America when it came to the politics of race. This chapter centres on British debates and developments, acknowledging interconnections with, and examples drawn from, America. These are helpful locations for developing new racial theories that have relevance elsewhere in multiethnic, multicultural and multiracial societies.

PAST DEBATES AND CONTEXTS

British, American, Canadian, Australian, New Zealand and South African debates and contexts, rendered through the (English-speaking) academy, are both specific and interconnected. While they illuminate conditions that are peculiar to each place and the ruminations of their local academies, theories and academics travel, revelations in one place are applied to another and published in international journals. In the end, the national origins of debates and theories are uncertain and their application inevitably extra-local. This section describes past debates and contexts relating to Britain, elements of which relate to other locations. There are numerous commentaries on the development of British theories of race and ethnicity with Mac an Ghaill (1999) and Alexander and Alleyne (2002) producing particularly useful overviews. Cutting a path through these commentaries, it is possible to give the briefest of outlines in contextualising the discussion of where we are now, and the directions in which things are developing.

Without the urban ecology of ethnic migration developed by the Chicago School in the early years of the twentieth century, British 'race relations' approaches of the 1960s were consumed with the implications of post-war migration.

This period was characterised by concern with weakening social and political cohesion resulting from poor social 'integration' in the face of growing, visible, bodily and cultural difference. These concerns are currently being recycled in a new, anti-Islamic context. As entrenched forms of white Britishness grappled with the logistics of peaceful multiracial co-existence and social scientists studied 'prejudice', Black power and civil rights were tackling the US political agenda against the backdrop of the Vietnam War. In line with the trends in sociological analysis at that time, the psycho-social dynamics of prejudice and cultural dislocation were overlain by more *systematic* concerns. Access and allocation systems in housing, jobs and education were assembled to form a broader picture of the *structural* forces at work in generating racial disadvantage, and an emerging sociology of 'race relations' was assembled by John Rex (1970), Robert Moore (1975) and others. As *structure* occluded *agency*, with its simplistic notions of racial prejudice as individualised flawed character, British *racism*[2] was conceptualised as a monstrous apparatus of racialised social distributions in the context of debates about whether *intention* or *outcome* was more significant in defining these forms of racism (Feuchtwang, 1982). Similar debates reverberated throughout other national contexts including the US and Canada. The research organised by these frameworks detailed racial access to social resources and provided important empirical evidence of systematic racism as exclusion and differential access. Although no longer fashionable, this evidence of racial disadvantage is still relied upon in arguments establishing the contemporary significance and ubiquity of race. At the height of 1960s' and 1970s' concern with social structure, Marxists (Miles, 1989; Cox, 1948) and Weberians (Banton, 1983; Banton and Harwood, 1975) operated this structural paradigm. They debated whether race was a subordinate form of inequality to class; the connections between Black struggle in Britain and anti-colonial struggles in developing countries (Sivanandan, 1976); and whether racism was an autonomous ideology from its referent, race (Miles and Torres, 1996). People, lives, feelings, routine social contexts and action didn't feature in structuralism; but it proffered concrete evidence of racism, a set of targets for social policy reform, and a constituency in black people and their supporters who could be mobilised in political struggles against racism.

Structuralist race theory became unfashionable as intellectual agendas in Britain, the US and elsewhere shifted in the 1980s to centre on the multiple subject positions concealed by the concept 'black'. The fragmentation of blackness was driven by the imperative of recognising different 'experiences' of oppression and led by African American feminists and their supporters in Britain (Carby, 1982; Parmar, 1982) who, rightly, pointed out that blackness was gendered and gender was a significant axis of differentiation. In the conceptual space opened by feminists, it was possible to consider manifestations of experience codified in identities. In Britain, the Birmingham Centre for Contemporary Cultural Studies (CCCS) set about articulating racial differences obscured by the starker binaries of blackness and whiteness, oppression and privilege. It redeployed ethnicity in

Hall's (1992) path-breaking 'New Ethnicities', hitherto material worked by anthropologists, now articulated in convergence with race. Hall (1992) declared the end of the essential black subject, and the *lost* Asian (Modood, 1988) and other historically migrant identities were reclaimed, articulated and acknowledged as part of the growing conceptual complexity of race. In Britain, these debates prioritised identities expressed in popular culture, in film and music as forms of aesthetic expression, articulated as discourse. Thus a preoccupation with 'identities' was established on both sides of the Atlantic. This was later refined in the US by Conyers (1999), Davis (1999) and others, articulating a plurality of African American voices liberated from the presumption of unitary experience in slavery.

While the fragmentation of this focus on identities is potentially library, it is, ironically, as uninterested in human agency as structuralism. The identities period of race theory is connected with the textual turn; with *representation* and *discourse*, not flesh-in-motion on the scenes of everyday life. Of course, earlier notions of black identities standardised by oppression and anti-racist struggle were an oversimplification. But the politics of identity that replaced it offered neither targets for social reform, nor a constituency mobilised in political struggle against racism. Indeed, racism became a secondary problem to the elaboration of racial identities. Paul Gilroy's (1987) imaginative work developed the intellectual ground established by the CCCS, concerned with 'discourse' rather than raced bodies, lives, social practices and social inequalities. While racism remained an urgent political problem, those who were preoccupied with discourse were able to claim that theorists concerned with race were reinforcing its common-sense meaning and the subjugation and exclusion this carried (Gilroy cited in St Louis, 2002: 659). Not only had race lost its connection with political struggle against racism, opposing racism simply sustained it. In this context, Gilroy declared an end to 'raciology'; the 'mythic morphology of racial difference' (cited in St Louis, 2002: 659).

These theoretical developments were by no means inevitable. In Britain alone there were at least two clear alternatives, one from within the CCCS itself. Solomos and Back's research on Black political activism in the town halls of the British Midlands 'develop(ed) a theoretically grounded analysis of the everyday processes through which race and ethnicity have become an integral part of political life' (1995: 17). They uncovered connections between political mobilisation and racial formation: 'While Hall and Modood were right to question simplistic notions of unitary and essential models of identity, it was still important to understand how "black" could serve as an organising category in contemporary political life' (pp. 212–213). Despite being abandoned in the refinements of the politics of identity, Black remained an important organising theme in national and local British politics. The second, equally unfashionable, alternative to the identities focus, came from a left antiracist political analysis set out in two edited collections; *Antiracist Strategies* (1990) and *Where You Belong* (1992) both edited by Cambridge and Feuchtwang. The result of a study group that met at

City University in London throughout the 1980s, these edited collections warned that it was important not to lose sight of the 'generality of racist forces and their effects and of the political implications of efforts to combat them' (Feuchtwang, 1990: ix). This notes two elements in the analysis of racism. First, it is important to be precise in identifying racism, rather than assume its existence in some general, less actionable, way. Second, it is vital to identify appropriate action to eliminate it (Feuchtwang, 1990: ix): racism after all was the reason why we needed to theorise race. Race in this analysis, maintains its connection with racism; and racism results from various conditions, calculations, practices and political forces – revealing Foucauldian deconstruction in the service of political activism – that produce exclusion and differential access. This approach supported neither unitary notions of blackness nor monolithic notions of racism, but this was overlooked in the retreat from 'blackness' and the anti-racist politics it sustained. Anti-racist struggle became a subordinate concern as more abstract, less material and socially grounded, theoretical concerns took priority over empirical and political ones.

WHERE ARE WE NOW? DEBATES AND NEW INITIATIVES

Race is over theorised and disconnected from social and political engagement. Elaborating *difference* provides complexity and depth, but is over-focused on identities and lacks political engagement. Yet, race politics are urgently needed. Racism continues in lethal attacks, in subtle discrimination, in differential opportunities, in bullying, in the treatment of new migrants and asylum seekers in a spectrum of nation states, and in political initiatives throughout Europe, and other places too, regarding integration. Similarly, new outbreaks of ethnic cleansing underscore the salience of ethnicity in the organisation of the modern world and its conflicts, from Iraq to Sudan. There is growing unease in academies at the disconnection between theoretical debate and political struggles addressing racism (Bulmer and Solomos, 2004: 8–10; St Louis, 2002). There is a gathering disenchantment with the focus on discourse in race scholarship. Underlying these concerns is an old argument that questions the usefulness of intellectual resources that cannot be levered into making the world a better, less violent and unjust place. This is a morally defensible and socially responsible position, even if intellectual engagement doesn't bring immediate social improvement. Bulmer and Solomos (2004: 10) insist on the importance of maintaining race as an object of sociological investigation *and* political action, and this is, I think, the key to developing a more theoretically informed, political engagement with race. This requires race to be explored for its social substance, using some quite conventional sociological tools. As St Louis (2002: 671) points out, 'the theorisation of race is neither the distillation nor transcendence of personal experience. ... Race is both material and ideal in lived and reflexive senses ...'. The gap between hyper-theorised conceptions of race and the social practices that operate around them, can be bridged by forms of social analysis that engage with the more mundane aspects of the social texture of life in racialised societies. And there are signs that things are moving in this direction.

There are, for example, signs of a willingness to tackle what Alexander (2002: 564) calls the 'rather messier, incommensurable realities' like school exclusions and racial murders and uses the resulting insights to generate new theoretical positions. This follows from a re-enchantment with people and their lives (Mac an Ghaill, 1999), from renewed interest in social texture – space, emotionality and social practice – conventional sociological concepts not usually deployed to theorise race. The excavation of difference has moved beyond identities fractured by religious and cultural markers, class gender and more (Alexander and Alleyne, 2002: 543; Alexander, 2002: 552), to focus on how difference plays out in people's lives. Race theorists are thinking about the impact of Islamophobia on social relationships; on the lives of British and American Muslims (Alexander, 2005); and on the global organisation of Islam. The 'complex' alchemy of difference is now centring on the complexity of *lives* instead of the complexity of *discourse* and *representation*. Gilroy's (1993: 223) powerful statements on black subjectivity stressing mutation, hybridity and intermixture, inspire a new generation of race scholars, on both sides of the Atlantic, exploring *lived dimensions* of mixity (Twine, 2006; Ali, 2005). Gunaratnam and Lewis (2001) and Vera and Feagin (2004: 75) explore the emotional dimensions of racialised life, and Montgomery (2004) examines routes through black neighbourhoods in Los Angeles, flesh-in-motion on the scenes of everyday life. This renewed enchantment with lives accompanies a renewed engagement with empirical research and its deployment in theory construction. It also signals a reconnection with classical sociological theory. These are signs that race no longer operates in a theoretical ghetto, but can become a focus in the mainstream of sociological theory.

The strength of this research is in its attention to detail and its elaboration of the minutia of social texture which place it in the traditions of micro-sociology. Moving in the opposite direction, joining-up some of these small contexts with the bigger structural reasoning that lies behind it, are other contemporary trends in race theory. Two trends, especially, organising the particular into broader circumstances and a re-engagement with macro-sociology, merit consideration. First, are prompts to revisit articulation of the social inequalities that lean on the alchemy of race, ethnicity and class (Bottero, 2005). This re-engagement with race as part of broader social structures and the organisation of social inequalities got sidelined during the 1980s. Second, from philosophical traditions, are (American) political theories conceptualising modern racialised states led by David Goldberg. These explain how race is part of the 'emergence, development and transformations' of modern states: conceptualising racial states as 'projects and practices, social conditions and institutions, states of being and affairs, roles and principles, statements and imperatives' (Goldberg, 2002: 5). This offers a clear understanding of social mechanisms through which racialised/ethnicised distinction are produced, and, exposes differential forms of citizenship *within* racial states. These are useful insights right now. Migration, displacement and differential access to nation states and their allocation systems, has produced a complicated mosaic of race, ethnicity and migration. The old axes of migration and racial alignment are overwritten by new systems, and we struggle to understand their racial grammar. The global inequalities produced by these new systems of migration pose urgent political questions about global dimensions of social justice and rights. These opposing tendencies, in which we deconstruct circumstances and grapple with their detail, as well as join things up and think about broader circumstances, are helpful. The micro/macro is a useful tension to maintain in developing our analysis of race, because it operates simultaneously at different levels of scope and scale.

There are other more recent trends that merit attention. First, is the application of race (and ethnicity) to those who used it to position others but not themselves. Scholars developing Critical White Studies argue that whiteness operates as a badge of racial privilege and a site of critical reflection on a racial past inflected with violence and exploitation. The best of this writing (Frankenberg, 2004; Back, 2004; Gallagher, 2003a, 2003b) grapples with everyday life and with the connections between whiteness and racism (Back, 2000). Their logic is that we are all raced and ethnicised, so the systems of advantage and disadvantage that produce race implicate everyone, expanding the constituency of anti-racist struggle.

Lastly, are theories concerned with global[3] dimensions of race. This is an important but problematic area of race theory. Race often features in the examination of globalisation as an 'addition' (Featherstone et al., 1995). Authors want us to take as axiomatic the fact that globalisation is raced without explaining how. Or, other times, race is the focus of analysis and globalisation and added as a *de facto* backdrop to racialisation (Bowser, 1995; Wilson, 1999). Both scenarios conceal the intersections between race and global social processes that need to be exposed. Conceptual schemes foregrounding interconnection (Sassen, 1990, 1991, 1996) are often framed in technical and economic (not social) terms, and so obscure the social texture of racialised global relationships. Massey (1999: 35) calls these 'iconic economics' because social features are treated as the consequence of formative technical and economic factors. These problems notwithstanding, conceptualising race in the intersections between networked social contexts, foregrounds spatial aspects of race as well as mobility and transcendence. These are productive avenues to explore in new conceptualisations of race. As the US theorist Winant (1994: 274) argues, the global geographies of race have made a new kind of comparative analysis possible: we can explore the global organisation of race and the racing of globalisation. This highlights the significance of social texture, social relationships and social practices; things we need to conceptualise as composing race.

MOVING FORWARD: WHERE DO WE GO FROM HERE?

These recent developments lead towards materialist analyses of race, grounded in the mechanisms composing and connecting social fabrics, and it is these that I want to develop a bit further in suggesting new directions in race theory. Clearly, race is not an objective condition of descent, it does not correspond with human gene pools; but neither is it a mythic, ideological or discursive construct. Of course it is mythical, ideological and discursive, but it is not *only* these things, and not primarily these things. What we need to focus on is the way in which these things become part of social practice and social relationships. To transcend the mantra that race is socially produced we need to say specifically *how*, and we need to do so in materialist terms – terms that concretise discourse, symbol and representation. Winant (2000: 183–184) argues that race has a salience in people's lives, in the ways in which people think about themselves and others. We can develop this further. Race is part of social relationships and social processes, part of the operation of global and local space and an inextricable part of the ways in which societies are organised. I want to pursue some of these thoughts and offer them as elements in a materialist analysis of race – with the texture of everyday life in which race is inextricably embedded. In what follows, I want to tease out a tangle of things composing everyday racial texture and so suggest some new directions to pursue: focused on doing, on action and social practice, race-making, rather than talking, discourse and symbolism. These directions include the production of subjectivity, social relationships, and relationships between people and places: conventional sociological concerns pursued – but not in connection with race – in the work of C. Wright Mills, Erving Goffman, Marcel Mauss, Henri Lefebvre and George Herbert Mead. In focusing on the production of race in spatially constituted social relationships, I think we can learn something about race-making; the production of race and the social inequalities – racism – it resources, and so restore connections between race and racism; and between theory, social relationships and politics.

PEOPLE, SUBJECTIVITIES AND COMPORTMENT

Racialised regimes, regimes where race (and ethnicity) resources social distinctions, are composed through human *being* and *action*: reflexivity, conviction and volition produce and sustain racial distinctions (Knowles, 2003). People are thus central actors in racial classification, and the forms of exclusion and (sometimes) untimely death, they support (Levi, 2000). In the Third Reich, German citizens drove trains and built gas pipes. The US segregation laws in the 1890s were similarly sustained through human initiatives. A mixed-race man named Plessy, who was counted as black in some states and white in others, was prosecuted for riding in a 'whites only' train carriage, thus violating the segregation laws of the State of Louisiana (Braman, 1999: 1394). This enforcement of the social boundaries distinguishing blackness and whiteness was made possible by Plessy's fellow passengers who were prepared to report him, the train guard who was prepared to enforce their objections and the personnel of the legal apparatus who were willing to pursue segregation by juridical means. Segregation broke down when these 'great and small complicities' (Levi, 2000: 49) were no longer viable. My point is that race is produced – activated as a resource in making social distinctions – through people's routine action. We are all involved in producing race for ourselves and others. These are personal matters, which are more than personal: racialised societies are sustained by racialised regimes and not just racialised individuals. The intersection between people and regimes is something sociologists need to better understand. What part do individuals play in sustaining racialised regimes with their complex tapestry of social differentiation of privilege and disadvantage? In what do individual complicities consist? Herzfeld (1992: 56) conceptualises complicity between regimes and its subjects as part of a broader problem. In the 'social production of indifference', in our 'destructive, routinised inaction' we are all, he says, *bricoleurs* working within and upon the system. Race, as sustainable classification, allocation, or subtle social difference, facilitating inequalities of social value and reward, is *made*, produced, in the interactions between people and regimes. In racialised regimes, our daily lives are lived through the production of race: our mundane actions contribute to racialisation. Focus on extreme racist parties or activists as the source of racism misses this point, revealed by conceptualising race's production through people, regimes and routine interactions.

It is not just action and its consequences that make race. Subjectivity and styles of being-in-the-world compose race too. We can think of these things as *people fabric*. Subjectivity is more fundamental than identity: it concerns the models in which personhood is cast – what it means to be a person, the general frame on which badges of identity are posted. This is partly existential and partly social: part corporeal and part consciousness. Begin with the social. Subjectivity is socially composed in this respect; the dialogical self can only exist among other selves in webs of inter-location (Taylor, 1989: 35–36 leaning on Mead) in the context of moral frameworks. We can think about personhood as social because it involves sociality, moral frameworks and engagement with the material details of everyday life (de Certeau, 1989): things which are already inflected with race in racialised societies. Social dimensions of subjectivity are inextricably intertwined with its existential dimensions; this includes things which are personal and connected with individual feeling and the casting of existence. Race is made here too, in a dialogical relationship with the (raced) social dimensions of subjectivity. Race is socially generated: it becomes personal through the existential/social intersections in the composition of subjectivity. This formulation borrows compositional approaches to subjectivity (Shotter, 1997: 13) in which selves are *made* in practical routine action and forms of knowing, in 'moment by moment' 'back and forth' processes. And. it extends compositional subjectivity to help us conceptualise race-making – the production of race in human fabric(ation). I propose that we consider these processes as the means by which race is made and transmitted as subjectivity.

Race is also made through corporeality and comportment, through bodily movement and intersections with space. In focusing on these components of race–making, I am neglecting consciousness: there is much to say about this but it is a subject of a bigger literature than corporeality and comportment. Space, which I will turn to later, is animated by lives and performances, by knowing how to act (Mason, 1996: 302–303). Techniques of the body, posture, attitude, movements and habits are also performances of ethnicity, race and hybridised cultural practices which lend their (orchestrated) mobile character to the architecture of the streets. I say also because they are much more than this. Movement, habit, performance, architecture and specialised commerce produce China Towns and Little Italys – the layered ethnic geographies of cities. We will return to these later. How people comport themselves is both enactment and composition of (raced) subjectivity: where we walk and how is significant. I want to suspend the 'where' for later consideration of mobility and focus now on 'how' people walk and act and thus compose the racialised relationships of space. Some historical examples from the US ground this point about race-making.

Smith's (2004: 120–121) *Photography on the Colour Line* shows postcards circulated in the 1920s depicting white people gathering at lynchings, unselfconsciously lined up, smiling, enjoying a day out. Their comportment composes and consolidates their whiteness, caught in the camera lens, in the act (crime) of racial annihilation. Compare the two forms of corporeality at a lynching; one at leisure, the other death, one smiling, the other ripped apart. This is an extreme example. Less murderous, more routine, forms of corporeality and comportment are equally significant, if less dramatic and deserve the attention of race theorists. Du Boise understood this. His America Negro Exhibition, shown at the 1900 Paris Exhibition depicting photographs (taken by African American photographer, Thomas Askew) of African American men sitting at desks, dressed in fine clothes, challenged the visual narratives of poverty and rural landscape in locating African Americans and with it the mutual constitution of race and visual culture in the white normative gaze (Smith, 2004: 10–11). Du Bois repositions blackness, usurping body poses and material circumstances appropriated by whiteness, to emphasise a common humanity, challenging nineteenth-century versions of racial hierarchy.

Routine corporeality and comportment also intersect with entitlement and territory. In hyper-white residential parts of US cities and small towns where people of colour form a tiny minority, white people walk with a sense of (historical) entitlement, an unchallengeable right to be there; and (because of this) people of colour tread more cautiously. Shift the spatial context to downtown Pittsburgh and a different set of circumstances appear: multi-racial proximities invoke a sharing of space without clear racial hierarchies. A sense of entitlement and territory – a right to be there – is more finely balanced. These are not just matters of numeric strength, but perceptions of being in or out of place in the contexts of specific territories and boundaries. In Johannesburg, white residents cluster in suburbs behind razor wire and high walls: theirs is a besieged entitlement, eroded by violence, a source of complaint. Black South Africans occupy the centre of a city, reshaped by white and business flight to the suburbs. American and British expats walk the streets of Hong Kong with a sense of difference from 'Chineseness', but with an unquestioned sense of a right to be there, and anywhere else they choose to settle, as part of a mobile global elite, entitled by their passports and qualifications.

These kinaesthetic versions of race (and ethnicity)-making are significant in filling-in and marking neighbourhoods. This is where race is walked, as bodies encounter other bodies on the street, moving through doors, negotiating the pavement, public transit or parking space. Assemblages of bodies and performances jostling each other in the same space is where some of the practical politics of multi-racial co-existence are played out, not in words, but bodily movements and the assumptions underpinning them. In summary then, I am suggesting that materialist analyses of race as race-making include subjectivity-production, corporeality and performance and the interface between people and regimes. Of course these themes deserve more detailed elaboration than they have been given in this chapter.

PLACES, SOCIAL RELATIONSHIPS AND ROUTES

Race-making is also about place, social relationships and routes, including global ones. Analytically, space[4] is at the centre of these concerns. People and their spatial practices provide a window to a rich archive of social differentiation, including race and ethnicity. Space is (socially) produced by *who* people are (subjectivities and identities), by *what they do* (social practices and activities) and *how they connect with other people* (social relationships). This framework is developed by Lefebvre (1996), and, although he doesn't do this, can be developed to think about race. I want to suggest that people's spatial practices reveal matrices of social differentiation in which race and ethnicity are entangled with other differences. You are not what you eat, but where you walk (or travel), the circumstances in which you walk and with whom you associate on the way. This position is also informed by Hesse (1999) and Massey's (1999) thoughts on globalisation and by Clifford's (1994) work on *Routes* which displaces the analytical centrality of *settlement* with the *dynamics* of movement. Race, it seems to me, is always in production on a moving landscape.

Race sociology acknowledges space; as urban ecology (Park, 1967; Farris and Dunham, 1965; Burgess, 1967); in patterns of residential segregation (Rex and Moore, 1967; Smith, 1993; Farrar, 1997; Smith and Torallo, 1993); in ethnic marking of place (Eade, 1997; Anderson, 1991); as architecturally encoded in territory (Farrar, 1997); in drawing battle lines in racial conflicts that periodically erupt in British and American urban centres (Feuchtwang, 1992; Kettle and Hodges, 1982); and in acts of commemoration and the production of popular imaginary (Cross and Keith, 1993). While these studies contain valuable insights that contribute to a materialist analysis of race as race-making, they don't conceptualise space in the way that I propose, following Lefebvre (1996), as constituted in, and expressed through, concrete raced *social practices* and *social relationships* in the dynamics of movement (Clifford, 1994).

Space acquires social – racial – significance in symbiotic relationship with the people using it. People refers to subjectivities, corporeality, comportment and so on, as the reader will be aware by this point in the chapter. It also includes the meaning associated with the social categories through which people are socially positioned and through which they understand themselves. Space is a general, abstract category. It is the meaning, use and character of space that makes *place* (Massey, 1994). Massey, guided by Lefebvre (1996), displays the instability of space in its ability to pick up new meanings, activities and people. Space is always being made, and has no essential or predictable relationship to race and ethnicity. This, of course, challenges essentialised notions of racial belonging to territories. Space makes, and is made by, race. This happens through the meaning attached to its occupants and users, through their activities and lives, and through the meanings attached to it and which make it a place. Space can be investigated, but not assumed. Places can be understood for their grammar, the forms of social practice to which they give rise and which are walked and talked by human bodies in routine activity. People's subjectivities, corporeality, comportment and social activities – dealt with earlier – are part of the spatial production of race. So too, is the architecture of the built environment, but in this section I want to draw attention to social relationships and practices and movement. I will argue that racially calibrated forms of social differentiation can be analysed through pathways and journeys both local and global.

If we think of places as constituted (racially and ethnically) in networks of social relationship and webs of social practice (Massey, 1994; Lefebvre, 1996), then we can differentiate places through their social relationships and practices. Social relationships differ in quality, scope and scale; they range from intimacy to the formal relationships connecting people with organisations and regimes. We could map people according to the nature and quality of the social relationships they form. Social-relationship maps would thus be adapted to log a whole range of social contacts, and hence provide a way of conceptualising social differentiation. For example, social relationships formed through work, forms of consumption, leisure activities and children's schools have a different character from social relationships formed through engagement with dispensers of social benefits, free school meals, social services, the police and agencies allocating social housing. Social relationships based on forms of violence, intimidation, raiding and competition have a different quality from those based on other more distant relationships of mutual respect or indifference. Social relationship maps of this sort would, of course, cross-cut simplistic notions of blackness, whiteness and so on; they would reveal subtleties in social circumstances. I suspect they would also reveal racialised concentrations and dispersals, broader patterns of social inequalities in which race and a raft of other social differences intersect. They would reveal which citizens deal with law-enforcement agencies and beauty therapists – who serves and who is served. They would expose the contributions of class and social position in race-making. We could discover which citizens living in the same neighbourhood live quite different or similar lives. Social-relationship maps would reveal fine social distinction between people; and suggest directions for political change to address them. Similarly, we could log the character of an area's social practices – the things people do. This, too, would reveal subtle social distinctions and we might expect social relationships and social practices to be closely interconnected. Race is made and displayed in a complex social process and the things I have suggested are ways of conceptualising this connect with politics.

Let's turn to pathways and movement and so disturb the notions of place as settled with the idea of places being constituted and threaded together in people's journeys. Lives are not fixed in place, although they compose place, but lived in journeys from one place to another. Space is etched by feet traversing it as pathways. This draws on Clifford's (1994) comments on the rhythms of dwelling and displacement. Small-scale, routine pathways are about jobs, home, shopping, facilities, social networks and social activities. Neighbourhoods are occupied and passed through, traversed or avoided on the basis of accumulated knowledge and habit. Who goes where and why – to borrow Hesse's (1999) and Massey's (1999) comments on migration – is socially significant. People's local maps reveal their use of an area and we can interrogate the rationale behind it. Where we walk – or drive – and why, contains important information about the operation of the world in which we live and its racial grammar, the forms of social practice to which race gives rise. Montmogery's (2004) research on black middle class parents' routes through Los Angeles neighbourhoods, threading together social resources and servicing social relationships on behalf of their children, grounds the kind of mapping I am suggesting with an example. Neighbourhoods may be used for cheaper housing, but avoiding certain parks, schools and children, parents navigate routes through an area, selectively assembling its resources and opportunities in self-production. This both logs and produces race and the forms of social practice and journeys to which race gives rise. This is a step beyond indices of segregation, which are traditionally used to reveal the racing of place, and which fail to include routes and movement; significant aspects of race's dynamism and production that should be included in its theorisation.

Bigger journeys, connecting locales within nation-states or traversing nation state boundaries in global movement, can also be mapped along the lines just suggested. The advantage of the approach I suggest is precisely its macro/micro application, particularly its connection with global dimensions of race. Migration routes (and circumstances) provide important information on the racial grammar of globalisation – the forms of social practice to which race gives rise on a global scale – and which Massey suggests (1999) reveal globalisation's deep social (racial) inequalities. Scholars have long suspected that the racial geography of globalisation is partly configured through the routes carved by mercantilism and empire (Winant, 1994: 271; Hesse, 1999: 127–129). MacGaffey and Bazenguissa-Ganga's (2000: 29–46) study of Congolese traders operating between Kinshasa and Brussels and Brazaville and Paris show how old routes are reactivated by new forms of global trading and social relationships. Their research reveals who goes where and why, on these particular routes. Traders trade African goods to migrant communities in Europe and designer, European-produced goods in Central Africa. Race is made in particular ways through these routes, as post-colonial migrants work their considerable resources and social relationships around new connections and schemes for making money. Under-development no longer underwrites, if indeed it ever did, the osmotic gradients of migration from less to more developed regions. The racial maps of contemporary globalisation are more complex. Sassen's (1990) research on the sources of migration to the US from Korea and similar locations shows that off-shoring and direct investment form important bridges between sending and receiving nations.

GLOBAL MIGRATION

Migration is only one place in which to examine race's global resonance. But given that migration is high on the political agenda of most nation-states, this is an important issue in its own right. The enlargement of the European Union (EU) to include Eastern European states sparked a lively political debate about European nations' capacities to absorb difference, and about rights and obligations, as asylum seekers are passed between nations and repatriated while Europe plans 'holding centres' in Albania. The US struggles with its Mexican border and the competing priorities of cheap labour and citizenship, while scrutinising its Northern boarder and approaching aircraft for terrorists. All countries, not just developed ones, are concerned with asylum seekers. Botswana, Mozambique and South Africa cope with Zimbabweans displaced by the collapse of agriculture and hyper-inflation. Those displaced by conflict and political persecution escape over the nearest border. As migration is such an important issue and because the political debates it prompts draw heavily on race (and ethnicity), I want to explore this a bit further in making an argument about the merits of theorising race as race-production. I also want to show the kinds of research agendas that might be developed around migration, particularly from Hesse's (1999) and Massey's (1999) arguments that we need to know who goes where and in what circumstances – ideas I have developed in my research on British lifestyle[5] migrants and South and South East Asian serving–class[6] migrants in Hong Kong. This is research particularly concerned with the circumstances of different migrants and migrations and offers, I think, a useful route into the maze of migration's racial grammar.

Tracking who goes where is complicated because not all countries collect statistics about arrivals, and still fewer count departures. Despite these limitations, mapping this data on a global scale would provide an overall picture of migration flows, identifying where people come from and where they go. We could thus determine whether migration had a distinctive racial grammar on the basis of empirical research. Scaling down a level we could then investigate the conduits that operate trans-nationally connecting people with places of new settlement and disconnecting them from old ones. Are these job opportunities, social relationships, lifestyle changes? Migration theory assumes that jobs and rational choice theory account for migration flows, but is this in fact the case? And how do we account for differences in who goes and who stays between people in the same circumstances? Scaling down again, and working within the systems of migration identified through world-wide mapping of movement, biographical research can identify fine differences in migration circumstances and topographies. My research in Hong Kong investigates (biographically) circumstances of departure and arrival for a range of different migrants. Serving-class migrants like Filipino maids and bar girls have substantially different circumstances of departure and arrival than British lifestyle migrants. Filipino maids leave so they can feed their children and send them to school. British migrants leave to earn more money or to live a more exciting life, in the sun. Filipino departure is calibrated by necessity. Circumstances of arrival include things like visas as well as friendship and family networks and employment and other opportunities. Filipino visas are tied to working as a maid and living with employers as well as being returned to the Philippines every two years, conditions which make it impossible to establish Hong Kong residence. British migrants can do a range of jobs and accumulate residence-status. Circumstances of arrival, of course, open onto conditions of new settlement and so the comments made above about the routes people carve connecting places in their everyday journeys apply to migrants, and reveal substantial differences between lives, too. White Britishness and Filipino-ness are made in migration and new settlement: race-making, and the ways in which this is cross-cut by the production of ethnicity in this example, is about social relationships, social (spatially calibrated) social practices, relationships between people and between people and places. White Britishness preserves and develops its accumulated advantages in migration to Hong Kong and to other places too. Migration works to produce race (and ethnicity) on a global scale in unequal terms demanding closer attention and research by race theorists. Race theorists in Britain have been slow to engage with migration since the obvious, seventies' connection between blackness, empire and immigration control was overwritten by the complexities of human mobility. Britain's migrants are no longer from its empire and frameworks centred on multiple forms of exclusion, into which the exclusion of immigrants neatly fit, no longer hold. Instead, migrants come from all countries and many of them are white. The US relationship to migration is similarly muddy and complicated. Hence we need new ways of theorising race that allow us to investigate multiple migration systems and micro-circumstances and expose patterns of racialisation.

CONCLUSION

In this chapter I have reviewed dominant trajectories of race theory, acknowledging differences, similarities and interconnections on both sides of the Atlantic. I have briefly explored current race writing and theorisation offering new initiatives and directions. These challenge dominant trends in race theory, which are overtheorised and divorced from empirical research and political engagement, at a time when political action is urgently needed. Building on exciting initiatives provided by contemporary race scholars, I have proposed a materialist conception of race that focuses on race-making. Race production, as I have demonstrated throughout this chapter, results from the routine actions and spatial contexts in which people comport themselves in everyday life. Approaching race in this way has a number of advantages. It highlights the significance of routine action. The routine has escaped analytical attention, as the spotlight focused on extreme expressions of racism and violence. Overt expressions of racism and racial violence exercised in white extremism, for example, are just one of whiteness' tactics. More sinister is the subtle centring of white existence, supplying the normative gaze and its racialised judgement, released in the production of whiteness itself. The approach I have outlined reveals the mechanisms of race production, and its dialogical operation. The racial production of self and otherness resonate unequally with regimes; this is the problem. White subjectivities are not inherently problematic; they are (unevenly) circumstantially problematic, in dialogue with white-dominated, regime-sanctioned, versions of racialised otherness, and in dialogue with non-whiteness. African American subjectivities, for example, are also circumstantially problematic. They are problematic in dialogue with white, European American subjectivities and the regimes sustaining them. Difference is dialogical and it furnishes (race) material articulated and activated in the production of social inequalities. This reiterates the (British) 1960s idea, that it's not race or racial difference that is problematic, but racial inequalities. I then take this a stage further, by exposing the production of race for providing the material for racial inequalities. It is the capacity of race to operate in this way, in furnishing the material substance of racial inequalities that is problematic. I show in this chapter, how race matters, and is made into matter, in space and through people and their activities and social relationships. The approach I suggest, then, has the added advantage of simultaneously foregrounding individual and systemic dimensions of race for analytic/political attention. Moreover, and this is its third advantage, it does so in ways that are open to political action in (small or more extensive) regime changes as well as in individual action. Race, then, becomes something we all contribute to, matters over which we have some control, over which we exercise agency and political decision-making. Fourth, the materialist approach I suggest incorporates global, as well as micro-dimensions of race-making. This is vital because race clearly operates on a global, as well as a national and a micro scale and needs to be so theorised. In an era of heightened mobilities, it is important to (re)connect race theory with migration and with new research agendas concerned with how migration operates, globally, biographically. Finally, the approach I suggest provides realistic and complex accounts of race, shaped through the intersections of multiple forms of social differentiation with which race coheres, based on empirical investigation of the social world. I am arguing that race should be theorised in 'positional' terms so that we end up with a scatter-graph of social circumstances: a fragmentation, not of identities, but social, spatially expressed, positions and circumstances. Of particular interest are the ways in which racially and ethnically conceived identifiers are distributed on these 'maps' of social circumstances. This, too, exposes how race works and makes it an actionable target of social reform. Race matters and is made into matter; it is concrete and part of who we are and what we do in the world. It is embedded in regimes, in social structures and inside people, traded and worked up in the dialogues between people conceived in racial terms, and in the dialogues between subjectivities and regimes. This is how we should theorise race, on the basis of social research, and in ways that support political action aimed at reducing and then eliminating its use as a resource in building social inequalities.

NOTES

1. The terms race and ethnicity have separate intellectual histories in sociology (race) and anthropology (ethnicity) and political commitments. While they do not mean the same thing – for intelligent discussion of ethnicity, see *Amit* (1996) and Verdery (1994) – they often operate in tandem and when I write race I am also writing about ethnicity, hopefully in a way which is less clumsy than always using both terms.

2. Deflecting from race to racism was itself the outcome of a political argument, in that this meant it was not race itself that was seen as significant but the system of social inequalities it supported. The meaning of race, as something supporting these inequalities, of course remained an object of intellectual inquiry and theorisation.

3. Theories of globalisation are diverse and the term is used here to indicate networks connecting distant locations and time space compression (Held and McGrew, 2004).

4. Place and space are not the same and Doreen Massey (1994) provides an excellent account of their differences. Broadly, space is the more general category from which places are made in more specific terms. In specifying a particular space, a neighbourhood, a building, we get place, a space with a specific set of identities.

5. I am using this term lifestyle migrant loosely to refer to those who weave together bits of what they 'need' or demand in life from different places, and who use this form of *bricolage* to think about belonging as the satisfaction of needs. Lifestyle migrants do not 'need' to move, they seek a change of place in order to upgrade their circumstances: they are economic migrants. Need is a problematic concept. You could say that even refugees do not *need* to move. Many stay put and suffer the consequences. But the concept of *need* has a different valency in their lives, which are organised by more basic forms of survival. All forms of migration ultimately bleed into each other as Clifford (1994) suggests.

6. This term is also being used loosely to refer to those whose migration status and other factors mark and maintain them in serving capacities as waiters, domestic helpers and so on, so that they have a profoundly unequal but symbiotic relationship with those who rely on their services. See Knowles and Harper (2009).

REFERENCES

Alexander, C. and Alleyne, B. (2002) 'Introduction: Framing difference: Racial and Ethnic Studies in Twenty-First Century Britain', *Ethnic and Racial Studies*, 25 (4): 541–551.

Alexander, C. (2005) 'Embodying Violence: "Riots", Dis/order and the Private Lives of "the Asian gang"', in C. Alexander and C. Knowles (eds) *Making Race Matter*. London: Palgrave.

Ali, S. (2005) 'Uses of the Exotic: Body, Narrative, Mixedness', in C. Alexander and C. Knowles (eds) *Making Race Matter*. London: Palgrave.

Amit-Talai, V. (1996) 'The Minority Circuit: Identity Politics and the Professionalisation of Ethnic Activism' in Vered Amit-Talai and Caroline Knowles (eds) *Resituating Identities: The Politics of Race, Ethnicity & Culture*, Peterborough: Broadview Press. pp. 89–114.

Anderson, K.J. (1991) *Vancouver's China Town*. Kingston: McGill-Queens University Press.

Back, Les and Solomos, J (2000) (eds) *Theories of Race and Racism*, London: Routledge.

Back, Les and Ware, Vron (2001) *Out of Whiteness*, Chicago: University of Chicago Press.

Banton, M. and Harwood, J. (1975) *The Race Concept*. Newton Abbott: David and Charles.

Banton, M. (1983) *Racial and Ethnic Competition*. Cambridge: Cambridge University Press.

Bottero, W. (2005) *Social Stratification*. London: Routledge.

Bowser, B. (1995) (ed.) *Racism and Anti-Racism in World Perspective*. Thousand Oaks: Sage.

Braman D. (1999) '*Of Race and Immutability*' *UCLA* Law Review 46. pp. 1375–1463.

Bulmer, M. and Solomos, J. (2004) (eds) *Researching Race and Racism*. London: Routledge pp. 1–15.

Burgess, E. (1967) 'The Growth of the City: An Introduction to a Research Project' in R.E. Park, M. Burgess and R.D. McKenzie (eds) *The City*. Chicago: University of Chicago Press [originally published 1925].

Cambridge, A. and Feuchtwang, S. (1990) (eds) *Antiracist Strategies*. Aldershot: Avebury.

Cambridge, A. and Feuchtwang, S. (eds) (1992) *Where You Belong*. Aldershot: Avebury.

Carby, H. (1982) 'White Woman Listen! Black Feminism and the Boundaries of Sisterhood' in Centre for Contemporary Cultural Studies *The Empire Strikes Back*. London: Hutchinson.

Clifford, J. (1994) 'Diasporas', *Cultural Anthropology*, 9 (3): 302–338.

Conyers, James L, (1999) (ed) *Black Lives: Essays in African American Biography*, New York: Armonk.

Cox, O.C. (1948) *Class, Caste and Race*. New York and London: Modern Reader Paperbacks.

Cross, M. and Keith, M. (1993) 'Racism and the Post Modern City' in M. Cross & M. Keith (eds) *Racism, the City and the State*. London: Routledge. pp. 1–30.

Davis, Olga Idriss (1999) 'Life 'aint been no crystal stair: the rhetoric of autobiography in black female slave narratives'. In Conyers, James L, (ed) *Black Lives: Essays in African American Biography*, New York: Armonk. pp. 151–59.

de Certeau, M. (1989) *The Practice of Everyday Life*. Berkeley: Los Angeles.

Eade, J. (1997) 'Reconstructing Places' in J. Eade (ed.) *Living the Global City*. London: Routledge. pp. 127–45.

Farrar, M. (1997) 'Migrant Spaces and Settlers' Time' in S. Westwood and J. Williams (eds) *Imagining Cities*. London: Routledge. pp. 104–24.

Feuchtwang, S. (1982) 'Occupational Ghettos', *Economy and Society*, 11 (3): 251–291.

Farris, R.E.L and Dunham, H.W. (1965) *Mental Disorders in Urban Areas: An Ecological Study of Schizophrenia and Other Psychoses*. Chicago: University of Chicago Press [originally published in 1939].

Featherstone M and Lash, Scott, 'Introduction' in Featherstone, M. Lash, S and Robertson, M (eds) *Global Modernities,* London: Routledge. pp. 1–23.

Frankenberg, R. (2004) 'On Unsteady Ground: Crafting and Engaging in the Critical Study of Whiteness' in M. Bulmer and J. Solomos (eds) *Researching Race and Racism*. London: Routledge.

Frankenberg, Ruth (2004) *White Woman Race Matters*, Minneapolis: University of Minnesota Press.

Gallagher, Charles, A (2003a) *Rethinking the Colour Line: Readings in Race and Ethnicity*, New York: McGraw Hill.

Gallagher, C. (2003a) 'Playing the White Ethnic card: Using Ethnic Identity to Deny Contemporary Racism' in A.W. Doane and E. Bonilla-Silva (eds) *White Out: The Continuing Significance of Racism*. New York: Routledge. pp. 22–37.

Gallagher, C. (2003b) 'Color-Blind Privilege: The Social and Political Functions of Erasing the Color Line in Post Race America', *Race, Gender and Class*, 10 (4): 22–37.

Goldberg, D.T. (2002) *The Racial State*. London: Routledge.

Gilroy, Paul (1987) *There Aint No Black in the Union Jack: The Cultural Politics of Race and Nation*, Chicago: University of Chicago Press.

Gilroy, P (1993) *The Black Atlantic: Modernity and Double Consciousness*, Cambridge Mass: Harvard University Press.

Guaratnam, Y. and Lewis, G. (2001) 'Racialising Emotional Labour and Emotionalising Racialised Labour', *Journal of Social Work Practice*, 2: 131–148.

Hall, S. (1992) 'New Ethnicities' in J. Donald and A. Rattansi (eds) *'Race', Culture and Difference.* London: Sage.

Held, D. and McGrew, A. (2004) (eds) *The Global Transformations Reader.* London: Polity.

Herzfeld, M. (1992) *The Social Production of Indifference: Exploring the Symbolic Roots of Western Bureaucracy.* Oxford: Berg.

Hesse, B. (1999) 'Reviewing the Western Spectacle: Reflexive Globalization through the Black Diaspora' in A. Brah, M. Hickman and M. Mac an Ghaill (eds) *Global Futures: Migration, Environment and Globalization.* London: Macmillan.

Kettle, M. and Hodges, L. (1982) *Uprising: The Police, The People and the Riots in Britain's Cities.* London: Pan Books.

Knowles, C. (2003) *Race and Social Analysis.* London: Sage.

Knowles, C. and Harper, D. (2009) *Hong Kong: Migrant Lives, Landscapes and Journeys.* Chicago: University of Chicago Press.

Lefebvre, H. (1996) *The Production of Space.* Oxford: Blackwell.

Levi, P. (2000) *The Drowned and the Saved.* London: Abacus.

Mac an Ghaill, M. (1999) *Contemporary Racisms and Ethnicities.* Buckingham: Open University Press.

MacGaffey, J. and Bazenguissa-Ganga, R. (2000) *Congo – Paris.* Bloomington: Indian University Press.

Mason, J. (1996) 'Street fairs: Social space, social performance', *Theatre Journal*, 48: 301–319.

Massey, D. (1994) *Place, Space and Gender.* Cambridge: Polity.

Massey, D. (1999) 'Imagining Globalization: Power Geometries of Time-Space', in A. Brah, M. Hickman and M. Mac an Ghaill (eds) *Global Futures: Migration, Environment and Globalization.* London: Macmillan.

Miles, R. (1989) *Racism.* London: Routledge.

Miles, R. and Torres, R. (1996) 'Does "Race" Matter? Trans Atlantic Perspectives of Racism after "Race Relations"' in V. Amit-Talai and C. Knowles (eds) *Resituating Identities: The Politics of Race, Ethnicity and Culture.* Peterborough: Broadview Press.

Modood, Tariq (1988) *"Black" Racial Equality and British Asian Identity,* New Community, 14(3): 397–404.

Montgomery, A. (2004) '"Living in Pockets": The Spatial Division of Public Goods and parenting Burdens in Los Angeles' ASA Conference Presentation.

Moore, R. (1975) *Racism and Black Resistance in London.* London: Pluto Press.

Park, R.E. (1967) 'The City: Suggestions for the Investigation of Human Behaviour in an Urban Environment' in R.E. Park, M. Burgess and R.D. McKenzie (eds) *The City.* Chicago: University of Chicago Press [originally published 1925].

Parmar, Pratibha (1982) '*Gender, Race and Class: Asian Women in Resistance*' in CCCS The Empire Strikes Back: Race and Racism in 70s Britain, London: Hutchinson. pp. 236–275.

Rex, J. (1970) *Race Relations in Sociological Theory.* London: Weidenfeld and Nicolson.

Rex, J. and Moore, R. (1967) *Race, Community and Conflict: A Study of Sparkbrook.* London: Oxford University Press for the Institute of Race Relations.

Sassen, S. (1991) *The Global City.* Princeton: Princeton University Press.

Sassen, S. (1990) 'US immigration policy towards Mexico in a global economy', *Journal of International Affairs*, 43 (2): 369–383.

Sassen, Saskia (1996) *Losing Control: Sovereignty in an Age of Globalization,* New York: Columbia University Press.

Shotter, J. (1997) 'The social construction of our inner selves', *Journal of Constructionist Psychology*, 10: 7–24.

Sivanandan, A (1976) *Race, Class and the State: The Black Experience in Britain.* London: Institute of Race Relations.

Smith, M.P. and Torallo, B. (1993) 'The Post-Modern City and the Social Construction of Ethnicity in California' in M. Cross and M. Keith (eds) *Racism, the City and the State.* London: Routledge.

Smith, S.J. (1993) 'Residential Segregation and the Politics of Racialization', in M. Cross and M. Keith (eds) *Racism, the City and the State.* London: Routledge.

Shawn Michelle Smith (2004) *Photography on the color line*; WEB Du bois, Race and Visual Culture, Duke University Press.

Solomos, J. and Back, L. (1995) *Race, Politics and Social Change.* London: Routledge.

St Louis, B. (2002) 'Post-race/post-politics? Activist Intellectualism and the Reification of Race', *Ethnic and Racial Studies*, 25 (4): 552–675.

Taylor, C. (1989) *Sources of the Self.* Cambridge: Cambridge University Press.

Twine, F.W. (2006) 'Visual ethnography and racial theory: Analysing Family Photograph Albums as Archives of Interracial Intimacies', *Ethnic and Racial Studies*, 29 (3): 487–511

Vera, H. and Feagin, J.R. (2004) 'The Study of Racist Events' in M. Bulmer and J. Solomos (eds) *Researching Race and Racism.* London: Routledge.

Verdery, K. (1994) 'Ethnicity, Nationalism and State-Making' in H. Vermeulen and C. Govers (eds) *The Anthropology of Ethnicity: Beyond Ethnic Groups and Boundaries.* Amsterdam: Het Spinhuis.

Wilson, W.J. (1999) 'When Work Disappears: New Implications for Race and Urban Poverty in the Global Economy', *Ethnic and Racial Studies*, 22 (3): 479–499.

Winant, H. (2000) 'The Theoretical Status of the Concept Race' in L. Back and J. Solomos (eds) *Theories of Race and Racism: A Reader.* London: Routledge.

Winant, H. (1994) *Racial Conditions.* Minneapolis: University of Minnesota Press.

Studying 'Race' and Ethnicity: Dominant and Marginalised Discourses in the Critical North American Case

Joe R. Feagin and Eileen O'Brien

Looking across the 'modern' world, a century ago W. E. B. Du Bois (1903 [1989]: 10) penned the famous line, the 'problem of the twentieth century is the problem of the colour line—the relation of the darker to the lighter races of men in Asia and Africa, in America and the islands of the sea'. Although the idea of 'race' as a biologically driven notion came into being long before Du Bois was writing, the century since his comment has clearly been the period during which most scholarship known today as 'race and ethnic studies' has been undertaken.

   The body of social science scholarship that has analysed 'racial relations' cannot be understood outside of the context of unequal racial-power relations that have characterised the world within which this scholarship developed. By the eighteenth century, a dominant white racial framing, with its racial ideology, inferiorised darker-skinned peoples in order to justify their colonisation and exploitation.[1] This rationalising white racial frame soon became very powerful in the minds of most self-defined 'white' people, and eventually in the minds of many colonised people of colour as well. Western scholars, especially from dominant groups, took centuries to divest themselves, even in part, of that dominant racial framing and ideology and to hone the critical tools necessary to question

deeply the deeply racialised socioeconomic and political realities of their societies. As a result, the story we tell of the development of racial and ethnic scholarship necessarily weaves dominant discourses and marginalised (resistance)
discourses, which relate to one other across the racial power barrier that has long
separated them.

This racial power inequality has for centuries allowed whites, especially those
in critical white elites, to develop stereotyped and obscured understandings of
marginalised racial groups whom they have historically exploited and dominated.
Due to great societal socioeconomic power, these distorted framings and understandings have typically passed for objective knowledge throughout most periods we analyse. Attempting to participate in the public sphere from behind the
imposed colour line, marginalised groups have been limited in the types of
knowledge they advanced about themselves and the dominant group, for their
own safety. As power imbalances shift to allow relatively greater freedom of
expression, however, we see over time the previously suppressed discourses
emerge, often in direct critique of dominant discourses that distort the experiences of people of colour. In each period we analyse, while dominant scholars
advanced particular models of racial–ethnic studies, scholars and activists from
marginalised groups often advanced much more critical analyses of those same
racial–ethnic realities.

Over this long era, there were undoubtedly many insightful social analysts of
racial–ethnic matters about whom we do not now know because those most bru-
talised by oppression – such as people of African descent – were barred from the
tools of writing, publishing and communication long held by powerful white
oppressors. The colour line still shapes what we currently advance as the state of
the field of 'racial and ethnic relations' today. Indeed, a major reason for this
chapter is to focus on people of African descent as the main group of contributors
to resistance or counter-framing discourses. This field of racial and ethnic
research and its major publishers have only recently acknowledged other (e.g.,
Latin American and Asian colonised peoples) groups that have contributed to
the resistance discourses. While our effort here is necessarily incomplete, we
provide the reader with insights into racial–ethnic matters that have come from
people of colour who overcame great obstacles to provide significant concepts
and empirical data for analytical use today. We do this by selecting key periods
where this contrast between dominant thinkers (who provide analyses that often
legitimise the racial status quo) and marginalised thinkers (who often counter
critique it) is most pronounced.

'SCIENTIFIC RACISM' AS A RATIONALE FOR SLAVERY

Few social scientists or popular analysts are willing to discuss the fact that
the 'modern world' arose on the back of a sustained, coercive and bloody
superexploitation of indigenous peoples in Africa and the Americas. European

capitalism and colonialism began just before the rise of the Atlantic slavery system, but took on their modern globalising and superexploitative wealthgenerating forms in concert with African and other indigenous enslavement and exploitation across the expanding north and south Atlantic economies. In this chapter, we note well a key dimension of this capitalistic colonialism, one that white social-scientists historically have not emphasised – the highly *racialised* reality of this brutal colonization of the Atlantic basin. The major groups that became central to early European accumulation of wealth in a globalising colonising system were *non-European*, and each of the latter soon were denigrated ('blackened') in an increasingly developed white racial framing of colonialism and the colonial societies thereby created.

With good reason we focus on the case of the United States. The US case is not just historically important, but since the sixteenth century constitutes a central case in creating European and European American wealth. The United States is a critical example of how European capitalism and colonialism were intertwined and heavily racialised from their inception. By focusing on this important case, we examine how racial framing and ideology influence knowledges produced in the modern world, in this case, the field of race and ethnic studies, as well as how oppressed peoples and marginalised scholars have contested those knowledges.

Before the mid-nineteenth century, European and US scholars did not think critically or in a systematic social science manner about this social world in which they lived. By that time, centuries of racialised enslavement for them to study had passed. England, France, the Netherlands and other European nations had colonised peoples in Africa, Asia, Central America and South America in a slavery or semi-slavery pattern. The concept of 'race' for people to study today exists because of this massive colonisation; European imperialists invented the concept of 'race' in rationalising oppressive exploits (Allen, 1994).

The first secular US intellectual and scientist, Thomas Jefferson, seems to have been the first major intellectual in the West to articulate at length a well-developed theory of the racial (biological) inferiority of African peoples, specifically African Americans, in his only book, *Notes on the State of Virginia* (1785 [1999]). Jefferson's influential analysis extended to readers overseas and averred that enslaved blacks were far inferior to whites in reason, imagination, and family sentiment, as well as in colour, beauty and odour. This rationalising racial framing and racist ideology grew out of the reality of many white American leaders (as well as many European leaders) holding Africans in slavery or being otherwise engaged in commerce in enslaved Africans or the agricultural products the latter produced (Feagin, 2006).

By the mid-nineteenth century, the dominant scientific figures in the West began to concern themselves systematically with societies around them; yet none was critical when it came to matters of 'race'. All accepted the 'scientific racism' of their day, a view dominating almost all social science until about the 1930s. Joseph Arthur de Gobineau (1970: 136), a very influential European intellectual writing on race in the nineteenth century, argued that whites were gifted 'with an energetic intelligence. … They have a remarkable, even extreme love of liberty, and are openly hostile to the formalism under which the Chinese are glad to vegetate, as well as the strict despotism which is the only way of governing the Negro'. De Gobineau's viciously racist writings made much use of American examples, especially black Americans, and his views soon migrated across the Atlantic to be used by US segregationists. They were widely used by European Nazis, including academics among them. Paul Broca, a French anatomist and founder of modern anthropology, was a leading thinker who measured head shapes, arguing that variations in shape were linked to racial differences. For most white physical and social scientists, the old white racial frame was much in evidence: Black skin still meant inferior intelligence, while white skin meant high intelligence, which they attempted to measure with their new scientific tools (Tucker, 1994: 23). By the late 1800s, a eugenics movement was spreading across the West, and leaders like Sir Francis Galton in England and Theodore Roosevelt in the United States opposed 'miscegenation' (a term coined by racist thinkers of the time) because it destroyed the racial 'purity' of the 'white race' (Higham, 1963: 96–152). Scientific racism encompassed, even celebrated, the notion of 'races' with different hereditary characteristics fitting into a natural hierarchy.

Yet from across the colour line, marginalised discourses have periodically emerged to challenge this biologically driven view of racial matters. Shortly after US intellectuals like Jefferson and James Madison – and European intellectuals like Immanuel Kant and G. W. F. Hegel – honed and extended an extensive antiblack, racist view of the world, early-nineteenth century African American thinkers like David Walker and Frederick Douglass developed and managed to publish a strong counter-perspective and framing of society that refuted much of this racist thought and pressed for real freedom and equality for Africans and African Americans. Prior to the Civil War's Thirteenth Amendment (1865) that officially freed enslaved African Americans, critical black abolitionists in the US and Europe researched and assessed well the effects of enslavement on those enslaved and their enslavers. A brilliant analysis of slavery and liberation from slavery was developed by formerly enslaved abolitionist, Frederick Douglass, whose lectures and writings offer a well developed sociological theory of oppression.

POST-SLAVERY RACIAL AND ETHNIC ANALYSES

After slavery was officially outlawed, first in Great Britain and much later in the United States, Western scholars grappled with the aftermath of incorporating peoples who had been barred from socioeconomic resources for centuries into the fabric of everyday social life. Analysts in both marginalised and dominant groups undertook studies that fall into two modes of thinking: (1) placing the onus of such incorporation onto members of previously excluded groups, or (2) placing the onus onto the dominant group that had oppressed them. The former approach is most often espoused by scholars from the dominant white group, while the latter, more critical approach is most often undertaken by scholars from marginalised groups of colour, though not exclusively. Analysis of scholarship in slavery's aftermath reveals clearly how a scholar's deep racial framing and ideological standpoint, coupled with power constraints under which one is operating, have a direct influence on the resultant knowledge.

By the late-nineteenth century, African American scholars like, the still active, Douglass and the younger Du Bois were among very few whose work countered the racism of leading white scientists and policymakers articulating racist views from political pulpits like the US Congress. Again, the ageing Douglass was on the cutting edge of the analysis of US racial matters. Before and after the Civil War, he (1999: 657–658) was the first serious analyst to place African Americans as the archetypal group in the development of white racist thought, law, and action in US society: 'Go where you will, you will meet with him [the black American]. ... To the statesman and philosopher he is an object of intense curiosity. ... Of the books, pamphlets, and speeches concerning him, there is literally, no end'. After the Civil War, under growing legal segregation (a type of neo-slavery), Douglass emphasised that African Americans had moved from slaves of individual white slaveholders to being the 'slaves of society' – a critical insight about the *systemic* character of racial oppression yet to be matched in much contemporary research.

After Douglass's death, W. E. B. Du Bois was the leading social scientist working with a deep structural analysis of US racial matters. He was the first trained (at Harvard) social scientist to develop a race-critical social science perspective for understanding the dynamics of racial oppression. Drawing on extensive research on slavery and antislavery rebellions, Du Bois cogently argued that without opportunities to create wealth (as their owners had done through them) African Americans could never prosper and be free. Researching the path-breaking *The Philadelphia Negro* (1998 [1899]), Du Bois shifted the focus from theorising about biological inferiority to the extensive racial discrimination that generated the unjustly deprived conditions under which African Americans lived.

While sociologist Emile Durkheim's *Suicide* (1897) has long been celebrated in social science as the first major empirical quantitative study, Du Bois's *The Philadelphia Negro* was published about the same time with equal attention to quantitative research methods, the first such book-length report on a systematic social science study of any urban community in the United States or overseas. Du Bois used data on black employment rates, wages, jobs and housing to show that antiblack discrimination involved more than oppression in the South. Black northerners were segregated out of good-paying jobs that allowed the white ethnic (many of them, new immigrant) groups to establish a major economic foothold in US cities. Discrimination was firmly grounded in economics because, although black urbanites were by then officially human beings under the US Constitution, theoretical equality meant nothing, since they could not participate fairly in sustenance-creating economic institutions.

Such pioneering analyses of what would later be known as *institutional* or *systemic racism*, produced by scholars from oppressed groups (or a few other black social scientists, including black women researchers, see Deegan, 1988), stand in stark contrast to the biologically based ways of racist thinking about racial group inequalities that characterised virtually all dominant scientific thinking in the United States and in Europe. If white mainstream scientists, including by 1900 many social scientists, had used their celebrated 'reason' and accepted Douglass's and Du Bois's well-reasoned and documented analyses, a radically different body of social science knowledge might have soon developed. What if these mainstream thinkers had turned the tools of the new biology or social science to the society-damaging peculiarities of most whites, to their apparent need to dominate the racialised others or pathological fear of those deemed racially inferior? Due to the imbalance of power in the relations of white and black Americans, critical analyses of the black thinkers could never have made it into the national public sphere. Yet, in numerous analyses written in this era by African American social scientists, such as Du Bois's 1910 essay 'The Souls of White Folk', later published in his book *Darkwater* (2003 [1920]), we observe that such critical questions apparently only existed in the minds of scholars of colour outside historically white institutions.

Beginning in the 1920s, US social scientists in the 'Chicago school of sociology' drew upon dominant paradigms to develop their well-known studies of race and ethnicity. In field studies, sociologist Robert E. Park (1950) and associates researched urban phenomena, including so-called slum and ghetto communities. In 1914, Park gave the first course on 'The Negro in America' by a white sociologist. Still, the otherwise racially liberal Park accepted some elements of the old scientific racism, for example, in suggesting that racial characteristics were 'innate biological interests' that determine the 'racial temperaments' characteristic of racial groups, with blacks viewed as having inferior characteristics to whites, indeed as the 'lady of the races' (Raushenbush, 1979: 67–84). In spite of acceptance of biologised stereotyping, Park was opposed to discrimination and viewed African Americans as eventually assimilating within mainstream institutions.

Observing Chicago's racial–ethnic mosaic, Park and his social science associates developed a stage theory of assimilation to explain processes by which immigrants (mainly of white-ethnic backgrounds) came to be incorporated into society. Well aware, like many US social scientists, of the global reality of US racial and ethnic contacts, they emphasised international migration in the creation of many such contacts. Park (1950) proposed a 'race-relations cycle' that involved stages: contact, competition, accommodation and assimilation. While this framework minimally accounted for the economic underpinnings of racial–ethnic exploitation by recognising that competition for jobs causes intergroup tensions, it proposes that eventually conflict subsides into accommodation and assimilation. Economic exploitation is only temporary because of unfamiliarity of incoming groups with dominant group ways. From this perspective, once the (typically white) immigrant group adjusts to the majority culture, economic inequality will soon disappear.

In contrast to this heavy accent by dominant social scientists on white ethnic groups and eventual assimilation, with its lingering scientific racism, several black and Jewish scholars managed to develop a much more critical approach to racial–ethnic issues in Western societies. During this era, black social scientists again led the way in studying the exclusion of Americans of colour from mainstream society, while white social scientists usually studied the inclusion of European immigrants into US society. Du Bois accented issues of US racism, in much sociological detail (e.g., Du Bois, 1920) and with an acutely honed orientation to the global context of such immigration. He assembled the first (internationally oriented) Pan-African Congress ever in 1919. Colonised peoples of African descent were thereby given an international voice and drew attention to their common racial oppression for a world audience. In the early 1900s, Du Bois also helped to create the National Association for the Advancement of Coloured People (NAACP), which drew on black scholarship to organise against US racism, an organisation that later became a model for black resistance to white oppression in a number of European countries.

In this era, Europe was experiencing growing racial oppression, much of it targeting Jews. The modern term *racism* appeared in a 1933 book of that title by the German Jewish scholar, Magnus Hirschfeld, who analysed well-scientific racists' notions about biologically determined 'races'. As Hirschfeld (1973 [1938]: 35–99, 266–318) saw it, German Nazis were successful in translating their racist ideology 'from theory into practice … with a ruthless consistency'. In its original meaning, *racism* thus entailed far more than racial prejudice and stereotyping; it included a racist framing and developed ideology of racial superiority and inferiority as well as racist practices in politics and even schemes for elimination of groups such as European Jews. During and after World War II, Jewish scholars, such as Ashley Montagu (1963) and T. W. Adorno and his associates begun in the 1940s (see below), accented the dangers of the ideological racism brought to the world's attention by German Nazis. Once again, the cross-Atlantic trade in ideas could be seen, this time anti-racist ideas. Germany's Adorno migrated to the United States and brought ideas about racial authoritarianism with him, and Hirschfeld's term 'racism' came to be used by increasing numbers of US scholars.

By the 1940s, scholars like Du Bois and Oliver Cromwell Cox were digging deeper into the character of US and overseas oppression of people of African origin. Both put US racism in international perspective. Though educated at the University of Chicago, Cox rejected what he saw as Park's weak racial analysis and developed the *first* book-length theory of racial oppression in the history of racial–ethnic studies. Considering the chicken–egg question of whether racial prejudice led to slavery or the reverse, Cox chose the latter in his pioneering book *Caste, Class and Race* (1948). To secure profit using this labour, chattel slavery was developed by white entrepreneurs and slaveholders, then rationalised ideologically using the most visible factor about Africans, skin colour.

Du Bois also used race-and-class lenses to look beyond racial oppression in the United States to its operation internationally. In his *The World and Africa* (1972

[1946]), whose social science insights are yet to be mainstreamed in racial–ethnic studies, Du Bois showed that the immense wealth Europeans gained from colonising Africa not only became the political-economic foundation of modern Europe, but came at a huge blood-price. As Africa was robbed of human and natural resources for European profit, Africans were left with the severe impact, including great impoverishment. Ironically, impoverishment became part of elite whites' rationalisation for the oppression they generated. People of African origin have long been painted by elite mythmakers and their rank-and-file followers in the West as lacking motivation and resourcefulness, but only because their resources have regularly been taken by colonisers. From the perspective of path-breaking scientists like Du Bois and Cox, modern racist ideology arises out of these imposed material conditions and the capitalist class's rationalisations of exploitation of darker-skinned peoples across the globe. Yet, it would take some time before this global economic framework would become recognised by mainstream social science, an unfortunate consequence of the marginalisation of scholars of colour in the society.

By the 1940s, in numerous countries, a wide gulf still existed between white colonisers or their descendants and oppressed people of colour on major socio-economic and political indicators. Official segregation, put in place in the United States soon after its Civil War, was still in operation. Until the 1940s, most social scientists, virtually all white, accepted scientific racism that viewed other peoples of colour as racially (biologically) inferior. Even where they examined situations of people of African descent, white scientists were cautious about challenging prevailing white-racist opinions. Still, with the growing scholarly and activist work examining oppression that was emanating from African American and Jewish scholars, mainstream scientists found it increasingly difficult to attribute racial differences to innate biological factors. By the 1940s and 1950s, a few white scholars were influenced to do more critical research on racism by the impact of Nazism, and by the work of black scholars and civil rights organisations. Growing numbers of whites in US elites were concerned about the negative US image overseas created by black lynchings and racial apartheid, an image aggressively circulated across the world's media by the Soviet Union (Feagin, 2000).

Given the racially conservative orientation of most white US social scientists, and the exclusion faced by black scholars in the United States (and Europe), unsurprisingly, the first comprehensive study of official racial segregation, the US case, was led by Swedish social scientist Gunnar Myrdal, who was funded by the Carnegie foundation. Once again the global character of racial oppression, and research on it, become clear. Prepared by Myrdal and his interdisciplinary team of white and black social scientists, *An American Dilemma* was a breakthrough in US and, indeed, Western social science. The scholars offered a detailed empirical analysis of discrimination facing African Americans, emphasising the US South. They provided a distinctive theoretical perspective accenting the contradiction between US ideals of liberty and the reality of extensive discrimination. Although grounded in an assimilation model of racial–ethnic relations, these scholars recognised that African Americans had not been able to reach the latter stages of the Park-type assimilation model – and not because of their own failings.

Yet, for all its pathbreaking research efforts and use of research (and even a few scholars) from the black anti-racist tradition, Myrdal and his social science colleagues did not assess how basic racial oppression was to the US politicaleconomic foundation. They accented instead a moral argument – racial discrimination represents a 'lag of public morals', a problem solved in principle but still being worked out in an ongoing assimilation process. Again, African American social scientists like Du Bois and Cox and humanities scholars like Ralph Ellison critiqued the limitations of an analysis that did not examine the economic-political foundation of oppression. As Ellison (1964: 313) noted, Myrdal actually accented a 'blueprint for a more effective exploitation of the South's natural, industrial and human resources'. While desegregation would free African Americans from extreme oppression, it would replace that with a more 'efficient and subtle manipulation of black and white relations' (Ellison, 1964: 314).

Also beginning in the late 1930s and 1940s, another social science group, led in part by the European refugee and Jewish scholar T. W. Adorno, undertook the first major sociopsychological study of racial prejudice in any country, *The Authoritarian Personality* (1950). Concerned about 'authoritarian personalities' linked to European and US Nazism, these social scientists developed innovative sociopsychological scales to measure racial prejudice, once again revealing the Atlantic trade in social science ideas on racial matters. They found that contemporary whites were intensely racist, views varying with conformity to the social milieu. This sociopsychological research soon led to a pioneering overview analysis by psychologist Gordon Allport, *The Nature of Prejudice* (1958), the first extensive conceptual treatment of racial–ethnic 'prejudice'. Allport continued the work of the Myrdal and Adorno groups by focusing on faulty reasoning processes that allow people to buy into stereotypical and prejudicial thinking about outgroups. Allport examined stereotypes and prejudices held about many racial–ethnic groups and urged the hypothesis that, the more equal-status contact people have across racial–ethnic lines, the less likely they are to hold prejudices about other groups. Like the Myrdal and Adorno groups, Allport broke with numerous other European and American social scientists, still holding to variations on scientific racism, by problematising dominant-group thought and behaviour, and his views soon travelled across the Atlantic to shape European thinking on racial and ethnic matters.

ASSIMILATION AND 'ETHNICITY' OR DISCRIMINATION AND 'RACE': RACIAL–ETHNIC PERSPECTIVES SINCE 1960

In recent decades, substantial analysis by mainstream scholars in the United States and in Europe has more or less continued in the Park tradition, with much attention given to ethnic groups, immigration and group assimilation. Influential sociologist Milton Gordon provided a still-used theoretical framework describing group-assimilation processes as centred in conformity-to-host-group pressures by new societal entrants. Gordon's (1964) authoritative typology recognises this conformity as occurring in regard to seven assimilation dimensions: cultural, structural, marital, identification, attitude-receptional, behaviour-receptional, and civic. He and his many US social science followers have applied this framework mainly to European immigrant groups, a common emphasis among scholars concerned with assimilation over the last few decades.

Since the 1960s, much racial–ethnic analysis has focused on migration and immigration. Emphasising ethnic groups like Jewish and Italian Americans, thus, sociologist Nathan Glazer and political scientist Daniel P. Moynihan (1965) questioned whether assimilation necessitates a complete melting of new groups into the dominant culture. They demonstrated that members of ethnic groups maintain ethnically distinct names, identities and primary group ties, even as they assimilate into dominant institutions. Andrew Greeley (1974) further developed a concept of 'ethnogenesis'. In most cases, he argued, there is a two-way adjustment process of dominant groups and new immigrant groups to each other rather than one-way conformity. Although still following an assimilationist approach, these scholars brought more agency into the adaptive responses of new racial and ethnic groups, a research strategy that took the latter's viable cultures seriously and rejected one-way assimilation models. Demonstrating continuing concern for international contexts of migration, Schermerhorn (1970) analysed major types of migration that generate racial–ethnic relations in all societies, suggesting a continuum from completely involuntary to completely voluntary migration.

Assimilation research accenting US immigrants and ethnicity is a major and continuing force in racial–ethnic research today. Building on the work of Gordon, sociologists Richard Alba and Victor Nee (1997) argue that Gordon's concept of core culture must be modified because cultures of immigrant groups have had an impact on that, especially in areas such as religion. Alba and Nee argue that skin colour may soon not be a barrier to structural assimilation; some US immigrant groups of colour may, like earlier white groups, be allowed by those whites in power to integrate completely into white-dominated institutions. Alejandro Portes (1995) and Min Zhou (1997) show that the outcomes of adaptation by immigrants to host institutions vary; some immigrants or their children remain confined to lower economic rungs of the societal ladder while others experience rapid economic development. Experiences of immigrant groups include upward and downward mobility – and thus variable ('segmented') assimilation.

In recent decades, scholars have varied considerably in their use of the key terms 'race' and 'ethnicity'. Anthropologist W. Lloyd Warner (Warner and Srole, 1945) was apparently the first to make significant use of the term 'ethnicity'; he distinguished ethnic groups as groups principally defined by cultural differences. These differed from racial groups socially defined principally by physical differences. Since then, numerous scholars (e.g., Pierre van den Berghe, 1967) have accented this narrower usage of the concept of 'ethnic groups' for those socially distinguished mainly in terms of their cultural characteristics, with 'racial groups' referring to those for whom phenotype is accented. This latter US tradition accents, as does that of numerous British sociologists (Banton, 1983; Rex, 1983), the central importance of power and resource inequalities in shaping societal designations of 'race' or ethnicity. From this perspective, various social groups accent ethnicity for relatively positive and group-inclusive reasons. In contrast, 'race' is accented by dominant groups seeking to oppress another group, thus rationalizing domination in racial terms.

Approaching 'race' as a social and political construction is a direct, albeit late, response to the long tradition of African American scholarship. Since the black civil rights movement of the 1960s, with its panoply of institutional-racism scholars (see below), much US racial–ethnic research has paid attention to the social construction of 'race'. Sociologists Michael Omi and Howard Winant (1994), as well as social historian Ronald Takaki (1990), have argued cogently that historically 'race' has been a fluid social and governmental construction that flexes over time in ways suiting the interests of those whites holding political and economic power. Such scholarship shows clearly the break with biologically driven theories of older scientific racism.

Nonetheless, some contemporary scholars (mostly white) have preferred to use 'ethnic group' and 'ethnicity' in the more-recent umbrella sense to cover all racial, ethnic and religious groups. Like many scholars since the 1960s, Gordon (1964; see also Barth, 1969) defined an ethnic group as one distinguished by race, religion, or national origin. Today, numerous social science and humanities scholars (e.g., Werner Sollors, 1989) catalogue religious, national origin and racial groups under the broad umbrella-phrase 'ethnic group'. Reviewing this generic usage of ethnic group, one sees that most such analysts give far more attention to issues of assimilation and immigration, and thus to the characteristics and adaptation of European-based or lighter-skinned (ethnic) groups than to darker-skinned groups and the racial oppression they face. For many, the use of ethnicity as the primary concept operates in order to play down the Western history of slavery, legal segregation and contemporary racism.

An alternative 'critical race' tradition (see below) accents slavery, official segregation and contemporary discrimination as central to Western history. Begun by Douglass and carried forward by black social scientists like Du Bois and Cox, this counter-racism research is best represented today in much 'critical race' theory and research by numerous black, Latino and white social scientists (Collins, 1991; Bonilla-Silva, 1997; Feagin, 2000), who pay much more attention to this history of racial oppression across the globe. In recent research work on US racism (see Feagin and O'Brien, 2003), the understanding of 'race' and racial groups as socially defined and linked to a long history of racial oppression has been much more satisfactory for empirical research on racial realities.

THE IMPACT OF THE CIVIL RIGHTS MOVEMENT ON SCHOLARLY RESEARCH

One force behind the emergence of critical analyses of contemporary racism is the civil rights movement, which expanded dramatically from the 1950s to the 1970s. New organisations like the Student Nonviolent Coordinating Committee (SNCC) emerged, and older organisations like the NAACP continued major legal struggles against racial discrimination, with the notable success of *Brown v. Board of Education* (1954) and other lawsuits against official segregation from the 1930s to the 1960s. Social scientists like Kenneth Clark (consulted for *Brown*) were asked to testify about the effects of racial segregation and other discrimination.

No serious social scientist could ignore the movement and its emancipatory impact. However, a great many social scientists were reluctant to change their thinking away from the old white-racist framing. Some withdrew from research in the area of racial and ethnic relations, while others worked to reinvigorate the old racist system. Indeed, as late as the 1980s, one social science survey (Reynolds, 1999: 141–145) found that *half* of all physical anthropologists still supported the idea of real, biologically differentiated 'races', compared to some 29 percent of cultural anthropologists, 40 percent of psychologists and 34 percent of sociologists surveyed. While the majority of social scientists no longer accepted the old biological racism, a significant minority still did. From the 1960s to the last decade, University of California social scientist, Arthur Jensen (1969: 1–123), received much attention for arguing that so-called 'intelligence test' data show that black Americans have less intelligence than white Americans. Biological determinism was central to the book, *The Bell Curve* (1990), by psychologist Richard Herrnstein and political commentator Charles Murray, who made a similar argument about white, black, and Latino 'intelligence test' data. Supported by arch-conservative groups like the American Enterprise Institute, Herrnstein and Murray suggested not only that their views were privately shared by many educated whites but also that such data brought into question the old ideal of equality (Stefancic and Delgado, 1996: 34).

Though most social scientists today no longer accept this sort of scientific racism, many still view African American families and communities as culturally inferior. Europeans and European Americans are seen as culturally modern, while black people (and other people of colour) in all countries are viewed as culturally primitive – a view US social scientists have long shared with European social scientists. During the 1960s, for example, political scientist (later, US Senator) Daniel P. Moynihan (1965) wrote a US government report reviewing demographic data on the poverty faced by black Americans. Theorising about causes, he argued for a self-imposed 'tangle of pathology' that supposedly existed in impoverished black communities. White patriarchal families were his standard, and he thus faulted what he saw as the pathological values of black parents as a major cause of negative family and community outcomes, mostly ignoring the impact of continuing racial oppression in those communities.

Moynihan later became a key advisor to President Richard Nixon, whose administration signaled a white conservative resurgence politically and intellectually. Since the Nixon era (1969–1974) all Republican administrations in the United States have, to varying degrees, pressed to end the government anti-discrimination policies of the 1960s, including affirmative action and school desegregation. Conservative politicians have accented the allegations of Americans of colour being responsible for their difficulties because of 'broken' families and a poor work ethic – a blaming-the-victim frame going back to slaveholders like Jefferson. Recurringly, major social science advisors to US officials, such as Harvard's influential Samuel Huntington (1997: 28), have insisted that US whites as a group have held to the 'universal ideas and principles articulated in the founding documents by American leaders: liberty, equality, democracy, constitutionalism, liberalism, limited government, private enterprise'. From this perspective, whatever problems remain for Americans of colour are mainly their responsibility.

A RENEWED ACCENT ON INSTITUTIONAL RACISM

However, breaking with this centuries-long white focus on cultures of people of colour as deficient, numerous intellectuals and activists in the 1960s civil rights movement celebrated black culture and identity ('black is beautiful'). They also resuscitated the critical idea of institutional racism, drawing on earlier African American thinkers like Du Bois. Activist Stokely Carmichael (later, Kwame Ture) and historian Charles Hamilton's powerful book *Black Power* (1967) articulated this scholarly perspective. This well-documented book accented concepts of internal colonialism and institutional racism – thereby showing systemic, not individual, antiblack prejudice and discrimination as responsible for racial inequality across the globe. Accenting the centrality of US racism to world racism, the great Caribbean scholar of the Africa diaspora, C. L. R. James (1993: 201), argued strongly that the oppressive situation of African Americans is the number one problem of racism in the modern world. For, if the problem of racism could not be solved in the United States, it could not be solved anywhere, because it was similar to oppression of African peoples in other societies.

The civil rights movement and its street-wise intellectuals had a major impact on social science. A rare critical white sociologist, Robert Blauner (1972), honed and expanded the increasingly influential concept of 'internal colonialism', making use of the sociological lens Du Bois had developed to analyse racial exploitation across the globe. Just as European imperial powers had used cheap labour in colonised lands, so the United States continued this colonial pattern for racially defined groups in its rural areas and cities. Slavery and legal segregation created an internally exploited colony of black Americans, and the labour, land, and other resources of groups such as Mexican Americans and Native Americans were also exploited by the US capitalist class in related versions of internal colonialism. Several scholars (e.g., Feagin and Hahn, 1973) showed how this pervasive internal colonialism triggered substantial anti-colonial resistance, such as hundreds of urban black revolts in the 1960s and 1970s. Internal colonialism and institutional racism models differ sharply from mainstream racial and ethnic scholarship, which has to this day mostly refused to make central this resistance to racial oppression.

Extending ideas from the black tradition, especially from Black Power theorists of the civil rights movement, by the 1980s social scientists like Molefi Asante (1988) were developing a distinctive black-centred perspective with a global focus. Arguing that much of the world, especially the West, is mired in a Eurocentric perspective and racist ideology, this innovative perspective is grounded in a vigorous Afrocentric plane of thought that makes sense of racial conflicts in Western societies. While the Eurocentric ideology stresses competition and dominance, Afrocentricity favours a community-centred, non-hierarchical way of relating. Afrocentric analysts accent Western dominance and the Eurocentric ideology as central to the degradation of peoples in the African diaspora globally. An important project of Afrocentricity is reclaiming and re-asserting ancient contributions made to human civilisation by African peoples, as well as accenting the origin of humanity in Africa.

Stimulated by 1960s protest movements, several scholars have developed critical social science perspectives assessing intersections of race with class and gender. Examining the intersection of race and class in the tradition of Du Bois and Cox, Edna Bonacich (1980: 11–14) developed the concept of a 'split labour market' to analyse the dynamics of how labour pools in Western countries get fragmented racially to the benefit of white workers. By excluding black workers from unions for decades, white workers and their union leaders helped create a split labour market where they had racially privileged access to better-paying jobs. Although white workers surely benefited, in the long run they lost out when job segregation created a 'reserve army' of nonunion workers of colour desperately willing to work for low wages. Significantly, the work of new, critical white scholars like Bonacich and Blauner demonstrate the recurring possibility that thinkers from the dominant group can diverge from dominant scientific traditions and make use of a lens originating from the other side of the racial barrier. This pattern, though still reserved for a minority of European-origin scholars, demonstrates that research and thinking of marginalised scholars has periodically been very influential in the sciences.

Similarly, stimulated by the civil rights movement and the (mostly white) feminist movements, distinctive black-feminist scholarship has accelerated since the 1970s. Humanities scholars like Bell Hooks (1981) and sociologists like Patricia Hill Collins (1991) have demonstrated that feminist analysis and movements are quite incomplete without a racially diverse analysis, as well as that racial–ethnic scholarship is incomplete without a gender analysis. Collins has examined hoary hostile stereotypes focused on black women: matriarch, mammy, Jezebel and Sapphire. Each is a controlling, white-imposed image designed to keep black women in inferior double-bind positions in society. Historians and activists like Angela Davis (1983) have brought in an economic lens to show how women of colour are exploited for their bodies and reproductive capacities as well as their labour. Referred to as multiracial feminism, this work contributes by expanding questions of race and class to questions of race, class and gender.

A few scholars have built on the institutional racism and internal colonialism ideas coming out of the 1960s and early 1970s, with a particular view on the *material* grounding of racial oppression, past and present. Feagin (Feagin and Vera, 1995; Feagin, 2000) and Bonilla-Silva (1997) have moved towards a rigorous development of an expanded institutional racism perspective that accents the continuing importance of deep racist structures and systems. They have developed a comprehensive systemic and structural approach to racism, emphasising that, because of the still-dominant racial hierarchy in the United States and overseas, whites of European descent have major political-economic *group interests* sharply different from the group interests of people of colour.

According to well-documented analyses by Feagin (2000, 2006), who uses historical and contemporary data, racial oppression in the US case is systemic and part of a centuries-old *foundation* of the society. The United States is the *only* leading industrialised nation founded deeply on racial oppression (racial slavery) and the only one today with an operational constitution made substantially by slaveholders. The profitable US slavery system lasted nearly two and a half centuries and was immediately followed by Klan-type terrorism and legal segregation, a type of near-slavery for black Americans. Most of US history is rooted in blatant oppression well designed to exploit the labour of black Americans in order to create affluence and wealth for whites in most economic classes, with the greatest economic benefits going to those at the top. Elites and rank-and-file whites have, from the beginning, been key actors in the creation and maintenance of this systemically racist society. Systemic racism has long been perpetuated by a social reproduction process constantly generating and regenerating patterns of racial hostility, individual and group discrimination and well-institutionalised racism. Systemic racism involves oppressors and oppressed – both groups with strong group interests because of divergent positions in the structure of oppression. These differences are more than ideological, for there are real material and power interests dividing oppressed from oppressor. Thus, a group like African Americans seeks to overthrow the racist system, while white Americans mostly seek to buttress it in blatant, subtle or covert ways.

While work from dominant-group scholars like Blauner, Bonacich and Feagin begins to show some breakdown of the segregating wall during this contemporary period, as they begin to adopt the more critical lens originating from the tradition of marginalised groups, especially African Americans, so does work from members of marginalised groups such as Carmichael and Hamilton, Asante, Bonilla-Silva and Collins adopt a more critical perspective than was acceptable (or widely publishable) in the social science or policy arenas before 1960. Nonetheless, new versions of the old scientific racism and its relative – the culture-of-poverty perspective – persist, largely (though not exclusively) thanks to dominant-group scholars, and perspectives that uphold dominant group interests continue to hold the attention of the mainstream media and governmental funding agencies in white-dominated countries worldwide.

CONTEMPORARY RACIAL AND ETHNIC SCHOLARSHIP: A MULTIPLICITY OF LENSES

The three periods we have just analysed often reveal a wall-like boundary between the thinking and research of dominant and marginalised group thinkers and researchers, often creating a dichotomy between the types of scholarship advanced by each side. Exceptions to this pattern, however, become greater in number with each subsequent period. In the current period, the major change seems to be more research that does not fit a simplistic dichotomy of dominant perspectives that support racial hierarchy versus marginalised perspectives that are critical of it – research reflecting a diversity of perspectives that seek to document what progress, if any, has been made to equalise the power imbalance between socially defined racial groups since the 1960s.

While the rise since the 1980s of white conservative political movements (and their allies) led to many popular and scholarly analyses (see D'Souza, 19??) characterising white racism as a thing of the past and antidiscrimination programmes such as affirmative action as unnecessary, numerous critical scholars have argued that neither is the case. This might be called the persistence-of-racism tradition. For example, humanities scholar Cornel West's *Race Matters* (1994) articulates a black perspective on discrimination as active and destructive for black Americans at all class levels. Using interviews with many middle-class black Americans, sociologist Joe Feagin and psychologist Melvin P. Sikes's *Living with Racism* (1994) was the first social science book to analyse thoroughly contemporary discrimination faced by African Americans in major aspects of their lives, from workplace to education to public places. Working with a smaller sample, and comparing experiences of US and European women of African origin, psychologist Philomena Essed (1991) documented the persistence of racism and gendered racism in both northern Europe and the United States.

Focusing more narrowly on economic effects of the racism's persistence, sociologists Douglas Massey and Nancy Denton's *American Apartheid* (1993) is a quantitative effort demonstrating that in housing, white behaviour does not match professions of equality. Analysing US housing, they showed that African Americans were more segregated from whites than any other group of colour. This segregation helps to generate the high concentration of poverty in many black communities. Housing researchers locate responsibility for this in a discriminatory real-estate industry and in views of white homeowners who prefer neighbourhoods with fewer neighbours of colour. Melvin Oliver and Thomas Shapiro's *Black Wealth White Wealth* (1995) and Dalton Conley's *Being Black,*

Living in the Red (1999) show glaring wealth discrepancies between black and white Americans – a 'sedimentation of racial inequality' that is a legacy of nearly four centuries of US slavery and official segregation.

While studies showing the persistence of white racism continue the critical tradition advanced by mostly marginalised thinkers in previous periods, other scholarship also adopts critical lenses, but in ways that accent alternative methods and realities. For example, in recent decades, a few innovative legal scholars have pioneered in 'critical race studies'. Scholars like Derrick Bell, Patricia Williams and Richard Delgado have used a unique style of crafting arguments about racial matters – weaving legal precedents, social science research, dialogues between fictional characters and personal experiences with discrimination together to provide deep analyses of contemporary racism and visionary proposals for its eradication. Critical race theorists have offered provocative methods to get readers' attention. Bell's essay, 'The Space Traders', in *Faces at the Bottom of the Well* (1992) imagines a time in which beings from another planet offer the white-controlled US government grand promises to save the country from destruction if whites will *trade* all black citizens over to this extraterrestrial society. This essay demands that the reader contemplate whether African Americans are indeed an expendable population whose labour and presence are no longer needed. Critical race theory is now an interdisciplinary approach to racial and ethnic issues and has developed some momentum in scholarly fields beyond the law.

A related interdisciplinary effort is critical white studies, whose scholars ask what specifically there is about whiteness and its dynamics that has allowed racial oppression to flourish for centuries. 'White studies' is today mostly a combination of psychological, historical and sociological scholarship; researchers examine whiteness as a social construct that has developed historically and that has psychologically impacted all members of a society. To note just a few key examples, Theodore Allen's *The Invention of the White Race* (1994), Noel Ignatiev's *How The Irish Became White* (1995), David Roediger's *The Wages of Whiteness* (1991) and Karen Brodkin's *How Jews Became White Folks* (1998) have outlined the historical development of whiteness and its association with white socioeconomic and political dominance in Western societies. Studies like these belatedly raise questions that marginalised scholars asked in earlier periods. For example, Allen, Ignatiev and Roediger ask what would have happened if the Irish immigrants had allied with enslaved or free black workers rather than with other European workers in their first decades in the United States? Also working in this white studies tradition, humanities and social science scholars like Beverly Daniel Tatum (1997), Ruth Frankenberg (1993) and Peggy McIntosh (1998 [2001]), among numerous others, have examined how whites' perceptions of themselves and racial 'others' have been privileged by membership in the constructed category of whiteness. Parallel work, such as that of Feagin and McKinney (2003), examines the negative psychological and physiological effects of racism on its targets. In addition, a few scholars of whiteness have investigated alternative models of whiteness developed by dissenting whites who are anti-racist activists (O'Brien, 2001).

In all periods of racial and ethnic analysis, scholarship is not divorced from what is being articulated in the public square about racial matters. In recent years, thus, much dominant-group media and popular commentary in several countries extol the virtues of a 'colourblind' approach as the route to racial progress (Carr, 1997). Contemporary social scientists like Ruth Frankenberg (1993) have examined white discourses on racial matters, including what Frankenberg calls essentialist, colour- and power-evasive, and race-cognizant discourses. 'Essentialist discourse', dominant from the eighteenth to the mid-twentieth centuries in the United States and Europe in the form of scientific racism, views human beings as marked by racial categories of innate superiority or inferiority and supports a society with a rigid hierarchy. Colour- and power-evasive discourse, in contrast, took hold in the US and much of Europe after the 1960s civil right movements forced essentialist discourse off much of the public stage. This discourse asserts that racism is dead and that modern societies should not take notice of race for any reason, legally or politically. In contrast, race-cognizant discourse is anti-racist and puts racial discrimination back into the public conversation, but by accenting 'race' as an oppressive category that continues to empower whites as a group and disempower people of colour across the globe.

As this contemporary colourblind perspective has silenced much public discussion of racial matters, several researchers (Carr, 1997; Bonilla-Silva, 2003) have examined it as a relatively new form of white racism. This colourblindness is more than white discourse; it allows racial discrimination to persist in subtle and covert ways that are often difficult to research by traditional methods. BonillaSilva and Forman (2000) compared white student responses to traditional survey questions asking about their racial views with white student responses to questions in lengthy interview conversations on similar racial themes. Answers to short survey questions tended to be much more liberal than answers in lengthy interviews. Thus, national surveys of rank-and-file white attitudes give a false reading of racial progress not borne out in the lengthier interviews with similar whites. Using colourblind I-am-not-racist language, whites portray themselves as racially unprejudiced while holding strikingly racist understandings that are revealed in more extended interviews or in active performances in private settings with white friends and relatives.

Bonilla-Silva (2003) suggests many whites have an abstract liberalism, which uses the language of equal opportunity to oppose concrete antidiscrimination policies. Whites often explain away patterns of housing segregation and segregated networks and marriages as people 'naturally' gravitating towards 'their own kind'. Whites also accent the old white racial framing of people of colour as lacking in family values or work ethic. As a result, whites view African Americans and other people of colour as often whining, complaining and exaggerating racism.

Yet other scholars have shown that, even though the dominant pattern in the United States and many European countries is to accent some colourblind discourse, such discourse misrepresents whites' real attitudes and their discussions and other persisting in backstage areas – in networks of white friends and relatives. Picca and Feagin (2007) examined how whites increase in overtly racist language, ideas, joking and other racist behaviour as they move from diverse public arenas to monoracial private networks. For their research project, some 626 white college students in various US regions kept journals for several weeks in which they recorded racial events in their lives. These journals provide more than about 7000 accounts of mostly old-fashioned, overtly racist thought, commentary and actions, three-quarters of it targeting African Americans. Whites' racist performances backstage seem to be ritualised drills in which some whites lead others in developing racist understandings of, and proclivities towards, racial outgroups. The contemporary period of research on racial matters includes multiple types of critical perspectives – all critical of racial hierarchies, but disagreeing on whether there is necessarily an altogether 'new' form of racism, or just the 'old' racism in a somewhat different guise or pattern of presentation.

In recent years, several scholars have argued that there is too little research on the racism targeting groups such as Latinos and Asian Americans. Elizabeth Martinez (2001) has sketched out how Asian Americans and Latinos face racism like that which targets black Americans. Martinez cautions that there are areas unique to nonblack groups of colour that mainstream (mostly white) scholars have not addressed, such as immigration policy, anti-immigrant racism and border patrol brutality. Scholars of colour have shown well the lack of research in the literature on the problems faced by other Americans of colour. In pioneering work examining these 'racial middle' groups by O'Brien (2008), discrimination and questions of citizenship loom large for groups like Latinos and Asians in ways not sufficiently addressed by traditional racial–ethnic ethnic scholarship.

A few scholars insist that the experiences of other people of colour with white oppression in the United States are mostly variations on a four-centuries-old white-racist theme. Using contemporary and historical data, Feagin (2000, 2006), for instance, shows that US society has not had an array of disconnected racisms affecting different people of colour, but instead has had a centuries-old, whitecreated system of oppression that maintains and sustains white dominance over all people of colour. The North American system of white exploitation and oppression was first developed for African Americans, after Native Americans were mostly killed off or driven beyond white-controlled lands. African Americans are the archetypal oppressed group within the new North American society created by European colonialism. Archetypal white-on-black oppression was thereafter extended to all non-European groups later brought into US society by whites (Feagin 2000, 2006). After the slavery system was in place for two centuries, from the 1840s forward, other non-European workers and their families – first the Mexicans and Chinese in the 1840s and 1850s, and later a long list including Japanese, Filipinos and many others – have been brought into this system of white-on-black oppression so that whites could exploit their labour for profit. Feagin uses the concept of the white-to-black continuum of privilege to analyse how such groups were usually placed, initially and most importantly by powerful whites in authority, somewhere between the highly privileged position of whites at one end and the oppressed position of blacks at the other. At times, and completely at the determination of those in power, whites have viewed lighter-skinned, or more assimilated, groups of colour as more socially acceptable than darker-skinned groups. Whites with determinative power in all major US institutions have thus periodically placed some Latino or Asian American subgroups in an intermediate status between the white and black ends of the socioracial continuum (Feagin, 2000: 203–234).

Bonilla-Silva has argued for an eventual 'Latin-Americanisation' of the US, whereby instead of only a white category and a black category in the dominant US racial hierarchy, there will eventually be a third intermediate category of 'honorary whites' (Bonilla-Silva, 2003). These and other scholars analyse how powerful whites periodically construct certain groups within the Latino or Asian categories as 'nearer-to-white' than to black Americans, and thus frequently designate the former as stereotyped 'model minorities', in the process keeping full control of the white-imposed racial hierarchy. However, this white-generated 'model minority' stereotype masks the great array of racial discrimination faced by Asian Americans (Chou and Feagin 2008), as well as the ethnic differences and array of socioeconomic circumstances within the umbrella category of 'Asian American'. The model minority stereotype was invented by a white social scientist, and has been used ever since by whites as a rhetorical tool to create divisions among groups of colour and thus reduce political alliances (Huhr and Kim, 1989). Asian American analyst Gary Okihiro (2000: 75) notes, whites have a sinister motive: They have 'upheld Asians as "near-whites" or "whiter than whites" in the model minority stereotype, and yet Asians experienced and continue to face white racism "like blacks" in educational and occupational barriers and ceilings and in anti-Asian abuse and physical violence'.

In the contemporary period, although scientific racism and culture-of-poverty arguments persist inside and outside social science, most recent scholarly debates have not been about whether institutional or systemic racism exists – this currently is accepted by most racial and ethnic researchers. Rather, the debates centre more upon why and how it exists, in what forms and to what extent – all this among scholars, of more varied racial and ethnic backgrounds, who increasingly owe their intellectual debts to earlier once-marginalised scholars in the race-critical tradition.

CONCLUSION

In Western societies like the United States, racial and ethnic researchers, especially those from the dominant white group, have only slowly come to recognise and research the deep-lying racist realities of these societies and their foundational racial hierarchies. These racialised hierarchies rank social groups with greatly divergent racial interests, which stem from long histories of dominant group oppression. Throughout each period analysed, we have seen that, while a wall of power has often separated dominant and marginalised thinkers, eventually that wall has become more permeable, allowing a greater degree of knowledge to flow between and through it and culminating in less of an explicit dichotomy between dominant and marginalised ways of knowing and researching racial and ethnic issues. However, deep, foundational, and systemic racism persists; this is an ongoing contemporary truth (if not in the public square, at least among some scholars discussed here). For that reason, powerful white forces inside and outside academia still operate to constrain what we currently accept as knowledge in the field and what can be researched without opposition. Thus, we can expect that future thinkers will further augment our racial and ethnic knowledge in ways we could not have known before.

As we have shown, there are at every turn, constant and recurring connections between the development of North American racial oppression – the rooted realities of 400 years of nothing but racial oppression in slavery, legal segregation, and contemporary racism – and the involvement and reaction of European states entrepreneurs and social scientists and other intellectuals. North American societies would not exist but for European colonialism and imperialism, which in turn produced the deeply racialised realities of whiteness and the white racial frame in all Western societies. To say 'race' and racism is to say the *white Atlantic* from the 1500s to the present.

NOTE

1. Throughout this essay we use the word 'white' to refer to a socially constructed category of peoples that only develops in this context of a worldwide system of power relations tied explicitly to this rationalisation function of 'race' that we articulate here.

REFERENCES

Adorno, T.W. ; Else Frenkel-Brunswik; Daniel Levinson; and Nevitt Sanford (1950) *The Authoritarian Personality*. New York: Harper.

Alba, R. and Nee, V. (1997) 'Rethinking Assimilation Theory for a New Era of Immigration', *International Migration Review*, 31: 826–874.

Allen, T.W. (1994) *The Invention of the White Race, Volume 1: Racial Oppression and Social Control*. New York: Verso.

Allport, G.W. (1958) *The Nature of Prejudice*. Garden City, NY: Doubleday.

Asante, M. (1988) *Afrocentricity: The Theory of Social Change*. Trenton, NJ: Africa World Press.

Banton, M. (1983) *Racial and Ethnic Competition*. Cambridge: Cambridge University Press.

Barth, F. (ed.) (1969) *Ethnic Groups and Boundaries: The Social Organization of Culture Difference*. Oslo: Universitetsforlaget.

Bell, D. (1992) *Faces at the Bottom of the Well*. New York: Basic Books.

Blauner, R. (1972) *Racial Oppression in America*. New York: Harper and Row.

Bonacich, E. (1980) 'Class Approaches to Ethnicity and Race', *Insurgent Sociologist*, 10: 11–14.

Bonilla-Silva, E. (2003) *Racism without Racists: Colour-blind Racism and the Persistence of Racial Inequality in the United States*. Lanham, MD: Rowman and Littlefield.

Bonilla-Silva, E. and Forman, T.A. (2000) '"I Am Not a Racist but…"': Mapping White College Students' Racial Ideology in the USA', *Discourse and Society*, 11: 50–85.

Bonilla-Silva, E. (2003) '"New Racism," Colour-Blind Racism, and the Future of Whiteness in America' in A.W. Doane and E. Bonilla-Silva, (eds.) *White out: The Continuing Significance of Racism*. New York: Routledge. pp. 271–284.

Bonilla-Silva, E. (1997) 'Rethinking Racism: Toward a Structural Interpretation', *American Sociological Review*, 62 : 465-480.

Brodkin, K. (1998) *How Jews Became White Folks and What That Says About Race in America*. Rutgers, NJ: Rutgers University Press.

Brown v. Board of Education, 347 US 483 (1954).

Carmichael, S. and Hamilton, C. V. (1967) *Black Power: The Politics of Liberation in America*. New York: Vintage.

Carr, L. (1997) *Colourblind Racism*. Thousand Oaks, CA: Sage.

Chou, R.S. (2007) 'Malady of the "Model Minority": White Racism's Assault on the Asian American Psyche' Master's Thesis, Texas A&M University, 2007.

Chou, R. S. and Feagin, J. (2008) *The Myth of the Model Minority*. Boulder, CO: Paradigm Books.

Collins, P.H. (1991) *Black Feminist Thought: Knowledge, Consciousness and the Politics of Empowerment*. New York: Routledge.

Collins, P.H. (1991) 'Rethinking Racism: Toward a Structural Interpretation', *American Sociological Review*, 62: 465–480.

Conley, D. (1999) *Being Black, Living in the Red: Race, Wealth and Social Policy in America*. Berkeley, CA: University of California Press.

Cox, O.C. (1970 [1948]) *Caste, Class and Race*. New York: Monthly Review Press.

Davis, A.Y. (1983) *Women, Race and Class*. New York: Vintage.

de Gobineau, A. (1970) 'Race and Intelligence' in M.D. Biddiss, (ed.) *Selected Political Writings*. New York: Harper & Row. pp. 136.

Deegan, M.J. (1988) *Jane Addams and the Men of the Chicago School, 1892–1918*. New Brunswick, NJ: Transaction Books.

Dinesh D'Souza (1995) *The End of Racism: Principles for a Multiracial Society*. New York: The Free Press.

Douglass, F. (1999) 'The United States Cannot Remain Half-Slave and Half-Free', in P.S. Foner and Y. Taylor, (eds.) *Frederick Douglass: Selected Speeches and Writings*. Chicago: Lawrence Hall Books. pp. 657–658.

Du Bois, W.E.B. (1989 [1903]) *The Souls of Black Folk*. New York: Bantam Classic Books.

Du Bois, W.E.B. (1972 [1946]) *The World and Africa: An Inquiry into the Part Which Africa Has Played in World History*. New York: International Publishers.

Du Bois, W.E.B. (1998 [1899]) *The Philadelphia Negro: A Social Study*. Philadelphia: University of Pennsylvania Press.

Du Bois, W.E.B. (2003 [1920]) *Darkwater*. Amherst, New York: Humanity Books.

Durkheim, E. (1951 [1897]) *Suicide*. Glencoe, IL: Free Press.

Ellison, R. (1964) *Shadow and Act*. New York: Random House.

Essed, P. (1991) *Understanding Everyday Racism: An Interdisciplinary Theory*. Newbury Park, CA: Sage.

Feagin, J.R. (2000) *Racist America: Roots, Current Realities and Future Reparations*. New York: Routledge.

Feagin, J.R. (2006) *Systemic Racism: A Theory of Oppression*. New York: Routledge.

Feagin, J.R. and Hahn, H. (1973) *Ghetto Revolts: The Politics of Violence in American Cities*. New York: Macmillan.

Feagin, J.R. and McKinney, K.D. (2003) *The Many Costs of Racism*. Lanham, Maryland: Rowman & Littlefield.

Feagin, J.R. and O'Brien, E. (2003) *White Men on Race: Power, Privilege, and the Shaping of Cultural Consciousness*. Boston: Beacon Press.

Feagin, J.R. and Sikes, M.P. (1994) *Living with Racism: The Black Middle-Class Experience*. Boston: Beacon Press.

Frankenberg, R. (1993) *White Women, Race Matters: The Social Construction of Whiteness*. Minneapolis: University of Minnesota Press.

Gordon, M. (1964) *Assimilation in American Life: The Role of Race, Religion, and National Origins*. Oxford: Oxford University Press.

Greeley, A. (1974) *Ethnicity in the United States*. New York: Wiley.

Gunnar Myrdal (1964, [originally published 1944]) *An American Dilemma*. New York: McGraw-Hill.

Higham, J. (1963) *Strangers in the Land*. New York: Atheneum.

Hirschfeld, M. (1973 [1938]) *Racism*. Port Washington, NY: Kennikat Press.

Hooks, b. (1981) *Ain't I A Woman: Black Women and Feminism*. Boston: South End Press.

Huhr, W.M. and Kim, K.C. (1989) 'The "Success" Image of Asian Americans: Its Validity, and Its Practical and Theoretical Implications', *Ethnic and Racial Studies*, 12: 512–538.

Huntington, S.P. (1997) 'The Erosion of American National Interests', *Foreign Affairs*, September/October, 1997: 28–35.

Ignatiev, N. (1995) *How the Irish Became White*. New York: Routledge.

James, C.L.R. (1993) *American Civilization*. A. Grimshaw, and K. Hart, (eds.), Cambridge, MA: Blackwell.

Jefferson, T. (1999 [1785]) *Notes on the State of Virginia*. F. Shuffelton, (ed.) New York: Penguin Books.

Jensen, A.R. (1969) 'How Much Can We Boost IQ and Scholastic Achievement?', *Harvard Educational Review*, 39: 1–123.

Martinez, E. (2001) 'Seeing More than Black and White: Latinos, Racism, and the Cultural Divides' in M. L. Andersen. and P. H. Collins, (eds.), *Race, Class and Gender: An Anthology*. Belmont, CA: Wadsworth. pp. 108–114.

Massey, D.S. and Denton, N.S. (1993) *American Apartheid: Segregation and the Making of the Underclass*. Cambridge: Harvard University Press.

McIntosh, M. (2001) 'White Privilege and Male Privilege: A Personal Account of Coming to See Correspondences through Work in Women's Studies' (1998) in M. L. Andersen and P. H. Collins, (eds.), *Race, Class and Gender: An Anthology*. Belmont, CA: Wadsworth. pp. 95–105.

Montagu, A. (1963) *Race, Science and Humanity*. Princeton, NJ: D. Van Nostrand.

Moynihan, D.P. (1965) *The Negro Family*. Washington, DC. US Government Printing Office

O'Brien, E. (2001) *Whites Confront Racism: Antiracists and Their Paths to Action*. Lanham, MD: Rowman and Littlefield.

O'Brien, E. (2008) *The Racial Middle: Latinos, Asians and the Future of Race*. New York: New York University Press.

Okihiro, G.Y. (2000) 'Is Yellow Black or White?' in T. P. Fong, and L. H. Shinagawa, (eds.), *Asian Americans: Experiences and Perspectives*. Upper Saddle River, New Jersey: Prentice Hall. pp. 75–79.

Oliver, M.L. and Shapiro, T.M. (1995) *Black Wealth/White Wealth: A New Perspective on Racial Inequality*. New York: Routledge.

Omi, M. and Winant, H. (1994) *Racial Formation in the United States*. 2nd edition. New York: Routledge.

Park, R. (1950) *Race and Culture*. Glencoe, IL: Free Press.

Picca, L.H. and Feagin, J.R. (2007) *Two-Faced Racism: Whites in the Backstage and Frontstage*. New York: Routledge.

Portes, A. (1995) 'Segmented Assimilation among New Immigrant Youth: A Conceptual Framework' in R. Rumbaut and W. Cornelius, (eds), *California's Immigrant Children*. La Jolla, CA: Center for Mexican American Studies, University of California. pp. 71–76.

Raushenbush, W. (1979) *Robert E. Park: Biography of a Sociologist*. Durham, NC: Duke University Press.

Rex, J. (1986) *Race and Ethnicity*. Milton Keynes: Open University Press.

Reynolds, L.T. (1999) *Reflexive Sociology: Working Papers in Self-Critical Analysis*. Rockport, TX: Rockport Institute Press.

Richard J. Herrnstein and Charles Murray (1994) *The Bell Curve: Intelligence and Class Structure in American Life*. New York: The Free Press.

Roediger, D. (1991) *The Wages of Whiteness: Race and the Making of the American Working Class*. New York: Verso.

Schermerhorn, R.A. (1970) *Comparative Ethnic Relations*. New York: Random House.

Sollors, W. (1989) *The Invention of Ethnicity*. New York: Oxford University Press.

Stefancic, J. and Delgado, R. (1996) *No Mercy: How Conservative Think Tanks and Foundations Changed America's Social Agenda*. Philadelphia: Temple University Press.

Takaki, R. (1990) *Iron Cages*. New York: Oxford University Press.

Tatum, B.D. (1997) *Why Are All the Black Kids Sitting Together in the Cafeteria? And Other Conversations about Race*. New York: Basic Books.

Tucker, W.H. (1994) *The Science and Politics of Racial Research*. Urbana, IL: University of Illinois Press.

Van den Berghe, P.L. (1967) *Race and Racism*. New York: Wiley.

Warner, W.L. and Srole L. (1945) *The Social Systems of American Ethnic Groups*. New Haven, CT: Yale University Press.

West, C. (1994) *Race Matters*. New York: Vintage.

Zhou, M. (1997) 'Growing up American: The challenge Confronting Immigrant Children and Children of Immigrants', *Annual Review of Sociology*, 23: 63–95.

Researching Race and Ethnicity: Methodological Issues

Nancy A. Denton and Glenn D. Deane

INTRODUCTION

Though race and ethnicity are important and often-used variables in social science research, methodological issues related to them are, somewhat surprisingly, rarely acknowledged despite being numerous, contested and complex. Despite the fact that biologists now tend to agree that there is as much genetic variation within races as between them, and intermarriage and migration increasingly complicate both ethnic and racial identities, race and ethnicity remain important concepts for social science research because groups so identified have recognisable disparities in health, wealth, residential location and many other aspects of life.

At the most basic level, even the distinction between race and ethnicity is not clear. Most introductory sociology texts point to the biological origins of race and the cultural origins of ethnicity. This perspective necessarily subsumes ethnicity within race, but there are certainly biological aspects to Jewish ethnicity. The fact that over 90 percent of those who identified as Some Other Race identifications in the US Census 2000 were respondents who also self-identified as Hispanic in the preceding question on ethnicity indicates that many are unwilling to accept the superordinate position of race. Despite the way in which we introduce students to the concepts of race and ethnicity, American social science research generally treats races as 'a special subset of ethnicity, in that race relates to classifications of ancestral origins for groups treated in especially distinct ways in the American past' (Perlmann and Waters, 2002: 3–4; see also Alba and Nee, 2005). But again the conceptual distinction is easily challenged when we consider, for example, that African Americans, dark-skinned Caribbeans and black Nigerians will identify (and be identified by others) as members of a shared race, essentially having their ethnicity racialised. African Americans experienced the same racialisation of their ethnicities when brought here as slaves (Frederickson, 2002: 155).

The conflation of race and ethnicity, and the link between racial categories and national history is not unique to the US. For example, in Canada, specific questions about race were added to the census in 1991 (Bourhis, 2003); prior to that race was inferred from ethnic identification, questions which are still the subject of some discussion (Jedwab, 2003). In France, data on race and ethnicity are not collected and are politically charged: all people are French (Body-Gendrot, 2004), though interest in collecting such data is increasing (Alba and Denton, 2008). The British Census asks about ethnic identity, but lists ethnicities (British, Irish) under racial categories: white, black, etc. (2001 Census Form).

Fundamental to understanding methodological issues surrounding race and ethnicity in social research is recognising that not only do the meanings of race and ethnicity vary across countries, their meanings have also changed over time, can change over the life course of an individual and continue to evolve in an era of global migration and accelerating rates of intermarriage. Since governments are major collectors of statistical data, they play a central role in influencing the way race and ethnicity is measured, especially insofar as they present fixed categories on benefit enrollment, census and survey forms. In this chapter, we frame many of the methodological challenges to researchers concerning race and ethnicity around the collection of federal data in the US following the implementation of the Federal Government's decision in 1997 to provide an opportunity for individuals to select one or more races when responding to agency requests (including the US Census Bureau) for data on race and ethnicity.

We begin with a brief review of current definitions of race and ethnicity and a short summary of how race and ethnicity was fundamental to early sociological inquiry into the dynamic interplay between individual and society. We then move to more in-depth discussions of what we consider to be the key methodological issues crucial to the use of race and ethnicity in current social science research, giving examples of each. We provide a summary of the influence of official measurement on race data, emphasising the government's role in creating methodological issues and close the chapter with some reflections on possible scenarios of future research on race and ethnicity.

DEFINING RACE AND ETHNICITY

As any elementary methods textbook notes, valid and reliable measurement of concepts begins with clear definitions of the concepts to be measured. And these definitions depend in turn on the intended use of the concepts. Some researchers who include race and ethnicity in their work are researching race and ethnicity *per se*, while others are researching the effect of race and ethnicity on some other outcome of interest. In other words, how researchers define and interpret the meaning of race and ethnicity depends on whether it is a dependent or independent variable for them. Those in the first group emphasise the fluidity of race and ethnicity over the lifecourse, space and time, viewing it as an important part of a person or group's identity, but one that is not fixed in stone or unchangeably determined at birth. Those who are interested in the effect that race and ethnicity have on some other outcome tend to view it as fixed, in much the same way that gender, age and education are fixed when one is dealing with adult populations. James (2001) explains this divide succinctly: those studying race as an outcome see it as fluid, dynamic and situational, while those using it as a control variable treat it as a fixed characteristic, or difference between populations (despite paying lip service to the fact that race is a social construct). That the latter is inherent in the control variable methodology does not eliminate the issue that it is not race *per se* that is the causal factor, but rather how race has led some groups to be treated in society.

It is important to point out this is not a theoretical dispute: both groups recognise that the biological origins of race are no longer viewed as real by the scientific community, and that both race and ethnicity are social constructs. However, when race or ethnicity is entered into a predictive equation, many in the latter group come under criticism for interpreting the effects of race as if it were fixed or essential, not variable (James, 2001). Fundamental to this issue is the fact that except in very limited circumstances, neither race nor ethnicity can be a cause or mechanism leading directly to some outcome (Zuberi, 2001: 95). Being black does not mean you do worse in school or earn less, it is the fact that being black means you often have poorer parents with less wealth, fewer well-trained teachers, attend poorer schools, are discriminated against in the labour market which causes the poor school and job performance. As a result, there is always the underlying question of exactly what race or ethnicity is measuring (Zuberi, 2001: 95–96).

Unlike social concepts such as age, sex and education, definitions of race and ethnicity are far from clear cut. At the most basic level is common usage, where race tends to refer in some way to physical differences such as skin colour or hair texture while ethnicity is linked to culture or geographical area of origin. Standard introductions to race and ethnicity in sociology textbooks tend to reinforce these emphases on physical differences and culture, while pointing out that these concepts are socially defined and influence people's lives. Even the dictionary definitions of the two terms have some overlap, something that has persisted over time (Rodriguez, 2000: 44–45). Scholars differ in their definitions, and while many researchers consider race as a subset of ethnicity (Alba and Nee, 2005; Perlmann and Waters, 2002), others argue that race is key (Omi and Winant, 1986; Winant, 2000). Certainly ethnicity has a more optional component than race (Waters, 1990) as it is not always immediately obvious to the observer.

Despite the link to biology, most scientists today consider race to be a social, rather than a biological construct (Hirschman et al., 2000; Hirschman, 2004; Omi and Winant, 1986; Skerry, 2000). As Angela James points out, 'to say that race is "socially constructed" means that it is neither "mere illusion" and thus irrelevant, nor something that should be viewed as "objective" and "fixed"' (2001: 238). James' conclusion was corroborated when an issue of the popular science magazine *Scientific American* devoted its lead article (as well as its cover illustration and letter from the editors, 'SA Perspectives') to the question 'Does Race Exist'? (*Scientific American*, 2003). The accompanying article by geneticist Michael J. Bamshad and science writer Steve E. Olson concludes that if races are defined as genetically discrete groups, then the answer is no; yet if the question is rephrased in practical terms 'does dividing people by recognised racial categories or by genetic similarities say anything useful about how members of those groups experience disease or respond to drug treatment?', the authors offer a qualified yes.

Increasingly, ethnicity is used as an inclusive term (Hirschman et al., 2000) and some expect that ethnicity may eventually supplant race. This expectation was given considerable momentum by a 1987 decision of the US Supreme Court wherein the Court ruled that ethnic groups could be considered races (and thereby be covered under provisions of the Civil Rights Act of 1965) because of the historical uses of these terms (*St. Francis College v. Al-Khazraji*, 1987). Taken together, all of these issues of definition, briefly sketched here and discussed more thoroughly in other chapters in this handbook, raise numerous measurement issues regarding the use of race and ethnicity as variables in social science research. Comparisons across different data sets, of respondents in different locales or with different immigration histories, to say nothing of across countries, are all problematic if the terms are the same but their meaning is different.

EARLY RACE RELATIONS RESEARCH

Though a detailed history of race relations research is beyond the scope of this chapter, a couple of points from that history in the United States deserves mention. It is important to note that the definitional issues just discussed have been important throughout the twentieth century as scholars studied race relations. Incorporating both race and ethnicity into one model was probably inevitable given that early scholars were studying cities, such as Chicago, populated by immigrants into which large numbers of African Americans were migrating. Thus the early Chicago School projects such as Robert Park's race relations cycle were known for their attempts to develop objective quantitative and qualitative research on race relations by actually getting out into the community. However, recent writing has questioned whether racial statistics are objective knowledge or would better be described as 'historically specific folk notions of socially constructed racial differences and their sociological, political and economic consequences'

(Stanfield, 1993b: 4). For example, Stanfield argues that Robert E. Park's 1950 race-relations cycle did not reflect a model based on empirically grounded reality as much as the racial idealism of the times, namely that blacks would eventually assimilate. This in turn influenced scholars such as Charles Johnson and E. Franklin Frasier, as well as William Julius Wilson, who continued to use Park's race-relations cycle even though Park had changed his mind.

A second point concerns the race of the scholars themselves. Prior to 1940, there were numerous African American sociologists working in the field of race relations; between 1940 and 1970 there were relatively few, then after 1970 there were more. Their absence in the 1950s and 1960s left a vacuum that was filled by white sociologists who were positioned to take advantage of opportunities resulting from Myrdal's project, the *Brown* decision, and government funding. Gunnar Myrdal's famous study was directed by whites, and the white and black scholars who provided him with notes, which became chapters published in his name, seldom saw much improvement in their careers, especially if they were black. When a similar strategy was tried in the 1980s by the National Academy of Science at the start of the production of *Common Destiny*, black scholars were included but not those who were prominent or had critical orientations. The resulting volume was not well received and reflected past rather than present empirical realities (Stanfield, 1993a: x–xxiii).

As Winant (2000) points out, if one looks at sociological theory, one can see the concept of race throughout, beginning with Herbert Spencer, but the sociological study of race has fluctuated in line with large-scale political developments. So in the early twentieth century, race was absolute according to scientific racism, but the increase in anticolonialism in Africa and Asia made the biological theories obsolete, leading to a more sophisticated concept of race evident in W. E. B. Du Bois's study of black life in Philadelphia. The racial concept was extensively challenged after World War II by new demands for inclusion. Exclusionary regimes were pressured to reform, and though while great gains were made, the twenty-first century begins with serious issues regarding racial inequality still to be faced.

INVARIANCE IN MEASUREMENT OVER TIME AND PLACE

Although we tend to think of race and ethnicity as stable, enduring characteristics, there is substantial evidence that a particular group's status as a race or an ethnic group changes over time and varies by place (Alba and Nee, 1995; Hollinger, 1995; Williams, 1999; Telles, 2004). In the United States, Irish, Jews and Italians made the transition from being considered races in the early part of the twentieth century to white ethnic groups by the century's end. Nineteenth-century caricatures of the Irish frequently gave them a distinctly simian cast, a perception now attributed to the fact that Irish immigrants lived, worked and socialised with African Americans in urban neighbourhoods (Lieberson, 1980).

Eventually the whiteness of the Irish was defined as they actively distinguished a clear social boundary between themselves and blacks (Alba and Nee, 1995: 133). That Italians tend to have an olive complexion or Jews have a particular nose shape still remains, but both are now definitely considered members of the white race. It is not surprising then that no single set of racial categories has been used on more than two US Census forms, and most were only used once.

Different cultures have different conceptions of race. For example, the racial categories recognised in Brazil are not the same as those in the US, even though its population also includes White Europeans and blacks of African descent. Marvin Harris (1964; Harris et al., 1993) described numerous racial categories, combined to create hundreds of different racial terms based primarily on physical characteristics in Brazil. But racial descent is not the rule: full siblings whose appearance differs are of different races. In addition, race is not a fixed characteristic of a person, rather it changes when a person achieves wealth. Edward Telles has recently explored racial ambiguity among the Brazilian population and the fact that early scholars have focused on the fluidity of definitions, while later ones focused on racial discrimination. He finds that these are two independent dimensions of race in Brazil, the first is a horizontal, interpersonal one, while the second is a vertical, economic and social mobility one. His analysis shows that the social class barrier keeping darker-skinned mulattos and blacks from rising into the middle class is firmly maintained, even as interpersonal relations are cordial and racial definitions fluid. But the bottom line is that there remains significant racial inequality in Brazil (Telles, 2004).

Another example comes from Puerto Rico, where race is strongly linked to socioeconomic status; so a person can be of different races at different times in his life. As status rises, race becomes lighter, ultimately white, a process known as blanqueamiento (Torres, 1998). Though this whitening has also been reported in Brazil, the pathways can be different: in some cases, class status improves first, then race, while in others, race changes first, then class, depending on whether the race or the class barrier is more permeable (Schwartzman, 2007).

A related issue is that of racial hierarchy. Song (2004) reports that while the racial hierarchy of whites at the top and blacks at the bottom is accepted among researchers in the United States, the same is not true in Britain, where they are dealing with people from their former colonies and some of the white immigrants do not get good jobs. Brazil (Warren, 2000) also denies having a racial hierarchy.

The variation across countries in racial 'systems' and definitions is of more than academic interest. New immigrants need to confront the meaning of race and ethnic terms in their new country. For example, in the US they learn how important umbrella terms such as Hispanic or Asian will be to their identity here. Since immigrants arrive with race/ethnic definitions, the extent to which they understand their usage in the context of their new country raises the issue of whether their self-identification means the same as a native born person's. Vickerman (1998) provides compelling evidence of this process. Based on interviews with

Jamaican immigrants in New York City, Vickerman documents how West Indian immigrants, who come from societies where race is downplayed and emphasis is placed on merit-based achievement, quickly learn that racial identity is consequential and how these immigrants strive to develop a distinct West Indian identity to counter the stigma placed on darker skin colour. As one respondent said 'Race was important [in Jamaica] but not on a day to day basis. The difference I find is that when you get to America, you have to start thinking about race when you walk into the store...' (1999: 95).

SELF VERSUS OTHER IN THE MEASUREMENT OF RACE AND ETHNICITY

Not only does the Census Bureau or other statistical agency define the racial and ethnic categories into which people are placed, they also determine how the data are collected, though this latter topic goes beyond just census enumerations. Sometimes race and ethnicity are self-reported, other times they are reported for each member of the household by the person filling out the form; on death certificates they are often reported by the coroner or funeral director; on birth certificates by the doctor, nurse, mother or father; and sometimes they are reported to a same-race person or to a different-race person. Each of these can be thought of as a variant on the complication that race and ethnicity measurement can be viewed from two vantage points, ego and alter (Hirschman, 2004).

The fluidity of identity

Self-identification became a major issue in 1970 when the US Census became mail out/mail back, meaning that people self-identify into particular races and ethnicities (Martin et al., 1990). This change in census-taking procedure meant that, from 1970 onwards, race was based on self-identification rather than enumerator identification. Research pointing to the disagreement in self-identified and observer-identified race (Hahn et al., 1992; Harris and Sim, 2000) anticipates the observation that, between the shift to self-enumeration and the Bureau's decision not to recode persons of Hispanic origin as white, the number of Hispanic origin persons classified as Other race rose from 700,000 in 1970 to 5.8 million in 1980 (Martin et al., 1990).

When inferring that there is self-identification of race and ethnicity in the completion of mail-back census questionnaires is important to be cognisant of the fact that the forms are often completed by a household informant rather than by each individual in the household. Though the household informant at least knows the person on whom they are reporting, there is still no guarantee that they would give the same response as the person themselves. This, then, adds another filter to validity in the measurement of race and ethnicity.

Discrepancies between the racial or ethnic identity that people select for themselves and the race assigned to them by observers have been documented in a variety of research. For example, in demographic research on births or deaths, it is necessary to calculate rates by using the number of births or deaths in the numerator, and an estimate of the population at risk of experiencing that event in the denominator. If the person's race is different as a result of being reported by a different person, then the rate will be wrong as well. Evidence of this kind of error on race/ethnic specific infant mortality rates is contained in Hahn et al. (1992). Rodriguez and Cordero-Guzman (1992) show that when Puerto Ricans were asked how they thought North Americans viewed them, the proportion responding black doubled, and those responding white decreased.

David Harris's study of observed race (2002) reveals the complex process by which observers' race and racial contexts affect perspectives on race. Observers' race, sex, and familiarity with racial groups each influence how they classify by race. Harris concludes that self-reported race is substantially more likely to be confirmed by observers when people self-identify with only one racial group, and especially if they self-identify as white or black. His results also illustrate some of the complex ways that race and gender affect observed race. For example, white men and Asian men consistently demonstrate a simplistic understanding of race. They take relatively little time to classify others, are the least likely to identify people as multiracial and the most likely to identify people as black. Multiracial observers are at the other extreme. They tend to take a long time to classify race and are far more likely than other observers to identify people as multiracial (Harris, 2002: 19). While self-definition clearly matters in socialpsychological aspects of one's identity, how others view us can have consequences in terms of discriminatory treatment.

There is also evidence that *where* one is asked about racial and ethnic classification matters. Harris and Sim (2002) provide evidence that multiracial adolescents tend to have fluid racial identities. By comparing responses to race questions on separate in-home and school surveys in the National Longitudinal Study of Adolescent Health (Add Health), Harris and Sim find that 10 percent of multiracial youths give inconsistent responses. In part this may be attributed to the school survey being self-administered while the home interview was administered by face-to-face interview, often observed by family members, but the inconsistency also reflects the difference in setting between the two surveys. Kanaiaupuni and Liebler (2003; Liebler, 2004) show that the racial identification of mixed-race Hawaiians varies according to the racial composition of their location, changing from a mixed-race identity in Hawaii to a single-race (white) identity on the US mainland.

Qualitative research foregrounds the situational nature of the response to a question on race or ethnicity. While survey research has noted that different responses are given in different situations, ethnographic research explains why: people answer a specific West Indian island if they feel the questioner will know it and give a more generic response if not (Waters, 1999: 57) or shift from a West Indian identity to a race identity if the situation in which they find themselves reflects discrimination against blacks, and not West Indians (Waters, 1999: 63).

Waters also explores the varied meanings behind West Indians' attempts to distance themselves from American blacks.

Reporting to interviewers

The fluidity of mixed-race identity is also supported in in-depth interviews. Rockquemore and Brunsma (2002) found that mixed-race adolescents identified themselves by the racial composition of their friendship networks and that identity changed as the composition of the friendship networks changed. Field (1996) also found that mixed-race adolescents reported that they take on the racial identity of their peer groups. Similarly, interviews fielded by Funderburg (1994) and Chideya (1999) consistently show that racial identity is dictated by neighbourhood and school peer-groups.

Qualitative researchers are increasingly questioning the idea that matching the race of the interviewer with that of the interviewee yields better data (Twine and Warren, 2000; Young, 2004). This work problematises the insider status in interviews and argues for the benefits of being an outsider in certain situations. According to Twine, race is not the only social signifier and it is not necessarily true that race will trump all other social statuses in all situations (Twine, 2000). One issue is that a same-race interviewer can lead to overidentification between the interviewee and the interviewed, such that the interviewee feels there is no need to explain things that the interviewer should know based on a common racial identification. Young (2004) reports this problem interviewing poor black males, and argues that being an outsider can stimulate interesting conversations. According to Blee (2000), a related issue arises as a white woman interviewing white female members of racist skinhead groups, where she was both an insider and an outsider simultaneously–white but not sharing the respondent's racial assumptions. Lamont (2004), a white woman interviewing working-class men, found that interviewing across class and gender made her respondents try harder to explain things to her. These points lead to the importance of taking social as well as physical geography into account when collecting, and interpreting, data on race and ethnicity. As Twine says 'The local calculus of color and race may thus determine which segments of the community the researcher can easily access, and the normative social roles and social scripts to which s/he is expected to conform' (2000: 18).

Another issue that emerges very clearly from qualitative research on race/ethnicity is how deeply a person's race/ethnic identity is intertwined with national and global history and politics, as well as with their residential and socioeconomic locations within a society, and that society's national identity. Keaton's study of Muslim girls in France provides an excellent example of the interplay among these. How young girls living in the outer-city try to navigate being French given their racial difference and headscarves is conditioned by the often-stated inclusive nature of France's ideology of national identity within which they have been raised but which is at odds with the reality of how their parents and they are treated on a day-to-day basis as a result of France's colonial heritage and general attitudes towards immigration. As she says

> After all, they are products of one common institution that begins at the formative age of two or three in France: national education. On the one hand, the French school teaches them that they are French through its ideology of a 'common culture' in a system whose gatekeepers are hostile to multiculturalism and change. On the other hand, young people are reared in segregated neighbourhoods and schools that clearly belie those very teachings. (Keaton, 2006: 13)

GOVERNMENT AND THE MEASUREMENT OF RACE/ETHNIC CATEGORIES

In countries where race and ethnic data are collected on the census, the government plays a major role in determining the terms used to denote race and ethnic categories. For example, blacks in the US have been referred to as Negroes and African Americans as well as blacks. In fact, only three racial terms – white, Chinese, and Japanese – have been on every census form in the last hundred years (Farley, 2002). Here we illustrate government's role with the US Census, the one we know best, though those of other developed countries could be used to the same effect (cf. Bulmer and Solomos, 2004; Bourhis, 2003; Nobles, 2000; Telles, 2004).[1] Khalfani and Zuberi (2001), writing about South Africa, argue that the nature of the state determines how race is defined, and how it is linked to stratification.

Measuring race

Although the fluidity of census racial classification underscores the arbitrary and popular basis of race reporting (Marshall, 1968), since the 1960s, the Federal Government, through the Office of Management and Budget (OMB), has recognised the need for compatible, nonduplicative race reporting. This led the OMB to issue Directive No. 15, *Race and Ethnic Standards for Federal Statistics and Administrative Reporting*, in May 1977. The Directive set forth a minimum set of categories for collecting and presenting data on race and Hispanic origin. Thus, for the first time, standard categories and definitions were to be used by all Federal agencies in both the collection and the presentation of data on race and ethnicity (Office of Management and Budget, 1997a, 1997b).

Beginning in the late 1980s and particularly since the 1990 Census, Directive 15 was criticised for not sufficiently reflecting the growing diversity of the US population resulting primarily from the growth in immigration and interracial marriages. In response to this criticism, in 1994, OMB established the Interagency Committee for the Review of the Racial and Ethnic Standards to undertake a comprehensive review of the categories for data on race and ethnicity. Following four years of review, research and testing of various proposed changes, and the very effective lobbying by small organisations of parents with mixed-race children, the Interagency Committee supported a method for reporting more than one race and recommended that the method for respondents to report more than one race should take the form of multiple responses to a single question and not a multi-racial category (Office of Management and Budget (OMB), 1997a, 1997b; see also Farley, 2002; Logan et al., 2004; Harrison, 2002). While this small change in wording seems innocuous enough, it presented new and important challenges in (1) tabulating the 2000 census, as well as data on race and ethnicity collected in surveys and from administrative records; (2) using data on race and ethnicity in applications such as legislative redistricting, civil rights monitoring and enforcement and population estimates; and (3) comparing data collected under the new standards with that collected under the prior standards when conducting trend analyses.

The 2000 census instructed respondents to 'mark one or more races to indicate what this person considers himself/herself to be'. Respondents were directed to choose among five major racial categories (American Indian or Alaska native, Asian, black or African American, native Hawaiian or other Pacific Islander, and white) and a sixth, residual, Some Other Race category. Analyses completed after the 1990 Census showed the multiracial population to be as large as 6.6 percent, leading some to expect the report in the 2000 Census to be on the order of 4–6 percent (Tafoya et al., 2004). While early tests expected that as many as 7–8 percent of Americans would choose a multirace option (Hirschman et al., 2000), Census 2000 counted far fewer: 2.4 percent, or about 7 million people (Tafoya et al., 2004). There were more multiracial people under the age of 18, 4.4 percent. In addition, a full 32.3 percent of the bi-racial people were 'white and other', reflecting the fact that 90.4 percent of those who checked the 'other' race box had previously chosen Hispanic ancestry despite the fact that the Hispanic ancestry question preceded the question on race (Farley, 2004).

Racial groups that are specifically listed on the form tend to have larger counts than groups that have to be written in, something that has led to the expansion of the number of specific Asian groups on the census form, as well as the separation of the Native Hawaiian and Other Pacific Islanders from Asians between 1990 and 2000 (Farley, 2002). The fact that groups listed have higher counts has led the Dominican population to want their group to be listed, along with Mexican, Cuban and Puerto Rican but so far this has not happened. The reason for privileging Hispanics is that the OMB requires that the population be divisible into the categories non-Hispanic white, non-Hispanic black, non-Hispanic Native American, non-Hispanic Asian and Hispanic. Thus the Census Bureau preserves the distinction between race and Hispanic ethnicity, which complicates their collection of race and ethnic data as many think of themselves as Hispanic only, not as a white or a black Hispanic.

Measuring ethnicity

In terms of the measurement of ethnicity, beginning in 1970, a distinct Hispanic identity question was included in the census. Thus, Hispanic origin is now conceptualised as an ethnic category independent of an individual's racial classification. Data on this population are collected on the short form, a distinct advantage as everyone fills out the short form while the long form is filled out only by a sample of the population. As Hirschman and colleagues (2000) point out, although Hispanic origin and race officially are independent classifications, administrative actions and popular understanding have created a social position for Hispanics almost equivalent to that of one of the major racial categories. The result is a five-category racial and ethnic classification (non-Hispanic whites, non-Hispanic blacks, non-Hispanic Asians, non-Hispanic Indians, and Hispanics) that is widely used to describe American society and was formally recognised by the OMB in its 1977 Statistical Directive 15 (2000: 382).

In addition to the Hispanic-origin question, since 1980, ethnic identification has been collected on the census long form by asking people to declare the ancestry or ancestries with which they most closely identify.[2] Since there are no directions (e.g., only go back to your grandparents origins), this question is quite subjective, and indeed, people who say they are Hispanic on the Hispanic origin question do not always choose a Hispanic ancestry, while non-Hispanics sometimes do. The Census Bureau codes and reports first- and second-ancestry, thus measurement of ethnicity through ancestry is subject to much the same difficulty as multiple race identification. Another feature in the measurement of ethnicity via ancestry is how much identifications vary according to the list of example ancestries. For example, in 1980, English was given as one example in the question wording, but German was not. In 1990, German was present but English was not. As a consequence, the percentage listing English ancestry declined by a large fraction in 1990, while the percentage identifying with German ancestry rose by a comparable amount and German replaced English as the largest reported ancestry group in the United States (Perlmann and Waters, 2002: 9–10). Other ancestry groups also rise and fall depending on whether they are in the list of examples. Lieberson and Waters (1993) document the simplification of ancestries across generations and the life course. It is clear, then, that for many Americans, this dimension of ethnic identification is quite weak and transient (Hout and Goldstein, 1994).

Data on race and ethnicity are also collected in other parts of the federal statistical system, and in other Census Bureau survey activities, and these efforts influence how the Bureau measures race and ethnicity in the decennial censuses. Examples of this are readily found in federal data collection that responded to the 1997 OMB directive prior to the 2000 census. The National Health Interview Survey (NHIS), conducted by the National Center for Health Statistics, was one of the first nationally representative surveys to collect and tabulate the more than one race categories (as well as the single race with which the respondent most closely identifies); and it was the first to confront disclosure limitation and confidentiality issues in the dissemination of data tabulated for unique multiple race respondents (Parker and Makuc, 2002). The Current Population Survey, administered by the Bureau of Labor Statistics and the Census Bureau, has been used to test a variety of questions concerning the wording and ordering of items about race, Hispanic-origin, and ancestry. The most comprehensive of the preliminary surveys was the 1996 Race and Ethnic Targeted Test (RAETT). RAETT used an experimental design to test the effects of eight possible changes in questionnaire format on racial and ethnic responses. Although each respondent answered only one version of the questionnaire, it is possible to measure the effects of different questionnaire formats because the different versions were assigned randomly to households within each targeted sample. A comprehensive examination of the RAETT responses is given by Hirschman et al. (2000).

It is important to realise that changing the racial categories is not something unique to the United States. Not only are censuses products of their time in the United States, but Nobles (2002) discusses how categories for reporting race have also changed in Brazil. The important point is that as the categories change, so do the choices made. Furthermore, many feel that fixed-response categories tend to reproduce racialised classification and imply a homogeneity within racial groups that simply is not there. Bradby (2003) makes this argument for Britain, as does Williams (1999) for the United States. Both point to the fact that this issue is particularly problematic in the United States because of the history of slavery and the fact that from the beginning, 'race has been a fundamental organizing principle of US society' (Williams, 1999: 124).

SAMPLING ISSUES AND RACE/ETHNIC DATA

It is often important to get statistics about selected subgroups of the population, but the cost of national samples that include representation of targeted racial and ethnic populations is generally prohibitive. As a result, large-scale surveys generally oversample targeted subgroups or restrict the sampling frame to areas that have high concentrations of the subgroups. The results of these common strategies should give pause to secondary data analysts for a variety of reasons. First, although it may seem intuitive and desirable to use high rates of oversampling to gain sufficient sample size from the rare population, the unintended consequence of high rate oversampling is a large increase in the variances for the total population and only marginal gain for the specific population targeted by the oversampling (Gonzalez and Waksberg, 1973; Waksberg et al., 1997; Morganstein and Marker, 2000: 310). In short, inferential statistics of racial and ethnic group differences (relative to the majority group) from surveys designed to target racial and ethnic groups are often conservatively biased towards no difference.

A second issue concerns coverage. As the cost of national samples that include representation of rare populations is generally prohibitive, survey samples of racial and ethnic populations often restrict sampling to areas that have high concentrations of the targeted groups. Description and inference from the analysis of these samples should be, but often isn't, restricted to the situation for groups living in areas that share the characteristics of the sampling frame. If the spatial locations of rare populations matter, and the well-known consequences of residential segregation (cf. Massey and Denton, 1993) generally assure that they do, then secondary data analysts who ignore the sampling frame are likely to make highly misleading attributions about race and ethnicity. In response, some targeted survey data derive sample weights to adjust beyond the areas included in the sampling frame (Morganstein and Marker, 2000: 310–311). But this solution has its own caveat: the adjustment is necessarily based on nonprobability methods which compromise the inferential properties of rigorous statistical analysis.

The impact of racial and ethnic residential locations can also affect conventional sampling methodology in unexpected ways. Skerry (2000: 64–66; see also Cresce et al., 2004) provides a notable example in the imputation of missing Hispanic identification in decennial census products. The Census Bureau has for many years imputed missing information based on a method known as hot deck allocation, the assignment of values from a set of stored values collected from other households. Skerry contends that the Bureau's hot deck allocation assigned Hispanic identity to non-Hispanic persons because Hispanics resided in more integrated neighbourhoods than other racial and ethnic groups. Thus a group that was not responsive to census enumeration ended up being overcounted!

THE STATISTICAL REDUNDANCY OF RACE AND NEIGHBOURHOOD SES

Although an appreciation of the interconnection of neighbourhood context and its racial and ethnic composition can be traced to the influence of the Chicago school sociologists such as Park and Burgess, Sutherland, Shaw and McKay through to the later work of Wilson and Sampson, a methodologically driven approach known as factorial ecology that emerged from the social area analysis of Shevsky and Bell in the 1950s has left an indelible imprint on how race and ethnicity enters into the search for, and interpretation of, neighbourhood effects. Factorial social ecology essentially involves the application of exploratory factor analysis or principal components analysis to identify the most salient underlying dimensions of neighbourhood context.

The conflation of race and class, the result of enduring residential segregation and high levels of racial and ethnic discrimination, consistently produces a factor scale of low neighbourhood socioeconomic status (SES) comprised of obvious socioeconomic indicators such as percentage of individuals who are poor and the percentage of families headed by females, but also of racial indicators such as the percentage of neighbourhood population that is black and the percentage that is white. While pointing to the highest positive loading on a factor interpreted as low neighbourhood SES of percentage black, and the second-to-highest negative loading of percentage white, Massey complained that when the SSRC commissioned two-volume study of neighbourhood poverty speaks of ' "low SES neighbourhoods," what it *really* means is neighbourhoods that are poor *and* black' (Massey, 1998: 572).

Massey argues that even though race and class may be empirically correlated across neighbourhoods, when race is treated as an inherent component of eco-logical structure, residential segregation disappears as an independent force and urban poverty is strangely deracialised. While it is easy to agree in principle with Massey's objection, the dictates of quantitative analysis of neighbourhood effects are not so easily amended. From the conventional methodological perspective, the ecological correlation of race and class is an issue of repetitiveness and redun-dancy in measurement that remains in the purview of multicollinearity and par-tialing fallacy (Gordon, 1968). Whether we object or not to the high ecological correlation of the racial and ethnic composition of neighbourhoods and obvious socioeconomic indicators such as the percentage of individuals who are poor and the percentage of families headed by females, the statistical consequences of ignoring highly correlated variables – inflated standard errors, unstable regres-sion estimates – are real and highly detrimental to the construction of social theory. Land et al. (1990) provide an excellent example of these consequences from the perspective of the structural covariates of crime. Shapiro (2004) pro-vides abundant ethnographic information on how race and class are connected for African Americans in the United States. The disentanglement of race and class, while satisfying conventional statistical properties, remains among the top methodological issues in the structural analysis of race and ethnicity.

THE IMPACT OF MULTIPLE-RACE MEASUREMENT

The newest methodological issue surrounding the official measurement of race in the US results from the adoption of the OMB's October 1997 *Standards for Maintaining, Collecting, and Presenting Federal Data on Race and Ethnicity*. As a follow-up to the OMB directive, the Tabulation Working Group of the Interagency Committee issued a guidance document to offer strategies for reas-signing multiracial counts to the single race categories used previously. This document, the *Provisional Guidance on the Implementation of the 1997 Standards for Federal Data on Race and Ethnicity* (Office of Management and Budget, 2001), included a Bridge Report in which Bridge Tabulation Methods were pro-duced for the assignment of the responses from individuals who identify with more than one racial group. The specific methods for assigning multiple race responses into single race categories are Deterministic Whole Assignment, Deterministic Fractional Assignment, and Probabilistic Whole Assignment. The distinction among these bridging methods is whether an individual's responses are assigned to a single racial category (termed whole assignment) or to multiple categories (termed fractional assignment), with whole assignment based on a set of deterministic rules or based on some probabilistic distribution.

Under the rubric of *Deterministic Whole Assignment*, the Bridge Report con-siders three assignment schemes. *Smallest Group* assigns responses with two or more racial groups into the group with the fewest number of individuals identifying that group as a single race. The second alternative, *Largest Group Other Than White*, assigns responses that include white with another race group to the other group, but responses with two or more racial groups other than white are assigned into the group with the highest single-race count. The third alternative, *Largest Group*, assigns responses with two or more racial groups into the group with the largest number of individuals reporting a single race. Typically this implies that any combination with white is assigned as white.

Deterministic Fractional Assignment uses fixed, deterministic rules for fractional weighting of multiple-race responses. This method shifts the unit of analysis from individuals to identifications, but *Deterministic Fractional Assignment* weights multiple responses in equal fractions to each racial group identified. For example, respondents identifying two racial groups are assigned to each of the two racial groups with a weight of 0.5, respondents identifying three racial groups are assigned to each of the three racial groups with a weight of 0.33 and so forth, whereas single-race respondents are assigned a weight of one. In this manner, the weighted count is equal to the number of respondents – rather than the number of identifications.

The final assignment method offered in the Bridge Report uses a random selection of one identity for each multiracial individual (single-race respondents retain their single-race identification) and is labelled *Probabilistic Whole Assignment*. This assignment scheme parallels the *Deterministic Fractional Assignment* method, except that, for a given set of fractions with equal selection probabilities, respondents with multiple race identifications are assigned to only one racial category. *Probabilistic Whole Assignment* will yield, in large samples or on average in repeated sampling, the same population counts as *Deterministic Fractional Assignment*.[3]

Each of these assignment schemes has something to recommend it, but the choice does matter. First, one can shrink or exaggerate the difference in majority and minority group sizes. The effects of the Deterministic Whole Assignments on group counts is obvious, Smallest Group assignments will flatten the racial distribution, while Largest Group and Largest Group Other than White assignments will skew the distribution by increasing the concentration in the largest racial group(s). The effects of Deterministic Fractional and Probabilistic Whole assignments are somewhat less obvious. The effects of Deterministic Fractional and Probabilistic Fractional assignments on relative group sizes is seen in the relation of the single-race groups that contain the multiracial population to other single-race groups. It is here that a bi-racial person is very much treated as a half person. If, for example, a population of 20 people is comprised of three racial groups, with ten people identifying as Group A and Group B and ten people identifying as Group C, Deterministic Fractional and Probabilistic Whole assignments show Group C to be twice as large as either Group A or Group B.

Determination of group size may be seen as a matter of taste or a matter of circumstance, though it is not clear why this should be left in the hands of the analyst rather than the respondent. The choice of assignment scheme matters because of the lack of uncertainty attributed to identifications. All of the assignment schemes to single-race groups fail to distinguish between individuals self-identified in a single-race group and the multiracial individuals allocated to single-race groups. In other words, there is no additional uncertainty, or randomness, attached to allocated individuals, even though to some extent their racial assignment is made-up by the analyst as he/she imposes a racial-stereotyped structure on multiple-race responses. It is not surprising then that Parker and Makuc (2002) have determined that the choice of bridge method will have a larger impact when the demographics and subsequent outcomes for a multiplerace group differ from those of its component single-race groups. In addition, Parker and Makuc find that the greater the association between socioeconomic profile and an outcome, the greater the effect of the assignment of multiple-race respondents to a single-race category on the subsequent estimate.

An additional concern is that simply putting all those who chose more than one race into a multi-race category will underestimate important population subgroups, something particularly problematic if the data are used in civil rights enforcement. As Goldstein and Morning (2002) point out, reassignment reinforces the old one-drop idea, violates the principle of self-identity, and risks making race-based policies even more controversial when reassignment increases the number of people in protected categories, thus *de facto* extending the coverage of policies already under attack. The problems of reclassification just described occur in both descriptive and multivariate statistics. Assigning the person to just one race disregards valuable information, while assigning fractional parts of the same person to multiple races yields statistical tables with fractional people in them and assigning people to all the races they choose leads to tables with more identifications than there are people.

OUR ALTERNATIVE TO REASSIGNMENT

While most analysts will resort to using some allocation scheme to deal with multiple races, the resulting analysis and statistical inference is conditional on the quality of the researcher's allocation scheme. We propose a more defensible alternative by allowing persons to contribute as many observations to the sample as necessary to exhaust their multiple racial identifications, effectively shifting the observational unit from a respondent to an identification, and then apply a post hoc correction to the violation of the *iid* assumptions, thus avoiding the problem that different analysts using the same data can obtain different answers if they use different allocation schemes for the multiple-race data.

In essence, this approach relies on well-established principles used to correct biases occurring as a result of cluster sampling. By allowing respondents to choose more than one race, respondents form natural clusters. The homogeneity exhibited within clusters will tend to increase the variance of sample estimators, while estimates of variance based on *iid* (residuals are independent and identically distributed) assumptions will be downward biased. Consequently, the standard errors of descriptive statistics will be too small and test statistics based on downwardly biased estimates of variance will appear to be more significant than is really the case. Generalised estimating equations (GEE) provide a computationally simple approach for estimating parameters in correlated data. In addition, GEE allow us to quantify how racial identifications are related to one another, and how those relations respond to model covariates, by imposing a variety of working correlation matrices (Hardin and Hilbe, 2003: 59).

The method proposed here is simple to implement, but more importantly it does not make arbitrary assignments of multiracial individuals to single race groups nor does it treat multiracial individuals as fractions of single-race people. Rather, it allows individuals to contribute as many observations as is necessary to exhaust their multiple identifications and uses the covariance structure among the explanatory variables to allocate the impact of the multiple identification individuals.

CONCLUSION

In this chapter we have tried to lay out some of the methodological issues social scientists face when they include race and ethnicity in their analyses. These included definitional issues, the role of government agencies in establishing categories, issues associated with the source of the racial or ethnic data, sampling issues and others. While our main focus was on measurement issues in quantitative research, we also highlighted some key examples of the contributions of qualitative research to the measurement of race and ethnicity for it can be argued that qualitative researchers inform quantitative researchers of the underlying problems in their measures of race and ethnicity (cf. Bulmer and Solomos, 2004 among others). Many of these issues are longstanding but still important. The newest methodological issue concerns multiple racial identities, an option allowed for the first time in the 2000 Census in the United States. Though the numbers who chose multiple races this time were small, it is expected that the numbers will increase in the future as people become more accustomed to the idea and as immigration and intermarriage proceed apace.

A major issue for the future is where the race/ethnic boundary will be drawn: are we moving towards white/non-white or black/non-black? The social structure of race relations in the United States rests on the black/white divide, but immigration is adding new groups, and these new groups bring with them new racial and ethnic understandings. Alba and Nee (2005) see us as moving towards a black/non-black divide as the new assimilation works better for immigrants than blacks. Bonilla-Silva (2002, 2006) argues that we are moving towards a tri-partite system of whites at the top, honorary whites in between and non-whites or collective blacks at the bottom. Herring (2002) shows that not all stratification outcomes conform to the tripartite model, in some cases, the former binary system is still important, as well as times when honorary whites or even blacks do better than whites, while Murguia and Saenz (2002) present evidence that there has always been a tripartite system. Frederickson (2002: 148) poses the question of whether the racial divide will be replaced by one based on faith or creed.

Regardless of where the line is drawn, there is little doubt that we are 'far from overcoming the tenacious legacies of colonial rule, apartheid and segregation' (Winant, 2000: 182) or appreciating the role of racism as part of the social structure, not just a characteristic of individuals (Bonilla-Silva and Baiocchi, 2001; Massey and Denton, 1993). Zuberi and Bonilla-Silva (2008) go further and challenge researchers to examine how racial considerations have influenced how their research is conducted in the first place, from conceptualisation to analysis, calling for a deracialisation of the analysis of studies of racial stratification and racial issues more generally. Issues of racial and ethnic inequality and conflict abound in the world and appear on the local and national news almost every night. Winant suggests that while race may not ever be transcended, the 'world still has a chance of overcoming the stratification, the hierarchy, the taken-for-granted injustice and inhumanity that so often accompanies the race concept' (2000:183).

So race and ethnicity are generally viewed today as social constructions not biological ones. Some argue that we would be better not classifying people by race and making decisions in a colourblind fashion. However, the ability of an outside observer to distinguish people based on skin colour, somatic features, and other ethnic identifiers remains obvious to all; so race and ethnicity are real in their consequences, regardless of their scientific grounding. The sometimes large disparities in health, wealth, education, employment and residential location between people of different races and ethnicities in the United States and around the world indicate the continuing significance of race and ethnicity and the importance of facing the methodological challenges they present us.

NOTES

1. As there are many fine histories of the US Census and federal data collection on race and ethnicity (Anderson, 1988; US Bureau of the Census, 1979; Nobles, 2000; Snipp, 2003), we do not cover this material here. Anderson (1988) gives a history of how race was counted in the United States from 1790 to the present. Both Rodriguez (2000: 83) and Tafoya et al. (2004) provide lists of terms used for race in all censuses.

2. This question replaced that on parents' place of birth, which had been on every census since 1870. Ironically, this change occurred just as it was becoming important to identify generations for the post 1965-immigrants, which the ancestry question does not allow.

3. The Bridge Report should not be interpreted as an exhaustive set of assignment schemes. For example, the National Health Interview Survey has had multiple-race options for a number of years, as well as a follow-up question asking the respondent for the race with which they most closely identify, information that can be used to make an assignment to a single category as well as to make assignments from a probability distribution. Another assignment scheme that involves the recoding of race and Hispanic origin has been suggested by the National Longitudinal Study of Adolescent Health (Bearman et al., 1997). This method is also a Deterministic Whole Assignment

method, but under this approach, Hispanic origin is treated as a racial classification rather than as a distinct identification of ethnicity. Any individual self-identified as Hispanic will be assigned to this race group, regardless of any additional identifications. Non-Hispanic blacks will be allocated as black, regardless of any additional identifications; any Non-Hispanic self-identified as Asian, SOR, or white, given that he/she did not also identify as black, will be allocated as Asian; any Non-Hispanic self-identified as SOR or white, given that he/she did not also identify as black or Asian, will be allocated as SOR; and only single-race Non-Hispanic whites will be remain as white. Still another method is to simply count all the people in all the racial categories, but this has the disadvantage of the sum of all the categories exceeding 100 percent, as well as not helping to bridge the present with the past. See also the review and allocation method given in Tucker et al. (2002).

REFERENCES

Alba, R.D. and Denton, N.A. (2008) 'L'expérience aux USA avec les données raciales et ethniques: Le bilan entre la connaissance scientifique et al politique des identités', *Revue Française de Sociologie*, 49 (1): 141–151.

Alba, R. and Nee, V. (2005) *Remaking the American Mainstream: Assimilation and Contemporary Immigration*. Cambridge: Harvard University Press.

Anderson, M.J. (2002) 'Counting by Race: The Antebellum Legacy' in J. Perlmann and M.C. Waters, (eds) *The New Race Question: How the Census Counts Multiracial Individuals*. New York: Russell Sage Foundation. pp. 269–287.

Bearman, P.S., Jones, J. and Udry, J.R. (1997) *The National Longitudinal Study of Adolescent Health: Research Design*. http://www.cpc.unc.edu/projects/addhealth/design.html.

Blee, K. (2000) 'White on White: Interviewing Women in U.S. White Supremicist Groups' in F.W. Twine and J. Warren, (eds) *Race-ing Research: Methodological and Ethical Dilemmas in Field Research*. New York: New York University Press. pp. 93–110.

Body-Gendrot, S. (2004) 'Race, a Word Too Much? The French Dilemma' in M. Bulmer and J. Solomos, (eds) *Researching Race and Racism*. London: Routledge. pp.150–161.

Bonilla-Silva, E. and Baiocchi, G. (2001) 'Anything but Racism: How Sociologists Limit the Significance of Racism', *Race and Society*, 4 (2): 117–131.

Bonilla-Silva, E. (2006) *Racism without Racists: Color-Blind Racism and the Persistence of Racial Inequality in the United States*. 2nd edition. Lanham, MD: Rowman & Littlefield Publishers, Inc.

Bonilla-Silva, E. (2002) 'We Are All Americans!: The Latin Americanization of Racial Stratification in the U.S'., *Race and Society*, 5 (1): 3–16.

Bourhis, R.Y. (2003) 'Measuring Ethnocultural Diversity Using the Canadian Census', *Canadian Ethnic Studies Journal*, 35 (1): 9–32.

Bradby, H. (2003) 'Describing Ethnicity in Health Research', *Ethnicity and Health*, 8 (1): 5–13.

Bulmer, M. and Solomos, J. (2004) *Researching Race and Racism*. London: Routledge.

Census 2001 Form, United Kingdom. http://www.statistics.gov.uk/census2001/pdfs/H1.pdf

Chideya, F. (1999) *The Color of Our Future*. New York: William Morrow & Co.

Cresce, A.R., Schmidley, A.D. and Ramirez, R.R. (2004) 'Identification of Hispanic Ethnicity in Census 2000: Analysis of Data Quality for the Question on Hispanic Origin'. Washington, DC: US Bureau of the Census, Working Paper No. 75. http://www.census.gov/population/www/documentation/twps0075/twps0075.pdf

Farley, R. (2002) 'Racial Identities in 2000: The Response to the Multiple-Race Response Option' in J. Perlmann and M.C. Waters, (eds) *The New Race Question: How the Census Counts Multiracial Individuals*. New York: Russell Sage Foundation. pp. 33–61.

Field, L.D. (1996) 'Piecing Together the Puzzle: Self-Concept and Group Identity in Biracial Black/White Youth' in M.P.P. Root, (ed.) *The Multiracial Experience: Racial Borders as the New Frontier*. Thousand Oaks, CA: Sage Publications. pp. 211–226.

Fredrickson, G.M. (2002) *Racism: A Short History*. Princeton, NJ: Princeton University Press.

Funderburg, L. (1994) *Black, White, Other: Biracial Americans Talk About Race and Identity.* New York: Harper Perennial.

Goldstein, J.R. and Morning, A.J. (2002) 'Back in the Box: The Dilemma of Using Multiple-Race Data for Single-Race Laws' in J. Perlmann and M.C. Waters, (eds) *The New Race Question: How the Census Counts Multiracial Individuals.* New York: Russell Sage Foundation. pp. 119–136.

Gonzalez, M.E. and Waksberg, J. (1973) 'Estimation of the error of synthetic estimates'. Presented at first meeting of the the the International Association of Survey Statisticians, Vienna, Austria.

Gordon, R.A. (1968) 'Issues in Multiple Regression', *American Journal of Sociology*, 73 (5): 592–616.

Hahn, R.A., Mulinare, J. and Teutsch, S.M. (1992) 'Inconsistencies in Coding of Race and Ethnicity between Birth and Death in US Infants: A New Look at Infant Mortality, 1983 through 1985', *Journal of the American Medical Association*, 267 (2): 259–63.

Hardin, J.W. and Hilbe, J.M. (2003) *Generalized Estimation Equations.* Boca Raton, FL: Chapman & Hall/CRC.

Harris, D.R. (2002) 'Does it Matter How We Measure? Racial Classification and the Characteristics of Multiracial Youth' in J. Perlmann and M.C. Waters, (eds) *The New Race Question: How the Census Counts Multiracial Individuals.* New York: Russell Sage Foundation. pp. 62–101.

Harris, D. and Sim, J. (2002) 'Who Is Multiracial? Assessing the Complexity of Lived Race', *American Sociological Review*, 67 (4): 614–627.

Harris, M. (1964) *Patterns of Race in the Americas.* New York: Walker.

Harris, M., Consorte, J.G., Lang, J. and Byrne, B. (1993) 'Who Are the Whites? Imposed Census Categories and the Racial Demography of Brazil', *Social Forces*, 72 (2): 451–462.

Harrison, R.J. (2002) 'Inadequacies of Multiple-Response Race Data in the Federal Statistical System' in J. Perlmann and M.C. Waters, (eds) *The New Race Question: How the Census Counts Multiracial Individuals.* New York: Russell Sage Foundation. pp. 137–160.

Herring, C. (2002) 'Bleaching out the Color Line? The Skin Color Continuum and the Tripartite Model of Race', *Race and Society*, 5 (1): 17–31.

Hirschman, C. (2004) 'The Origins and Demise of the Concept of Race', *Population and Development Review*, 30 (3): 385–415.

Hirschman, C., Alba, R. and Farley, R. (2000) 'The Meaning and Measurement of Race in the U.S. Census: Glimpses into the Future', *Demography*, 37 (August): 381–393.

Hollinger, D.A. (1995) *Post-Ethnic America: Beyond Multiculturalism.* New York?: Basic Books.

Hout, M. and Goldstein, J.R. (1994) 'How 4.5 million Irish Immigrants Became 40 million Irish Americans: Demographic and Subjective Aspects of the Ethnic Composition of White Americans', *American Sociological Review*, 59 (1): 64–82.

James, A. (2001) 'Making Sense of Race and Racial Classification', *Race and Society*, 4 (2): 235–247.

Jedwab, J. (2003) 'Coming to Our Census: The Need for Continued Inquiry into Canadians' Ethnic Origins', *Canadian Ethnic Studies*, 35 (1): 33–50.

Kanaiaupuni, S. and Liebler, C.A. (2003) 'Pondering Poi Dog: The Importance of Place to the Racial Identification of Multi-Racial Native Hawaiians'. Honolulu, HI: Kamehameha Schools, PASE Working Paper 02-03:24. http://www.ksbe.edu/pase/reports-year.php#2003

Keaton, T.D. (2006) *Muslim Girls and the Other France.* Bloomington: Indiana University Press.

Khalfani, A.K. and Zuberi, T. (2001) 'Racial Classification and the Modern Census in South Africa, 1911-1996', *Race and Society*, 4 (4): 161–176.

Lamont, M. (2004) 'A Life of Sad, but Justified, Choices: Interviewing across (too) May Divides' in M. Bulmer and J. Solomos (eds) *Researching Race and Racism.* London: Routledge. pp. 162–171.

Land, K.C., McCall, P.L. and Cohen, L.E. (1990) 'Structural Covariates of Homicide Rates: Are There Any Invariances Across Time and Social Space?', *American Journal of Sociology*, 95 (3): 922–963.

Lieberson, S. (1980) *A Piece of the Pie: Blacks and White Immigrants Since 1880.* Berkeley: University of California Press.

Lieberson, S. and Waters, M.C. (1993) 'The Ethnic Response of Whites: What Causes Their Instability, Simplification, and Inconsistency?', *Social Forces*, 72 (2): 421–450.

Liebler, C.A. (2004) 'Ties on the Fringes of Identity', *Social Science Research*, 33 (4): 702–723.

Logan, J.R., Stults, B.J. and Farley, R. (2004) 'Segregation of Minorities in the Metropolis: Two Decades of Change', *Demography*, 41 (1): 1–22.

Marshall, G. (1968) 'Racial Classifications: Popular and Scientific' in M. Mead, T. Dobzhansky, E. Tobach, and R. Light (eds) *Science and the Concept of Race*. New York: Columbia University Press. pp. 149–164.

Martin, E., DeMaio, T.J. and Campanelli, P.C. (1990) 'Context Effects for Census: Measures of Race and Hispanic Origin', *Public Opinion Quarterly*, 54 (4): 551–566.

Massey, D.S. (1998) 'Back to the Future: The Rediscovery of Neighbourhood Context', *Contemporary Sociology*, 27 (6): 570–572.

Massey, D.S. and Denton, N.A. (1993) *American Apartheid: Segregation and the Making of the Underclass*. Cambridge: Harvard University Press.

Morganstein, D. and Marker, D. (2000) 'A Conversation with Joseph Waksberg', *Statistical Science*, 15 (3): 299–312.

Murguia, E. and Saenz, R. (2002) 'An Analysis of the Latin Americanization of Race in the United States: A Reconnaissance of Color Stratification among Mexicans', *Race and Society*, 5 (1): 85–101.

Nobles, M. (2002) 'Lessons from Brazil: The Ideational and Political Dimensions of Multiraciality' in J. Perlmann and M.C. Waters, (eds.) *The New Race Question: How the Census Counts Multiracial Individuals*. New York: Russell Sage Foundation. pp. 300–317.

Nobles, M. (2000) *Shades of Citizenship: Race and the Census in Modern Politics*. Stanford, CA: Stanford University Press.

Office of Management and Budget (OMB), Executive Office of the President. (1997a) 'Revisions to the Standards for the Classification of Federal Data on Race and Ethnicity', *Federal Register*, 62 (10): 58782–58790.

Office of Management and Budget (OMB) (1997b) 'Recommendations From the Interagency Committee for the Review of the Race and Ethnic Standards to the Office of Management and Budget Concerning Changes to the Standards for the Classification of Federal Data on Race and Ethnicity', *Federal Register*, 62 (131): 36873–36946.

Office of Management and Budget (OMB) (2000) 'Provisional Guidance on the Implementation of the 1997 Standards for Federal Data on Race and Ethnicity'. Federal Register (because of its length, this document is not reproduced in the Federal Register, but is available electronically from the OMB web site: www.whitehouse.gov/omb/fedreg/index.html [OMB Federal Register 2001]).

Omi, M. and Winant, H. (1986) *Racial Formation in the United States: From the 1960s to the 1980s*. New York: Routledge.

Parker, J.D. and Makuc, D.M. (2002) 'Methodologic Implications of Allocating Multiple-Race Data to Single-Race Categories', *Health Services Research*, 37 (1): 201–213.

Perlmann, J. and Waters, M.C. (eds) (2002) *The New Race Question: How the Census Counts Multiracial Individuals*. New York: Russell Sage Foundation.

Rockquemore, Kerry Ann and Brunsma, D.L. (2002) 'Socially Embedded Identities: Theories, Typologies, and Processes of Racial Identity among Biracials', *The Sociological Quarterly*, 43 (3): 335–356.

Rodriguez, C.E. (2000) *Changing Race: Latinos, the Census, and the History of Ethnicity in the United States*. New York: New York University Press.

Rodriguez, C.E. and Cordero-Guzman, H. (1992) 'Placing Race in Context', *Ethnic and Racial Studies*, 15 (4): 523–542.

Schwartzman, L.F. (2007) 'Does Money Whiten? Intergenerational Changes in Racial Classification in Brazil', *American Sociological Review*, 72 (6): 940–963.

Shapiro, T.M. (2004) *The Hidden Cost of Being African American: How Wealth Perpetuates Inequality*. London: Oxford University Press.

Skerry, P. (2000) *Counting on the Census?: Race, Group Identity, and the Evasion of Politics*. Washington, D.C.: Brookings Institution Press.

Snipp, C.M. (2002) 'American Indians: Clues to the Future of Other Racial Groups' in J. Perlmann and M.C. Waters, (eds) *The New Race Question: How the Census Counts Multiracial Individuals*. New York: Russell Sage Foundation. pp. 189–214.

Song, M. (2004) 'Racial Hierarchies in the USA and Britain: Investigating a Politically Sensitive Issue' in M. Bulmer and J. Solomos, (eds) *Researching Race and Racism*. London: Routledge. pp. 172–186.

St. Francis College v. Al-Khazraji 481 U.S. 604 (1987).

Stanfield, J.H. II (1993a) *A History of Race Relations Research: First Generation Recollections*. Newbury Park: Sage.

Stanfield, J.H. II (1993b) 'Methodological Reflections: An Introduction'. in J.H. Stanfield II and M.D. Rutledge, (eds) *Race and Ethnicity in Research Methods*. Newbury Park: Sage Publications. pp. 3–15.

Statistics Canada. (2006) Census Questionnaire. http://www12.statcan.ca/english/census06/reference/questions/index.cfm.

Tafoya, S.M., Johnson, H. and Hill, L.E. (2004) *Who Chooses to Choose Two?* New York: Russell Sage Foundation and Washington, DC: Population Reference Bureau.

Telles, E.E. (2004) *Race in Another America: The Significance of Skin Color in Brazil*. Princeton, NJ: Princeton University Press.

Torres, A. (1998) 'La Gran Familia Puertorriquena 'Ej Prieta de Belda' (The Great Puerto Rican family is really really Black)'. in A. Torres and N.E. Whitten, Jr. (eds) *Blackness in Latin America and the Caribbean: Social Dynamics and Cultural Transformations*. Volume II: Eastern South America and the Caribbean. Bloomington: Indiana University Press. pp. 285–306.

Tucker, C., Miller, S. and Parker, J. (2002) 'Comparing Census Race Data under the Old and the New Standards' in J. Perlmann and M.C. Waters, (eds) *The New Race Question: How the Census Counts Multiracial Individuals*. New York: Russell Sage Foundation. pp. 365–390.

Twine, F.W. (2000) 'Racial Idoeologies and Racial Methodologies' in F.W. Twine and J.W. Warren, (eds) *Racing Research Researching Race*. New York: NYU Press. pp. 1–34.

Twine, F.W. and Warren, J.W. (eds) (2000) *Racing Research Researching Race*. New York: NYU Press.

US Bureau of the Census (1979) *Twenty Censuses: Population and Housing Questions 1790–1980*. Washington, D.C.: US Government Printing Office.

Vickerman, M. (1998) *Crosscurrents: West Indian Immigrants and Race*. New York: Oxford University Press.

Waksberg, J., Judkins, T. and Massey, J.T. (1997) 'Geographic-Based Oversampling in Demographic Surveys of the United States', *Survey Methodology*, 23 (1): 61–71.

Warren, J.W. (2000) '"Masters in the Field" White Talks, White Privilege, White Biases' in F.W. Twine and J.W. Warren, (eds) *Racing Research Researching Race*. New York: NYU Press. pp. 135–164.

Waters, M.C. (1999) *Black Identities: West Indian Immigrant Dreams and American Realities*. Cambridge and New York: Harvard and Russell Sage.

Waters, M.C. (1990) *Ethnic Options: Choosing Identities in America*. Berkeley: University of California Press.

Williams, D.R. (1999) 'The Monitoring of Racial/Ethnic Status in the USA: Data Quality Issues', *Ethnicity and Health*, 4 (3): 121–137.

Winant, H. (2000) 'Race and Race Theory', *Annual Review of Sociology*, 26: 169–185.

Young Jr., A.A. (2004) 'Experiences in Ethnographic Interviewing about Race: The Inside and the Outside of It' in M. Bulmer and J. Solomos, (eds) *Researching Race and Racism*, London: Routledge. pp. 187–202.

Zuberi, T. (2001) *Thicker Than Blood: How Racial Statistics Lie*. Minneapolis: University of Minnesota Press.

Zuberi, T. and Bonilla-Silva, E. (eds) (2008) *White Logic, White Methods: Racism and Methodology*. Lanham, MD: Rowman and Littlefield.

5

The Spirit Lives On: Races and Disciplines

Chetan Bhatt

INTRODUCTION

Though the biological validity of race was rejected after World War II, racial discourse and race-thinking continue to thrive in Euro-American academia. While the nature of racial discourse varies substantially between the UK and North America, and across Europe, certain themes are common in academic writings about race and racism. Indeed, writing abstractly about race is about engaging with a series of constant repetitions about the existence and non-existence of race, about the utility of the concept of race for social justice or for explaining biological difference and about the need to abandon this concept for the social sciences and humanities. The act of repetition promises a finality that fails to arrive since race appears to escape any theoretical discourse that seeks to contain, map or invalidate it.

The 'impasse of race' thus continues to reproduce itself in various academic disciplines in different Euro-American nations. The impasse often takes the form of a disavowal within biological science of the existence of races, together with a sociological and anthropological renunciation of scientific ideas of race. But at the same time, there is an acknowledgement in social science of race as 'merely' a Durkhemian social fact, a reification that requires analysis and rejection, critique and refutation. In this way racial discourse – and the idea of race – proliferates through their disavowal. The impasse of race often depends on issues such as whether race does or does not exist, and whether race should or should not be used academically (St. Louis, 2005: 30). Hence, the utterance of race advances it as a genuine concept that has a real referent, or the utterance knowingly promotes the use of an illegitimate concept.

In the social sciences, race is acknowledged to be a 'myth', but racial and ethnic classifications are readily instrumentalised to remedy discrimination and disadvantage: the lie about the existence of races is sustained so that the injustices arising from this lie can be ameliorated. A similar impulse is present in contemporary biomedical sciences – the use of racial categories is considered essential for the medical well-being of minorities. (A different rationale appears in forensic science and in the physical anthropology of victims and criminals.) The abundance of racial and ethnic classifications in health and social policy areas is a consequence of the logic of partition inherent in race-thinking, an unrelenting taxonomic imperative that exists partly because there is no stable content to the idea of race. In this way, much contemporary anti-racism can also reify and proliferate further the racial categories that it says are not valid (Guillaumin, 1995; Solomos and Back, 1996; Gilroy, 2001). No claim of moral equivalence between racism and anti-racism is being made here. But if racism is a fantasy of purity, it is also a discourse of existential anxiety, and both of these themes can inform the efforts of anti-racists. For example, it is significant that many of the meta-languages of contemporary anti-racism can mimic the biosocial, moral and religious hygiene and sanitation metaphors of older racisms: both racism and the victims of racism represent the 'cancer', 'virus', 'poison' or 'evil' that is to be 'stamped out' or 'eradicated'. In this way, both racism and anti-racism can be pesticide or exorcism. This sharing of language is not accidental. As seen later, this common language can have profound moral consequences and can allow seemingly cosmopolitan anti-racist discourse to mystify some of the most powerful and violent forms of state racism that exist today.

The critique and refutation of race and racism is a synchronised deconstruction–reproduction of racial ideas and identities such that it is impossible to refute race without in *some way* affirming the field of intelligibility that allows race to exist in the first place. We might claim that in analytically 'racing' a social process, we are revealing, and so refuting racial ideologies within it; yet our 'racing' may unleash a variety of open-ended effects that escape us, and are beyond our command. 'Racing research' might be undertaken with genuine anti-racist motives but can lead to the reification of races at the same moment at, and through the same processes through, which racism is rejected. 'Reification' is a somewhat blunt term for a series of manifest and subtle effects that escape us and are not captured wholly by the treating of an idea as if it is an object.

If race acquires very different and unpredictable meanings in specific social and historical events, processes and circumstances (Solomos and Back, 1996: 209, 213–14), it is also worth asking: what is it about the intensities of race that allow it – as if it was an agential concept – to conduct, regulate and synthesise such a diversity of meanings in particular socio-historical situations? One argument explored throughout the chapter is that modern ideologies of race are dependent on a range of metaphysical ideas: about time, bodies and violence; inherited virtue and arcane consciousness; ingathering, co-presence and empyrean hierarchy; and original purity and inerrancy. The essential task of refuting or invalidating race in specific circumstances therefore may fail to address the broader metaphysical potentials that configure the way race descends into and supplies meanings for particular social circumstances or, conversely, how the latter generate new meanings of race for future historical events.

For anti-racists, the problem of race is that it is a 'concept' that cannot reify or hypostasise whatever its referent (including its self-referent) might be, since that is its *inherent* peril. Anti-racism is after all based on a genuine conviction that races do not exist. But many forms of especially communal anti-racism,[1] in challenging racism, generate other race concepts. Yet, it can still feel as if the academic performance of risk in using the term 'race' is as real as it is a *frisson* of danger, the actual danger residing within a different economy of academic production. There is adjacently a frequently acknowledged confusion regarding the academic use of race in the United Kingdom and the United States, though it is one of the properties of race-thinking that this confusion should exist. The terms we use – race, racism, racialisation, anti-racism – are viscous, adhesive ones. We escape race only to preserve a particular 'black' identity; we refute the existence of race and in the process of doing so, end up finding it everywhere.

One way of thinking about these areas is as a movement from the particular 'species' of race that must be rejected for the universal 'genera' of a common humanity. However, a generic humanity (Badiou, 2005) cannot be grasped imaginatively, except in rare or extreme political circumstances (including ones where violence is unleashed in the name of humanity.) Beyond its rhetorical power, 'humanity' rarely has specific utility in academic disciplines and fragments readily into intra-human groups. Hence, in the name of (a receding horizon of) humanity, the particularism of race reasserts itself, as indeed it must do in academic fields concerned with populations, majorities, minorities, groups, identities, beliefs and cultures. The broader point is that philosophical humanism does not seem to exist independently of the metaphysics of the fragment or group.

In the light of recent molecular biology, the 'impasse of race' seems somewhat outmoded, and yet this impasse is a historically vigourous and productive one that seems unlikely to be superceded in a putative postracial future. If biological, sociological and anthropological debates tend to hover around the ontology of race as real presence or void, they are also concerned with its epistemic qualities, its analytical status, its usefulness for the discipline and the various hermeneutic and moral snares that race creates. Hence, we tend to concern ourselves with issues such as the instabilities in the meaning of race, the invisibility of a stable referent for race, its ceaseless proliferation of connotations, its generation of myriad chains of signification, its omnivorous ability to act as a signifier for the most divergent of events and phenomena, its inexplicably powerful association with politics or philosophy, the vicious regressions and circularities that bedevil its cognate terms. However, these issues do not indicate problems with the meaning of race but instead *give* race its meanings. Similarly, the question of whether race is a social fact or is instead a determinate object in biology is not one that demands an answer but is instead a fount of meanings. There is truth in the claim that, during most of the postwar period, the social sciences have laboured far more intensively to promote race-thinking than have the natural sciences, and have done so precisely through the claim that it is biology that illegitimately continues to promote the idea of races (see Murji and Solomos, 2005: 9–10). This asymmetry is significant: it allows the social sciences (and humanities) to repetitively censure the biological sciences for harbouring a concept of race while ceaselessly promoting it themselves, the propagation of race through the maintenance of vigilance on biological racism. Hence, problems regarding the meaning of race are not problems as such, but generate a wider field of understanding that brings together aesthetics with rationality, politics with mythology, the scientific with the mystical and the ideological with the affective.

These binaries indicate some key antinomies in racial thinking and these areas are explored below by considering a deliberately diverse range of issues from eighteenth-century philosophy, nineteenth-century anthropology, twentieth-century molecular genetics and finally the so-called Israel–Palestine conflict. These xamples, two historical and two contemporary, are explored in an open-ended way, but link to three main frictions or tensions: between cosmopolitan and communal varieties of racism and anti-racism; between rationalist and 'mystical' influences in racial thinking; and between continuity in modern racial thinking on the one hand, and the ways in which discontinuities are 'given' coherence.

The approach of this chapter might suggest that there is a much stronger continuity in racial ideas than actually exists across the four main examples explored. Indeed, histories of race and racism can inadvertently provide the latter with a rationality and coherence they do not possess: the 'history of ideas usually credits the discourse it analyses with coherence' (Foucault, 1972: 149). It is largely accepted in the humanities and social sciences that the history of the idea of race followed a fairly clear path from the emergence of systematic race-thinking from the mid-eighteenth-century natural historical and philosophical discourse to the ideas and practices in the nineteenth-century that initiated the rise of scientific racism (Banton, 1977, 1987; Barkan, 1992; Augstein, 1996; Tucker, 1994; Hannaford, 1996). Alongside this, there is the parallel history of race in transatlantic slavery, colonialism and imperialism, including the first mobilisations of scientific racism against abolitionists. The historical trajectory then moves from the 'high period' of scientific racism and eugenics in the later nineteenth and early decades of the twentieth-century, to the seeming suspension of the idea of race following the Holocaust. The idea of race emerges again in comparative analyses of the racial state (South Africa during apartheid, segregation in the southern states of America) and of the position of minority groups in Western societies. The nineteenth-century consolidation of scientific racism is also located in a postcolonial theoretical approach to the enumeration, cataloguing, classification and representation that took place in the administration of the Empire, particularly in South and South-East Asia, but having precedents in eastern and central Africa. These are diverse histories of race-thinking and yet their narrativisation can provide a coherent frame of reference for understanding race and racism. The coherence of race-thinking can also be over-informed by the histories of scientific racism and its emphasis on the rationalist and positivist aspects of racial enumeration and classification.

The assumption of coherence is significant and allows race and racism to be understood primarily through organised, rational systems and processes. Hence, race and racism are often related to modernist enumeration, the calculus of populations and geometries of hierarchy and power. They are seen as systematic ideologies of division and conflict, social facts that can be identified, elaborated, mapped and understood or which can be dismantled by *Ideologiekritik* or by raw statistics of discrimination and disadvantage. Some dominant academic vocabularies relating to race are also interestingly *technological*: race is associated with systems, processes, formations, institutions and structures; hence, racism can seemingly be 'dismantled'. One result can be that many contemporary discussions tend to circumvent the metaphysical cosmology of race and instead focus on what are seen as coherent, rational systems of racism, ones which can be thus associated with modernity. One consequence is how the mystificatory qualities of race, racism and communal anti-racism can be politically instrumentalised so as to disguise racial states and racial conflicts.

While acknowledging the risk of assuming continuity and coherence in racial thinking across the main examples used in this chapter, some broader similarities are nevertheless argued for. Fantasies of purity and the will towards inerrant classification ('a war against ambiguity') are vital to racial discourse and these ideas are present in each of the examples below. One further aim of this chapter is to show certain continuities regarding the '*mystemes*' of race – metaphysical, mystical and affective ideas intrinsic to the race concept – across these highly diverse historical examples. Such ideas seem as important to the most rationalist forms of race-thinking (as in Kantian philosophy or molecular biology) as they do to, for example, mystical Aryanism. The essay also discusses how other metaphysical ideas – particularly ideas of violence, perhaps even an ethic of violence – travel across the boundaries that otherwise rigourously separate racism and anti-racism. The so-called 'Israeli–Palestinian conflict' and its dominant popular and academic rendition is discussed in order to show how anti-racist ideas (in the form of the claim of antisemitism as it is used by some contemporary pro-Israel groups) can be used to justify racially based discrimination and violent occupation by the state. In this example, claims based on cosmopolitan anti-racism merge with forms of communal racism. This example also demonstrates the transversal nature of many of the languages of race, racism and anti-racism, ones that can lend to an ethically diminished anti-racism. The aim of the essay is not to develop a general theoretical approach to race and racism but to explore some usually under-discussed ways in which race and its associated terms are and have been used.

THE MORAL AND THE RACIAL

It is a commonplace view that race-thinking and racism are key features of *modern* societies and institutions (Goldberg, 1993; Solomos and Back, 1996). One aspect of this view is about demonstrating that race and racism are endogenous to Enlightenment philosophy and emerge fairly clearly and naturally from it (Eze, 1997a; Mills, 1998). The embedment of racism in modernity can be thus concluded. Kant is a recurring target of attempts to show that racism and modernity are associated inextricably with each other. Kant's race-thinking and his racism are quite evident from his writings. His ideas are considered in opposition to those of Johann Gottfried Herder, himself a formidable race thinker, in order to draw out the broader ideas that both share and which appear today in many racial discourses.

It is also necessary to ask why we might wish to show *today* that 'Enlightenment' and 'modernity' are irrefutably racist, that their very essence is rotten, that race is philosophically imbricated in modernity as an evil that manifested in the Middle Passage, chattel and plantation slavery, colonisation and imperialism, and the Holocaust. The academic and political conditions of possibility that make this task an important one can subsume other ways of understanding 'Enlightenment' and 'modernity'.

If, in the past, racism sanctified racists, then in an existential reversal, race can sacralise today the descendents of victims of the brutal horrors of past racisms. This is an issue of vital moral consequence, since it can result in an elision of other democides and politicides that 'have accompanied modernity' but which cannot carry the symbolic and political resonance of those deemed 'racial' within Euro-America. Contemporary discourses about who one is can bestow virtuousness, ethical gnosis and a moral rectitude that cannot be extended to those who do not exist other than through what they think or what they do. Ideas of race and racism certainly have led to monstrous crimes, racial crimes, but this observation can lead to a moral partitioning of the sufferings and violence that modern humanity has endured. As we see later, the cleaving apart of humanity through certain understandings of 'morality', 'character' and even 'virtue' has been an essential feature of some kinds of humanist race-thinking, but the immediate issue here is that anti-racism can also demonstrate this kind of moral partitioning of humanity and a moral partiality towards identitarian and communal politics – which re-invigorates the idea of race and racial victimology in a different form.

Race and culture

If Kant produced the first systematically modern articulation of race (Kant, 1950), this was challenged by Johann Gottfried Herder (Herder, 1969) who proposed instead a common global humanity and its diverse, dense cultures (though Kant did of course refer to 'the human race'.) Significantly, Herder saw cultural differentiation as resulting from the 'genetic force' of nature as well as from other environmental and aesthetic modes through which cultures flourished. Herder believed in universal attributes shared by all humanity (such as reason and religion) but he also opposed a simple unitary idea of human nature (since 'human nature under diverse climates is never the same' (Barnard, 1969: 382) see also Herder, 1997).

While this might seem 'presentist', Herder's view about environment and cultural difference was as resistant in its implications about the cultural fixedness of human groups as views about the innate natural differences between races. Moreover, this view of his can be held in place next to his apparently contrary position that there is not necessarily any unchangeable human nature (Barnard, 1969). Hence, cultural density – the result of the genetic and organic forces that create nations – is a property manifested by individuals who, from a different perspective, are the same.

Without wishing to collapse their views, Kant, like Herder, used an idea of latent powers (which for Kant related to the potential of the 'germ', the primordium or *Anlagen*). For Kant, these were predetermined by nature to explain both variation and fixity (Lovejoy, 1910; 1911: 42). Significantly, both Kant's latent power and Herder's genetic force provided for the possibility of world history – a history of 'civilisation' within a largely 'teleological' understanding of human development. Similarly, in both Kant and Herder, there is the importance of rationality as a key criterion for evaluating cultures, despite Kant and Herder's differences about which peoples do, or do not, possess the (full) capacity for reason and morality. An 'aesthetic' apparatus in Kant (from his philosophical anthropology, and owing in critical respects to Hume) and Herder (in his early racial psychology and apparent in his vulgar assessments of Africans and Asians) forms the basis for judgement of Europeans and non-Europeans such that it seems impossible to separate the judgement of moral qualities and virtues from the 'aesthetic' judgement of somatic appearances, characteristics and climates. In Herder's case, this position can again be held together with a contrary one that can propose positive characteristics for non-Europeans – indeed, even the view that the 'culture of man is not the culture of the *European*; it manifests itself according to place and time in *every* people' (Barnard, 1969: 63). Put otherwise, in both Kant and Herder's work, ideas that are 'cosmopolitan' and ideas that are 'communal' generate a *constitutively* important tension.

Now, if Herder's rigid cultures can seemingly allow all humans to share the common essence of what it means to be human, does Kant's 'race' limit 'cultural development' for some? A fundamental issue in Kant's work is whether the 'limits of race' are permanent, or whether the non-European races can be dragged into a 'cultivated' state so as to achieve fully the 'stage' of cultured advancement and moral detachment equivalent to that seemingly possessed by Europeans. Partly, this is because of Kant's incorporation of earlier taxonomic ideas that sought to identify the lowest possible limit of human existence.

Kant's races

For Kant, human races were based on the 'invariably inherited' characteristic of skin colour rather than the 'alternatively inherited' characteristics of, say, hair colour, the latter resulting not in races but *varieties* (Lovejoy, 1911: 42). Kant's human races (European, African, Mongoloid and Hindu) were manifestations of latent powers in which nature had anticipated for perpetuity all the foreseeable environments in which such manifestations 'would out' (ibid). Races are 'fixed' in some important way that varieties are not. Hence, there is a seeming paradox: primordial 'fixedness' exists with the inexhaustible diversity of the species.

Kant would not accept (entirely) the obvious monogenist resolution to this contradiction (which was available in his day and pre-existed Darwin), that all human species had a common origin. He argued that species were *originally* partitioned, but he also allowed for the idea that all human races originated from one 'stock' (*Stamm*) (Lovejoy, 1911: 38–39). This holding together of deeply contrary positions (in both Kant's and Herder's work) regarding sameness and difference, common and differential origins, permanence and transformation is a key attribute of many forms of modern humanism, whether 'rationalist' or 'romantic'. From this perspective, the sharp differences between Kant and Herder, in their respective racial and (largely) cultural understanding of human groups, become less important than the broader epistemological similarity they share.

Kant, race and philosophy

It is worth exploring Kant's ideas about race a little more deeply. Of significance for Kant's racial ideas is how homogeneity (*genera*) and specification (species) co-exist and at which scale of abstraction can one subsume the other (Kant, 1929 [1781–1787]: 539–42). How can the unities of nature be reconciled with its diversities, and how are both subsumed under the overall unity of nature itself? It is from considering *genera* and species and the associations between them that Kant elaborated (synthetic *a priori*) principles of unity, manifoldness and affinity (ibid: 544–545). This shows a movement in Kant's *Critique of Pure Reason* from a consideration of species to the laws of *genera*, specification and continuity, and from there to the core edifice of Kant's philosophical system, namely certain categories of quantity that organise how nature's manifoldness is given to us as objects of our experience. We might claim that the core of Kant's philosophical system derives from his ideas about genera and species, ideas that are, in an empirical way, also associated with his ideas about the human species and human races. So we might claim to have gleaned racial ideas at the core of his philosophy. Detractors would wish to find ways of dismissing these claims.

But, race does become *philosophically* significant in several ways. There is not *one* theory of race in Kant, one simply related to skin colour. While Kant certainly somatised race, it is not defined solely by the epidermis. Instead, several theoretical moves can be discerned that associate the outer body (skin) with what would, in his philosophy, be unwarranted hierarchies in inner morality, character (and virtue) or faculties. These extend further to ideas regarding the immutability of race in accordance with the laws and purposiveness ('without purpose') of nature. This implies an association between race and the capacity for reason (Eze, 1997b), morality and aesthetic judgement; it also implies a relation between race, history and civilisation.

Race and variety

It seems to require a great deal of work by Kant (and, it seems, by 'nature') to uphold these opposing ideas: of human races as relatively fixed, but human varieties as changeable; of race as a fundamental primordial division of the human species that had nevertheless originated from a single 'stock'. Kant had to allow for a common origin of the human races while holding on to the original partition of the races. He allowed for the variation (as 'varieties') of humans, and yet did not consider the racial characteristics he identified as outwardly changeable in anything like the way that human varieties were. Racial predispositions did not produce new forms, whereas the predispositions that led to human varieties indicated the inexhaustible production of new inner and outer *characters* (Lovejoy, 1911: 44–45). Hence, while humans grouped within a specific race would demonstrate variety, the partitioning out of race by Kant as a particularly resistant, relatively unchanging and primordial aspect of human differentiation – in a way that his human varieties seemed not to be – is important in several respects. It reveals the fantasy of eternal purity that afflicts race-thinking. For Kant, nature had already determined the 'end goal' of race (and every possible manifestation of racial differentiation) from a primordial point that had also anticipated, and had therefore already visited, every possible future (ibid: 44). It seems reasonable to presume that the varieties exhibited within one 'race' cannot be sufficient to breach the boundaries of outer and inner character or the virtues manifested within a race, otherwise there seems to be no reason for race's existence. If so, this also implies a natural racial boundary to the possible variety of inner characters, the conduct of thinking, the virtues and morality.

This fixedness of race for all time is important because of the seeming implication of morally 'differential ends' for different races, a position radically at odds with Kant's moral philosophy as a whole. It might be argued that ours is an illegitimate argumentative move from the empirical to the transcendental, not least around an area that Kant's philosophy precludes. Seeing race in Kant's writings as more than empiricism may appear to confuse an empirical area with Kant's moral philosophy. Nevertheless an ambiguity exists here (one related to *a posteriori* and *a priori* judgements.) It links to a broader issue about the division of the empirical and transcendental, the suggestion being that race has an ambiguous position within this binary.[2] Hence, while Kant's ideas of nature, species and morality apply universally, there is also the possibility of a metaphysical racial idea of considerable power. Given Kant's association of the universal laws of nature with reason and morality, the reason for the existence of race is, indeed, 'reason'. Put in a different way, the reason race exists in nature at all is a mystery of nature, since we cannot venture into knowing nature's (or, if you like, reason's) reasons.

Kant, race and judgement

This is also significant for race in another way, since Kant's idea of the 'purposiveness without purpose' of nature is inextricably associated with his philosophy of moral judgement. We can suggest that race associates with his teleological thinking in an extraordinary way in which reason and mystery become combined. It is not simply that 'race is nature' in Kant, a characteristic primarily relevant for non-Europeans, whereas for the European, human variety combines with cultivated morality in some way that is seemingly precluded for non-Europeans. Race is different from human variation, but seemingly must retain a powerful association with nature's teleology. Race appears as the most purposively fixed element that nature originally bestowed upon humans, and it must exist fixed and fairly bounded in its manifestations for all times. Yet the 'purposiveness without purpose' of nature leads to moral cultivation and the capacity for aesthetic judgement since the latter are prefigured within original, latent powers and capacities. How do the limits of race defined primordially by nature relate to the direction towards morality that is an inherent part of nature's telos, a direction which, it seems, Kant has limited for some humans? We can suggest that race defeats nature's teleology: race, while a part of nature, does not seem to follow nature's nature but is contrary to it, since it prevents (differentially for some humans) a certain direction towards morality that appears as an inherent aspect of nature's 'purposiveness without purpose'. Race, similarly, halts movement, history and thus time. Race seems to present a pre-ordained limit to moral development, whereas variety might exhibit an unlimited capacity for change and development. Hence, race extends beyond an anthropological concept or an empirical issue subsidiary to Kant's grand philosophy (Kant, 1978; Eze, 1997a; 1997b).

Certainly, Kant's advancement of racial (or national) character is intertwined with a moral hierarchy in which judgement about the moral and the beautiful appear inseparable from the natural capacity of different races to make such judgements. The key issue is not whether all humans belong to same or different groups by virtue of their physical differences, but concomitantly, whether they possess the indwelling power that provides them with the capacity to become cultivated, and so become moral agents (agents that are within *society* as the latter was understood in eighteenth-century Europe, those who have entered the field of cultivated sociality.)

The idea of *particular* moral groups would, of course, be an abomination to the transcendental aspects of Kant's philosophy (since this idea does not distinguish practical anthropology from the transcendental conditions for abstract morality and judgement). Hence the charge that Kant's ideas of race determine whether or not all humans belong to the same 'moral groups', share the same moral history and whether they are travelling in time towards the same goal of universal morality can be dismissed as inconsequential for his transcendental philosophy. It might also be argued reasonably that the 'universal' and 'particular' (say, the human species and human races) are held in a functionally important tension in Kant's philosophy in a way that cannot be dismissed easily. It could then be argued that what is required to remedy Kant's racism is the injection into his moral and political philosophy of a dose of contemporary multiculturalism, one that can be metabolised by a hopeful cosmopolitanism. However, this would avoid the reasons for why there is in Kant's philosophy no natural or transcendental space for (a non-anachronistic) 'multiculturalism' of a kind that had been articulated in his time, nor why he laboured to create the space for differentiated races precisely against such an *immoral* 'multicultural' possibility (Kant, 1991 [1785]: 219–220).

It would thus appear that some non-European races do not have the comprehensive capacities of will and reason and do not exist fully within the class of 'all rational beings' who can know, will and judge. Nor do they seem to exist fully within the species that characterises humans such that the latter as a whole might 'retire' in the kingdom of ends. It does not require from Kant the explicit elaboration of the idea of race as a transcendental (Eze, 1997b), a synthetic *a priori*, to also suggest that the Kantian division between particular bodies and universal morality lends to a dominant race-thinking.

Similarly, the powerful association in Western philosophy between aesthetics and the affective, an association intimately linked to morality and judgement in Kant's third *Critique* (Kant, 1951 [1790]), can also lead to a different consideration of race and judgement in Kant's philosophy. Here the capacity for moral judgement resulting from a particular kind of cultivated and therefore disinterested feeling in the presence of the sublime, is unavailable, or unavailable fully for the non-European 'races' (Spivak, 1999). An inherited hierarchy of morality, character and virtue associates with racial (or national) belonging. This hierarchy is naturally bestowed, primordial, eternal, but we cannot venture into its mysterious origins. Hence, several issues present themselves from Kant's writings: race as original mystery; race as an excision of some non-European groups from the possibility of morality, judgement, civilisation and history; race as an inherent limit and boundary; and race as the halting of time. The latter two ideas in particular pose further difficulties for followers of Kant. This is especially because of his writings about why certain groups, such as the happily indolent inhabitants of Tahiti, limited by a natural threshold immanent from within themselves and thus immobilised in time, should even exist – or be allowed to exist (Kant, 1991 [1785]).

Those who wish to stress Kant's cosmopolitanism or simply the majesty of his pure philosophy might consider the above arguments as selective over-interpretation, or even that Kant's racism is irrelevant to his pure philosophy or is trumped by his cosmopolitan desires. Those who wish to highlight Kant's racism could point to more complex philosophical arguments. It is one of the qualities of race- thinking in academia that both possibilities exist, since they sustain the idea of race as concealed and indwelling (genetic code, elusive sprite, that 'bur-iedness' within from which emerges everything of relevance without) that we might feel morally compelled to reveal and deny: race as truth as *aletheia*, and race as a vital absence. For some academic tendencies, the most terrible thing that can be revealed about Kant, and which ultimately discredits his philosophy and, somehow, the underpinnings of Western civilisation, is his racism. This is a way of reminding ourselves that Euro-American societies are foundationally racist, or at least carry the enduring potential to be so. These claims may well have valency. But it is also possible to make such claims not because they are dangerous to Western philosophy or 'civilisation', but because the performance of academic risk or danger is an inherent element of the claims themselves. The economy here is a largely academic rather than political one. Hence, a revelation about Kant's racism can also be one about the intellectual and political economy of anti-racist or diasporic Euro-American academia. This can highlight an affec-tive 'co-presence' across time of the anti-racist or diaspora academic working in the West today who wishes to foreground an emotional association with the 'ancestral' victims of the past. This can also result in a rejection of Kant's racism in a way that leaves the imperial desires of Kant's contemporary rainbow cosmo-politans largely unruffled.

SKULLS AND FOLKLORES

It is not surprising, given his stature, that in the wake of Kant's advancement of races, formalised race-thinking became widely established in Europe. In the nineteenth-century, race-thinking acquired both a scientific (anthropological) footing and expanded its specifically metaphysical reach. Much of this related to varieties of the Aryan hypothesis that started to emerge from the late eighteenth and early nineteenth centuries and which later led to the horrific exterminations of the majority of the Jewish populations of East and West Europe.

The science of culture

Some of the dynamics between science and metaphysics can be illustrated in deliberations about races during the second half of the nineteenth-century among the Ethnological Society of London, its competitor, the Anthropological Society of London, and the successor to both, the Anthropological Institute of Great Britain and Ireland. These few decades from the 1850s to the 1880s saw contesta-tion around (but also the eventual coalescence of) ideas of cultural, civilisational or racial evolution, racial monogenism and polygenism, racial taxonomies and ordering. The late-nineteenth-century tracts produced by ethnologists, anthro-pologists and folklorists ('the science of folklore' being the cultural studies of its time) readily yield foul prejudices that jostle claims about scientific veracity. In the contributions of especially the Anthropological Society of London (Stocking,

1971, 1982), the elements of brutish racism are vividly present and range from practical justifications for the violence of chattel slavery to the Aryan hypothesis of racial-civilisational advancement (Hunt, 1864, Guppy, 1864 and the interestingly titled Farrar, 1864 provide a fair sample for that year.) More sophisticated Victorian racial ideas about comparative morality and civilisation complement these cruder deliberations, and both rest on a generalised white supremacist *doxa*. But the racism is not simply an infelicity that soils here and there the otherwise pristine discoveries of noble science: it is rather that the cultural field provides intelligibility and coherence to the projects of racial science in a way that shows the process of the mythmaking of a pure racial science untainted by cultural preconceptions.

Race, culture and civilisation

What is called 'racialisation' today is as relevant to figures such as Edward Burnett Tylor, one of the 'fathers' of modern cultural anthropology who, while assiduously deploying the language of (low and high) human races, is usually seen as rejecting physical or intellectual racial hierarchy. Tylor worked within many of the languages of race-thinking of his day even as he appeared to reject the ruder racism of his adversaries. However, Tylor's anthropological science did not preclude support for physical race differences or the role of anthropology in colonial governance (Tylor, 1893: 381). His progressive evolutionism regarding cultures was directed against (mainly polygenist, mainly theological) degeneracy theorists who believed in differential origins for the races (Stocking, 1982). Against such views he wished to propose – provocatively for his time – a unity or 'uniformity' of the human mind that he discovered in studying primitive cultures. His observations on mythologies, language and animism provided the empirical ground from which he articulated a cultural holism among humankind, moreover one in which physical and mental racial difference could apparently be rejected, '... the facts collected seem to favour the view that the wide differences in the civilisation and mental status of the various races of mankind are rather differences of development than of origin, rather of degree than of kind' (Tylor, 1878: 372).

Here, civilisation is linked to evolution, a development from the savage to the barbarian to the civilised races of humankind (Tylor, 1867). While situated in Darwinian ideas of evolutionary progress, Tylor's work shows interesting analogies with both Kant's moral telos and its implied culturcide, and Herder's universalism of partitioned cultures. Cultures are the universal possession of humanity and their ethnological analysis reveals intricate webs of myth and language connecting the most diverse of peoples on the globe. In its laws, myths or rituals, the most advanced of civilisations contains traces or survivals of the most savage or barbaric. Yet cultures evolve, progress and advance and, as he says in the last words of volume two of his *Primitive Culture*, it is the harsh and painful office of the ethnographer to mark out for destruction the harmful and superstitious remnants of crude cultures (Tylor, 1891: 453).

For his mechanism of cultural progress, Tylor does not present a factor as elaborate as Herder's genetic force of nature or Kant's latent powers; instead there is a Darwin-influenced *spirit* of progress applied to human civilisations. As with Kant, who could make brutal evaluations about the worth and even the necessity of existence of the inhabitants of Tahiti, we have in Tylor's scholarship the comparative measurement of groups based on whether they are judged to have advanced to the moral state that is believed by the most powerful to be their possession. This is a state of moral being from which unfolds the direction of all humankind such that present moral existence is unthinkable without the invocation of future moral ends. Such ideas lend to imperialism, to be sure. While culture and civilisation are intimately related, these ideas also foreground a difference between culture as the field of myths and civilisation as the efflorescence of technology. This difference between culture and civilisation can lead to a symbolic division of the world that looks and feels like it is a racial one, and yet the idea that it could be so can be gently pushed away.

This civilisation idea is of key importance since it is indefinable as 'racial', can even appear to neutralise race, even if its purely cultural form seems to leak race-thinking and ideas of racial hierarchy from all sides. Here, the racial histories of humankind are broadly homologous with the histories of its differential cultural and civilisational achievements. Yet there is no requirement to signify explicitly 'the white', 'the brown' and 'the black' in the 'scale' of their respective contributions to 'civilisation'. These classifications are already understood in connotation, but in such a way that their explicit signification might invoke rebuke and recoil. We are not in Gobineau's sinister landscape of racial civilisation here. This is instead a subtler field of thought, one that – like that of Samuel Huntington's (1996) cosmology of clashing civilisations – does not require a fully fledged theory of rational racism to become operative and can disavow such a theory, and yet its objects of culture, character, values, morality and civilisation harbour a metaphysic that seems to have the capacity to rouse an imprecise racial feeling.

It is worth asking here whether it is strictly *racism* of the religious, scientific or cultural kind that we are even speaking about anymore, or whether these ideas are about a different group of xenologies based on character, morals, virtues and their associated civilisations and cultures – not strictly who one is but what qualities and burdens of a particular civilisational history have been deposited over time into the depths of one's character. Such xenologies might invoke ideas from scientific or religious racism, but they do not necessarily have to. Conversely, the stricter historiographical separation of religious, scientific and cultural racism (Banton, 1987; Barker, 1981) can be destabilised by broader civilisation-based xenologies, since the latter can mobilise in a flexible and syncretic way religious, scientific and cultural racism. We might also speak of a parallel genealogy of racism that is based on largely under-theorised aspects, such as civilisation, virtue, character, morals, tastes, aesthetics, spirits, cosmogonies – the 'physiognomy' of personality, character and the cultivated self, rather than the body, its hue and its shape.

These earlier ideas about culture and civilisation, and their elusive but often symbiotic association with more formal varieties of race-thinking, provided resources from which it later became possible to claim that cultures are simply different *such that* it is already understood that some cultures are superior and more advanced than others, and that this understanding is in some ineffable way about 'racial' belonging. Yet, it is not necessary to make an explicit claim that some cultures are superior to others or that this has anything to do with 'race'. In this sense, contemporary 'new racism' (Barker, 1981) or 'cultural racism' (Goldberg, 1993) can appear to have shed vestiges of racial hierarchy and supremacy while reproducing them in novel, global forms. Here, it is the metonymic power of race (Solomos and Back, 1996: 27) that allows it to be discovered, concealed and denied everywhere; the suspicion of its presence and its power to drive motivations appears to be simultaneously credible and deniable. (The disavowal of the idea of race as causal in social events *and* the simultaneous suspicion of its explanatory presence can form a lethal circuit that is obscured by but continues to empower the evident public discourse that avowedly refuses racial explanations. In this sense, race is not the 'unsayable' of the tremulous liberal sensibility fearing public mortification: in such circumstances, it has already been articulated in the full sense.)

Metaphysical racism

Now, even assuming the Victorian cultural milieu, a figure like Tylor's 'savage' is still excessive to the traditional-scientific figure of 'the hunter-gatherer' placed on or outside a moral and civilisation scale. What is the nature of the excess that it represents? What kind of metaphysics associates Kant's racism with his apparently universal moral philosophy, Herder's universalism with his racial vulgarities, or Tylor's uniformity of the human mind with his evolutionary hierarchy of cultures? Though it might seem warranted, it seems too simple to see a fullfledged *rationalist* racism operative here. There appears instead a much more numinous form of xenological-racial thinking, one that mysteriously, surreptitiously connects together disparate fragments, activities, elements, discoveries and gives them a unity of sorts. It is a spiritual racism, but that phrase carries the risk of assuming an organised systematicity of thought that is not present, and so should not be too hastily described. But we can suggest that xenological systems of civilisation, character, virtue, morality and culture owe to a different consciousness, more effective than rational, more faith-driven than scientific, a spiritual xenology that animates the knowledge quests of these scholarly men, and vitalises the moral reckoning of cultures that they advance.

THE ARYAN SECRET

It is in Aryanist thinking that the mysteries of race were perhaps most revealed and celebrated. Little theoretical attention has been focused on the metaphysical and affective dimensions of race and racism, though this is also a truism. It is not implied here that there is a social object called race which is in itself a mystical object; rather that race-thinking elicits rationalities and intuitions, 'logic' and gnosis, knowledges that are exoteric and arcane. The supernatural aspects of race-thinking characteristically exhibit a transcendental polarisation and violence, a typically foundational threat to the *existential* body. The metaphysics of race is unthinkable outside a cosmology of hostility, aggression, conquest, extermination or an interminable war whose origins are primordial. While attention has rightly focused on the technical, instrumental and means–ends rationality through which the industrial genocide of Europe's Jewish populations was undertaken (Hilberg, 1985; Bauman, 1989), as important ideologically is a vicious metaphysics of violence, exemplified not only by the 'political religion', rhetoric and symbols of Nazism, but by other metaphysical ideas in and around it (Mosse, 1964). Examples of the latter included Dietrich Eckhart's philosophical Aryanism in which Jewishness *within* as well as without had to be expunged, the adversarial cosmology of Carl Schmitt, and Heidegger's futurity of self-hood in which Volk and Dasein had an over-familiarity with each other in a way that acted as a rebuke to technological scientism.

The argument here is not that race and violence become subsequently linked; rather a metaphysics of violence has been endogenous to the formation of key ideas of race and arguably remains so. (This metaphysics of violence does not necessarily vanish at the point at which racism becomes anti-racism, or right becomes left.) It is this kind of metaphysics which silently stirs Kant's casually 'genocidal' remarks about the dwellers of Tahiti or Tylor's imaginary ethnograper whose task it is to destroy the ruder cultures in order to safeguard what is valuable for the advancement of humankind.

The patterns of violence in race-thinking are not illustrated through one Aryan/ non-Aryan formula but are demonstrated in a multitude of late-eighteenth and nineteenth-century demotic forms. These included theories of polarity that divided the globe into (two main) peoples, cultures, civilisations, environments, morals and tastes, two 'genders' of civilisation and culture. Such ideas were best elaborated in the early-nineteenth-century by the librarian and collector of ethnological artefacts, Gustav Klemm, and taken up in various fields and disciplines. Aside from its impact on figures like Gobineau and the antisemitism of Arthur Schopenuauer, Richard Wagner and Houston Stewart Chamberlain (Rose, 1992), an Aryanist civilisational world-view also influenced aspects of the formation of the discipline of political science and its empirical theory of the state, as exemplified in the work of Johann Kaspar Bluntschli and his American disciples (Bluntschli, 1971).

Aryanism had precedents in post-revolutionary aristocratic thinking in France (Mosse, 1964; Arendt, 1973). Other European ideas of nobility were also intermingled with early Aryanism in a variety of ways prior to Gobineau's bleak contribution during the mid-nineteenth-century (Biddiss, 1970). Aryanism also had a strong mystical precedent, a peculiarly Catholic one, in Frederich Schlegel's early-nineteenth-century speculative philology and comparative mythology.

Aryanism can be seen as a protean form that was expanded and diversified. It gave rise to or merged with supremacist and chauvinist projects regarding the Anglo-Saxon, Saxon, Teuton, Norse, Gaul, Celt, Hamite, Persian, Brahmin. These projects proliferated their own remarkable variants, some of which continue to this day and include Hutu supermacism and the Rwandan genocide, and Hindutva fascism in India, both of which owe in some way to an original Aryan versus Anaryan design.

Aryanism typically contained a story of a monumental primordial conflict between two global armies, and so it made internationalist claims and came to inhabit a nation-state from the mid-1930s. (As indeed did some varieties of Marxism and their imagination of an elemental conflict of two global armies. It is significant that it was mainly these exceptional ideologies of primordial planetary conflict that had managed to capture a state until 1979, when another 'cosmogony' took hold in Iran.) The archaic war that is central to Aryanist thinking is the cleansing battleswarm, the equalising 'democracy of war', that is as important to Aryanism as is the natural hierarchy of static races. As critical to Aryanism's magical allure is the lore of the folk, those common nostalgias that travel backwards from the present to earlier wars and heroes, to original folk gods and their mythologies (Mosse, 1964), and from there to an elemental cosmic power, one that can signify the grim shadow and the blaze of light. To be Aryan was to be in a meaningful way miraculous, such was the sanctifying power of race-thinking. (A mirror image of this idea exists in contemporary communal anti-racism.)

Racial folk

If Aryanism provides a racial cosmology that has both mystery and violence at its core, then a dispute between folklorists and philologists during the last two decades of the nineteenth-century furnishes us with some further elements about how racial consciousness was thought to maintain itself. Fredrich Max Müller, the British German Indologist who promoted the term 'Aryan' (after Frederich Schlegel), had made use of Tylor's studies of folklore and mythology in his deliberations about religious myths. While Aryanism had initially emerged from comparative philology, it was soon joined by the 'sciences' of mythology and later by ethnology. (It is significant for the meanings of race that race-thinking in the eighteenth and nineteenth centuries was intimately linked to the systematic study of mythology.) By using comparative mythology, rather than solely philological discoveries, Müller asserted the links among Aryan peoples based on comparisons between (mainly) archaic Greek, Sanskrit and Latin mythology. The coherence of Aryan mythology, he argued, related to the solar myths of Aryan groups. The solar myths provided the Aryan unity that Müller sought to advance (Dorson, 1955).

However, he – and the status of Aryan-solar mythology as *Ur-mythus* – came under attack from British folklorists organised through the Folk-Lore Society, the latter founded by Tylor among others (ibid). The cultural evolutionists, in Tylorian mould, asserted the proto-stratum of savage and primitive myths. This deep structure of myth and its association with diverse world mythologies provided a primordial unity for humankind while also explaining the 'temporal unity' between contemporary advanced civilisations and primitive cultures. This suggests an evolutionist universalism realising itself against chauvinistic Aryanist claims. But Tylor-influenced folklore studies, while seeing itself as superseding Aryanism, generated its own varieties of subtle racial thinking. For example, Alfred Nutt, a key British folklorist argued that the 'practical elements' of the lore of the folk might not evince a necessarily racial or pre-racial stratum (Nutt, 1910). However, he argued that the artistic elements of the common people, their bodies of belief and legend, demonstrated pre-eminently the racial consciousness of the folk.

Beyond the purely practical sciences of anthropology, behind even the rituals of folklore, one can find a powerful racial consciousness in the folk aesthetics that animate the common people's beliefs and stories (even if these are preserved fully only by the elite bard or priest.) Race interestingly elevates what might otherwise have been considered the raw, unrefined cultures of the poor (and indeed a rather different pedigree and future was assigned to these same folk and their stories by early twentieth-century British eugenics.) In this example, race can be seen to escape the empiricism of the sciences. The science of comparative mythology does not complete it, nor does 'scientific' Aryanism capture it. Yet race vitalises the story, fairy-tale, legend; its primeval form drifts and glides in the collective imagination of the folk. This idea of race as an imagined quality residing in and vivifying the reservoirs of myth within an idealised folk community is significant (and is at the root of the political strategies of racial populists and neo-Nazis today). The British folklorists may not have strictly adhered to the kind of racial thinking that Aryanism proposed, may not have even believed in the veracity of races. Yet an appreciation of the qualities of race is created since it enervates the vernacular imagination, glints in the otherwise unworldly folk consciousness. There is an interestingly metaphysical texture to the existence of racial consciousness as a social fact, even as the existence of race might be disavowed.

RACE, MYSTERY AND ORIGIN

If, in this admittedly obscure example, both 'Aryanists' and 'savagists' (to put it crudely) appear to mobilise something which looks like Herder's *Geist des Volkes*, this should not be a surprise. Mystical ideas of race infuse the most civil and abstract of discussions that Victorian science produced, and yet they are frequently overlooked in favour of a focus on the rising scientific claims about race. The 'genius' of a race, a dominant theme in eighteenth and nineteenth-century scientific, romantic or dilletantist race-thinking is an incorporeal entity based on the sentinel spirit that activates human capacities, appetites, character and desires: if the racial Völksgeist is the inner spirit, the racial genius is its phantasmatic companion. In such ideas, it was the *mythos* and *poesis* of race that gave race its *affective* rhythms and repertoires. But emotions are not there to be felt subsequent to the expression of the mythic or poetic. They are already part of the assemblage of racial meanings. The archaic cry of the race has already elicited sadness or disgust or pride, already invoked the discriminating taste, already cultivated a repertory of appreciation and lament, and invoked the qualities of being that makes one and binds one to others. Our flourishes here are not inappropriate ones, nor, strictly, are we even in sight of the realm of the purely romantic as opposed to the stoically scientific. A nineteenth-century magisterial survey of great Anglo-Saxon achievements may be a scientific treatise, but it is also reflects a orientation that acquaints the ethnologist with his (and occasionally her) mythic ancestry and a hopeful destiny. In this way, race also provides an emotional chronography of time that allows those in the present to feel the victories – and vitally, the failures, defeats and sorrows – of the past.

Nineteenth-century ideas of race presented a great deal more than taxonomies of human subspecies. Here, the mystical and scientific were not systematized couplings but reflected the coalescence of disparate strands and ideas (Guillaumin, 1995). To call these Victorian ventures simply pseudo-scientific, as if there was the possibility of a greater scientific veracity, is to misapprehend the importance of race's mythical, mystical qualities. This excessive 'mythicism' was not simply a reflection of the cultural milieu of Victorian England, nor was its 'function' simply to become instrumentalised in the power/knowledge that governed and administered the Empire. Instead, race carried the qualities of affect and mystery that continue to empower it today and enable it to conduct, synthesise, regulate and vitalise an array of social and political conflicts in Euro-America.

The mystery of the void

Perhaps the most potent 'mysteme' of race arises from the void at the heart of race, the postulated germ plasm whose repeated absence from the performance did not put the idea of race to rest but vitalised it even more. This is the hidden cipher of race, that fugitive code that refuses to reveal itself. The 'secrecy' of race's truth is a key element in the mythmaking of race. It relates both to the mystery of the origin of races and the mysterious absence at the core of race's vitality. The 'mystery' in racial discourse can shift from origin to absence. For example, Kant said we cannot entertain enquiry into race's origins since this is venturing into an area of knowledge about nature that must remain beyond us; and yet, for Kant, races must rationally exist; and yet further we do not know anything about the 'germ' that animates races. In a parallel way, as we see later, some of these same aspects, hovering between origin and absence, continue to resonate powerfully in contemporary racial genetic science and its mathematical defences.

The absence at the core of race cannot be seen as the absence of a real referent for what race signifies. The non-existence of an organising core is necessary for the meaning of race itself, such that this meaning does not require final revelation of its hidden code, even as the quest for it necessarily continues. Prior to the emergence of racial science, this void was filled with many myths, spirits, and humours. Philosophical anthropology (and ethnology) provided a content of sorts in the absence of the germ plasm in a way that reflected an extraordinary relation between racial appearance and racial essence. Appearance (in today's terms, the phenotype) overwrites the missing essence, inserts itself not just as body, but as morality, intellect, genius, civilisation, character and 'nature'.[3] The absence of a stable centre to race, the quest for its permanently inadequate 'referent', was precisely the cause of early disputes about race or culture, mono-genism or polygenism, heredity or environment, (sub-)species or ordinary variety. With the possible exception of race as subspecies (though this requires qualification) each of these disputes exists in some form today.

GENES, DEMES AND SOCIAL FACTS

If Kant's postulated 'germ' could not tell us about race and racial belonging, genetic science – which is after all wholly concerned with 'the germ' – seems to promise otherwise. This area is explored not because we might seek from it the truths of race, but because even the most advanced defences of the race 'concept' demonstrate the surprising emergence of older metaphysical ideas that are sup-posed to have been discarded by hard positivism.[4]

Though genetics announced emphatically the death of race in the 1970s, what can legitimately be called 'racial science' is resurgent today in a form perhaps unimaginable even a few years ago. Today, the scientific existence of races can be claimed with full acknowledgement of the history of scientific racism and of the social and political consequences of race and racism. It is possible to make such claims from within mainstream genetic and biological science without any reference to the bone collectors of earlier periods or their contemporary propo-nents who huddle around *Mankind Quarterly* or can be found in the recesses of physical and biological anthropology. That intoxicating eighteenth-century meta-physical idea of 'genius' continues to appear intermittently in investigations of racial IQ differences. The kind of racial psychology prefigured by Herder and elaborated by Steinthal in the mid-nineteenth-century as *Völkerpsychologie* (Kalmar, 1987) re-appears in sociobiology and its offspring, evolutionary psy-chology.[5]

Virtually all defences of the race concept are vigourously opposed by other molecular biologists, geneticists, physical anthropologists, biogeographers, psychologists and clinicians – those who read the molecular runes differently, who discover a gene-shaped void at the heart of race, who find nothing but impu-rity, admixture and minor variations of human geography that show up in the genetic indicators of the paleohistory of human beings. Yet there is little question that racial science has emerged again, moreover in a form that often looks like nineteenth-century racial science while claiming resolutely to be based on the rejection of the latter.

Substances and boundaries

Through activities associated with the Human Genome, HapMap and other projects, new claims about race and racial differences have become possible. Key aspects of population genetics, biological anthropology, historical genomics, biomedicine, forensic science and other allied fields are clustering around an emergent defence of race concepts. The scientific ideas of race that have reappeared can dovetail neatly with, even as they usually oppose, popular knowledges about the decisive association between races and genes. It seems racial science can proceed happily with a scepticism about its own discoveries. Racial science repeatedly claims there is 'confusion' about the meaning, classification, taxonomy or applicability of the term 'race'. (The word 'confusion' is so ubiquitous in discussions about defining race that its presence cannot be accidental and must be a constitutive one; perhaps this highlights the confounding nature that race is meant to have rather than the confusion that the 'proper' use of race is meant to eliminate.) Hence, racial science can debunk earlier scientific racism while also claiming that races exist in some form. Most commonly, contemporary racial science can claim that races do and do not exist, that the idea of race is vacant and has utility, that race has no significance and has operational purpose (Burchard et al., 2003; Jorde and Wooding, 2004). Such oscillations between presence and absence, inerrant classification and nebulous boundary organise how race is to be thought.

Races, it is said today, can be described by genetic variation, often measured as genetic distance, without *having* to make a second claim about ordinal scales and hence racial hierarchies (see especially Templeton, 2003 for a critical overview of genetic race-thinking). In other words, there exist genetic racial differences but, as with 'cultural differences', they do not imply inferiority or hierarchy – at most, they indicate geographical separation and what is termed 'ancestry' (though even terms like 'ancestry' and 'heritage', while intended to be neutral, fizz with potent meaning.) In genomics, the absence of a stable centre to race is not simply a missing gene or set of genes. No 'racial gene' is available for to us to ponder which consistently, uniquely and unequivocally identifies in a non-*a priori* fashion groups formerly known as races. There are several (discovered and hypothesised) genes that are responsible for differing levels of epidermal melanin. There also exist a variety of genes (alleles) linked to diseases whose prevalence is associated with particular groups (Mountain and Risch, 2004), though there is no known 'racial' boundary that can prevent the occurrence of those genes in other groups in future generations through 'admixture' or because of other factors, including environmental ones (the classic example being the presence of the malarial parasite).

Drift, distance, trees

However, especially following the various Human Genome (and HapMap) projects, race (and ethnicity and linguistic group) are increasingly claimed to be identified through DNA polymorphisms, changes at locations in the genome (typically resulting from genetic drift) that can be different between individuals and show different frequencies between populations (Keita et al., 2004). Most of the variation measured is in non-genetic (non-functional) areas of the human genome. Several mathematical measures of frequencies of sets of polymorphisms within groups of people can be undertaken that provide a statistical value of genetic distance between groups (Cavalli-Sforza et al., 1994; Templeton, 2003). Polymorphisms can be searched for and selected *a priori* so as to stand in for racial differences between groups if those groups are already defined as different racial or ethnic groups and the selection undertaken on that basis (Bamshad et al., 2006: 600). (In principle, DNA polymorphisms can probably be found that can differentiate groups of people defined *a priori* by the cities they live in or by whether or not they believe in the existence of races.) It is unclear whether qualitatively meaningful and unique groups broadly homologous with groups formerly identified as races would independently emerge if sets of DNA polymorphisms are selected randomly and in a non-*a priori* way and correlations measured between the frequencies of (sets of) polymorphisms. However, it appears possible that populations separated geographically would emerge naturally (Rosenberg, 2002). Since geographical distance is readily used as a metonym for race (or ethnicity or 'tribe' or linguistic group), some would argue that the genetic distance so measured refers essentially to race, even if they reject the use of this concept.

Genetic distance between groups can be represented by an evolutionary tree diagram (and in various other ways.) This diagrammatic representation can be claimed to indicate an underlying population structure and a genetic lineage – typically characterised as 'treeness' – for which a 'root' can be hypothesised, assumed or indicated by software (Templeton, 2003). 'Treeness', of course, cannot but invoke the evolutionary trees of nineteenth-century racial science and their specific connotations regarding human evolutionary hierarchy. However, today, treeness is said to represent an underlying structure of correlation between frequencies of, for example, sets of DNA polymorphisms and the differences (distances) between these sets of frequencies between different groups. This mathematical structure of correlation is of significance for how race is imagined today; in key respects, it *is* the race concept. But it is also conversely claimed (in relation to human 'races') that 'all genetic distance data sets that have been tested fail to fit treeness' (Templeton, 2003: 244). Instead, treeness (or other representations) can be interpreted as the isolation-by-distance of groups: the underlying structure of correlation represents little more than an expected measure of geographical distance between populations.

Fuzzy boundaries and reified people

Despite this, the existence of biological or genetic races is still stated, even though the number of genetic races said to exist vary (from 3 or 5 to 30 or over 60). Genetic boundaries between races are also acknowledged to be highly nebulous and indistinct, such that races cannot exist as nominal categories without an arbitrariness that insults the genetic data. However, advocates of race-thinking have little problem in foregrounding the irreducibly statistical, probabilistic nature of racial ascription or categorisation (Sarich and Miele, 2004). Nor does the measure of genetic 'gradation' (cline) across the putative boundaries of races appear to matter: today, races are claimed to be really fuzzy and permeable and 'really real'. Races can also be claimed to exist though the commonly used value of the statistic that measures the genetic distance between races reaches nowhere near the usual (and arbitrary) threshold values used for non-human subspecies differentiation (see Templeton, 2003: 238–239).

Molecular genetics has also claimed (since at least the mid-1990s) not only that races exist biologically but their historical provenance can be described phylogenetically (Cavalli-Sforza et al., 1994; Levin, 2002 – the former claims to reject race while using it, the latter is a vigourous defence of the phylogenetic and biological race concept). Molecular phylogeny (empowered by that ancient, potent word 'phylon') fuses together older, distinct ideas of race as lineage, type and subspecies to create new ideas of 'diachronic' and 'synchronic' races. However, the genetic paleohistory of humans also appears to illustrate repeated processes of so-called 'admixture' instead of a linear origin 'out of Africa' followed by separation and relatively stable differentiation into 'races' that can be genetically characterised (Templeton, 2003: 247–248). Just as genetic distance measures fail to fit 'treeness', it also seems that the 'out-of-Africa replacement hypothesis', the seemingly last gasp of a somewhat polygenetic quest, is a deeply problematic and repeated 'admixture' among human populations has taken place since the early migrations 'out of Africa' (ibid: 244, 248).

Hence, where one might have thought that genetic discoveries would have led to deracialisation or to different, unpredictable and arbitrary genetic configurations of groups, racial categories from the past continue to re-emerge forcefully. More insidiously, it can be claimed that races do not exist genetically while the older categories of racial classification are deployed for groups defined genetically (Cavalli-Sforza et al., 1994). As in the past, associations between language (formerly philology), physical anthropology (formerly ethnology), geography (formerly landscape and climate) and genes (formerly germ or germ plasm) can be stated. The remnant taxonomies of old ethnology, physical anthropology and philology are combined with modern population administration categories of ethnicity, and these are then reified in order to find genetic differences between them that confirm the reification.

Similarly, what was to prove to be a disastrous coupling of philology and ethnology in the nineteenth-century occurs today in elaborate and pretty maps that compare linguistic variation with genetic variation – such that it is assumed, in a now classic study (ibid; see also Cavalli-Sforza, 2001) based on the selective sampling of *aboriginal* populations, that the movement and spread of languages is homologous with the flows of human genetic material. However, the processes by which a language (or dialect) spreads and becomes the dominant one in a region (or the way it supplants or interpolates other languages) cannot be the same as those that 'govern' genes – consider English or Spanish – unless the sampling is designed *a priori* to select for this finding. Hence, those who appear to reject the claim that there are races nevertheless use in an *a priori* way linguistic, anthropological or ethnic criteria to group 'aboriginal' populations and 'tribes' from which genetic distances are calculated and phylogenetic trees mapped. The result of the 'delineations of populations using DNA polymorphisms' appears not very different to the traditional categories of European, African and Asian, and yet the frequent claim is that this has little or nothing to do with nineteenth-century physical anthropological classifications such as 'Caucasoid', 'Negroid' and 'Mongoloid'–see Figure 5.1.

The health of the race

As in the past, the idea of genetic races has a moral dimension, but today this morality is avowedly about the biomedical therapeutic dividend for minorities (Bamshad et al., 2003; Mountain and Risch, 2004). It is rare to find a contemporary research article on racial genetics that does *not* make a routine claim to advance the welfare of minority groups – though this sometimes seems to be a sliver of over-concern, an alibi for the serious work of racial genetic discovery. The most mendacious of contributions to racial science also happily make claims about the well-being of minority populations while maintaining the multifaceted genetic inferiority of the latter (Sarich and Miele, 2004).

However, claims about medical benefits for black populations have been challenged on medical and health grounds. Some empirical and theoretical arguments claim that the operationalisation of racial genetics in biomedical science can work to the detriment of the health and welfare of black populations (Rotimi, 2004). It is striking how discourses of *health* have historically maintained such a powerful affinity with discourses of *race*. Hence, genetic disease markers are critically important for the genetic science of race. It is also fairly common (and revealing) to find a gene for skin colour listed together with genes associated with disease or disease resistance (malarial and other parasites, HIV, lactase persistence, drug and alcohol metabolism, among others (Tishkoff and Kidd, 2004: S25)).

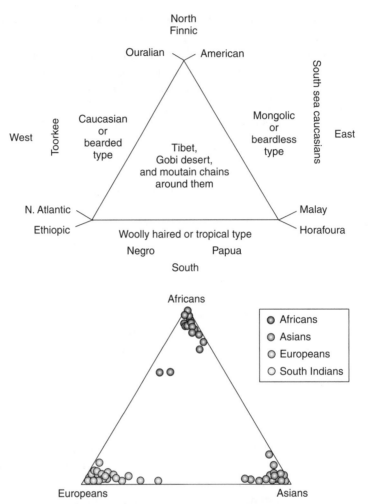

Figure 5.1   Human races – Charles Hamilton Smith's eighteenth-century and today's molecular genetic depictions (Sources: Banton, 1987: 53; Bamshad et al., 2001: 600).

Race and mathematics

One of the strongest arguments for the defence of human genetic races is an interestingly *mathematical* one (Edwards, 2003) that claims to refute the now famous findings of Richard Lewontin in the 1970s that genetic variations between individuals within defined human groups ('races') are always far higher than 'average' genetic variations between any two such groups, and that the overwhelming amount (from about eighty-five percent to much higher) of all human genetic variation can be found within any one group usually characterised as a race (Lewontin, 1974; Lewontin et al., 1990). The claim against Lewontin, however, is emphatic:

> It is not true that 'racial classification is…of virtually no genetic or taxonomic significance'. It is not true, as *Nature* claimed, that 'two random individuals from any one group are almost

as different as any two random individuals from the entire world', and it is not true, as the *New Scientist* claimed, that 'two individuals are different because they are individuals, not because they belong to different races' and that 'you cannot predict someone's race by their genes'. (Edwards, 2003: 801)

The mathematical argument is based on an assumed non-independence of measured characteristics and it is worth dwelling on this briefly, since it links directly to arguments advanced earlier in this essay about the metaphysics of race.

If there are correlations between the characteristics measured such that the characteristics are not truly independent of each other, then Lewontin's conclusions are flawed in a fundamental sense, since his method was based on assuming that each characteristic (e.g., a polymorphism at one locus) for which variations between groups were measured was independent of another similarly measured characteristic (say, another polymorphism at another locus).[6] When correlations between characteristics being measured exist – for example, if the length of a skull correlates with its width and appears to indicate an overall property such as 'faceness' – then the 'average' distance between groups can be shown to increase dramatically and groups can be identified clearly and distinctly. The clear analogy is with a putative property such as 'race'.

It is also claimed that an underlying structure of correlation will emerge irrespective of whether or not there is an *a priori* racial classification (Edwards, 2003: 800). But studies based on such a non-*a priori* method appear to confirm Lewontin's findings and characteristically infer geographical clustering, as might be expected (Rosenberg et al., 2002). However, several studies also show that 'self-inferred ancestry' (a euphemism for race) and language spoken corresponds well with 'genetic ancestry' (as defined through multilocus markers). But more mundanely, this means people who come from a particular geographical area and speak a particular language can also share particular patterns of polymorphisms or allele frequencies. The latter can be markers of geographical distance (or relative isolation) such that one might consider such an argument to be circular, since it is a measure of (primarily) genetic drift and so it is also largely an indirect measure of geographical distance and separation. A measure of geographical distance is transformed into a measure of a qualitative property called 'race'. Moreover, measures of genetic distance also place Europeans *between* Africans and other racially characterised populations, including Asians and descendents of the original inhabitants of Australia – the distance between the latter and Africans being the greatest genetic distance, as might be expected due to geographical separation and drift (Templeton, 2003).

Racial likeness

But this still does not get to the heart of the objection to Lewontin's findings. The seemingly conclusive demolishing of 'Lewontin's fallacy' rests on a different, older argument from the mathematics of racial science. It is one of the curiosities of the way that empirical positivism is taught today that the history of its statistical techniques – and the racial and eugenic logic which led to their discovery or invention – is rarely elaborated. That history is thoroughly imbricated in exactly the racial sciences of the late-nineteenth and early centuries discussed earlier. In 1926, Karl Pearson (of the chi-squared test, the product-moment correlation coefficient, and linear regression and correlation) attempted to define mathematically the 'coefficient of racial likeness' which could be applied to craniometric and other biometric (physical anthropological) measures so as to provide a measure of racial similarity (and, in effect, racial difference, though criticisms of its use for the latter were also made) (Pearson, 1926). Pearson noted that 'the fundamental weakness of the Coefficient of Racial Likeness lies in the fact that it neglects the correlations between the characters dealt with' (ibid: 111). His coefficient was based on the assumption that each (racial) characteristic being measured was independent of every other characteristic being measured, a weakness also noted by Ronald Aylmer Fisher (of the F-distribution and the exact test) (Fisher, 1936).

For advocates of genetic races, the key issue rests on the meaning of the hidden structure of correlation between polymorphism frequencies and how this hidden structure relates to a putative measure of 'race'. Whether the sampling populations are defined *a priori* or not, if sets of DNA polymorphisms can be found such that there are significant differences between groups regarding the frequencies of these sets of polymorphisms taken together, what *precisely* is the quality or property, beyond the fact of geographical distance, that associates the frequencies of these bits of (mostly non-functional) DNA? What *substantive* property or quality associates these frequencies of polymorphisms?

In other words – significantly but tediously – *what is race*? There are in biological discipline several quantitative and qualitative criteria, including arbitrary ones, for what counts as non-human subspecies differentiation ('race'). The fact of their existence is not in itself a reason to accept them since they are largely systems of taxonomy. Nevertheless, no distinct human 'race' meets these various criteria (Templeton, 2003). Similarly, with some exceptions (including the Old Order Amish), there appear to be no 'localised breeding groups' or demes that share a distinct genetic pool. If such a thing as race exists in the mathematical way proposed, it does so in and through the nature of the *arrangement* that apparently associates a variety of allele or haplotype frequencies within different populations such that the populations can be distinguished unambiguously from each other as 'races'. That is, the definition of race that appears to be emerging is a probabilistic one that cannot be qualitatively characterised and given meaning to, yet exists causally in the *hidden structure* of correlations among frequencies of sets of polymorphisms. Race as a distinct attribute emerges holistically in the overall configuration of, say, allele frequencies and yet its qualitative meaning remains hidden somewhere in (or as) the arrangement of that configuration. Nor can it be qualitatively described in a way that avoids circular description. Nevertheless, what is insidiously advanced is the property of race as the theoretical and explanatory cause governing the observed correlations. Given its malevolent history, we might wonder why the designation 'race' continues to be thus invoked. It is moreover significant that the quest for race continues in the concealed factor behind the pattern of correlations, that inexplicable 'raceness' that provides a necessary and excessive coherence to the otherwise unexciting findings of geographical distance. Race refuses to remain mundane, contained, finally explained. Even in the most technically advanced of modern sciences, race emerges as real obscurity, again as a mystery.

SUFFERING AND THE ETHNOSUPREMACIST STATE

If contemporary racial genetic science appears to return us to older problems and issues regarding race and racism, then several other themes discussed earlier in the essay are relevant to what is referred to as the 'Israel–Palestine conflict', including tensions between cosmopolitan and communal varieties of race-thinking, as well as the moral mystifications that associate with racial thinking about civilisation, culture and history. The example of 'Israel/Palestine' is also focused on because it demonstrates some metahistorical properties of race, the complex moral economies that are generated in race discourse and the highly mystificatory nature of racist and much anti-racist political discourse. If, as was implied earlier, the association in dominant strands of Western humanist philosophy between the moral, the aesthetic and the affective is not a necessary but a fantastical one that coheres a strong humanism through which the violent potentials of race are arranged, then one consequence is that the moral arrangement of the self that allegedly results from extreme suffering might be able to give us no practical knowledge about the moral arrangement of the self that can cause extreme suffering. It is not argued that the victimised can or should bear a moral knowledge or a 'higher' moral knowledge through their suffering. The assumption of such moral intensities that associate with suffering is not necessarily a warranted one. Much is also apparent from Western (and other) philosophy about the architecture of the moral self, how it is packaged together as a moral subject, how it coalesces under humanist empathy and discharges its moral duty; but there is little about how it unpacks itself, how the infrastructure of morality dismantles and can unravel rapidly. Modern humanism contains within itself the enduring capacity for its own moral subversion (a dangerous capacity that Kant discovered in a transcendental form and parcelled away as 'radical evil'). But we can suggest that the architecture of the moral self can co-exist and be coextensive with moral annihilation.

It is often considered tendentious to focus on issues of racial discrimination and violence relating to Israel and the occupied Palestinian territories without comparing Israel favourably with what are termed 'Arab states' and their treatment of minorities. Similarly, 'minorities' within Israel are often said to be best compared with ethnic minorities in the United States or European countries. Similarly, Israel's racism, if acknowledged, is claimed to be of the kind familiar from the broad racial history of most nationalisms or nation-states - if anything, it is Israel that is the victim of a vicious global racism.

Such arguments are part of the exceptionalising approach to Israel that varieties of both communal and cosmopolitan anti-racism make possible and through which Israel as a nation-state or polity, and Zionism as an ideology become 'normalised' as liberal–democratic. The independent critical intellectual process is damaged and at the moment it services and shores up the political ideologies and agendas of nation-states, nationalism and racism. The ethical responsibility for independent academics in challenging, demystifying and opposing genuine antisemitism is indisputable because it is equivalent to the ethical responsibility to challenge advocates of a violent metaphysical nationalism who mystify their racism through a claim to racial victimhood.

In 'the Israel–Palestine conflict', virtually every epistemic and moral claim made by Israel is controverted by Palestinians, and vice versa. Nevertheless, the term 'conflict' and its invocation of 'two sides' disguises enduring and systematic ethnic cleansing, state terrorism against and 'politicide' of Palestinians (Kimmerling, 2003; Pappé, 2006). Beyond the largely illegal so-called 'anti-terrorist security' wall, the West Bank is internally divided into three main Palestinian cantons under a military controlling regime such that the 'autonomy' conferred upon the South African bantustans under apartheid might even seem a luxury. Gaza is little more than a punitive prison camp for Arabs. Comparisons between Israel's occupation and South African racial apartheid are now fairly evident in the academic literature, and contested by those who would wish to highlight Israel's largely benign liberal–democratic and apparently non-racial nature (e.g., see Glaser, 2003 on the apartheid argument; Ben-Rafael, 2003 for a response.)

However, the systematic brutality in the 'occupied territories' (and regularly in Lebanon) are hardly contingent matters of Israeli 'foreign policy'. They are outcomes of what has been called the 'ethnocratic regime' (Yiftachel and Ghanem, 2004) or '*Herrenvolk* democracy' (Kimmerling, 2003: 39). Israel's founding and governing ideologies are rightly seen as racially informed in a number of complex ways. They have had mystifying dimensions, but have figured from their inception a shifting but largely ideologically coherent view of Arab inferiority (by no means restricted to cultural inferiority) and Jewish supremacism. In some respects, the ideological racism directed against Arabs in general and Palestinians in particular is similar in its content and imagery to the European antisemitism directed against eastern and western European Jews in the nineteenth and first half of the twentieth-century, though this analogy can also be extremely misleading. As apparent are contemporary tropes that should be familiar to scholars of racism and eugenics: the enduring obsession with Palestinian or Arab demographic fertility and the 'demographic threat' or 'demographic aggression' resulting from nothing other than the bare existence of Palestinians both in the occupied territories and as infracitizens of Israel.

Hence, the claim that Israel, within the Green Line, manifests the kind of 'institutional racism' and unintended discrimination that exists in Euro-America is a highly immoral mystification. Israel is a racial or ethnosupremacist state in its basic and nationality and immigration laws, its policies (and operations) relating to the systematic expropriation of land and resources from its Palestinian Arab citizens, its planned destruction of Palestinian Arab citizens' homes and communities, its laws on marriage with Palestinians 'outside Israel', its violent operational policies regarding Palestinian Arab political protest, the dismally low state expenditure on (and budgets for) resources towards Palestinian Arab areas, education or communities, and its policies on Palestinian Arab birth rates (Cook, 2006: 122–23 and *passim*). There is furthermore an increasingly vocal and instrumentalised political logic of 'population transfer'. This clinical term masks ethnic cleansing of both Palestinians in the occupied territories and potentially (some or all) Palestinian infracitizens of Israel, and represents the political context in which Ariel Sharon's Gaza 'disengagement' took place (ibid).

Hence, the claim that Israel is simply a liberal democracy elides the absolutist racial and ethnic thinking that prevents the basic laws of Israel from allowing it to be a state for all its legal citizens or a state in which all its citizens are regarded as equal. It is factors such as this that controvert comparisons with, for example, the legal status of minorities in the US who may face racial discrimination. (Indeed, the statements that all Israeli citizens be considered wholly equal before the law and that the state should exist for all of its citizens have been construed as both antisemitic and effectively seditious (ibid: 23.)) Similarly, the fact of the universal adult franchise for Palestinian citizens of Israel is severely constrained within a hard boundary of majority Jewish political supremacy. The nature and extent of the organisation of the racial state and of concomitant Palestinian oppression is elided by dominant terms of reference: 'the Israel/Palestine conflict', 'security', 'defence', 'pre-emption', 'Arab terrorism', 'antisemitism' and the threat of a 'second Holocaust'. There is also a ubiquitous idea of an 'existential threat' to the existence of Jews in Israel that invokes so powerfully the memory of the mass extermination of Jews in Europe.

Horror languages

The Gaza Strip has been referred to as the largest 'concentration camp' to have existed (Kimmerling, 2003: 169). This reference, as well as the references above to 'racial state' and 'Herrenvolk', are important for this essay because they highlight the way symbols and languages of National Socialism, antisemitism and the Holocaust, and thus of race and racism, manifest in transversal, complex and instrumental ways. The 'concentration camp' allusion has been made with full knowledge of the horrors of the Nazi camps that organised for systematic destruction of the Jewish 'lives not worth living' (Hilberg, 1985; Agamben, 1998: 138). The identification of Israel with Nazism is a feature of some strands of political discourse, ones said to demonise Israel. There exists a strong ideological current in several middle-eastern countries, much of it directly related to Israel's occupation of Gaza and the West Bank, some of it owing to antisemitic ideas that include the classical imagery of European antisemitism and Holocaust denial. This form of ideological–political racism directed against Jewish people has a history that is largely independent of that of European antisemitism, though it may marshal key symbols from the latter.

What, in Euro-America, has been far less visible, let alone stirred much academic concern, is the nature and history of a coherent political and ideological anti-Arab racism promoted by Israel and its supporters. This has ranged from the early equivalence of Arabs with Nazis to the idea of an international, malicious, exterminatory Arab (today, 'Islamist' or 'jihadi') movement, network or conspiracy, one soon to acquire nuclear capabilities. This movement has the sole intention of 'driving Jews into the sea' or destroying Jewish people with nuclear bombs. This is a coherent racial cosmology that requires much fuller elaboration than can be provided here. It harbours an extensive repertoire of dehumanising ideas, images and symbols about Palestinians, Arabs or Muslims. It is often articulated with the claim of the existence of a new antisemitism, and it is in such instances that anti-racist and racist ideas merge into a singular claim. The arguments of Norman Finkelstein, among others, that claims of a new antisemitism occur when Israel behaves aggressively or is in a war may seem stark but are convincingly documented (Finkelstein, 2000, 2005).

Antisemitism – old and new

The equivalence throughout Israel's history of Arabs with Nazis (Zertal, 2005) includes the characterisation of Arabs as harbingers of a second Holocaust, of Arabs as motivated by the same antisemitism that existed in Europe in the 1930s and 1940s, and of the necessity of pre-emptive wars to prevent a second modern catastrophe against Jews. Hence, the statements, antisemitic and otherwise, of some middle-eastern leaders (who have ranged from the secular Nasser to the anti-secular Ahmedinejad) are taken to be equivalent to the conduct of Nazi Germany. In this way, criticisms of Israel's actions are removed from a historical register and relocated within a grander narrative of an essentially timeless, transcendental antisemitism.

There is, in the vision of a new antisemitism, a global antisemitic movement, centred on the Arab or Iranian middle-East and, through Muslim minorities in Europe, aligned with the European political left. (In Europe and America today, the charge of antisemitism is characteristically marshalled against the political left.) This global antisemitic movement is portrayed as having the exterminationist vision and intention of the kind possessed by National Socialism. A dominant Israeli view of Arabs as an inhuman mass, a swarming multitude that signifies threat and extermination, has intensified greatly following the so-called 'war on terror' and an overpowering discourse of 'security' both within and outside Israel.

If this appears to be a mystificatory moral and political belittling of the Holocaust, as well as an elision of the ethical power of its necessarily disordered and complex memories, it can also legitimise a brutality and demonisation where discourses about an impending genocide muddle with ones about Israel's humanism and democracy, propelling a moral rectitude that is coextensive with moral subversion.

Idith Zertal has highlighted how dominant Israeli discourses about the 'Nazi Arab' were already present around 1948 but expanded after the trial and execution of Adolf Eichmann (1961–1962) and the 1967 war by Israel against its neighbours (Zertal, 2005: 98). Zertal's discussion refuses to contain under political simplicities the serious moral and ethical dimensions that are unleashed through the association between the Nazi exterminations of the Jewish populations of Europe and the instrumentalised political discourses of the state of Israel regarding the exterminations. The systematic Nazification of the Arab was occurring while the survivors of the death and slave labour camps were largely silenced in Israel, partly because as victims they did not fit into the mould of Zionism's heroic pioneer-soldier (ibid: 93–94).

Much academic attention has rightly focused on the nature and limits of ethical and moral conduct among both victims and perpetrators and, for the victims, under the terror and the most extreme of conditions they suffered and died under, not only in the death and slave camps (Arendt, 1977; Todorov, 1999) but in the monumental genocide in the east which was conducted systematically outside the camps (Browning, 1992).

One element that Zertal discusses relates to the actions of a few of the survivors in the formative period of the Israeli state. It raises formidable difficulties about the moral apprehension of findings of the kind that in some of the massacres of entire villages of unarmed, white-flag-waving Arabs (during the mass ethnic cleansings of Palestinians in the late 1940s) some survivors of the Nazi camps were said by other soldier-witnesses to be the most eager perpetrators (Zertal, 2005: 171–172). Clearly, the argument associates such actions to the characterisation of Arabs as Nazis. These are not issues beyond nuanced ethical judgement, or within the moral expansiveness that might be brought to bear in comprehending such actions in the context of the horrors that had (mostly) ended barely three years before in Europe. The brutality was opposed by some other soldiers but, as Zertal says more generally of Zionist pioneer-soldiers during the 1948 massacres,

> The role reversal had now been completed. The licensed heirs of the Holocaust had transformed themselves into efficient and murderous 'Germans', while the 'reincarnation' of the Nazis, according to Israeli Holocaust discourse, simple Arab villagers, became by this deed the total victims of the misdeed of transposing the Holocaust into the local conflict. (ibid: 173)

Within an extensive history of anti-Arab racism and its ideological equivalence of the Arab and the Nazi, Kimmerling's 'concentration camp' allusion becomes significant in a different way, since it challenges Israel's mobilisation of

Holocaust symbols for political and military purposes, just as it symbolically controverts academic and political claims about the ahistorical uniqueness of the Holocaust or, indeed, of a transcendental antisemitism. Anti-racism – in the form of the ubiquitous charge of antisemitism and a constrained and instrumentalised memorialisation of the Holocaust – is the most powerful ideological weapon used to justify Israel's brutalities, to subdue its critics and disperse whatever moral courage they might have otherwise mustered in the face of Israel's systemic racism. Anti-racism here allows for an inverted ethical universe, where victims of the racial state are racist aggressors (the entire continuum from the Arab foetus in the womb to stone-throwing Arab children to adult Arab suicide-bombers), and the aggressors morally innocent victims of racism. Indeed, the charge of 'new antisemitism' often includes any potential conflation of Jewish victims with Jewish perpetrators (Finkelstein, 2005: 87).

The Holocaust has often been described as an incomprehensible industrialised genocide outside rational comprehension, or as an incorrigible, transcendental evil, perhaps the absolute intensity of human evil by which all other evils past, current or ones to come have to be judged. There are other ethically sensitive approaches that neither seek to 'externalise' the Holocaust out of history, rationality and cognisance, nor render it extraneous to thought (Hilberg, 1985.) But they attempt to preserve in all of its brutal complexity the extensive and compounded moral and political challenges that the Nazi extermination poses, including ones that may exceed or subvert moral or affective understandings we may seek to impose so as to contain their meanings under rational concepts. This is indeed different to the political instrumentalisation of the Holocaust, an externalisation beyond history, but nevertheless within a specific temporality of memory, affect and evil. This can signal a sanctifying imagination, one neither strictly religious nor entirely secular, neither simply ahistorical nor located within the histories of nations and societies.

The externalising views of the Holocaust have significant metaphysical, non-secular dimensions related to exceptional suffering through a uniquely evil event that exists on the edges of historical time. They can erase from the moral universe the sufferings of the Palestinians and other victims of Israel's racial projects. The careless comparison of the scale and horror of the Nazi Judeocide with the current situation of the Palestinians is at best a morally deceitful one. But by any serious moral reckoning, the situation of Palestinians is a contemporary horror.

In the United States and United Kingdom, defenders of Israel's supremacism or its actions regularly invoke the charge of anti-Jewish racism against critics of Israel (even when they claim not to be doing so). This translates the situation of Palestinians into an entirely different set of issues about Jewish diaspora politics and representation, thus diminishing the importance of the occupation. Critics of Israel are said to be invoking, knowingly or otherwise, the blood libel, the characterisation of Jews as child-killers, a world Jewish conspiracy, global Jewish power and control, secret Jewish influences, inherently malign or disloyal Jewish intentions, among various other such elements from European medieval and modern antisemitism. Similarly, anti-racism is mobilised to claim that critics who demand that Israel be accountable under international law are singling out specifically the 'Jewish democratic' state for censure and concomitantly evading other human rights violations committed by other nations. (The frequent charge is that Israel is being singled out, exceptionalised or characterised as a unique evil; hence, critics *cannot but* be motivated by antisemitism, irrespective of whatever moral claims they might otherwise make.) These charges mobilise anti-racism to shield from criticism Israel's systematic and intentional violations of human rights, its war crimes and crimes against humanity, and its extra-judicial assassinations or routine killings of Arabs, including children, through regular military offensives against civilian populations. They imply that the precondition for criticism of Israel has to be prior remedy of every other global human rights violation first (Rose, 2005: xix). They also act to shelter the significance of the relation between Israel and America, as well as the relative power of pro-Israeli political lobby organisations in the United States. As importantly, the charge is often made of collusion with – or even equivalence to – genuine antisemites (neo-Nazis, antisemitic Islamist tendencies, 'jihadis', advocates of global Jewish conspiracies and sundry Holocaust deniers.) It may be morally and empirically irrelevant to whether or not Israel is a racist state or a violator of human rights that other racist states and human rights violators also exist. Yet apologias for Israel's atrocities characteristically combine anti-racism with varieties of Kantian cosmopolitanism. There are, for reasons outlined earlier, regressive problems with this kind of cosmopolitanism anti-racism. But in these various ways, anti-racism is mobilised to prevent criticism of a racial state and the charge of racism against critics acts to sustain the racism of that state.

CONCLUSION

In each of the examples discussed above, one consistent issue has been how discourses of race slip easily and readily across divergent and even opposed or contrary phenomenon, such that seemingly anti-racist discourse can be used for chauvinistic purposes and cosmopolitan languages merge with communal ones – such is the pliability of race. Race similarly evades theoretical attempts within the social and natural sciences, arts and humanities to define, describe, delimit or stabilise it. The concept of race readily subverts efforts that seek to abandon or expunge it from academic labour. Its political resonances outside the university – the work that race does for politics in Euro-America, and that politics does to keep race alive and vital – continually sabotage affectations about value-free inquiry. Race similarly disrupts emic-etic distinctions created to trap it within the methodological rules of academic research. The meanings and utility of race as an analytical concept are regularly contested, but new definitions are proffered and their analytical legitimacy and use defended. This, however, re-energises the hermeneutic cycles around race, ones that are vicious in their regression and remain unsettled in their meanings.

There is equally severe disagreement about the meanings and value of each of the terms that make up the current chain of signification regarding race – race, racialisation, racialism, racism, anti-racism – and which form the currency of many academic disciplines (see Murji and Solomos, 2005). The movement from studying race or 'race relations' to studying processes of racialisation – how events and populations come into existence or are made intelligible through abstract discourses of race – cannot prevent the furtherance of race-thinking. Equally problematically, race appears in unpredictable forms through the dialectic of elite external ascription and the subaltern's 'group consciousness' of itself as a race, such that the subaltern can meaningfully valourise languages of race that it comes to share with the elite and so, in an Hegelian way, bears and sustains the consciousness of race possessed by the elite racist (Gilroy, 1993). Conversely, the idea of race is seemingly dispensed with by racists who are anti-racist in order to be more effective in their racism (St. Louis, 2005: 32), a conceptual Möbius strip that makes race meaningless and meaningful in the same move.

Even if we ignored the identitarianism that is often invoked at the same time that the call is made to expunge race from academic disciplines, the call arguably remains within the racial logics explored above. Hence, every utterance of race (including this essay) knowingly advances a fiction within an academic economy while willing the academic disciplines to reject the concept. In this sense, race is neither concept nor idea but bears resemblance to a catachrestic entity, one that we cannot not use, yet one without an adequate referent (Spivak, 1999: 14). If we follow through this application of Spivak's important idea, it also implies that the 'space' occupied by race constitutes an inherently destabilising one, such that an analysis of race as a rational phenomenon cannot be sufficient, nor, consequently is any general definition or theory of race and racism possible (Gilroy, 1987).

There are further, imprecise difficulties in rejecting the race concept because of the existence of infrastructures of race in many legal, state and political institutions (Guillaumin, 1995). The response to the latter cannot persist through an even further, deeper or global 'raceing' that propels academic anti-racism into its own fictions about political commitment, ethical importance or alliance with the oppressed. Euro-American academic anti-racism and its forms of race-thinking and reification can become embedded within and exported as imperial projects for the 'global South' to ponder. Dominant Euro-American academic ideas of race can become explanatory discourses for states, institutions and conflicts outside Euro-America that cannot be considered 'racial'. But, conversely, the same global academic hegemony can also mean an elision and exclusion of other racial conflicts and states, precisely because of the mystificatory qualities of some forms of Euro-American racial and anti-racist thinking. As important is an academic 'treaty of victimhood' with diaspora elites in Euro-America who have a different political investment in preserving discourses of race, a kind of diaspora imperialism. Like the *revenant*, race refuses to die even though it kills and even though it has been killed many times, and that, perhaps more than anything else, says everything that is genuinely significant about it.

ACKNOWLEDGEMENTS

I would especially like to thank Nick Denes, Alberto Toscano, Stephen Cross and the Editors for their critical comments. Some of the ideas relating to the metaphysics of violence owe to useful discussions with Dilip Simeon.

Figure 5.1 reprinted by permission, M. Banton, *Racial Theories*, 1987, Cambridge University Press; reprinted by permission from Macmillan Publishers Ltd: NATURE REVIEWS GENETICS, Bamshad, M. et al. Deconstructing the relationship between genetics and race. 5(8), 598–609, © 2006.

NOTES

1. The terms 'communal' and 'cosmopolitan anti-racism' are not used in opposition to each other – the later sections on Kant and Herder and Israel–Palestine show how close they can become, or how the former can be used to justify the latter.

2. What, in Foucauldian terms, is conceived as the empirical-transcendental double as a component of a post-Renaissance episteme can elide arrangements of knowledge that are not captured fully in this binary (Foucault, 1970: 320).

3. This is the genuine significance of Hume's famously gratuitous footnote on Africans (see Eze, 1997a: 33; Immerwahr, 1992).

4. This links to a broader argument about the association between metaphysics and empiricism/positivism; it is not an accident that ultra-Darwinian empiricists sound absolutist about their truths and religious in their zeal.

5. Scholarly contributions from the latter teach us about 'race encoding', which is caused by 'computational mechanisms whose operation is automatic and mandatory'. We are relieved to learn that the 'inferential machinery' of race encoding is not a by-product of the brain's 'ethnicity module'. Instead, our views about people's races may be based on a 'living kinds' template or 'inferential machinery' that is designed through evolution to track 'coalitional alliances' (see Cosmides et al., 2003). We might want to dismiss this particular guff, but the merging of genetics, psychology and metaphors from engineering and information technology has resulted, across several disciplines, in a new, proliferating form of what used to be called 'biological reductionism'.

6. The reason they would be flawed is that, effectively, if correlations exist between (frequencies of) several characteristics measured among (say) random samples from two populations, then there is a rapidly decreasing probability that the populations are the same; this is a consequence of mathematical techniques, including principal components analysis.

REFERENCES

Agamben, G. (1998) *Homo Sacer: Sovereign Power and Bare Life.* Stanford, CA: Stanford University Press.
Arendt, H. (1973) *The Origins of Totalitarianism.* New York: Harcourt Brace and Company.
Arendt, H. (1977) *Eichmann in Jerusalem: A Report on the Banality of Evil.* London: Penguin.
Augstein, H.F. (ed.) (1996) *Race: The Origins of an Idea, 1760–1850.* Bristol: Thoemmes Press.
Badiou, A. (2005) *Metapolitics.* London: Verso.

Bamshad, M., Wooding, S., Salisbury, B. A., Stephens, J. C. (2006) 'Deconstructing the Relationship between Genetics and Race', *Nature Review Genetics*, 5 (8): 598–609

Banton, M. (1977) *The Idea of Race*. London: Tavistock.

Banton, M. (1987) *Racial Theories*. Cambridge: Cambridge University Press.

Barkan, E. (1992) *The Retreat of Scientific Racism: Changing Conceptions of Race in Britain and the United States between the World Wars*. Cambridge: Cambridge University Press.

Barker, M. (1981) *The New Racism: Conservatives and the Ideology of the Tribe*. London: Junction Books.

Barnard, F.M. (1969) 'Culture and Political Development: Herder's Suggestive Insights', *The American Political Science Review*, 63 (2): 379–397.

Bauman, Z. (1989) *Modernity and the Holocaust*. Cambridge: Polity Press.

Ben-Rafael, E. (2003) 'Where Stands Israel?', *Ethnic and Racial Studies*, 27 (2): 310–316.

Biddiss, M. D. (1970) *Father of Racist Ideology: The Social and Political Thought of Count Gobineau*. London: Weidenfeld & Nicolson.

Bluntschli, J.K. ([1895] 1971) *The Theory of the State*. 2nd edition. Freeport NY: Books for Libraries Press.

Browning, C. (1992) *Ordinary Men: Reserve Police Battalion 101 and the Final Solution in Poland*. New York: Harper Collins.

Burchard, E. G., Ziv, E., Coyle, N., Gomez, S. L., Tang, H., Karter, A. J., Mountain, J. L., Pérez-Stable, E. J., Sheppard, D., Risch, N. (2003) 'The importance of race and ethnic background in biomedical research and clinical practice', *New England Journal of Medicine*, 348(12): 1170–1175. Cavalli-Sforza, L.L. (2001) *Genes, Peoples and Languages*. London: Penguin.

Cavalli-Sforza, L.L. (2001) *Genes, Peoples and Languages*. London: Penguin.

Cavalli-Sforza, L.L., Menozzi, P. and Piazza, A. (1994) *The History and Geography of Human Genes*. Princeton, NJ: Princeton University Press.

Cook, J. (2006) *Blood and Religion: The Unmasking of the Jewish and Democratic State*. London: Pluto Press.

Cosmides, L., Tooby, J. and Kurzban, R. (2003) 'Perceptions of Race', *Trends in Cognitive Science*, 7 (4): 173–179.

Dorson, R.M. (1955) 'The Eclipse of Solar Mythology', *Journal of American Folklore*, 68 (270): 393–416.

Edwards, A.W.F. (2003) 'Human Genetic Diversity: Lewontin's Fallacy', *Bioessays*, 25 (8): 798–801.

Eze, E. (ed.) (1997a) *Race and the Enlightenment: A Reader*. Oxford: Blackwell.

Eze, E.C. (1997b) 'The Color of Reason: The Idea of 'Race' in Kant's Anthropology' in E.C. Eze (ed.) *Postcolonial African Philosophy: A Critical Reader*. Oxford: Blackwell. pp. 103–40.

Farrar, F.W. (1864) 'On Hybridity', *Journal of the Anthropological Society of London*, 2: ccxxiii–ccxxix.

Finkelstein, N.G. (2000) *The Holocaust Industry: Reflections on the Exploitation of Jewish Suffering*. London: Verso.

Finkelstein, N.G. (2005) *Beyond Chutzpah: On the Misuse of Anti-semitism and the Abuse of History*. Berkeley: University of California Press.

Fisher, R.A. (1936) '"The Coefficient of Racial Likeness" and the Future of Craniometry', *Journal of the Royal Anthropological Institute of Great Britain and Ireland*, 66 (Jan–Jul): 57–63.

Foucault, M. (1970) *The Order of Things: An Archaeology of the Human Sciences*. London: Tavistock.

Foucault, M. (1972) *The Archaeology of Knowledge,* London: Tavistock.

Gilroy, P. (1987) *There Ain't no Black in the Union Jack: The Cultural Politics of Race and Nation*. London: Routledge.

Gilroy, P. (1993) *The Black Atlantic: Modernity and Double Consciousness*. London: Verso.

Gilroy, P. (2001) *Between Camps: Nations, Cultures and the Allure of Race*. London: Penguin.

Glaser, D. (2003) 'Zionism and Apartheid: A Moral Comparison', *Ethnic and Racial Studies*, 26 (3): 403–421.

Goldberg, D.T. (1993) *Racist Culture: Philosophy and the Politics of Meaning*. Oxford: Blackwell.

Guillaumin, C. (1995) *Racism, Sexism, Power and Ideology*. London: Routledge.

Guppy, H.F.J. (1864) 'Notes on the Capabilities of the Negro for Civilisation', *Journal of the Anthropological Society of London*, 2: ccix–ccxiv.

Hannaford, I. (1996) *Race: The History of an Idea in the West*. Baltimore: The Johns Hopkins University Press.

Herder, J. G. (1997 [1784-1791]) *J. G. Herder – On World History*, H. Adler and E. A. Menze (eds). New York: M. E. Sharpe.

Herder, J.G. (1969) *J.G. Herder on Social and Political Culture*. Trans. F.M. Barnard. Cambridge: Cambridge University Press.

Hilberg, R. (1985) *The Destruction of the European Jews*. 2nd edition. New York: Holmes & Meier.

Hunt, J. (1864) 'On the Negro's Place in Nature', *Journal of the Anthropological Society of London*, 2: xv–lvi.

Huntington, S. (1996) *The Clash of Civilisations and the Remaking of World Order*. New York: Simon & Schuster.

Immerwahr, J. (1992) 'Hume's Revised Racism', *Journal of the History of Ideas*, 53 (3): 481–86.

Jorde L.B. and Wooding S.P. (2004) 'Genetic Variation, Classification and "Race"', *Nature Genetics*, 36 (11 Supplement): S28–33.

Kalmar, I. (1987) 'The Volkerpsychologie of Lazarus and Steinthal and the Modern Concept of Culture', *Journal of the History of Ideas*, 48 (4): 671–690.

Kant, I. (1929 [1781-1787]) *Critique of Pure Reason*. Trans. N.K. Smith. Basingstoke: Macmillan.

Kant, I. (1951 [1790]) *Critique of Judgement*. Trans. J.H. Bernard. New York: Hafner Press.

Kant, I. (1978 [1796–97]) *Anthropology from a Pragmatic Point of View*. Trans. V.L. Dowdell. Carbondale & Edwardsville: Southern Illinois University Press.

Kant, I. (1991 [1785]) 'Reviews of Herder's Ideas on the Philosophy of the History of Mankind' in H. Reiss (ed.) *Kant: Political Writings*. Cambridge: Cambridge University Press.

Kant, I. (1950 [1775]) 'On the Different Races of Man' in E.W. Count (ed.), *This is Race*. New York: H. Schuman. pp. 16–24

Keita, S.O.Y., Kittles, R. A., Royal, C. D. M., Bonney, G. E., Furbert-Harris, P., Dunston, G. M., Rotimi, C. N (2004) 'Conceptualizing Human Variation', *Nature Genetics*, 36 (11 Supplement): S17–20.

Kimmerling, B. (2003) *Politicide: The Real Legacy of Ariel Sharon*. London: Verso.

Levin, M. (2002) 'The Race Concept: A Defense', *Behaviour and Philosophy*, 30: 21–42.

Lewontin, R.C. (1974) *The Genetic Basis of Evolutionary Change*. New York: Columbia University Press.

Lewontin, R.C., Rose, S. and Kamin, L.J. (1990) *Not in Our Genes: Biology, Ideology and Human Nature*. London: Penguin.

Lovejoy, A.O. (1910) 'Kant and Evolution I', *Popular Science Monthly*, 77: 538–553.

Lovejoy, A.O. (1911) 'Kant and Evolution II', *Popular Science Monthly*, 78: 36–51.

Mills, C.W. (1998) *Blackness Visible: Essays on Philosophy and Race*. New York: Cornell University Press.

Mosse, G.L. (1964) *The Crisis of German Ideology: Intellectual Origins of the Third Reich*. New York: Howard Fertig.

Mountain, J.L. and Risch, N. (2004) 'Assessing Genetic Contributions to Phenotypic Differences among "Racial" and "Ethnic" Groups', *Nature Genetics*, 36 (11 Supplement): S48–53.

Murji, K. and Solomos, J. (2005) 'Introduction: Racialization in Theory and Practice' in K. Murji and J. Solomos (eds) *Racialization: Studies in Theory and Practice*. Oxford: Oxford University Press. pp. 1–27

Nutt, A. (1910) 'How Far is the Lore of the Folk Racial?', *Folklore*, 21 (3): 379–384.

Pappé, I. (2006) *The Ethnic Cleansing of Palestine*. Oxford: Oneworld.

Pearson, K. (1926) 'On the Coefficient of Racial Likeness', *Biometrika*, 18 (1-2): 105–117.

Rose, J. (2005) *The Question of Zion*. Princeton, NJ: Princeton University Press.

Rose, P.L. (1992) *Wagner: Race and Revolution*. London: Faber.

Rosenberg, N. A. et al. (2002) 'Genetic Structure of Human Populations', *Science*, 298 (5602): 2381–2385.

Rosenberg, N. A., Pritchard, J. K., Weber, J. L., Cann, H. M., Kidd, K. K., Zhivotovsky, L. A., Feldman, M. W. (2002) 'Genetic Structure of Human Populations', *Science*, 298 (5602): 2381–2385.

Rotimi, C.N. (2004) 'Are Medical and Nonmedical Uses of Large-Scale Genomic Markers Conflating Genetics and "Race"?', *Nature Genetics*, 36 (11 Supplement): S43–47.

Sarich, V. and Miele, F. (2004) *Race – The Reality of Human Differences*. Boulder, CO: Westview Press.

Solomos, J. and Back, L. (1996) *Racism and Society*. Basingstoke: Macmillan.

Spivak, G.C. (1999) *A Critique of Postcolonial Reason: Towards a History of the Vanishing Present*. Cambridge, MA: Harvard University Press.

St. Louis, B. (2005) 'Racialization in the "Zone of Ambiguity"' in K. Murji and J. Solomos (eds) *Racialization: Studies in Theory and Practice*. Oxford: Oxford University Press. pp. 29–50.

Stocking, G.W. (1971) 'What's in a Name: The Origins of the Royal Anthropological Institute (1837–1871)', *Man*, 6 (3): 369–390.

Stocking, G.W. Jr (1982) *Race, Culture and Evolution: Essays in the History of Anthropology*. Chicago: University of Chicago Press.

Templeton, A.R. (2003) 'Human Races and the Context of Recent Human Evolution: A Molecular Genetic Perspective' in A.H. Goodman, D. Heath and M.S. Lindee (eds) *Genetic Nature/Culture*. Berkeley, CA: University of California Press. pp. 234–257.

Tishkoff S.A. and Kidd K.K. (2004) 'Implications of Biogeography of Human Populations for "Race" and Medicine', *Nature Genetics*, 36 (11 Supplement): S21–7.

Todorov, T. (1999) *Facing the Extreme: Moral Life in the Concentration Camps*. London: Weidenfeld & Nicolson.

Tucker, W.H. (1994) *The Science and Politics of Racial Research*. Urbana, IL: University of Illinois Press.

Tylor, E.B. (1867) 'Phenomena of Higher Civilisation: Traceable to a Rudimentary Origin among Savage Tribes', *Anthropological Review*, 5 (18/19): 303–314.

Tylor, E.B. (1878) *Researches into the Early History of Mankind*. 3rd edition. London: John Murray.

Tylor, E.B. (1891) *Primitive Culture: Researches into the Development of Mythology, Philosophy, Religion, Language, Art and Custom*, Volume II. London: John Murray.

Tylor, E.B. (1893) 'Anniversary Address', *Journal of the Anthropological Institute of Great Britain and Ireland*, 22: 376–385.

Yiftachel, O. and Ghanem, A. (2004) 'Towards a Theory of Ethnocratic Regimes: Learning from the Judaization of Israel/Palestine' in E.P. Kaufmann (ed.) *Rethinking Ethnicity: Majority Groups and Dominant Minorities*, London: Routledge. pp. 79–98.

Zertal, I. (2005) *Israel's Holocaust and the Politics of Nationhood*. Cambridge: Cambridge University Press.

Race, Ethnicity and Social Hierarchy

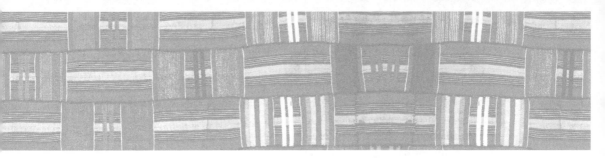

Introduction

In Part II of the handbook we move on from the overarching accounts in the previous part to explore the complexities of the way that race and ethnicity have shaped social hierarchies. The role of race and ethnicity as a force in the making of social hierarchies is an issue that is touched upon throughout this volume, and from a diverse range of national, policy, political and cultural contexts. In this part of the handbook, however, the focus is very much on developing more substantive accounts of the intersections between race, ethnicity and evolving forms of social hierarchy.

The key question addressed by all the chapters is on how the study of race and ethnicity informs scholarship on other comparable social inequalities and, conversely, how these areas might inform the study of race and ethnicity. In this section, we focus on class, nation, gender and sexualities because they are four important social hierarchies that have garnered considerable scholarly attention. Each of these areas of inquiry has established research traditions and groups of practitioner s who historically have differentially incorporated the study of race and ethnicity into their paradigms and methodologies. Moreover, each of these areas is experiencing considerable change in its theoretical frameworks, research questions and practices.

The first chapter by Satnam Virdee is framed by the relationship between race, racism and class. Virdee draws extensively on Marxist and other critical accounts of the interface between racism and class in order to articulate and develop what he terms an agent-centred account of racism and antiracism. Much of his analysis is influenced by the need to redefine the accounts of race and class to be found both in mainstream sociology and Marxism in order to move towards an analytical frame that allows for a more dynamic understanding of the intersections between race and class in both historical and contemporary societies. Drawing on a range of both theoretical and empirical accounts (including the work of

Bonacich, Gilroy and Miles) Virdee also foregrounds the role of material relations in the structuring of race and ethnicity through processes of class formation and social division. A recurrent theme in his analysis is the argument that we need to broaden the terms of analysis of class to allow for a stronger emphasis on agency and social action.

The next chapter in this part by Margaret Andersen is more specifically focused on the nexus of race and gender relations. Andersen's starting point is the emergence in the United States in the aftermath of the Civil Rights Movement of studies that took as their analytical focus the exploration of the complex relations between race, class and gender. Andersen's account is inflected with the debates and political controversies that emerged from the 1970s onwards about the importance of linking the study of race and ethnicity to a more grounded analysis of gender relations. The debates from this period focused attention on the need to explore the nexus of race and gender inequalities more fully, and in many ways this is an argument that is still being worked through in both theoretical discussion and in empirical terms. Andersen also argues forcefully that studies that look at the intermeshing of gender, class and race can highlight similarities in forms of domination and subordination and allow for a policy agenda that deals with multiple forms of social inequality. It is also interesting to note, however, that she also draws attention to the research and scholarship that have emerged from all over the world to this field of scholarship and research.

The historical and contemporary interfaces between ethnicity, race and sexuality are the focus of the next chapter by Joane Nagel. It links up in a number of interesting ways with the accounts of both Virdee and Andersen, drawing as it does on the core idea of the intersections between ethnicities and sexualities. Nagel, however, takes the analysis in the direction of exploring specifically how 'race is sexed' and in turn 'sex is raced'. By exploring the complex processes that underpin the social construction of racial and ethnic boundaries she also seeks to outline the ways in which sexual boundaries are part of the way in which what she defines as ethnosexual frontiers are negotiated and given meaning. This also involves a discussion of the role of sexual violence and conflict in the formation of patterns of ethnic domination and violence. This is an important avenue of new scholarship and research in race and ethnic studies as well as related sub-fields such as nationalism and gender.

The concluding chapter in this part of the handbook is by Floya Anthias and it is framed by the analysis of the ways in which the construction of the nation is shaped by both racial and gender boundaries. Anthias's point of departure is the argument that it is best to see current debates and preoccupations about the nation as part of wider processes of boundary making in our increasingly globalising world. She highlights this line of analysis through a critical review of the ways in which the idea of 'belonging' to a nation has been socially constructed through ideas of nationhood, gender, racialisation and related processes. Anthias's account is influenced by the intersectional frame of analysis that is also evident in other chapters in this volume (notably Andersen, Nagel and Mutua) and this is reflected in her discussion of the role of forms of identity formation shaped by cosmo-politanism and multiculturalism. Her discussion of these issues foregrounds the growing impact of forms of diasporic and translocational belongings that result from the increasing impact of globalised movements of people and social and cultural identities.

Racism, Class and the Dialectics of Social Transformation

Satnam Virdee

We cannot go forward unless we know our yesterdays.

Alfred Rosmer

Marxism is a revolutionary worldview that must always struggle for new revelations. Marxism must abhor nothing so much as the possibility that it becomes congealed in its current form.
Rosa Luxemburg

Since the 1960s, successive waves of sociologists have referred to the inherently debunking character of their discipline (Berger, 1963) whose task it is to demystify social relations (Rex, 1973). Most recently, Michael Burawoy, in his presidential address to the American Sociological Association in 2004 called on his colleagues to rediscover their radical edge and return to the early promise of sociology as the 'angel of history' that seeks to 'salvage the promise of progress' (Burawoy, 2005: 5). While Burawoy's call is laudable enough, it rests on a highly questionable assumption that the founding figures of sociology ever performed such a progressive role. Indeed, when it comes to offering an assessment of the knowledge produced by prominent US sociologists like William Graham Sumner, Lester Ward and Edward Ross regarding race, it would be more accurate to contend that their social Darwinian, cultural evolutionary and eugenicist perspectives added further layers of obfuscation that served to rationalise the discriminatory practices employed against African Americans and other so-called 'inferior races' (Frazier, 1949; Hofstadter, 1967).

Of course, there were individuals who rejected such racist perspectives and wanted as Reed (1997: 44) argues 'to rectify racial misconceptions by means of enlightenment'. Foremost amongst them was W. E. B. Du Bois and it was Du Bois' monumental *The Philadelphia Negro* published in 1899 that first challenged the dominant racist consensus in the academy by systematically demonstrating that the black ghetto was the result of poverty and racism rather than innate inferiority and the allegedly criminal tendencies of African Americans. While Burawoy (2005) clearly has Du Bois in mind when calling on contemporary sociologists to renew their commitment to the radical sociology of their predecessors, what he fails to reveal is the shoddy treatment meted out to Du Bois by *fin de siècle* American sociologists who weren't ready to take on board the intellectual insights and understandings of his early Fabian-inspired work (Reed, 1997).

It was another African American scholar, Oliver Cromwell Cox (1970) – from a later generation than Du Bois – who first advanced in a systematic fashion a Marxist-class analysis of racism and grounded its evolution in the development of the capitalist system, and Atlantic slavery in particular. For Cox, racism or what he refers to as 'race prejudice' was an ideology formulated by ruling elites to justify the exploitation of non-European labour. Racism is 'a social attitude propagated amongst the public by an exploiting class for the purpose of stigmatising some group as inferior so that the exploitation of either the group itself or its resources may be justified' (Cox 1970: 393). Cox contended that racism served the additional purpose of keeping workers divided and thereby blunted any 'interracial' challenge to elite domination by perpetuating amongst the white working class 'an attitude of distance and estrangement mingled with repugnance, which seeks to conceptualise as brutes the human objects of exploitation … race prejudice is the socio-attitudinal concomitant of the racial exploitative practices of a ruling class in a capitalistic society' (Cox, 1970: 475).

Cox's careful spatial and temporal embedding of racism in the formation of capitalist modernity contrasts favourably with the analysis produced by some of his more renowned contemporaries in the Chicago School such as Robert Park who, working under the narrower philosophical remit 'of how social science could be used to realise liberal values and goals in modern American society' (Smith, 1988: 5) could only offer in response that racism had existed since the 'immemorial periods of human association' (Park, 1950).

Despite the production of *Caste, Class and Race* and an additional three-volume work on world capitalism that preceded Wallerstein's world-systems approach by two decades, Cox, like Du Bois before him, found himself ostracised and marginalised by the predominantly white sociological community of the 1950s and early 1960s – in his case largely because of the 'anti-leftist imperatives of the time' (Reed, 2000). Concerns about Macarthyite witchhunts constituted sufficient reason for many leading sociologists to steer clear of Cox's impressive body of work and thereby silence it through non-engagement. Howard Becker, for example, refused to write an introduction to *Caste, Class and Race* because of its 'communist leanings' (Hier, 2001). As Hier notes,

> Cox had introduced a text which was highly critical of capitalism into a postwar social-political climate, characterised by relative affluence and harmony. The economic prosperity brought on by the end of the war left Americans optimistic where their future was concerned, and sociological theory reflected this optimism in a functionalist mirror.

Consequently, this kind of Marxist-inspired analysis that Cox had penned, centred on class conflict and racial exploitation, was met with utter hostility or outright rejection. (2001: 71)

It was only in the 1970s, in the slipstream of the world revolution of 1968 (Wallerstein, 2004) which undermined the racist liberal geoculture that had held the world-system together for so long that Du Bois and Cox were rediscovered by activists and academics alike.

In Britain and the United States, heated debates took place between liberal supporters of Martin Luther King advocating integrationist strategies and revolutionary black nationalists like Malcolm X who questioned the legitimacy of the 'white power structure' and advanced the right to 'black autonomy'. These debates took an even sharper turn in the United States with the formation of the Black Panther Party who, in their 10-Point Plan, demanded 'an end to the robbery by the capitalists of our black and oppressed communities' and the Detroit Revolutionary Union Movement (DRUM) who explicitly linked black liberation with the abolition of capitalism (Geschwender, 1977).

Sociologists, or at least some of them, couldn't help but be inspired by such powerful resistance and it was this dramatic wave of emancipatory politics that first sparked academic interest in questions relating to the origins and reproduction of racism in capitalist society (see e.g. Hall, 2002: 451). Participants active in emancipatory struggles against racism brought into sharp focus questions that had hitherto remained masked by the intellectual veneer provided by the sociology of race relations (e.g., Park, 1950; Banton, 1967) such as how was racism reproduced in a post-holocaust world? In what ways was racism related to class relations and the workings of capitalism, and, significantly, due to the politically engaged character of much of the work, it inevitably raised questions about how racism could be most effectively countered?

In this chapter, I outline and critically evaluate the contributions made to racism studies by a number of key intellectuals including Michael Reich, Edna Bonacich, Stuart Hall, Paul Gilroy, Robert Miles and David Roediger. While the work of Reich (1972, 1978, 1981) and Bonacich (1972, 1976, 1980) sought to embed explanations of contemporary racism in segmented or split labour markets, it was Hall (1980, 1996), Gilroy (1982) and Miles (1982, 1989, 1993) through their productive engagement with the structuralist Marxism of Althusser and Poulantzas that forced class analyses of racism beyond the world of work to assess the significance of culture, ideology and politics. The chapter also maps and interprets the retreat from class analyses of racism through a consideration of the later work of Gilroy (1987, 2000) and Omi and Winant (1994) and suggests ways in which historical materialism could be renewed through a critical engagement with this and other poststructuralist work.

Much of the academic writing informed by the materialist conception of history since the 1940s comes under the rubric of what Perry Anderson (1976) refers to as 'western Marxism'. A key characteristic of this otherwise impressive body of work has been its relative detachment from any form of emancipatory political project. From the miserable Marxism of the Frankfurt School's Theodor Adorno and his claims of working-class incorporation through the culture industry through to the structuralist Marxism of Louis Althusser and his termination of the emancipatory subject via the ideological state apparatus, this body of work has expressed a deep pessimism about the possibility of progressive social change in late capitalism. In this sense, it contrasts sharply with the classical Marxism or praxis philosophy (Habermas, 1987) of Luxemburg, Gramsci and Marx himself, who conceived the materialist method as not only providing the means of understanding history, but also of making it through political interventions (Hook, 2002). This essay is informed by a commitment to developing a non-dogmatic, critical historical materialism that views the production of critical, scholarly knowledge as indivisible from the struggles for progressive social change.

'BLACK AND WHITE, UNITE AND FIGHT': MICHAEL REICH AND THE THEORY OF LABOUR MARKET SEGMENTATION

Observing the durable, empirical facts of labour-force fragmentation and the disproportionate representation of racialised minorities (and women) in secondary labour markets, Reich (1973, 1981) and his colleagues (Reich et al., 1973) developed one of the first systematic accounts of how racism was reproduced in late capitalist society. Grounded in a theory of labour market segmentation defined as 'the division of the labour market into separate submarkets or segments, distinguished by different labour market characteristics and behavioural rules' (Reich 1973: 359), Reich offered a complex historical account mapping how the processes associated with early-twentieth-century US capitalism produced a homogenous and proletarian class that was increasingly conscious of its material class interests and significantly, was pursuing them in ways that threatened to undermine capitalist hegemony. Faced with this threat of worker militancy and growing support for revolutionary socialist political parties like the IWW and the SP, Reich (1973: 361) contends that the US political and economic elites consciously fostered labour market segmentation as a way of dividing the working class and thereby regaining social control over a precarious political situation.

Significantly, racism was one of the key mechanisms by which this process of labour market segmentation was effected. Employing African Americans as strikebreakers and cheap labour in predominantly white worker plants, the resultant activation of racist sentiment amongst this latter group was sufficient to divert its anger away from the white elites and towards black workers, thus ensuring the continued maintenance of capitalist-class rule. For Reich et al. (1973: 364), this type of labour market segmentation 'arose and is perpetuated because it is *functional* – that is, it facilitates the operation of capitalist institutions. Segmentation is functional primarily because it helps reproduce capitalist hegemony'. According to Reich and his colleagues, the *only* beneficiary of racism is the capitalist elite; who retain power by virtue of working class divisions resulting from the process of racist labour market segmentation.

Additionally, while African Americans lost most as the victims of racist labour market segmentation, Reich (1972, 1983) is careful in making clear that white workers also failed to derive material benefits through their embrace and articulation of racist sentiment '...the divisiveness of racism weakens workers strength when bargaining with employers; the economic consequences of racism are not only lower incomes for blacks but also higher incomes for the capitalist class and lower incomes for white workers' (Reich, 1972: 316–317). Indeed, it has been demonstrated by others (e.g., Perlo, 1976; Symanski, 1976; Leiman, 1993) that there was a positive correlation between the degree of working class unity and the wages of black and white workers such that the incomes of both groups tended to rise significantly when they engaged in united action.

If racism didn't result in economic gains for white workers, then one is immediately confronted with the question of why racism had such purchase among white workers? Unlike Oliver Cox (1970) who argued that white workers suffered from false consciousness because they had been duped by ideologies propagated by the ruling elites, Reich contended that working class racism represented a form of nihilistic, psychological outlet for white workers frustrated by the problems caused by the division of labour under capitalism. This racism '... provides some psychological benefits to poor and working class whites. For example, the opportunity to participate in another's oppression compensates for one's own misery ... In general, blacks provide a convenient scapegoat for problems that actually derive from the institutions of capitalism' (Reich, 1972: 319–320).

Rather than attempt to integrate this potentially significant motivating factor into his explanation for racism, Reich unnecessarily closes down this line of inquiry by classifying such motivation as irrational, rationality having been defined narrowly in economic terms. In large part, this was due to Reich's theoretical framework, which showed little interest in understanding the white working class as a social actor. The resultant consequences for political practice emanating from this theoretical standpoint are disappointing with the struggle against racism, and therefore capitalism, narrowly conceptualised within the workplace and an abstract call for black and white solidarity accompanied by union growth.

'DIVIDED WE FALL': EDNA BONACICH AND THE THEORY OF SPLIT LABOUR MARKETS

A clear difficulty with Reich's theory was his contention that the white working class had no material interest in perpetuating racism. This left him vulnerable to the charge that the white working class were either cultural dopes suffering from false consciousness (e.g., Cox, 1970) or that they were economically irrational actors; either way, for someone attempting to advance a historical materialist understanding, it was not a particularly encouraging description of a key segment of the primary agent of radical social transformation.

Edna Bonacich, on the other hand, avoids such a damaging charge when formulating her explanation for the reproduction of racism in late capitalist society. Like Reich, Bonacich 'stresses the role of a certain kind of economic competition in the development of ethnic antagonism' (Bonacich, 1972: 548). However, unlike Reich, Bonacich contends that the white working class were not only the primary perpetrators of racism but actually had a material interest in reproducing racism as well.

In Bonacich's model, the labour market is characterised by conflict between three classes: capitalists who want the cheapest labour, regardless of ethnicity so that they can reduce their labour costs to a minimum; higher priced labour which is fearful of this employer strategy and use their strength to exclude the third class of cheaper labour, often deploying racism as an ideological rationale for such action. As Bonacich (1972: 553) argues:

> This class is very threatened by the introduction of cheaper labour into the market ... If the labour market splits ethnically, the class antagonism takes the form of ethnic antagonism. It is my contention ... that, while much rhetoric of ethnic antagonism concentrates on ethnicity and race, it really is in large measure (though probably not entirely) an expression of this class conflict.

Hence, in Bonacich's model, the primary class responsible for reproducing racism in late capitalist society was the white working class fearful of being replaced or undercut by cheaper black or immigrant labour that capitalists wished to employ to maximise their surplus value. While clearly an impressive theoretical model that firmly located the reproduction of racism in economic competition generated by split labour markets, there are some challenging questions that can be posed of this theoretical frame.

First, Bonacich's approach gives the impression that elites played little part in perpetuating racism in contemporary capitalist society. Such a position is directly contradicted by the evidence provided by Reich (1973) (see above). Perhaps even more damaging however, is the failure to account for the part played by the elites in the historical formation of ethnically split labour markets. This invites a whole set of questions about the role of Western capitalist elites in the uneven development of the capitalist world economy since the sixteenth century, and in particular, the significance of Atlantic slavery, colonialism, imperialism and labour migration to the 'core countries' in the postcolonial world. In a much neglected but important essay, Bonacich (1980) has sought to embed the ethnically split labour market thesis firmly within a world-systems approach (Wallerstein, 1974) as a way of theoretically negotiating the concerns raised above, particularly those relating to the origins of racism and the part played by the elites in perpetuating it.

However, by the early 1980s, it would be fair to surmise that the debate between segmentation and split labour market theorists had reached an impasse.

However, it has recently been revived, most significantly by the work of Phillip Cohen (e.g., 2001). Employing sophisticated quantitative analysis, Cohen demonstrates conclusively, contra the early Bonacich, that white capitalist elites derive economic benefits from racism. And contra Reich, he shows that white workers also benefit economically from racism such that it represents a 'purposive reaction in defense of a privileged status' (Cohen, 2001: 148):

> In the process of creating divisions within the working class, racism may also play a unifying role for white workers, who can apply pressure to protect job boundaries. Therefore, even if racism retards the development of unions, contributes to stagnated overall wages, or fuels public policy that favours capital over labour, there may be a simultaneous tendency to widen the gap between black and white workers. (Cohen 2001: 148)

Cohen also goes onto problematise abstract appeals for black and white solidarity that Reich and others invoked as a way of transforming capitalism and therefore racism. For Cohen, the white working class have rather more to lose than their chains, and, if socialists are to realise their goal of black/white solidarity, they need to acknowledge the unequal distribution of economic capital between the two groups and that the white working class would have to give up some of the material advantage they have accrued directly from racism and discriminatory practices:

> Paying white workers more and black workers less may be a means of dividing workers, but it is not done at an equal cost to black and white workers....The white working class may be able to improve its class position by uniting with black workers, but those who would promote such efforts should recognize that in so doing they threaten their racial advantage. (Cohen 2001: 164)

While Cohen's insights help to shift the debate beyond the zero-sum thinking of elite gain/ working class loss characteristic of the 1970s, it nevertheless remains the case that the explanations for racism considered thus far have remained narrowly grounded within the organisation of work and labour market inequalities. Hence, they remain open to the charge of economic reductionism, that is, the tendency to reduce the distinctively racialised character of certain social divisions to economic processes and questions of class inequality. It was Stuart Hall (1980, 1996) writing from the early 1980s, who first redressed this major weakness in class analysis by giving greater consideration to the political, ideological and cultural dimensions structuring and manufacturing racialised social divisions.

THE TWO SOULS OF STUART HALL: A STRUCTURALIST–HUMANIST PERSPECTIVE ON RACISM

Some influential scholars like David Theo Goldberg (1993: 93) have claimed that Marxism is inherently reductionist. It's certainly not difficult, superficially at least, to substantiate such a claim as the following excerpt from a letter by

Engels testifies: 'Though the economic factor is not the "*sole* determining factor," ... the production and reproduction of real life constitutes in the *last instance* the determining factor in history' (Letter to Joseph Bloch, September 21, 1890 cited in Wilson, 1972: 219). Significantly, these economistic and reductionist tendencies were strengthened further as a result of the mechanical Marxism institutionalised within the 2nd International under the auspices of the 'Pope of Marxism', Karl Kautsky, and then, within the Third International under the deadening hand of Stalinism.

Nevertheless, I want to resist arguments like Goldberg's that point to Marxism's inherent reductionism. Indeed, Goldberg fails to acknowledge that the founders of Marxism were more than aware of the economistic misinterpretation of the materialist method already underway in their own time, as well as their attempts at combating such problematic readings. Hence, Engels acknowledges that whilst Marx and he were:

> ... partly responsible for the fact that at times our disciples have laid more weight upon the economic factor than belongs to it. We were compelled to emphasize its central character in opposition to our opponents who denied it, and there wasn't always time, place and occasion to do justice to the other factors in the reciprocal interactions of the historical process. (cited in Wilson, 1972: 214)

Despite this important corrective, it is nevertheless the case that due to the ossification of Marxist theory under the 2nd and 3rd Internationals, the versions of Marxism that most academics were likely to encounter in western Europe and the United States in the 1970s were those that stressed the primacy of the 'economic' and not the 'reciprocal interactions of the historical process'.

It is against this background that a critical assessment of Stuart Hall's (1980, 1996) important contribution to the study of race and racism must be undertaken. The publication of his hugely influential essay 'Race, Articulation and Societies Structured in Dominance' in 1980 moved the epicentre of the race/class debate firmly across the Atlantic to Britain. In this essay, Hall transformed the existing debate on questions of race and class by advancing a set of highly influential, yet programmatic arguments that effectively shifted it beyond the labour market and the site of economic relations, to consider the role of the state and the importance of politics and ideology/culture.

Hall, at least in the 1970s and early 1980s, was unwilling to write off historical materialism as a method for analysing and capturing the specificity of racialised relations in different national societies. Instead, he proposed that through an engagement with the structuralist-Marxism of Althusser and the Marxist-humanism of Gramsci (Hall, 1980), a more intellectually fruitful and non-dogmatic Marxist approach to understanding racism could be developed which was: '...capable of dealing with both the economic and the superstructural features of such societies, while at the same time giving a historically-concrete and sociologically-specific account of its distinctive racial aspects' (Hall, 1980: 336).

Recalling Marx's own repudiation ('je ne suis pas Marxiste') of those individuals and organisations who claimed allegiance to Marxism but had failed to

grasp its materialist and dialectical underpinnings, Hall's aim was nothing short of intellectually 'saving' Marxist theory from the ills associated with orthodox Marxism:

> What I have tried to do...is to document the emergence of a new theoretical paradigm, which takes its fundamental orientation from the problematic of Marx's, but which seeks, by various theoretical means, to overcome certain of the limitations – economism, reductionism, 'a priorism', a lack of historical specificity – which have beset certain traditional appropriations of Marxism, which still disfigure the contributions to this field by otherwise distinguished writers, and which have left Marxism vulnerable and exposed to effective criticism by many different variants of economistic monism and sociological pluralism. (Hall, 1980: 336)

From Althusser, Hall borrowed the key concept of articulation which allowed him, among other things, to heuristically conceive of society as a complex structured totality (made up of the economy, politics, ideology–culture) 'each with a degree of "relative autonomy" from one another – yet linked into a (contradictory) unity' (Hall, 1980: 326). In this theoretical model, no part of society was reducible to another or corresponded to another; rather the focus was on studying how the different parts of society operated on the 'terrain of articulation' to 'provide the conditions of existence of any conjuncture or event' (Hall, 2002: 450). By deploying articulation as a middle-range conceptual tool to analytically distinguish and capture the specific linkages between different parts of society, Hall was successfully able to avoid falling prey to the traditional Achilles heel of orthodox Marxist theory of reducing or privileging one part of society over another.

The implications of this structuralist approach were profound and contributed to a genuine paradigm shift in understanding the causes of racism (see CCCS, 1982; Gilroy, 1987; Solomos, 1988). In particular, it was clear that race could no longer be seen as an epiphenomenon, a mere phenomenological expression of the underlying social reality of class but rather was relatively autonomous and needed to be given its own specificity. Relatedly, a key implication of race not being reducible to the economic sphere, was that Hall helped to turn our sociological gaze towards the study of how racism 'worked' at the political and ideological–cultural levels of society. Hence, one of the key conclusions to be derived from Hall's Althusserian-inflected approach was that there were additional layers of explanation that required excavation if one was to fully account for the reproduction of racism in contemporary society.

To equip himself with the conceptual tools necessary to accomplish such a task, Hall turned to the work of the Italian Marxist, Antonio Gramsci (Hall, 1980, 1996) who was especially useful in generating 'new concepts, ideas and paradigms pertaining to the analysis of political and ideological aspects of social formations … the much neglected dimensions of the analysis of social formations in classical marxism' (Hall, 1996: 415). In particular, Hall, borrowed the concept of hegemony, defined as a 'state of total social authority' (Hall, 1980: 331–332), to analytically capture how in modern societies, elites secured their right to rule primarily through the manufacture of consent rather than coercively. Relatedly, Hall followed Gramsci in understanding that such hegemony was exercised over the whole of society, including over the working class, and:

> ...not only at the economic level, but also at the level of political and ideological leadership, in civil, intellectual and moral life as well as the material level: and over the terrain of civil society as well as in and through the condensed relations of the State. (Hall, 1980: 331)

Finally, hegemony is: '... not a given *a priori* but a specific historical moment ... a state of play in the class struggle which has, therefore, to be continually worked on and reconstructed in order to be maintained, and which remains a contradictory conjuncture' (Hall, 1980: 332).

This 'reading' of Gramsci proved immensely productive for Hall and enabled him to offer a number of invaluable insights about understanding the reproduction of racism in late capitalist societies. First, there could no longer be a general theory of racism along the lines offered by Cox (1970), only historically specific racisms:

> One must start, then, from the concrete historical 'work' which racism accomplishes under specific historical conditions – as a set of economic, political and ideological practices, of a distinctive kind, concretely articulated with other practices in a social formation...In short, they are practices which secure the hegemony of a dominant group over a series of subordinate ones, in such a way as to dominate the whole social formation in a form favourable to the long-term development of the economic productive base. (Hall, 1980: 338)

Second, a key factor that helped explain why ruling elites were so successful in securing hegemony was their effectiveness in fragmenting the working class in the political and ideological–cultural spheres. One manifestation of this was how the working class tended to reconstitute itself as belonging to separate races such that:

> ... the class relations which ascribe it, function as race relations. Race is thus, also, the modality in which class is 'lived', the medium through which class relations are experienced, the form in which it is appropriated and 'fought through'. This has consequences for the whole class not specifically for its 'racially defined' segment. (Hall, 1980: 341)

In this formulation, Hall offers us a productive and non-reductionist way out of the disabling impasse of the orthodox race versus class debate where both Marxists (e.g., Miles, 1982) and Weberians (e.g., Rex, 1970) treat race and class as discrete and dichotomous variables. Instead, Hall suggests that at the level of politics and ideology, race works through class such that it would be more appropriate to re-conceive this relationship as the racialisation of class and the classification of race.

The dangers of interpellation for Hall's 'Marxism without guarantees'

Hall's work in this period represents a genuine *tour de force* which helped to re-shape thinking within the discipline of sociology and beyond. Specifically, it represented the intellectual high point of scholarly work that was sparked by the mass protest movements of the 1960s and 1970s. However, I want to draw attention to possible flaws in Hall's project of attempting to renew Marxism as a non-dogmatic method of analysis and action – a 'Marxism without guarantees' – because ultimately they have serious implications for his analysis of race and racism using the materialist conception of history.

The source of the problems lies in Hall's attempt to introduce human agency into his theoretical frame. Hall was acutely aware of E. P. Thompson's (1978) polemical attack on Althusser's attempt to square structuralism with Marxism, and especially, his charge that it had resulted in the construction of a flawed theoretical apparatus – an 'orrery of errors' – which had banished the idea of human subjectivity from Marxism. Indeed Hall, because he engaged with Althusser's work seriously, was the object of Thompson's ire in a now (in)famous debate held at Ruskin College Oxford in December 1979 (Samuel, 1981: 375–408). Hall, while rejecting many of Thompson's substantive criticisms, nevertheless had independently begun to turn to Gramsci as a way of re-introducing the 'historically concrete' and human subjectivity into his theoretical frame. As he retrospectively acknowledged: 'Gramsci is where I stopped in the headlong rush into structuralism and theoreticism. At a certain point, I stumbled over Gramsci, and I said, "Here and no further!"' (Hall, 1988: 69).

The additional analytic purchase Hall achieved by introducing a notion of subjectivity that had hitherto been missing from his work enabled him to demonstrate how the ascription of racist identities could also be appropriated by the racialised and infused with a new ideology of resistance to counter racism and discrimination:

> The racist interpellations can become themselves the sites and stake in the ideological struggle, occupied and redefined to become elementary forms of an oppositional formation – as where 'white racism' is vigorously contested through the symbolic inversions of 'black power'. The ideologies of racism remain contradictory structures, which can function both as vehicles for the imposition of dominant ideologies, and as the elementary forms for the cultures of resistance. Any attempt to delineate politics and ideologies of racism which omit these continuing features of struggle and contradiction win an apparent adequacy of explanation only by operating a disabling reductionism. (Hall, 1980: 342)

However, his attempt to bring the subject back into history through the work of Gramsci is flawed because Gramsci is read through a structuralist-Marxist lens. In particular, the root of the problem lies in Hall's use of interpellation, a concept derived from Althusser and Laclau, and employed to denote the process by which individuals are constituted by ideologies, and so become subjects of ideology (Hall, 1996). Two corollaries of this understanding are that interpellated individuals believe that such subjectivities or identities are self-generated and so freely accept, even embrace their subjection, thereby contributing to the continuation of the capitalist system, and second, even when subjects do resist, they remain interpellated individuals.

Consequently, in Hall's conceptual framework, because the working class are always interpellated, the prospect of this class reaching 'beyond ideology' or piercing the veil of ideology, and moving towards a higher form of (class) consciousness in explicit recognition of their objective, material interests is lost. Such an understanding of subjectivity and human agency is at odds with Gramsci's (and Marx's) theory of working class self-emancipation and the understanding that the working class could, under definite social conditions, break free from such ideologies of domination. The outcome is that despite his well-intentioned attempt at rethinking Marxism, Hall ends up offering a portraiture of the white working class that, like the Utopian Socialists before him (Marx and Engels, 1977; Draper, 1978), reduces this class to mere victims of the degradations inflicted by the capitalist system, a class with little capacity to resist the power of ideology in fragmenting and dissipating resistance to elite rule.

This is not to claim that Hall's approach, demonstrating the power of ideology in integrating the working class, and thereby, fragmenting opposition to the capitalist state, is wholly inconsistent with Marx's approach and the emphasis he placed on ideologies shaping working class conceptions of the world. After all, it was Marx and Engels (1987: 45) in *The German Ideology* who claimed famously that:

> The ideas of the ruling class are in every epoch the ruling ideas, i.e. the class which is the ruling *material* force of society, is at the same time its ruling *intellectual* force. The class which has the means of material production at its disposal, has control at the same time over the means of mental production, so that thereby, generally speaking, the ideas of those who lack the means of mental production are subject to it.

Significantly, however, Marx – unlike Hall – explicitly juxtaposed such an understanding of ideology and its impact on working class consciousness with a conception of this same class as the eventual 'gravedigger of capitalism' (Marx and Engels, 1977). Indeed, it could be contended that what distinguished Marx's Marxism from other philosophical and theoretical traditions was not its emphasis on socially produced inequalities or political economy, nor even its focus on class struggle and capitalism, but instead, its conception that the working class was *the* universal class – the class whose own particularist interests, under given historical conditions, would synchronise with the transformation needed by society as a whole. It was in this sense, that Marx, 'nominated the proletariat as the universal class … [and] hence, the agent of revolution' (Draper, 1978: 71).

Marx himself was acutely aware of the theoretical and practical dilemmas posed by what others have rather lazily interpreted as this 'contradiction' in his work. How then did Marx set about resolving the dilemma of a class that, on the one hand, was so thoroughly dehumanised in capitalist society and politically divided on the grounds of nationalism, racism, sexism and other ideologies of domination, with, on the other hand, a simultaneous conception that it was *only* this class that had the capacity to transform capitalist social relations and so release the full potential of humanity? Or as the young Sidney Hook (2002: 157) succinctly puts it, 'how is it possible for human beings conditioned by their cultural education and environment to succeed in changing that environment?'

Marx solved this dilemma by introducing the concept of class struggle, broadly understood as encompassing forms of collective working class resistance to the multifarious forms of capitalist exploitation and oppression. For Marx, it was only through struggle that the working class could change politically and reject what he memorably termed the 'old crap' and thereby become fit to rule. That is, it was only through struggle that attachments to deeply held ideological positions would become unsettled and open up a political as well as ideological space from within which those articulating an internationalist working class standpoint could attract an audience and begin the process of manufacturing the necessary preconditions for the socialist transformation of society. Thus, for Marx, it was in the course of struggles against capitalist exploitation and oppression that the working class would begin to loosen their attachments to long-held reactionary sentiments and thereby begin the process of self-transformation.

> Both for the production on a mass scale of this communist consciousness, and for the success of the cause itself, an alteration of men on a mass scale is necessary, an alteration which can only take place in a practical movement, a revolution; the revolution is necessary, therefore, not only because the ruling class cannot be overthrown in any other way, but also because the class overthrowing it can only in a revolution succeed in ridding itself of the 'old crap' and become fitted to found society anew. (Marx cited in Draper, 1978: 74)

This dialectically informed solution to the question of how those who are dehumanised by capitalist society are simultaneously the ones who are also most likely to transform it that Marx brings to bear on the question of social change is absent in the body of work produced by Hall. The outcome is while Hall very successfully takes us beyond the economistic and reductionist Marxism of the 2nd and 3rd Internationals, it is at the cost of expunging the beating heart of Marxism – the conception of the working class subject as the gravedigger of capitalist society. In doing so, Hall abandons, albeit unwittingly, the revolutionary standpoint that was central to Marx's life and thought.

In contrast, for Marx, class struggle was the central concept by which he understood history and its major transitions; it was the motor of history, and its intensification (across all levels of society) was the key mechanism by which changes in consciousness took place. The absence of the concept of class struggle in Hall's schema means that he is unable to analyse societal developments in their totality. The implications for his theoretical frame are deeply problematic because he is simply unable to capture analytically, how the class struggle, especially its intensification, *may* contribute to the destabilisation of well-entrenched interpellated racialised subjectivities. Hence, while he usefully analyses how state racism 'works' in 1970s Britain, especially in relation to the issue of mugging (Hall et al., 1978), and identifies the growth of anti-racist protest around the identity 'black' (Hall, 1980), there is little analytical space to capture anti-racism amongst the white working class who are largely seen as individuals increasingly adopting racist interpellated identities.

FROM MARXISM TO POSTMODERNISM: PAUL GILROY AND THE RETREAT FROM CLASS

Stuart Hall's development of a non-reductive Marxist approach to the study of racism proved intellectually fruitful and attracted a great deal of attention, both within British academia and beyond (Nelson and Grossberg, 1988). In particular, Hall's conception of race being relatively autonomous from class, and other valuable theoretical and conceptual insights inspired a generation of former students to carry out historically concrete studies assessing the role of racism in the cultural and political life of postcolonial Britain (e.g., CCCS, 1982; Gilroy, 1987; Solomos, 1988). In the course of these studies, Gilroy, Solomos and others helped to further refine and develop the original insights giving rise to what can retrospectively be termed the CCCS school.

Briefly, these studies showed how the relationship between race and nation was re-configured with the arrival of migrant labour from the Caribbean and Indian sub-continent in the 1950s and 1960s giving rise to an explicit indigenous racism that viewed a previously external presence as threatening the imagined British way of life from within. This new racism emerged onto the national political scene most significantly during the late 1960s and 1970s when, as part of the New Right project, it was employed by parts of the State to re-assert its authority amidst the organic crisis of British capitalism (Solomos et al., 1982). According to Gilroy (1987: 55–56), a key outcome of this new racism was that blackness and Britishness were reproduced as mutually exclusive categories, as neatly captured in the title of his influential book *There Ain't No Black in the Union Jack*. As a result, a more critical and multi-dimensional materialist analysis of the phenomenon was developed during the 1980s that demonstrated conclusively that racism was not just the result of class inequalities in the 'economic' sphere of society but also the product of state actions and nationalist ideologies.

For the purposes of this chapter, I want to focus critically on the important contribution made by Paul Gilroy (1982, 1987), one of the key individuals who helped shape and develop a neo-Marxian understanding of racism, but yet someone who subsequently went onto make an explicit break with a materialist conception of history.

There is a sense in which Gilroy's work represents both an organic continuation of Hall's impressive oeuvre and an innovative departure. The continuities can be seen in how Gilroy, through a study of the cultural politics of race and nation, is able to demonstrate convincingly how nationalism in postcolonial Britain became intimately entwined with racism such that the white working class' allegiance to a racist nationalism overrode any attachment to fellow class members subjected to racism:

> It may be that the benefits of imperialism have determined that 'the people' will always tend towards 'the race' in this country, at any rate 'The British Nation' and 'The Island Race' have historically failed to, and cannot at present, incorporate black people. Indeed their alieness and externality to all things British and beautiful make it hard to imagine any such discourse which could accommodate their presence in a positive manner and retain its popular character. The popular discourse of the nation operates across the formal lines of class, and has been constructed *against* blacks. (Gilroy, 1982: 278)

According to Gilroy (1982: 305–306), central to the construction and maintenance of this racist division within the working class were the institutions of the working class who have:

> ... failed to represent the interests of black workers abroad and at home, where black rank-and-file organization has challenged local and national union bureaucracy since the day the 'Empire Windrush' docked. We are disinclined to the pretence that these institutions represent the class *as a class* at all ....

For Gilroy, such historical and contemporary developments undermined those political strategies advocated by Stalinists and Eurocommunists alike in 1970s Britain that premised anti-racist interventions on the idea of an already existent unified class subjectivity. It is here, concerning questions of how political practice is organically derived from theoretical understanding that Gilroy's differences with Hall become most marked with his innovative attempt to rethink Marxism in such a way as to re-encompass questions of class subjectivity. Thus, for Gilroy, the pressing analytic (and strategic) question becomes that of establishing the processes by which racism can be challenged and the working class unified around a class subjectivity: 'Our premise is the problem of relating "race" to class, ... for socialist politics' (Gilroy, 1982: 276).

The key concept that Gilroy employs to analytically grasp this dynamic process of social change is class struggle, defined in such a way as to include 'the relentless processes by which classes are constituted – organised and disorganised – in politics, as well as the struggles between them once formed' (Gilroy, 1982: 284). Here, Gilroy opens up a theoretical and political space by which to re-conceive autonomous black struggles against racism, in the community as well as within the workplace, as forms of class struggle. The theoretical implications of such a position are clear; if black struggles are class struggles, then these struggles contribute to a process of class formation within which a consciousness of class becomes synchronised with a consciousness of race.

> Though for the social analyst 'race' and class are necessarily abstractions at different levels, black consciousness of race and class cannot be empirically separated. The class character of black struggles is not the result of the fact that blacks are predominantly proletarian, though this is true. It is established in the fact that their struggles for civil rights, freedom from state harassment, or as waged workers, are instances of the process by which the class is constituted politically, organized in politics. (Gilroy, 1982: 302)

By locating the analysis of racism at the heart of processes of class reformation (and dissolution), the black working class, far from being peripheral to working class politics was now brought centrestage and imputed with a vanguard role that Marx had attributed to the working class as a whole:

> In our view of class formation, the racist ideologies and practices of the white working class and the consequent differentiation of 'the blacks' are ways in which the class as a whole is disorganized. The struggles of black people to refuse and transform their subjugation are no simple antidote to class segmentation, but they are processes which attempt to constitute the class politically across racial divisions – 'that is which represent it against capitalism, against racism' ... these struggles do not derive their meaning from the political failures of the classically conceived, white, male working class ... it appears that autonomous organiza- tion has enabled blacks ... to 'leap-frog' over their fellow workers into direct confrontations with the state in the interest of the class as a whole. (Gilroy, 1982: 304)

Remarkably, however, these influential statements on the workings of contempo- rary racism and emancipatory politics, rather than representing a key moment in the historical renewal of the materialist method, actually marked Gilroy's depar- ture to more postmodern forms of social thought. Hence, just five years after the publication of the collectively authored *The Empire Strikes Back* (1982) where he began the intellectually fruitful task of rethinking the relationship between race and class, Gilroy published *There Ain't No Black in the Union Jack* (1987) which saw him effecting a divorce between race and class. Hence, the reconception of black struggles as class struggles, constituting one moment in the historical unification of the working class was now rejected with such strug- gles disengaged from any type of class analysis:

> If these struggles (some of which are conducted in and through 'race') are to be called class struggles, then class analysis must itself be thoroughly overhauled. I am not sure whether the labour involved in doing so makes it either a possible or desirable task. (Gilroy, 1987: 245)

Instead, drawing on social movement theory emerging out of western Europe (during a period of working class defeat), Gilroy moved to settle his account with Marxism by reconceiving black struggles against racism (or what remained of them by the late 1980s) as one of the burgeoning social movements alongside those of the feminist, ecology and youth movements. This breach with his previ- ous Marxist approach was made explicit with his conclusion that:

> The Proletariat of yesterday, classically conceived or otherwise, now has rather more to lose than its chains. The real gains which it has made have been achieved at the cost of a deep-seated accommodation with capital and the political institutions of corporatism. It's will, as Calhoun has also pointed out 'is apt to be a reformist will'. (Gilroy, 1987: 246)

Principally, there are two factors that help to understand the remarkable turn- around in Gilroy's theoretical and political position. First, were the decisive defeats suffered by antisystemic movements that had their origins in the world revolution of 1968. In particular, the political exhaustion of the militant workers movement in western Europe and the antiwar, anti-racist and feminist movements in Europe and the US, coupled with the fall of the Stalinist bloc of eastern Europe (including the Soviet Union itself in 1991), effectively extinguished the utopian sentiments that had been sparked in the late 1960s. Against this unfavourable political backdrop, Marxist approaches to racism and other phenomena, with their concern for making history as well as understanding it, found themselves marginalised in the academy for the more esoteric concerns of postmodernism and poststructuralism. It is clear that academics, even those as intellectually impressive as Gilroy, could not fail to be affected by such developments.

Second, however, such an intellectual shift away from a materialist conception of history was made easier because of some of the weaknesses associated with Gilroy's theoretical framework, in particular, his failure to conceptualise the concept of class struggle in its totality. Gilroy used it only to reconceptualise the struggles of black workers as class struggles but not as an overarching concept that could help to uncover and interpret the struggles of white workers and their dialectical relationship with those of the racially demarcated black class fraction (see Virdee, 2000). The resultant abstraction of racist and anti-racist struggles from the historical rhythms of the class struggle and a historically concrete assessment of their impact in shaping and changing white working class consciousness and identities is entirely missing from his work. The outcome is that whilst Gilroy produces a dynamic analysis of anti-racist politics and black culture and its racialisation, the portraiture of the white working class is static, ahistorical and generally shorn of any subjectivity across time and space.

The implications of reconnecting the racialised class struggles of black workers to the class struggles of white workers and analysing their significance in their totality are disastrous for Gilroy's theory of race and class as Virdee (2000, 2002) demonstrates with respect to 1970s Britain – the period that Gilroy uses to formulate his theoretical standpoint. Rather than the white working class being defined as a racist class fraction devoid of any subjectivity across time and space, we actually find that under conditions of militant class struggle and major political and industrial unrest, the attachment to racist and nationalist identities became unsettled, creating a space for the emergence of a stronger class identity amongst parts of the organised working class which lead to the formation of a fragile but real class solidarity across 'racial' lines at a specific historical conjuncture. This was evidenced most clearly in the mass support provided by white workers in the dispute involving Asian women at the Grunwick film processing plant in north London but also entailed significant working class involvement in the mass anti-racist movements of Rock Against Racism, the Anti-Nazi League and the trade unions.

The most visible manifestation of rank and file 'inter-racial' working class solidarity and the rejection of racist ideologies took place between 1976 and 1978 during the Grunwick dispute when thousands of white (and black) workers, including miners, dockers and transport workers heeded the call for secondary picketing in support of the South Asian women on strike (Rogaly, 1977; Sivanandan, 1982; Ramdin, 1987). Additionally, local post office workers stopped the delivery of mail coming in or out of Grunwick against the wishes of their union leadership in the Union of Post Office Workers (UPW) whilst contracted TGWU drivers, working for the police on picket duty at Grunwick refused to drive them into the premises of the firm (Rogaly, 1977; Ramdin, 1987). Ramdin (1987: 292) describes how the local people of the London Borough of Brent also responded with 'donations from the Millner Park Ward, the Rolls Royce Works Committee, Express Dairies, Associated Automation (GEC), the TGWU and the UPW Cricklewood Office Branch'. Particularly significant was the solidarity action of the London dockers who, in 1968, had marched to the Houses of Parliament in support of Enoch Powell's racist 'rivers of blood' speech and the end of black immigration (Sivanandan, 1982; Miles and Phizacklea, 1984). Only one docker, Terry Barrett, a member of the Leninist International Socialists (IS), had publicly opposed the march then (Socialist Review, April 1998: 31). However, less than a decade later, on 11 July 1977, there was a marked change in the attitudes of these same dockers towards racialised minorities as evidenced by the 'Royal Docks Shop Stewards banner heading a mass picket of 5,000 over-whelmingly white trade unionists in support of the predominantly Asian workforce' (Callinicos, 1993: 61).

There is a tendency in much of Marxist writing, including that by Marx him-self (see the discussion above) to view struggle as somehow inevitably leading to the formation of a progressive (class) consciousness. Hook (2002: 212) also claims that a 'class is not always critically conscious of what it really is fighting for. It is the shock and consequence of the struggle which brings it to self-consciousness'. However, this teleological outlook ignores the possibility, especially in our post-Holocaust epoch, that other more reactionary, nihilistic ideas might fill the vacuum left by the disintegration of capitalist hegemony. It was Walter Benjamin (2006) who first warned Marxists of the dangers of assum-ing the inevitable victory of socialism with his pertinent observation that 'Nothing has corrupted the German working class so much as the notion that it is moving with the current'. Of course, Benjamin was attuned to the dangers of teleology and fatalism because he tragically witnessed firsthand the political capitulation of the Stalinised German Communist Party (KPD) to the Nazis so potently captured by their defeatist political slogan 'After Hitler, Us'.

Virdee's (2000, 2002, forthcoming) work demonstrates that movement towards progressive, anti-racist solidarities was not inevitable as both Marx and Hook claimed; instead, returning to 1970s Britain, he demonstrates concretely how anti-racist internationalists and racist nationalists competed politically for the soul and support of the white working class. Critical to the formation of united working class action was direct human intervention that transcended the racist colour line in the form of black workers engaged in independent anti-racist action and black and white socialist activists who recognised that racism served to divide the working class, something the working class could ill afford while trying to defend their class interests against employer and state attacks. Hence, key fractions of the working class were ideologically won to anti-racist ideas because black and socialist activists from a multiplicity of political parties were able to successfully synchronise the struggle against racism with the struggle against employer attacks on the working class.

A hegemonic bloc, involving parts of organised white labour and the black population, around the programme of militant resistance to working class exploitation and racism was constructed in the 1970s which was only defeated in the early 1980s by the counter hegemony manufactured around the 'authoritarian populist' agenda of Thatcherism involving a different component of the working class. This 'historically concrete' re-reading of events is important because it allows us to derive one further point about the relationship between race and class from the critical historical materialist perspective advanced by Virdee (2000, 2002).

Under conditions of intensifying class struggle, the possibility arises by which particularist identities around race and nation can be unsettled and mutate into a more universalist identity of class. Yet, because of his problematic conception of the relationship of race to class at the level of theory, Gilroy misses out entirely on analytically capturing these important changes in the consciousness of white workers, including towards racism. Having written off the trade unions as irretrievably racist, he is unable to analyse the important process of anti-racist racialised black formation in trade unions throughout the 1980s and 1990s (see Virdee and Grint, 1994) which has lead some to predict that when we witness the 'fire next time' and the resulting intensification of the class struggle, black workers will be an indispensable component of the struggle of organised labour against capitalist exploitation and that trade unions by virtue of the leading presence of black workers will play a crucial part in combating racism.

Gilroy's neglect of the class struggles of white organised labour and the implications for consciousness and the presumption of their unchanging racism across time and place, helps us to understand his attribution of a vanguard role to the black proletariat and the subsequent reconception of it as one movement among many social movements. However, with the decline of black politics from the mid-1980s, Gilroy loses even this diminished conception of human agency and is reduced to making an abstract appeal for a liberal planetary humanism to counter the growing array of racist absolutisms in the global era (Gilroy, 2000) – a demand almost wholly devoid of any systematic understanding of the inequalities produced by contemporary capitalist social relations.

ROBERT MILES, THE RACE CONCEPT AND THE MISSING HUMAN AGENT

Unlike Gilroy, and eventually Hall too (e.g., 1989), there was one individual – Robert Miles (1982, 1989, 1993) – who resisted the allure of poststructuralist and postmodern forms of social thought in the late 1980s and early 1990s and continued to vigorously defend and also elaborate further on his original and explicitly Marxist informed account of racism. Writing against the dominant currents of the day, especially from the mid-1980s, Miles found himself engaged in an often heated and highly contentious debate with individuals working within both the liberal (e.g., Rex, 1970) and radical (e.g., Gilroy, 1982, 1987) sociology of race relations paradigms.

Miles' starting point was his wholesale rejection of the liberal sociology of race relations paradigm and especially its use of race as an analytical and descriptive concept (Miles, 1982). For Miles, the subject of study was not race or race relations but how and why parts of the human population came to be constructed and defined as members of different races with different levels of cultural endowment. By employing a conceptual distinction between essential and phenomenal relations characteristic of Marxist approaches, he attempted to sideline the 'race versus class' debate by claiming that race and class occupied different analytical spaces. In particular, race was employed to refer to a social and historical construction, an effect of ideology masking real social relations based on class.

Also, since Miles was keen to distance himself intellectually and politically from the concept of race, he analytically captured the process of race-making using the concept of racialisation defined as referring to 'those instances where social relations between people have been structured by the signification of certain human biological characteristics in such a way as to define and construct differentiated social collectivities (Miles, 1989: 75). For Miles, such a process of racialisation was almost always followed by that of racism defined as an 'ideology which signifies some real or alleged biological characteristic as a criterion of other group membership and which also attributes that group with other, negatively evaluated characteristics' (Miles, 1993: 60).

Substantively, Miles (1982, 1989, 1993) claimed that the genesis of race-making was intimately entwined with the projects of Atlantic slavery, colonialism and nationalism. Through these large-scale social processes, large parts of Africa, Asia and South America came to be economically underdeveloped at the expense of the economic development of the European nation-states of Western Europe and later North America. It was against this backdrop that ideas about race began to have some analytic purchase as a way of ideologically rationalising the rule of Western capitalist elites, and, thereby, the process of capitalist accumulation.

While slavery and colonial regimes were politically overthrown in a wave of nationalist-inspired revolutions (Nairn, 1977), racism continued to be reproduced because of the continuing economic dominance exercised by the departing powers. Specifically, the continuing uneven development of the capitalist world economy meant that international labour migration to the former colonial powers became an essential element of the postcolonial world-system such that when the demand for labour couldn't be met within the confines of the national state, individual employers and the state secured labour from beyond its national boundaries. It was at this historical moment that racism came to be replenished, with international migration being politically refracted by the State through the historical and ideological lens of racism (and nationalism).

Employing a structuralist-Marxist conceptualisation derived from Nicos Poulantzas, Miles concluded that the effect of such racism and the exclusionary practices arising thereof, were felt across 'all three levels of a social formation: economic, political and ideological. These effects can, in combination, cohere to lead to the formation of fractions within classes' (Miles, 1982: 157).

This summary of Miles' key theoretical and substantive insights allows us to draw several conclusions about how he moved the debate about racism forward in the social sciences. First, any theory about the historical formation of racism and its reproduction, had to be grounded in a theory of the capitalist world-system. Second, by also embedding his account of racism in a theory of nationalism he opened up the scholarly debate to conceiving of racism not only as a colour-coded problem relating to non-European others but also as one that encompassed the racialisation of the European interior. Third, through his rejection of the dubious concept of race, Miles provided subsequent generations of scholars – both Marxist and non-Marxist – with an alternative vocabulary by which to understand and analytically capture the phenomenon of racism which didn't contribute to the further racialisation of social relations.

However, it was precisely one of the strengths of Miles' framework – his objection to the employment of the concept of race in either description or analysis – that was, simultaneously the cause of the most serious weakness in his work. While conceding that individuals may be forced to organise against racism independently around racialised identities due to the racism of the white working class, Miles remained unwilling to accommodate such anti-racism within his Marxian frame because of his concern that the continued use of race only served to sustain the conditions for the reproduction of racism within society:

> … as a result of reification and the interplay between academic and common sense discourses, the "use" of race as an analytical concept can incorporate into the discourse of antiracism a notion which has been central to the evolution of racism. As a result, anti-racist activities then promote the idea that 'races' really exist as biological categories of people. Thus, while challenging the legitimacy of unequal treatment and stereotyping implicit and explicit in racism, the reproduction within anti-racist campaigns of the idea that there are real biological differences creating groups of human beings sustains in the public consciousness a notion which constitutes an ideological precondition for stereotyping and unequal treatment. (Miles and Torres, 1999: 26)

While entirely consistent with his theoretical position, Miles' failure to accommodate anti-racist action constructed around the racialised identity of black in 1970s Britain within his theoretical perspective created immense problems relating to political practice. In particular, in the context of the state racism unleashed against Britain's racialised minority populations in the 1970s and 1980s (see CCCS, 1982; Solomos, 1988), Miles was left advocating support for an idealised and unified class subjectivity which he hoped would evolve out of a shared class position in the process of production providing a 'material and political basis for the development of anti-racist practice within the working class'. Such an abstract political and theoretical standpoint appears to be wholly at odds with the understanding of historical materialism outlined in this essay which conceives of the materialist method of history as one that helps to inform the making of history as well as understanding it. The undialectical and potentially reactionary nature of this position was made explicit by Gilroy (1987: 23) in no uncertain terms when he contended that:

> This position effectively articulates a theoretical statement of the 'black and white unite variety'. The consciousness of groups which define themselves in, or organize around, what becomes racial discourses is rendered illegitimate because of its roots in ideology. It is consistently counterposed to the apparently unlimited potential of an ideal category of workers. This group, the repository of legitimate and authentic class feeling, is able to transcend racial particularity in political practice uncontaminated by non-class subjectivity.

Miles' later collaborative work (e.g., Miles and Torres, 1999) did eventually concede the power of such a critique: 'the strongest case made in favour of the retention of the notion of "race" as an analytical concept arises from the fact that it has been used by the victims of racism to fashion a strategy and practice of resistance to their subordination' (Miles and Torres, 1999: 3). However, his belated attempt to incorporate anti-racist mobilisations around a racialised identity into his theoretical framework as examples of what he termed racialised formation (Miles and Torres, 1999: 30) only led to further conceptual difficulties and the unravelling of his theoretical and political perspective.

Miles quite rightly notes that the process of racialization is a dialectical process such that by racialising an individual or group as the 'other', one is also simultaneously racialising the `self'. Both these dimensions of racialization can be treated as examples of racialised formation. The problem in Miles' later work is that he has no intellectual strategy to analytically distinguish between projects of racialised formation that are motivated by racism and those that are motivated by anti-racism. Hence, the implications for his theoretical framework are, for example, that both white supremacists demonstrating against the arrival of Hispanic migrants in the United States and Hispanic Americans countering such mobilisations constitute instances of racialised formation. This fundamental failure to accommodate anti-racism around a racialised identity means that the theoretical promise of Miles' original intellectual framework remains only partially fulfilled.

It could be contended that this is not an isolated failing but integral to his problematic conception of historical materialism which over-emphasised the structural forces shaping the lives of racialised minorities whilst at the same time underestimated the creative self-activity of racialised minorities in reshaping the adverse circumstances they found themselves in. This type of historical materialist approach which became hegemonic in Western academic circles in the 1970s and 1980s was, as has already been shown in this essay, heavily informed by the work of French theorists like Althusser and Poulantzas. Through their 'reading' of Marx, they came to advance an understanding of human development which allowed little room for human agency and where the abstract 'laws of society' were impervious to human will and action (Althusser, 1994).

In Miles' structuralist theoretical schema, this manifested itself in how capital and capitalist elites were conceived as omnipotent whilst migrant labour, emptied of any capacity for agency, was reduced to a mere object, a compliant cog in the wheel of capitalism moved from one nation to another by the all-powerful and anonymous 'law of capital accumulation'. While not wishing to deny the undoubted strengths of this approach, especially the way in which it highlighted the importance of labour migration to the capitalist world economy, the neglect of human agency made it impossible for Miles to envisage a scenario where racialised minorities might actually counter and *successfully* resist the allegedly omnipotent interests of capitalist elites and thereby re-shape their lives under capitalism. This leads to the conclusion that whilst Miles's migrant labour approach is useful in identifying the initial mechanisms triggering racism, namely, the uneven development of the capitalist world economy and international migration, it loses much of its analytic and explanatory purchase when the focus turns to post-migration developments, especially those relating to anti-racism, subjectivity and identity formation.

Critically integrating concepts developed within poststructuralist racial formation theory offers the most productive way of theorising anti-racist subjectivities within a revised historical materialist frame. Its founders, Michael Omi and Howard Winant (1994: 55), deploy the concept of racial formation to refer to the 'sociohistorical process by which racial categories are created, inhabited, transformed, and destroyed'. Crucial to this formulation is the treatment of race as a central axis of social relations which cannot be subsumed or reduced to some other category like class. Against the neo-Marxists who sought to abolish the race concept from the sociological lexicon, Winant (2000: 184) contends:

> ... this fails to recognise that at the level of experience, of everyday life, race is a relatively impermeable part of our identities: US society is so thoroughly racialized that to be without racial identity is to be in danger of having no identity. To be raceless is akin to being genderless. Indeed, when one cannot identify another's race, a microsociological crisis of interpretation results ....

This conception of race is therefore underpinned by an understanding that it is rooted neither in biology as scientific racists claim, nor, is it a fiction as many Marxists contend; rather race is a 'concept which signifies and symbolises social conflicts and interests by referring to different types of human bodies' (Omi and Winant 1994: 55). This understanding of race has clear similarities to the position advanced by the CCCS school of Hall and Gilroy outlined earlier in this essay. However, Omi and Winant's theory of racial formation takes us beyond the debate in Britain; indeed, it may even help to resolve this sometimes heated and contentious debate because unlike the CCCS school, Omi and Winant go on to offer a way of analytically distinguishing between racist and anti-racist usages of the race concept.

Omi and Winant (1994: 56) define a racial project as involving 'simultaneously an interpretation, representation, or explanation of racial dynamics, and an effort to reorganise and redistribute resources along particular racial lines' and go on to claim that it can only be understood to be racist 'if and only if it creates or reproduces structures of domination based on essentialist categories of race' (Omi and Winant 1994: 71). This approach offers a strategy of analytically capturing and distinguishing between racist and anti-racist movements that are underpinned by the idea of race in ways that overcome the conceptual difficulties associated with structuralist Marxist perspectives such as that of Miles.

If we take the examples of the 1960s US Civil Rights movement and the black anti-racist movement of 1970s Britain – both cases would be understood by Miles to be 'problematic' because they attempted to combat racism using ideological categories of thought invented by racists. However, following Omi and Winant, such movements can now be understood as cases of anti-racist racialised projects since they were not seeking to replace white supremacy with black supremacy but trying to challenge white supremacy by invoking demands for citizenship and equal rights.

Further, racial formation theory draws out into the open, the previously neglected study of white racist identities or whiteness by allowing us to study racist racial formation projects. Both the race relations and the racism problematics tended to focus on the processes by which subordinated racialised minority groups were subject to racism. However, Omi and Winant direct our sociological gaze towards how black and white races are produced and reproduced in changing political and historical circumstances. Finally, racial formation theory makes the valuable point that there are some racial projects, especially at the level of micro-social relations that cannot be understood with reference to macro-sociological theories. A class approach to race and racism they claim 'hardly begins to inquire into the sources and contours of racial dynamics' (Omi and Winant, 1994: 35) associated with what labour historians have termed the 'social equality' question.

However, whilst clearly advocating a critical engagement with poststructuralist racial formation theory as a way of renewing and also circumventing some of the conceptual difficulties associated with existing historical materialist approaches towards racism, racial formation theory in and of itself is clearly a partial and sometimes problematic way of understanding the material bases of racism. In particular, attempts by their founders to actualise a divorce between the study of racial formation processes and capitalist modernity and reduce class to race are deeply problematic (e.g., Omi and Winant, 1994: 34–35). The adoption of racialised identities also brings with it the danger of such labels becoming the basis for suppressing claims to alternative political strategies within the group. And finally, the perspective has a tendency to fall into the trap of objectifying race and thereby reinforcing the belief that race is real such as when Winant (2000) claims 'To be raceless is akin to being genderless' and that 'when one cannot identify another's race, a microsociological crisis of interpretation results'. A historical materialist perspective in contrast is predicated on achieving the deracialisation of social relations as an essential precondition to the realisation of the full potential of each human being, and thereby, has no interest in institutionalising race-thinking in society from an anti-racist perspective.

'RACE TRAITORS': DAVID ROEDIGER, NOEL IGNATIEV AND WHITENESS STUDIES

By the late 1980s, the intransigence of structuralist Marxist accounts of racism in addressing questions of subjectivity and identity formation raised by poststructuralist critiques coupled with the political exhaustion of the social forces associated with the world revolution of 1968, contributed to a decisive retreat away from class analyses of racism. By the 1990s, Marxist theories of racism and their focus on questions of class, inequality and the politics of redistribution had been largely replaced by a growing concern about questions relating to identity, culture and the politics of recognition. Amidst this general retreat, it was mainly in history, and more specifically, the new labour history, that groundbreaking, historical materialist accounts of racism continued to be developed by individuals like David Roediger (1991, 1994), Theodore Allen (1994a, 1994b), and Noel Ignatiev (1995, 1996).

From the landing of Englishmen at Plymouth Rock in the early seventeenth century to the mass migration of Italians and Jews in the late nineteenth and early twentieth centuries, these authors demonstrated how racism was intimately entwined with processes of class formation in the United States. Whilst it is beyond the scope of this essay to undertake a thorough review of this prolific and intellectually rich body of work, by focusing on the work of Roediger and Ignatiev, I hope to draw attention to the key theoretical points made by the new labour historians.

The primary questions explored by Roediger (1991, 1994) were how and why did white workers come to view their whiteness as meaningful, or to put it another way, why did they settle for being white. For Roediger (1991), the processes of working class formation and development of whiteness were inextricably entwined in the US. Yet, Marxism has been unable to analytically capture this linkage because of its tendency to naturalise whiteness and oversimplify race such that 'Race disappears into the "reality" of class' (Roediger, 1991:8). To avoid this perennial problem of reductionism, and, echoing the work of Stuart Hall outlined earlier in this essay, Roediger (1991), treats race as relatively autonomous from class in his account. A second problem facing Marxists like Cox (1970) was their focus 'on the ruling class's role in perpetuating racial oppression, and to cast white workers as dupes … The workers, in this view, largely receive and occasionally resist racist ideas and practices but have no role in *creating* those practices' (Roediger, 1991: 9). Rejecting this capitalist conspiracy/working class false consciousness dualism and injecting a much-needed element of human agency into his theoretical frame, Roediger (1991: 9) contends that white workers are 'historical actors who make (constrained) choices and create their own cultural forms'.

While these critical insights may in and of themselves be considered fairly modest, and perhaps merely echo the conclusions drawn by Hall and others a decade earlier, it is how Roediger synthesises them with the theoretical insights drawn from the psychoanalytical frame of Fanon and Kovel and the critical sociology of W. E. B. Du Bois on whiteness, especially the latter's most radical work, *Black Reconstruction* (1978), that makes Roediger's theoretical perspective original. In particular, Du Bois's focus on whiteness as a status category enabled him to demonstrate how whiteness functioned as a wage for white workers; a compensatory 'public and psychological wage' that benefited Southern white workers and made them forget their 'practically identical interests' with the black poor and accept stunted lives for themselves and for those who are more oppressed than themselves' (cited in Roediger, 1991: 13).

In a series of essays tracing the evolution and outcome of that wage in nineteenth century America, Roediger (1991) demonstrates conclusively how whiteness was the product of the white working class's attempts to come to terms with the traumatic process of proletarianisation. It was this that led them to place on African Americans, the mantle of the racialised other, 'as embodying the preindustrial, erotic, careless style of life the white worker hated and longed for' (Roediger, 1991: 14).

Ignatiev (1995) demonstrates how this racist logic proved particularly attractive for the Irish worker, newly arrived in the United States. After an initial period of co-operation, Ignatiev maps how the Irish worker through institutions as diverse as the trade unions, the Democratic Party and the Catholic Church, as well as racist riots, distanced themselves from the black population, and, thereby convinced the ruling elites of their worthiness to become white Americans.

While these arguments are illuminating and original in understanding the history of racism and the formation of a racist, white working class subjectivity, I want to focus briefly on the implications of their assessment for political practice. Ignatiev (1996: 10) contends that:

> The key to solving the social problems of our age is to abolish the white race ... The existence of the white race depends on the willingness of those assigned to it to place their racial interests above class, gender or any other interests they hold. The defection of enough of its members to make it unreliable as a determinant of behaviour will set off tremors that will lead to its collapse.

Hence, his advice to whites is to 'dissolve the club' because 'treason to whiteness is loyalty to humanity' (Ignatiev, 1996: 10). Whilst such a proposal appears to be radical, even revolutionary in its intention, it is in actual fact, hugely problematic, because it lends weight to the argument that racism could be abolished simply through a rejection of whiteness. Such an idealist standpoint ignores entirely the structures that produce and re-produce everyday racism in capitalist society. Even, if the majority of white individuals were to reject their whiteness, they would still psychologically and materially derive enormous benefits from being white simply because such a white abolitionist project had left untouched the racism and inequality wired into the project of capitalist modernity for half a millennia (Frankenberg, 1993).

Historically, as the work of authors like Kelley (1990) and Virdee (2000) unequivocally demonstrate, an alternative and more effective strategy to challenging racism has been that of racialised 'black' formation where African Americans in the United States and South Asians and Caribbeans in Britain engaged in autonomous action. Indeed, history confirms, at least in Britain, that such independent self-organisation was a precursor to the formation of a fragile but meaningful class solidarity involving parts of white organised labour who subsumed (at least temporarily) their attachment to a long-held white racial identity for a deracialised working class identity (Virdee, 2000).

CONCLUSION

This essay set out to critically evaluate the contribution made by Marxist class analyses to our understanding of racism. Collectively, this body of work produced since the 1970s has provided a complex and multi-layered account of the economic, political and cultural forces that drive the production and reproduction of racism in the social system referred to as capitalist modernity. However, it is only when this body of work is contrasted to what preceded it, both in European and North American sociology, that one can truly grasp the immense intellectual achievement of these scholars. With social Darwinian and interactionist perspectives merely serving to reproduce everyday understandings of race for much of the twentieth century, it was only with the arrival of Marxist scholars in the academy – in the slipstream of the 1968 world revolution – that such conceptions were banished from the sociological vocabulary (at least for a time) and the material foundations of racism explained.

This essay has not just engaged in an academic exercise of evaluating the relative merits of competing theories of racism but has tried consistently to understand and map under what historical and political conditions such sociological knowledge was produced. It is this understanding of the relationship between social science and politics that helps to explain how and why the intellectual dominance of Marxist accounts of racism was eventually undermined. First, was the political exhaustion of the social forces unleashed by the 1968 world revolution which manifested itself politically in the defeat of the workers movement throughout Europe, and the defeat, but also partial accommodation with the State of the anti-racist and antisexist movements of both the United States and Europe. Against this backdrop of political retreat and defeat, Marxist intellectuals lost their key public or social base – the exploited and oppressed striving for human emancipation. Second, however, were the internal theoretical and conceptual contradictions within the accounts of racism produced by scholars working within the structuralist Marxist tradition, especially their failings in addressing questions of identity formation and subjectivity. By the late 1980s, this process of intellectual and political fragmentation was complete such that most Marxist intellectuals had moved decisively in the direction of poststructuralist, post-modern accounts of racism (e.g., Gilroy, 1987, 2000).

Yet, as with earlier generations of sociologists who attempted to settle their accounts with Marxism (e.g., Weber, 1993; Dahrendorf, 1959; Giddens, 1981), historical materialism has proved difficult to silence. Despite the dark days of the 1990s, there appears to be a growing interest in historical materialist accounts of society as evidenced by the establishment of not only a number of new journals like *Cultural Logic* and *Historical Materialism* but also the publication of origi-nal works focusing on Marxist theory (e.g., Wood, 1995; Nimtz, 2000; Lih, 2005). More substantively, this essay and other works (e.g., Virdee, 2000; Meyerson, 2001, Dardar and Torres, 2004) demonstrate that there is a process of intellectual renewal of historical materialist accounts of racism underway in the early twenty-first century. Through a critical engagement with sociological and postcolonial theory, concerns about identity formation, subjectivity and human agency are being addressed by drawing on the intellectual resources of hegelian-inflected Marxism, as well as realism (see Carter, 2000).

However, significant themes like that of gender oppression and its relationship to race and class remain relatively unexplored by historical materialists and post-structuralists alike. A useful starting point would be to engage more systemati-cally with intersectionality theory (e.g., Crenshaw, 1994; Hill Collins, 1998) whose proponents claim that it 'may shed light on the mutually constructing nature of systems of oppression, as well as social locations created by such mutual constructions' (Hill Collins, 1998: 153).

Underpinning this essay philosophically has been the understanding that intellectual renewal is bound up with the process of political renewal. Influential and politically engaged intellectuals such as Immanuel Wallerstein (2004: 77) have recently warned of the final, impending crisis of the capitalist world-economy, even going so far as to predict its demise sometime in the middle of the twenty-first century. Yet, the articulation and support for emancipatory projects that seek to transform our existing social relations and free us from exploitation and oppression remain marginal, especially in the West, leading one to recall Gramsci's pertinent observation that whilst 'The old order is dying ... the new is powerless to be born, and in this interregnum arises a great morbidity of symptoms' – including manifestations of racist absolutism. The importance of developing an agent-centred materialist account of racism (and anti-racism) has never been more important and remains integral to any universalist project for human emancipation. As Rosa Luxemburg remarked at the start of the twentieth century, human beings are faced with a political choice – to accept a descent into barbarism or to take up the challenge of creating a democratic socialist society free of exploitation and oppression. To avoid the horrors of the former, we must renew our commitment to the latter.

ACKNOWLEDGEMENTS

I thank my colleagues Stephen Ashe, Bob Carter, Bridget Fowler, Robert Gibb, Patricia Hill Collins, Andy Smith, John Solomos, Rodolfo D. Torres, Matthew Waites and Erik Olin Wright for their critical comments and discussions of earlier drafts.

REFERENCES

Allen, T.W. (1994a) *The Invention of the White Race.* Volume 1. London: Verso.

Allen, T.W. (1994b) *The Invention of the White Race.* Volume 2. London: Verso.

Althusser, L. (1994) *The Future Lasts a Long Time.* London: Vintage.

Anderson, P. (1976) *Considerations on Western Marxism.* London: Verso.

Banton, M. (1967) *Race Relations.* London: Tavistock Publications.

Benjamin, W. (2006) 'On the Concept of History' in H. Eiland and M. W. Jennings (eds) *Selected Writings of Walter Benjamin* Vol. 4. Cambridge, MA: The Belknap Press of Harvard University Press. pp. 389–400.

Berger, P.L. (1963) *Invitation to Sociology.* New York: Anchor Books.

Bonacich, E. (1972) 'A Theory of Ethnic Antagonism: The Split Labour Market', *American Sociological Review,* 37 (5): 547–559.

Bonacich, E. (1976) 'Advanced Capitalism and Black/White Race Relations in the United States: A Split Labour Market Interpretation', *American Sociological Review,* 41 (1): 34–51.

Bonacich, E. (1980) 'Class approaches to Ethnicity and Race', *The Insurgent Sociologist,* 10 (2): 9–23.

Burawoy, M. (2005) 'For Public Sociology', *American Sociological Review,* 70 (1): 4–28.

Callinicos, A. (1993) *Race and Class.* London: Bookmarks.

Carter, B. (2000) *Realism and Racism.* London: Routledge.

Centre for Contemporary Cultural Studies (CCCS) (1982) *The Empire Strikes Back.* London: Hutchinson.

Cohen, P. N. (2001) 'Race, Class and Labor Markets: The White Working Class and Racial Composition of U.S. Metropolitan Areas', *Social Science Research,* 30 (1): 146–169.

Cox, O.C. (1970) *Caste, Class and Race.* New York: Monthly Review Press.

Crenshaw, K.W. (1994) 'Mapping the Margins: Intersectionality, Identity Politics and Violence Against Women of Colour' in M. Fineman and R. Mykitiuk, (eds) *The Public Nature of Private Violence.* New York: Routledge. pp. 93–118.

Dahrendorf, R. (1959) *Class and Class Conflict in an Industrial Society.* London: Routledge and Kegan Paul.

Darder, A. and Torres, R.D. (2004) *After Race: Racism after Multiculturalism.* New York: New York University Press.

Draper, H. (1978) *Karl Marx's Theory of Revolution.* Vol. II. New York: Monthly Review Press.

Du Bois, W.E.B. (1899 [1967]) *The Philadelphia Negro.* New York: Schocken.

Du Bois, W.E.B. (1978) *Black Reconstruction in America 1860–1880.* New York: Free Press.

Frankenberg, R. (1993) *White Women, Race Matters: The Social Construction of Whiteness.* Minnesota: University of Minnesota Press.

Frazier, E.F. (1949) 'Race Contacts and the Social Structure', *American Sociological Review,* 14 (1): 1–11.

Geschwender, J. (1977) *Class, Race and Worker Insurgency.* Cambridge: Cambridge University Press.

Giddens, A. (1981) *A Contemporary Critique of Historical Materialism.* Vol. 1. Berkeley: University of California Press.

Gilroy, P. (1982) 'Steppin' out of Babylon: Race, Class and Autonomy' in CCCS (ed.) *The Empire Strikes Back.* London: Hutchinson. pp. 276–314.

Gilroy, P. (1987) *There Ain't No Black in the Union Jack*. London: Hutchinson.

Gilroy, P. (2000) *Between Camps*. London: Allen Lane.

Goldberg, D. T. (1993) *Racist Culture*. Malden, Massachusetts: Blackwell.

Habermas, J. (1987) *The Philosophical Discourse of Modernity*. Cambridge MA: MIT Press.

Hall, S. (1980) 'Race, Articulation and Societies Structured in Dominance' in UNESCO (ed.) *Sociological Theories: Race and Colonialism*. Paris: UNESCO. pp. 305–345.

Hall, S. (1988) 'The Toad in the Garden: Thatcherism amongst the Theorists' and 'Discussion' in C. Nelson and L. Grossberg, (ed.) *Marxism and the Interpretation of Culture*. Chapel Hill: University of North Carolina Press. pp. 35–73.

Hall, S. (1989) 'New Ethnicities' in Mercer, K. (ed.) *Black Film, British Cinema*. London: Institute of Contemporary Arts.

Hall, S. (1996) 'Gramsci's Relevance for the Study of Race and Ethnicity' in D. Morley and K. Chen (eds) *Stuart Hall: Critical Dialogues in Cultural Studies*. London: Routledge. pp. 411–440.

Hall, S. (2002) 'Reflections on "Race, Articulation and Societies Structured in Dominance"' in D.T. Goldberg and P. Essed (eds) *Race Critical Theories*. Malden, MA: Blackwell. pp. 449–454.

Hall, S., Critcher, C., Jefferson, T., Clarke, J. and Roberts, B. (1978) *Policing the Crisis*. London: Hutchison.

Hier, S. (2001) 'The Forgotten Architect: Cox, Wallerstein and World-System Theory', *Race and Class*, 42 (3): 69–86.

Hill Collins, P. (1998) *Fighting Words: Black Women and the Search for Justice*. Minneapolis: University of Minnesota Press.

Hofstadter, R. (1967) *Social Darwinism in American Thought*. Boston: Beacon Press.

Hook, S. (2002) *Towards the Understanding of Karl Marx*. New York: Prometheus.

Ignatiev, N. (1995) *How the Irish Became White*. New York: Routledge.

Ignatiev, N. (1996) 'Abolish the White Race' in N. Ignatiev and J. Garvey (ed.) *Race Traitor*. New York: Routledge.

Kelley, R. (1990) *Hammer and Hoe*. Chapel Hill: University of North Carolina Press.

Leiman, M. (1993) *The Political Economy of Racism*. London: Pluto Press.

Lih, L.T. (2005) *Lenin Rediscovered: What Is to Be Done? In Context*. Leiden: Brill Publishers.

Marx, K. and Engels, F. (1977) *The Communist Manifesto*. Beijing: Foreign Languages Press.

Marx, K. and Engels, F. (1987) 'The German Ideology' in *Marx, Engels, Lenin on Historical Materialism*. Moscow: Progress Publishers.

Meyerson, G. (2001) 'Rethinking Black Marxism', *Cultural Logic*, 3 (2). http://clogic.eserver.org/3-1&2/meyerson.html (date accessed 8/10/09)

Miles, R. (1982) *Racism and Migrant Labour*. London: Routledge and Kegan Paul.

Miles, R. (1989) *Racism*. London: Routledge.

Miles, R. (1993). *Racism after 'Race Relations'*. London: Routledge.

Miles, R. and Phizacklea, A. (1984) *White Man's Country*. London: Pluto Press.

Miles, R. and Torres, R. D. (1999) 'Does "Race" Matter: Transatlantic Perspectives on Racism after "Race Relations"' in R.D. Torres, L.F Miron and J.X. Inda, (eds) *Race, Identity and Citizenship*. Malden, Massachusetts: Blackwell. pp. 19–38.

Nairn, T. (1977) *The Break-up of Britain*. London: New Left Books.

Nelson, C. and Grossberg, L. (1988) *Marxism and the Interpretation of Culture*. Chapel Hill: University of North Carolina Press.

Nimtz, A. (2000) *Marx and Engels: Their Contribution to the Democratic Breakthrough*. New York: State University of New York.

Omi, M. and Winant, H. (1994) *Racial Formation in the United States*. New York: Routledge.

Park, R. (1950) *Race and Culture*. C. Everett-Hughes (ed.). New York: Free Press.

Perlo, V. (1976) *Economics of Racism USA*. New York: International Publishers.

Ramdin, R. (1987) *The Making of the Black Working Class in Britain*. Aldershot: Gower.

Reed, A. (1997) *W.E.B. Du Bois and American Political Thought*. New York: Oxford University Press.

Reed, A. (2000) 'Introduction' in O. C. Cox (ed.) *Race: A Study in Social Dynamics*. New York: Monthly Review Press. pp. ix–xvii.

Reich, M. (1972) 'The Economics of Racism' in R.C. Edwards, M. Reich and T.E. Weisskopf, (eds) *The Capitalist System*. Englewood Cliffs, NJ: Prentice Hall. pp. 314–321.

Reich, M. (1978) 'Who Benefits from Racism? The Distribution among Whites of Gains and Losses from Racial Inequality', *Journal of Human Resources*, 13 (4): 524–544.

Reich, M. (1981) *Racial Inequality: A Political-Economic Analysis*. Princeton: Princeton University Press.

Reich, M., Gordon, D.M. and Edwards, R.C. (1973) 'A Theory of Labour Market Segmentation', *The American Economic Review*, 63 (2): 359–365.

Rex, J. (1970) *Race Relations in Sociological Theory*. London: Routledge and Kegan Paul.

Rex, J. (1973) *Sociology and the Demystification of the Modern World*. London: Routledge and Kegan Paul.

Roediger, D. (1991) *The Wages of Whiteness*. London: Verso.

Roediger, D. (1994) *Towards the Abolition of Whiteness*. London: Verso.

Rogaly, J. (1977) *Grunwick*. London: Penguin.

Samuel, R. (1981) *People's History and Socialist Theory*. London: Routledge and Kegan Paul.

Sivanandan, A. (1982) *A Different Hunger*. London: Pluto Press.

Smith, D. (1988) *The Chicago School: A Liberal Critique of Capitalism*. Basingstoke: Macmillan.

Solomos, J. (1988) *Black Youth, Racism and the State*. Cambridge: Cambridge University Press.

Solomos, J., Findlay, B., Jones, S. and Gilroy, P. (1982) 'The Organic Crisis of British Capitalism and Race' in CCCS *The Empire Strikes Back*. London: Hutchinson. pp. 9–46.

Szymanski, A. (1976) 'Racial Discrimination and White Gain', *American Sociological Review*, 41 (3): 403–414.

Thompson, E.P. (1978) *The Poverty of Theory and Other Essays*. London. Merlin.

Virdee, S. (2000) 'A Marxist Critique of Black Radical Theories of Trade-Union Racism', *Sociology*, 34 (3): 545–565.

Virdee, S. (2002) 'Gewerkschaften und Antirassismus in England: eine replik auf Paul Gilroy and Ambalavaner Sivanandan', *1999: Zeitschrift fur Sozialgeschichte des 20. und 21. Jahrunderts*, 17 (1): 153–186.

Virdee, S. (forthcoming) *Racism, Resistance and Radicalism*. Basingstoke: Palgrave Macmillan.

Virdee, S. and Grint, K. (1994) 'Black Self-Organisation in Trade Unions', *Sociological Review*, 42 (2): 202–226.

Wallerstein, I. (1974) *The Modern World-System*. New York: Academic Press.

Wallerstein, I. (2004) *World-Systems Analysis*. Durham: Duke University Press.

Weber, M. (1993) *From Max Weber*. London: Routledge and Kegan Paul.

Wilson, E. (1972) *To the Finland Station: A Study in the Writing and Acting of History*. London: Penguin Books.

Winant, H. (2000) 'The Theoretical Status of the Concept of Race' in L. Back and J. Solomos (eds.) Theories of Race and Racism. London: Routledge. pp. 181–190.

Wood, E.M. (1995) *Democracy against Capitalism*. Cambridge: Cambridge University Press.

The Nexus of Race and Gender: Parallels, Linkages, and Divergences in Race and Gender Studies

Margaret L. Andersen

> When, now, ... two of these movements—woman and colour—combine into one, the combination has deep meaning.
>
> W. E. B. Du Bois, *Darkwater: Voices from Within the Veil*,
> pp. 181 (also cited in Aptheker 1982: 81)

In 1982, Gloria Hull and Barbara Smith in the presciently titled anthology, *All the Women Are White, All the Men Are Black, but Some of Us Are Brave* (Hull et al., 1982), wrote that simply noting the existence of Black women was 'in direct opposition to most of what passes for culture and thought on the North American continent' (1982: xvii). They added that even to acknowledge that fact was a radical act of political courage. As they wrote, 'Our condition as autonomous beings and thinkers in the white-male run intellectual establishment is constantly in question and rises and falls in direct proportion to the degree to which we continue to act and think like our Black selves, rejecting modes of bankrupt white-male Western thought' (Hull and Smith, 1982: xxiv). What was needed, they argued, was the development of Black women's studies – studies that would put Black women, along with other women of colour, in the centre of social and cultural thought.

Throughout the 1970s, Women's Studies and Black American Studies were developing along parallel, only occasionally, intersecting, paths in the United States. There was a renaissance of Black women's literature occurring, even while women of colour remained highly marginalised in the academy. And, Women's Studies, although rapidly expanding, was fundamentally founded on the experiences of white women. At the same time, studies of race and ethnic studies were anchored primarily in the experiences of men. Women of colour would appear in discussions of female-headed households and, occasionally, in statistics on race and income equality. Rarely were they studied in their own right. Most of the classic studies of race, from the period, ignored women altogether. A womanless, all-white curriculum was the norm. Knowledge in the academy was centred in the experiences and perspectives of an exclusive few thereby 'legitimat[ing] a view of the world for our students which sees men's experiences as central, women's as peripheral, white experience as the norm, and all 'others' as deviant or exceptional' (Andersen, 1988: 123).

Since then (indeed, over a relatively short time span), studies of both race and gender have been fundamentally altered by a more inclusive perspective that incorporates analyses of race, class, and gender (Andersen and Collins, 2007). Race, gender, and class in this framework are conceptualised as fundamental social structures – located in society, but influencing all dimensions of social life and ranging from immediate face-to-face social interactions to the formation and articulation of social consciousness and to macro-level social organisation and stratification. The new race/gender/class paradigm is specifically framed around the *social structural intersections* of race, class and gender.

This new paradigm has now been elaborated and expanded in the academy, but its origins in the pioneering work of women of colour cannot be ignored. There were many who early criticised the exclusionary frameworks of white feminist studies and articulated the need for a more inclusive perspective. Their early theoretical, empirical and political work constitutes the foundation for contemporary race/class/gender studies. (See, as early examples, Aptheker, 1982; Baca Zinn, 1982; Bambara, 1970; Combahee River Collective, 1979; Davis, 1981; Dill, 1979; Gilkes, 1980; Glenn, 1980; Higginbotham, 1981; Hull et al., 1982; Jordan, 1985; Ladner, 1971; Lewis, 1977; Lorde, 1984; Moraga and Anzaldúa, 1981; Myers, 1975; Reagon, 1983; Rodgers-Rose, 1980; Smith, 1983; Wilkinson, 1980)

Within the United States, the emergence of this new paradigm was rooted in the politics of the civil rights movement, the feminist movement and the activism of women of colour. These social movements spawned a new critical consciousness that strongly influenced thinking within the academy. Moreover, at the same time, the number of women attending college and graduate school was increasing, as was the number of African American men and women entering higher education. The presence of these new social groups within the academy, coupled with the critical consciousness that emerged from the social movements of the day, led to the development of both Women's Studies and Black American (later, African American and Africana) Studies programmes and, then, Ethnic Studies programmes. The political activism and awareness of the time, as well as the token treatment of women and people of colour in the higher educational curriculum, meant that a critical group of thinkers were encountering systems of knowledge from which they were largely excluded or, if included, were presented in highly stereotyped terms. Using their own intellectual skills and questioning systems of thinking that were exclusionary, yet taken for granted, people of colour and women produced new ways of thinking about both race and gender. As the field of race/class/gender studies developed, race, class and gender were seen as together constituting not just the experiences of women of colour, but the experiences of all social groups. In other words, the confluence of race class, and gender structures systems of both privilege and subordination.

As race/class/gender studies have developed, several themes have guided this new paradigm. This chapter identifies the themes that emerge from seeing gender, race and class as intersecting social structures. A second section examines some of the parallels in studying race and studying gender. The chapter concludes by criticising the idea that race, class and gender are analogous social processes. Throughout, the implications for how studying gender and studying race each transform our understanding of the other form the texture of the chapter.

From the outset, it is important to understand that there is no unidirectional line from gender studies to race studies nor from race to gender, as if the social construction of knowledge proceeds along a carefully laid down route. Rather than coming from a single line of influence, knowledge develops from sometimes overlapping points of discussion, sometimes parallel paths, and sometimes crossing tracks. Studies of the intersecting influence of gender, race and class emerge from a wide community of scholars who are examining the lives of women of colour, as well as how race and gender – and class and sexuality – influence the lives of all groups, including members of dominant groups whose race, gender, class and sexual privilege have previously been taken for granted. As scholarship has moved from a womanless, all-white curriculum to one of greater complexity and inclusion, scholars have come to see that even the most privileged groups are situated in the nexus of race, class and gender. And, although seldom thought of through these frames, dominant groups are as much influenced by their race, class and gender location as are those more subordinated by these social factors. Thus, it has become important to study even all-male groups to understand how gendered social and cultural structures influence men *as* men. Likewise, new studies show how whiteness situates white people in a system of racial stratification (Andersen, 2003; Doane and Bonilla-Silva, 2003). Race and gender are important to study not just when studying subordinated groups, but also when studying dominant groups.

While much of the work on race, class and gender has developed in the United States, scholars in other nations are also contributing to this new paradigm. Their work is expanding the understanding of race, class and gender beyond the borders of the United States and raises new questions about social relations of ethnicity, gender, race and class (see, e.g., Anthias, 2001; Stoetzler and Yuval-Davis, 2002; Anthias and Yuval-Davis, 1992). Especially because the social meaning of race varies in different historical and cultural contexts, the international scholarship brings different insights to how race, class and gender are manifested in particular cultural contexts (Solomos and Back, 1996; Telles, 2002). As just one example, thinking about race in some cultural contexts also requires an analysis of ethnicity and its intersections with class and gender. This point underscores the idea that the social meanings of race, gender, class and ethnicity – and, therefore, their interconnections – emerge in particular social and historical locales.

GENDER, RACE AND CLASS: A NEW PARADIGM

This more inclusive way of studying the influence of gender, race and class has been guided by several themes. Here, I identify several.

(1) First is that race and gender, along with class, are *interlocking systems* of inequalities, subordination and domination (Andersen and Collins, 2007; Collins, 1990, 1998). People – both women and men – experience these interlocking systems *simultaneously*. Thus, women of colour experience their race *and* their gender – not as separate categories – but as intricately linked in their experience. Although one factor may be more salient at a given moment than at another, it is their linkage that shapes the experiences of women of colour – not just one or the other added together (Andersen and Collins, 2007; Baca Zinn and Dill, 1996; Collins, 1990, 1998; Combahee River Collective, 1982; Moraga and Anzaldúa, 1981). Furthermore, each shapes the others. Race is manifested differently depending on gender just as class and race intertwine. Thus, an African American man may have some privileges associated with his gender, but may be disadvantaged by virtue of his racial-ethnic status and, perhaps, his social class. Race/class/gender studies recognise the complexity of these intersecting hierarchies – at all levels of experience, as we will see below (Andersen and Collins, 2007; Baca Zinn and Dill, 1996; Glenn, 2002).

(2) A second theme is that *neither race class, nor gender can be subsumed analytically under any one of the others*. Though each can be conceptualised as a major axis of social stratification, each changes in relationship to the others. Thus, while many scholars conceptualise class as the major axis of social stratification, such an analysis incorrectly assumes that race and gender are somehow secondary or peripheral systems of inequality. Instead, race/class/gender scholars see race, class and gender as equally primary in shaping social, economic and political relations. No one is derived from the other; all are equally central in the formation of society (Glenn, 2002).

This also means that, when studying a given group, it is important to look at differences within groups, as well as across groups. Thus, class differences within racial, ethnic or gender groups can be as significant as differences across such groups (Anthias and Yuval-Davis, 1992). Focusing solely on one social factor can obscure the workings of others within a given social category.

(3) Third, gender, race and class *operate at multiple levels of social life*. Race, class and gender are embedded in social institutions, but they are also part of our immediate social interactions, social identities and social consciousness. Analysing three contexts (from 1870 to 1930) – Whites and Blacks in the American South, Anglos and Mexicans in the American Southwest and Haoles and Japanese in Hawaii – Evelyn Nakano Glenn (2002) describes race, class and gender relations as involving three realms of social life: representation, micro-interaction and social structure. Representation includes 'the deployment of symbols, language and images to express and convey race/gender meanings'; micro-interaction is 'the application of race/gender norms, etiquette and spatial rules to orchestrate interaction within and across race/gender boundaries'; and, social structure refers to the 'rules regulating the allocation of power and resources along race/gender lines' (Glenn, 2002: 12). Thus, race, class and gender have *both* a material *and* an ideological basis. Studies of race, class and gender require understanding the economic and political facts of people's lives, as well as understanding how these are manifested in representational systems, such as stereotypes and ideology (Andersen, 2006a).

This point has also been made in the British context wherein Floya Anthias and Nira Yuval-Davis (1992) argue that race, class and gender involve differential access to resources as well as involving systems of representation. The important thing is to see that no one of these realms can be studied in isolation from the others. Moreover, no one of them, including class, is based on material and economic activity alone. Each involves systems of representation and meaning – systems that shape group identity and intergroup social relations.

(4) Race, class and gender have differential effects in all people's lives which operate through hierarchies of power and privilege, even though *invisible systems of privilege* are not usually apparent to members of dominant groups. Still, it is essential to examine the lives and experiences of dominant groups as they are shaped by the social structure of race, class and gender, although differently from subordinated groups. Thus men, including men of colour, can be understood as gendered subjects. Stated differently, women are not the only gendered subjects. And, white people can be studied through a lens that does not take race for granted (Andersen, 2003; Doane and Bonilla-Silva, 2003). As scholars have thought more inclusively about race, class and gender as intersecting systems, they have interpreted the experiences of all groups in a new light. Think of the process of taking a photograph. For years, scholars simply kept women and people of colour – and especially women of colour – totally outside their frame of vision. But, as the angle of sight moves to the so-called margins of society, new subjects come into sight. This is more than a matter of sharpening one's focus (although that is required for clarity). Instead, it means actually seeing things differently, perhaps even changing the lens we look through – thereby removing the filters that dominant groups bring to their observations. These filters are rooted in stereotypes, misconceptions and incomplete vantage points.

(5) *Systems of privilege are the unexamined norm* from which all others are judged. In a system of racial stratification, whiteness is culturally hegemonic; its hegemony is maintained by seeming natural or just not being questioned. Likewise, masculinity in a gender-stratified society is hegemonic, crafting normative judgements about both men and women, even while being taken for granted.

That systems of privilege are hegemonic does not mean that they are uniform, a point recently made by Connell and Messerschmidt (2005) in an article revising Connell's original formulation of hegemonic masculinity. As they point out, masculinity takes various forms – both across and within cultures. Drawing from studies of masculinity in places as diverse as Japan, Mexico, Chile and southern Africa, they note that multiple masculinities can exist within a given culture or given time, even while men as a social class remain dominant. It would also be true that other forms of hegemonic power may entail diverse forms (such as in multiple ways of identifying as 'white'). Moreover, not all groups within a hegemonic group have the same degree of power. Still, the largely invisible character of hegemonic power (at least to those in positions of privilege) is one way that systems of domination maintain their legitimacy.

(6) Gender, race and class focus on the *socially constructed basis* of these analytical categories. The significance of each comes from their development as socially created categories. Thus, the actual meaning of race changes over time, both as it is contested by oppressed racial groups and as the society changes in how race operates in social institutions and social relationships. Race is both a fluid category and one that has a concrete location in social institutions – such as in laws that define people in racial categories or in the income brackets that differentiate the class status of different racial-ethnic groups. Saying that race is socially constructed does not mean that it is not less real, only that *it is the social reality of race that makes it meaningful in society* (Andersen and Taylor, 2006). Likewise, gender is a social concept – one that some have argued is a social structure in its own right (Risman, 2004). Although marked and ideologically believed to be a biological category, the significance of gender, like race, comes from the social and historical treatment of groups identified in gender categories.

(7) A further theme in these studies is that the study of race, class and gender is not just about *victimisation*, although certainly people are victims of this interwoven system of oppression. But, race, class and gender studies see that people contest and challenge the systems of subordination and representation that oppress them. Understanding that there is 'interplay of social structure and … agency' (Baca Zinn and Dill, 1996: 328) means that even the most oppressed groups are not merely passive objects onto which are poured the abstract forces of social structure. Even under oppressive conditions, people exercise human agency, acting and thinking in ways that construct a meaningful social existence. This may take the form of accommodating oneself to oppressive social forces, but it also takes the form of resisting oppression – or at the very least, adapting to the conditions one faces. The focus on human agency in race/class/gender

studies has especially highlighted the active and creative ways that groups resist oppression even at times when oppression seems overwhelming (Baca Zinn and Dill, 1996).

(8) Race, class, and gender studies *challenge various forms of dichotomous thinking*. Race, gender and class construct groups in binary opposition to each other (Collins, 1998). Dehumanising traits are used to identify the subordinated group and they become defined as 'other'. At the same time, the assumption that groups are posited in oppositional terms mystifies the complex relationship of groups to systems of power. The implications of this are especially evident in thinking about gender in relationship to race. To explain, collectively, men hold power over women, but when you introduce a race/class/gender perspective into the picture, you see that power does not accrue equally to all men, as if a group is either all powerful or not. As Michael Kimmel has stated, 'aggregate power in the world does not translate to individual men feeling powerful' (Kimmel in Andersen et al., 2004). Race/class/gender studies reveal the multiple dimensions of structural power, explaining how some groups of men can feel and be powerless (or at least less powerful) because of their class, race or even sexual status, even when there is a rigid patriarchal system operating at the structural level.

(9) Analysing gender, race and class simultaneously *discovers the parallels in diverse group experiences*. Understanding, for example, how racial stereotyping influences White people's perceptions of Black and Latino people also helps us understand how gender stereotypes operate. Or, analysing the historic exploitation of Black women's labour as domestic workers helps us see similar processes at work in the segregation of immigrant Latinas and Asian American women in contemporary domestic labour in the United States. This can also be seen in the international context where domestic labour, for example, by West Indian, Asian and Cypriot women, is central to understanding the connections between gender, ethnicity and class (Anthias and Yuval-Davis 1992).

Seeing the similarities in the experiences of diverse groups does not mean however that the groups' experiences are the same – a point elaborated below. Race, class, gender studies not only call attention to similar and interrelated processes in history and social structure, but also reveal the unique experiences of different groups. The interplay between common experiences and differences is important in analysing the race, class and gender dimensions of group life. Race, class, gender studies are *both* about untangling the race, class and gender dimensions within the experiences of a given group *and* untangling the racialised, gendered, and class processes that shape structures of domination across groups.

(10) Finally, race, class and gender studies are *more than just recognising diversity* within society. Race, class and gender are social structures – located in society and experienced as social facts. But this is not just a matter of recognising difference – as if the only thing to understanding a plurality of views and life experiences. This point emphasises that race, gender and class are built into the institutional fabric of society, forming a system of power that advantages and

disadvantages groups based on their social location in this hierarchical structure. Thus, studying race, class and gender is not just about studying difference. Indeed, it is about studying how they are linked in a system of social stratification. Although they form the basis for group identities and can also engage cultural differences, their significance lies in their interrelationship in a system of power and inequality.

Given these new themes in race/class/gender studies, how then does gender matter in studying race and what can we learn about race by examining gender studies?

HOW GENDER MATTERS IN STUDYING RACE

Scholarship on the intersections of race, class and gender has taught us many things, not the least of which is avoiding *false generalisation*. False generalisation comes from only thinking about one group even when making general claims. Feminists have criticised scholars for seeing only men, but it is equally problematic when thinking about gender to 'see' only white women – as if their experience represented that of women as a whole. For example, gender scholars in the United States typically make the claim that women earn less than men, partially evidenced in the fact that there is an income gap between women and men ($32,515 versus $42,261 for US women and men, respectively, working year-round and full-time in 2006; DeNavas-Walt et al., 2007, US Census Bureau, 2008). But, considering gender and race together, new facts emerge. Thus, among year-round, full-time workers, White, non-Hispanic women and Asian women actually *earn more* than both Black and Hispanic men. Additionally, Black women earn more than Hispanic men. Thus, including both gender *and* race reveals a very different picture than what is found by looking at gender alone – or race alone, for that matter.

Furthermore, the oft-cited 23 percent gender gap in income between US men and women is only true when generalising from women as a whole and men as a whole. Only true when comparing *all* women in the aggregate to *all* men, this gap is often used to point to the significance of gender in the economic disparity between men and women, But, the gender gap in income *within* racial-ethnic groups is very different. Thus, comparing year-round, full-time workers shows that in the United States, White women earn 73 percent of White men's earnings and Asian American women earn 75 percent of Asian American men's earnings. But, Black women earn 82 percent of Black men's median earnings and Hispanic women, 87 percent of Hispanic men's median earnings—likely a reflection of the fact of low wages attenuating by virtue of race in and of itself. Furthermore, if you compare the earnings of Black and Hispanic women to those of White men, the gender gap is much larger than the usually cited 76 percent figure. Black women earn only 59 percent of White men's median income; Hispanic women, 50 percent of White men's earnings (US Census Bureau, 2008).

This relatively simple example shows how an analysis of gender *and* race results in different or incomplete truths when you ignore their interactive effects. Simply adding gender to the race picture – or vice versa – shows the significance of considering both social facts together – even in the most straightforward, descriptive examples. Looking at race and gender interactively avoids the false generalisation of assuming a 'universal woman' or 'universal man'. Furthermore, these examples show how ignoring race when looking at gender and ignoring gender when looking at race reveal only partial truths – truths that are misleading when generalised to a whole.

Another way to approach the significance of gender in studying race is to consider the consequences of the actual *omission* of gender. Just as claims about gender that ignore race are misleading and incomplete, so are analyses of race that ignore gender. Such studies risk not only forgetting the very presence of women in racial and ethnic populations, but they also start from a vantage point that assumes men's lives are representative of the whole of society. This assumption (usually implicit) obscures social processes that are gendered in their very nature – even when the subject of study is men. For example, rich as their work is in ethnographic detail about race and urban street life, neither Elijah Anderson (1990, 1999) nor Mitchell Duneier (1992, 1999) analyse gender as a central fact in the lives of the urban street men they study. As rich in detail and sociological observation as their studies are, both largely miss the significance of gender in constructing life on the street and in shaping social relations among men. And, to the small extent that women are present in these studies, they tend to be seen through the eyes of men. But, equally important, neither are men portrayed as gendered subjects, giving the impression that gender is only important when studying women – a fact belied by the rich new studies of masculinity as a gendered identity and social structure (Connell, 2005; Kimmel, 2005).

Thus, studying gender when studying race raises new questions – not just about the lives of women, but also about the lives of men. For example, in Anderson's and Duneier's studies, how do the men construct an identity of themselves *as men*? How does the social construction of gender shape their relationships with each other and with the women in their lives? How does it configure space on the street? How do the men interact with women – women who are their mothers, sisters, friends, lovers, or and even strangers passing them by? Granted, no research scholar can answer all questions about any subject matter, but ignoring gender altogether in such otherwise rich ethnographies makes it seem as though gender has no place in the lives of these men.

Another classic example of the risks of ignoring gender is found in the work of William Julius Wilson. Wilson takes a more structural approach than Anderson and Duneier, analysing the relationship between race and class. In one of his well-known conclusions, one frequently used by social policymakers and politicians, Wilson argues that the rise of poor, female-headed households in the United States can be attributed to the 'long term decline in the proportion of black men, and particularly young black men, who are in a position to support a family' (1987: 83). According to Wilson, with the decline in the *male marriage-able pool index* – itself attributable to young men's joblessness – female-headed households increase as does poverty because of the shortage of financially stable men. Wilson reached this conclusion, as his critics have often pointed out, without an analysis of the gender relations that structure the lives of low-income, unmarried women in the post-industrial period he examines.

In subsequent research that is more attentive to the dynamics of race, class and gender (in particular, research centred on women's, not just men's, experiences) we now know that young, poor women in the United States highly value marriage, but they also want to be able to support themselves, and they fear being in relationships that put them at risk of economic dependence, domestic violence and possible divorce (Edin and Kefalas, 2005). This is not contrary to Wilson's argument, but it augments his work by seeing more than men's structural un-employment as the major reason for poverty. Rather, women's own socio-economic condition – including their disadvantage in the labour market and the value they place on marriage – helps explain the rise of female-headed households.

This point has implications beyond the United States, given international trends of an increase in the number of female-headed households in many of the industrial nations. In these post-industrial economies, structural supports for the nuclear family have eroded; yet social policies, certainly in the United States, continue to rely on a model touting marriage as the solution to women's poverty. Without understanding the actual conditions of women's lives, such policies are likely to fail (Jones-DeWeever, 2002).

To summarise, in studying race, gender matters and it matters a lot. It matters because without understanding the connections between gender and race as social phenomena, you get only a partial perspective on either. Yet, seeing the connections between them does not mean they are the same as social phenomena, even though the study of one can reveal much about the workings of the others. The following section examines how we can learn about race by studying gender and vice versa, given the similar social processes each engages. This section is followed by a concluding section cautioning researchers about seeing race and gender as equivalent social phenomena.

CONNECTING GENDER, RACE AND CLASS

Revealing the significance of both gender and race has led many to see them as involving common processes and similar consequences. Are the processes of race and gender relations in society similar? How are they related to class? Are race and racism like gender and sexism? By asking these questions, similarities in the social realities of gender and race can be examined.

Early on, for instance, conceptualising women as a minority group (Hacker, 1951) revealed how prejudice and discrimination operate in the lives of women, similar to the way they work in the lives of racial and ethnic minorities. What are the common processes of gender, race and class relations? They can be categorised in the following way: (a) race, class and gender as social constructions; (b) race, class and gender as ideological frames; (c) race, class and gender as stratifying mechanisms; (d) race, class and gender as systems of social control; and, (e) race, class and gender as sources of resistance and cultural formation. The following section examines each in turn, before returning to the final question of whether race and gender are equivalent processes.

Race, class and gender as social constructions

Race, class and gender are each conceptualised in the social sciences as social constructions, meaning that their significance comes not from some essential characteristic, but from the social and historical treatment of social groups. Understanding race, class and gender as social constructions means that their very meaning emerges from the particular historic and social treatment of groups – a premise that has been quite clear in discussions of class formation. Although few now think of class in biological or natural terms, the social constructionist perspective on race and gender emerges from explicit criticisms of biological determinism – as if race were a matter of genetics or skin colour and gender, a matter of reproductive organs. But, beyond biological determinism, the social constructionist approach also departs away from considering race, class and gender as individual attributes or static 'variables' that differentiate fixed categories of people. Rather, each is understood as carrying *social* significance – significance that emerges in the context of group power relations and from social institutions that are themselves founded on race, class and gender stratification. This point, long established in the sociological literature, is becoming even more crucial to understand in the contemporary context where there is a resurgence of biological determinism associated with race and genetics (Duster, 2006, Duster, in Dreifus 2005). In studies of race and gender, the social constructionist perspective also emphasises the fluidity of race and gender categories and questions how race and gender boundaries are maintained and surveilled.

New scholarship on race goes even further than the longstanding emphasis on the social construction of race by studying the specific social and historical processes by which racial categories are actually formed. Thus, Michael Omi and Howard Winant's (1994) now classic concept of *racial formation* has changed how scholars conceptualise the social construction of race. Omi and Winant anchor the process of racial formation in the political–economic practices and structures of racially stratified societies. They also explore the process of *racialisation* – that is, the process by which groups become defined in racial terms. Based on Omi and Winant's work, contemporary scholarship shows how the processes of racial formation and racialisation are found not only in the practices and policies of the state, particularly the law, but also in other state institutions. And, at the same time, Omi and Winant argue that race is articulated through ongoing political struggles between state institutions and the social movements that contest racially unjust social orders.

Gender scholars have yet to seize the idea of gender formation, at least not in the same terms as developed by Omi and Winant. But the theoretical framework of racial formation offers gender scholars a conceptual path that would part from the tendency in gender scholarship to see gender mostly through an individualistic lens. Although recent gender scholarship has moved towards seeing gender as a social structure in its own right (Martin, 2005; Andersen, 2006b; Risman, 2004), there is still a pervasive tendency to conceptualise gender as an individual attribute – granted, a learned one, but an individual attribute nonetheless. This is especially evident in research that emphasises gender socialisation as the most significant social process in producing gendered subjects.

Although feminist theory sees the meaning and significance of gender as emerging from social institutional practices, compared to studies of race there has been less attention in gender studies to the role of state power in framing social constructions of gender. This would be a fruitful direction for feminist theory, whereby feminists could learn from the scholarship on race. For example, state-based laws regarding sexuality reinforce and recreate dichotomous gender categories – a point that could be elaborated in the context of current debates about same-sex marriage. Furthermore, building from Omi and Winant's argument that there is a complex and interrelated social process between social movements and state institutions, gender scholars could examine how social movements challenge state-based constructions of gender and sexuality.

The parallel view of race and gender as social constructions reveals that they are not 'natural' or fixed categories of being. In contemporary gender studies, this has resulted in a fascination with 'performing gender' – that is, how gender is produced through social interaction and how gender is 'displayed' in everyday social interaction. Understanding that people 'do gender' (West and Zimmerman, 1984) means theorising gender as an accomplished activity – one that is enacted in social interaction. This theoretical formulation of gender conceptualises it as a highly fluid category – a point that is articulated especially well in the new paradigm of queer theory and studies of transgender identities (Seidman, 2003; Stein and Plummer, 1994). The doing gender perspective also suggests that crossing gender boundaries is a tactic for challenging the social structures of gender. That is, by refusing to comply with the dominant gender order, people contest the presumed fixedness and stability of the gendered social order (Lorber, 2005).

Studies of race have not emphasised fluidity as much – most likely because studies of race have been more consistently anchored in a materialist approach. Unlike gender, people seldom think of race in terms of performance, although studies using this idea are becoming more numerous (Jackson, 2001; Willie, 2003). For example, in an analysis of women of colour in the sciences, Maria Ong shows how women of colour manage their racial-gender identities in a context where they are perceived as outsiders (Ong, 2005). Her work utilises the concept of performance to capture how women of colour in the sciences negotiate their race *and* gender identity in a context where they are accountable to an 'audience' of white, masculinist scientists. Conceptualising women of colour's identities as fragmented, an insight derived from W. E. B. Du Bois, Ong shows the straddling that women of colour must do by virtue of being both insiders and outsiders in a dominant white, male world (Collins, 1990).

Others have examined the social construction of categories in a more global context, especially as related to the construction of ethnic and national identities. Thus, Yuval-Davis and Stoetzler, using autobiographical material from women in 25 different nations, argue that people create imagined communities and draw collective boundaries based on their different social locations positioned by 'ethnicity, class, gender, and other social divisions' (2002: 331). In related research, Yuval-Davis et al. (2005) examine how British national identity is constructed vis-à-vis the surveillance of immigrants and through state practices that construct a collective definition of national identity. As they suggest in an analysis especially appropriate in the post-9/11 politics of terrorism, 'Surveillance is being directed against anyone who might be seen to be 'different' and has enhanced the racialization of the "Others" in Western countries and affected constructions of national boundaries' (2005: 516–517). In this context, they continue, '"secure borders" are a pre-condition for "secure boundaries" of a national collectivity and identity' (2005: 517). Taken in this global context, the concept of racial formation can be extended to show how national identities – and other forms of social identity – are framed through the operation of state institutions.

Race, class and gender as ideologically linked

A second common process found in studies on race, class and gender is in the realm of attitudes and ideology. It is here where scholars have most emphasised not just the parallels in studying race, class and gender, but how they intersect and overlap. Parallels between race and gender are easy to see when examining social attitudes. Prejudice based on race and gender is deployed in ways that similarly diminish and devalue both women and racial-ethnic groups. When combined, race and gender prejudice also produce particular stereotypes for different race-gender groups. Volumes of scholarship have examined both race and gender prejudice with some showing the similarities in how gender and race stereotypes work (Biernat and Manis, 1994; Dovidio, 2001; Dovidio et al., 2002).

Some also point to *stereotype interchangeablility* as a way that race and gender similarly label social groups based on either race or gender. Stereotype inter-changeability refers to the idea that stereotypes, particularly negative ones, are perceived as transferable from one subordinate group to another. In other words, the same stereotypes (being dumb, lazy, violent and so forth) that are applied to a given racial or ethnic or gender group may also be used in reference to other social minorities (Andersen and Taylor, 2006).

Prejudice and stereotypes are situated, however, in the larger realm of ideology. Some of the most interesting work linking gender and race examines how ideological systems engage *both* race and gender, such that they are intertwined and mutually reinforcing systems of meaning. Many have long noted that race and gender reinforce and support each other in historically specific ways (Jordan, 1968). Ideologies of race and gender also intertwine around ideas about sexuality. Thus, Joane Nagel (2003) details how ideological systems surrounding race, ethnicity, gender, sexuality and nationalism produce perceived boundaries between dominant and subordinate groups. As she states, 'Ethnicity and sexuality blend together to form sexualized perimeters around ethnic, racial, and national spaces' (2003: 1). These perimeters are what Patricia Hill Collins calls called *controlling images* – a concept meant to emphasise that representations of groups subordinated by race and gender are not just free-floating images. Rather, they emanate from specific relationships of power (Collins, 1990) – relations of power that engage both race, gender *and* class – and, in some contexts, ethnicity, as well.

Studying race, class and gender ideology shows that power relationships of race and gender not only target subordinate groups, but also produce belief systems that construct the dominant group as normative. At the same time, subordinate groups are constructed as 'other', 'alien', or 'different'. Creating groups who are perceived as 'other' reinforces social distinctions between dominant and subordinate groups and leads to a heightened sense of belonging for dominant group members. In other words, 'otherness' creates boundaries and obscures systems of power and privilege, at least for the dominant group. Studies of whiteness and studies of hegemonic masculinity have been especially compelling in pointing this out. Thus, just as race constructs whiteness as a dominant, but invisible, system of power, so does hegemonic masculinity construct manhood as an invisible, but assumed, system of power. Likewise, heterosexism constructs sexual power as an assumed, though taken for granted, system of norms, values, beliefs, and behaviour – all of which are centred in the presumption of heterosexuality. And, in the British context, Anthias also shows how the experiences of exclusion of young people of Asian and Cypriot backgrounds, is connected to their narrations of belonging and not belonging (Anthias, 2002).

Race, class and gender as stratifying mechanisms

A third common thread in studies of race, class and gender is to study them as opportunity structures. Scholars who liken race, class and gender stratification notice that patterns of discrimination and exclusion position groups differently in labour markets and other social locations (such as the healthcare system, the criminal justice system, schooling and so forth). Volumes of research document the ongoing practices and consequences of discrimination and institutionalised inequality by race and by gender (Browne and Misra, 2003). Various parallel arguments can be found in the research literature on class stratification.

One strand of such research is in the argument that dominant group use their power to maintain group advantage. First articulated in the context of racial inequality (Lieberson, 1980), this argument has also been used by gender scholars to show how gender inequality can stem from the particular actions of men working to preserve their group advantage (Reskin, 1988).

Other work examines the role of dual labour markets in fostering patterns of occupational segregation and wage inequality for both racial-ethnic groups and for white women and women of colour. Both women and people of colour – and women of colour, in particular – are segregated in the workforce, concentrated in occupations with low wages, given less opportunity for advancement, receive poor employment benefits and have little job protection (Amott and Matthaei, 1996). Studies of employer perceptions of people of colour – and sometimes women – also show how persistent attitudinal frames can be in perpetuating inequality in the labour market (Kennelly, 2002; Moss and Tilly, 2001).

Seeing the parallels in the experiences of white women and men and women of colour has also produced work noting the link between race and gender as stratifying mechanisms. Studies have routinely conceptualised this link in terms of 'double jeopardy', meant to show the multiplying effect if experiencing simultaneous systems of inequality. Thus, women of colour are said to experience the double jeopardy of being both a racial and a gender minority; lesbian women of colour are seen as experiencing triple jeopardy; older, lesbian women, quadruple jeopardy and so forth. Accurate as is the multiple jeopardy metaphor is in terms of its ability to explain compounding forms of discrimination, it is nested in an additive model of inequality.

The additive model of inequality shows how the effects of race, gender, class and other social minority statuses 'add up', both over time and in intensity of impact. But just adding various 'differences' together can miss the social structural connections between different social factors, like race and gender, giving the impression that they operate independently of one another. Moreover, the additive model of thinking can create hierarchies of difference in which groups compete for recognition as victimised minorities. Thus, while intending to show the cumulative effects of experiencing multiple forms of oppression, the additive model inadvertently reproduces a hierarchical system in which a dominant group remains normative and all others remain, deviant or 'different'. Moreover, as we will see below, an additive model of thinking can foster the idea that different group characteristics can be just added on to others, as if they were all the same. Thus, ethnicity, sexuality, religion, age and ability all can be 'added on' to race, class and gender in ways that suggest that any of these forms of difference are equivalent to race, gender and class inequality. This use of difference fosters a view of all forms of oppressions as equivalent. Furthermore, adding on various forms of difference is a neverending process. After all, there are as many forms of difference as there are people in the world. Ironically, this form of recognising difference can obscure the workings of power just as it claims to recognise 'diversity' (Andersen and Collins, 2007).

Race, class and gender as systems of social control

Race, class and gender inequality are all buttressed by systems of social control that range from everyday norms and behaviours to extreme forms of violence. At the level of everyday practice, as engaged in by individuals, race, class and gender structure social interaction. This is revealed in simple, everyday practices where racial and gender etiquette, for example, signifies group power relations and reproduces – even if inadvertently – norms of domination and subordination. Thus, social control occurs along a two-tiered continuum with the two tiers ranging from individual to collective action and from mild, often taken for granted forms of behaviour to overt violence.

Whether committed by individuals (such as rape, sexual assault, sexual harassment, hate crime, lynching and so on) or via state-based violence (such as the death penalty, honour killings or other state-sponsored forms), race and gender violence operate as systems of social control. Subordinated racial and gender groups are subjected to various forms of harassment, intimidation or even death as a means of maintaining the race and/or gender hierarchy.

The enforcement mechanisms of class also show how social control need not be overt to be effective. Class ideology, whereby groups are defined as succeeding only because of their moral virtues, buttresses a system of class inequality by making success and failure seem to be within individual's control. Thus, despite the enormous power and advantage bestowed on those who benefit from the intergenerational transmission of wealth, the belief that 'anyone can make it' – common certainly in the United States – serves to justify a system of vast inequality – class inequality that, at least within the United States, is currently growing.

Race, class and gender as sources of resistance and cultural formation

Finally, because race and gender involve relations of domination and subordination, they also produce forms of resistance both at the individual and collective level. The focus on victimisation that permeates much race and gender scholarship, although accurate in detailing the consequences of race and gender stratification, tends to view subordinate groups in passive terms. While certainly race and gender victimise people, seeing only this dimension of race and gender relations overlooks the many ways that people resist oppression – both individually and collectively. The new emphasis on human agency in contemporary scholarship on gender and race shows that systems of domination also produce forms of resistance, whether in individual forms of resistance or in large-scale social movements for social justice.

While one might criticise the process of racial formation as producing identities based on a system of subordination and domination, at the same time, such identities also can become the basis for collective resistance to racism. This has been articulated in the case of Pakistanis in Britain. Thus, while Pakistanis have their origins in as a national group, within the British context, they are constructed in terms of ethnicity and can even become racialised. But this same phenomenon provides the basis for the construction of a community identity and can thus become the basis for collective resistance (Anthias and Yuval-Davis, 1992). Likewise, groups whose difference is derived from other ethnic distinctions – Muslims in London, Jews in the Soviet Union, or people of mixed race in South Africa, may be constructed as having common origins (whether religious, ethnic, or national) and thus use this presumed common identity as the basis for collective resistance.

Indeed, Anthony Marx (1998) has argued that in Brazil, the fluidity of racial categories mitigates against the formulation of a collective resistance because people do not identify as Black in a way that cuts across the various forms of 'blackness' that are found in this society. Marx concludes that, ironically, that by not socially collapsing diverse groups into a single category of black there is less chance for the genesis of a collective movement for racial progress. The opposite can occur when groups of diverse national, ethnic, or religious origins, such as Asian Americans in the United States, are treated as a monolithic group (that is, 'Asian American') and thus develop a pan-ethnic consciousness which can itself become the basis for collective mobilisation (Espiritu, 1992).

These various examples show the significance of human agency in the analysis of race, class and gender. While race, class and gender studies need to emphasise the material basis of race, class and gender relations, seeing them solely as stratifying mechanisms can obscure the various ways that social groups use their identities and social locations to context the existing social order.

CONCLUSION: PROBLEMS IN ARGUING BY ANALOGY

To summarise, connecting gender, class and race studies reveals many similarities in the social processes of domination and subordination involving each and their interconnection. Race, class and gender relations are social constructions, are supported by overlapping belief systems, have similar social and economic consequences, are maintained via systems of social control and produce movements for social justice. Yet, seeing these common processes can lead one to conclude that gender, class and race oppression are equivalent social processes—an assumption often built into 'diversity workshops' where 'trainers' encourage different groups to see the commonalities in their group experiences.

In part, this work comes from the impetus to recognise and include the diverse experiences of multiple groups – experiences that for multiple social groups have been largely excluded, overlooked and devalued. Noting the parallels in diverse group experiences has opened new inquiries into different group experiences based on different social factors such as race, gender, sexuality, disability, nationality, age, religion and so forth. In other words, seeing the common realities in subordinated group experiences has called attention to the various ways that different groups experience oppression. But similar and intersecting as these diverse group experiences are, race and gender (nor class, sexuality, age and so forth) are not exactly analogous. The last section of this paper discusses problems in assuming that race and gender are equivalent social processes.

As many have noted, race and gender, along with systems of class and sexuality, are mutually reinforcing systems of power. For instance, Lynn Weber writes, that race, class, gender, and sexuality 'are power hierarchies where one group exerts control over another, securing its position of dominance in the system, and where substantial material resources ... are at stake ... They are not completely independent but rather are interdependent, mutually reinforcing systems' (2001: 91). Weber is not equating them, in that she points out that each is a specific system of oppression. But others have taken this point further, arguing that because these various systems of oppression operate as master statuses (whether race, gender, disability, sexuality and so forth), they produce common forms of difference or group oppression.

The term *analogy of 'isms* can be used to refer to arguments that equate race oppression with gender oppression or class oppression with sexual oppression or racism with heterosexism and sexism with racism and so forth. Arguing by analogy does reveal some of the similar processes involved in race and gender relations, (as well as similar processes between things such as race discrimination and discrimination against the disabled, etc.), as has been noted above. But making race and gender or other forms of oppression analogous is misleading, theoretically and empirically.

To begin with, an argument by analogy is based on an additive model of inequality. That is, arguing by analogy suggests that you can substitute the analysis of any one social factor for the other – as if all oppressions were equivalent or the same. Although such an argument can reveal common processes and consequences, it tends to obscure the specific ways that race and gender as systems of inequality and power work (Andersen and Collins, 2007). Moreover, arguments by analogy overlook the historically unique conditions that different groups have faced and the particular ways that race, gender and other social factors overlap in these experiences (see Andersen, 2005, 2008; Daniels, 2008).

As this chapter shows, looking at race and gender together can prevent false generalisation, can reveal the overlapping influences of race and gender inequality and can show how race and gender intersect with other social factors. Thus, developing an intersectional perspective on race and gender opens up new ways of understanding each and how they interrelate. Understanding the intersection of gender and race is not the same as arguing that these are analogous forms of oppression. Analogous arguments continue to treat race and gender as if they were discrete social phenomenon. And, while each plays a role in shaping the other and both share some similar social patterns, studying both is about understanding the *connections between* them, *not* making one equivalent to the other.

The point is to see that race and gender are not experienced as separate social phenomenon, as the experience of women of colour directly shows. Rather, race and gender, along with social class, sexuality, age and so forth, are part of an entire fabric of group relations. The point is not to isolate a given social factor, even though there are times to observe the specific effects of any given factor. Rather, studying gender and race together is more likely to reveal the social structural connections that continue to give both gender and race social significance. Neither can be reduced to the other. Nor can either be seen in isolation from the other. But, as W. E. B. Du Bois suggests in the opening quotation for this chapter, combining the two – understanding their mutually reinforcing influence, how they merge, their material basis and their manifestation in the experiences of diverse groups – is a powerful way to understand society.

ACKNOWLEDGEMENTS

The author thanks Maxine Baca Zinn, Patricia Hill Collins, Elizabeth Higginbotham and the editors of this volume for their very helpful comments on an earlier draft.

REFERENCES

Amott, T. and Matthaei, J. (1996) *Race, Gender, and Work: A Multi-Cultural Economic History of Women in the United States.* Boston: South End Press.

Andersen, M.L. (2008) 'Thinking about Women Some More', *Gender & Society*, 22 (February): 120–125.

Andersen, M.L. (2006b) *Thinking about Women: Sociological Perspectives on Sex and Gender.* 7th edition. Boston, MA: Allyn & Bacon.

Andersen, M.L. (2005) 'Thinking about Women: A Quarter Century's View', *Gender & Society*, 19 (August): 437–455.

Andersen, M.L. (2003) 'Whitewashing Race: A Critical Review' in W. Doane and E. Bonilla-Silva (eds), *Whiteout: The Continuing Significance of Race.* New York: Routledge. pp. 21–34.

Andersen, M.L. (1988) 'Moving Our Minds: Studying Women of Colour and Reconstructing Sociology', *Teaching Sociology*, 16 (April): 123–132.

Andersen, M.L. (2006a) 'Race, Gender, and Stereotypes: New Perspectives on Ideology and Inequality'. *Norteámerica, revista académica*, Centro de Investigaciones sobre América del Norte.

Andersen, M.L., Bowler, A. and Kimmel, M. (2004) 'Do We Still Need Feminist Theory?' in C. Valentine and J. Spade (eds) *The Gender Kaleidoscope: Prisms, Patterns, and Possibilities.* Belmont, CA: Wadsworth Publishing Co. pp. 544–550.

Andersen, M.L. and Hill Collins, P. (eds.) (2007) *Race, Class, and Gender: An Anthology.* 6th edition. Belmont, CA: Wadsworth.

Andersen, M.L. and Taylor, H.F. (2006) *Sociology: Understanding a Diverse Society*, 4th edition. New York: Wadsworth.

Anderson, E. (1999) *The Code of the Street: Decency, Violence, and the Moral Life of the Inner City.* New York: W.W. Norton.

Anderson, E. (1990) *Streetwise: Race, Class, and Change in an Urban Community.* Chicago, IL: University of Chicago Press.

Anthias, F. (2001) 'The material and the symbolic in theorizing social stratification: Issues of gender, ethnicity, and class', *Signs*, 52 (September): 367–390.

Anthias, F. (2002a) 'Beyond Feminism and Multiculturalism: Locating Difference and the Politics of Location', *Women's Studies International Forum*, 25 (3): 275–286.

Anthias, F. (2002b) 'Where Do I Belong? Narrating Collective Identity and Translocational Positionality', *Ethnicities*, 2: 491–514.

Anthias, F. and Yuval-Davis, N. (1992) *Racialized Boundaries: Race, Nation, Gender, Colour and Class and the Anti-Racist Struggle.* London: Routledge.

Aptheker, B. (1982) *Woman's Legacy: Essays on Race, Sex, and Class in American History.* Amherst, MA: University of Massachusetts Press.

Baca Zinn, M. (1982) 'Mexican-American Women in the Social Sciences', *Signs*, 8 (Winter): 259–272.

Baca Zinn, M. and Thornton Dill, B. (1996) 'Theorizing Difference from Multiracial Feminism', *Feminist Studies*, 22 (Summer): 321–331.

Bambara, T.C. (ed.) (1970) *The Black Woman: An Anthology.* New York: New American Library.

Biernat, M. and Manis, M. (1994) 'Shifting Standards and Stereotype-Based Judgments', *Journal of Personality and Social Psychology*, 66 (January): 5–20.

Browne, I. and Misra, J. (2003) 'The Intersection of Gender and Race in the Labour Market', *Annual Review of Sociology*, 29: 487–513.

Collins, P.H. (1990) *Black Feminist Thought: Knowledge, Consciousness, and the Politics of Empowerment.* New York: Routledge.

Collins, P.H. (1998) *Fighting Words.* Minneapolis: University of Minnesota Press.

Combahee River Collective (1979) 'A Black Feminist Statement' in Z. Eisenstein (ed.) *Capitalist Patriarchy and the Case for Socialist Feminism.* New York: Monthly Review Press. pp. 13–22.

Connell, R.W. (2005) *Masculinities.* Berkeley, CA: University of California Press.

Connell, R.W. and Messerschmidt, J.W. (2005) 'Hegemonic Masculinity: Rethinking the Concept', *Gender & Society*, 19 (December): 829–859.

Daniels, J. (2008) 'Beyond Separate Silos: Andersen Symposium Introduction', *Gender & Society*, 22 (February): 83–119.

Davis, A. (1981) *Women, Race, and Class.* New York: Random House, Inc.

DeNavas-Walt, Proctor, C.B.D. and Smith, J. (2007) *Income, Poverty, and Health Insurance Coverage in the United States 2006.* Washington, DC: U.S. Census Bureau.

Dill, B.T. (1979) 'The Dialectics of Black Womanhood', *Signs*, 4 (Spring): 543–555.

Doane, W. and Bonilla-Silva, E. (eds) (2003) *Whiteout: The Continuing Significance of Race.* New York: Routledge.

Dovidio, J.F. (2001) 'On the Nature of Contemporary Prejudice: The Third Wave', *Journal of Social Issues*, 57 (Winter): 829–849.

Dovidio, J.F., Kawakami, K. and Gaertner, S.L. (2002) 'Implicit and Explicit Prejudice and Interracial Interaction', *Journal of Social Psychology*, 82 (January): 62–68.

Dreifus, C. (2005) 'A Sociologist Confronts the Messy Stuff of Race, Genes, and Disease: A Conversation with Troy Duster', *The New York Times*, October 18, Section F, page 2.

Du Bois, W.E.B. (1921) *Darkwater: Voices from within the Veil.* New York: Harcourt.

Duneier, M. (1992) *Slim's Table: Race, Respectability and Masculinity.* Chicago, IL: University of Chicago Press.

Duneier, M. (1999) *Sidewalk.* New York: Farrar, Straus and Giroux.

Duster, T. (2006) *Race and Reification in Science.* New York: Social Science Research Council. www.ssrc.org

Edin, K. and Kefalas, M. (2005) *Promises I Can Keep: Why Poor Women put Motherhood before Marriage.* Berkeley: University of California Press.

Espiritu, Y.L. (1992) *Asian American Panethnicity: Bridging Institutions and Identities.* Philadelphia, PA: Temple University Press.

Gilkes, C.T. (1980) '"Holding Back the Ocean with a Broom": Black Women and Community Work' in L.F. Rodgers-Rose (ed.) *The Black Woman.* Beverly Hills: Sage. pp. 217–232.

Glenn, E.N. (1980) 'The Dialectics of Wage Work: Japanese American Women and Domestic Service, 1905-1940', *Feminist Studies*, 6 (Fall): 432–471.

Glenn, E.N. (2002) *Unequal Freedom: How Race and Gender Shaped American Citizenship and Labour.* Cambridge, MA: Harvard University Press.

Hacker, H. (1951) 'Women as a Minority Group', *Social Forces*, 30 (1): 60–69.

Higginbotham, E. (1981) 'Is Marriage a Priority? Class Differences in Marital Options of Educated Black Women' in P.J. Stein (ed.) *Single Life: Unmarried Adults in Social Context*. New York: St. Martin's Press. pp. 259–267.

Hull, G.R., Bell Scott, P. and Smith, B. (eds) (1982) *All the Women are White, all the Blacks are Men, but Some of us are Brave*. Old Westbury, CT: The Feminist Press.

Hull, G.T. and Smith, B. (1982) 'Introduction: The Politics of Black Women's Studies' in Gloria T. Hull, P. Bell Scott, and B. Smith (eds) *All the Women Are White, all the Blacks are Men, but Some of us Are Brave*. Old Westbury, CT: The Feminist Press. pp. xvii–xxxi.

Jackson, J.L. Jr. (2001) *Harlemworld. Doing Race and Class in Contemporary America*. Chicago, IL: University of Chicago Press.

Jones-DeWeever, A. (2002) 'Marriage Promotion and Low-Income Communities: An Examination of Real Needs and Real Solutions'. Briefing Paper, Institute for Women's Policy Research, Paper #D450. www.iwpr.org

Jordan, J. (1985) *On Call: Political Essays*. Boston: South End Press.

Jordan, W.D. (1968) *White Over Black: American Attitudes Toward the Negro 1550–1812*. Chapel Hill, NC: University of North Carolina Press.

Kennelly, I. (2002) '"I Would Never be a Secretary": Reinforcing Gender in Segregated and Integrated Occupations', *Gender & Society*, 5 (October): 603–624.

Kimmel, M.S. (2005) *The History of Men: Essays in the History of American and British Masculinities*. Albany, NY: State University of New York Press.

Ladner, J. (1971) *Tomorrow's Tomorrow*. Garden City, NY: Doubleday.

Lewis, D. (1977) 'A Response to Inequality: Black Women, Racism, and Sexism', *Signs*, 3 (Winter): 339–361.

Lieberson, S. (1980) *A Piece of the Pie*. Berkeley, CA: University of California Press.

Lorber, J. (2005) *Breaking the Bowls: Degendering and Feminist Change*. New York: W.W. Norton.

Lorde, A. (1984) *Sister Outsider*. Freedom, CA: Crossing Press.

Martin, P.Y. (2004) 'Gender as a Social Institution', *Social Forces*, 82 (June): 1249–1273.

Marx, A. (1998) *Making Race and Nation: A Comparison of the United States, South Africa, and Brazil*. New York: Cambridge University Press.

Moraga, C. and Anzaldúa, G. (eds) (1981) *This Bridge Called My Back: Writings by Radical Women of Colour*. Watertown, MA: Persephone Press.

Moss, P.I. and Tilly, C. (2001) *Stories Employers Tell: Race, Skills, and Hiring in America*. New York: Russell Sage Foundation.

Myers, L.W. (1975) 'Black Women and Self Esteem' in M. Millman and R. Moss Kanter (eds) *Another Voice: Feminist Perspectives on Social Life and Social Science*. Garden City, NY: Anchor Press/Doubleday. pp. 240–250.

Nagel, J. (2003) *Race, Ethnicity, and Sexuality: Intimate Intersections, Forbidden Frontiers*. New York: Oxford University Press.

Omi, M. and Winant H. (1994) *Racial Formation in the United States: From the 1960s to the 1990s*. New York: Routledge.

Ong, M. (2005) 'Body Projects of Young Women of Colour in Physics: Intersections of Gender, Race, and Science', *Social Problems*, 52 (June): 593–617.

Reagon, B.J. (1983) 'Coalition Politics: Turning the Century' in B. Smith (ed.) *Home Girls – A Black Feminist Anthology*. New York: Kitchen Table Press. pp. 358–368.

Reskin, B. (1988) 'Bringing the Men back in: Sex Differentiation and the Devaluation of Women's Work', *Gender & Society*, 2 (March): 58–81.

Risman, B.J. (2004) 'Gender as a Social Structure: Theory Wrestling with Activism', *Gender & Society*, 18 (August): 429–450.

Rodgers-Rose, L.F. (ed.) (1980) *The Black Woman*. Beverly Hills: Sage.

Seidman, S. (2003) *The Social Construction of Sexuality*. New York: W. W. Norton.

Smith, B. (ed.) (1983) *Home Girls – A Black Feminist Anthology*. New York: Kitchen Table Press.

Solomos, J. and Back, L. (1996) *Racism and Society*. New York: St. Martin's Press.

Stein, A. and Plummer, K. (1994) '"I Can't Even Think Straight": Queer Theory and the Missing Sexual Revolution in Sociology', *Sociological Theory*, 12 (July): 178–187.

Stoetzler, M. and Yuval-Davis, N. (2002) 'Standpoint Theory, Situated Knowledge and the Situated Imagination', *Feminist Theory*, 3: 315–333.

Telles, E.E. (2004) *Race in Another America: The Significance of Skin Colour in Brazil*. Princeton, NJ: Princeton University Press.

Weber, L. (2001) *Understanding Race, Class, Gender, and Sexuality: A Conceptual Framework*. New York: McGraw Hill.

West, C. and Zimmerman, D. (1987) 'Doing Gender', *Gender & Society*, 1 (2): 125–151.

Wilkinson, D. (1980) 'Minority Women: Social-Cultural Issues', in A. Brodky and R. Haremustin (eds) *Women and Psychotherapy*. New York: The Guilford Press. pp. 285–304.

Willie, S.S. (2003) *Acting Black: College, Identity, and the Performance of Race*. New York: Routledge.

Wilson, W.J. (1987) *The Truly Disadvantaged: The Inner City, The Underclass, and Public Policy*. Chicago: University of Chicago Press.

US Census Bureau (2008) *Income: Detailed Historical Tables*. www.census.gov

Yuval-Davis, N., Anthias, F. and Kofman, E. (2005) 'Secure Borders and Safe Haven and the Gendered Politics of Belonging: Beyond Social Cohesion', *Ethnic and Racial Studies*, 28 (May): 513–535.

Yuval-Davis, N. and Stoetzler, M. (2002) 'Imagined Boundaries and Borders: A Gendered Gaze', *European Journal of Women's Studies*, 9 (3): 329–344.

Ethnicities and Sexualities

Joane Nagel

INTRODUCTION

This chapter explores the intersection of ethnicity and sexuality. Sexuality is a core constitutive element of race, ethnicity and the nation.[1] Sexual stereotypes are powerful components of ethnic stereotypes. Sexual fears and loathing underlie racial terror and hatred. Sexual rules and protocols are part of the ideological apparatus for imagining nations. It is impossible to understand fully the dynamic and enduring nature of ethnicity without acknowledging its intimate partner – sexuality. It is no accident that many incidents of ethnic violence around the world are accompanied by assertions of sexual misconduct by the victim or the victim's community. For instance, throughout US history, the lynching of African American men has been justified as punishment for sexual misdeeds, most often for 'disrespecting' or raping white women (Hodes, 1997; Brundage, 1993; Tolnay and Beck, 1995). In colonial India, the British torture and execution of hundreds of Indian men in the 1857 'Sepoy' war was spurred, in part, by reports that the Indians had raped women and girls prior to killing them (Ward, 1996; Paxton, 1992; Roy, 1994). Various forms of sexual violence during national and international conflicts (rape, sexual slavery, sexualised torture) frequently are justified by ethnocentric ideologies about the sexual impurity of enemy women, the sexual perversion or impotency of enemy men and the moral and physical sexual superiority of aggressors. Japan's sexual enslavement of Korean and other mainly Asian 'comfort women' during World War II reflected Japanese imperial claims to national superiority and ethnocentrism towards more 'backward' peoples (Watanabe, 1995; Henson, 1999; Hicks, 1995). The mass rape of Bengali women during the Bangladesh war of independence from Pakistan in 1971 was committed by fellow Muslims of different ethnic backgrounds amidst claims that the Bengalis were not following proper religious doctrine (Brownmiller, 1975; Mascarenhas, 1986). An atmosphere of ethnic denigration also served as the context for US sexual exploitation and rape of Southeast Asian women during the Vietnam war in the 1970s; and theories of Arab male sexuality guided the prison abuses of detainees during the US-led Iraq war beginning in 2003 (Lawson, 1991; Williams, 2006; Massad, 2007; Margulies, 2006; Hunt and Rygiel, 2006; Kahlili, 2008).

We will focus in this chapter on the common, yet commonly disregarded sexual dimensions of ethnicity. We will draw on *social constructionist* theories of ethnicity and sexuality to show how the construction of each depends upon and informs the other. We will examine the ways that race is sexed, and sex is raced; we will show how ethnic and sexual *boundaries* are erected to divide populations and build communities; and we will explore the *ethnosexual* terrain located at the intersections of sexualities and ethnicities.[2] The chapter begins with a discussion of the social construction of ethnicity, then outlines developments in sexuality studies to illuminate the often obscured coupling of ethnicity and sexuality and finally surveys a number of *ethnosexual frontiers* to document the ways that sexuality shapes ethnic boundaries and relations in the United States and in the global system.

THE SOCIAL CONSTRUCTION OF ETHNICITY

The international system of sovereign states provides many examples of the social construction of ethnicity. The second half of the twentieth century was marked by the rise of nation states out of the colonial empires of Eastern and Western Europe and Japan. By the early twenty-first century, the number of countries with membership in the United Nations (UN) had grown from 51 at the UN's founding in 1945 to 192 in 2006 (United Nations, 2006). Against the expectations of many social scientists, this consolidation of land and people into an unprecedented number of national units did not result in a parallel development of corresponding national identities to unite linguistically, religiously and culturally diverse populations in new states. Although independence movements generated new national consciousness, especially in urban cosmopolitan centres, in many of the new states of Asia and Africa and in the more established states of Europe and the Americas, national unity frequently was eclipsed by new or resurgent ethnic mobilisations, increases in ethnic identification and heightened levels of ethnic violence.[3]

For instance, ethnic groups enclosed in the newly independent states of Africa often formed ethnoregional political parties that competed for national office and control over national resources; interethnic competition resulted in civil wars in a number of states including Nigeria, Angola, Rwanda, and Sudan, and occasionally, as in the case of Ethiopia, led to the creation of a new state (Eritrea).

In India, the process of independence and its aftermath generated ethnic conflict that produced two new states: Pakistan and Bangladesh. In post-World War II Europe, when former colonial subjects and migrant laborers grew in numbers and visibility and mobilised to obtain rights, they were greeted by anti-immigrant nationalist backlashes; the result was new interethnic violence in many relatively ethnically homogenous countries such as Germany, Sweden, France, and England.

During the same period in the United States, a variety of ethnic rights movements, most notably the African American civil rights movement, inspired parallel mobilisations among other groups, both ethnic (e.g., Latinos, Asian Americans, Native Americans) and non-ethnic (e.g., women, gays and lesbians, the disabled), and launched renewed interest in ethnic ancestry among whites (Waters, 1990; Bakalian, 1993). At the close of the twentieth century, the collapse of the Soviet empire generated two dozen new states as the former Soviet republics became independent, as Czechoslovakia split in two, and as Yugoslavia 'Balkanised', splintering into many smaller sovereign units (Caplan, 2005), including, in 2008, the new state of Kosovo (BBC, 2008).

The durability of ethnicity as a source of tension around the world has produced ongoing debates in both new and old states about immigration, minority rights and the feasibility of constructing national identities out of diverse native-born and immigrant populations. The ubiquity and continuing volatility of ethnicity has led social scientists to question the inevitability of assimilation and to a search for a more accurate, less evolutionary means of understanding not only the *resurgence* of longstanding differences among peoples, but also the actual *emergence* of historically new ethnic groups.[4] The result has been the development of a *social constructionist model of ethnicity* which stresses the fluid, situational, volitional and dynamic character of ethnic identification, organisation, and action. The social constructionist model of ethnicity emphasises the ways in which ethnic identities and the boundaries that divide ethnic groups are negotiated and defined through social interaction inside and outside ethnic communities.[5] According to this view, ethnicities reflect the creative choices of individuals and groups as they define themselves and others in ethnic ways.[6] Ethnicity is built out of the material of language, religion, culture, appearance, ancestry or regionality. Through the actions and designations of ethnic groups, their antagonists, political authorities, and economic interest groups, ethnic boundaries are built dividing some populations and unifying others. The location and meaning of particular ethnic boundaries are continuously negotiated, revised and revitalised both by ethnic group members themselves as well as by outside observers. Sexuality is a major ingredient in ethnic construction projects.

To assert that ethnicity is socially constructed is not to deny the historical basis of ethnic conflict and mobilisation. A constructionist view of ethnicity poses questions where a historical view begs them. For instance, to argue that the ethnic conflicts between Serbs, Croats and Bosnian Muslims in the former Yugoslavia simply are the result of longstanding historical antagonisms built on centuries of distrust and contention, asserts a certain truth, but answers no questions about when and where conflicts will erupt, about their intensity or about the prominent and sometimes disturbing place of sexuality in interethnic relations. In fact, scholarship shows that Yugoslavs from many ethnic backgrounds lived closely and peacefully together during most of the post World War II period and frequently intermarried in urban areas, such as Sarajevo. The reasons for the resurgence of ethnic differences and antagonisms in Yugoslavia during the 1990s can be traced to the withdrawal of Soviet influence which led to political competition among Yugoslavian ethnic groups resulting in a re-construction of ethnic differences marked by widespread ethnically motivated rapes and executions (Stiglmayer, 1994; Allen, 1996; Munn, 2008). Yugoslavia was an ethnosexual frontier in which warfare and sexual violence were used by ethnic entrepreneurs to reassert the importance of linguistic or religious differences and construct new national identities (Serbs, Croats, Bosnians, Macedonians, Montenegrins, Slovenians and Kosovars).

Similarly, to view black–white antagonism in contemporary American society simply as based in history – albeit a powerful and divisive history – is to overlook demographic, political, social and economic processes that prop up this ethnic boundary, reconstructing it, and producing tension along its borders and within the two bounded racial groups. For instance, Lemann's (1991) study of the post World War II demographic shift of African Americans from the South to the North and from rural to urban areas reveals a reconfiguration of the black–white ethnic boundary in northern and southern cities. This 'great migration' magnified urban ethnic segregation, stratified black society, increased interracial tensions, promoted ethnic social movements among both blacks and whites and helped produce a black urban underclass. All of these changes reflect the dynamic, constructed character of black ethnicity in American society (Wilson, 1987; Best, 2005; Massey and Denton, 1993; Morris, 1984). Always haunting the black–white racial divide in the United States is the spectre of sexuality – the sexual dangerousness of black men in the white imagination and the sexual predations and appetites of white men in black history (see Hooks, 1992; Collins, 2004).

Sexual violence is a prominent feature of the ethnic violence in the Darfur region of Sudan. Social scientists have been studying the relationships among various ethnic groups occupying this region since the 1940s (see Barth, 1969), and documented a reasonably placid, exchange relationship among herding and agricultural groups of Baggara and Fur peoples (Haaland, 1969). After independence from Britain in 1956, ethnoregional competition for control of the central government and Sudanese economic resources (mainly access to land, oil, water), led to a succession of governments controlled mainly by northern 'Arab' groups and a militarised resistance by southern 'African' groups in the Darfur region. The civil political and economic conflict was exacerbated by ideological and resource shifts in the 1970s and 1980s when the rise of a regional pan-Arab movement seen as exclusionary by Darfur groups was complicated by a sustained drought and subsequent famine that killed nearly one-third of the population of the Darfur region (Prunier, 2005). In the 1990s, the organisation of resistance movement in Darfur brought the region into direct conflict with the Sudanese government and state-sponsored militias, including the notorious 'janjaweed' militia, whose sustained campaign of pillage, rape and ethnic cleansing has brought international attention to the role of sexual violence in the logic of intimidation and 'othering' characteristic of much ethnic conflict (Daly, 2007; Nielsen, 2008).

CONSTRUCTING ETHNIC BOUNDARIES

Race, ethnicity and nationalism are not simply historical legacies of migration or conquest. The continuous ebb and flow of ethnic identification and contention shapes and reshapes ethnic boundaries in political, economic, cultural, social and moral time and space. By using the imagery of ethnic boundaries, ethnicity can be seen as external to individuals – not so much a property of appearance or community, but rather a feature of the social landscape. According to this perspective, ethnicity is a series of moving boundaries that crisscrosses populations, shifting to divide people into different categories at different times in different social spaces. The ethnic boundary model was developed in the early work of anthropologist Fredrik Barth (1969) who deemphasised the importance of cultural differences as the main determinant of ethnic differences, and argued instead that ethnicity is better understood as a set of markers in both physical and symbolic space that signifies who is and who is not a member of an ethnic group – ethnicity is a matter of who is inside and who is outside an ethnic boundary.

Conceiving of ethnicity as a system of boundaries that divides a population into different groups provides us with a way to think about ethnicity in terms of its structure rather than its content, that is, its presumed genetic or cultural bases. Instead of assuming that ethnic differences inevitably lead to segregation or conflict, we can ask questions about the conditions under which ethnic boundaries will be erected and defended versus the conditions under which boundaries will be dissolved to promote ethnic integration and tranquility. We can ask questions about why particular group characteristics (language, religion, appearance) become the building blocks for barriers that separate people and groups. When we see violence erupt between ethnic groups, we can think of explosions occurring along particular ethnic boundaries, and we can ask when boundaries will become volatile. When we see people reaching over walls, making connections across ethnic boundaries – intermarrying, forming friendships, living next door to one another, we can ask about the conditions that weaken ethnic boundaries, allowing individuals to pass through, over or around these differences. When we see people pull away from one another, speaking words and enacting deeds of hatred and intolerance, we can envision them peering suspiciously over ethnic boundaries, taking aim and tossing grenades over the walls that separate ethnic groups. The notion of ethnic boundaries allows us to imagine ethnic police guarding ethnic borders, patrolling ethnic frontiers, erecting ethnic checkpoints, demanding ethnic identification and turning away or rounding up non-members; once again we can ask when this will happen and when it will not.

The boundary model suggests a kind of ethnic cartography in which we can chart the ethnic landscape by tracing lines in the geographic, legal, cultural, social, economic, political, moral and/or sexual sand.[7] These lines are drawn by ethnic insiders and outsiders, and both the lines (ethnic boundaries) and the terrain they surround (the membership and meaning of various ethnicities) are social constructions. The boundary trope permits us to survey the ethnic world through a number of different lenses. We can envision ethnic boundaries as *spatial* boundaries – the borders of national states in the global system or of ethno-cultural regions enclosed within or spanning national borders, or spatial boundaries can mark the edges of ethnic neighbourhoods or ghettos in segregated cities. We also can see ethnic boundaries imbedded in the law, *legal* boundaries – instantiated into formal definitions of who is and is not a member, citizen, white, black, and as a result, dictating who has which rights and who is subject to what kinds of treatment. Ethnic boundaries also are detectable as *cultural* markers – seen in tastes in food, fashion, furnishings, film, music, art, and other forms of recreational consumption, as well as in styles of demeanour and talk marked by body language, accents, dialects, jargon and linguistic differences. Ethnic boundaries are evident in *institutions* – marked by affiliations such as religion, education, clubs and organisations. Ethnic boundaries also are *social* – reflected in patterns of friendship and association, *economic* – seen in business transactions, investments, partnerships, and *political* – revealed in patterns of support for political candidates, policies, or positions. Ethnic boundaries are *ideational*, imaginary, in the mind, in the consciousness – reflected in notions of self and others, in the texture of feelings, intuitions, comfort levels, trust, affinity, and in the sense one has of connectedness, familiarity, safety, membership and of being 'home' or 'among friends'. Finally, and most important for the agenda of this chapter, ethnic boundaries are *sexual* – manifesting themselves in patterns of dating, childbearing, marriage and sexual relations, including sexual assault, rape and sexual slavery, as well as in sexual cosmologies – theories of ethnosexual attributes, practices, preferences and perversions.

CONSTRUCTING SEXUAL BOUNDARIES

The same insights gained from considering the socially constructed aspects of ethnicity can be applied to sexuality. Just as we can conceptualise ethnicity as a series of boundaries dividing a population according to various characteristics such as language, religion, culture or colour, sexuality can be seen as a set of boundaries dividing a population according to sexual practices, identities, orientations, labels and desires. In any society, we can identify divisions of the population along sexual lines. We can observe differences in levels of sexual activity (celibate, active, occasional, promiscuous), social organisation of sexuality (monogamous, polygamous, polyamorous), types of sexual partners (same, opposite, both), kinds of sexual desire, practice, intensity (fetishists, exhibitionists, sado-masochists, conservatives, experimentalists), sorts of sexual identities (gay, straight, bisexual, transgendered). Sexuality, like ethnicity, is a highly charged aspect of personal and collective life. Individual and group sexual characteristics are the subjects of strong moral judgements and strict social control, and sometimes sexual differences, like ethnic differences, become the basis for identification, discrimination, mobilisation and violence.

If we approach an analysis of sexuality as a series of boundaries, we obtain a somewhat different set of questions and ultimately a different set of answers from those generated from models of sexuality stressing biology, nature versus nurture, or as a matter of the relative morality of one form of sexuality over another. The sexual boundary model emphasises and raises some interesting questions about the *spatial* and *temporal* aspects of sexuality. For instance, we can ask where and when sexuality is enacted and accomplished – where are the boundaries of various sexualities and sexual events located in time and space?[8] By mapping sexual boundaries, we can plot the placement and timing of sexual practices, sexual desires, sexual identities and sexual communities.

In any geographic location, we can imagine a number of sexual zones – places identified and/or designed for particular sexualities and their enactment. In a city there are 'red light districts' for prostitution, 'gay districts' for homosexuals, singles bars (presumably for straights), areas zoned for 'adult entertainment', neighbourhoods which are defined as places for families, or for singles, or for gay men or lesbians or both, places where particular types of sexuality are desired or practiced (leather, sado-masochism, sexual performances). Some of these sex zones are ethnically segregated – separate spaces for sex workers, clients and sexual contact for different ethnic groups; some of these erotic spaces are integrated and serve as ethnosexual frontiers where members of different ethnic groups meet for sex for profit or recreational sexual interludes.

Sexual boundaries are not only spatial and temporal. Like ethnic boundaries, sexual boundaries can be *cultural*, involving spectacles, music, literature, art and all of the paraphernalia of cultural production such as gay pride parades and carnivals, sexual recreation or performance clubs, sexual websites, straight and queer erotic art, films and pornography; *legal*, involving the regulation of sexual practice such as laws certifying heterosexual marriage and outlawing sodomy, same-sex marriage, divorce; *economic*, involving the production and consumption of sexual products and services such as contraceptives, fashion, sex aids, toys, and pharmaceuticals, prostitution, tourism; *political*, involving restrictions on immigration or debates over discrimination based on sexual orientation or accommodating domestic partners; and *racial, ethnic, or national*, involving sexual stereotypes of particular ethnic groups, the marginalisation or exclusion of homosexuals from ethnic communities, nationalist calls for compulsory heterosexuality and sex for procreation – designed to reproduce the nation.

THE SOCIAL CONSTRUCTION OF SEXUALITY

Like ethnic boundaries, sexual boundaries give the appearance of naturalness and timelessness. They seem and feel inborn, unchanging, and stable, and while a majority of social and natural science researchers have dismissed the validity and feasibility of biologically distinct races, the idea that sexuality is a physical phenomenon that is almost exclusively a feature and function of the body has been more durable. The traditional study of sexuality – 'sexology' – has focused primarily on heterosexuality, but not in order to question its naturalness or physicality. Rather sexology has confined itself mainly to documenting the practices of heterosexuals (frequency of coitus, orgasm, or masturbation, age at first sexual intercourse, number of sexual partners, etc.), in part to establish the boundaries of 'normal' sex (Kinsey et al., 1948, 1953; Masters and Johnson, 1966; Michael et al., 1994; Laumann et al., 1994, 2004). Historically, sexuality studies also have examined 'deviant' sexualities, such as homosexuality, prostitution, unconventional sexual desires, practices, and sites (Reiss, 1961; Humphreys, 1970; Masters and Johnson, 1970). This interest in the 'margins' of normative heterosexuality has reinforced rather than challenged the centre. Instead of questioning the naturalness of conventional heterosexuality, both sexology and sexual deviance research have documented and distinguished between the sexually 'normal' and the sexually 'pathological'.

Despite the pioneering sexual constructionist work of John Gagnon and William Simon (1973) on 'sexual scripting' in the early 1970s, as well as much research on the social construction of gender since that time (Lorber, 1994; Connell, 1995; Prugl, 1999), social constructionism has not been a dominant paradigm for social science understandings of sexuality. In the past two decades, however, things have changed. There has been a great deal of interdisciplinary research examining heterosexuality as a social construction, questioning the universality and biological imbeddedness of heterosexual exclusivity, inquiring into the origins of 'compulsory heterosexuality', challenging the norms governing what are defined as acceptable and conventional sexual practices, examining the purposes served by the widespread institutionalisation of heterosexuality into the law and into everyday life, and criticising prevailing definitions of normal sexuality and normative sex acts (Rich, 1980; Fuss, 1989; Warner, 1993; Ingraham, 1994; Katz, 1995; Stychin, 1998; Seidman, 2003; Johnson, 2005; Hill, 2008).

This work has developed a critical vocabulary: *phallocentric*, *heteronormativity*, queer.[9] When queer theorists make the discursive move from 'sexuality' to 'sexualities', they are *queering* (twisting and turning on its head) heteronormative assumptions and challenging conventional assertions and expectations of universal opposite sex desire and practice. Queer theory has its work cut out for it since heteronormative, socially approved enactments of sexuality are perhaps the most embedded and enforced norms in human societies. The challenge is especially great for scholars who contest the validity and universality of the heterosexual–homosexual binary since critiques of heteronormativity confront deeply held, widespread beliefs in the naturalness of heterosexuality. Besides the assumed naturalness of heterosexuality, another prominent feature of hegemonic or dominant sexual formation in contemporary US society is the expectation that sexual practice is necessarily tied to sexual identity.[10] According to this thinking, individuals do not have the choice *not* to have a sexual orientation and identity. One is presumed to be 'gay' or 'straight', if not in deed, then surely in mind. The connection between sexual behaviour and sexual identity, however, has not always been so clear or assumed. Historians have situated the connection between sexual practice and sexual identity in the West sometime in the last two hundred years. In fact, Michel Foucault (1978: 43) actually identifies a specific moment in 1870 when homosexuality became something someone *was* rather than something someone *did*, although some historians have dated the construction of homosexuality as a social category and identity somewhat earlier, in the eighteenth century (Trumbach, 1991; Ramet, 1996).[11]

Whatever the exact time and place that homosexuality became an identity and a socially defined kind of person, the invention of homosexuality led to the crowning of heterosexuality as the *normal* form of sexual desire, identity and behaviour. Like all hegemonies, heterosexuality is not without its detractors and its sceptics. Feminist and queer theory challenge the essentialist sexual division of the population into males and females and question whether *men* and *women* exist. Gender theorists have consistently acknowledged that the content and meaning of gender roles and gendered bodies are local constructions that vary across time and space. Queer theorists have gone a step further positing that the male/female binary and the sexed body are utterly unreal except as social conventions or 'performatives'. In this assertion, queer theorists follow in the footsteps of ethnicity theorists who question the validity of 'race' as a biological or real human characteristic.

PERFORMANCE AND PERFORMATIVITY

Just as the raced body is a site of ethnic attributions and stereotypes flung across racial boundaries, the gendered and sexualised body is a major location for the social construction of men and women, masculinity and femininity and male and female sexuality. The body, thus, is an instrument of *performance* and a site of *performativity*. Ethnicity, gender and sexuality are performed and performative – conscious and unconscious, intended and unintended, explicit and implicit. These two concepts deserve some attention because of their usefulness in understanding social construction processes in general, for their increasingly common usage among researchers and theorists of gender and sexuality, and for their applicability to other socially constructed roles and categories of interest here, namely race, ethnicity and nationalism.

The role of performance in social life was explicated by Erving Goffman (1959) in the 1950s, and his 'dramaturgical' approach has been widely used in sociology and beyond, including in contemporary performance studies (Roach, 1996; Phelan, 1993; Carlson, 1996; Phelan and Lane, 1998). Gender theorists examine how we perform gender in the ways we walk, talk, sit, defecate, have sex, through our costuming, hair styling, hand gestures, patterns of eye contact, touching, movement, body language in general, topics and styles of conversation, by the cars we drive, jobs we work at, games we play, etc. These are all gendered activities. In US society, some activities are more masculinised (warfare, camouflage patterned clothing, hunting) or feminised (childcare, the colour pink, quilting) than others (being a student, wearing blue jeans, swimming), and the gender meanings of all of these vary across time and cultures. Racial performances parallel gender performances – styles of dress, speech, body language, food, drink, leisure pursuits, for instance, all can be employed to denote racial difference or mimicry. Whatever the prevailing norms at any time or place, these and other ethnic and gendered behaviours and ways of being comprise the repertoire of performances we give as ethnically distinct straight and gay men and women as we move through the day and through life. We evaluate, refine, reevaluate, and revise our ethnic, gender and sexual enactments based on the positive and negative feedback we receive from the audiences we encounter. But ethnicity, gender and sexuality are not only performed, they are also performative.

The notion of performativity has its roots outside the social sciences in the humanities,[12] and recently has been circulated more widely by queer theorists, in particular in the work of philosopher Judith Butler (1990). Performativity refers to the ways in which we affirm and reaffirm, construct and reconstruct hegemonic social roles and definitions. We participate, for instance, in performative constructions of gender by our daily repetitive acts of accepted gender performance, by our tacit or implicit approval of the proper gender performances of others, by what we take for granted, assume, expect, demand from ourselves and others in terms of gender appearance and behaviour. We become agents reinforcing the performative gender order very often without thinking, only noticing when a rule is violated, an expectation is not met, and especially when we unthinkingly are repelled by or shun unsuccessful or nonconforming gender performances. Performativity is a powerful mechanism of social construction and social control, all the more so because it tends to go unnoticed, be invisible and operates at the level of intuition. Performatives just seem to *feel* right or wrong. They are difficult to identify or think about because they are so ingrained, presumed and seemingly natural. The invisible and comfortable character of ethnic, gender and sexual performatives contribute to their durability and pervasiveness.

To emphasise the symbolic, ideational, assumptive nature of performatively constructed gender or racial or sexual systems is not to overlook the importance material and structural factors play in the construction, enforcement and perpetuation of social orders. By social 'order' I refer to systems of social control over class, power and status in which some groups are valued and privileged relative to others, but in which all groups are subjected to disciplinary regimes and ideological hegemonies. Even those who benefit from a particular ethnic, or gender, or sexual order are constrained by its assumptions and regulatory apparatus. Even though everyone in a social order is subject to it, some subjects are more equal than others. For instance, Gayle Rubin (1975) describes a 'political economy' of gender and sexuality around the world. She notes that many different types of societies are characterised by the 'traffic in women'—in which men exchange women and their productive and reproductive labour (symbolically enacted as a father 'giving away the bride'). The political economy of gender is both formal (inscribed into law, policies, business protocols) and informal (ingrained in ways of interacting, notions of worth and dignity and ways of 'doing business'). Both men and women are ruled by these political economies, but men are relatively advantaged by them. The same is true of ethnicity. There is a political and moral economy of ethnicity, characterised by racial formations and racial systems of privilege and domination, that makes the uneven distribution of respectability, resources and power along ethnic lines seem natural, just and deserved both by those who win and by those who lose (Feagin, 2006; Bonilla-Silva, 2003).[13]

Just as the mere presence of female or male bodies does not constitute socially meaningful 'men' or 'women', and just as differences in sexual practice or sexual desire do not always produce stable sexual identities and boundaries, differences in skin colour, language, religion or ancestry do not inevitably generate strong ethnic identities or interethnic conflict. Ethnic differences are created and reinforced by performative expectations about racial behaviour and authenticity, by intentional ethnic performances such as 'acting black' and 'acting white', and by boundary recognition and regulation, such as the admonition to 'stick to your own kind' (Boyd, 1997; Julien, 1992; Childs, 2005). Ethnic boundaries are anchored in performative assumptions about ethnic differences, the resonance of certain ethnic stereotypes, the 'intuitive' appeal of some ethnic groups and aversion to others, or by the inconceivable – neighbourhoods one doesn't consciously avoid, but where it simply does not even occur to one to look for housing; churches, clubs, restaurants or shops one doesn't *choose* not to visit, but which one simply would never even think to enter.

The 'unthinkable' in social life provides us with one window through which to view what is performative. In fact, most understandings and conceptualisations of performativity stress that it is mainly unconscious and thus not easily accessible to us in our everyday actions and thoughts. Social performances arising out of performative systems, whether they are gender, sexual, racial/ethnic or situated in some other social order (political, economic, cultural, class, age), often are automatic or habitual. Even when performances are intentional, such as trying to be a sexually attractive man or woman, attempting to display class reputability by speaking or dressing according to expectations, or acting in accordance with norms governing proper racial or ethnic performance such as 'being a devout' Jew or Catholic or Muslim, still can reflect little conscious choice since they 'feel' right or comfortable, and since they are rooted in unexamined, assumed performative systems. Social change can occur when the performative becomes problematic. Revolutionary thinking is that which, by definition, exposes and defies performative processes and assumptions. 'Black is beautiful'. 'Workers of the world unite'. 'We're here, we're queer, get used to it'. Such challenges tend to be resisted both consciously and unconsciously, however. As a result, hegemonic shifts are rare historical events.

SEXUAL AND ETHNIC INTIMATE INTERSECTIONS

Ethnic boundaries typically rest on an ideological foundation of ethnocentric superiority that celebrates 'Us' and denigrates 'Them'. Ethnocentrism almost always is ethnosexual, when groups define members of other ethnicities as sexually different from, usually inferior to, their own moral and proper ways of being sexual. These ethnic 'Others' might be seen to be over-sexed, under-sexed, perverted, exotic or dangerous. For instance, many ethnicity and sexuality scholars argue that in contemporary US society, dominant notions of acceptable femininity, masculinity and gendered sexuality reflect the behaviours and desires of white middle-class heterosexuals (Hooks, 1992; Crenshaw et al., 1995; Espiritu, 1997; Halberstam, 1998; Ignacio, 2005; Collins, 2006). These race-based sexual standards define white heterosexual sexuality as normal and respectable and the sexualities of non-whites and non-heterosexuals as abnormal and disreputable. The result is an ethnosexual imaginary, a performative order in which, for instance, African American and Latino men are seen as excessively masculine and over-sexed or 'hypersexual', or Asian women are fetishised as sexually submissive and available, or African American women are characterised as sexually promiscuous and irresponsibly fertile, or Asian men are labelled insufficiently masculine and under-sexed or 'hyposexual'.

This pattern of contrasting valorised in-group sexuality with devalued out-group sexuality is not purely an American invention, but can be found in descriptions of ethnic relations around the world. Sexual stereotypes commonly depict 'us' as sexually vigorous (usually our men) and pure (usually our women), and depict 'them' as sexually depraved (usually their men) and unchaste (usually their women). For instance, during World War II, it is well known that the Nazis forced Jews to wear a yellow six-sided Star of David on their sleeves – an insignia that reflected the ethnic intolerant face of nationalism. Less familiar than the Star of David is the pink triangle that homosexuals in Germany and Nazi-occupied territories were forced to wear – a stigma that reflected the more hidden heteronormative, sexually intolerant face of nationalism. Pink triangles and Stars of David not only served to distinguish publicly outcast non-Aryan Others from true Aryans, these symbols also attributed potent and degenerate sexualities to their wearers. In fact, discredited sexuality is an important part of Nazi anti-Semitism and racism. George Mosse (1985) summarises the assertions of sexual degeneracy made in articulations of fascist and European racism: 'Blacks, and then Jews, were endowed with excessive sexuality, with a so-called female sensuousness that transformed love into lust. They lacked all manliness. Jews as a group were said to exhibit female traits, just as homosexuals were generally considered effeminate' (p. 36).

Not only were Jewish men seen as hypersexual or sexually defective in Nazi discourse, so also were Jewish women. Johanna Gehmacher's (1998) review of Nazi-era Austrian nationalist propaganda documents a similar denigration of Jewish women's sexuality, and a depiction of Jewish women as procurers of Aryan victims for their men's sexual exploits. Gehmacher quotes an early German National Socialist (Nazi) party propaganda leaflet warning Austrian girls and women about the seductive power of Jews – both women and men:

> Aryan girls, be on your guard against Jewish girls as friends. The Jewish community has ordered them to prepare you for the sin against your blood. They will lead you to dances, bars, etc., that are Jewish contaminated, alien to the Volk, where you will become helpless victims of Jewish playboys and lecherous Jews. You will be lost to your German people from the day you become captivated by those lechers. As women you will [be]get only Jewish children. (p. 206)

African Americans also were the targets of Nazi World War II propaganda. In his study of family politics in West Germany, Robert Moeller (1993) reproduces a World War II Nazi military recruitment poster featuring a racist caricature of an African American soldier in a First World War US Army uniform dragging a white woman by the hair. The German text on the poster reads: 'German! Should this once again become a reality?' Moeller (1993: 109) described the propagandist's intent: 'This Nazi poster was intended to evoke racist memories of black troops, who were among the Allied forces of occupation in the Rhineland after Germany's defeat in the First World War. In the background looms a caricature of a Jew'.

Such ethnosexual constructions and regimens of sexuality shape ethnic relations, conflicts and boundaries and underline the importance of sexuality in all things racial, ethnic and national. Definitions of ethnicity are imbued with sexual meanings and expectations resulting in an ethnosexual performative order which attributes powerful, 'intuitive' sexual stereotypes to other ethnic groups. The construction of ethnic boundaries depends on the establishment and enforcement of rules and regulations governing sexual demeanour, partners and reproduction. The domestic and international politics of ethnicity revolve around the defense of ethnic homelands from sexual invasion and strategies for dominating and sexually controlling ethnic Others' bodies and territories. The notion of *ethnosexual frontiers* illustrates interrelatedness of the ethnicity and sexuality.

ETHNOSEXUAL FRONTIERS

As I have argued in this chapter, ethnic boundaries are also sexual boundaries. Ethnicity and sexuality join together to form a barrier to hold some people in and keep others out, to define who is pure and who is impure, to shape our view of ourselves and others, to fashion feelings of sexual desire and notions of sexual desirability, to provide us with seemingly 'natural' sexual preferences for some ethnic partners and 'intuitive' aversions to others, to leave us with a taste for some ethnic sexual encounters and a distaste for others. Despite the visceral power of sexual matters in general, especially those involving race, ethnicity or the nation, the connection between ethnicity and sexuality often is hidden from view. Sex is the whispered subtext in spoken racial discourse. Sex is the some-times silent message contained in racial slurs, ethnic stereotypes, national imag-inings and international relations. Although the sexual meanings associated with ethnicity may be understated, they should never be underestimated. Sexual performatives are imbedded in ethnic, racial and national imaginings; sexual aspects of racial, ethnic or national performances are the bases of intergroup stereotypes, cultural enactments and conflict: sultry blues singers, sexy Latin dancers, loose American women, sexually dangerous American GIs (Hardin, 1997; Keyso, 2000).

Ethnicity and sexuality are strained, but not strange bedfellows. The territories that lie at the intersections of racial, ethnic or national boundaries are *ethnosexual frontiers* – erotic locations and exotic destinations that are surveilled and super-vised, patrolled and policed, regulated and restricted, but that are constantly penetrated by individuals forging sexual links with ethnic Others across ethnic borders. Ethnosexual frontiers are the borderlands on either side of ethnic divides; they skirt the edges of ethnic communities; they constitute symbolic and physical sensual spaces where sexual imaginings and sexual contact occur between members of different racial, ethnic and national groups. Some of the sexual con-tact across ethnic boundaries is by *ethnosexual settlers* who establish long-term liaisons, join and/or form families, and become members of ethnic communities 'on the other side'. Some sexual contact is by *ethnosexual sojourners* who arrange for a brief or extended stay, enter into sexual liaisons, but eventually return to their home communities. Some sexual contact is by *ethnosexual adven-turers* who undertake expeditions across ethnic divides for recreational, casual or exotic sexual encounters, often more than once, but who return to their sexual home bases after each excursion. Some sexual contact is by *ethnosexual invaders* who launch sexual assaults across ethnic boundaries, inside alien ethnic territory, seducing, raping and sexually enslaving ethnic Others as a means of sexual dom-ination and colonisation. Ethnosexual frontiers are sites where ethnicity is sexualised, and sexuality is racialised, ethnicised and nationalised. All ethno-sexual boundary crossing has the capacity to generate controversy since ethnic groups almost always encourage members to 'stick to your own kind', and since ethnic ideologies often contain negative sexual stereotypes of outsiders.

ETHNOSEXUAL SETTLERS AND SOJOURNERS: MIGRATION AND IMMIGRATION

Ethnosexual settlers and sojourners migrate around the globe or simply travel across town to make social, emotional and sexual contact with local populations.

Settlers and sojourners often try to blend into the host community within which they seek to establish sexual liaisons. These individuals can be seen to 'go native', discarding an old ethnicity or nationality for a new one. They often adopt local customs, court acceptance by local people, attempt to 'pass' as members and seek to establish lasting relationships with locals. Sexual contact is a major means of cultural transmission since intimate relationships facilitate language acquisition, provide detailed cultural knowledge and expand social networks. By dating and marrying locals, ethnosexual settlers and sojourners can become members of local communities. If these relationships produce children, settlers and sojourners become further integrated into local society. Sexual relationships between migrants and locals can become controversial in both origin and host communities. Ann Stoler's (1990, 1992, 2002) research on the role of sexuality in Europe's colonisation of Africa, Asia and the Americas reveals both high rates of ethnosexual contact between colonists and the colonised as well as high levels of official and informal disapproval about the liaisons. For instance, French and Dutch colonial authorities often turned a blind eye to the sexual exploits of military and other official personnel stationed in Indochina and Indonesia. Over time, however, the growing numbers of mixed race offspring resulting from European–Asian sexual relationships became an embarrassment to the authorities concerned with maintaining a superior moral position and troubled by vexing questions of racial and national classification – were these children French or Dutch citizens, should they be educated and sent to colonial homelands, what was the proper relationship between these children and the families, especially the wives and offspring left at home while the men philandered in the colonies?

The contemporary global system is not insulated from such questions. Hsiu-hua Shen's (2003, 2005) research on Taiwanese investments in mainland China documents similar controversies resulting from Taiwanese businessmen's ethnosexual sojourning and settling in China. Public opinion on both sides of the Taiwan Strait has condemned these 'dangerous liaisons', especially when children are the result, and both the Chinese and Taiwanese governments have passed laws attempting to regulate this ethnosexual dimension of international commerce. Shih (1998) describes similar contacts and controversies associated with ethnosexual sojourning between Hong Kong and the Chinese mainland which are separated not by the 100-mile stretch of ocean comprising the Taiwan Strait, but only by the three quarters of a mile long Ting Kau bridge. The differences in salaries and standards of living in Taiwan and Hong Kong on the one hand, and mainland China on the other, make modern concubinage attractive and affordable for many Taiwanese and Hong Kong businessmen.

Ethnosexual settlers and sojourners' intimate relationships can open the door to assimilation. Thus, assimilation – the incorporation or integration of an individual or group into another group or society – can be seen as a live sex act, though scholarship on migration or assimilation seldom details the ethnosexual aspects of either except when examining rates of intermarriage. Intermarriage is a measure of formalised sexual relations across ethnic boundaries. Researchers often compare rates of intermarriage among ethnic groups as indicators of relative rates of assimilation (Spickard, 1989; Joyner and Kao, 2005). The intense interpersonal involvement associated with sexual intimacy pulls willing partners towards one another on many social and cultural fronts, blending their lives and biographies, and creating conditions conducive to assimilation. As a result of extended contact over time, ethnic settling or sojourning can lead to dramatic forms of assimilation such as 'ethnic conversion' or 'ethnic switching' – instances where an individual changes ethnicity (Kelly, 2000).

However, ethnic conversion or passing are not 'ethnic options' for everyone, since some ethnic boundaries are more permeable than others (Waters, 1990). Race can serve as a solid barrier to assimilation. In the United States, the practice of 'hypodescent' or the 'one drop rule', for instance, classifies all people with African ancestry as 'black' whether they are race-identified or not (Davis, 1991). The contradictions, tensions and sometimes absurdities resulting from hypo-descent classification schemes have led to debates about racial data collected by the US Census Bureau, in particular about the decision to include a 'biracial' category for individuals of mixed African, European, Asian, Native American or other 'racial' backgrounds in the 2000 Census (Anderson and Feinberg, 1999). The *existence* of individuals of mixed racial ancestry is the direct result of ethno-sexual contact, but the *meaning* and *classification* of such individuals involve the politics of colour and continuing controversies associated with sexually crossing the US colour line (Loveman and Muniz, 2007).

Rigid racial classification systems are not the only reason why migration does not always result in ethnic assimilation. In some cases, ethnic identities are strengthened in immigrant communities, and ethnic boundaries become effective barriers to extensive intimate contact. For instance, the influx of ethnically distinct migrants into a neighbourhood or region can create new ethnic awareness on both sides of an ethnic boundary. Rather than assimilating, immigrant groups can become new ethnic groups when they settle and establish ethnic associations such as churches, businesses and restaurants. Locals in host communities can develop ethnic consciousness in response to the presence of new migrants with their different religions, languages and cultures. Researchers have documented, for instance, an ethnic political economy in south Florida where a Cuban American/Latin American ethnic enclave has formed (Portes and Rumbaut, 2001; Stepick et al., 2003; Pedraza, 2007). Non-Latinos – both white and black Anglos as well as Haitians – have reacted to the Latinoisation of Miami culture (music, food, religion) and social life. Although Cuban-Americans, like many of their fellow Latinos are quite likely to marry outside the ethnic group, adopt the English language, and embrace American culture, the presence in south Florida of large numbers of Cuban and Latin Americans, many of whom are bilingual, and some of whom speak Spanish exclusively, was greeted by the rise of an official English language, 'English Only' or 'English First' movement in the 1980s that reflected heightened ethnic awareness by resident Anglos (Baron, 1990).

Despite tensions associated with immigration, interethnic sexual contact remains an inevitable feature of migration. One reason for this is the gendered character of much international migration. Although the migration of entire families occurs, until the recent upsurge in women's international migration (Parrenas, 2001, 2005), most internal and international migrants have been men, often young men. This gender imbalance in immigration has resulted in a shortage of co-ethnic women in many destination communities. Even when migrant men have wives and children back home, sexual relationships that cross ethnic boundaries often are established in immigrant settings. Another reason for both short-term and sustained ethnosexual contact is the ethnic character of sexual desire and desirability. Individuals gazing across racial, ethnic and national boundaries are often attracted by what they see. Like all sexual attractions, the desire for intimate contact with ethnic Others may not last, but when it develops into a long-term relationship, it is likely to contribute to reshaping ethnic identities. Yet another factor contributing to ethnosexual settling and sojourning, even where there are co-ethnic partners available, is generational. The children of immigrants – second generation and beyond – are considerably more likely than their parents to cross local ethnic boundaries to establish amorous alliances (Joyner and Kao, 2005). Intergenerational ethnosexual drift frequently is defined as a threat to ethnic group vitality and the stability of ethnic boundaries.

ETHNOSEXUAL ADVENTURERS AND INVADERS: RECREATION AND DOMINATION

Sexual contact across ethnic boundaries is not always a long-term affair, nor is it always a welcome advance. Recreational sex with, and sexual exploitation of, members of other ethnic groups are the specialties of ethnosexual adventurers and invaders. These forms of hit-and-run ethnosexuality, especially adventuring because of its relative ease and casualness, are at least as common, possibly even more common, historically than are ethnosexual settling and sojourning for several reasons. First, ethnosexual adventurers and invaders are less likely to be penalised or stigmatised for having sex with sometimes reviled ethnic Others since often they keep their border crossings a secret, they deny their liaisons, or their acts officially are overlooked or approved. These are in contrast to the situations faced by ethnosexual settlers or sojourners whose interethnic intimacies are public, and who can encounter family resistance and social disapproval. Secrecy, deniability and official approval are especially important in interethnic sexual relations because intimate encounters across ethnic boundaries have been historically, and remain quite likely to be, sources of gossip, disapproval or condemnation, and in some cases ethnosex is against the law.

Ethnosexual adventuring and invasion also are more common than settling or sojourning because they are relatively easier and more convenient. Ethnosexual adventures and invasions are short-term and noncommittal enterprises, involving little investment of time or resources. Even in highly segregated settings, adventurers easily can find different-raced partners since the ethnic geography of sexuality generally permits opportunities for mixing – in entertainment areas, 'red light' prostitution districts or border towns (Hubbard et al., 2008). Illicit interethnic encounters are made possible in these liminal spaces situated in the borderlands between racial, ethnic or national communities. For instance, Julia Davidson (1998) argues that race and eroticism are important intertwined features of international 'sex tourism'. Both ethnosexual adventuring and invasion can be 'wink and nod' activities associated with masculine coming-of-age or solidarity rituals. Ethnosexual adventurers can be socially defined simply as young men 'sowing their wild oats' or displaying evidence of sexual bravery or *sangfroid*. A visit to a brothel staffed by members of a different racial, ethnic or nationality group might be accepted or even applauded, where a dating relationship across ethnic boundaries would be censured.

Ethnosexual adventuring and invasion are common features of political economies of desire which depend on stereotypes of the sexual talents or characteristics of members of particular races, ethnicities or nationalities. Assertions of the impurity, inferiority or hypersexuality of ethnic Others are useful justifications for ethnosexual invasions including rape, forced sexual servitude and trafficking in women or children for sexual purposes (Barstow, 2000; Skrobanek et al., 1997; Richard, 1999; Williams, 1999; Ticktin, 2008). As researchers have documented, part of the allure of commercial sex destinations is the alleged ethnically specific sexual features of those working there (Kempadoo and Doezema, 1999; Manderson and Jolly, 1997; Bishop and Robinson, 1999; Thorbeck and Pattanaik, 2002). Such ethnosexual mythologies include visions of Others with large or exotic genitals who are possessed of unusual sexual prowess or skill or who are exceptionally attractive or beautiful. The promise of exotic sex offered for sale by men, women and children of different races, ethnicities and nationalities is a main attraction of sex tourism around the world.

Ethnosexual adventuring and invasion are not without their costs to adventurers and invaders as illustrated by the ethnosexual dimensions of the US military presence around the world. A number of critics of the US global military presence point out the economic and moral costs associated with the militarisation of US foreign policy and the expansion of American military bases around the world (Enloe, 2000; Johnson, 2004; Bacevich, 2005, Elias, 2008). Chalmers Johnson (2000) asserts that the presence of the US military is deeply resented in many countries, not the least because of the local presence of American culture and consumers, especially militarised sexual consumers.

> Few Americans who have never served in the armed forces overseas have any conception of the nature or impact of an American base complex, with its massive military facilities, post exchanges, dependents' housing estates, swimming pools, and golf courses, and the associated bars, strip clubs, whorehouses, and venereal disease clinics that they attract ... They can extend for miles, dominating localities and in some cases whole nations. (p. 35)

In such cases, the American presence can be experienced by locals as an occupation by foreign men, women, equipment, vehicles, buildings, war machinery and materièl, as an invasion of Western culture, ideas, and desires and as a source of pollution and corruption. Johnson links anti-American sentiment and actions, such as attacks on US military and civilian targets, to the 'blowback' from America's international presence and foreign policy that, he argues, are hidden from or conveniently denied by most Americans and by the US government.[14]

QUEERING ETHNOSEXUAL BOUNDARIES

Just as collective sexual cosmologies designate the approved race, ethnicity or nationality of sexual partners for various purposes (dating, marriage, recreation, domination), a related set of rules dictates ethnic group members' acceptable sexual orientation and sexual practices. Heterosexuality plays an important role in defining racial, ethnic and national group boundaries by designating who is a member in good standing and who is an outsider or traitor. Ideologies of fertility and purity celebrations of hyper-heterosexuality are central to many nationalist movements focused on populating the nation and can be heard in contemporary fascist and racist ideology. Scholars note that present-day white supremacists and white nationalists speak a familiar language of virile men and fertile women fervently coming together in the service of their race and nation (Ferber, 1998; Daniels, 1997; Swain, 2002), resonating with earlier twentieth century fascist discourses that used sexualised racism, homophobia and misogyny as foils against which to contrast their claims to superior morality and virile, but proper sexuality – a sexuality dedicated to reproducing the race. In the words of the Italian fascist, Filippo Tommaso Marinetti, writing in 1919 in *Democrazia Futurista*:

> We speak in the name of the race, which demands ardent males and inseminated females. Fecundity, for a race like ours, is its indispensable defense in times of war, and in times of peace, its wealth of working arms and genial heads ... we futurists condemn the spreading feminine idiocy and the devoted imbecility of males that together collaborate to develop feminine extravagance, prostitution, pederasty, and the sterility of the race. (Spackman, 1996: 12; Marinetti, 1994)

Homosexuals contradict the core nationalist project of reproducing the nation, and both feminists and homosexuals tend to be seen by nationalists as potential sources of disloyalty, since their commitment to gender and sexual equality raises doubts in the minds of nationalists about the strength of their allegiance to the nation as their primary unit of identification. In recent years, lesbian and gay rights groups around the world, but particularly in the West, have mounted assaults on exclusionary policies, claiming equal rights to be members of the ethnic community or nation. During the past few decades, both straight and queer sexual rights advocates have asserted equal rights and membership in ethnic and national communities around the world (Jones-Yelvington, 2008). The integration of Europe is playing an interesting and emerging role in efforts to liberalise conservative nationalism inside European states. In the Republic of Ireland, for instance, both feminist and gay rights groups appealed *outside* Irish national boundaries, to the European Union, to claim rights within the Irish state.

The notorious case of a pregnant Irish teenager denied an abortion in Ireland in 1997 led feminists opposed to Ireland's restrictions on abortions to seek support in the more liberal arenas of European legal and public opinion (Clarity, 1997; Conrad, 2000). Irish gay and lesbian rights groups have appealed to the European Convention on Human Rights to force the decriminalisation of same-sex acts between consenting adults in Ireland (Stychin, 1998:,137). The anti-homosexual legal codes of many Eastern European countries seeking admission has become a volatile, but as yet unresolved issue although in 1995 the European Parliament resolved to forbid discrimination on the basis of sexual orientation in member states and extended certain same-sex partner employment benefits to its employees (Sanders, 1996: 84).

Despite such efforts, heterosexuality continues to set the standard for approved ethnosexual identities and practices in ethnic groups and nations around the world, and homophobia continues to dominate the discourses of racial, ethnic and national politics. It is not only dominant racial, ethnic or national groups that police sexual boundaries to identify and punish those whose partners or practices are judged improper. Virtually all communities define and enforce sexual rules governing with whom their members should have sex and what kind of sex they should have. Many lesbians and gay men in the United States and abroad have noted with much irony and bitterness that they are erased at best, stereotyped and demonised at worst, both inside and outside their ethnic communities and nations. For instance, lesbian and gay African Americans report that a variation on the admonition not to mix race and sex often greets them in their home communities: don't mix race and sexualities (Collins, 1990; Hemphill, 1991; Reid-Pharr, 2001).

One important feature of ethnic boundaries involves questions of membership – who *is* and who *is not* a bonafide member of the group; in the case of African Americans, it is about who *is* and who *is not* black (Davis, 1991). In *Soul on Ice*, black power activist Eldridge Cleaver articulated the meaning of black macho as exclusively heterosexual when he attacked James Baldwin's homosexuality as 'somehow un-black' (Page, 1996: 101) and equated both heterosexual and homosexual black/white sexual crossings as reflecting a 'racial death wish' (Cleaver, 1968: 102). Researchers identify widespread support in the work of black scholars and in the discourse in African American communities for Cleaver's assertions about the incompatibility of blackness and homosexuality (Collins, 2004; Nero, 1991; Chateauvert, 2008). An example is Frantz Fanon's (1968: 84) psychoanalytically based conclusion in *White Skin, Black Masks* that homosexuality was 'an attribute of the white race' and did not exist in the Caribbean because blacks there don't experience the oedipal tensions that putatively give rise to same-sex desire. Joseph Beam (1986: 231) laments the exclusion of black homosexuals in their own communities in the United States, commenting:

> When I speak of home, I mean not only the familial constellation from which I grew, but the entire Black community; the Black press, the Black church, Black academicians, the Black literati, and the Black left. Where is my reflection? I am most often rendered invisible, perceived as a threat to the family, or I am tolerated if I am silent and inconspicuous.

Homophobia in the black community combines with the racism of gay whites to further isolate black homosexuals. Essex Hemphill (1991: xviii) argues that 'the contradictions of "home" are amplified and become more complex when black gay men's relationships with the white gay community are also examined'. The writings of Native American, Asian American and Latino gay men resonate with those of African Americans reporting feelings of exclusion from home communities and from the white gay world (Vidal-Ortiz, 2008). Cherrie Moraga (1983, 1997) and Audre Lorde (1984, 1985) have similar analyses of the isolation of lesbians of colour and criticise white lesbians and feminists for insensitivity to the differing needs of lesbian and straight women of colour.

CONCLUSION

In the preface of the 1999 edition of *Gender Trouble*, Judith Butler reflects on the social changes of the 1990s and on the critiques and extensions of her original work (Butler, 1990). She comments on what she would have changed had she written the book a decade later: 'If I were to rewrite this book under present circumstances, I would ... include a discussion on racialized sexuality and, in particular, how taboos against miscegenation (and the romanticization of cross-racial sexual exchange) are essential to the naturalized and denaturalized forms that gender takes' (p. xxvi).

Butler's ruminations about social change and the intersections of ethnicity and sexuality are central to understanding the importance of sexualities in understanding race and ethnicity. Just as ethnicity is sexualised, sex is itself racialised, ethnicised, and nationalised. Race and sex each reinforce and magnify the other. Sexual descriptions and enactments of race, ethnicity and nationalism are seductive or threatening depending on the cultural content evoked. Racialised depictions of sexual purity, dangerousness, appetites, desirability and perversion are part of the performative construction of sexual respectability and disreputability, normalcy and deviance. Ethnosexual frontiers are exotic, but volatile social spaces, fertile sites for the eruption of violence. Racial, ethnic or nationalist defence and enforcement of in-group sexual honour and purity strengthens ethnic boundaries and disciplines members enclosed inside ethnic borders. Both positive and negative stereotypes about the sexuality of ethnic Others reinforce ethnic differences and sustain ethnic segregation. Negative images or accusations about Other sexualities contribute to the creation of disreputable and toxic outgroups and can be used to justify their exclusion, oppression, exploitation or extermination.

Ethnic boundaries, then, are both constituted by and constitutive of sexual boundaries. Part of the reason for the enduring colour line in the United States is the sexual meaning attached to race. Sexualised racial depictions distinguish black Americans from white Americans. Hegemonic white sexual claims and attributions enhance white sexual self-imaginings and devalue black sexuality, play on white sexual fears of blacks, and reflect white racialised sexual desires. Counter hegemonic black sexual claims and attributions challenge these stereotypes with unflattering sexual images of whites; conservative black sexual performativity reproduces white homophobia designating whites as the sources of queerness and embracing standards of hyper-respectability (Hooks, 1992; Hansberry, 1970; Hine, 1999; Chupa, 1990). The sexual ideologies of both hetero-sexuals and homosexuals contain racialised images and stereotypes of erotic others, cataloguing, for instance, the sexual anxieties of white men, the sexual submissiveness of Asian women, the sexual looseness of white women and the sexual potency of black men. Heterosexual masculine and feminine performances and performatives constitute gender/sexual regimes that lie at the core of ethnic cultures.

It is the sexualised nature of things ethnic, racial and national that heats up the discourse on the values, attributes and moral worth of Us and Them, that arouses anger when there are violations of sexual contact rules, that raises doubts about loyalty and respectability when breaches of sexual demeanour occur, that pro-vokes reactions when questions of sexual purity and propriety arise and that sparks retaliations when threats to sexual boundaries are imagined or detected. Sex-baiting can be as provocative as race-baiting in conjuring up a vision of ethnosexual threat. In fact, sex-baiting is a mechanism of race-baiting when it taps into and amplifies racial fears and stereotypes, and when assertions of sexual dangerousness are employed as a strategy to create racial panic. Sex-baiting and race-baiting often are used together by defenders of particular ethnosexual orders to maintain the status quo. There is a sexual message imbedded in ethnic stereotypes and categories, a sexual undercurrent that runs through many ethnic conflicts and controversies, an ethnosexual subtext in many economic and polit-ical debates. There is no more potent an image to justify violence and repression than the 'rape' of one's homeland or women, and no more convincing an argu-ment for military intervention to civilise or pacify ethnic Others than to accuse them of ethnosexual misbehaviour, excesses or violence. Appeals for protection against sexual threats are extremely durable weapons in the wars of words that accompany conflicts. When those threats are seen to be *ethno*sexual, their power to mobilise a response is greatly enhanced.

Ethnosexual boundaries represent an interesting and important paradox – even when they are crossed, they remain in place. This permanence in the face of per-meability has puzzled researchers. When social scientists and policymakers search for evidence of any kind of social change relating to race or ethnicity, one of the first places they look is in the bedroom. Sexual contact is the most intimate of ethnic boundary crossings, and intermarriage is perhaps the most controversial ethnosexual act since it tends to be public, officially recognised and reproductive. The reasoning goes – if individuals are crossing forbidden frontiers to marry one another, aren't those frontiers becoming less fraught with danger, less forbidden?

Indeed, tracing the rates of intermarriage among different ethnic groups over time is one way to map the ethnic landscape in a society. Intermarriage rates tend to indicate which ethnic boundaries are strongest and weakest. The examination of intermarriage rates over time and space point to the times in a country's history when ethnic boundaries are most defended or the parts of a country where ethnic boundaries are most relaxed. US intermarriage rates can serve as indicators of whether race or religion are as important as they used to be as sources of ethnic division or if the black/white colour line in the South is as strongly defined as in the past or as in the North. International comparisons of intermarriage rates allow us to extend the maps further: Is religion as important an ethnic division in the United States as it is in Canada or Lebanon or Switzerland? How is race defined in the United Kingdom compared to the United States; is the colour line equally fixed in both countries? Sexual contact and intermarriage reveal a great deal about ethnic relations across space and time and illustrate the power of sexuality to shape racial and ethnic relations.

Members of most American racial groups are still quite likely to marry a partner from the same race. Despite this stable pattern of racial endogamy, intermarriage within the US racial pentagon has been slowly, but steadily increasing in the past few decades. The US Census Bureau reports that in 1960, 99.6 percent of Americans married within their own race; in 1970 that figure had decreased slightly to 99.3; in 1980 there was a further decline in intraracial marriages to 98.0 percent; in 1990 there was further decline to 95.0 percent; and in 2000, 94.6 percent married within their own race (US Census Bureau, 1998, 2001). US intermarriage rates vary by ethnic group: in 2000, 6.1 percent of whites married non-whites, 10.9 percent of blacks married members of another race, 26.3 percent of Asian Americans outmarried, 26.1 percent of Hispanics married non-Hispanics and 67.0 percent of American Indians married non-Indians (US Census Bureau, 1998, 2001).[15] Gender also matters. In 2000, in three-quarters of black–white marriages, the husband is black and the wife is white (US Census Bureau, 2001). The reverse is true in Asian–white marriages, where two-thirds of husbands are white and wives are Asian. These patterns are consistent with long-standing ethnosexual cosmologies of desire and desirability in the United States and the West.[16]

Like all ethnic boundaries, racial boundaries are mutable and flexible. One caveat that should be noted when trying to understand the implications of increased ethnosexual contact for assimilation, however, is the capacity of ethnic boundaries to remain in place despite high rates of sexual contact across them. One means by which boundaries appear stable in the presence of cross-boundary sexual connections is racial reclassification. A factor not to be underestimated when examining intermarriage rates across time is the elasticity of whiteness. The 'white' racial category historically has absorbed many immigrant and ethnic groups once considered as racial Others (Irish, Italians, Armenians and Jews). Rising rates of intermarriage between whites and Latinos, American Indians and Asian Americans raise questions about the stability of the durability of the 'non-white' racial classification and identification of some members in these categories (e.g., middle and upper class Latinos, mixed race children of Asian–white couples). For instance, Qian and Cobas (2004) find differences in patterns of intermarriage between Latinos who identify themselves as 'white' and those who do not:

> When Latinos marry outside their own national-origin groups, [Latino] Whites tend to marry non-Latino Whites, but [Latino] Nonwhites tend to marry other Latino Nonwhites. This may imply two paths of integration in American society: Latino Whites assimilation into American society and Latino Nonwhites formation of Latino pan-ethnicity. (p. 225)

The stability of the black–white colour line in comparison to white absorption of many European and other national groups, reminds us of the power of history to shape contemporary race relations and the relatively impervious nature of the performative assumptions that prop up racial boundaries – despite performances that violate those same colour lines. Until the Civil War ended slavery in the United States, white men's sexual access to and exploitation of black women was unchallenged and widespread; even long after the war ended, black women remained vulnerable to white men's sexual demands (see Hooks, 1992, especially Chapters 2 and 4). The diversity of skin tones among African Americans today is visible evidence of those centuries of black–white sexual contact. It is an interesting historical fact that sex across the colour line has reversed its gender structure in the past century and a half, shifting from sex, often coerced sex, primarily between white men and black women to sex and marriage primarily between black men and white women. Despite a long history of interracial sex, the colour line dividing blacks and whites remains the most stable and dangerous ethnic boundary in American society. Ironically, sex across the colour line may do as much or more to strengthen the boundary as to weaken it. This apparent contradiction raises some interesting questions about race and sex: how is it that blacks and whites have had forced and consensual sex throughout US history, yet the colour line between these two 'races' remains the most visible and volatile American ethnic boundary? Why is it that sex-baiting, especially in the black/white case, seems to retain its strategic power to reinforce racial boundaries? The answer to these questions lies in the capacity of ethnicity to sexually attract and repel, in the success of sexuality as a performative ideology of superiority and inferiority, and in the power of sexuality as an instrument of racial formation – as a means of domination or resistance, as a badge of honour or shame.

Having sex with an Other might reflect a heartfelt longing or an act of rebellion or a way to demean and defile another person or group. No motivation is likely to be entirely pure since it is hard to untangle the desire from the disdain. Even when we try to step outside local ethnosexual hegemonies, the racial, ethnic and national meanings that we know they embody are difficult to ignore. Even when we reach across ethnic boundaries, we remain part of an ethnosexual ideological, legal and social system that is seldom colour-blind, religion-blind, language-blind or nationality-blind. We may feel that our actions and decisions are our own, but they are imbued with meanings over which we have little control. Such is the power of sexuality as the performative bedrock upon which racial, ethnic and national boundaries rest and reproduce themselves. To ignore sexuality in the study of race, ethnicity and nationalism is to overlook one of the most durable and dangerous bricks in the walls that separate groups. Not to hear the sexual subtext of racism and nationalism is to be deaf to the powerful discourses deployed to justify discrimination, domination and genocide.

ACKNOWLEDGEMENTS

My thanks to Eve Clark, University of Kansas and the editors of this volume for their insightful and constructive feedback on an earlier version of this chapter; this research was supported, in part, by the Institute for Policy and Social Research, University of Kansas.

NOTES

1. I see race, ethnicity and nationalism as different faces of the same social phenomenon. Race tends to be based on colour differences, what David Hollinger (1994) calls the 'US racial pentagon': black, white, yellow, brown and red. Ethnicity tends to be based on language and/or religious and/or cultural differences (e.g., French vs. English speakers in Quebec, Malays vs. Chinese in Malaysia, Catholics vs. Protestants in Northern Ireland, Muslims vs. Christians in Nigeria). Nationalism is commonly viewed as a particular kind of ethnically based social identity or mobilisation generally involving claims to statehood or political autonomy, and most often rooted in assertions of cultural distinctiveness, a unique history and ethnic or racial purity (Connor, 1990; Hobsbawm, 1990; Smith, 1989). Cornell and Hartmann (1998) note the interrelatedness of race and ethnicity, but distinguish them in terms of power and choice: race is more likely to be an assigned attribute and ethnicity is more likely to be volitional. Power differentials are not restricted to racial boundaries, however, since much ethnic differentiation and conflict involve uneven power relations, and often in the absence of racial (colour) difference – for example, in Rwanda, Northern Ireland, and the former Yugoslavia in the 1990s (see Denitch, 1996; McGarry, 1995; Smith 1998). Although I often use 'race' and 'ethnicity' interchangeably, I acknowledge the preeminence of race both in US history and contemporary society.

2. By *ethnosexual*, I refer to the intersection and interaction between ethnicity and sexuality and the ways in which each defines and relies on the other for its meaning and power (see Nagel, 2003).

3. I define ethnic mobilisation as the organisation of groups along ethnic lines for collective action.

4. An ethnic group can be seen as 'new' or 'emergent' when ethnic identification, organisation, and collective action is constructed around previously nonexistent identities, such as 'Latino' or 'Asian-American'. An ethnic group can be seen as 'resurgent' when ethnic identification, organisation, or collective action is constructed around formerly quiescent historical identities, such as 'Basque' or 'Serbian' (see Yancey et al., 1976).

5. See Berger and Luckmann (1967) and Spector and Kitsuse (1977) for general discussions of the social constructionist model; see Holstein and Miller (1993) for a recent assessment of social constructionism.

6. For a discussion of the dialectical process whereby ethnic identities are negotiated, see Nagel (1996: Ch. 2).

7. Gieryn (1999) uses the idea of a 'cultural cartography' in his analysis of science and credibility.

8. For example, certain buildings and parts of buildings are defined as 'appropriate' sexual sites (private residences, bedrooms inside private residences, massage parlors, brothels, motels, hotels),

and that sex outside of these designated areas can be risky, illegal and exciting; similarly, time itself can be sexually mapped – when is sexual activity most likely, what are the conventions in any society about when should sex occur – at night, in the morning, in the afternoon, on weekends, during weekdays; should sexual activity and conformity be different during adolescence, young adulthood, middle age, old age?

9. *Phallocentric* refers to the emphasis on the penis (phallus) and penile penetration as the central pillar of sexuality in theory and practice. *Heteronormativity* refers to the assumption that everyone is heterosexual and the recognition that all social institutions (the family, religion, economy, political system) are built around a heterosexual model of male/female social relations.

10. By *hegemonic* I refer to both coercive and ideological domination. Coercive domination is easier to see; it refers to the actual use of power – in laws, courts, police, military to enforce specific rules for behaviour (who can marry whom, when, and where, who serves in military combat, who controls childbirth and child rearing). Ideological domination can be more or less subtle; it refers both to explicit propaganda or 'messages' contained in political discourse, commercial marketing or popular culture, as well as to popular beliefs that are so ingrained, so assumed, so unconsciously held that they are taken-for-granted, 'feel' right, seem 'natural'. Ideological domination shapes public opinion and epistemologies (ways of knowing and understanding the world) so powerfully that alternative ways of knowing become unthinkable, unimaginable or fail to 'resonate' with one's sense of what is intuitively 'true'. Hegemonic ideologies are hard to even think about; the alternatives seem so inconceivable. Revolutionary thought challenges hegemonies.

11. As Foucault (1978:43) writes:

> the psychological, psychiatric, medical category of homosexuality was constituted from the moment it was characterized—[Carl] Westphal's famous article of 1870 [*Archive fur Neurologie*] on 'contrary sexual sensations' can stand as its date of birth—less by a type of sexual relations than by a certain quality of sexual sensibility, a certain way of inverting the masculine and the feminine in oneself. Homosexuality appeared as one of the forms of sexuality when it was transposed from the practice of sodomy onto a kind of interior androgyny, a hermaphrodism of the soul. The sodomite had been a temporary aberration; the homosexual was now a species.

12. The early use of 'performativity' is attributed to linguist and philosopher J.L. Austin (1975), and is further developed in literary theory by Shoshana Felman (1983).

13. The production of ethnic, gender and sexual differences requires social and often political recognition, definition and reinforcement as well as individual and collective assertion and acceptance to become socially 'real'. Ethnic, gender and sexual identities, meanings, cultures and social divisions between ethnic groups, men and women, and heterosexuals and non-heterosexuals are social constructions, arising out of historical conditions, power relations and ongoing social processes (Hartsock, 1983; Ortner, 1972, 1996; MacKinnon, 1989; Scott, 1988).

14. As its 2000 publication date indicates, Johnson's book was written before the September 11, 2001 attacks on New York and Washington, but he does link the 1996 bombing of the Khobar Towers apartments in Saudi Arabia, an attack that has been attributed to the same perpetrators of the 2001 attacks, to the presence of US military in Saudi Arabia, a presence that was invited by the Saudi government in the early 1990s following Iraq's invasion of Kuwait, but which is resented by 'devoutly Muslim citizens of that kingdom [who] see [US] presence as a humiliation to the country and an affront to their religion' (p. 92); my thanks to Norm Yetman, American Studies, University of Kansas, for bringing this book to my attention.

15. The relatively high rate of outmarriage by American Indians is part of a historic trend towards exogamy among Native Americans; see Snipp (1989). Harris and Ono (2005) argue that racial imbalance in marriage markets shapes rates of intermarriage as much or more than do social distance norms governing race relations; their research (Harris and Ono, 2000) also shows that interracial cohabitation rates are considerably higher than intermarriage.

16. For instance, Lynn Thiesmeyer (1999: 81) argues that the imaginary construction of Asian women's sexuality is accomplished by 'discourses of seduction' in which the Asian female body is characterised by servile sexual availability. She argues that this longstanding, performative Western sexual stereotype of Asian women works to silence dissident discourses and mask inconvenient realities of Asian women's physical abuse, forced servitude and sexual exploitation both by Western

and non-Western men; see also, Chapkis (1986: 53–45). Lisa Lowe (1996: 178) argues that there is not a unified Euro-American ahistorical imagining of Asian women, rather there are similarities between regional and historical different 'orientalisms'.

REFERENCES

Allen, B. (1996) *Rape Warfare: The Hidden Genocide in Bosnia-Herzegovina and Croatia*. Minneapolis: University of Minnesota Press.
Anderson, M.J. and Feinberg, S.E. (1999) *Who Counts? The Politics of Census-Taking in Contemporary America*. New York: Russell Sage Foundation.
Austin, J.L. (1975) *How to Do Things with Words*. Cambridge, MA: Harvard University Press.
Bacevich, A. (2005) *The New American Militarism: How Americans Are Seduced by War*. New York: Oxford University Press.
Bakalian, A.P. (1993) *Armenian-Americans: From Being to Feeling Armenian*. New Brunswick (USA): Transaction Publishers.
Baron, D. (1990) *The English-only Question: An Official Language for Americans?* New Haven, CT: Yale University Press.
Barstow, A.L. (2000) *War's Dirty Secret: Rape, Prostitution, and Other Crimes against Women*. Cleveland: Pilgrim Press.
Barth, F. (1969) *Ethnic Groups and Boundaries*. Boston: Little, Brown and Company.
Beam, J. (1986) *In the Life: A Black Gay Anthology*. Boston: Alyson Publications.
Berger, P. L. and Luckmann, T. (1967) *The Social Construction of Reality: A Treatise in the Sociology of Knowledge*. London: Penguin Press.
Best, W.D. (2005) *Passionately Human, No Less Divine: Religion and Culture in Black Chicago*, 1915–1952. Princeton: Princeton University Press.
Bishop, R. and Robinson, L.S. (1998) *Night Market: Sexual Cultures and the Thai Economic Miracle*. New York: Routledge.
Bonilla-Silva, E. (2003) *Racism without Racists: Colour-Blind Racism and the Persistence of Racial Inequality in the United States*. Lanham, MD: Rowman and Littlefield.
Boyd, T. (1997) *Am I Black Enough For You? Popular Culture From the 'Hood and Beyond*. Bloomington: Indiana University Press.
British Broadcasting Company (BBC) (2008) 'Kosovo's MPs proclaim independence'. BBC News (Sunday, February 17). Accessed online at: http://news.bbc.co.uk/2/hi/europe/7249034.stm (February 26, 2008).
Brownmiller, S. (1975) *Against Our Will: Men, Women, and Rape*. New York: Bantam Books.
Brundage, W.F. (1993) *Lynching in the New South: Georgia and Virginia, 1880–1930*. Urbana: University of Illinois Press.
Butler, J. (1990) *Gender Trouble: Feminism and the Subversion of Identity*. New York: Routledge.
Caplan, R. (2005) *Europe and the Recognition of New States in Yugoslavia*. Cambridge: Cambridge University Press.
Carlson, M. (1998) *Performance: A Critical Introduction*. New York: Routledge.
Chapkis, W. (1986) *Beauty Secrets: Women and the Politics of Appearance*. Boston: South End Press.
Chateauvert, M. (2008) 'Framing Sexual Citizenship: Reconsidering the Discourse on African-American Families', *Journal of African American History*, 93 (2): 198–222.
Chateauvert, M. (2008) 'Introduction: Discourses on Race, Sex and African-American Citizenship', *Journal of African American History*, 93 (2): 149–152.
Childs, E.C. (2005) *Navigating Interracial Borders: Black-White Couples and Their Social Worlds*. New Brunswick, NJ: Rutgers University Press.
Chupa, A.M. (1990) *Anne, the White Woman in Contemporary African-American Fiction: Archetypes, Stereotypes, and Characterizations*. Westport, CT: Greenwood Press.

Clarity, J.E. (1997) 'Top Irish Court Lets Girl, 13, Have Abortion in England', *New York Times*, (December 2), A6–7.

Cleaver, E. (1968) *Soul on Ice*. New York: Dell Publishing Company.

Collins, P.H. (1990) *Black Feminist Thought: Knowledge, Consciousness, and the Politics of Empowerment*. New York: Routledge.

Collins, P.H. (2004) *Black Sexual Politics: African Americans, Gender, and the New Racism*. New York: Routledge.

Collins, P.H. (2006) *From Black Power to Hip-Hop: Racism, Nationalism, and Feminism*. Philadelphia: Temple University Press.

Connell, R.W. (1995) *Masculinities*. Berkeley: University of California Press.

Connor, W. (1990) 'When Is a Nation?', *Ethnic and Racial Studies*, 13 (1): 92–103.

Conrad, K. (2000) 'Domestic Queers: Home and Nation in Ireland'. Paper presented at the Hall Center for the Humanities, University of Kansas, Lawrence, Kansas.

Cornell, S. and Hartmann, D. (1998) *Ethnicity and Race: Making Identities in a Changing World*. Thousand Oaks, CA: Pine Forge Press.

Crenshaw, K., Gotanda, N., Peller, G. and Thomas, K. (1995) *Critical Race Theory: The Key Writings that Formed the Movement*. New York: New Press.

Daly, M.W. (2007) *Darfur's Sorrow: A History of Destruction and Genocide*. Cambridge; New York: Cambridge University Press.

Daniels, J. (1997) *White Lies: Race, Class, Gender, and Sexuality in White Supremacist Discourse*. New York: Routledge.

Davidson, J.O. (1998) *Prostitution, Power and Freedom*. Ann Arbor: University of Michigan Press.

Davis, J.F. (1991) *Who Is Black? One Nation's Definition*. University Park: Pennsylvania State University.

Denitch, B.D. (1996) *Ethnic Nationalism: The Tragic Death of Yugoslavia*. Minneapolis: University of Minnesota Press.

Elias, J. (2008) 'Introduction: Hegemonic Masculinities in International Politics', *Men and Masculinities*, 10 (3): 383–388.

Enloe, C. (2000) *Maneuvers: The International Politics of Militarizing Women's Lives*. Berkeley: University of California Press.

Espiritu, Y.L. (1997) *Asian American Men and Women: Labor, Laws, and Love*. Thousand Oaks, CA: Sage Publications.

Fanon, F. (1968) *Black Skin, White Masks*. New York: Grove Press.

Feagin, J. (2006) *Systemic Racism: A Theory of Oppression*. New York: Routledge.

Felman, S. (1983) *The Literary Speech Act: Don Juan with J.L. Austin, or Seduction in Two Languages*. Ithaca, NY: Cornell University Press.

Ferber, A.L. (1998) *White Man Falling: Race, Gender, and White Supremacy*. Lanham, MD: Rowman and Littlefield.

Foucault, M. (1978) *The History of Sexuality*. New York: Pantheon Books.

Fuss, D. (1989) *Essentially Speaking: Feminism, Nature, and Difference*. New York: Routledge.

Gagnon, J. and Simon, W. (1973) *Sexual Conduct: The Social Sources of Human Sexuality*. Chicago: Aldine.

Gehmacher, J. (1998) 'Men, Women, and the Community Borders: German-Nationalist and National Socialist Discourses on Gender, "Race," and National Identity in Austria, 1918–1938' in R.R. Pierson and N. Chaudhuri (eds), *Nation, Empire, Colony: Historicizing Gender and Race*. Bloomington: Indiana University Press. pp. 205–219.

Gieryn, T.F. (1999) *Cultural Boundaries of Science: Credibility on the Line*. Chicago: University of Chicago Press.

Goffman, E. (1959) *The Presentation of Self in Everyday Life*. New York: Doubleday.

Haaland, G. (1969) 'Economic Determinants in Ethnic Processes' in F. Barth (ed.), *Ethnic Groups and Boundaries*. Boston: Little, Brown and Company. pp. 58–74.

Halberstam, J. (1998) *Female Masculinity*. Durham, NC: Duke University Press.

Hansberry, L. (1970) *To Be Young, Gifted, and Black*. New York: Signet.

Hardin, M. (2002) 'Altering Masculinities: The Spanish Conquest and the Evolution of the Latin American Machismo', *International Journal of Sexuality and Gender Studies*, 7 (1): 1–22.

Harris, D.R. and Ono, H. (2000) 'Estimating the Extent of Intimate Contact between the Races: The Role of Metropolitan Area Factors and Union Type in Mate Selection'. Annual meeting of the Population Association of America, Los Angeles.

Harris, D.R. and Ono, H. (2005) 'How Many Interracial Marriages Would There Be if All Groups Were of Equal Size in All Places? A New Look at National Estimates of Interracial Marriage', *Social Science Research*, 34: 236–251.

Hartsock, N. (1983) *Money, Sex, and Power: Toward a Feminist Historical Materialism*. New York: Longman.

Hemphill E. (1991) *Brother to Brother: New Writings by Gay Black Men*. Boston: Alyson.

Henson, M.R. (1999) *A Filipina Woman's Story of Prostitution and Slavery under the Japanese Military*. Lanham, MD: Rowman and Littlefield.

Hicks, G.L. (1995) *The Comfort Women: Japan's Brutal Regime of Enforced Prostitution in the Second World War*. New York: W.W. Norton and Company.

Hill, R. (2008) 'Interval, Sexual Difference: Luce Irigaray and Henri Bergson', *Hypatia*, 23 (1): 119–131.

Hine, D.C. (1997) 'Rape and the Inner Lives of Black Women in the Middle West: Preliminary Thoughts on the Culture of Dissemblance', in R.N. Lancaster and M. di Leonardo (eds), *The Gender/Sexuality Reader: Culture, History, and Political Economy*. New York: Routledge. pp. 434–439.

Hobsbawm, E. (1990) *Nations and Nationalism Since 1780: Programme, Myth, Reality*. Cambridge: Cambridge University Press.

Hodes, M. (1997) *White Women, Black Men: Illicit Sex in the Nineteenth-century South*. New Haven, CT: Yale University Press.

Hollinger, R. (1994) *Postmodernism and the Social Sciences: A Thematic Approach*. Thousand Oaks, CA: Sage.

Hooks, B. (1992) *Black Looks: Race and Representation*. Boston: South End Press.

Holstein, J. and Miller, G. (1993) *Constructionist Controversies: Issues in Social Problems*. New York: Aldine de Gruyter.

Hubbard, P., Matthews, R., Scoular, J. and Agustin, L. (2008) 'Away from Prying Eyes? The Urban Geographies of "Adult Entertainment"', *Progress in Human Geography*, 32 (2): 363–381.

Humphreys, L. (1970) *Tearoom Trade: Impersonal Sex in Public Places*. Somerset, NJ: Aldine Transaction.

Hunt, K. and K. Rygiel (2006) *(En)gendering the War on Terror: War Stories and Camouflaged Politics*. Aldershot, England and Burlington, VT: Ashgate.

Ignacio, E. (2005) *Building Diaspora: Filipino Cultural Community Formation on the Internet*. New Brunswick, NJ: Rutgers University Press.

Ingraham C. (1996) 'The Heterosexual Imaginary: Feminist Sociology and Theories of Gender' in S. Seidman (ed.) *Queer Theory/Sociology*. New York: Blackwell. pp. 168–193.

Johnson, Chalmers (2000). *Blowback: The Costs and Consequences of American Empire*, New York: Henry Holt.

Jones-Yelvington. T. (2008) 'A Half-Dozen Things That We Are: Collective Identity in Intersectional LGBT/Queer Social Movement Organizations: Part I', *Theory in Action*, 1 (1): 23–47.

Jones-Yelvington. T. (2008) 'A Half-Dozen Things That We Are: Collective Identity in Intersectional LGBT/Queer Social Movement Organizations: Part II', *Theory in Action*, 2 (2): 83–105.

Johnson, C. (2000) *Blowback: The Costs and Consequences of American Empire*. New York: Henry Holt.

Johnson, C.A. (2004) *Blowback: The Costs and Consequences of American Empire*. New York: Henry Holt.

Johnson, P. (2005) *Love, Heterosexuality and Society*. New York: Routledge.

Joyner, K. and Kao, G. (2005) 'Interracial Relationships and the Transition to Adulthood', *American Sociological Review*, 70 (3): 563–581.

Julien, I. (1992). *Looking for Langston.* New York: Waterbearer Films.

Katz, J.N. (1995) *The Invention of Heterosexuality.* New York: Dutton.

Kelly. M. (2000) 'Ethnic Pilgrimages: People of Lithuanian Descent in Lithuania', *Sociological Spectrum*, 20 (1): 65–92.

Kempadoo, K. and Doezema, J. (1999) *Global Sex Workers: Rights, Resistance, and Redefinition.* New York: Routledge.

Keyso, R.A. (2000) Women of Okinawa: Nine Voices from a Garrison Island. Ithaca, NY: Cornell University Press.

Khalili, L. (2008) 'Monstering: Inside America's Policy of Secret Interrogations and Torture in the Terror War and One of the Guys: Women as Aggressors and Torturers', *Feminist Review*, 88 (2): 164–167.

Kinsey, A.C., Pomeroy, W.B., Martin, C.E. and Gebhard, P.H. (1948) *Sexual Behavior in the Human Male.* Philadelphia: W.B. Saunders.

Kinsey, A.C., Pomeroy, W.B., Martin, C.E. and Gebhard, P.H. (1953) *Sexual Behavior in the Human Female.* Philadelphia: W.B. Saunders.

Laumann, E.O., Ellingson, S., Mahay, J., Paik, A. and Yim, Y. (eds) (2004) *The Sexual Organization of the City.* Chicago: University of Chicago Press.

Laumann, E.O., Gagnon, J.H., Michael, R.T. and Michaels, S. (1994) *The Social Organization of Sexuality: Sexual Practices in the United States.* Chicago: University of Chicago Press.

Lawson, J.E. (1991) '"She's a Pretty Woman ... for a Gook": The Misogyny of the Vietnam War' in P.K. Jason (ed.), *Fourteen Landing Zones: Approaches to the Literature of the Vietnam War.* Iowa City: University of Iowa Press. pp. 15–37.

Lemann, N. (1991) *The Promised Land: The Great Black Migration and How It Changed America.* New York: A.A. Knopf.

Lorber, J. (1994) *Paradoxes of Gender.* New Haven, CT: Yale University Press.

Lorde, A. (1984) *Sister Outsider: Essays and Speeches.* Trumansburg, NY: Crossing Press.

Lorde, A. (1985) *I Am Your Sister: Black Women Organizing across Sexualities.* Latham, NY: Kitchen Table, Women of Colour Press.

Loveman, M. and Muniz, J.O. (2007) 'How Puerto Rico Became White: Boundary Dynamics and Intercensus Racial Reclassification', *American Sociological Review*, 72 (6): 915–939.

Lowe, L. (1996) *Immigrant Acts: On Asian American Cultural Politics.* Durham, NC: Duke University Press.

McGarry, J. (2001) *Northern Ireland and The Divided World: The Northern Ireland Conflict and The Good Friday Agreement in Comparative Perspective.* Oxford: Oxford University Press, 2001.

MacKinnon, C. (1989) *Toward a Feminist Theory of the State.* Cambridge, MA: Harvard University Press.

Manderson, L. and Jolly, M. (1997) *Sites of Desire, Economies of Pleasure: Sexualities in Asia and the Pacific.* Chicago: University of Chicago Press.

Margulies, J. (2006) *Guantanamo and the Abuse of Presidential Power.* New York: Simon and Schuster.

Marinetti, F.T. (1994) *Democrazia Futurista in the Untameables.* Trans. Jeremy Parzen. Los Angeles: Sun and Moon Press.

Mascarenhas, A. (1986) *Bangladesh: A Legacy of Blood.* London: Hodder and Stoughton.

Massad, J. A. (2007) *Desiring Arabs.* Chicago: University of Chicago Press.

Massey, D.S. and Denton, N.A. (1993) *American Apartheid: Segregation and the Making of the Underclass.* Cambridge, MA: Harvard University Press.

Masters, W. and Johnson, V. (1966) *Human Sexual Response.* Boston: Little, Brown.

Masters, W. and Johnson, V. (1970) *Human Sexual Inadequacy.* Boston: Little, Brown.

Michael, R.T., Gagnon, J.H., Laumann, E.O. and Kolata, G. (1994) *Sex in America: A Definitive Survey.* Boston: Little, Brown.

Moeller, R.G. (1993) *Protecting Motherhood: Women and the Family in the Politics of Postwar West Germany*. Berkeley: University of California Press.

Moraga, C. (1983) *Loving in the War Years: Lo que nunca pasó por sus labios*. Boston: South End Press.

Moraga, C. (1997) *Waiting in the Wings: Portrait of a Queer Motherhood*. Ithaca, NY: Firebrand Books.

Morris, A. (1984) *The Origins of the Civil Rights Movement*. New York: The Free Press.

Mosse, G.L. (1985) *Nationalism and Sexuality: Middle Class Morality and Sexual Norms in Modern Europe*. Madison: University of Wisconsin Press.

Munn, J. (2008) 'The Hegemonic Male and Kosovar Nationalism, 2000–2005', *Men and Masculinities*, 10 (3): 440–456.

Nagel, Joane (1996) *American Indian Ethnic Renewal: Red Power and the Resurgence of Identity and Culture*. New York: Oxford University Press.

Nagel, J. (2003) *Race, Ethnicity, and Sexuality: Intimate Intersections, Forbidden Frontiers*. New York: Oxford University Press.

Nero, C.I. (1991) 'Toward a Black Gay Aesthetic: Signifying in Contemporary Black Gay Literature' in E. Hemphill (ed.), *Brother to Brother: New Writings by Gay Black Men*. Boston: Alyson Publications. pp. 229–252.

Nielsen, E.S. (2008) 'Ethnic Boundaries and Conflict in Darfur: An Event Structure Hypothesis', *Ethnicity*, 8 (4): 427–462.

Ortner, S. (1972) 'Is Female to Male as Nature Is to Culture?', *Feminist Studies*, 1 (1): 5–31.

Ortner, S. (1996) *Making Gender: The Politics and Erotics of Culture*. Boston: Beacon Press.

Page, C. (1996) *Showing My Colour: Impolite Essays on Race and Identity*. New York: Harper.

Parrenas, R. (2001) *Servants of Globalization: Women, Migration and Domestic Work*. Stanford, CA: Stanford University Press.

Parrenas, R. (2005) *Children of Global Migration: Transnational Families and Gendered Woes*. Stanford, CA: Stanford University Press.

Paxton, N.L. (1992) 'Mobilizing Chivalry: Rape in British Novels about the Indian Uprising of 1857', *Victorian Studies*, 36 (1): 5–30.

Pedraza, S. (2007) *Political Disaffection in Cuba's Revolution and Exodus*. New York: Cambridge University Press.

Phelan, P. (1993) *Unmarked: The Politics of Performance*. New York: Routledge.

Phelan, P. and Lane, J. (1998) *The Ends of Performance*. New York: New York University Press.

Portes, A. and Rumbaut, R.G. (2001) *Legacies: The Stories of the Immigrant Second Generation*. Berkeley: University of California Press.

Prugl, E. (1999) *The Global Construction of Gender: Home-Based Work in the Political Economy of the 20th Century*. New York: Columbia University Press.

Prunier, G. (2005) *Darfur: The Ambiguous Genocide*. Ithaca, NY: Cornell University Press.

Qian, Z. and Cobas, J.A. (2004) 'Latinos' Mate Selection: National Origin, Racial, and Nativity Differences', *Social Science Research*, 33 (2): 225–247.

Ramet, S.P. (1996) *Gender Reversals and Gender Cultures: Anthropological and Historical Perspectives*. New York: Routledge.

Reid-Pharr, R.F. (2001) *Black Gay Man: Essays*. New York: New York University Press.

Reiss, Jr., A.J. (1961) 'The Social Integration of Peers and Queers', *Social Problems*, 9 (1): 102–120.

Rich, A. (1980) 'Compulsory Heterosexuality and Lesbian Existence', *Signs*, 5: 631–660.

Richard, A.O. (1999) *International Trafficking in Women to the United States: A Contemporary Manifestation of Slavery and Organized Crime*. Central Intelligence Agency, Center for the Study of Intelligence. Washington, DC: Government Printing Office.

Roach, J. (1996) *Cities of the Dead: Circum-Atlantic Performance*. New York: Columbia University Press.

Roy, T. (1994) *The Politics of a Popular Uprising: Bundelkhand in 1857*. New Delhi: Oxford University Press.

Rubin, G. (1975) 'The traffic in women: Notes on the "political economy" of sex' in R.R. Reiter (ed.), *Toward an Anthropology of Women*. New York: Monthly Review Press. pp. 157–210.

Salvador Vidal-Ortiz, (2008) 'Transgender and Transsexual Studies: Sociology's Influence and Future Steps', *Sociology Compass*, 2 (2): 433–450.

Sanders, D. (1996) 'Getting Lesbian and Gay Issues on the International Human Rights Agenda', *Human Rights Quarterly*, 18 (1): 67–106.

Scott, J. (1988) *Gender and the Politics of History*. New York: Columbia University Press.

Seidman, S. (2003) *The Construction of Sexuality*. Albany: State University of New York Press.

Shen, H.H. (2003) 'Crossing the Taiwan Strait: Global Disjunctures and Multiple Hegemonies of Class, Politics, Gender, and Sexuality'. Unpublished PhD dissertation, University of Kansas, Lawrence, Kansas.

Shen, H.H. (2005) '"The First Taiwanese Wives" and "the Chinese Mistresses:" The International Division of Labour in Familial and Intimate Relations across the Taiwan Strait', *Global Networks*, 5 (4): 419–437.

Shih, S.M. (1998) 'Gender and a New Geopolitics of Desire: The Seduction of Mainland Women in Taiwan and Hong Kong Media', *Signs: Journal of Women in Culture and Society*, 23 (2): 287–319.

Skrobanek, S., Boonpakdee, N. and Jantateero, C. (1997) *The Traffic in Women: Human Realities of the International Sex Trade*. London: Zed Books.

Smith, A. (1989) *The Great Rift: Africa's Changing Valley*. New York: Sterling Publishing Company.

Smith, D.N. (1998) 'The Psychocultural Roots of Genocide: Legitimacy and Crisis in Rwanda', *American Psychologist*, 53 (7): 743–753.

Snipp, C.M. (1989) *American Indians: The First of This Land*. New York: Russell Sage Foundation.

Spackman, B. (1996) *Fascist Virilities: Rhetoric, Ideology, and Social Fantasy in Italy*. Minneapolis: University of Minnesota Press.

Spector, M. and Kitsuse, J. (1977) *Constructing Social Problems*. Hawthorne, NY: Aldine de Gruyter.

Spickard, P.R. (1989) *Mixed Blood: Intermarriage and Ethnic Identity in Twentieth-Century America*. Madison: University of Wisconsin Press.

Stepick, A., Grenier, G., Castro, M. and Dunn, M. (2003) *This Land Is Our Land: Power and Interethnic Relations in Miami*. Berkeley: University of California Press.

Stiglmayer, A. (1994) *Mass Rape: The War against Women in Bosnia-Herzegovina*. Lincoln: University of Nebraska Press.

Stoler, A.L. (1990) 'Making Empire Respectable: The Politics of Race and Sexual Morality in 20th Century Colonial Cultures' in J. Breman, (ed.), *Imperial Monkey Business: Racial Supremacy in Social Darwinist Theory and Colonial Practice*. Amsterdam: Vu University Press. pp. 35–70.

Stoler, A.L. (1992) 'Sexual Affronts and Racial Frontiers: European Identities and the Cultural Politics of Exclusion in Colonial Southeast Asia', *Comparative Study of Society and History*, 24 (2): 514–551.

Stoler, A.L. (2002) *Carnal Knowledge and Imperial Power: Race and the Intimate in Colonial Rule*. Berkeley: University of California Press.

Stychin, C.F. (1998) *A Nation by Rights: National Cultures, Sexual Identity, Politics, and the Discourse of Rights*. Philadelphia: Temple University Press.

Swain, C.M. (2002) *The New White Nationalism in America: Its Challenge to Integration*. New York: Cambridge University Press.

Thiesmeyer, L. (1999) 'The West's "Comfort Women" and the Discourses of Seduction' in S.G. Lim, L.E. Smith, and W. Dissanayake, (eds), *Transnational Asia Pacific: Gender, Culture, and the Public Sphere*. Urbana: University of Illinois Press. pp. 69–92.

Thorbeck, S. and Pattanaik, B. (2002) *Transnational Prostitution: Changing Patterns in a Global Context*. London: Zed Books.

Ticktin, M. (2008) 'Sexual Violence as the Language of Border Control: Where French Feminist and Anti-Immigrant Rhetoric Meet', *Signs*, 33 (6): 863–889.

Tolnay, S.E. and Beck, E.M. (1995) *A Festival of Violence: An Analysis of Southern Lynchings, 1882–1930*. Urbana: University of Illinois Press.

Trumbach, R. (1991) 'Sex, Gender, and Sexual Identity in Modern Culture: Male Sodomy and Female Prostitution in Enlightenment London', *Journal of the History of Sexuality*, 2 (3): 186–203.

United Nations (2006) 'Growth in United Nations Membership, 1945–2006'. Accessed online at: http://www.un.org/Overview/growth.htm (July 31, 2006).

US Census Bureau (1998) 'Race by wife by race of husband: 1960, 1970, 1980, 1991, and 1992 (6/10/98)'. Accessed online at: http://www.census.gov/population/socdemo/race/interractab1.txt) (March 30, 2002).

US Census Bureau (2001) 'America's Families and Living Arrangements', March 2000 (June 29, 2001), Table FG3: Married Couple Family Groups, by Presence of Own Children Under 18, and Age, Earnings, Education, and Race and Hispanic Origin of Both Spouses: March 2000. Accessed online at: http://www.census.gov/population/socdemo/hh-fam/p20-537/2000/tabFG3.txt (March 30, 2002).

Vidal-Ortiz, S. (2008) 'Transgender and Transsexual Studies: Sociology's Influence and Future Steps', *Sociology Compass*, 2 (2): 433–450.

Ward, A. (1996) *Our Bones Are Scattered: The Cawnpore Massacre and the Indian Mutiny of 1857.* New York: H. Holt and Company.

Waters, M.C. (1990) *Ethnic Options: Choosing Identities in America.* Berkeley: University of California Press.

Warner, M. (1993) *Fear of a Queer Planet: Queer Politics and Social Theory.* Minneapolis: University of Minnesota Press.

Watanabe, K. (1995) 'Trafficking in Women's Bodies, Then and Now: The Issue of Military Comfort Women', *Peace and Change*, 20 (1): 501–514.

Williams, K. (2006) *American Methods: Torture and the Logic of Domination.* Boston: South End Press.

Williams, P. (1999) *Illegal Immigration and Commercial Sex: The New Slave Trade.* London: Frank Cass.

Wilson, W. J. (1987) *The Truly Disadvantaged: The Inner City, the Underclass, and Public Policy.* Chicago: University of Chicago Press.

Yancey, W. Erickson, E., and Juliani, R. (1976) 'Emergent Ethnicity: A Review and Reformulation', *American Sociological Review*, 41 (3): 391–403.

Nation and Post-Nation: Nationalism, Transnationalism and Intersections of Belonging

Floya Anthias

INTRODUCTION

In what has often been referred to as the post-September 11th and post-July 7th world and in the aftermath of the Iraq war, we have seen terror, violence and the dehumanisation of categories of people on the basis of colour, class and faith growing to a terrifying extent. From the point of view of academic and political debate, these developments have reinforced the recognition that forms of violence based on ethnic, religious and national group boundaries share many characteristics. Boundaries of 'nation', and the related ones of ethnicity and racialisation, are as important today as they ever were, despite the growing complexity of forms of otherness we find in our globalising world. However, a critique of methodological nationalism (Beck, 2002; Wimmer and Glick Schiller, 2002) has evolved to show the problems of 'naturalising' the nation and seeing it as the main analytical category for exploring a range of inter-related issues in modern society around boundaries and hierarchies of belonging. This position also mirrors developments in more intersectional forms of social analysis (e.g., see Collins, 1993, 1998; Anthias and Yuval Davis, 1983, 1992; Anthias, 1998a, 2005), calling for a new paradigm for understanding social boundaries and divisions.

In this chapter I will examine the concept of nation within the context of a range of other boundary-making processes such as 'race' and gender boundaries.

I will look at the connections between nation and racism and then look at various challenges to the nation state, focusing on debates on multiculturalism, diaspora, hybridity and cosmopolitanism. I will then look at how nation and gender may be related, and provide a critical reflection on the uses of an intersectional lens for understanding boundary formations.

CONCEPTS OF THE NATION

There are many different definitions of nation and it is not my intention to review them here. Rather, I want to point to some central areas of debate.

The view that nations pre-existed states, and that they are the basis of state formation, has been a central plank in the literature. This is found in a range of positions, ranging from those of primordialists (like Van den Berge, 1979) to those of ethnicists (like, for example, Smith, 1986; Connor, 1994), as well as being found in some of the ideas of Stalin (1929/1976) in constructing historical versus non-historical nations. Much discussion of 'nation' has been premised on the assumption of a generic right to territory and political representation by a people constructed as sharing a pre-given cultural or historical commonality. There is also a view that citizenship in a political community would, or indeed should, coincide.

It is not possible to discuss nations without discussing nationalism inasmuch as nation formation is part of a political project entailing the consolidation of political rule by the incipient 'nation' over a given territory. Gellner (1983: 36) has defined nationalism as: 'a theory of political legitimacy which requires that ethnic boundaries should not cut across political ones, and in particular, that ethnic boundaries within a given state...should not separate the power holders from the rest ... and therefore state and culture must now be linked'.

However, not only has this never been fully achieved but increasing movements of population in the modern era have made this achievement more or less impossible. There is an ongoing discourse and practice around 'who' has the right to enter and stay within a nation-state. This is usually premised on criteria such as possessing the right attributes of birth, descent, religion or culture (or a mixture), or in terms of being adopted as having the equivalent to these through a process of deracination and reracination, or acculturation and adaptation. Such a process demands that minorities without entitlements to national belonging are also excluded from full citizenship. They are assumed to lie outside the 'normal' boundaries of the nation, thereby being excluded, or their participation as full members of society being delimited.

Currently, much has happened to make indentations, indeed serious indentations, in the hegemony of the nation-state paradigm as a form of political and cultural entity. This includes the development of transnational phenomena such as the European Union (EU) and the European Court of Human Rights, as well as increasing international co-operation. The big blocs of West and Soviet power have arguably given way to new blocs around the West and 'the rest'. The 'rest' is not only the developing world but increasingly being identified as the 'Muslim world'; in this, threats to national or Western security are seen as central. There is also the emergence of the economic giants of China and India as forces in their own right.

Rampant globalisation, on a range of scales and types, forges ahead to make 'the national' increasingly a small cog in a larger machine. And yet the power of national ideologies and practices, and the local and vernacular attachments and cultural solidarities that underpin them, as well as at times undermining them, are continuing forces in the world. Anti-racist struggles of different types, the growth of multiculturalist and other discourses and practices that recognise diversity, as well as increasing hybridisation and transnational relations, have to be seen in the context of the continuing importance, situationally, of the national paradigm and the nation-state form. This is also manifested in what some have called methodological nationalism (Beck, 2002; Wimmer and Glick-Schiller, 2002).

The equation of nation with state is an important issue in relation to the nation-state form in the modern era. Although this chapter is not concerned with theorising the state, it is important to note that tendencies in state theory have worked in two directions. First, the concept of the state has been expanded to include all major ideological and organisational elements in a society, such as schools, the family and social policy provisions (an early account is the classical structuralist Marxist position found in Althusser, 1971 and Poulantzas, 1978). Second, the state has been seen as the place where a constellation of effects take place (see Jessop, 1982). In 1989, Nira Yuval Davis and I defined the state as a body of institutions that are centrally organised around the intentionality of control, with a given apparatus of enforcement as its basis. Different forms of the state involve different relationships between the coercion/control twin which is the residing characteristic of the state. A range of forces, ideological, juridical and repressive among others, may be used by the state in this process. The control of forms of violence, particularly through the military and legal apparatus, underpins state, and indeed nation-state power, in the modern world. Education and the media are also prime institutional forms for ideological production in the modern liberal democratic state, but it is not useful to treat them as identical with the state (such a position treats the state as all too encompassing and it thereby becomes synonymous, by default, with society). The state is also characterised by nationalist and ethnic projects of dominant ethnic and class elites and the coincidence between them, as well as those of gender, despite ideologies and practices of diversity, plurality and gender-sensitive projects.

There has been much written on what constitutes a nation, and the extent to which it is a particularly modern, or even Western phenomenon. On the one side lie the so-called primordialists (Shils, 1957; Van den Berghe, 1979) that regard nations as natural and universal manifestations of social organisation or as flowing from bonds of kinship. On the other side are 'the modernists', who see

nationalism and nations arising out of the development of modernity and particularly the growth of capitalism (Althusser, 1969; Hobsbaum, 1990). Marxists
who share the modernist paradigm have developed a range of approaches. For
example, Otto Bauer (1907/2000), Samir Amin (1978) and Tom Nairn (1977),
regard nationalism and nations as social, rather than 'natural', phenomena, but
not necessarily as products of capitalism. Samir Amin, for example, understands
the growth of the nation as a result of a strong state bureaucracy, and claims that
'a nation' was present in pre-modern societies with strong centralised states (like
ancient Egypt).

'Modernist' approaches include those of Anderson (1983) and Gellner (1983)
who regard nations as a product of social developments from eighteenth-century
Europe onwards. Nationalism, for Anderson, was fostered through the discovery
and use of print technology which revolutionised communication and spread cultural forms, leading to the forging of what he calls, famously, 'imagined communities' (Anderson, 1983). Gellner (1983) provides a more functionalist version,
seeing the development of nationalism as a product of societal needs for cultural
homogeneity, with the culturally excluded seeking to form their own national
state forms. While Marxists and others give importance to the role of state
bureaucracy, elites or to capitalism, these theorists of nationalism focus on the
role of intellectuals in the creation and reproduction of nationalist ideologies.
Collective sentiments, traditions and memories are used by intellectuals to promote a glorious historical past of culture, thus fuelling calls for entitlement to
separate state formations on this basis.

On the other hand, Anthony Smith (1986) is concerned with the 'ethnic origins
of nations', arguing that while the nation-state is a modern phenomenon, it incorporates premodern ethnie (1986: 18). The particularity of ethnie is found in a
'myth/symbol complex' rather than in more structural features. This is disputed
by Sami Zubaida (1989) who agrees with the view that ethnicities are durable,
but believes that this is precisely because they are a product of their social, economic and political contexts. He argues that ethnic homogeneity is a product of
pre-modern centralised governments and 'was not given but was achieved precisely by the political processes which facilitated centralization' (1989: 13).

Some of these ideas are reiterated and developed in a range of other work. For
example, Walker Connor (1994) sees states and nations as separate phenomena.
His work also argues against the distinction between ethnic and civic nationalisms. Indeed, he treats nationalism *per se* as always linked to ethnic formations
(echoing Smith) and argues that the tendency towards ethnic solidary formation
increases rather than reduces over time.

Paul Brass (1991), on the other hand, is concerned to argue a strong link
between state actions and projects and the political emergence of both ethnic and
national categories and politics. Unlike Walker Connor, these are not treated as
generic phenomena, but as socially and politically constructed. He develops an
approach that treats ethnicity and nationalism as outcomes of particular kinds of

relationships amongst powerful elites within dominant and non-dominant groups within the state.

Rogers Brubaker (1996) tries to differentiate between different forms of nationalism and points to the complex and diverse progenies and outcomes involved between political state formations and nationalist projects. He is concerned with the reframing of nationalism which is treated therefore as a diverse range of '"nation"-oriented idioms, practices, and possibilities that are continuously available or "endemic" in modem cultural and political life' (p. 10). He suggests that the idioms and claims of 'nation' are used heterogeneously in terms of different political projects.

In Anthias and Yuval Davis (1992), it is argued that it is difficult to disentangle nation and ethnicity as they are part of a complex relating to boundaries around collectivities which are seen to share an inalienable origin around stock, culture or territory. The specificity of the 'national' within this complex of discourses and practices lies in the claim made for a separate political representation for the 'group', which usually means a separate territorial presence and a separate state. However, like Brubaker, the emphasis is on the deployment of particular narratives and idioms which essentially function as political tools, thereby emphasising the political dynamics of both ethnic and national phenomena (see also Cohen, 1974; Hechter, 1987).

Such a position is far removed from an earlier discourse, worth noting here, about real 'nations' who should have rights to their own states, and false ones who shouldn't. How is a claim to separate political representation or separate territory to be judged? Who should be given the right to self-determination? Marx and Engels argued for the existence of 'historical nations' (which had the right) and 'history-less' nations which didn't. Lenin, on the other hand used much less historicist ideas, relying on the nature of the claims in relation to struggle against oppression. Those who were fighting against their oppression by others should be supported by socialists, (Lenin, 1913/1972). Stalin made a distinction between proletarian nations and bourgeois nations (1929/1976) but nonetheless had a culturalist version of national entitlement relating to the existence of 'a community of culture'.

Indeed, ideas of common culture and common fate are found in the work of some theorists (e.g., Bauer, 1907/2000) relating to the future as well as the past. A vision of the future as a collective future links to ideas of common experience and has been picked up by others, such as Stuart Hall (1990), in theorising common struggles around ethnic or racial categories. The idea of 'common solidarity', is also found in the work of Renan (1882) who states:

> A nation is therefore a large-scale solidarity, constituted by the feeling of the sacrifices that one has made in the past and of those that one is prepared to make in the future. It presupposes a past; it is summarized, however, in the present by a tangible fact, namely, consent, the clearly expressed desire to continue a common life. A nation's existence is, if you will pardon the metaphor, a daily plebiscite, just as an individual's existence is a perpetual affirmation of life.

Martha Nussbaum (1998) treats ethnic and national categories as part of a range of social forms which structure community and solidarity, rather than prime ones. Her view is that we should see ourselves as part of circles which include the family, the locality, the region, the nation and the world. These are circles which define us and which we operate within. Moreover the emphasis on humanity in her work treats patriotic zeal as dangerous and indeed contradictory in terms of some of the worthier goals of patriotism, that is, as counterproductive because the tendency is to create divisive communities. She espouses a cosmopolitan imagery as opposed to a nationalist one and argues for education into cosmopolitan values (which we shall turn to later on in this chapter).

One of the primary aspects of national categories is the setting up of boundaries between those who can have and those who are excluded from national belonging and the next section will turn to this important issue with reference to the issue of racialisation.

WHO BELONGS TO THE NATION?: PROCESSES OF RACIALISATION

A classic distinction has been made between national belonging defined by *culture* and national belonging being defined by *state* membership or nationality/citizenship. This, broadly speaking, is a distinction between a sociological membership and a *juridico* legal one. An assumption in Eurocentric theory is that there is an identification and overlap, as stated earlier, between culture (language, values and, at times, religion) and state membership or nationality. With regard to the latter, the question of *who* is entitled to state membership may depend classically on one of two criteria: those of origin and assimilation, culturally and structurally, with the polity (seen as the embodiment of the dominant ethnic group). An example of this difference is found in the German concern with 'volk', a people united by supposed origin and blood relations reincarnated as a cultural and political community, and the French conception of the importance of assimilation and integration with the political community.

Many writers on Europe have connected the rise of nationalism with new forms of racism. The 'new racism' (classically noted by Barker, 1981) was regarded as characterised by the use of notions of cultural difference rather than those of biological inferiority to justify exclusion from citizenship. Ideas about immigrants or asylum holders constituting a national threat is not new and range from Margaret Thatcher's 'fears of being swamped' to more subtle notions (see Solomos, 1989). For example, these are concerned with fears for the English national culture from immigrants and minorities, a national culture whose claims rest on being the core of the 'real' British nation. More recently, there have been political initiatives in Britain relating to the importance of migrants being taught and accepting 'British' values of democracy and so on, thereby giving an inferior value to those who cannot claim to be 'British', particularly non-European and Muslim groups in Britain (see *Ethnic and Racial Studies*, special issue 2005).

Of course, the discussion here depends very much on how racism is defined. For some writers (e.g., Banton, 1983), racism involves hierarchical racial typologies which specify generic biological differences. Other writers argue that racism occurs when racial categories are imbued with negative meaning (Miles, 1993). Racism, however, is not dependent always on explicit racial typologies. The ideologies and practices that migrant ethnic groups, refugees and so on are subjected to construct them as inferior, but not always on the premise of a supposed racial categorisation, but as cultural, political or national outsiders and undesirables. However, it is possible to go even further – notwithstanding the dangers of over-inflation of the concept (see Mason, 1994; Jenkins, 1994) – and define racism as a set of discourses and practices that inferiorise, subordinate and lead to outcomes relating to exclusionary group boundaries and hierarchies (Anthias and Yuval Davis, 1992; Anthias, 1992).

There is increasing recognition that there can be no definitive definition of racism as it comes in many forms. Although racisms as forms of discourse come in different guises, they are underpinned by a notion of a natural relation between an essence attributed to a human population, whether biological or cultural, and social outcomes that do, will or should flow from this. There is a large range of repertoires from which racism can draw, including those of ethnicity. Racism is opportunistic, it is relational to other social processes and it is therefore a fluid and shifting phenomenon which evades clear and absolute definition in a once and for all type of way. Moreover, racism as a discourse and racism as a practice do not always go together; it is possible to behave in ways which have racist outcomes without necessarily using an explicitly racist discourse. Racist ideas may not necessarily be accompanied by race hatred or race violence, although such practices generally are bolstered by such ideas. Alternatively, racist ideas become emergent in new ways through practices, that is, through enactment and response.

In the context of the growth of Islamophobia in Europe, on the one hand, and anti-asylum forms of exclusion and disadvantage on the other, there is a question mark about the continuing importance of 'race' markers. However, I think we can be too quick to dismiss them, for race markers constitute only one of a variety of situational and local contexts for the mobilisation of 'othering' and exclusionary group boundaries. Local particularities and identities, ethnic violence and extreme nationalist ideologies such as neo-fascism may provide refuge for marginalised populations who claim rights to territory and national belonging. Over the past decade, within a global context of increased ethnic conflict, we have seen alarmingly high levels of racist violence, physical attacks on asylum seekers and electoral support for the extreme right (in Austria, Belgium and France for instance). These developments are often concentrated when large numbers of young men come together, for example, in violence between football supporters.

There have been fundamental shifts in the view that racism is what white people do to black people, a particularly dominant view in the British race relations tradition. Partly this has been a product of inflows of new migrants and asylum seekers on the one hand and Islamophobia on the other which focuses on culture and religion rather than 'race' ascriptions. As suggested before, racism in fact can use all kinds of signifiers or markers. These serve to deny full participation in economic, social, political and cultural life. Racism in this sense uses various means for the setting up and legitimisation of exclusions. These involve projects that are, at different times, informed by nationalist, class or other struggles for dominance. However, racisms cannot be adequately understood as emanating from ethnic or race phenomena. This requires an analysis of wider social relations that include those of class, gender and the state (Anthias and Yuval-Davis, 1992). Racism also involves the ability to impose beliefs or world views as hegemonic, and as a basis for a denial of rights or equality. Racism is thus embedded in power relations of different types All those exclusionary practices that are formulated on the basis of the categorisation of individuals into groups, whereby ethnic or 'racial' origin are criteria of access or selection, may become racist. Further, racist practices are also those whose outcome, if not intention, is to produce systematic exclusions on the basis of such categorisations.

Much recent debate has focused on issues of immigration controls and citizenship, linking this directly to the policing of national boundaries. As far back as 1991, Miles and Rathzel (1991) noted that, since 1974, immigration law and migration processes continue to be shaped by 'racialised conceptions of national identity and citizenship' (1991: 23). The cases of Britain, France and Germany raise the issue of the importance of the different criteria used by nations to determine who its members are. In Britain, until 1981 (when the Nationality Act introduced for the first time the criterion of birth to a parent born on British soil), any person who was born on British sovereign territory had a right to British citizenship. Recent redefinitions of citizenship and increased immigration controls serve to effectively deny full citizenship to black and other migrants from the developing world as well as to new migrants from third country states. At the same time, a managed migration system focusing on a points system relating to the 'needs' of the British economy, functions to exclude the poorest and most disadvantaged in the world.

In France, the 'civilising' mission of the great universal republican nation could embrace all its ex-colonials in its arms irrespective of creed, colour or religion as long as they agreed to integrate with the polity. However, the differential treatment of those that are seen to pose a threat to supposed universalising values, like Islamic populations, has opened up the essential flaw in the fabric of universalism to reveal what Balibar has called 'racisme differentialiste' (Balibar, 1991).

Belonging to the nation is more than being merely a passport holder. In Britain, Black or Muslim citizens are not regarded as properly being true British subjects. In Germany, the majority of the population treat immigrant passport holders as foreigners. Miles and Rathzel note: '... We anticipate the construction of new conceptions of "belonging" by means of a renewed problematisation of migrant workers as an Islamic presence' (Miles and Rathzel, 1991: 22). This has certainly happened, particularly since the Rushdie affair, which was linked to the growth of racialisation of Muslims in Britain and the importance given to religion as a marker of undesirability. This has taken even more virulent forms after the attacks of Sept 11th in New York and July 7th in London. Anti-Islamism presents a new face to racisms, no longer dependent on supposed physiognomic, biological or cultural difference, but a religious difference defined as an essence and demonised.

Although not all constructions of national identity are racist, nonetheless this always depends on criteria of belonging which over the last 30 years have become increasingly rooted in notions of cultural *desirability* and not just cultural *difference*. The growth of 'fortress Europe' as it has been called, albeit a growing fortress with new member states who themselves can be divided in terms of centre and periphery, constructs the dominant ethnicities of the respective European nations as essentially acceptable and denoting a benign European commonality, despite difference. The undesirables are the Others from the outside, the ex-colonials (even those who have lived for centuries within) marked out by their different skin colours or their different religions, third country nationals and asylum seekers.

It is difficult to maintain that there are 'real' or 'essential' nations as opposed to false ones. Ethnic, racial and national groups are all attributed and proclaimed from the outside and from the inside using various claims to difference and identity such as history, culture, biology, territory, etc. (this does not however make them merely 'ideological' inasmuch as the attributions and proclamations are embedded in concrete practices and relations). These claims are dynamic and shift over time just as ethnic groups can come to redefine themselves or be re defined as national, racial or religious groups.

Can there be, then, a general relationship between nationalism and racism? Whilst we can distinguish between nationalisms which are struggles for emancipation and those that are exclusionary, all border controls set up by nationalist discourse, whether of the former or the latter are potentially racist in their effects. Tom Nairn (1977) describes nationalism as a Janus, with two opposite facets. Eli Kedourie (1960), on the other hand, sees nationalism as always inherently illiberal and in constant tension with universalism. Anderson (1983) separates absolutely between nationalism and racism. For him nationalism and racism are opposite sentiments. He views nationalism as a positive sentiment, 'which thinks in terms of historical destinies', while racist discourse is negative – 'racism dreams of eternal contaminations, transmitted from the origins of time ... On the whole, racism and anti-semitism manifest themselves, not across national boundaries but within them' (p. 136).

Anderson's dichotomy is problematic because wherever a delineation of boundaries takes place, processes of exclusion and inclusion are in operation. If only for these reasons, we should treat seriously the fundamental processual link between ethnicity, nationalism and racism.

One primary role of national borders has centred on a basic right: the right to enter, or, once having entered, the right to stay. Boundaries are constructed according to various inclusionary and exclusionary criteria, which relate not only to ethnic and racial divisions but also to those of class and gender. This central arena of struggle concerning citizenship remains completely outside the agenda of Marshallian theories of citizenship (Anthias and Yuval Davis, 1992). The 'freedom of movement within the European community' for example, is an instance of ideological and racist constructions of boundaries which allows unrestricted entry to some but blocks others completely.

Racist boundaries with regard to national entitlements and citizenship are found against both those defined as immigrants and internal minorities (e.g., against indigenous people). Cases include Australian Aboriginals (who only received the right to citizenship in 1967), and Black South Africans who have gained this more recently. In addition, the entry and incorporation of migrants may be a result of two sets of rules: those of their country of origin on the one hand, and those of their country of destination, on the other. Some countries allow dual citizenship with certain countries but not with others. Differential access to the state and its resources can also exist in relation to different ethnic and racial minorities within the same state just as their location within the labour market can be very different.

I would argue that national and ethnic processes need to be understood within a framework which also recognises the ways in which gender and class categories (which the same individuals are divided into) function to place, exclude and inferiorise and some of the contradictions and overdeterminations this results in. This presents particular problems for anti-racism, anti-sexism and equal opportunities programmes – a cultural practice that is fostered as anti-racist may be sexist and vice versa. We shall turn to this issue later on in the chapter but first, the issue of whether the 'nation' may be transcended through transnational processes will be discussed.

BEYOND THE NATION: TRANSNATIONALISM AND A GLOBAL WORLD

Up until now we have concentrated on issues of nation in relation to the cross-cutting links to racism. We need to go beyond the nation-state, however, because globalisation processes indicate a greater transnational and international movement of culture, capital, modes of communication and of course labour. The debate on borders and societal mechanisms of exclusion and belonging cannot, and should not, be using the paradigm of the nation since they take place within increasingly global transnational contexts. Not only is migration *per se* one that challenges national borders but increasing flows of people, commodities, cultures and economic and political interests turn our attention to a range of social processes broadly identifiable as 'translocational' (see Anthias, 2001, 2002) as well as global and transnational (or cosmopolitan, e.g., Beck, 2006).

Transnationalism itself involves the crossing and challenging of borders. However, it is often accompanied by increased expressions of inequality, uncertainty, ethnic conflict and hostility (Bulmer and Solomos, 1998). It is not therefore the case that the dismantling of national or ethnic borders of particular types leads to the dismantling of all borders. A good example is that of Europe and Islam. New borders achieve prominence in particular constellations of political and economic practice. New enemies emerge or may be resurrected in new ways. The ways the violence or hatred is expressed may also be reconfigured.

Globalised networks certainly now characterise modern societies at all social levels, including the cultural and the economic. Although this does not minimise the importance of ethnic and cultural ties, it does mean that these ties operate increasingly at a transnational rather than merely national level. Groups involved are also at the leading edge of the emergence of new more transcultural forms on the one hand, and communication flows around racist hatred and insularity on the other. Diasporic groups have been thought of as particularly adaptable to a globalised economic system (Cohen, 1997). However, such depictions rely on a *national* imaginary of social location (Anthias, 1998b). The more violent, dislocating and 'othering' practices that they are subjected to cannot be ignored. Awareness of the broader international frameworks of racist imaginings, and racist violence, also involves the need to include asylum seekers and forced migrants. Recently arrived migrant, asylum-seeking and refugee groups suffer from social and economic insecurity, instability in their lives as well as increasing victimisation.

In the following sections, I will focus on a number of different ways that the movement of peoples and the transnational arena are challenging the primacy of the nation-state border.

MULTICULTURALISM

Just as ethnicity is not merely a question of culture and identity and has a political component, so also nations are political entities primarily constructing a basis for solidarity often using ethnic articulations of common origin or common fate, although not necessarily, as Zubaida (1989) reminds us, originating from prior ethnic communities. The idea of a coincidence of ethnicity and nation (although nowhere fully attained) has been very much problematised by the growth of multi ethnic and multicultural societies in the West – they have always existed in the East where state formation was more a product of colonialism and imperialism. The idea of a transnational state, found in the Single European Act has not been without its tensions and contradictions such as those of the growth of nationalism, as well as divisions within the EU itself. For example, we find tensions in the unification of Germany with new forms of nationalism and racism emerging in the wake of economic fears and destabilisation of the old order. In the old Soviet Block and in former Yugoslavia, particularly we have seen the emergence of new claims to nationhood by previously submerged nationalities (groups with an ancient and historic notion of a national, not merely ethnic, claim to their own territory) who have now resurrected themselves as 'nations' with their own political autonomy.

First, I want to cast a critical eye on multiculturalism and diversity or what has recently been called super-diversity (Vertovec, 2007). One central difficulty of multiculturalism is the assumption that all members of a specific 'cultural' group are equally committed to that culture, or the view that culture is a commodity or a normative system which is statically present and is 'possessed' by people from specific national or territorial regions. Culture is seen as articulated in terms of peoples ethnicity or identity. In this way, members of minority 'cultures' are homogenised. In one sense this may be because the voices of the culturally different have to be treated as working in unison otherwise they cannot be easily distinguished from the majority or the 'normal' dominant 'self'. Such constructions do not have space for 'diversity within' or conflicts of interest. For example, those of class and gender become invisible. The notion of multiculturalism has tended to assume definite, static, ahistorical and essentialist units of 'culture' with fixed boundaries and with little space for growth and change (Modood, 2007, challenges this recently).

Moreover, claims of minority groups have tended to be treated as 'cultural' claims when indeed they may be less motivated by a concern with culture and more motivated with a concern for equal opportunity. For example, when asked about their involvement in such claims (such as for Muslim schools), many see themselves as attending to the educational opportunities for their children and making their life easier than explicitly being concerned with cultural preservation (Pecenka, 2007).

Defining the limits of difference in a multiculturalist context is problematic. Which 'cultures', or elements of 'cultures', would be 'legitimately' included in the multiculturalist vision and which would not, is essentially a political question decided by the dominant group in the state. Outlawing cultural systems like polygamy, female genital modification, the ritual use of drugs or forced marriages immediately come to mind. The differential degrees of tolerance of the dominant towards social practices is central here and these are related to what Western thinkers often regard as universalistic rules which themselves have a social and cultural base. The limits of multiculturalism are also determined by struggles over the allocation of resources and the prioritisation of different cultural 'needs' relating to an identification of so-called 'private needs' and 'public needs'. The boundaries between public and private are socially determined, within specific cultural, class and gender contexts. In this regard, whether or not provisions for specific religious needs, childcare facilities for working mothers or cultural activities are provided, depends, among other factors, on definitions of what constitute core cultural needs of groups to be attended to in the public arena.

Critiques of multiculturalism have come from both the right and the left often echoing the same problems, particularly the idea of 'parallel' or separate lives which are seen as the cause of disharmonious 'race' relations, rioting, crime and indeed a potential and fertile ground for terrorism, particularly that fostered by Muslim dissentors in the wake of Sept 11th and July 7th events. Critiques of multiculturalism (e.g., Phillips, 2004; Goodhart, 2006) have pinpointed the unintended consequences of segregating communities on the basis of cultural needs and cultural commonalities. Multiculturalism's strategy of paying attention to cultural needs is not only about unambiguously respecting the wishes of communities, for it has resonances with segregationist politics, where it has led to separation of culturally or ethnically defined groups.

Multiculturalist policies have also tended to fail to acknowledge the gender-specific, and indeed at times sexist, elements of ethnic culture or the ways in which both ethnic and race boundaries are exclusionary. Critiques of identity politics, too, are very powerful in this regard (e.g., MacLaren and Torres, 1999).

The recent concern in Britain, using the vocabulary of social cohesion, is also part of the backlash against multiculturalism and its problems. Recognising the fetishisation of cultural attributes and claims has been important in this new politics of social cohesion. The old multicultural style has the pitfalls of putting cultures in little boxes thereby reifying and fixing them. Social cohesion politics refuses such essentialising. However, the new politics of social cohesion reasserts the idea of the primacy of the 'national' collective, in its more recent forms in Gordon Brown's concern with British values: Britain has claimed ownership of democratic and egalitarian values of tolerance and caring for others. Such a politics has the danger of throwing away some of the achievements of multicultural policies and of reasserting the view that the progress of groups away from racism and disadvantage lies in convincing them to go mainstream by adopting the language and culture of the white English (defined as British). This is despite the fact that the inherent problems of class are equally well known in New Labour's take on widening educational participation.

Exhorting minorities to take on the cultural and other symbols of so-called mainstream society also hides the concern with tighter border controls in the interest of national security in the wake of Sept 11th and July 7th events and the ideological and political aftermath. It constructs 'the stranger' (who may be a British citizen or even second or third generation locally born) as the root cause of social and political alienation. This is found most recently in Britain in the Path to Citizenship Green paper (Home Office, 2008) which sets out a *conditional citizenship* based on ideas of it being earned through proving knowledge of, and embeddedness within, a British way of life and a *tiered citizenship* process with, for a first time, the setting up of a probationary period.

However, we critique multiculturalism for reifying culture and failing to deal with issues of equality, leading to parallel lives and new calls for 'social cohesion' (reasserting the rights of the dominant group to have 'integration' on its terms), the problem still remains of a balance between valorising difference and the cherished traditions of people from different backgrounds or different values, and finding a common space of civic participation and agreement on core social aims. This is far from easy, particularly where there are divisions in terms of economic and other material resources and a different commitment to dominant structures.

There is also the debate on the twin aspects of the representational needs of people defining themselves in terms of different group boundaries (religious, ethnic or territorial, amongst others) and the pursuit of a politics of redistribution of resources. In this connection, these become pitched against each other only on the assumption that they are indeed alternatives and therefore not inextricably linked.

The pursuit of representation can, however, also be seen as the pursuit of a form of social capital in its broadest sense and therefore may also enter into the pursuit of redistribution of a range of cultural, symbolic and material resources (Anthias, 2002, cf Fraser, 2000). Forms of representation, as indeed ethnicity is in its mobilised form, may constitute a resource (e.g., see Barth, 1969).

A liberal multiculturalist framework has meant that the dominant group within the state can set the terms of the agenda for participation by minority ethnic groups has meant that the premises themselves are not be open to negotiation. However, the identification of the fault lines of multiculturalist policies should mean reframing the agenda and not ditching it in the name of a spurious notion of social cohesion (see Yuval-Davis et al., 2005). A starting point may be found in a move away from the idea of one dominant culture that sets out the frame of reference, and which sees the issue as a question of tolerance towards other cultures. The reframing of the debate has been too polarised in terms of either cultural diversity *or* social cohesion.

I will now look at some related debates on belonging. Hybridity, diaspora and cosmopolitanism problematise the idea of belonging as emanating mainly from a national or ethnic position. These are important in the context of the development of multiculturality and an engagement with framing the debate away from the polar conception of societies as either diverse or cohesive.

BEYOND NATIONAL BELONGINGS

The concepts used to understand identity formations such as diaspora, hybridity, and cosmopolitanism provide different ways by which culture and ethnic identity are seen to be affected by translocation processes or population movements and set out a challenge to national exclusivity and particularisms. Critiques of notions of ethnicity and identity that are fixed, stable, monolithic and exclusionary have led scholars and activists to embrace new ideas of hybridity and diaspora. Cosmopolitanism, despite the difficulties, or indeed the refusal to give it a precise definition, is also a claim towards a broader cultural and justice-related framework, beyond national exclusivity, and a more global liberal understanding of difference and cultural values. Cosmopolitanism has been more an outcome recently of debates on globalisation and citizenship (e.g., Held et al., 1999) while debates on hybridity and diaspora have been more tied to transnational flows of people and cultures. I will begin by commenting on hybridity and diaspora and then turn to examining cosmopolitanism.

Hybridity and diaspora (for critiques of these concepts see also Anthias, 1998b, 2001) are used to counter the essentialism found in many traditional approaches to ethnicity and racism. They both postulate shifting and potentially transnational and transethnic cultural formations and identities. These new identities are seen to be tied to a globalised and transnational social fabric rather than one bounded by the nation-state form. If one of the most virulent forms of racism is to be found in the very nature of modern exclusivist ethnicity and nationalism with its culture of fixed boundaries, then we might envisage that progress can be made with forms of cultural identity that are more fluid and synthetic, such as those that have been characterised as hybrid and diasporic. This can be seen similarly, with cosmopolitanism that paints a world where ethnic and national spectacles are abandoned in favour of one-world ones. In the following sections, I will focus on each of these in turn in order to show some of the difficulties they face in providing a worked-through alternative.

Hybridity

The modern use of the concept of hybridity seeks to argue against a mono-culturalist view of identity, depicting identity as syncretic and changeable rather than static and essentialised (Bhabha, 1994). It is often used alongside what may be regarded as its sister notion, that of diaspora. Hybridity is often linked to globalisation processes. These have been characterised as political, economic and cultural. It is the latter that is most relevant to the arguments found in current formulations of diaspora and hybridity (although diaspora has been used to denote political economy and political processes) in the work of Cohen (1997), Segal (1995) and Said (1979), from both a traditional sociological and political economy framework. Globalisation has been seen as a challenge to the nation-state, although also seen as generating ethnic and cultural parochialisms and localisms or glocalisation in Roland Robertson's own 'hybrid' term (Robertson, 1995). Diasporic and hybridisation processes have been related to all of these processes. It has also been claimed that the global cultural is constituted in and through hybridisation (Pieterse, 1995). In these respects, Giddens's emphasis on the global cosmopolitanism of the modern world and the self-reflexivity of its individual and institutional actors (1991) reverberates with some of the themes of post-colonial cultural studies.

Not all aspects of culture have been equally malleable to globalisation, how-ever, if that, as it often does, implies homogenisation particularly around Western values and actions. This is particularly the case with regard to family organisa-tion, gender relationships and religion. The mixed cultural patterns of second and third generation underplays the ways in which gender and religion, for example, serve different ends in different contexts (e.g., see Afshar, 1994). In other words, the bringing together of different cultural elements syncretically may transform their meaning but need not mean the breakdown of the central or core cultural values espoused.

It may be the case that there is an intermingling of cultural styles and values, producing new and innovative forms, but this need not necessarily lead to changing ethnic solidarities or the diminution of ethnocentrism and racism which is often implied by hybridity theorists. For example, young white adolescents have been seen as synthesising the culture of their white English backgrounds with the new cultures of minorities. New cultural forms are forged in music and inter-racial friendship networks and movements (Hewitt, 1986; Back, 1996). The pick and mix of cultural elements, denoted by the term hybridity, does not necessarily signify, however, a shift in identity or indeed the demise of identity politics of the racist or anti-racist kind.

Diaspora

The popularity of new notions of diaspora identities and experiences (e.g., Hall, 1990; Gilroy, 1993; Cohen, 1997; Clifford, 1994; Brah, 1996) can be related to the attempt to overcome some of the criticisms made of the 'race and ethnic relations' tradition (e.g., Miles, 1993; Anthias, 1990; Anthias and Yuval Davis, 1992; Hall, 1990; Gilroy, 1993; Brah, 1996). However, the term 'diaspora' itself relies on a nation-based imaginary for it refers to a connection between groups across different nation-states whose commonality derives from an original homeland. Although the term is often limited to population categories which have experienced 'forceful or violent expulsion' processes (classically used about the Jews), it may also denote a *social condition* entailing a particular form of 'consciousness' which is particularly compatible with globalisation. However, one danger of using the concept too uncritically is that this may overemphasise transnational as opposed to trans-ethnic processes (i.e., not focus enough on common experiences amongst different ethnic groups).

Globalisation involves a growth in the amount of movement, which both intensifies strangeness and normalises it. The condition of 'overall strangeness' becomes the condition par excellence of global society. The importance of 'asymmetry', together with hegemonic cultural discourses in this process, needs to be considered by the new approaches to interculturality found in the idea of cultural hybridities and diasporic imaginations. We must be careful, therefore, not to treat hybridity and diasporic formations outside the parameters of unequal power relations that exist between and within cultures (Anthias, 2001).

It is equally important to attend to differentiations within 'diasporic' groups, such as those of gender and class, as well as differences between different 'diasporas', thereby treating them situationally and contextually. Whilst diasporic groups have been thought of as particularly adaptable to a globalised economic system (Cohen, 1997) it is important not to think that they are essentially constituted in this way. It is also important to continue examining the more violent, dislocating and 'othering' practices that they are subjected to. The existence of group boundaries and the ways we think about our belonging are crucial elements in these practices but the forms they take are products of positionalities and contexts that do not themselves originate from these identity formations. We must be careful that the focus on belongings in terms of diasporic attachments does not foreclose a concern with differences of gender, class and generation within diasporic groups.

I would propose that it is difficult to encapsulate the processes relating to translocation through the terms available today (for a critique of diaspora see Anthias, 1998b). Migrants and their descendants have complex relationships to different locales. These include social networks involving social, symbolic and material ties between homelands and destinations and relations between destinations. Many nation-states wish to retain the ethnic identity of their diaspora populations and encourage their reproduction as well as their return to the homeland (unrecognisable for those who were born outside it; a home no longer 'a home' or a place where they may feel 'at home'). All these present us with a multiplex reality and a shifting landscape of belonging and identity.

Cosmopolitanism

Like diaspora (as well as some versions of multiculturalism) the term 'cosmopolitan' sees people belonging to a range of social relations and political and cultural communities across nation-states. There are a range of approaches to cosmopolitanism, however, ranging from the idea that it is the consciousness of frequent travellers (Calhoun, 2002) to the idea that it is the refusal to be rooted within an ethnic or nationalist space, (e.g., Nussbaum, 1998). John Urry (1995) sees the belonging attached to cosmopolitanism as unfixing and fluid, at home both nowhere and everywhere – a kind of cultural nomad. The role of local attachments extending beyond the local is found in the work of Held (2000). For Beck 'The central defining characteristic of a cosmopolitan perspective is the '*dialogic* imagination'. By this I mean the clash of cultures and rationalities within one's own life, the '*internalized* other' (2002: 18).

Cosmopolitanism is antithetical to local cultures and traditions and particularly to forms of ethnoculturalism. There is however, the issue of whether solidarity can be understood through cosmopolitanism. Since we are national actors, involved in national or even local practices at any one time (with often local attachments as well as sometimes more global ones), how is this compatible with a cosmopolitan orientation?

Cultural cosmopolitanism is associated with the middle class urban intellectual/business elite familiar with a range of cultures, who travel frequently and who feel 'at home' everywhere . Normative cosmopolitan additionally questions the value and meaning of national identity and belonging and longs for a wider social space to imagine belonging to. The citizenship or transnational citizenship strand of this is concerned with the formation of new forms of governance and political arrangements that diminish the importance of national borders and is dedicated to a world political system. However, Calhoun (2002) warns against dismissing the strength and validity of peoples more local belongings and attachments and questions the extent to which solidarity is attainable without these, unlike Nussbaum (1998). As Held (1995: 233) says with regard to the notion of cosmopolitan citizenship: '... People would come, thus, to enjoy multiple citizenships – political membership in the diverse political communities which significantly affected them'. One particular difference between cosmopolitanism and multiculturalism is that the former does not engage with collectivities, culture or claims of culture. Indeed, quite the opposite since the focus is on the individual, divested of 'group' solidarities whose aim is the attainment of rights across (rather than within) the nation-state form.

Kofman (2005) rightly notes that the positive conception of the moving subject who is at home everywhere and belongs to nowhere becomes negative for particular categories of persons, depending on their ethnic origin. One could argue that it is not just a question of ethnic origin but that whether it is imbued with positive or negative value depends on their social location within the world. Western individuals are regarded positively (on the whole) and yet migrants who travel and are involved in multiple sites of destination over time are regarded as problematic, even though they may have acquired some of the cultural baggage of the cosmopolitan ideal: many languages, extensive travel, familiarity with a range of cultural norms and values and being able to negotiate these. Eurocentric views of cosmopolitanism, therefore, exclude the transnationalism of migrants, particularly economic and poor migrants. For example, there is the issue of the class nature of the concept as the term cosmopolitan is often not seen as appropriate for describing the global pathways of working-class migrants (Werbner, 1999).

Cosmopolitanism (like transnationalism, diaspora or hybridity) does not attend to asymmetry or inequality. However, the idea of a 'free-floating' cosmopolitan without a social base is problematic. Even free-floating intellectuals (to coin Mannheim's term 1929/1936) have a social base. Similarly, there are no classless cosmopolitans.

One issue faced by the exhortation to cosmopolitanism (as cosmopolitan individualism) lies in the question of how societies achieve a solidarity that doesn't also relate to either a class based, ethnic based or universal human interest. As cosmopolitanism is about transcending interest, it thereby refuses to engage with local class or political interests even of a non-ethnic kind. It purports to be universalist but of particular kind, that is, having particularistic values around the global rather than the local. However, as individuals are socially and cultural embedded, it is important to make a distinction between a cosmopolitan orientation and a locally embedded form of practice in relation to this orientation.

Cosmopolitanism could involve the formation of new forms of citizenship, away from national democracy, there is an assumption that globalised or cosmopolitan citizenship is consensual. However, there is no singular cosmopolitan politics or social and cultural system of values. Indeed, cosmopolitanism is merely itself – an empty glass waiting to be filled. It could potentially involve a fascist system as much as participatory democracy. Laying claims to a cosmopolitan politics doesn't give us the detail of social arrangements necessary. It is better at being set as an opposition to forms of ethnic or national boundaries at a number of different levels, depending on its object of reference, rather than as a specific political alternative.

The cosmopolitan specificity is to oppose an ethnic and nation-based lens for seeing the world and as such is important. It potentially asserts a world without borders of national and ethnic violence and is proscriptive rather than prescriptive. It knows what it doesn't want but does not attend to inequalities and non-national/ethnic boundaries. However, it is difficult to discuss cosmopolitanism as a breaking of boundaries without thinking through the other boundaries of class and gender as well as political values.

Cosmopolitanism as an orientation is inimical to ethnic solidarities but need not be opposed to using such solidarities to achieve more universalising ends such as striving for greater representation or participation or greater social equality. Calhoun (2002) asserts the continuing relevance of solidarity and of culture but tends to confuse culture with attachment as previously was done by many (particularly the hybridity theorists who have tended to equate culture with identity).

Identities or belongings can be fixed or fluid under different conditions and for different groups. However, it is important not to confuse ethnicity with community. You can have ethnicity, in the sense of a conscious political assertion of ethnic boundaries, without feeling that you fully belong to such a community (e.g., second-generation migrants). You can also treat ethnicity as purely a matter of fact, as something you can't avoid being purely because of background and family, without necessarily according it a central place in your sense of belonging (Anthias, 2002).

Nussbaum (1998) promotes a universal human subject with commonalities beyond nations. Held (2000) promotes the moderate who espouses a world political order and citizenship but with associational and organisational roles at the local level – with the idea of multiple citizenships.

The debates on multiculturalism and different forms of transnational identity (e.g., hybridity, diaspora and cosmopolitanism) all point to the difficulties of thinking about the contemporary world as bounded by national boundaries alone. And yet, within all discussions of these processes and social imaginaries, there is a crucial stumbling block in terms of a continuing core of 'ethnic' and national' commitments, solidarities and power relations. None of these positions focus on social locations in their broader sense and this constitutes a significant shortcoming. Both local and less local forms of belonging and position cannot be disassociated from a range of bounded social relations through the other categorical formations of gender and class, for example, their processes and their effects.

This brings me to the issue of the ways in which gender links to nation and the debate on intersectionality.

INTERSECTIONS: THE NATION AND GENDER

In most analyses of the formation of nationalist sentiments or developments of nationhood, as we have seen earlier, there has been an absence of reference to women. Given the centrality of notions of belonging to the debates on the nation, it is worth noting those approaches that see belonging as a gendered process. Gender has been treated as central to the boundary formation which characterises ethnic, national and state formation and transformation (e.g., see Anthias and Yuval Davis, 1989, 1992; Yuval Davis, 1997; Collins, 1993). It is easy to forget that it is over 20 years since some of us have been thinking and writing about the intersections of gender, ethnicity and class. We argued that women carried the burden of the reproduction of national discourse and imagery and practice, with men taking a different role in national processes. Women were important in the reproduction of the ideology and culture of the nation and in producing nationalised subjects through the transmission of national ideologies and practices as well as ethnic ones. They were symbolic of the nation. Often the nation was represented as a woman, particularly in appealing for rights (Anthias and Yuval Davis, 1989). For example, in Cyprus, after the 1974 war and invasion of Cyprus, there were a lot of posters on the island of Cyprus with the picture of a woman clothed in black – with the words underneath 'our martyred Cyprus'. Cyprus was this woman in black, mourning. Women play specific roles in institutional and other arrangements of the nation-state such as labour markets and the military. Women are often the cornerstone of ethnic transmission, cultural transmission and reproduction, as well as the reproduction of patriarchy. Women also participate in national projects and struggles either as members of national liberation movements (see Anthias, 1989) or as mothers of patriots.

The relationship between gender and nation has been a relatively uncharted area partly because academic concern with the nation has often come from political theorists who do not generally consider gender relations as part of the public political arena. Of course, gender, in any case has been marginal with respect to academic discourse. It was feminist practice and theory that placed gender on the academic map and feminist political theorists have been important in discussing forms of gendered citizenship (e.g., Pateman, 1988). Equally, the discussion of gender within feminist thought charted patriarchal relations (considered as the domination of men over women) or alternatively class domination (Marxist feminists have looked extensively at gender and economic processes). It was particularly through the work of Black and anti-racist feminists that gender, ethnicity and racialisation were linked (e.g., Hooks, 1981; Collins, 1993; Anthias and Yuval Davis, 1983, to name a few pioneers in this field).

Women play a central role as transmitters of the cultural stuff of ethnicity as part of their mothering role. They help to produce gendered ethnic and national subjects, such as good male patriots and women who can play appropriate ethnically specific gender roles, for example, as sexually pure and obedient in some societies. The definition of a true ethnic or national subject may be tied to conforming to sexually appropriate rules (examples from different societal contexts of the many roles women play in national processes can be found in Yuval Davis and Anthias, 1989).

One of the ways in which the relationship between nation and other categories which construct populations has been conceived is through an intersectional lens and I will turn to looking at this and its implications for the understanding of 'nation'.

Intersectionality

Since the early 1980s, the triad of gender, race and class, has been the subject of a great deal of social debate and commentary (e.g., see McCall, 2005). Triple oppression, interconnections, interplay, multiple oppressions, fractured identities, overlapping systems, simultaneous oppressions are all terms that have been used to signify the processes highlighted (Anthias, 2005).

Put simply, intersectionality argues that it is important to look at the way in which different social divisions inter-relate in terms of the production of social relations and in terms of people's lives. In the earlier debates, particularly in the Marxist feminist concern with gender, one way in which different social divisions were connected was to argue that one of them was most determining (for a review see Anthias and Yuval Davis, 1992). This found its currency in debates on 'race' and class, and gender and class, where the tendency was to use a reductionist model, whereby gender and 'race' were determined by class. Gender and 'race' were treated as epiphenomena, as super-structural elements built upon a real foundation, which was to do with class relations. A further (and opposite) formulation was in terms of ideas about a triple burden faced by ethnic minority women. Here class, gender and 'race' inequalities were treated as separate but as being experienced simultaneously. This position can be criticised as being too mechanistic and entailing an additive model of the oppression of gender, race and class.

Intersectional approaches have tried to move away from this additive model by treating each division as constituted via an intersection with the others (e.g., Collins, 1993, 1998; Anthias and Yuval Davis, 1992; Crenshaw, 1994; McCall, 2001; Anthias, 2002a, 2005, to name a few). In this way, classes are always gendered and racialised and gender is always classed and racialised and so on.

In trying to do this, the tendency has been to look at processes of disadvantage emanating from the conjuncture between two or more different categorisations or identities such as those combining race and gender or race, class and poverty/ unemployment/ exclusion (e.g., Black poor mothers or Black unemployed, criminalised men). The intersections are therefore formulated in terms of the different positions people hold in relation to gender, race and class and other social categories. According to this approach, the unity of two minority traits constitutes in fact a distinct single-minority entity. Cross-cutting identity categories may also be regarded as hybrid but this might already assume the distinctive categories in the first place to be pure forms. What this type of 'intersectionality' does recognise, however, is that the syncretic character of social divisions leads to a transformation.

There are clearly rather different foci within the 'intersectionality' framework. Gender, race and class may be treated as different ideological (e.g., Collins, 1993) or discursive practices that emerge in the process of power production and enablement (as would be suggested in the work of Foucault, 1972). Treating them as historically contingent, as Foucault's work suggests, whilst being necessary may also fail to address some of the most persistent and universally salient features of the processes involved.

On the other hand, gender, race and class can be regarded as distinctive systems of subordination (Weber, 2001) with their own range of specific social relations and how these systems interact. Using this framework, however, one could argue that there is an endorsement of identity concepts and therefore forms of identity politics (using more hybrid identities) in its political arm in more complex ways.

Another view is that social divisions refer to social ontologies around different material processes in social life, all linked to sociality and to the social organisation of sexuality, production and collective bonds, all features which arguably societies entail (Anthias, 1998a). This position leaves a great deal of space for the development of different and changeable forms, produced in their cross-cutting and mutual effectivities in specific locales and times, which relate to wider social relations in terms of overall structures of dominance and conflict over resource allocation more generally.

The political and policy dimensions raised by intersectionality are also important. A particularly influential account of intersectionality in the United States (e.g., around human rights) is that categories of discrimination overlap and individuals suffer exclusions on the basis of race and gender, or any other combination (Crenshaw, 1994). Using this account, for example, the understanding of the positioning of domestic workers from Eastern Europe in Britain cannot be seen as either a gender problem (about the position of women) or a migration or racist problem (about the position of eastern Europeans in Britain). Clearly important is that this approach leads to an interest in the production of data or policy research and practice that recognises specific problems of this social category and which cross references the divisions within formulated groups.

However, the very act of already presupposing the groups *per se* as useful classificatory instruments, as opposed to groups who are positioned in a particular relation to the state (e.g., focusing on Eastern Europeans rather than working class or poor migrant women who are located in British society in a particular way) has the danger of placing too much emphasis on the origin of the migrant and not enough on a shared terrain of disadvantage across region background or lines based on country of origin (or those of religion, etc).

A related issue is the extent to which cross-cutting categories can be multiplied; potentially there could be an infinite number of cross-cutting categories.

Of course, one could argue that the relevance of the category is a product of its social saliency but there may be equally important categories which are invisible in social practice (as women or non-black minorities such as the Roma have been). The political salience of a category doesn't always exhaust its social saliency or the importance of forms of oppression (experienced and unseen).

Arguably, one danger with the notion of intersections is found in constructing people as belonging to fixed and permanent *groups* (e.g., ethnic, gender and class groups) which then all enter, in a pluralist fashion, into their determination. This undermines the focus on *social processes, practices and outcomes* as they impact on social categories, social structures and individuals.

This is further complicated by the fact that, despite the danger of seeing people as belonging to fixed groups, groups exist at the imaginary or ideational level as well as at the juridical and legal level. Therefore, the membership of people in groups is important in two ways. One is in terms of attributions of membership and the consequences that flow from these attributions. For example, being labelled as a member of a national or racialised group may affect how one sees oneself and ideas of belonging and otherness. This may have an important role in determining forms of social engagement and participation and in the construction of claims about belonging that may be vehicles for a range of political, cultural and economic resource struggles.

One could argue that the intersectionality focus doesn't go far enough in its deconstructionist project. Looking at the concrete experiences and positions of subjects in terms of a multiplicity of identities, for example, black working class women or white middle class men, may be useful. However, this cannot pay attention to the range of social processes, that is, the multiple situational elements that produce social outcomes. These cannot be encapsulated by sex/gender, race/ethnicity and class and their intersections and raise broader issues of social organisation and representation.

It could also be argued that it can go too far, thereby leading to the failure to identify systematic forms of oppression. In the attempt to say that each individual has a unique position in terms of the triad of gender, race and class (e.g., Collins 1993: 28) and that each person is simultaneously oppressor and oppressed (ibid) the danger is the steady disappearance of systematic forms of subordination and oppression in terms of categories of people who suffer them.

A simple model of descriptive intersectionalities, denoting hybrid categories (such as black working class women) has the danger of race, class and gender becoming taken for granted categories for social analysis. Issues emerge about the power of definitions and who makes them here. The question of the political nature of claims and attributions at the intersectional level is also raised. Identities of legitimisation and identities of resistance are useful ways of thinking about this (Gimenez, 2001). Contradictory locations where dominant and subordinate ones intersect (Anthias, 1998a) may also be usefully thought through.

Despite the difficulty of the notion of intersections, it may be possible to see ethnicity/nation, gender and class as involving processes relating to a range of economic, political and social interests and projects and to distinctive (and variable) forms of social allegiance and identifications which are played out in a nuanced and highly context-related fashion. These may construct multiple, uneven and contradictory social patterns of identity and belonging (as well as domination and subordination). The political questions opened up here go beyond an auditing of hybrid positions in the social structure and have direct relevance in terms of how inequalities, identities and political strategies are conceptualised and assessed. Such implications undermine identity politics on the one hand and raise issues about contextual and conjunctural coalitions around specific issues as well as more general questions about wider frameworks for integrating approaches to inequality. They also problematise the view of inalienable and primary boundaries round the categories of ethnic and national phenomena and reinsert the role of cross-cutting allegiances of gender and class as well as, potentially, a range of other social constructions.

CONCLUDING REMARKS: TRANSLOCATIONAL BELONGINGS

I have attempted to show the importance of examining the links between nation and other ethnic and racial phenomena, and explored various types of transnational belonging which act as challenges to the paradigm of 'the national' and 'national belonging' in our increasingly global yet divided world. I then turned to the links between nation and gender, briefly reviewing interesectionality frameworks. It is vital to consider the links to other social relations and particularly those that produce structures of differentiation and identification and structures of exclusion and inclusion.

There are a range of social locations that people occupy and it is not easy to disentangle them or to treat them separately from each other. These dimensions of social life are also linked to categories of difference which entail power and hierarchical difference. These are intertwined with political strategies for representation and for exclusion which construct such categories as meaningful. There is often contestation or political struggle around who belongs and what criteria individuals should have in order to count as fully belonging. Sometimes this includes cultural criteria, sometimes legal entitlement (as in nationality) and sometimes religious faith or gender roles such as behaving in appropriate ways (e.g., women within ethnic groups).

Borders play a central role in the discourse of states and nations. As Sahlins (1989: 271) claims, borders are 'privileged sites for the articulations of national distinctions', and therefore, of national belonging. The socially constructed nature of borders and their political nature contrasts with the naturalised view of nations as embodying singular identities and cultures. Many borders of nations today have been imposed by international treaties in the aftermath of wars and do not relate to national imaginings of peoples or cultures. National borders however, acquire and lose their significance under different conditions, whether in terms of embodying the 'ethnic group' or as significant political communities with international legitimacy or forms of primary social solidarity. Despite the growth of supranational and transnational realities, they are still a significant part of the social landscape of the modern world. They constitute a significant, albeit contested, arena where issues of otherness and belonging are played out, reproduced and transformed. However, as I have argued, in order to understand them better, we need to pay attention to their location within broader structures of dominance and constructions and practices relating to other boundary-forming phenomena and identities such as those of gender and class which also relate to contradictory locations and translocational belongings (Anthias 2002).

I have also argued that the challenges coming from multiculturalism and transnational forms of solidarity that link 'home and away' (diaspora), mixed cultural forms (hybridity) and cosmopolitanism are themselves problematised by persisting ethnocentric and ethnic-based power structures. In the case of multiculturalism, there has been a failure to consider multiculturality in terms of equalisation of position and it has functioned within the parameters of the dominant ethnicity in the state. In relation to diaspora, hybridity and cosmopolitanism, there has been a failure to fully consider the role of asymmetries of power and differentiations in terms of the experience of these transnational processes by actors in different social locations, which include those of gender, class and generation. A promising perspective, found in intersectionality approaches, requires even further the development of more integrated social theorisations of unequal power relations within our globalising world.

REFERENCES

Afshar, H. (1994) 'Women and the Politics of Fundamentalism in Iran', *Women against Fundamentalism Journal*, 5: 15–20.

Althusser, L. (1969) *For Marx*. London: Allen Lane.

Althusser, L. (1971) *Lenin and Philosophy and Other Essays*. New York: Monthly Review Press.

Amin, S. (1978) *The Arab Nation*. London: Zed.

Anderson, B. (1983) *Imagined Communities*. London: Verso.

Anthias, F. (1989) 'Women and Nationalism in Cyprus' in N. Yuval-Davis and F. Anthias (eds) *Woman, Nation, State*. Basingstoke: Macmillan.

Anthias, F. (1990) 'Race and Class Revisited – Conceptualising Race and Racisms', *Sociological Review*, 38 (1): 19–42.

Anthias, F. (1992) 'Connecting "Race" and Ethnic Phenomena', *Sociology*, 26 (3): 421–438.

Anthias, F. (1998a) 'Rethinking Social Divisions: Some Notes Towards a Theoretical Framework', *Sociological Review*, 46 (3): 506–535.

Anthias, F. (1998b) 'Evaluating Diaspora: Beyond Ethnicity?', *Sociology*, 32 (3): 557–580.

Anthias, F. (2001) 'New Hybridities, Old Concepts: The Limits of Culture', *Ethnic and Racial Studies*, 24 (4): 617–641.

Anthias, F. (2002) '"Where Do I Belong?" Narrating Collective Identity and Translocational Positionality', *Ethnicities*, 2 (4): 491–515.

Anthias, F. (2005) 'Social Stratification and Social Inequality: Models of Intersectionality and Identity' in R. Crompton, F. Devine, J. Scott and M. Savage (eds) *Rethinking Class: Culture, Identities, and Lifestyle*. London and Basingstoke: Palgrave.

Anthias, F. and Yuval Davis, N. (1983) 'Contextualising Feminism – Ethnic Gender and Class Divisions', *Feminist Review*, 15: 62–75.

Anthias, F. and Yuval-Davis, N. (1989) 'Introduction' in N. Yuval-Davis and F. Anthias (eds) *Woman, Nation, State*. Basingstoke: Macmillan.

Anthias, F. and Yuval Davis, N. (1992) *Racialised Boundaries – Race, Nation, Gender, Colour and Class and the Anti-Racist Struggle*. London: Routledge.

Back, L. (1996) *New Ethnicities and Urban Culture*. London: UCL Press.

Balibar, E. (1991) 'Racism and Nationalism' in E. Balibar and L. Wallerstein (eds) *Race, Class, Nation: Ambiguous Identities*. London: Verso.

Banton, M. (1983) *Racial and Ethnic Competition*. Cambridge: Cambridge University Press.

Barker, M. (1981) *The New Racism*. London: Junction Books.

Barth, F. (1969) *Ethnic Groups and Boundaries*. New York: Little, Brown and Co.

Bauer, O. (1907/2000) *The Question of Nationalism and Social Democracy*. Minnesota: University of Minnesota Press.

Beck, U. (2002) 'The Cosmopolitan Society and Its Enemies', *Theory, Culture & Society*, 19 (1–2): 17–44.

Beck, U. (2006) *Cosmopolitan Vision*. Cambridge: Polity.

Bhabha, H. (1994) *The Location of Culture*. London: Routledge.

Brah, A. (1996) *Cartographies of the Diaspora*. London: Routledge.

Brass, P. (1991) *Ethnicity and Nationalism: Theory and Comparison*. London: Sage.

Brubaker, R. (1996) *Nationalisms Reframed: Nationhood and the National Question in the New Europe*. Cambridge: Cambridge University Press.

Bulmer, M. and Solomos, J. (1998) 'Introduction: Rethinking Ethnic and Racial Studies', *Ethnic and Racial Studies*, 21 (5): 819–837.

Calhoun, C. (2003) 'Class Consciousness of Frequent Travellers: Towards a Critique of Actually Existing Cosmopolitanism', *South Atlantic Quarterly*, 101 (4): 869–897.

Clifford, J. (1994) 'Diasporas', *Cultural Anthropology*, Summer.

Cohen, A. (ed.) (1974) *Urban Ethnicity*. London: Tavistock.

Cohen, R. (1997) *Global Diasporas: An Introduction*. London: UCL Press.

Collins, P.H. (1993) 'Toward a New Vision: Race, Class and Gender as Categories of Analysis and Connection', *Race, Sex and Class*, 1 (1): 25–45.

Collins, P.H. (1998) 'Intersections of Race, Class, Gender, and Nation: Some Implications for Black Family Studies', *Journal of Comparative Family Studies*, 29.

Connor, W. (1994) *Ethnonationalism: The Quest for Understanding*. Princeton University Press.

Crenshaw, K. (1994) 'Mapping the Margins: Intersectionality, Identity Politics and Violence against Women of Color' in M.A. Fineman and R. Mykitiuk (eds) *The Public Nature of Private Violence*.

Ethnic and Racial Studies (2005) Special Issue: Migration and Citizenship, 28.

Foucault, M. (1972) *The Archaeology of Knowledge*. London: Tavistock.

Fraser, N. (2000) 'Rethinking Recognition', *New Left Review*, May–June: 107–120.

Gellner, E. (1983) *Nations and Nationalism*. Oxford: Blackwell.

Giddens, A. (1991) *Modernity and Self-identity*. Oxford: Polity.

Gilroy, P. (1993) *The Black Atlantic*. London: Verso.

Gimenez, M. (2001) 'Marxism and Class, Gender and Race: Rethinking the Trilogy', *Race, Gender and Class*, 8 (2): 23–33.

Goodhart, D. (2006) 'Progressive Nationalism', *Demos pamphlet*, May 2006 http://www.demos.co.uk/publications/progressivenationalism

Hall, S. (1990) 'Cultural Identity and Diaspora' in J. Rutherford (ed.) *Identity: Community, Culture, Difference*. London: Lawrence and Wishart.

Hall, S., Held, D. and Mcgrew, T. (eds) (1992) *Modernity and Its Futures*. Cambridge: Open University/Polity.

Hechter, M. (1987) 'Nationalism as Group Solidarity', *Ethnic and Racial Studies*, 10 (4): 415–426.

Held, D. (1995) *Democracy and Global Order: From the Modern State to Cosmopolitan Governance.* Cambridge: Polity.

Held, D, (2000) *A Globalizing World? Culture, Economics, Politics.* London: Routledge.

Held, D., McGrew, A., Goldblatt, D. and Perraton, J. (1999) *Global Transformations: Politics, Economics, Culture.* Cambridge: Polity.

Hewitt, R. (1986) *White Talk, Black Talk: Inter-Racial Friendship and Communication amongst Adolescents.* Cambridge: Cambridge University Press.

Hobsbawm, E. (1990) *Nations and Nationalism since 1780.* Cambridge: Cambridge University Press

Home Office (2008) *The Path to Citizenship: Next Steps in Reforming the Immigration System.* London: Border and Immigration Agency.

Hooks, B. (1981) *Ain't I a Woman.* London: South End Press.

Jenkins, R. (1994) 'Rethinking Ethnicity', *Ethnic and Racial Studies*, 17: 2.

Jessop, B. (1982) *The Capitalist State.* London: Martin Robertson.

Kedourie, E. (1960) *Nationalism.* London: Hutchinson.

Kofman, E. (2005) 'Figures of the Cosmopolitan', *Innovation: The European Journal of Social Sciences*, 18: 1.

Lenin, V. (1913/1972) *Collected Works.* Volume XX. London: Lawrence and Wishart.

MacLaren, P. and Torres, R. (1999) 'Racism and Multicultural Education: Rethinking "Race" and "Whiteness" in Late Capitalism' in S. May (ed.) *Critical Multiculturalism.* London: Falmer Press.

Mannheim, K. (1929/36) *Ideology and Utopia.* London: Routledge.

Mason, D. (1994) 'On the Dangers of Disconnecting Race and Racism', *Sociology*, 28: 845–859.

McCall, L. (2001) *Complex Inequality: Gender, Class and Race in the New Economy.* New York: Routledge.

Miles, R. (1993) *Racism after Race Relations.* London: Routledge.

Miles, R. and Rathzel, N. (1991) 'Migration and the Homogeneity of the Nation State' in S. Bolaria (ed.) *World Capitalism and the International Migration of Labour.* London: Garamond Press.

Modood, T. (2007) *Multiculturalism.* Cambridge: Polity.

Nairn, T. (1977) *The Break Up of Britain*, London: New Left Books.

Nussbaum, M. (1998) 'For Love of Country: Debating the Limits of Patriotism', *Journal of Value Inquiry*, 32 (3).

Pateman, C. (1988) *The Sexual Contract.* Stanford: Stanford University Press.

Pecenka, J. (2007) 'Recognition and Redistribution Struggles: An Empirical Contribution', paper given to Conference on Ethnicity, Biography, Belonging and Ethnography, University of Gottingen, December 7–9, 2007.

Phillips, T. (2004) Interview in *The Times* London, 3 April 2004.

Pieterse, J. N. (1995) 'Globalisation as Hybridisation' in M. Featherstone, S. Lash and R. Robertson (eds) *Global Modernities.* London: Sage.

Poulantzas, N. (1978) *State, Power, Socialism.* London: New Left Books.

Renan, E. (1882) 'What Is a Nation?', Sorbonne Lecture, March 11, 1882, http://www.tamilnation.org/selfdetermination/nation/renan.htm

Robertson, R, (1995) 'Glocalisation: Time–Space and Homogeneity–Heterogeneity' in M. Featherstone, S. Lash and R. Robertson (eds) *Global Modernities.* London: Sage.

Said, E. (1979) *Orientalism.* London: Routledge.

Sahlins, P. (1989) *Boundaries: The Making of France and Spain in the Pyrenees.* Berkeley: University of California Press.

Segal, R. (1995) *The Black Diaspora.* London: Faber and Faber.

Shils, E. (1957) 'Primordial, Personal, Sacred and Civil Ties', *British Journal of Sociology*, 7.

Solomos, J. (1989) *Race and Racism in Britain.* Basingstoke: Macmillan.

Smith, A. (1986) *The Ethnic Origin of Nations.* Oxford: Blackwell.

Stalin, J. (1929/1976) *The National Question and Leninism.* Calcutta: Mass Publications.

Urry, J. (1995) *Consuming Places.* London: Routledge.

Van den Berge, P. (1979) *The Ethnic Phenomenon.* New York: Elsevier.

Vertovec, S. (2007) 'Super Diversity and Its Implications', *Ethnic and Racial Studies*, 30 (6): 1024–1054.

Weber, L. (2001) *Understanding Race, Class, Gender and Sexuality: A Conceptual Framework*. Boston: MacGraw-Hill.

Werbner, P. (1999) 'Global Pathways: Working Class Cosmopolitans and the Creation of Transnational Ethnic Worlds', *Social Anthropology*, 7 (1): 17–35.

Wimmer, A. and Glick Schiller, N. (2002) 'Methodological Nationalism and beyond: Nation State Building, Migration and the Social Sciences', *Global Networks*, 2 (4): 301–334.

Yuval Davis, N. (1997) *Gender and Nation*. London: Sage.

Yuval-Davis, N., Anthias, F. and Kofman, E. (2005) 'Secure Borders and Safe Haven and the Gendered Politics of Belonging: Beyond Social Cohesion', *Ethnic and Racial Studies*, 28 (3): 513–535.

Zubaida, S. (1989) 'Nations: Old and New', *Ethnic and Racial Studies*, 12: 329–339.

PART III

The Social Organisation of Race and Ethnicity

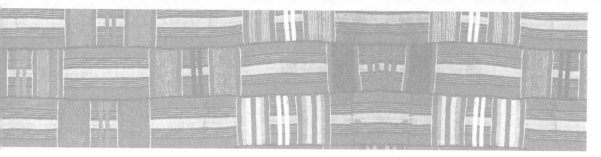

Introduction

In Part III of the handbook, we move on to a series of interlinked chapters that are focused on a recurrent theme in contemporary studies of race and ethnicity, namely the ways in which race and ethnicity are organised via major social institutions and/or social processes as well as how these institutions and social processes construct actual patterns of race and ethnicity. We approach this question of the organisation and construction of race and ethnicity by focusing on important sites where these phenomena occur. As numerous sites might illustrate these concepts, we have only included selected cases.

The opening chapter is by Peter Kivisto and his subject matter ranges over the role of the state as a social institution and its impact on the development of multiculturalism and forms of racial democracy. Kivisto's analysis is organised around a historical excavation of the meanings that have been attached to the notions of racial democracy and multiculturalism, an account of how to develop a better theoretical understanding of these notions and an exploration of the political and policy implications of these debates. His focus throughout the chapter is on the changing modalities through which migrants and minorities are incorporated within political relations and state policies. Given the controversies about the question of multiculturalism and social cohesion that are raging in a number of countries at the present time, Kivisto's account provides a useful reminder of the need to situate modes of minority incorporation and exclusion in a historical frame.

This is followed by Athena Mutua's chapter, which is a more focused overview of the contribution of what is referred to as critical race theory (CRT) to the understanding of racism and the ways in which racism and its institutional forms can be overcome. Mutua's initial account of CRT seeks to explore its intellectual and political origins, looking at its roots in critical legal theory, feminism and theorists of race and racism. Moving on from this intellectual origin, however, Mutua also places a strong emphasis on the political and oppositional character of CRT. In doing so, she highlights a recurring issue in much research and scholarship on race and ethnicity, namely the ways in which the boundaries between scholarship and political engagement are often blurred. While many contemporary theorists of race and ethnicity situate themselves as working within a sociological frame, the bulk of critical race theorists have been drawn from departments of law. This has led to CRT developing is some ways in dialogue but separate from the mainstream of the field. As Mutua seeks to show, however, the key questions raised by CRT are ones that are at the heart of contemporary discourses about how to understand the historical roots of racism as well as its contemporary forms.

The next chapter by Ralph Premdas takes up the issue of ethnic conflict and its impact on contemporary societies. Premdas's chapter is focused on a typology of the key patterns of ethnic conflict, namely the interaction between nationalism and forms of self-determination, plural societies and post-colonial societies, democratic transition and ethnic division and the role of globalisation and migration. In developing his analysis, he discusses in some detail the types of ethnic conflict that have shaped contemporary societies as well as the emergence of new forms of ethnic tension and conflict in the past three decades or so. Premdas's account provides both an overview of research and scholarship in this rapidly evolving area and a suggestive agenda for developing new research directions for understanding the ethnic dimensions of conflict in various parts of the globe.

The concluding chapter of this part by Liza Schuster is a detailed overview of the role of global migration in reshaping our understandings of both race and migration studies. Schuster's analysis is a masterful overview of trends and approaches in scholarship on this issue in contemporary Europe as well as more generally. She begins her account by pointing to the tendency in some of the literature to see the study of migration as almost separate from the study of race and ethnicity. In contrast to this approach, she argues forcefully that scholars and researchers need to pay close attention to the interrelationships between global patterns of migration and patterns of racialisation and anti-immigrant mobilisation. Drawing on extensive research on this issue in a range of European countries, she highlights the role of social and political constructions of migrants in terms of race, colour, ethnicity and religion. From these examples, she then moves on to outline the need for weaving the study of migration and mobilities together with a systematic understanding of racism.

10

Multiculturalism and Racial Democracy: State Policies and Social Practices

Peter Kivisto

According to some recent commentators focusing on the major liberal democracies in the world, the multicultural moment is over as state policy, social practice, and perhaps as theoretical construct as well (Joppke, 2004; Wolfe, 2003), while other commentators concentrating on the post-colonial nations of Latin America contend that racial democracy is a myth, based on what G. Reginald Daniel refers to as 'the illusion of inclusion' (Daniel, 2006: 79; see also Twine, 1998; Daniel, 2005). If true, these assessments signal a radical departure from the earlier purchase of these terms in both the academic and public arenas.

Multiculturalism, in particular, has generated, during the past two decades, a veritable cottage industry of scholarly and popular publications, primarily but not solely focusing on the advanced industrial nations of the globe. It has been widely used in various ways during the past two decades, including the depiction of interethnic relations, the defense of group rights, as a valorisation of difference, and as a rationale for new state policies of incorporation. It has also generated intense ideological debates. Not long ago, Nathan Glazer (1997) proclaimed that 'we are all multiculturalists now', and others have argued that however fitfully and fraught with conflict and unease, the world's liberal democracies have imbibed what might be seen as a multicultural sensibility, even if they have not instituted official policies or offered explicit endorsements of multiculturalism (Kivisto, 2002; Pearson, 2001; Joppke and Morawska, 2003; Modood, 2007;

Parekh, 2008). If the critics are correct, these assessments merely managed to capture a fleeting moment that we have now moved beyond.

Meanwhile, racial democracy has had a far more circumscribed conceptual trajectory insofar as it has been primarily associated with the racial politics of Latin America in general, and Brazil in particular (Twine, 1998; Andrews, 2004; Telles, 2004; Daniel, 2006). Once seen as an apt characterisation of the presumed harmonious racial relations in these nations, in stark contrast to the conflictual character of race relations in North America and many other nations, racial democracy has more recently been criticised as an ideological construct that has blinded Latin Americans and outside observers alike to the continuing legacy of subordination and marginalisation of dark-skinned citizens, and prevented them from generating a constructive dialogue about this reality.

One conclusion that might be drawn from these potential reversals of fortune is that both terms have been the victims of a certain intellectual fashion consciousness. One can, for instance, point to current efforts to find what are depicted as alternatives to multiculturalism such as cosmopolitanism (Vertovec and Cohen, 2002) or conviviality (Gilroy, 2005: 121–151). Another reasonable conclusion that might be drawn is that both terms are so tainted by ideological baggage that they can no longer reasonably be assumed to offer the sort of conceptual clarity needed to be constructive guides to theory construction and empirical research programmes. Yet another possible conclusion related directly to multiculturalism and more implicitly to racial democracy is that after 9/11, we have entered an 'age of terror' that affects a sharp break with the recent past, and therefore renders obsolete calls for a politics of difference or for the recognition of group rights.

While clearly plausible accounts, one might question the bottom line conclusion, which contends that these two terms have outlived their intellectual utility. Such is the position advanced herein. This paper argues that both of these terms have the potential to play significant roles as theoretical constructs shaping research agendas in the study of modern multiethnic nations, but only if they are seen as what Giuseppe Sciortino (2003) describes as 'fields for claim-making'. In doing so, it calls into question each of these critical assessments, while remaining cognisant of the fact that there is a kernel of truth in all of them. While there is compelling evidence that both concepts have been used profitably by scholars and have contributed to our understanding of the significance of citizenship and the capacity or incapacity of racial and ethnic groups to participate as relative equals in civic life, there is nonetheless a need to engage in a process of conceptual clarification if scholars are to be able to employ a shared vocabulary. Such a vocabulary is a prerequisite for comparative research programmes that have recently begun. To accomplish this task, the chapter is divided into the following parts: (1) a brief and necessarily partial review of the historical careers of these terms is undertaken with the goal being to deconstruct them in order to separate the ideological encrustation from the potentially useful conceptual core; (2) an effort at theory clarification that builds on that core to construct coherent theoretical accounts of both terms independently and in relation to each other; and (3) a brief concluding comment about the moral and political implications of this theoretical perspective.

HISTORICAL CONTEXTS: ORIGINS AND TRAJECTORIES

If we pursue a chronological approach to the origins of multiculturalism and racial democracy, we begin with the second term since its initial appearance dates to the 1930s, while multiculturalism only emerged on the scene in a significant way during the 1960s.

Racial democracy

Racial democracy was first developed as an explanatory device to depict race relations in Brazil by anthropologist (and former student of Franz Boas) Gilberto Freyre, who in *Master and Slave* (1963a [1933]) and its sequels, *The Mansions and the Shanties* (1963b [1936]) and *Order and Progress* (1970 [1959]) sought to distinguish the situation in his nation from the *Herrenvolk* democracy of the United States. In part, he painted an idyllic portrait of the Brazilian past where white masters lived in close proximity to, and in general harmony with, the vast slave population. Racial interdependency, high rates of miscegenation and the greater ease by which Brazilian slaves could obtain their freedom signalled for Freyre factors contributing to the conclusion that Anglo-American racism was a virtual impossibility in the Brazilian context. Although slavery ended later in Brazil (1888) than in any other country in the Americas, the assumption was that by the early part of the twentieth century, the legacy of slavery had for all intents and purposes been overcome and therefore by the time he began writing, Brazil could not be characterised as having a racial problem.

  Part of the reason for drawing this conclusion was linked to the claim that the state historically tended to avoid playing a direct role in defining race relations. Thus, advocates of this position note, after slavery the state did not establish a legal basis for segregation and exploitation in a manner akin to Jim Crow laws. Nor did it seek to define race in stark dichotomous terms, such as employing the 'one-drop' rule. Nor did it prohibit marriages across racial lines. Indeed, inter-marriage was extremely common and a large self-identifying 'brown' (*pardo, Moreno*) population emerged. Thus, race was defined more informally and in terms of a continuum consisting of a complex range of colour gradations. Add to this the fact that Brazil did not experience racial violence as a mode of social control the way that the United States did after the failure of Reconstruction, and one gets an idea of the basis for Freyre's formulation of Brazil's racial democracy. His thesis was not entirely original, but constituted a codification and elaboration of an ideological claim that began to be advanced shortly after the abolition of slavery and the creation of the Republic in the late nineteenth century (Reichmann, 1999: 7; Skidmore, 1974: 24). From this time forward, writes David Theo Goldberg (2002: 214), 'Brazil was reconstructed discursively as a tropical racial paradise. It projected itself as the laboratory of racial modernity and democracy through miscegenizing mixture...'. Moreover, contrary to the claim of an uninvolved state, in fact it played a significant role in projecting this image of national identity.

Nevertheless, Howard Winant (2001: 226–228) has pointed out that Freyre was the individual most responsible for providing the nation with a myth of national origins, one that 'abandoned in part the previously taken-for-granted superiority of whiteness and the principles of racial hierarchy, substituting for these a new racial nationalism that vindicated and glorified miscegenation and hybridization'. In his formulation, what emerged in Brazil's relatively relaxed racial climate was the so-called 'new man (sic) of the tropics'. Racial democracy, thus, constituted a form of assimilation predicated on the creolisation of the population – in effect a racial melting pot.

This portrait of Brazil as a polar opposite of the United States' racial formation and as an exemplary model of harmonious race relations took root in the academic community for the next three decades at least (Degler, 1986 [1971]; Hoetink, 1971; Pierson, 1942; Tannenbaum, 1992 [1947]). It also became deeply embedded in the national consciousness of the Brazilian people, across racial lines. However, when this idea entered the public sphere, it was recast by elites who fused it, somewhat ironically, with the idea of 'whitening', particularly as it was advanced by the last significant exponent of scientific racism in Brazil, Oliveira Vianna (Skidmore, 1974: 200–203). The idea was that the social circumstances of darker-skinned Brazilians would improve as they biologically merged with whites. Race mixing was thus construed as an 'escape hatch' for those trapped at the bottom of the class structure. Freyre was highly critical of Vianna and the elite rearticulation of racial democracy that sought to fuse a democratic ideal to the racial upgrading of the population as a whole. Rather than the creolisation of society, they envisioned a progressive lightening of the population. This is a rather stark contrast to white elites in the United States, who despite the fact that they had been as sexually predatory as their Brazilian counterparts when it came to black females, were intensely opposed to the idea of race mixing. Rather than a progressive upgrading of the racial stock as a consequence of miscegenation, they feared that racial mixing would pose a threat to the future of the superior white race. In their view, mixing of the races spelled the progressive degeneration of the nation's racial stock. Thus, the idea of 'whitening' was impossible for them to comprehend.

In both scholarly and popular form, the idea of racial democracy took root, not only in Brazil, but throughout the Latin American and Caribbean nations with colonial histories similar to that of Brazil, resulting in what some have referred to as Iberian exceptionalism, which attributes the presumed racial egalitarianism of this part of the Americas to three factors. First, the experience of living under Moorish rule for centuries prevented the Spanish and Portuguese from viewing dark-skinned peoples as inferior (Briggs, 2004). Second, Catholics were seen as more willing than Protestants to view the racial other as having a soul. Finally, colonisers from the Iberian Peninsula tended to be single men, in contrast to the intact families of many early colonial settlers in North America. The consequence for unmarried colonisers was the stimulation of sexual and emotional contacts with indigenous and slave women (Peña et al., 2004).

This argument has come under increased scrutiny in recent years. In particular, critical race theorists have made the argument that Brazil and similar nations cannot accurately be described as racial democracies, contending that the concept is a myth, and a pernicious one at that (Guimarães, 2001a; Hanchard, 1994; Twine, 1998; Warren, 2002; Winant, 1999, 2001). One part of the critique focuses on a historical question about the nature of the Spanish and Portuguese colonial pasts, challenging the racial democracy perspective, which viewed these pasts as essentially benign. The reality, critical race theorists point out, is that all of the colonisers in the Americas were brutal, the only significant differences being in regard to varying degrees of brutality. In comparative terms, it is not at all clear that the Iberians were the least brutal. It is clear, however, that they were brutal. The second part of the critique calls attention to the fact that darker-skinned people are far from equal in these nations. Indeed, Brazil exhibits the second highest level of inequality in the world (after Sierra Leone), and patterns of class inequality parallel racial inequality. Moreover, not only are darker-skinned people socio-economically disadvantaged, but they are also marginalised and excluded from full participation in social, cultural and political life. It has often been said in Brazil that money whitens. Luisa Schwartzman's (2007: 942) research concludes that the reverse is also true: 'poverty darkens'.

This leads to the third prong of the argument, which points to the presumed pernicious character of the racial democracy myth. In Brazil and elsewhere in Latin America, organised social movements devoted to promoting the civil rights and social circumstances of racially disadvantaged groups have historically been few in number, and those organisations that did exist had relatively small memberships. The claim of critical race theorists is that the myth of racial democracy has served to deny, in Winant's (2001: 228) words, 'both black difference and black inequality'. In other words, it has served as an ideological mask that in the name of national unity has affected what amounts to censorship about existing racial disparities, with the result being that anti-racist struggles have been stymied (Twine, 1998; Hanchard, 1994). Thus, racial democracy served the same ideological function in Brazil as colourblindness did in the United States. It is an odd formulation, in which Brazilian society was simultaneously highly conscious of colour differences while denying that racial disparities existed or mattered. This resulted in a formulation that Goldberg (2002: 201) has succinctly characterised as 'raced racelessness'.

While this may have been the case in the past, even before the return to democracy in 1985, commencing during the two decades of military dictatorship, social movement organisations arose that were devoted to anti-racism and to the politics of black culture. This includes O Movimento Negro Unificado (MNU), which Daniel (2005: 94) contends, 'comes the closest to being a national civil rights organization', with an estimated 25,000 members. In addition, particularly during the administration of Fernando Henrique Cardoso, the state began to assert itself by instituting both anti-discrimination and affirmative action policies, some of the specifics of which we turn to shortly (Andrews, 2004: 186–187).

In this light, it is not surprising that, as Stanley Bailey (2004) has pointed out, some scholars have begun to reconsider the idea of racial democracy, contending that its earlier critics have tended to be overly negative in their evaluations. Thus, Fry (2000) and Sheriff (2001) have argued that as a concept, racial democracy functions in Brazilian society less as an ideology and more as an ideal by which to measure and judge present reality. Bailey's research lends support to this position by providing empirical evidence for the idea that ordinary Brazilians do not share the elite ideology of a racial democratic paradise. Rather, they are quite aware of the existence of racial inequality and racism, and thus for them racial democracy serves as the basis of a counter-hegemonic critique of the existing racial formation. This perspective constitutes what can be viewed as the 'racial commonsense' of most Brazilians (Bailey, 2004: 729), which shapes how they come to engage in egalitarian claims making in what they perceive to be an unequal world shaped to a significant extent along racial lines (Guidry, 2003). This, I suggest, should become the starting point for developing the idea of racial democracy as a useful concept in the arsenal of race and ethnic studies scholars.

An alternative might be to simply call for the abandonment of the idea of racial democracy as failed ideology. However, as is the case with so many sociological concepts employed in the study of race and ethnicity (beginning with these very words [Cornell and Hartmann, 2004]), we inherit a language of everyday usage and find it difficult, if not impossible, to replace such terminology with an 'objective' language free from the tarnish of everyday life. Moreover, self-reflexive critical theorists are justifiably suspicious of such a quest for a pure language of science, viewing it as scientistic chimera. Thus, the task becomes one of transforming the concept in accordance with the racial commonsense of ordinary people. The fact that critical race theorists have argued that Brazil is not a racial democracy suggests two things: (1) there is such a thing as a racial democracy – as a real or ideal typical construct; and (2) criteria can be articulated to determine which societies do and which do not qualify as racial democracies. Thus, the task becomes one of describing what a racial democracy would look like and developing the metrics for ascertaining how close to or far removed any particular society is from that definition.

While a more robust definition is necessary, one that specifies the meaning and significance of a just and egalitarian society, this is a task that goes beyond what can be accomplished herein. For our purposes, *a racial democracy can be defined as a racially diverse nation that recognises racial differences but is not characterised by inequalities predicated along racial lines.* This construct is an ideal type. This chapter is also not the place to develop the metrics, but the substantial body of empirical research on intersecting inequalities certainly provides ample evidence essential to making such determinations. In so reconfiguring the idea of racial democracy, it would no longer be characterised as a raced racelessness. On the contrary, by the interjection of the adjective 'racial' before the noun 'democracy', there is an expectation that democracy will be shaped within the parameters of a racially diverse society whose legitimacy is predicated on both recognition of self-defined racial groups and on the absence of inequalities and exclusions along racial lines.

This conceptual transformation – in effect turning the original idea on its head – parallels what is occurring in current social practices. Thus, in the past, Brazil was defined in such a way that race was invisible, while at the same time – and rather paradoxically – it was highly colour conscious. However, as Guimarães (2001b: 39) has pointed out, the above-noted anti-racist movement challenged the received ideology, and to do so it required 'the mobilisation of black identity', which became a 'component fundamental to the Brazilian democratic process'. As mentioned earlier, the state followed suit with the implementation of an ambitious programme of affirmative action. At the end of the Cardoso administration, the government published a document that was intended to summarise its accomplishments. In reviewing its efforts aimed at promoting racial equality via affirmative action, *Brazil 1994–2002: The Era of the Real* (2002: 72) begins with the following statement:

> By recognizing racial discrimination as a major obstacle to the exercise of citizenship, the Federal Government has opened a new phase in the fight against racism. At the same time as the government recognized the existence and severity of the problem, it also recognized the black movement in Brazil as a partner in dialogue and reaffirmed the need for affirmative action.

It then proceeds to indicate what specific steps have been taken, which included establishing employment quotas for blacks in various government ministries and for businesses under contract to the government. It also implemented preferential investment programmes to address matters related to education, health, housing, sanitation and potable water, and environmental concerns in areas predominantly inhabited by blacks. In this, neither the movement nor the state called for the abandonment of the notion of racial democracy, preferring instead to use this deeply embedded idea as an ideal or goal rather than as a depiction of current realities. It is in this light that it, too, can become a serviceable concept for social analysis.

Multiculturalism

Multiculturalism as a concept widely used in the social sciences (and elsewhere in the academy), a term employed in public policy discourse and as a flashpoint of political contestation reveals itself to be a word of widely disparate meanings. In its typical articulation, it is generally presented in a fashion that manages to blend or blur its utility as an analytic concept with its expression as a normative precept.

David Pearson (2001: 129) also notes the significance of context in coming to terms with the particular meaning attached to this 'highly contested and chameleon-like neologism whose colours change to suit the complexion of local conditions'. This is evident in a cursory glance at the major sites where multiculturalism has emerged as a significant factor.

Although multiculturalism's origins are perhaps more nationally varied than that of racial democracy, it is generally agreed that the first nation to sketch out the contours of what has come to be defined as multiculturalism is Canada. As with racial democracy in Brazil, multiculturalism in Canada was conceived as an alternative to the assimilationist model of the United States. Multiculturalism's ideological roots are located in the popular understanding of the nation as a mosaic – with the idea of an identity based on discrete tiles constituting the constituent elements of a national portrait – rather than a melting pot (Porter, 1965; Kivisto, 2002: 85–101). The underlying historical context involved policy efforts on the part of the Canadian government to respond to an increasingly restive and militant Québecois nationalist movement.

Canadian national identity had been defined in terms of the distinctive identities of the nation's two 'charter groups', the English and the French. According to Gilles Bourque and Jules Duchastel (1999: 185) the bifurcated model 'made very poor use of the concept of nation; rather, it focused on the idea of a *community of citizens*', which contained an understanding of a shared system of universal entitlements brought about by the welfare state. However, the bifurcation was based on an asymmetrical relationship wherein the Anglophone community occupied a superordinate position vis-à-vis the Francophone community. This was the context wherein the mobilisation of the Francophone community began first with a movement of civil rights known as the Quiet Revolution that in effect was a counterpart to the civil rights movement in the United States and moved in short order to a more militant phase that called for the independence of Quebec. The left-of-centre Canadian government reacted to this incipient ethnonationalist movement by promoting a policy of biculturalism. This included downplaying the hegemony of British influence in various symbolic forms, such as changing the Canadian flag from a modified Union Jack to an innocuous maple leaf. It also involved more substantive policy initiatives aimed at elevating the status of French–Canadian culture, seen most explicitly in the inauguration of policies promoting official bilingualism.

Biculturalism was, however, short-lived due to the combined impact of mobilised First Nations people and the new immigrants arriving in Canada during this time who revitalised what had become known as the Third Force – immigrant groups other than the English and French. The latter had until the 1960s chiefly been composed of European immigrants, including large numbers of 'displaced persons from Eastern Europe' who arrived in Canada in the immediate aftermath of World War II. However, a new wave began to arrive from the nations of the South and they transformed the ethnic dynamics of the nation, particularly its major cities. Thus, Canada was confronted not only by an ethnonationalist movement with a separatist agenda embraced by many Francophones, but by an aboriginal rights movement and the presence of new immigrants demanding integration policies that respected their cultural backgrounds. In short order, biculturalism gave way to multiculturalism, particularly under the Trudeau administration (Breton, 1986).

Canada became the first nation in the developed world to officially enshrine multiculturalism into its constitution, doing so in 1982. In 1988, this multicultural provision took legislative form in the Multiculturalism Act. As part of a national identity-building project, multiculturalism meant that the official stance of the Canadian government was to repudiate the earlier valorisation of a homogeneous Anglophone culture in favour of a plurality of cultures. To this end, unlike the United States, Canada appeared prepared to promote ethnic group rights as well as individual rights. However, from the point of view of elected officials and government bureaucrats, the purpose of multiculturalism was not to Balkanise the nation, but rather to find a new *modus vivendi* for achieving national unity. At its most elemental, it was intended to insure that Québecois nationalism did not result in the break-up of Canada, but beyond ethnonationalism, it saw in multiculturalism a way of dealing with what the left-of-centre sector of the dominant culture saw as the legitimate grievances advances by First Nation's advocates and the need to find new tools to integrate the current wave of immigrants (Harles, 1997).

Thus, multiculturalism in practice has meant that ethnic groups are permitted to maintain aspects of their ancestral heritages, and that at times the state will play an interventionist role in protecting ethnic group claims. Such has been the case in terms of federal legislation designed to elevate the status of French as one of the nation's two official languages. Multiculturalism led to the ill-fated effort to have Quebec defined as a 'distinct society' in the Meech Lake Accord. On the other hand, it has provided the rationale for funding of a wide range of ethnic cultural pursuits, particularly symbolic practices such as ethnic festivals and the promotion of ethnic art, music and so forth. In the case of aboriginal peoples, it led to the creation of Nunavut, a new political jurisdiction for the Inuit carved out of the Northwest Territories.

Canada was not alone in becoming a multicultural nation. Australia, though lacking an ethnonationalist separatist movement, was similar to Canada insofar as it confronted an increasingly restive Aboriginal rights movement and the impact of mass immigration, particularly the migration of non-whites, particularly Asians. Patterning their legislation after the Canadian model, Australia became the second, and to date, only other developed nation to develop an official multicultural policy. In doing so, it replaced the short-lived policy of integration. While there were similarities between integration and multiculturalism, there were two significant differences. First, based on the assumption that multiculturalism necessitated a reduction in racism, the government assumed a more proactive role in the protection of rights of individual minority members than it had in the past. Second, multiculturalism meant not merely tolerating the presence of difference, but viewing the core of Australian national identity as embedded in the notion of diversity. This implied that national identity was not to be construed as fixed in the past, but rather as fluid and future-oriented.

Stephen Castles (1997: 15) has pointed out that multiculturalism in Australia did not promote minority group rights, but rather was articulated at the level of individual rights and obligations and was premised on a commitment to the nation and its legal system, along with 'the acceptance of basic principles such as tolerance and equality, English as the national language and equality of sexes'. As the New Agenda of 1997 made clear, multiculturalism was to be understood in relationship to 'civic duty', which is the term used to locate cultural diversity within a framework of shared values and orientations as citizens. If we accept Russel Ward's (1978) thesis, underlying this articulation of democratic citizenship and solidarity is the frontier-based myth of 'mateship'. Multiculturalism in the Australian version encourages cultural pluralism or diversity, accepts structural pluralism and necessitates civic assimilation (Galligan and Roberts, 2003).

Although the United States did not become an officially, state-sanctioned multicultural society, due to a number of causal variables, it increasingly came to exhibit a multicultural sensibility. Like Australia, the United States did not confront an ethnonationalist challenge, while it was forced to deal with an increasingly mobilised indigenous population and a major new migratory wave. What made the US case distinctive was the emergence of a civil rights movement from within the black community – a movement created by the only involuntary migrants in the nation. This movement originally pressed for equality and integration, but a more militant Black Power phase would question the desirability of the latter.

Criticism of Anglo-conformity as the appropriate model of incorporation into American society grew from the 1960s, when it was challenged both by white ethnics from Southern and Eastern Europe (the 'unmeltable ethnics' of Michael Novak's title) and by the rise of Black Nationalism. The Red Power and Chicano movements would also play roles in critiquing it. Even without multicultural legislation, the federal government, paralleling the attitudes of the general public, was increasingly willing to tolerate and even support manifestations of symbolic ethnicity (the proactive role of the federal government became especially evident with the passage of the Ethnic Heritage Studies Act in 1972).

However, multiculturalism was not merely advanced symbolically. Rather, it took a more substantive form in policies that came to constitute 'the minority rights revolution', which John Skrentny (2002: 4) depicts as rising very quickly during the 1960s as a result of a congeries of 'federal legislation, presidential executive orders, bureaucratic rulings, and court decisions that established nondiscrimination rights'. The minority rights revolution was generally not equated with multiculturalism, though the parallels to policies elsewhere that were so designated is quite clear. A distinctive feature of these efforts, Skrentny (2002: 4) went on to note, was that they 'targeted groups of Americans understood as disadvantaged but not defined by socioeconomic class'. While many accounts of multiculturalism view it as promoting identity politics in contradistinction to interest politics, this example provides compelling evidence that it is a mistake to treat 'identity' and 'interest' as antithetical (see, e.g., Sciortino, 2003).

Two particular policies stand out as being of singular importance: affirmative action and bilingual education. At least from the perspective of state intent – however difficult it is to specify state intentionality – these policies resemble those enacted in Australia insofar as the focus is on individual members of disadvantaged groups, and not the groups themselves. Thus, the legislative purpose of affirmative action was to assist minority individuals to obtain university admission, employment slots and business ownership opportunities through a variety of administrative devices. In other words, its purpose is to assist individual upward social mobility. Likewise, the Bilingual Education Act of 1968 was conceived as assisting individual immigrants – chiefly Latinos and Asians – in making the transition from their native languages to English language proficiency. Lawmakers did not see the act as designed to protect or preserve native languages over time. Perhaps the only significant exception to this focus on minority individual rights was the gerrymandering of electoral districts to enhance the likelihood of increasing minority membership in Congress.

Turning to a non-settler nation, during the second half of the past century, Britain became a site of both ethnonationist movements and, coincident with the collapse of empire, the mass immigration of residents from various Commonwealth nations. Regarding the former, three movements arose with differing goals and approaches to pursuing those objectives: (1) the irredentism and violence of the republicans in Northern Ireland; (2) the peaceful pursuit of greater political autonomy and perhaps independence by Scottish nationalists; and (2) the equally peaceful culturalist preservation efforts of Welsh ethnonationalists. Regarding the latter, the initial reaction of exclusionary British politicians and citizens was that the arrival of blacks (the then blanket term for virtually all immigrants) would lead to, in Enoch Powell's hyperbolic phrase, 'rivers of blood'. The response of the British government to ethnonationlism varied depending on the particular movement and in part whether the Tories or Labour were in power. Dealings with the IRA ranged from the use of massive force to seeking a negotiated settlement, while the Scottish and Welsh nationalists were variously ignored, challenged and accommodated (the last with 'New Labour' via a policy of 'devolution'). Meanwhile, the response to the new immigrants was twofold. First, highly restrictive immigration policies were enacted to stem the flow of new arrivals. Second, there was a concerted effort – grounded in the Race Relations Act and administratively promoted by the Commission for Racial Inequality and Race Relations Councils – to reduce racism and intergroup tensions (Favell, 1998; Solomos, 2003).

None of this was viewed as advancing a multicultural agenda, but as with the United States, Britain increasingly exhibited a multicultural sensibility. In part, this was because many of the initiatives advancing multiculturalism took place in educational instututions, which had been an important site for the percolation of a multiculturalist agenda (Modood, 2005: 171). Despite the persistence of racism, the social exclusion of immigrants and ethnic-based inequalities in socio-economic well-being, the lead author of a Runnymede Trust study on multi-cultural Britain concluded that it is possible to conceive of a 'relaxed and self-confident multicultural Britain with which all its citizens can identify' (Parekh, 2000a: x). Indeed, the rationale for the report, *The Future of Multi-Ethnic Britain*, was to identify the chief obstacles to achieving this state and to lay out a wide range of policy initiatives concerning topics such as policing and the criminal justice system, education, the media and entertainment, health and welfare, employment, political representation and religious pluralism. What is clear from this report is that the advocates of multiculturalism thought it possible and desirable to both promote and sustain diversity while forging a shared sense of what it meant to be British.

As these examples indicate, whether as official state policies or as implicit approaches to ethnic diversity, multiculturalism in practice has meant that at the same time that differences were to be not only tolerated but valorised, there was also an expectation that such an approach would serve the interests of the state insofar as it simultaneously constitutes what Jeffrey Alexander (2001; see also 2006; Kivisto, 2007) calls a 'mode of incorporation'. Alexander treats modes of incorporation in general as processes that bring heretofore excluded, margina-lised, and oppressed groups into civic life in terms that make them the relative equals of established members and at the same time facilitate the emergence of new patterns of societal solidarity. Multiculturalism represents but one possi-ble mode of incorporation. As the experiences not only in the above-noted advanced industrial nations, but in many other similar nations as well as poorer nations (Sieder, 2002) indicate, the logic of such an approach is predicated on the assumption that multiculturalism threatens neither the core values of liberal democratic societies nor the incorporation of ethnically marginalised groups – both 'multinational' and 'polyethnic' ethnics, to use Kymlicka's (1995: 17) terminology.

CHARTING MODES OF INCORPORATION

If there is a lesson to be learnt from existing practice-related formulations of racial democracy and multiculturalism, it is that they are designed to serve a dual purpose. On the one hand, they are a response to the demands on the part of marginalised ethnic groups for collective rather than merely individualistic solutions to inequality and exclusion. In other words, they are responses to the claims-making efforts of mobilised groups for recognition and/or redistribution. On the other hand, at least from the perspective of decision-makers, policy-formulators and most of the political advocates of some version of group rights, the other objective is to bring heretofore-marginalised groups into the societal mainstream. Moreover, as Alexander and Smelser (1999: 14–15) observe about the United States, but I would argue is more generally applicable, 'Although the radical multicultural position advocated by many spokespersons for minority groups seems to contradict [the sense of] connectivity, the actual political and social movements advocating multiculturalism consistently employ a civil-society discourse'. In other words, multiculturalism in a racial democracy constitutes a 'mode of incorporation' that is characterised by a particular type of civil partici-pation. In this formulation, multiculturalism constitutes a complex of strategies pursued by social movement actors, the state or both, in an effort to move towards an ideal of society framed by the idea of racial democracy.

What follows in this section is an effort to sketch out what is distinctive about this particular mode of incorporation. At the outset, it is important to note that what follows builds on theoretical discussions explicitly concerned with multi-culturalism and not with the idea of racial democracy. To my knowledge, efforts aimed at theoretically clarifying what is meant by racial democracy similar to the two discussed below that deal with multiculturalism have not been undertaken. That being, said, my intent is to suggest how these two terms used in tandem can be valuable, with the idea of racial democracy usefully complementing the idea of multiculturalism insofar as it stresses the need to connect diversity discourse to social inequality and in turn relate inequality to citizenship.

It should be noted that this is not the way multiculturalism is construed by many commentators. Critics of multiculturalism seldom consider the possibility that it constitutes a mode of democratic inclusion. Such critics are varied and can be found across the political spectrum, though those on the political right are more inclined to be hostile to multiculturalism both as an ideal and as policy. The arguments of those opposed to multiculturalism fall into several broad catego-ries. The first argument is that multiculturalism is divisive and as such threatens national unity. This was the thesis advanced by historian Arthur Schlesinger, Jr., advocate for the 'vital center', in his highly influential *The Disuniting of America* (1992). Counterparts to this thesis have been advanced for other developed nations, such as Reginald Bibby's critique of Canadian multiculturalism in *Mosaic Madness* (1990). The inverse of this argument is that multiculturalism serves to ghettoise marginalised populations rather than assist them to enter the mainstream (Bissoondath, 2002; Malik, 2002).

Another critique of multiculturalism emanates from the political left. Although often intertwined, this critique contains two complaints. First is the charge that the differentialist focus of multiculturalism results in the erosion of the possibil-ity of progressive alliances and coalitions. A particularly influential argument along these lines is Todd Gitlin's (1995) contention that multiculturalism has contributed to the 'twilight of common dreams'. This argument parallels that of Schlesinger insofar as the concern is that multiculturalism divides rather than unites – in this case dividing not the nation, but the progressive political left. The second aspect of the left's concerns with multiculturalism is that one of the unin-tended consequences of the promotion of a politics of recognition (Taylor, 1992) is that in the process, a politics of redistribution is ignored or placed on the back burner (Fraser, 1995).

It is necessary to move beyond these and related polemics and to similarly move past the philosophical controversies surrounding multiculturalism in its varied forms, ranging from, to use the distinction employed by Kwame Anthony Appiah (2005: 73–79), 'hard pluralism' (e.g., Iris Marion Young and John Gray) to 'soft pluralism' (e.g., Will Kymlicka and Joseph Raz), if a distinctly socio-logical theoretical framework for multiculturalism is possible. Two such efforts at mapping the terrain offer particularly useful guideposts: Jeffrey Alexander's (2001) essay on modes of incorporation (which receives further empirical elabo-ration in Alexander, 2006) and Douglas Hartmann and Joseph Gerteis' (2005) article on 'mapping multiculturalism' (which builds on Alexander's work). We turn to these two efforts.

Alexander's thesis, which is intended to offer a theoretical rejoinder to both multiculturalism's conservative critics and to radical multiculturalists (here his exemplar is Young's *Justice and the Politics of Difference* [1990]), is structured around the centrality he accords the civil sphere, which is portrayed by his concept of 'fragmented civil societies' (which, as Patricia Hill Collins [2006] has pointed out, is similar to the idea of 'imagined communities). 'An impartial civil sphere', he contends, 'does not necessarily rest upon the kind of undifferentiated, homogeneous, melted social values that conservatives recommend and radicals deplore'. His definition of the civil sphere locates it squarely within the para-meters of a modern liberal democratic society, as is evident in his emphasis on the individual over the group, and on the reciprocal notions of respect and trust. Thus, he writes that this sphere:

> is organised around a particular kind of solidarity, one whose members are symbolically represented as independent and self-motivating persons individually responsible for their actions, yet also as actors who feel themselves, at the same time, bound by collective obliga-tions to all the other individuals who compose this sphere. The existence of such a civil sphere suggests tremendous respect for individual capacities and rationality and also a highly idealistic and trusting understanding of the goodwill of others. For how can we grant a wide scope for freedom of action and expression to unknown others—as the democratic notion of civil society implies—if we did not, in principle, trust in their rationality and goodwill? (Alexander, 2001: 239–240)

In this scenario, incorporation entails the permitting of out-group members to move into the civil sphere. This occurs in one of two ways, either because core group members become convinced that the out-group members share a 'common humanity' and are thus 'worthy of respect' or because they have been required by wielders of power to act as if this was the case (reminiscent of Merton's idea of prejudiced non-discriminators). Alexander writes:

> Incorporation points to the possibility of closing the gap between stigmatized categories of persons—persons whose particular identities have been relegated to the invisibility of private life—and the utopian promises that in principle regulate civil life, principles that imply equality, solidarity, and respect among members of society. (Alexander, 2001: 242)

He identifies three incorporation regimes, which he treats as ideal types: assimilation, ethnic hyphenation and multiculturalism. The first two have had lengthy histories in the United States and elsewhere, while multiculturalism is a historically novel mode of incorporation. By assimilation, Alexander (2001: 243) means that individuals are admitted into the civil sphere only when and insofar as they are willing and able to shed their ethnic cultural heritages – in his language, replacing their 'polluted primordial identities' with the 'civilising' identity of the core group. In this scenario, there is no intercultural dialogue between the centre and the periphery. Instead, the out-group remains forever the alien 'other', while its members opt to engage in a strategy of exit in order to obtain an admission ticket to the centre. Assimilation thus defined requires that the ticket can only be purchased once the deracination of those traits associated with the marginalised ethnic group has been accomplished.

In contrast, the ethnic hyphenation model allows for greater fluidity insofar as it permits to varied degrees the maintenance of certain 'primordial' features as the individual ethnic is also taking on the cultural characteristics of the core. This mode became increasingly viable as the civil sphere gains strength and the core society is less inclined to see itself threatened by the presence of the other. Although he does not use the term, what he appears to have in mind is that in this model, the members of the core exhibit greater tolerance of an individual, from an out-group, who manifests both out-group and core-group traits. This is an instance of hybridisation, but one that is quite different from cosmopolitanism, which treats as equals the different cultural components that come to comprise a 'common collective identity' (Alexander 2001: 245). The difference is a consequence of the fact that in the ethnic hyphenation model, the hierarchy of cultural values is maintained, with the centre constituting the benchmark by which all out-groups are evaluated. Here ethnic identities can be maintained as long as they are confined to the private realm, thus making 'outsider qualities invisible' (Alexander 2006: 432). In his view, American history during the first part of the twentieth century can be described as one in which European immigrants from the great major wave that occurred between 1880 and 1924 were incorporated chiefly via this mode, while in the case of ethnic minorities, exclusion rather than incorporation characterised their relationship to the core.

Multiculturalism arose as a response to – indeed a rejection of – both of these modes of incorporation. Alexander (2001: 246) views it as a new mode of incorporation, one that 'remains in its infancy'. What differentiates it from the other two modes is that rather than individuals extirpating themselves from their particularistic ethnic identities, those identities are revalorised and permitted to enter the civil sphere. In the process, the separation between the private and public realms becomes increasingly blurred. Although he does not put it this way, what Alexander's argument suggests is that it is not only individuals who enter the civil sphere, but particularistic groups do too. The result is a more complex, fragmented and heterogeneous civil society that makes possible the expansion of democratic participation. The result is a new relationship between the universal and the particular, which in the other two modes were seen as antithetical. In a multi-cultural society, 'incorporation is not celebrated as inclusion but as the achievement of diversity. When universal solidarity is deepened in this way, particularity and difference become guiding themes of the day' (Alexander, 2001: 246). This then makes possible a politics of difference in place of the traditional politics of a unified and homogeneous core.

In their effort to map multiculturalism sociologically, Douglas Hartmann and Joseph Gerteis (2005) build on Alexander's framework, but elaborate it to identify four rather than three varieties of incorporation. They do so by considering both the social and cultural bases of societal cohesion. To use Durkheimian language, they do so by distinguishing between social integration and moral regulation. With these two dimensions in place, they constructed a two-by-two grid containing four distinct types of incorporation: assimilation, cosmopolitanism, fragmented pluralism, and interactive pluralism. From their perspective, the last three can all appropriately be considered as types of multiculturalism. Although Hartmann and Gerteis intend their model to be useful in distinguishing competing theoretical perspectives on multiculturalism rather than existing incorporation regimes, I would suggest that it sheds light on the latter, too.

Social integration – or association – occurs either via the singular interactions of autonomous individuals or through the activities of mediating groups. Moral regulation occurs either due to the existence of substantive moral bonds or procedural norms. The former constitutes a 'thick' form of regulation, while the latter is a 'thin' form (Gregg, 2003). Factored into this framework is the need to consider the respective strengths of both internal group boundaries and of external boundaries that out-groups confront.

With this in mind, their view of assimilation parallels that of Alexander. This mode of incorporation stresses the individual rather than the mediating group. At the same time, it involves a thick form of regulation based on 'mutual responsibilities' that connect the individuals to the centre while detaching them from the ethnic group. This type is possible insofar as internal group boundaries are sufficiently weak to permit individuals to exit, while the boundaries of the society as a whole (read: the nation) are strong enough to keep individual members bounded and bonded to shared values. As with Alexander, Hartmann and Gerteis contend that this assimilative incorporation regime demands the absence of particularism in the civil sphere, but is generally prepared to permit it in the realm of private life. They are speaking about theories and not real-world examples of their types. However, based on their description, it would be reasonable to conclude that France is perhaps the exemplar of this particular type of society – its republican ideal being antithetical to multiculturalism (Kivisto, 2002: 170–184).

Cosmopolitan multiculturalism is akin to Alexander's interstitial category, ethnic hyphenation. A cosmopolitan multiculturalism is one that values diversity. As with assimilation, the individual rather than the mediating group serves as the basis of association, and therefore in this version of multiculturalism, neither group rights nor the constraining impact of groups over individuals is endorsed. Instead, the operative terms characterising such a society are fluidity and hybridity as individuals exercise their ethnic options, picking and choosing which aspects of their ethnic cultures to embrace and which to discard. This occurs in a dialectical process whereby both newcomers and existing core members of the civil sphere exhibit a willingness to change as a result of interacting with others. This is a society where ethnic attachments are thin and the manifestations of ethnicity are typically symbolic rather than instrumental. Again, if one were to point to an existing society that most closely resembles this type, the United States or Britain could be identified.

By contrast, fragmented pluralism is depicted as being furthest removed from the assimilation model. Here the centre does not hold as mediating groups take on a salience not evident in the other models. Incorporation means inclusion into group membership, or as Hartmann and Gerteis (2005: 231) put it, fragmented pluralism is 'assimilation *into* group difference'. This type is far removed from Bhikhu Parekh's (2000b: 219; see also 2008) claim that, 'Like any other society, a multicultural society needs a broadly shared culture to sustain it'. It is also a prospect that Alexander would object to on both moral and empirical grounds.

At the theoretical level, they (concurring with Alexander) depict Iris Marion Young's work as perhaps most reflective of this perspective. They also point to Afrocentrism. However, their empirical example derived from the idea of 'segmented assimilation' is problematic. They depict segmented assimilation as amounting to entry into distinctive sectors of society that both in terms of related patterns of cultural values and social interaction function in isolation from other sectors. In the first place, I think this is a misreading of what Portes and others associated with the idea of segmented assimilation meant. Furthermore, as the work of Elijah Anderson (2000) makes clear, the adversarial culture of the streets exists in dialectical relationship and tension with the culture of 'decent people'. Likewise, for scholars of the new immigrants, while the civil society they enter is fragmented, there are nonetheless linkages that prevent the society's sectors from being totally isolated from each other. There is no existing society among the world's liberal democratic regimes that fits this model. Indeed, to the extent that multiculturalism is a product of elite decisionmaking – political and/or cultural elites – it is inconceivable that any elites would actively endorse or promote such societal Balkanisation.

The third type of multiculturalism is dubbed 'interactive pluralism'. Hartmann and Gerteis (2005: 231–235) consider this type to be what both Alexander and Taylor mean when they speak about multiculturalism. One might add that it also appears to be the form most closely resembling the perspectives advanced by Will Kymlicka and Bhikhu Parekh. Here, mediating groups play a central role in defining associative patterns, but in such a society not only do group members interact with non-members, but the groups themselves enter into dialogue and interaction with other groups. Not only is such a society characterised by the politics of recognition, but groups like individuals open themselves to being influenced and changed by the very process of intergroup interaction. Interactive pluralism shares with assimilation a premium placed on substantive moral bonds as a basis of societal cohesion. It differs insofar as those bonds – indeed, the character of the core culture itself – are subject to redefinition through what Hartmann and Gerteis (2005: 232) refer to as a 'democratic hermeneutics in which understanding the "other" involves a new understanding of the self'. The two nations that come closest to this version of multiculturalism are Canada and to a somewhat lesser extent Australia.

CONCLUSION: CITIZENSHIP AND THE TERMS OF ENGAGEMENT

Multiculturalism, in either of its two viable forms – cosmopolitan or interactive – constitutes a political project. Whether and to what extent the project is realised in any particular society depends on the outcome of the dialectical tension between the competing demands of outsiders seeking incorporation and states seeking to manage diversity on their own terms. There is nothing inevitable about multiculturalism and it ought not to be construed as an achievement that once settled is permanent. Rather, if it exists, it does so only as long as it is an ongoing accomplishment, revised and reconstituted in response to historical contingencies. In this regard, Kymlicka (2007) has recently pointed out that the institutionalisation of multiculturalism has been increasingly influenced by the role of international intergovernmental organisations.

Both Alexander and Hartmann and Gerteis point out that liberal democratic states have an older mode of incorporation available to them: assimilation or ethnic hyphenation. It may well be the case that some states, like France, will continue to resist multiculturalism in favour of assimilation (despite the shock of the events in that nation during the Fall of 2005) while others who took steps towards becoming multicultural will retreat and return to assimilation (Brubaker, 2001; Kivisto, 2005), witnessed in the Netherlands, for example, after the murder of Theo van Gogh. What they don't mention, but which is yet another option is the development of policies that result in the exclusion and/or marginalisation of the racial or ethnic other. Such a course of action would ratchet up the level of societal conflict (Esman, 2004). In other words, states can resist pursuing any mode of incorporation altogether. For their part, the ethnic or racial outsider may decide to reject or resist incorporation because the society is viewed as unjust, illegitimate or morally suspect. If this was an avowed group or partial group claim, it could be seen as the quest for fragmented pluralism.

While the main task of this article has been to lay out a conceptual framework for making sense of incorporation regimes, it should be noted at the end that there is a moral dimension to the argument. Alexander (2001: 247) concludes his discussion of multiculturalism by asserting, 'Multiculturalism is a project that can be attempted only in a situation of increasing, not diminishing, feelings of common humanity'. The recognition of individuals not only *qua* individuals, but as members of distinct groups, along with the desire to create more just and egalitarian societies constitutes the moral basis of multiculturalism. The idea of racial democracy points to the fact that it is as citizens interacting in the public sphere that we are best equipped to achieve the aspirations of both recognition and redistribution (Kivisto and Faist, 2007). Whether or not citizens acting in concert – in co-operative and conflictual situations – manage to advance the ethos of a common humanity characterised nevertheless by differences that can be respected and valorised, will prove to be crucial to the prospects of the project.

ACKNOWLEDGEMENTS

Patricia Hill Collins and John Solomos provided remarkably detailed and thoughtful comments on an earlier draft. I would like to thank them for their sage advice. I have benefited from conversations on multiculturalism with Jeffrey Alexander, Thomas Faist and Giuseppe Sciortino. In addition, I am appreciative of the helpful suggestions offered by two of my colleagues, Margaret E. Farrar and Mariano Magalhães, and by my friend John Guidry.

REFERENCES

Alexander, J.C. (2001) 'Theorizing the "Modes of Incorporation": Assimilation, Hyphenization, and Multiculturalism as Varieties of Civil Participation', *Sociological Theory*, 19 (3): 237–249.

Alexander, J.C. (2006) *The Civil Sphere.* New York: Oxford University Press.

Alexander, J.C. and Smelser, N.J. (1999) 'Introduction: The Ideological Discourse of Cultural Discontent' in N.J. Smelser and J.C. Alexander (eds), *Diversity and Its Discontents: Cultural Conflict and Common Ground in Contemporary American Society.* Princeton, NJ: Princeton University Press. pp. 3–18.

Anderson, E. (2000) *Code of the Street: Decency, Violence, and the Moral Life of the Inner City.* New York: W.W. Norton.

Andrews, G.R. (2004) *Afro-Latin America, 1800–2000.* New York: Oxford University Press.

Appiah, K.A. (2005) *The Ethics of Identity.* Princeton, NJ: Princeton University Press.

Bailey, S.R. (2004) 'Group Dominance and the Myth of Racial Democracy: Antiracism Attitudes in Brazil', *American Sociological Review*, 69 (5): 728–747.

Bibby, R. (1990) *Mosaic Madness: Pluralism without a Cause.* Toronto: Stoddart.

Bissoondath, N. (2002) *Selling Illusions: The Cult of Multiculturalism in Canada.* Toronto: Penguin.

Bourque, G. and Duchastel, J. (1999) 'Erosion of the Nation-State and the Trans-Formation of National Identities in Canada' in J.L. Abu Lughod (ed.), *Sociology for the Twenty-first Century: Continuities and Cutting Edges.* Chicago: University of Chicago Press. pp. 183–198.

Brazil 1994–2002: The Era of the Real. 2002. Brasília: SECOM.

Breton, R. (1986) 'Multiculturalism and Canadian Nation-Buildings' in A. Cairns and C. Williams (eds), *The Politics of Gender, Ethnicity, and Language in Canada.* Toronto: University of Toronto Press. pp. 27–66.

Briggs, X. de S. (2004) 'Civilization in Color: The Multicultural City in Three Millennia', *City and Community*, 3 (4): 311–342.

Brubaker, R. (2001) 'The Return of Assimilation? Changing Perspectives on Immigration and Its Sequels in France, Germany, and the United States', *Ethnic and Racial Studies*, 24 (4): 531–548.

Castles, S. (1997) 'Multicultural Citizenship: A Response to the Dilemma of Globalization and National Identity', *Journal of Intercultural Studies*, 18 (1): 5–22.

Collins, P.H. (2006) Personal communication with the author, March 23.

Cornell, S. and Hartmann, D. (2004) 'Conceptual Confusions and Divides: Race, Ethnicity, and the Study of Immigration' in N. Foner and G.M. Fredrickson (eds), *Not Just Black and White: Historical and Contemporary Perspectives on Immigration, Race, and Ethnicity in the United States.* New York: Russell Sage Foundation. pp. 23–41.

Daniel, G.R. (2005) 'White into Black: Race and National Identity in Contemporary Brazil' in P. Spickard (ed.), *Race and Nation: Ethnic Systems in the Modern World.* New York: Routledge. pp. 87–113.

Daniel, G.R. (2006) *Race and Multiraciality in Brazil and the United States: Converging Paths?* University Park, PA: The Pennsylvania State University.

Degler, C. (1986 [1971]) *Neither Black nor White: Slavery and Race Relations in Brazil and the United States.* Madison: University of Wisconsin Press.

Esman, M.J. (2004) *An Introduction to Ethnic Conflict.* Malden, MA: Blackwell Publishing.

Favell, A. (1998) *Philosophies of Integration.* Basingstoke, UK: Macmillan.

Fraser, N. (1995) 'From Redistribution to Recognition? Dilemmas of Justice in a Postsocialist Age', *New Left Review*, 212 (July/August): 68–93.

Freyre, G. (1963a [1933]) *The Masters and the Slaves.* New York: Alfred A. Knopf.

Freyre, G. (1963b [1936]) *The Mansions and the Shanties.* New York: Alfred A. Knopf.

Freyre, G. (1970 [1959]) *Order and Progress.* New York: Alfred A. Knopf.

Fry, P. (2000) 'Politics, Nationality, and the Meanings of "Race" in Brazil', *Daedalus*, 29: 83–118.

Galligan, B. and Roberts, W. (2003) 'Australian Multiculturalism: Its Rise and Demise'. Paper presented at the Australasian Political Association Conference, University of Tasmania. Hobart, Tasmania.

Gilroy, P. (2005) *Postcolonial Melancholia.* New York: Columbia University Press.

Gitlin, T. (1995) *The Twilight of Common Dreams: Why America is Wracked by Culture Wars.* New York: Metropolitan Books.

Glazer, N. (1997) *We Are All Multiculturalists Now.* Cambridge, MA: Harvard University Press.

Goldberg, D.T. (2002) *The Racial State.* Malden, MA: Blackwell Publishing.

Gregg, B. (2003) *Thick Moralities, Thin Politics: Social Integration across Communities of Belief.* Durham, NC: Duke University Press.

Guidry, J.A. (2003) 'Being Equal in an Unequal World: Citizenship, Common Sense, and Social Movements in Brazil'. Unpublished manuscript.

Guimarães, A.S. (2001a) 'The Misadventures of Nonracialism in Brazil' in C. Hamilton, L. Huntley, N. Alexander, A. Guinarães, and W. James (eds), *Beyond Racism: Race and Inequality in Brazil, South Africa, and the United States.* Boulder, CO: Lynne Rienner Publishers. pp. 157–185.

Guimarães, A.S. (2001b) 'Race, class and color: Behind Brazil's "racial democracy"', *NACLA Report on the Americas*, 34 (6): 38–39.

Hanchard, M.G. (1994) *Orpheus and Power: The Movimento Negro of Rio de Janeiro and Sao Paulo, Brazil, 1945–1988.* Princeton, NJ: Princeton University Press.

Harles, J.C. (1997) 'Integration before Assimilation: Immigration, Multiculturalism, and the Canadian Polity', *Canadian Journal of Political Science*, 30 (4): 711–736.

Hartmann, D. and Gerteis, J. (2005) 'Dealing with Diversity: Mapping Multi-Culturalism in Sociological Terms', *Sociological Theory*, 23 (2): 218–240.

Hoetink, H. (1971) *Caribbean Race Relations: A Study of Two Variants.* New York: Oxford University Press.

Joppke, C. (2004) 'The Retreat of Multiculturalism in the Liberal State: Theory and Policy', *British Journal of Sociology*, 55 (2): 237–257.

Joppke, C. and Morawksa, E. (eds) (2003) *Toward Assimilation and Citizenship: Immigrants in Liberal Nation States.* New York: Palgrave.

Kivisto, P. (2002) *Multiculturalism in a Global Society.* Malden, MA: Blackwell Publishing.

Kivisto, P. (2005) 'The Revival of Assimilation in Historical Perspective' in P.Kivisto (ed.), *Incorporating Diversity: Rethinking Assimilation in a Multicultural Age.* Boulder, CO: Paradigm Publishers. pp. 3–29.

Kivisto, P. (2007) 'In Search of the Social Space for Solidarity and Justice', *Thesis Eleven*, (91): 110–127.

Kivisto, P. and Faist, T. (2007) *Citizenship: Discourse, Theory, and Transnational Prospects.* Malden, MA: Blackwell Publishing.

Kymlicka, W. (1995) *Multicultural Citizenship.* New York: Oxford University Press.

Kymlicka, W. (2007) *Multicultural Odysseys.* New York: Oxford University Press.

Maik, K. (2002) 'Against Multiculturalism'. *New Humanist* (Summer). http://www.Rationalist.org.uk/newhumanist/issue02summer/malik.shtml

Modood, T. (2005) *Multicultural Politics: Racism, Ethnicity, and Muslims in Britain.* Minneapolis: University of Minnesota Press.

Modood, T. (2007) *Multiculturalism.* Cambridge: Polity Press.

Parekh, B. (2000a) *The Future of Multi-Ethnic Britain: The Parekh Report.* London: Profile Books.

Parekh, B. (2000b) *Rethinking Multiculturalism: Cultural Diversity and Political Theory.* Cambridge, MA: Harvard University Press.

Parekh, B. (2008) *A New Politics of Identity: Political Principles for an Interdependent World.* Basingstoke, Hampshire: Palgrave Macmillan.

Park, R.E. (1914) 'Racial Assimilation in Secondary Groups, with Particular Reference to the Negro', *American Journal of Sociology*, 19 (5): 606–623.

Pearson, D. (2001) *The Politics of Ethnicity in Settler Societies: States of Unease.* New York: Palgrave.

Peña, Y., Sidanius, J. and Sawyer, M. (2004) '"Racial Democracy" in the Americas: A Latin and U.S. Comparison', *Journal of Cross-Cultural Psychology*, 35 (6): 749–762.

Pierson, D. (1942) *Negroes in Brazil: A Study of Race Contact at Bahia.* Chicago: University of Chicago Press.

Porter, J. (1965) *The Vertical Mosaic: An Analysis of Social Class and Power in Canada.* Toronto: University of Toronto Press.

Reichmann, R. (1999) 'Introduction' in R. Reichmann (ed.), *Race in Contemporary Brazil: From Indifference to Inequality.* University Park: The Pennsylvania State University Press. pp. 1–35.

Schlesinger, A. Jr. (1992) *The Disuniting of America: Reflections on a Multicultural Society.* New York: W.W. Norton.

Schwartzman, L.F. (2007) 'Does Money Whiten? Intergenerational Changes in Racial Classification in Brazil', *American Sociological Review*, 72 (6): 940–963.

Sciortino, G. (2003) 'From Homogeneity to Difference? Comparing Multiculturalism as a Description and a Field for Claim-Making', *Comparative Social Research*, 22: 263–285.

Sheriff, R. (2001) *Dreaming Equality: Color, Race, and Racism in Urban Brazil.* Piscataway, NJ: Rutgers University Press.

Sieder, R. (ed.) (2002) *Multiculturalism in Latin America: Indigenous Rights, Diversity and Democracy.* New York: Palgrave Macmillan.

Skidmore, T.E. (1974) *Black into White: Race and Nationality in Brazilian Thought.* New York: Oxford University Press.

Skrentny, J.D. (2002) *The Minority Rights Revolution.* Cambridge, MA: The Belknap Press of Harvard University Press.

Solomos, J. (2003) *Race and Racism in Britain.* 3rd edition. London: Palgrave Macmillan.

Tannenbaum, F. (1992 [1947]) *Slave and Citizen: The Negro in the Americas.* Boston: Beacon Press.

Taylor, C. (1992) *Multiculturalism and the 'Politics of Recognition.* With commentary by A. Gutmann, S.C. Rockefeller, M. Walzer, and S. Wolf. Princeton, NJ: Princeton University Press.

Telles, E. (2004) *Race in Another America: The Significance of Skin Color in Brazil.* Princeton, NJ: Princeton University Press.

Twine, F.W. (1998) *Racism in a Racial Democracy: The Maintenance of White Supremacy in Brazil.* New Brunswick, NJ: Rutgers University Press.

Ward, R. (1978) *The Australian Legend.* Melbourne: Oxford University Press.

Warren, J. (2002) *Racial Revolutions: Antiracism and Indian Resurgence in Brazil.* Durham, NC: Duke University Press.

Winant, H. (1999) 'Racial Democracy and Racial Identity: Comparing the United States and Brazil' in M. Hanchard (ed.), *Racial Politics in Contemporary Brazil.* Durham, NC: Duke University Press. pp. 98–115.

Winant, H. (2001) *The World Is a Ghetto: Race and Democracy Since World War II.* New York: Basic Books.

Wolfe, A. (2003) 'The Costs of Citizenship: Assimilation v. Multiculturalism in Liberal Democracies', *The Responsive Community*, 13 (3): 23–33.

Young, I.M. (1990) *Justice and the Politics of Difference.* Princeton, NJ: Princeton University Press.

11

Law, Critical Race Theory and Related Scholarship

Athena D. Mutua

One of the most significant developments in law on issues of race and ethnicity in the last 20 years is the development of critical race theory (CRT) and related scholarship.[1] The name, CRT was coined in the late 1980s by Kimberle Crenshaw who explained that the theory represented a racial analysis, intervention and critique of traditional civil rights theory on the one hand, and a critique of critical legal studies insights on the other (Crenshaw et al., 1995). Its basic premises are that race and racism are endemic to the American normative order and a pillar of American institutional and community life. Further, it suggests that law does not merely reflect and mediate pre-existing racialised social conflicts and relations. Instead law, as part of the social fabric and the larger hegemonic order, constitutes, constructs and produces races and race relations in a way that supports white supremacy. (Harris, 2002: 1216–1217). CRT, as Cheryl Harris explains, 'coheres in the drive to excavate the relationship between the law, legal doctrine, ideology and racial power ... [but the] ... motivation [of critical race theory is] not merely to understand the vexed bond between law and [white] racial power but to change it' (p. 1218).

CRT rises during the ascendance of and as a challenge to the ideology of colourblindness in law, which asserts that race, like eye colour, is and should be irrelevant to the determination of individuals' opportunities. A noble sentiment perhaps, but CRT, while maintaining that race is not like eye colour,[2] argues that legal colourblindness operates as if a colourblind society already exists in the United States; and in doing so, ignores and cements the oppressive conditions and lack of opportunities for subordinated groups that continue to be structured by the historical and modern use of race in law and throughout the society.[3]

Colourblindness, or more specifically, 'colourblind individualism'[4], as an ideology applied in law, fully emerges after the civil rights movement in the United States. Though the civil rights movement is commonly celebrated in the United States and throughout the world as a movement that challenged racial oppression and broadened American concepts of equality and democracy, its broad egalitarian democratic agenda remains largely unmet. That is, its agenda for economic, social and cultural rights in addition to civil and political rights went unfinished.

Specifically, while the movement succeeded in removing laws, which explicitly permitted black oppression through, for example, segregation, it failed to alter the concrete accumulated oppressive social and economic conditions that structure black life even in those areas where specific laws for change were specially targeted. So, for instance, today, more than 50 years after the Supreme Court decided the *Brown v. Board of Education* case in which it declared segregation in schools illegal, schools in the United States remain as racially segregated and disadvantaging for black and other racial minorities as they had been before the case. These kinds of outcomes were structured by new laws and policies (built on the old), which, while not racially explicit, had racial effects. For instance, housing laws, policies and practices perpetuated in a new form the old pattern of racial residential segregation that in the context of neighbourhood schooling perpetuated racially segregated schools. But racial segregation is just the tip of the iceberg. Today, disproportionate numbers of blacks and other non-whites remain economically and socially disadvantaged and subordinated, as evidenced by high unemployment rates, high infant mortality rates, poor health outcomes and extraordinary incarceration rates that are often double those for whites, despite the election of Barack Obama, the first African American president of the United States. Said differently, the system of racial hierarchy, which structures white privilege and non-white disadvantage and which is informed, structured and shaped by the racial caste system of old, remains alive and well.

The result of continuing and persistent black oppression and subordination in the face of profound change in the United States is not new. The United States has grappled with changing a social order built on white supremacy foundations on only two significant occasions and thus committed to the oppression of black and other non-white people. These two moments in history were the period of Reconstruction after the abolition of black slavery in 1865 and during the civil rights movement at mid-twentieth century, mentioned earlier. After Reconstruction, the same pattern of continuity in the face of change occurred. After the slaves freed themselves and society capitulated to this state of affairs (Du Bois, 1935), white people, through law and practice and in government and civil society, recreated a labour peonage system that resulted in black people often being bound to, and working on, the same slave plantations from which they had been freed. That is, the society, through law, culture, the economy and custom, recreated essentially the same system but in a new form. They complemented this system with the enactment of segregation laws, which explicitly sought to maintain blacks as a subordinated class, on a theory of white superiority and black inferiority.

In the face of these laws and practices, black people, free enough to escape, but barely free enough to survive, began to flee the rural areas they occupied, migrating to central cities across the country. Consequently, what had been a predominately rural population, over 60 years, became a predominately urban population. Unsurprisingly, blacks in these urban spaces not only continued to face oppression but also faced laws, policies and practices that occasioned the dis-investment of resources in the very cities they then found themselves in, while encouraging and subsidising the development of white suburbs, recreating a new form of residential segregation. Nevertheless, it is from these urban spaces and in the process of these events that the civil rights movement was born. Significantly, the civil rights movement eliminated the formal and explicit features of Jim Crow segregation. But long before new laws and practices could begin to dismantle the deeply embedded social structure of black oppression, colourblind individualism rose, in law and other places, to halt black empowerment and maintain black and non-white subordination in the same way that the peonage system and Jim Crow laws had been erected to halt black emancipation and progress after slavery and Reconstruction (Mutua, 2010).

Though colourblind individualism emerged after the civil rights movement, it had historical roots even in the law itself. One of its earliest and clearest articulations is found in the dissent of the infamous US Supreme Court case, *Plessy v. Ferguson* (1896). In *Plessy*, the Court declared that the 14th Amendment to the US Constitution, enacted as part of the civil war amendments that abolished slavery, provided for the separate but equal treatment of racialised people. *Plessy* thus made legal the practices of racial, 'Jim Crow' segregation in the United States that the civil rights movement, almost 70 years later, would challenge. Justice Harlan, the lone dissenter in the case rejected the holding and asserted the clearly aspirational colourblind claim: 'In the eye of the law, there is in this country no superior, dominant, ruling class of citizens … Our Constitution is colorblind, and neither knows nor tolerates classes among its citizen'. The separate but equal legal doctrine of *Plessy* was overturned in the case of *Brown* in 1954, making segregation in schools illegal.

The re-discovery in the 1980s of colourblind notions *in law*, appropriated and misapplied some of the language of the civil rights movement, inspired in part by Martin Luther King's 1963 speech. In it, King aspired to a time when his children would be judged by the content of their characters rather than the colour of their skin. However, while King believed, worked and died fighting for peace, racial and economic justice, the application of legal colourblindness has worked to undermine that dream.[5] A central theme of CRT, therefore, is to explore the ways in which legal colourblindness, in supplanting overt legal racial ordering, has not only allowed law to ignore the social and institutional structures of oppression created historically and recreated presently in law and practice but also has blunted efforts to dismantle the racial caste system, working instead to maintain it. CRT's main goal is the liberation of minorities and other socially subordinated people; its stance is one of 'antisubordination'.

CRT supports its claims by analysing cases, laws and legal patterns that unearth the many ways in which law constitutes and/or supports the status quo of white racial power and black and non-white subordination. For example, CRT scholars have examined the ways that past naturalisation laws together with cases such as *Dred Scott* (1856) both constructed whiteness and defined it as a condition of citizenship (Uniform Naturalization Act of 1790; *Ozawa v. United States*, 1922; *Scott v. Sandford*, 1856). They have examined how current laws legitimate racial profiling of non-white peoples thereby reinforcing elements of the caste system developed throughout the nation's history (Cooper, 2002). And they have analysed the ways in which race-neutral housing laws facilitated white flight and suburban sprawl after the *Brown* decision (Calmore, 1993). From this perspective, CRT rejects the conventional claims of lawyers, judges and others that law, through the professional processes of reasoned analysis of abstract rules such as equality, is neutral, objective and distinct from and outside the realm of politics and political choices (Harris, 1994; Phillips, 1999; Houh, 2003: 1058–1059). Having emerged from a critique of civil rights, critical race theorists initially focused on constitutional and civil rights issues. However, they now explore the relationship between white racial power and law in a range of topics from business law (see e.g., Aoki, 1998; Houh, 2003) to international law (see e.g. Richardson, 2002, 2004, 2008; Iglesias 1996).

In addition, CRT helped spawn the development of the Latina and Latino Critical Theory (LatCrit) and Asian American critical legal analyses and movements (Valdes, 1999; Chang, 1993, respectively). By shifting the CRT lens to racialised groups other than African Americans, these analyses brought into the discourse important discussions of both historical and contemporary issues of citizenship and immigration law as sources of racial and ethnic subordination, as well as, for example, language suppression and stereotypes such as the model minority myth. These issues were less visible in the context of CRT's employment of the white over black paradigm and the particularities of the African American experience as analytical frameworks.

The LatCrit movement is particularly interesting because it explicitly incorporates and builds upon feminist legal insights and queer theory as foundational philosophies, explores international issues and explicitly and consciously articulates the social justice position of antisubordination – a stance against all forms of oppression. Further, LatCrit scholars have established an institutional framework for the future development of LatCrit and other CRT scholarship.[6]

While feminist theory, particularly feminist legal theory and black feminist theory, were inherent in the original CRT scholarship through the work of people like Crenshaw and Harris (Crenshaw et al., 1995; Harris, 1990), critical race feminism, a term coined originally by Richard Delgado, and a field adopted and promoted specifically by Adrien Wing, has taken off as a separate, newly developing theory and body of scholarship (Wing, 1997, 2000). Critical race feminism builds on critical race theory as well as insights specifically from black feminist theory and is also a leftist legal critique that primarily focuses on the intersections of race, ethnicity and/or colonialism on the one hand and gender on the other. It also explores the international manifestations of racialised gender oppression. The exploration of the sex/gender system, generally, its relationship to the racial order, and the living reality of sexual minorities of colour, coupled with CRT's embrace of the larger social justice project of working towards the liberation of all, has resulted in many critical race theorists also examining the ways in which law subordinates sexual minorities (Hutchinson, 1999; Valdes, 1997a).

Together, these issues have led to insights about the ways in which identity is multidimensional. For instance, critical race theorists, among others, point out that people are not simply raced (black, white, yellow or 'Hispanic'), they are also gendered (masculine, feminine or transgendered), and possess sexual identities (heterosexual, homosexual, or bisexual), etc. From this perspective, every person's identity is multidimensional (Truyol, 1995; Hutchinson, 2001). This insight of multidimensionality goes further. The social structures of race, gender, sexuality and class as systems of power are interrelated and mutually reinforcing. They create multiple and intersecting positions of subordination for members of the groups they disadvantage. So for example, racism in the United States is patriarchal and patriarchy in the United State is racist. As Dorothy Roberts points out, some of the first laws passed in America involved changing the legal/social practice of children inheriting the status of their fathers, to children inheriting the status of their mother if their mothers were [black] slaves, while patrolling and later prohibiting sexual relations between white women and black men. 'Black women [were forced to] produce children who were legally black to replenish the master's supply of slaves [while] white women [were compelled to] produce white children to continue the master's legacy' (Roberts, 1993: 8). The racism that both black men and women experienced was thus, also gendered. To these analyses, scrutiny of the specific relations of class could be added as well as analyses of compulsory heterosexuality. As such, the structure of black oppression was and has remained multidimensional.

Below, I expand on these themes. Although I present CRT as a 'fully unified school of thought', this is not the case, as CRT remains a work in progress (Crenshaw, 2002: 1362). Finally, although I present what are commonly agreed to be the 'tenets' of CRT, not every precept presented here is held valid by every self-described critical race scholar.

Part one of this paper discusses CRT's intellectual antecedents. Part two lays out its basic tenets and methodological fingerprints. Part three builds upon the context developed in these sections and applies critical theory insights and methods to a historical analysis of race and U.S. law. In doing so, it provides a counter-narrative to the dominant story about race and law. The dominant story suggests that the struggle for racial justice, though long and incremental, is nevertheless forward moving, progressive and eventually triumphant, given commitment to the America's creed and precepts (Delgado and Stefancic, 2001; Bell, 2004: 22). The counter-narrative challenges this, suggesting in part, that the law's commitment, on matters of race, is primarily to white supremacy and its continuation. Part three, thus, seeks to *do* CRT and is followed by a theory of law from a CRT perspective. Part four outlines the basic conceptual frameworks of multidimensionality and antisubordination praxis, suggesting that these theories, augmented and in part developed by scholarship related to CRT necessarily informs the CRT project. Part five concludes the paper probing a broader application of CRT insights.

INTELLECTUAL ANTECEDENTS

Many scholars have described the origins of CRT. They suggest that it owes its intellectual genesis to three intellectual movements. The first is the civil rights movement and the critical assessments of its effects in changing the actual conditions of black life. Second, CRT builds upon the themes and critical understandings of law exposed by the critical legal studies movement (Crenshaw et al., 1995; Delgado and Stefancic, 2000). And third, it incorporates many of the insights and theorising of feminist legal and other feminist scholars (Delgado and Stefancic, 2000).

Richard Delgado traces CRT's genesis to the early 1970s when several legal scholars began to express doubts about the effectiveness of the civil rights movement's legal strategy in pursuit of racial justice. For instance, Derrick Bell, considered a forefather of CRT, in an essay in 1976, suggested that civil rights attorneys' approach to litigating school cases for purposes of desegregating entire school districts (and balancing them racially) might be at odds with their clients' – African American families – very real hopes and concrete goals of immediately improving their children's education (Bell, 1976). In another article, Bell argued that the result in the 1954 *Board v. Brown* decision, although heralded as a triumph of the civil rights legal strategy, might be better explained by what he called 'interest convergence' (Bell, 1980), a theme that has become a mainstay of critical race analysis. *Brown*, he suggested, came about not because of some belated realisation by whites of the harms that black children suffered under segregation, but rather, because of its value to whites – a value and interest that converged with black aspirations for freedom and well-being. The decision, he suggests, was intended to and 'helped to provide immediate credibility to America's struggle with communist countries to win the hearts and minds of emerging third world people' (Bell, 1980: 524). The implication of Bell's analysis that the goal of the US government in advocating for the decision in *Brown* had little to do with improving the education or life chances of black children, rang particularly accurate in 2004 when 50 years after the decision, education in the United States was found to be as segregated (and disadvantaging) in terms of race as it had been at the time of *Brown*.[7] Bell later argued that racism was pervasive in the American social order, that law was imbued with it and that racism was a permanent feature of American society including its legal system (Bell, 1989, 1993, 2004).

At about the same time, the critical legal studies movement based in the legal academy was growing. This movement questioned the entire edifice of law as an objective arbiter of social conflict distinct from the messiness of politics and political choices. This movement, which included scholars such as Alan Freeman, Peter Gabel, Duncan Kennedy and Mark Tushnet, successfully demonstrated the ways in which legal rules were, in and of themselves, not determinate of a particular result (Kairys, 1982).[8] They showed that for any given rule, there were multiple, contrasting and conflicting rules whose resolution required actors to make choices. These choices were political ones that generally reflected, supported and legitimised the social power of dominant classes (Kairys, 1982; Rabinowitz, 1982).

However, they rejected what they termed 'vulgar instrumentalist' or 'structuralist' accounts of law that understand it as merely a tool and reflection of bourgeoisie/elite interest and ideas of a superstructural phenomenon determined by the underlying economic base. Rather, drawing in part on the Italian philosopher Antonio Gramsci's idea of hegemony, critical legal studies scholars understand law as a complex system with many functions, one of which is to exercise and simultaneously *legitimate* the use of institutional violence within the *prevailing* social arrangements in a way that gains the consent and acquiescence of the subordinated to their conditions (Cover, 1986). Law does this political work by deploying a distinct and elaborate discourse and body of knowledge (which while constraining choice does not eliminate it, but is nonetheless popularly perceived as objective and apolitical) to justify its decisions. These decisions sometimes actually restrain the exercise of power and occasionally provide justice to ordinary people. In doing so, however, they lend legitimacy to law and to many of the existing social arrangements and institutions of which law is a part. Thus, while there may indeed be 'a difference between arbitrary power and [the] rule of law', law may also be 'in some part sham' (Rabinowitz, 1998: 688, citing E.P. Thompson).

So, for example, in a path-breaking article on antidiscrimination law, Alan Freeman argued that anti-discrimination law offered a credible measure of tangible progress without in any way disturbing the basic class structure of the American society (Freeman, 1990). This was accomplished by the anti-discrimination law using concepts such as intent, fault, colourblindness and formal equality, which over time, ultimately located the problem of racism in the intentional actions of bad actors instead of the established caste system that included the conscious and unconscious habitual human and institutional practices of racial ordering. The remedy to the problem, defined in this manner, was to compel the bad actors to act differently instead of changing or dismantling the caste system of embedded racial arrangements.[9] Thus, although judges declared that law would treat everyone the same, they did so without regard to and so without changing the conditions that stratified people(s) socially and materially in the first place. As such, anti-discrimination law outlawed the obvious and explicit manifestations of racism (the 'white only' signs of the 'Jim Crow' segregation era) and thereby provided credible evidence that the law and the basic structure of society were fair, without disturbing the society's structures and systems within which racism was deeply embedded.

And finally, though perhaps not initially perceived, CRT owes a debt to yet another school of thought: feminism. As Delgado notes, CRT builds upon feminist 'insights into the relationship between power and the construction of social roles, as well as the unseen, largely invisible collection of patterns and habits that make up patriarchy and other types of domination' (Delgado and Stefancic, 2001: 5). In addition, the idea of antisubordination, the central stance of 'race crits', can be traced not only to race scholars but also to feminist scholarship.[10]

CRT TENETS AND METHODOLOGY

The basic tenets of CRT remain true to the original ideas discussed in the 1990 CRT workshop, which was established in 1989 and continued until 1997. With little modification, critical race theory:

- holds that racism is pervasive and endemic to, rather than a deviation from, American norms;
- [rejects] dominant claims of meritocracy, neutrality, objectivity and colorblindness;
- [rejects] ahistoricism, and insists on contextual, historical analysis of law;
- challenges the presumptive legitimacy of social institutions;
- insists on recognition of both the experiential knowledge and critical consciousness of people of color in understanding law and society;
- is interdisciplinary and eclectic (drawing upon, inter alias, liberalism, poststructuralist, feminism, Marxism, critical legal theory, postmodernism, and pragmatism) with the claim that the intersection of race and the law overruns disciplinary boundaries;
- works toward the liberation of people of color as it embraces the larger project of liberating all oppressed people (Phillips, 1999: 1249–1250).

The purpose of CRT, its *raison d'être*, is twofold. First, its purpose is to demonstrate the many ways in which white supremacy is endemic to American society by 'exposing the facets of law and legal discourse that create racial categories and legitimate racial subordination' (Crenshaw et al., 1995: xiii). Second, its purpose is to destabilise and change this relationship, in part by challenging or proposing alternative laws, among other things, in order to contribute to the liberation of oppressed people. As Jerome Culp notes, CRT may mean many different things to different people but 'there is a common belief in an opposition to oppression' (Culp, 1999: 1638). And, CRT scholars such as Matsuda and Hutchinson, as well as LatCrit and others have issued a clarion call that *Antisubordination,* a stance against all forms of oppression and subordination, be both the commitment of race scholars and the *principle* upon which racial justice, particularly *equality*, be understood and practiced (Matsuda, 1999; Hutchinson, 2003).

These tenets and the overall commitment to antisubordination that CRT scholars evidence also provide crucial insight into CRT methodological tendencies. CRT is said to have no single, unifying methodology. Rather it is eclectic, drawing from various schools, disciplines and approaches. Harris, in providing some examples of the different methodologies employed by race crits, notes that they include structuralism, historical, doctrinal (legal), empirical and economic analyses (Harris, 2002: 1218 n.6).

CRT approaches can, however, be said to possess some unifying themes or methodological tendencies. These include a particular focus on context and history. CRT suggests that a rule or principle may mean different things in different contexts and/or historical periods. So, for instance, they have argued that the idea of colourblindness, first expressed in Justice Harlan's 1896 dissent in *Plessy v. Ferguson*, can be understood as a progressive idea in the context of a society in which law sanctioned the explicit and systematic oppression of blacks after slavery. However, a colourblind approach to race in the current era when the subordination of blacks is no longer explicit but remains systematic is no longer a progressive approach. Thus, as an abstract principle its meaning and progressive potential is neither universal nor trans-historical. CRT, therefore, pays particular attention to the specificity of context in order to understand the meanings of a particular concept or practice, to evaluate a particular position and to render additional information and ideas. Further, CRT argues that as rules and principles mean different things in different contexts, they *should* mean different things in different contexts. So, for instance, equality might mean symmetrical or 'same treatment' in a society without vast racial, gender and class inequalities but might mean and require affirmative practices to bring about equality for historically disadvantaged groups, treating them differently from the privileged, in a society with these alarming disparities.

In addition, CRT scholars listen to and scrutinise the voices, understandings and experiences of marginalised and oppressed peoples to situate, test and inspire the examination of particular and/or novel approaches to law. The idea of distinctive minority voices, recognises, for example, that not every Native American thinks critically about celebrating Columbus's 'discovery of America' as a US holiday or has a sceptical opinion of it. But it does understand that given Native American history, the conditions of oppression, and the cultural nature of their resistance, Native Americans, as a group, might find the idea of Columbus *discovering* America, problematic, and not exactly a cause for *celebration*. This understanding has led CRT scholars to excavate forgotten or overlooked histories, rules and cases, as well as, the cultural practices, stories and perspectives of marginalised groups as sources for grounding their analysis.

In this vein, race crits have often successfully employed storytelling or narrative to explore alternative meanings, insights and perspectives on an issue. Some of the leading legal storytellers include, Derrick Bell (*And We Are Not Saved* (1989) and *Faces at the Bottom of the Well* (1993)), Richard Delgado, in his *Rodrigo series* (1996) and Patricia Williams in the *Alchemy of Race and Rights* (1991). Legal storytelling has garnered significant critique, including criticism 1) that such stories are not subject to empirical or other typical methods of evaluation; 2) that challenge the idea of a particular minority voice or perspective; and 3) that charge that such stories tend to distort the 'truth' (Farber and Sherry, 1993), a truth understood by many CRT theorists, as simply the common sense understandings that arise under the current hegemonic ideologies and practices. It has further led to the suggestion, as Dorothy Brown points out, that CRT stands against empiricism as a form of argumentation and verification because it arguably negates narrative.[11] This idea is buttressed by CRT's embrace of CLS's critique of the Law and Economics movement, a scholarly tradition that often employs empirical data. While most law is viewed from the liberal perspective of individual rights perceived as neutral and objective, the Law and Economics School, like CLS, is critical of that approach. Law and Economics, however, is a conservative approach, which according to crits, simply replaces law's claims of impartially and neutrality with similar claims for the field of economics. Economics, however, is neither neutral nor objective. Rather, it too involves political choices both at the level of practice and study. And, arguably, both are replete with the values, assumptions, presumptions and dictates about human behaviour and the operation of society as shaped by and understood within the current reigning capitalist economic order (White, 1987).

Harris, however, notes that CRT scholars have employed both empirical data and economic analysis. Nevertheless, an argument based on empiricism or economic analysis, according to CRT, is just that, a form of argumentation. Similar empirical data could presumably be used, like various rules, to support contrary and alternative arguments and interpretations. Ultimately, the question from a CRT perspective is: how useful are these tools in representing reality and promoting social justice. Finally, the tendency of CRT to deconstruct and expose the racial meanings of law betrays its postmodern sensibilities and contradicts its commitment to modernist ideals of justice? truth and dignity. However, in view of the dual vision that Du Bois located in the oppressed, and the dual respect and disdain that oppressed people have shown for the law (Williams, 1991), scholars have encouraged race crits to inhabit the tension between its postmodern insights and its modernist ideals of justice because within that tension lies CRT's creative potential (Harris, 1994).

LAW AND THE CONSTRUCTION OF RACE

Below I provide a brief structural history of the relationship between race and law focusing primarily on US case law, and drawing on, and applying, some of the insights and methodological tendencies of CRT. Specifically, I employ historical analysis and narrative to tell the story of this relationship between law and race.

The narrative emphasises the longevity of American racial ordering and practice, the breadth of that racial ordering, and its depth in regulating American life. It does so to demonstrate the ways in which law both constructs and produces races and racism and to demonstrate the deeply structured nature of race in US society. Further, it is meant to show how law has aided in building race into the institutions, systems and processes of the society as well as into the very psychics and patterns of behaviour of its inhabitants. In doing so, it provides a counter-narrative to the dominant and ever-popular American story about race and law that suggests that the struggle for racial justice, though long and incremental is nevertheless forward moving, progressive and eventually triumphant, given the American creed and precepts (Delgado and Stefancic, 2001; Bell, 2004: 22). Instead, it suggests the continuity of the underlying structures of white supremacist thought, operation and social arrangements, though, accomplished through new and changing forces and rationalisations.

I then provide a simplified theory of law, its functions and the way it operates in the United States, from a CRT perspective. Here I emphasise the law's power to aid in crafting social arrangements while simultaneously justifying or telling a story about what it is doing. I highlight a couple of cases to illustrate what judges say they are doing in reference to race in contrast to what they through their decisions actually make concretely and structurally of race.

Brief structural history

Throughout most of its history, legislators, legal practitioners and judges have made and interpreted various legal doctrines, rules and procedures to define, construct, produce and preserve white privilege and black subordination, as well as the subordination of other people of colour. Throughout most of its history, American law has been decidedly race conscious and specifically white supremacist whenever it has encountered what it, itself, has often defined as Other. For instance, in order to perpetuate a white state, judges defined whiteness through cases to determine whether a Japanese man was white for purposes of citizenship, whether a Chinese person was Black or Indian for the purpose of determining whether he could testify against a white, and whether Mexicans were white and thus entitled to serve on juries (*Ozawa v. United States*, 1922; *People v. Hall*, 1854; *Hernandez v. Texas*, 1954). American law facilitated, defined and established white privileges by limiting the rights of Indians to their land and facilitating white appropriation of the same land (*Johnson v. McIntosh*, 1823). It did so using slave laws, black codes and Jim Crow laws to exploit black labour and maintain black subordination for the purposes of white wealth accumulation and white racial class consolidation (*Dred Scott*, 1856; *Plessy v. Ferguson*, 1896). It has constructed race for the purposes of determining who might vote, the manner in which those who presumably were entitled to vote could do so, and whether such people could actually and effectively vote (e.g., Texas Statute, Art. 3093a;[12] *Breedlove v. Suttles* (1937)).[13] It delineated a range of businesses practices affecting everyone from labourers to professionals including who could be treated by a doctor or a nurse. It has used racial categories to the detriment of people of colour to determine questions concerning where people can live, who they can marry, what schools they can attend, and where they sit on a train, in a cafeteria, and in a theatre (e.g. *Kraemer v. Shelley*, (1946);[14] *Jackson v. State,* (1954);[15] *Sweat v. Painter*, (1948);[16] and *Plessy*).

From a CRT perspective, the movement from overt racial oppression sanctioned by law to law's racial neutrality or colourblindness has done little to undo the systemic and accumulated conditions of racial oppression created by and through law over several hundred years. For that matter, except for two very brief though significant periods, American law has been, and remains, a bulwark of white supremacy. The first period followed the promulgation of the Emancipation Proclamation, and the ratification of the 13th, 14th, and 15th Amendments. Wrenched from a civil war, these laws helped radically change the status of blacks from slaves to free people and might have held the promise of providing the economic, social and political rewards of citizenship and belonging. The promise was short lived as the country's political leadership capitulated to the southern elites' efforts to reassert white control over black life, and various legal actors including judges, enacted laws and interpreted legal doctrine, to narrow the rewards of citizenship based on race helping to legitimate the Jim Crow era of racial segregation, as exemplified in *Plessy*.

The second period, almost 70 years later, sparked in part by cases such as *Hernandez* and *Brown*, ushered in the civil rights movement and renewed the promise of equality. The highlight of this period was the passage of the Civil Rights Act of 1964, the Voting Rights Act of 1965, the Fair Housing Act of 1968 and the decision in *Griggs v. Duke Power Co.*, (1971). The latter case involved hiring practices, based on standards not related to job performance, which had the effect of disqualifying disproportionate numbers of blacks relative to whites. In *Griggs*, the Supreme Court took an approach to race (not the colourblind approach) that might have engendered actions that would result in actual changes in the conditions of black lives in terms of poverty, wealth accumulation, health, etc. This was so because it potentially rendered successful, suits brought on evidence of racial disparities and the impact of laws (demonstrated largely through statistical evidence of continuing disparities), instead of on proof of some individual's intention to discriminate. However, like the earlier period of Reconstruction, courts began to narrow these laws, thereby stabilising and legitimising the prevailing order of white privilege and non-white disadvantage. So for example, though the desegregation (integration) of secondary schools in the United States had only begun in earnest in 1964 due to the Courts initial hesitancy and massive white resistance; the Court had already signalled its retreat from desegregation by 1973 allowing a school board to potentially escape the imposition of desegregation (integration) orders if it could show that segregation had occurred owing to acts other than the board's *intentional* activities. (Brown, 2005 discussing *Keyes v. School District No. 1, Denver, Colorado*).[17]

The courts narrowed the laws not only by focusing primarily on identifiable intentional acts of discrimination but also by focusing on the individual and virtually banning the use of racial categories arguably long before affirmative uses of these categories could effect any significant change in the social arrangements and structure of white racial power. In essence they took a colourblind approach that prohibited almost all uses of racial categories regardless of whether they were being used to subordinate black and other non-whites ('invidious discrimination') or redress systemic white racial oppression ('benign discrimination'). And, in focusing on the individual, the courts have been able to ignore or trivialise societal wide racial ordering engrained for several hundred years in the institutional and human decisionmaking throughout the country at all levels. Further, given the success of the civil rights movement in pressing for the removal of obvious signs of black racial oppression, the colourblind individualist approach has been applied to and primarily targets the *measures* and *remedies* meant to attack non-white subordination and discrimination (measures often opposed by whites), even as minorities have sought to expand these. While the Supreme Court has not interpreted the equal protection clause as requiring a colourblindness approach, it has largely and increasingly accomplished this effect by applying various procedural and other standards drawing on the logic of colourblind individualism.[18]

For example, in 1978, in a suit bought by a white student denied medical school admission, the Court struck down a medical admission programme that reserved a number of seats for minority students in the entering class. The Court noted, 'the guarantee of equal protection cannot mean one thing when applied to one *individual* and something else when applied to a person of another color' (*Regents of Univ. of Cal v. Bakke*: 289–290). The Court thus struck down a programme meant to undo the racial ordering of white privilege and non-white subordination arguing that equality protected the individual regardless of his 'colour', despite societal oppression of groups that rendered admissions into the medical school overwhelmingly white in the first place. In addition, the Court expressed concern for 'innocent persons', (referring to white people) noting that it was impermissible for them to be forced 'to bear the burdens of redressing burdens not of their making',[19] while blind to the fact that the *decision left blacks bearing the burdens of exclusion, subordination and discrimination not of their own making.*

Further in 1986, the Court struck down provisions of a collective bargaining agreement that in response to past integration, litigation provided black teachers greater protection against layoffs than it provided to white teachers with higher levels of seniority. In absence of the agreement, an agreement, again, meant to undo the racial ordering of white privilege and non-white subordination, black teachers would have been the first fired because they were the last hired, their hiring presumably occasioned in the first place by affirmative action measures. Brought by white teachers seeking to protect their positions through the seniority plan, the Court, referring to whites, noted that the level of scrutiny did not alter 'because the challenged classification operates against a group that historically had *not* been subject to governmental discrimination,' (*Wygant v. Jackson Board of Education*: 273). Equality was thus blind to the color, context, and circumstance of the differently racialized groups in a white supremacist ordered society even if the society was not. Further, commenting on 'societal wide discrimination' against blacks as a basis for striking down the agreement, the Court notes:

> Societal discrimination, without more is too amorphous a basis for imposing a racially classified remedy ... No one doubts that there has been serious racial discrimination in this country. But as the basis for imposing discriminatory legal remedies that work against *innocent people*, societal discrimination is insufficient and over-expansive emphasis mine.

Apparently, it was acceptable for blacks and other non-whites to suffer the cost of societal discrimination operating to the benefit of whites, but inappropriate and over-expansive for whites to bear any costs in eliminating this same societal discrimination from which they benefitted and in which they played a role in maintaining.

Continuing this trend, in 1989, the Court struck down a plan by the city of Richmond requiring those who received city contracts to subcontract thirty percent of the contract's value to businesses owned by minorities. The city passed the plan to remedy past discrimination in the construction industry based on a number of factors including, 1) testimony about discrimination in the industry; 2) the fact that although black residents constituted almost fifty percent of the city, they received less than one percent of public contracting funds; 3) that there were almost no minority contractors in local and state contractors' associations; and 4) that 'in 1977, Congress [had] made a determination that the effects of past discrimination had stifled minority participation in the construction industry nationally' (*Richmond v. J.A. Croson Co.*: 499). Nevertheless, the Court explained that these facts did not 'taken singly or together provide a basis for a prima facie case of a constitutional or statutory violation by anyone in the city's construction industry'. In fact, the court reasoned that the wrong was so 'ill-defined' that 'relief' – apparently incredulously and impermissibly – 'could extend until the percentage of public contracts awarded to minority-controlled businesses in Richmond mirrored the percentage of minorities in the population as a whole'[!][20]

The Supreme Court, however, in *Grutter v. Boiling* (2004), a case involving a white student denied law school admission, ultimately allowed applicants' 'race' to be considered in the limited area of admissions in higher educational institutions. But it came on the heels of lower court decisions and statutes applying colourblind approaches to similar affirmative action cases. The effects of these laws were that fewer black and brown students gained admission into these institutions, leaving them overwhelmingly white (see e.g., *Hopwood v. Texas* and California Proposition 209). These events revealed not only the social embeddedness of white supremacist racial ordering but demonstrated the way in which colourblindness policies were a proxy for and a mechanism for maintaining white access and privilege. Further, though *Grutter* permitted the use of race in admissions on a theory of diversity, it abstracted the meaning of diversity in a way that disconnected it from exclusionary practices and social justice concerns,[21] while simultaneously proclaiming the benefits of diversity as teaching, presumably white students that 'there is no minority view', and 'visibly' lending *legitimacy* to the social system by signifying that the 'path to leadership is open to talented and qualified individuals of every race and ethnicity', whether it is or not.

However, it is in the complicated area of voting where the colourblind ideology seems to have received its greatest boost. Here, despite the fact that the 15th Amendment was initially enacted to provide the newly emerging slaves a right to vote and there has been a long and appalling struggle to ensure meaningful enfranchisement, the Court, according to Bell had established a new constitutional injury. First articulated in the case of *Shaw v. Reno* (1993), the injury seems to be that of a state by 'a predominate use of race in redistricting' impermissibly sending the message 'that racial identity is and should be a salient political characteristic' (Bell, 2004: 516). Rather, redistricting should be race-blind. Unsurprisingly, the case involved and blocked efforts to create a voting district that would render black votes meaningful, while ignoring the pervasive historical and current reality of racial bloc voting by whites, who only occasionally elect black representatives and rarely elect officials who will effectively represent black or other non-white interests.

The ultimate effect of these interpretations is that law, while denying blacks and other non-whites justice, has protected vested white interests accumulated over time, such as seniority systems, educational advancement, wealth, and/or or white expectations, through the racialised orderings of the society, *first on a theory of white superiority and increasingly on the theory of colourblindness.*

Until the job of racial justice is done, CRT theorists might argue, CRT will expose the whiteness of colourblindness, the white supremacist effects of colourblind laws and rulings, and the white consciousness of American society and power. And CRT theorists will do so, from inside the experiences, consciousness and perspectives of black, Native American, Latina/o, Asian American people, etc., using these essentialised categories that white power created to oppress, strategically, as sources of solidarity, empowerment and analysis. These efforts have been supplemented by the work of critical white studies scholars who analyse, among other things, white privilege (see e.g., Frankenberg, 1993; Lipsitz, 1998; McIntosh, 1988; Roediger, 1998).

Law: telling a story, structuring reality

CRT understands law as having a number of systemic functions. These functions, though simplified, are, on the one hand, creating and interpreting rules, regulating behaviour and mediating conflict through providing incentives and penalties to enforce compliance. In this way law contributes to the structure of the society. On the other hand, law functions to legitimate this power. It does so by justifying a decision or rather telling a story about the way the rules and decisions are necessary, neutral, pre-ordained or otherwise correct. Law thus has the power both to frame a debate and to enshrine parts of its determinations in the social structure.

The various legal tasks in the United States are divided among different institutions with their own internal logic and theories of justification. For instance, the legislature is supposed to make laws in support of the public welfare (function) as democratically elected representatives of the populace (justification). The courts are to interpret rules and decide conflicts in accordance with the law – (function), and act as a check against the potential 'tyranny of the majority' inherent in democracy as practiced by the United States, among other things (justification) (Hutchinson, 2003; Ely, 1980).

Then, there are the people, who inhabit the roles of judges, legislators, executors, administrators, attorneys, etc. They tend to come from the dominant class or are educated into their 'proper roles'. As such, they are taught the logics of the various legal systems and processes though educational processes that sensitise and link them to the appropriate hierarchal roles they are to play (Kennedy, 1982).

Law not only makes decisions about race or has racial impact, it also tells a story about race. It does so through its own legal discourse involving the analysis of abstract principles. A story from within this discourse emerges that mirrors the popular story in society about the incremental but nevertheless forward-moving progress on racial matters. However, the stories that law tells about itself and the decisions it enshrines into the social structure do not exhibit a one-to-one correspondence. Often judges may say the law finds racism odious even as the very cases being decided, relied on and/or cited as precedent in many ways demonstrate the contrary by continuing to construct and cement the racial caste system even as they justify the case's outcome as natural, necessary or correct.

For instance, the court quoted in the passage below provides its own legal history on the issue of race. 'Over the years, this Court has consistently repudiated "distinctions between citizens solely because of their ancestry" as being 'odious to a free people whose institutions are founded upon the doctrine of equality' *Loving v. Virginia* (1967).

In this case, the Supreme Court struck down a Virginia anti-miscegenation law essentially outlawing such laws in the United States. Ironically, while stressing the way it has 'consistently repudiated distinctions between citizens, it relies on a case in which it upheld curfew laws that applied specifically to people of Japanese descent, many of whom were Americans (*Hirabayashi v. United States*, 1943) Further, this curfew case was later used to rationalise the *Korematsu* decision upholding the executive order that ordered the interment of Japanese Americans in American interment camps during World War II (*Korematsu v. United States*, 1944). Further, these two decisions were rendered while the doctrine of 'separate but equal' still reigned supreme.

Consider also the Court's language in *McClesky v. Kemp* (1987). The case involved the Georgia sentencing system. While the system appears race-neutral, it nonetheless has a disparate and disadvantaging impact on blacks. Georgia's capital sentencing system had been invalidated three times by the Supreme Court within the previous 15 years, in which on one occasion, race was specifically mentioned. In addition, Georgia had a long history of a 'dual system'. In the case, *McCleskey*, a black man was sentenced to death for murdering a white police officer. He challenged the death sentence in his case based on a sophisticated statistical study, finding that prosecutors in Georgia sought the death penalty in 70 percent of cases involving a black defendant and white victim, compared to only 32 percent of the time where both defendant and victim were white. It also showed that the death penalty was imposed in 22 percent of cases involving black defendants and white victims, as compared to only 8 percent in cases involving both whites. While rejecting the use of the statistical report to document discriminatory effect in the absence of proof of intentional discrimination, the Court nevertheless stresses its efforts to overcome racism in the criminal justice system. It notes: 'Because of the risk that the factor of race may enter the criminal justice process, we have engaged in "unceasing efforts" to eradicate racial prejudice from our criminal justice system' (McClesky, 1987: 309).

But the Court undercut this assertion near the outset of the case by limiting the examination. It states:

> Our analysis begins with the basic principle that a defendant who alleges an equal protection violation has the burden of proving 'the existence of purposeful discrimination.' ... Thus, to prevail under the Equal Protection Clause, [the defendant] must prove *that the decision makers in his case acted with discriminatory purpose.* (p. 292) [emphasis mine]

The Court's *unceasing efforts* to eradicate racial prejudice in the criminal justice system stopped at the door of proof of intent against and in an individual defendant's case without an examination of the *systemic* context in which the case was decided.

In these ways, judges tell a story about law and its role in pushing the ever-forward progress toward racial justice while rationalising decisions that often effectively stunt its progress on the basis of highly manipulative legal concepts such as intent.

MULTIDIMENSIONALITY AND ANTISUBORDINATION PRAXIS: CRT-RELATED SCHOLARSHIP BROADENING THE CRT PROJECT

The development and proliferation of other scholarship such as LatCrit, Asian American legal scholarship, critical race feminism and the writings of sexual minorities of colour to explore race, law and other systems of oppression, raised concerns about the fragmentation of the CRT project. The development of this related scholarship, and for instance the separate institutionalisation of the LatCrit project, also raised concerns over the multiplication of identity-based groups and thus the elevation of identity politics as opposed to the formation of a broad political movement. However, though a broad political movement is yet to emerge, this 'fragmentation' has actually deepened and broadened the CRT project by providing the necessary intellectual expansion and theoretical bridges between identity politics and a politics of solidarity that values difference. So, for instance, these bodies of scholarship broadened the lens through which the workings of white racial privilege were revealed by, for example, exploring the racialised experiences of Latina/os through LatCrit, in addition to the racialised experiences of African Americans. At the same time, it deepened the commitment to and the project of antisubordination by focusing on other systems of social subordination in additional to racial subordination, such as exploring the patriarchal gendered oppression of women through critical race feminism.

In addition, it has spurred the development of other theories through which to analyse these systems of subordination. Multidimensionality is one such emerging theory and methodology. It draws on a number of theoretical strands but is grounded in the theoretical insights and practical experiences of two related notions, those of anti-essentialism and intersectionality. Both of these insights not only laid the foundation for multidimensionality theory, they also played a significant role in the way much of the CRT-related scholarship was conceptualised and formed.

Anti-essentialism and intersectionality as building blocks in the formation of CRT-related scholarship and multidimensionality

Essentialism and anti-essentialism had engendered substantial prior debate in CRT, feminist and other intellectual circles. It recognises, for example, that black people have no coherent collective identity, that no single experience or perspective could reflect the common interests of the people constituting *the group* 'without acknowledging the intra-group differences and relations of subordination and domination that are organized around differences such as [gender], sexual orientation, language proficiencies, national origin, and age' (Iglesias, 2006). This insight in many ways exposes the illusion of group identity by rendering visible the divisions and fragmentedness of group identity. Nonetheless, anti-essentialist insights were foundational to the formation of LatCrit, Asian American, critical race feminism and sexual minorities of colour projects (in more ways than had been apparent in CRT's initial focus on the African American experience). This is so in part because though these projects were based on identities historically seen, shaped and oppressed as biologically (and racially) essential and monolithic, these identities encompassed people of differing nationalities, cultures, and sometimes even 'races'. For instance, critical race feminism, which focused on the experiences of women of colour both nationally and internationally (Wing, 1997: 4) drew on feminism, which had long challenged the category of 'woman' in feminist writings as largely reflecting the interest and priorities of white middle class women in the United States and thus not representative of *all* women's experience – a quintessential anti-essentialist claim (e.g., Harris, 1990). But the disaggregation of the group called women created space to explore the distinct and various experiences of women of colour. Anti-essentialism was also foundational in many of the writings of sexual minorities of colour who initially had to fight, in the context of CRT workshops, to have their struggle against heterosexist oppression embraced as part of the antisubordination commitment within CRT (Phillips, 1999). This experience highlighted, for instance, the heterogeneity of black experiences and confirmed the anti-essentialist insight.

Anti-essentialism also became crucial and foundational for LatCrit and Asian American Legal scholarship. LatCrit consciously saw itself as a first cousin of CRT and was committed to building on its strengths while focusing on issues germane to the Latina/o community and Latina/o identity (Valdes, 1996, 1997b). This was a challenge in part because though Latina/o identity was historically constructed in the US as a monolithic 'Hispanic' group, it, as a practical matter, embraced people representing a host of different nationalities with different cultural perspectives and historical experiences, and who were raced differently, as black, white and/or mestizo, among other differences. Valdes, a founder of LatCrit, envisioned a larger pan-Latina/o identity but one which both respected and explored the diversities within the group while building solidarity among the differently positioned individuals and groups within the larger pan-ethnic collectivity. LatCrit thus strategically used a non-essentialised Latino identity to bring people together in order to engage critical legal analyses that often delineated the histories and differences among Latino groups such as Cuban Americans and say those of Mexican Americans, while also demonstrating shared commonalities of oppression, such as the way ethnic characteristics such as the Spanish language had been racialised to both stigmatise and materially disadvantage all Latinos. So, for example, LatCrit scholars demonstrated the way the term 'spic' is a racial epithet stigmatising Latina/os on the basis of language (Ruiz Cameron, 1997: 1365). They also analysed language in the context of the 'English Only Movement' in the United States, which in complicated ways mixed racial imagery using terms such as 'rampant bilingualism' and 'moguls' to stigmatise Spanish-speaking people as part of a process meant to exclude and deny them information, government services and opportunities on the basis of English language ability (Serrano, 1997). In this way the political use of Latino identity for LatCrit both expanded analysis of the connection between the different 'Latina/o groups' and expanded analyses of the connection between law and white racial power while challenging it.

Asian American legal scholarship faced similar challenges. It focused on the unique and varied experiences of Asian Americans in US society. Asian Americans, like Latina/os, consist of people originating historically from widely varying Asian communities and nationalities. Like Latina/os they experience a racialised ethnicity that often flattens and misunderstands their differing ethnic diversities. Their experiences often include an American view of them as perpetually foreign, which thereby legitimates their exclusion and subordination while simultaneously holding them up as model minorities, as against other minorities (Chang, 1993; Saito, 1997; Gotanda, 1992).

Thus while the development of critical race feminism, LatCrit, Asian American legal scholarship, etc. seemed to fragment the CRT project, the anti-essentialist insight seemed internally to fragment all of the group identities that informed the foci of the different analyses. However, in the process of forming these collectivities, the anti-essentialist critique made it apparent that these groups were *political* associations organised in part to demonstrate through analysis their shared current and historical experiences of oppression and ultimately to propound common goals to resist this oppression and transform society. In other words, though CRT and related scholarship took an anti-essentialist approach to the categories of blacks, Latina/os, Asian Americans and/or women, specifically with regard to the dynamics and definition of the groups, their formation was simultaneously premised on the pragmatic idea that the individuals and the subgroups that constituted these various collectives have a shared history of oppression based on essentialised group identities. These essentialised identities had been and could be used strategically, politically and consciously to fight oppression.

The development of intersectional theory demonstrated a similar dynamic of highlighting fragmentation but ultimately uniting groups though it did so *across* racial and ethnic lines. It did so by demonstrating the links between different systems of subordination such as racism and sexism through a focus on the location and social position of racial subgroups, such as black or Asian American women. It thus highlighted the particularities of intra-race difference, as in the difference between black men and black women, while also exposing the connections between a variety of subgroups across the various racial collectives, as in women of colour, a term that represents women who are differentially racialised.

Intersectional theory, first articulated as a theory by Kimberele Crenshaw, again, drew upon black feminist thought. It had consistently argued that black women were not only oppressed by the white supremacist system of racism but were also oppressed by the patriarchal practices and system of sexism. The theory thus explored the experiences of black women at the intersection of racism and sexism, rejecting a single-axis framework (race or gender) for understanding black women's conditions. Crenshaw, for example, demonstrated the way courts in using a single-axis framework limited legal remedies available to black women by, for instance, denying them representative status in class action suits where the actions were based on charges of racial discrimination but involved circumstances (presumably around sexism) that were held not to apply to disadvantaged black men. At the same time, where an action was based on gender, if white women were not equally disadvantaged (presumably because it had racial elements), then courts again denied black women representational status. These single-axis frameworks denied the experiences of black women, which were shaped at the intersection of both racism and sexism (Crenshaw, 1990).

LatCrit scholars and sexual minorities of colour, in particular, further expanded the analysis of intersectionality recognising that it applied to all individuals and to a variety of identity-based groups, connecting them in multiple ways. Together, these insights led to the emerging theory known as multidimensionality (LatCrit and sexual minorities: Iglesias and Valdes, 2001; Valdes, 1998; Hernandez-Truyol, 1995, 1996; CRT and sexual minorities: Hutchinson, 2001).

Key insights of multidimensionality theory

Multidimensionality captures three separate ideas implicit in anti-essentialist and intersectional analyses (Mutua, 2006). First, it recognises that an individual has many dimensions, some of which are embodied human traits such as skin colour, sex, ear-lobe length, eye colour; and others which are expressive, such as being Methodist or Catholic, a cat owner or dog owner, etc. Second, multidimensionality identifies some of these dimensions as materially relevant,[22] meaning that a particular society has taken some dimensions such as colour, sex or a particular religious belief (but not ear-lobe length or owning a cat or a dog) and constructed meanings about the groups that possess them. It then allocates or denies both material and status-related resources through systems of racism, sexism, and anti-semitism, for example, which operate through multiple sites, including law. These systems operate on the individuals who belong to groups that inhabit or express a particular trait producing a host of experiences, rewards or demerits. Said differently, multidimensionality captures the way society disadvantages people or benefits them primarily on the basis of their possessing a particular group trait, linking, in many ways the material distribution of resources and the materiality of embodiment to the expressive and cognitive meanings that construct or are constructed upon materiality. Thus, the second idea of multidimensionality is a focus on systems of subordination or privilege (Hutchinson, 2004: 1199). In so focusing, it allows analysts to see the patterns woven by these systems as well as allows them to organise a politics against these patterns and systems. Third, multidimensionality recognises that these systems intersect, inter-relate and are mutually reinforcing so that, for example, racism in the US is patriarchal and patriarchy is racist. This example exposes the links between sexism and racism and potentially exposes the political coalitions that could be built between anti-racist's and anti-sexist's justice struggles.

In addition, as these systems are mutually reinforcing and intersecting, two or more systems of disadvantage or privilege often produce unique categories and experiences. So, for example, intersectional theory has been interpreted as suggesting that black men are privileged by gender and oppressed by race. But this does not sufficiently explain, for example, racial profiling as a phenomenon that happens most frequently to black men. Multidimensionality, however, might better capture not only the idea that black men are both black and men but that because systems intersect, race colours the way in which patriarchy functions with regard to black men and vice versa. It thus begins to capture the insight that black men are sometimes oppressed because they are 'blackmen' one word, one position, one socially, multidimensionally constructed oppressed group of people (Mutua, 2006). The positionality of blackmen – one word, could be further analyzed by looking at the class or other materially relevant statuses of those who are, in this example, racially profiled. In this sense, it replaces an approach that is additive, one that says for instance that poor black men are poor + black+ men, to one that allows analyst to explore the way that axes of classism, racism, gender oppression, etc., mutually construct unique positions for individuals and groups, while simultaneously demonstrating that these same forces are implicated in all identity categories.

And finally, multidimensionality is also an approach. In recognising, for example, that racial oppression is also gendered, sexualised and classed, a multidimensional approach conceptually links the struggles of racial justice, gender justice and class justice, for example; and it has the potential to link the differing groups fighting for these different types of justice projects. As such a multidimensionality approach is an approach to building solidarity and potential coalitions (Valdes, 1998).

Multidimensionality thus guards against uncritical essentialism calling instead for specificity and a contextual analysis while also allowing for analysts to make generalisations, to identify patterns, and thus to produce theory.[23] It focuses on the way in which systems such as racism and sexism link the material and the expressive.

Antisubordination praxis

While the development of CRT-related scholarship could be understood as a process of fragmentation, it can be seen as a period of intense contextualised study that deepened the CRT project of exposing the connections between race and law from a variety of perspectives. Further, it can be seen as constituting a move from '"color" to consciousness' (Valdes, 1996), from biology, and perhaps even culture, to politics, informed by the understanding and appreciation of difference, and arguably allowing the multidimensionality of oppression to be analysed and potentially attacked from a number of vantage points, ventures and enterprises.

However, all of these analyses are meant to service the goal of antisubordination – a stance against all forms of subordination, and a goal to which CRT and its related scholarship adhere. While these theories may service the commitment to antisubordination, critical race theorists suggest that this commitment must be practiced by both producing scholarship that can be used to advance antisubordination practice and by engaging in practice that would advance antisubordination theory. This engagement with struggle and the dynamic of theory-informed practice and practice-informed theory is captured by what Eric Yamamoto calls a 'critical race praxis' (Yamamoto, 1997). I refer to the idea as 'antisubordination praxis' to encompass the many justice projects that inform the antisubordination commitment.

Yamamoto has been involved in justice struggles that have brought different minority groups into conflict with each other. Aoki and Chon summarise his notions of critical race praxis as:

> [Combining] critical, pragmatic, socio-legal analysis with political lawyering and community organizing to practice justice by and for racialized communities. Its central idea is that

racial justice requires antisubordination practice. In addition to ideas and ideals, justice is something experienced through practice ... It requires, in appropriate instances, using critiqu[e], and moving beyond notions of legal justice pragmatically to heal disabling inter-group wounds and to force intergroup alliances. It also requires, for race theorists, enhanced attention to theory translation and deeper engagement with frontline practice; and for polit-ical lawyers and community activists, increased attention to a critical rethinking of what race is, how civil rights are conceived, and why law sometimes operates as a discursive power strategy. (1999: 36)[24]

While this definition raises a number of provocative issues, two seem particularly relevant for this discussion. The first is the recognition that justice is experienced through practice and that racial justice in particular requires an antisubordination practice. As such, this requires groups to work through intergroup wounds and conflicts to promote healing. This action may represent a justice project in and of itself but also may be the key for different groups to work in coalition in pursuit of shared justice goals.

Second, Yamamoto emphasises that CRT theorists should translate theory into practical use for activists and legal practitioners and that practitioners should think critically and theoretically about what their work means and the ways it may be limited. This is best accomplished by these groups working together, theorist and activist, to mutually inform one another's work, and more importantly, to do so on behalf of and in conjunction with communities of colour. Critical race theorists believe that engaged community work and practice as well as attention to this work should dictate and inform the contours of CRT theorising, grounding it and potentially rendering it more useful for community advancement. Many critical race theorists have embraced this idea as does much CRT- related scholarship.

CONCLUSION

This essay has touched on a number of themes central to critical race theory such as critiques of colourblind individualism, antisubordination, intersectionality and multidimensionality. Yet the question arises: what might the contributions of CRT mean for the study and politics of race and ethnicity outside the discipline of law and what is its impact in other societies?

CRT's origins and focus is the American situation and its emphasis is a contex-tual approach to any examination of social phenomenon. Due to this, it pays par-ticular attention to the American legal setting. Thus, its application to other disciplines and other countries may first appear to be limited. The reality suggests otherwise, particularly with regard to its spread to other disciplines within the United States. For instance, while scholars in fields such as sociology, psychology and philosophy, among others in the United States engage CRT and related schol-arship, it appears to have had its biggest impact in education where its insights and methodology have been widely explored (see e.g., Solorzano and Yasso, 2001; Ladson-Billings, 1998; Parker, 1998; Parker and Lynn, 2002). However, the breath its impact on scholarship and thought globally seems more limited.

So, for instance, in law, CRT's natural home, Mathias Moschel has argued that CRT and related scholarship has had limited impact in Europe.[25] He notes that less than a dozen books and articles have been written in a European language about CRT or which apply CRT precepts to Europe. However, while he explains the various obstacles to CRT's adoption in Europe, he argues that a number of CRT precepts are applicable to the European context. In addition, while scholars from places as diverse as Africa, Australia and New Zealand, Eastern Europe, India and Latin America too have engaged CRT and related scholarship, particularly critical race feminism and LatCrit, these scholars have often done so in the context of publications primarily written in the United States.[26] However, this may be changing and two brief points suggest that CRT may have much wider application.[27]

The first point is with regard to CRT and other disciplines. CRT draws from many other disciplines in crafting its legal arguments and ideas. Scholars and activists who work in other fields such as anthropology, economics, psychology, sociology, postcolonial studies, feminist theorising and organising, etc., will see many of the ideas central to modern studies of their disciplines implicit in the legal arguments and insights that CRT makes. For instance, feminists may see similarities in the way that colourblindness reproduces some of the same fault lines of gender blindness in that it tends to reinforce a hidden norm, whiteness on the one hand, maleness on the other. At the same time, many understand that colourblindness is not simply a legal or law-related policy and phenomenon but a more generalised aspiration of many in American society. To the extent that CRT builds on these other disciplines, it may also contribute to them.

Makau Mutua has made clear the second point on the application of CRT to the international legal realm and to studies of societies outside of the United States. He argues that though CRT flows out of a particular and specific context and concerns 'itself with the struggles of various minority groups in the United States, its 'particularity and specificity' belies its universality. This universality lies in its emancipatory potential located in its antisubordination stance, which he understands as condemning powerlessness and oppression around a host of identity categories. He suggests that no category or identity of people 'should be left out in understanding or fighting against exploitation and subordination' (Mutua, 2000: 848). As many countries consist of categories of people who are powerless, the analysis focuses attention on these peoples and groups – on their stories, perspectives, and experience. But equally important, he suggests, is the universality of what he calls CRT's 'theoretical method[s]' of multidimensionality and intersectionality. These tools, he argues, aid the scholar and activist in acknowledging and accounting 'for many of the indicia of subordination in the struggle against powerlessness'. He notes:

> multidimensionality and intersectionality …frees analysis from the strictures and blindness of single category/identity analysis…. It seeks to take into account many of the variables that create powerlessness, marginalization, debilitating and degrading social hierarchies and exclusion. In effect what [CRT] does is to universalize and globalize – by its holistic method – the struggles against subordination. Its specific location belies the universal tools of analysis

that it has contributed to the desegregation of complex social and legal phenomenon. ....
Because many of these categories [of oppressed identity] exist in societies outside the United
States, it would be useful for social, political and legal scholars and activists elsewhere to
study the CRT method and explore what aspects of it might inform or advance their own
struggles. (pp. 848–849)

In short, the CRT insights and method may aid those in other disciplines and
other places to call attention to and to disaggregate, for purposes of study and
remedy, the phenomena that create and support subordination.

ACKNOWLEDGEMENT

A version of this paper also appears as 'The Rise, Development, and Future
Directions of Critical Race Theory', 84 *Denver University Law Review*, pp. 329–394
(2006). While this version seeks to place CRT in its broader historical context, the
Denver version explores in more detail CRT's formation and institutionalisation
as well as the issues and people involved in that formation.

NOTES

1. See generally, Crenshaw et al. (1995); Delgado and Stefancic (2000); Perea et al. (2000);
Delgado and Stefancic (2001); Harris (2002); Valdes et al. (2002); Delgado and Stefancic (1998); Wu
(2002); Aoki (1996); Saito (1997); Chang (1993).

2. Critical race theorists would argue that race is socially constructed in a process, in which social
and materially relevant meanings are assigned to certain biological traits; whereas eye colour is a
biological trait to which no overriding social meaning has been assigned. For good treatments of the
social construction of race, see Omi and Winant (1994) and Haney-Lopez (1994).

3. In other words, colourblindness perpetuates the racial inequalities of the status quo. It has to
forbid any consideration of race, any real look at the racial situation, because to consider race
exposes the current character and organisation of society as racially unequal and informed by
current and historical practices of white supremacy. The goal of colourblindness is to hide as much
of this inequality as possible and forbid its correction, thereby perpetuating white privilege and
power.

4. This term is used to capture both the ideas of race neutrality and the emphasis in American
law on the individual. For instance, Kevin Brown (2005) uses this term to capture these two different
dynamics in discussing the demise of school desegregation efforts in the United States.

5. As Michael DeHaven Newson (2004: 346) explains, '[t]he objective of the Civil Rights struggle
has never been colorblindness. Rather, it has been the elimination of racial oppression'. Colourblind
rhetoric was a mere argument, a tactic, not the goal.

6. LatCrit literature is readily available at the LatCrit website, http://biblioteca.uprrp.edu/
LatCritCD/default.htm

7. This point was made during celebrations marking the 50th anniversary of *Brown*. See, for
example, *USA Today*, April 28, 2004, at A1 entitled 'Integrated schools still a dream 50 years later'.

8. David Kairy's (1982) edited book provides a good overview of critical legal studies' themes.
This book has been revised several times, the first edition in 1982 was updated and followed by a
publication in 1990, and then again in 1998. I like each of these editions but find the 1982 publication the best for introducing many of the basic CLS concepts and initial ideas. In this edition, the
ideas tend to be more fully explained whereas in later publications some key insights are merely
summarised. The later editions however, introduce new thinking developed in a covered area and
introduce additional essays that explore a wider breadth of legal fields.

9. Freeman also suggests that the Court's momentary flirtation with attacking the actual structural conditions of subordination through ordering school desegregation lent support to its rhetoric of change.

10. For instance, antisubordination ideas and concepts also can be traced to Catherine MacKinnon's theory of domination (1987) and Ruth Colker's articulation of the idea of antisubordination (1986).

11. Dorothy Brown (2004) in the symposium, *Critical Race Theory: The Next Frontier: Fighting Racism in the Twenty-First Century*, suggested that CRT rejects numbers as neutral, that the privileging of numbers refutes narrative, and thus empirical research may be incompatible with CRT. I disagree. But she argues that empirical evidence is necessary to reach out to white America. See also Darren Hutchinson (2004: 1213–1214) arguing that CRT theorists usually rely on law and legal reasoning but could buttress their arguments by also relying on political science data that, for instance, has used polling to demonstrate that the Supreme court largely responds to majoritiarian concerns in its decisionmaking and facilitates majoritarian interests.

12. In 1924, the Texas statute, Art. 3093a, afterwards numbered Art. 3107 (Rev. Stat. 1925) declared 'in no event shall a Negro be eligible to participate in a Democratic Party primary election in the State of Texas'. *Smith v. Allwright*, 321 U.S. 649,658 (1944) (citing *Nixon v. Herndon*, 273 U.S. 536 (1927)) .

13. In *Breedlove v. Suttles*, 302 U.S. 277 (1937), the Supreme Court upheld a Georgia provision requiring the payment of a poll tax as a prerequisite for voting. Though a white man brought the case, establishment of poll taxes was one of the many ways in which blacks were prohibited from voting. Breedlove was overruled in *Harper v. Virginia State Bd. of Elections* (1966).

14. This case upheld restrictive covenants in housing. It was overturned by the Supreme Court in *Shelley v. Kraemer*, (1948). But see Bell (2004) describing subsequent history and current problems of housing discrimination. For other discussions of housing segregation see Calmore (1993), Perea et al. (2000: 646–754) and Massey and Denton (1993).

15. Bell, notes that '[a]ccording to one study, 38 states had miscegenation statutes at one time or another during the nineteenth century; and as late as 1951, 29 statutes were still on the books' (2004: 256). The Supreme Court in *Loving v. Virginia* (1967) struck down these laws.

16. The Supreme Court in *Sweat v. Painter*, (1950) ruled that a black student could attend a white university. However, while the Court granted relief in this case, it did not address the constitutionality of the separate but equal doctrine. Rather, this doctrine was finally overturned in *Brown*.

17. Kevin Brown argues that the *Milliken v. Bradley* case decided a year later, in 1974, dealt the 'deathblow to the [nation's] ability to successfully integrate public schools'. It effectively made US suburbs a safe haven for whites who did not want their children to attend integrated schools with black children, and in doing so contributed to 'white flight' to these suburbs (2005: 210).

18. These include providing remedies for only those practices that can be specifically identified and proven as the product of intentional actions, ignoring societal wide racial ordering and applying the Court's highest and toughest level of scrutiny, strict scrutiny, to all cases, even though it previously had been primarily applied in cases where the government had used racial identification to disadvantage minorities. Prior to 1995, the Supreme Court had been divided as to whether strict scrutiny should apply to all cases involving racial classifications. Strict scrutiny had been applied to 'invidious' discrimination, discrimination meant to disadvantage minorities. But the Court had applied a more lenient level of scrutiny to remedies that relied on race to undo past discrimination and as such benefited minorities. This had been termed by the Court as 'benign' discrimination. However, in 1995 a solid majority of the Court held in favour of applying strict scrutiny to all uses of race-specific laws. *Adarand Constructors, Inc v. Pena* (1995).

19. Id. at 298.

20. Justice O'Connor also seemed concerned by the fact, in a section of the opinion lacking a majority, that Richmond was 50 percent black and five of the nine council officials that passed the ordinance were black. She suggested that this presented a stronger need for the application of strict scrutiny since it was not a majority of whites acting in a way that burdened themselves but was the act of minorities doing so (Croson, 1989).

21. Frank Wu and Charles Daye made these points in the 2004 James McCormick Mitchell Lecture at the University at Buffalo. The transcript is of the proceedings are published in

'Who Gets In: A Quest for Diversity after Grutter', *University at Buffalo Law Review*, 52: 531–596. Other panelists included Athena Mutua, Shedon Zedeck, Maragaret Montoya and David Chambers.

22. This insight comes from Francisco Valdes.

23. Iglesias and Valdes in listing the early guideposts for LatCrit scholarship include the idea to 'balance specificity and generality in LatCritical analysis to ensure multidimensionality' (2001: 1263).

24. They are summarising Yamatoto's text found on pages 829–830, see Yamamoto (1997).

25. One of the books Mathias (2007) cites is John Solomos and Liza Schuster, (2002).

26. For instance scholars such as Mai Chen from New Zealand and Zorica Mrsevic from Serbia, both published articles in Adrien Wing's book (2000). On the other hand see, Mahmood (2000), a collection of articles not only from scholars primarily in Africa but also from India and the United States that was published in South Africa. The African American experience and a number of insights from CRT inform this discussion of rights and culture.

27. CRT's impact may be growing. For instance a conference entitled 'Critical Race Theory in the UK: What is to be learnt? What is to be done?' organised by the Higher Education Academy subject Network for Sociology, Anthropology, Politics (C-SAP) was scheduled for June 25, 2009 at the Institute of Education, University of London. Dr. Kevin Hylton organised it and he is the author of '"Race," Sport and Leisure: Lessons from Critical Race Theory', *Leisure Studies*, 24: 81–98 (2005), which discusses sports in the UK.

REFERENCES

Adarand Constructors, Inc. v. Pena, 515 U.S. 200 (1995).

Aoki, K. (1996) 'The scholarship of reconstruction and the politics of backlash', *Iowa Law Review*, 81 (5): 1467–1488.

Aoki, K. (1998) 'The Stakes of Intellectual Property Law' in D. Kairys, (ed.), *The Politics of Law: A Progressive Critique*. 3rd edition. New York: Pantheon. pp. 259–278.

Aoki, K. and Chon, M. (1999) 'Nanook of the Nomos: A Symposium on Critical Race Praxis: Introduction: Critical Race Praxis and Legal Scholarship', *Michigan Journal of Race and Law*, 5: 35–52.

Bell, D. (1976) 'Serving Two Masters: Integration Ideals and Client Interests in School Desegregation Litigation', *Yale Law Journal*, 85 (4): 470–517. Reprinted in: Delgado, R. and Stefancic, J. (eds) (2000) *Critical Race Theory: The Cutting Edge*. 2nd edition. Philadelphia: Temple University Press.

Bell, D. (1980) '*Brown v. Board of Education* and the Interest-Convergence Dilemma', *Harvard Law Review*, 93 (3): 518–533.

Bell, D. (1989) *And We Are Not Saved: The Elusive Quest for Racial Justice*. San Francisco: Harper.

Bell, D. (1993) *Faces at the Bottom of the Well: The Permanence of Racism*. New York: Basic Books.

Bell, D. (ed.) (2004) *Race, Racism and American Law*. 5th edition. New York: Aspen.

Breedlove v. Suttles, 302 U.S. 277 (1937)

Brown v. Board of Education, 347 U.S. 483 (1954).

Brown, D. (2004) 'Critical Race Theory: The Next Frontier: Fighting Racism in the Twenty-First Century', *Washington and Lee Law Review*, 61 (4): 1485–1500.

Brown, K. (2005) *Race, Law and Education in the Post-Desegregation Era: Four Perspectives on Desegregation and Resegregation*. Durham: Carolina Academic Press.

Calmore, J. (1993) 'Spatial Equality and the Kerner Commission Report: A Back-to-the Future Essay', *North Carolina Law Review*, 71 (5): 1487–1518. Reprinted in part in: Mahoney, M., Calmore, J., and Wildman, S. (eds) (2003) *Social Justice: Professionals, Communities, and Law*. St. Paul: West Group.

Chang, R. (1993) 'Toward an Asian American Legal Scholarship: Critical Race Theory, Post-Structuralism, and Narrative Space', *California Law Review*, 81 (5): 1241–1323.

Colker, R. (1986) 'Anti-Subordination above All: Sex, Race, and Equal Protection', *New York University Law Review*, 61 (6): 1003–1066.

Cooper, F. (2002) 'The Un-balanced Fourth Amendment: A Cultural Study of the Drug War, Racial Profiling and Arvizu', *Villanova Law Review*, 47 (4): 851–895.

Cover, R. (1986) 'Violence and the Word', *Yale Law Journal*, 95 (8): 1601–1629.

Crenshaw, K. (1990) 'A Black Feminist Critique of Antidiscrimination Law and Politics' in D. Kairys, (ed.), *The Politics of Law: A Progressive Critique*. 2nd edition. New York: Pantheon Books. pp. 195–218.

Crenshaw, K. (2002) 'The First Decade: Critical Reflections, or "a Foot in the Closing Door"', *UCLA Law Review*, 49 (5): 1343–1372.

Crenshaw, K., Gotanda, N., Peller, G. and Kendall, T. (eds.) (1995) *Critical Race Theory*. New York: The New Press.

Culp, J. (1999) 'To the Bone: Race and White Privilege', *Minnesota Law Review*, 83 (6): 1637–1679.

Delgado, R. (1996) *The Rodrigo Chronicles: Conversations about America and Race*. New York: New York University Press.

Delgado, R. and Stefancic, J. (eds) (1998) *The Latino Condition: A Critical Reader*. New York: New York University Press.

Delgado, R. and Stefancic, J. (eds) (2000) *Critical Race Theory: The Cutting Edge*. 2nd edition. Philadelphia: Temple University Press.

Delgado, R. and Stefancic, J. (2001) *Critical Race Theory: An Introduction*. New York: New York University Press.

Dred Scott v. Sandford, 60 U.S. 393 (1857).

Du Bois, W.E.B. (1935) *Black Reconstruction in America: 1860–1880*. New York: The Free Press

Ely, J. (1980) *Democracy and Distrust: A Theory of Judicial Review*. Cambridge: Harvard University Press.

Fair Housing Act, 42 U.S.C. 3601 (1968).

Farber, D. and Sherry, S. (1993) 'Telling Stories out of School: An Essay on Legal Narratives', *Stanford Law Review*, 45: 807–854.

Frankenberg, R. (1993) *White Women, Race Matters: The Social Construction of Whiteness*. University of Minnesota Press.

Freeman, A. (1990) 'Antidiscrimination Law: The View from 1989' in D. Kairys, (ed.), *The Politics of Law: A Progressive Critique*. 2nd edition. New York: Pantheon Books. pp. 121–150.

Gotanda, N. (1995) 'Asian American Rights and the "Miss Saigon Syndrome"' in L. Bender, and D. Braveman, (eds), *Power, Privilege and Law*. St. Paul, Minn: West Publishing Co. pp. 106–110.

Griggs v. Duke Power Co., 401 U.S. 424 (1971).

Grutter v. Bollinger, 539 U.S. 306 (2003).

Haney Lopez, I. (1994) 'The Social Construction of Race: Some Observations on Illusion, Fabrication, and Choice', *Harvard Civil Rights – Civil Liberties Law Review*, 29 (1): 1–62.

Harper v. Virginia State Bd. of Elections, 383 U.S. 663 (1966)

Harris, A. (1990) 'Race and Essentialism in Feminist Legal Theory', *Stanford Law Review*, 42 (3): 581–616.

Harris, A. (1994) 'Forward: The jurisprudence of Reconstruction', *California Law Review*, 82: 741–785.

Harris, C. (2002) 'Critical Race Studies', *UCLA Law Review*, 49 (5): 1215–1240.

Hernandez,Truyol, B. (1995). Symposium: Women's Rights as International Human Rights: Concluding Remarks Making Women Visible: Setting an Agenda for the Twenty-First. *St. John's Law Review*, 69 (Winter-Spring), p. 231-254.

Hernandez-Truyol, B. 'Women's Rights as Human Rights – Rules and Realities and the Role of Culture: A Formula for Reform', *Brooklyn Journal of International Law*, 21: 605–677.

Hernandez v. Texas, 347 US 475 (1954).

Hirabayashi v. United States, 320 U.S. 81 (1943).

Hopwood v. Texas, 78 F.3d 932 (1996).

Houh, E. (2003) 'Critical Interventions: Toward an Expansive Equality Approach to the Doctrine of Good Faith in Contract Law', *Cornell Law Review*, 88 (4): 1025–1096.

Hutchinson, D. (1999) 'Ignoring the Sexualization of Race: Heteronormativity, Critical Race Theory, and Anti-Racist Politics', *Buffalo Law Review*, 47 (1): 1–116.

Hutchinson, D. (2001) 'Identity Crisis: "Intersectionality," "Multidimensionality," and the Development of an Adequate Theory of Subordination', *Michigan Journal of Race and Law*, 6 (2): 285–317.

Hutchinson, D. (2003) '"Unexplainable on Grounds Other Than Race": The Inversion of Privilege and Subordination in Equal Protection Jurisprudence', *University of Illinois Law Review*, 2003 (3): 615–700.

Hutchinson, D. (2004) 'Critical Race Histories: In and out', *American University Law Review*, 53 (6): 1187–1215.

Iglesias, E. (2006) 'Toward Progressive Conceptions of Black Manhood, LatCrit and Critical Race Feminist Reflections: Thought Piece, May 2001' in A. Mutua, (ed.), *Progressive Black Masculinites*. New York: Routledge. pp. 55–59.

Iglesias, E. (1996) 'Human Rights in International Economic Law: Locating Latinas/os in the Linkage Debates', *University of Miami Inter-American Law Review*, 28: 361–386.

Iglesias, E. and Valdes, F. (2001) 'Afterword to LatCrit V Symposium; LatCrit at Five: Institutionalizing a Postsubordination Future', *Denver University Law Review*, 78 (4): 1249–1330.

Jackson v. State, 37 Ala. App. 519, 72 So. 2d 114, cert. denied, 348 U.S. 888 (1954)

Johnson v. McIntosh, 21 U.S. 543 (1823).

Kairys, D. (ed) (1982) *The Politics of Law: A Progressive Critique*. New York: Pantheon Books. pp. 40–61.

Keyes v. School District No. 1, Denver, Colorado, 1413 U.S. 189 (1973).

Kennedy *(1982). Legal Education and the Reproduction of Hierarchy*, J. Leg. (ed.), *32: 591.*

Korematsu v. United States, 323 U.S. 214 (1944).

Kraemer v. Shelley, 355 Mo. 814, 198 S. W. 2d 679 (1946).

Ladson-Billings, G. (1998) 'Just What Is Critical Race Theory and What's It Doing in a Nice Field Like Education?', *Qualitative Studies in Education*, 11 (1): 7–24.

LATCRIT: Latina and Latino Critical Theory. Retrieved September 6, 20a08, from http://biblioteca.uprrp.edu/LatCritCD/default.htm

Lipsitz, G. (1998) *Possessive Investment in Whiteness*. Philadephia: Temple University Press.

Loving v. Virginia, 388 U.S. 1 (1967).

MacKinnon, C. (1987) *Feminism Unmodified*. Cambridge: Harvard University Press.

Mahmood, M. (ed.) (2000) *Beyond Rights Talk and Culture Talk*. South Africa: David Phillips Publishers.

Massey, D. and Denton, N. (1993) *American Apartheid*. Cambridge: Harvard University Press.

Matsuda, M. (1991) 'Voices of America: Accent, Antidiscrimination Law, and a Jurisprudence for the Last Reconstruction', *Yale Law Journal*, 100 (5): 1329–1399. Reprinted in part in: Perea, J., Delgado, R., Harris, A., and Wildman, S. (eds) (2000) *Race and Races: Cases and Resources for a Diverse America*. St. Paul: West Group. pp. 551–561.

Mathias, M. (2007) 'Colour Blindness or Total Blindness? The Absence of Critical Race Theory in Europe', *Rutgers Race & the Law Review*, 9 (1): 57–127.

McCleskey v. Kemp, 481 U.S. 279 (1987).

McIntosh, P. (1988) White Privilege and Male Privilege: A Personal Account of Coming to See Correspondences through Work in Women's Studies. Working Paper #189, Wellesley College Center for Research on Women, Wellesley, MA 02181.

Milliken v. Bradley , 418 U.S. 717 (1974)

Mutua M. (2000) 'Symposium: Keynote Address, Critical race theory and international law: A view of an insider-outsider', *Villanova Law Review*, 45 (5): 841–853.

Mutua, A., (2004) "Introduction" to Mutua, A. Zedeck, S., Wu, F., Daye, C., Montoya, M. and Chambers, D. (2004) 'Who Gets In? The Quest for Diversity after Grutter', *Buffalo Law Review*, 52: 531-596.

Mutua, A. (2006) 'Theorizing Progressive Black Masculinities' in A. Mutua, (ed.) *Progressive Black Masculinites*. New York: Routledge. pp. 3–41.

Mutua, A. (forthcoming, 2010) Restoring Justice to Civil Rights Movement Activists?: New Historiography and the 'Long Civil Rights Era' at http://works.bepress.com/athena_mutua/1/; and http://papers.ssrn.com/sol3/papers.cfm?abstract_id=1133130

Newson, M.D. (2004) 'Clarence Thomas, Victim? Perhaps, and Victimizer? Yes – A Study in Social and Racial Alienation from African-Americans', *St. Louis Law Journal*, 48 (2): 327–424.

Nixon v. Herndon, 273 U.S. 536

Omi, M. and Winant, H. (1994) *Racial Formation in the United States from the 1960s to the 1990s*. New York: Routledge.

Ozawa v. United States, 260 U.S. 178 (1922).

Parker, L. (1998) '"Race Is Race Ain't": An Exploration of the Utility of Critical Race Theory in Qualitative Research in Education', *Qualitative Studies in Education*, 11 (1): 43–55.

Parker, L. and Lynn, M. (2002) 'What's Race Got to Do with It?: Critical Race Theory's Conflicts with and Connections to Qualitative Research Methodology and Epistemology', *Qualitative Inquiry*, 8 (3): 7–22.

People v. Hall, 4 Cal. 399 (Sup. Ct. 1854).

Perea, J., Delgado, R., Harris, A. and Wildman, S. (eds) (2000) *Race and Races: Cases and Resources for a Diverse America*. St. Paul: West Group. pp. 551–561.

Phillips, S. (1999) 'The Convergence of the Critical Race Theory Workshop with LatCrit theory: A History', *University of Miami Law Review*, 53: 1247–1256.

Plessy v. Ferguson, 163 U.S. 537 (1896).

Rabinowitz, V. (1982) 'The Radical Tradition in the Law' in D. Kairys, (ed.), *The Politics of Law: A Progressive Critique*. New York: Pantheon Books. pp. 310–318.

Rabinowitz, V. (1998); The Radical Tradition in the Law. In Kairys, D. (3rd Ed.), *The Politics of Law: A Progressive Critique*. New York: Basic Books. pp. 680–690.

Regents of Univ. of Cal. V. Bakke, 436 U.S. 265 (1978).

Richardson, H. (2002) 'Dinner and Self-Determination' in F. Valdes, J. Culp, and A. Harris, (eds) *Crossroads, Directions, and a New Critical Race Theory*. Philadelphia: Temple University Press. pp. 288–301.

Richardson, H. (2004) 'Imperatives of culture and race for understanding human rights law', *Buffalo Law Review*, 52 (2): 511–530.

Richardson, H. (2008) *The Origins of African-American Interests in International Law*. Durham, North Carolina: Carolina Academic Press.

City of Richmond v. J. A. Croson Co., 488 U.S. 469 (1989).

Roberts, D. (1993) 'Racism and the Patriarchy in the Meaning of Motherhood', *American University Journal of Gender and the Law*, 1 (1): 1–38. Reprinted in: Olsen, F. (ed.) (1995) *Feminist Legal Theory: Foundations and Outlooks* New York: New York University Press. pp. 535.

Rodriguez v. San Antonio Independent School District, 411 U.S. 1 (1973).

Roediger, D. (1999) *The Wages of Whiteness: Race and the Making of the American Working Class*. Revised edition. London and New York: Verso Books.

Ruiz Cameron, C. (1997) 'How the Garcia Cousins Lost Their Accents: Understanding the Language of Title VII Decisions Approving English-Only Rules as the Product of Racial Dualism, Latino Invisibility, and Legal Indeterminacy', *California Law Review*, 85 (5): 1347–1393.

Saito, T. (1997) 'Alien and Non-Alien Alike: Citizenship, "Foreignness," and Racial Hierarchy in American law', *Oregon Law Review*, 76 (2): 261–345.

Serrano, S. (1997) 'Rethinking Race for Strict Scrutiny Purposes: Yniguez and the Racialization of English only', *University of Hawaii Law Review*, 19 (1): 221–263.

Shaw v. Reno, 509 U.S. 630 (1993).

Shelley v. Kraemer, 334 U.S. 1 (1948).

Smith v. Allwright, 321 U.S. 649 (1944).

Solomos, J. and Schuster, L. (2002) 'Hate Speech, Violence, and Contemporary Racisms' in The Even Foundation (ed) *Europes New Racism: Causes, Manifestations, and Solutions*.

Solorzano, D. and Yosso, T. (2001) 'Critical Race and Latcrit Theory and Method: Counter-Storytelling', *Qualitative Studies in Education*, 14 (4): 471–495.

Sweat v. Painter, 210 S. W. 2d 442 (1948).

Uniform Naturalization Act of 1790, 1 Stat. 103 (repealed 1795).

Valdes, F. (1996) 'Foreword–Latina/o Ethnicities, Critical Race Theory and Post-Identity Politics in Postmodern Legal Discourses: From Practices to Possibilities. *Berkeley La Raza Law Journal*, 9 (1): 1–31.

Valdes, F. (1997a) 'Queer Margins, Queer Ethics: A Call to Account for Race and Ethnicity in the Law, Theory and Politics of "Sexual Orientation"', *Hastings Law Journal*, 48 (6): 1293–1341.

Valdes, F. (1997b) 'Under Construction: LatCrit Consciousness, Community, and Theory', *California Law Review*, 85 (5): 1087–1142.

Valdes, F. (1998) 'Afterword–beyond sexual orientation in queer legal Theory: Majoritarianism, Multidimensionality and Responsibility in Social Justice Scholarship – or, Legal Scholars as Cultural Warriors', *Denver University Law Review*, 75 (4): 1409–1464.

Valdes, F. (1999) 'Afterword: Theorizing 'OutCrit' Theories: Coalitional Method and Comparative Jurisprudential Experience – RaceCrits, QueerCrits and LatCrits', *University of Miami Law Review*, 53 (4): 1266–1322.

Valdes, F., Culp, J. and Harris, A. (eds) (2002) *Crossroads, Directions, and a New Critical Race Theory*. Philadelphia: Temple University Press.

White, J. (1987) 'Economics and Law: Two Cultures in Tension', *Tennessee Law Review*, 54 (2): 161–202.

Williams, P. (1991) *The Alchemy of Race and Rights*. Cambridge: Harvard University Press.

Wing, A. (ed.) (2000) *Global Critical Race Feminism: An International Reader*. New York: New York University Press.

Wing, A. (ed.) (1997) *Critical Race Feminism: A Reader*. New York: New York University Press.

Wu, F. (2002) *Yellow*. New York: Basic Books.

Wygant v. Jackson Bd. of Ed., 476 U.S. 267 (1986).

Yamamoto, E. (1997) 'Critical Race Praxis: Race Theory and Political Lawyering Practice in Post-Civil Rights America', *Michigan Law Review*, 95: 821–900.

Ethnic Conflict

Ralph Premdas

INTRODUCTION

During the last decade of the twentieth century, a particularly virulent form of social conflict seemed to have set siege to the survival of humanity. The new scourge was labelled 'ethnic conflict' and its surge to unprecedented proportions by the early 1990s had evoked cataclysmic and apocalyptic portents expressed by terms such as 'pandemonium' (Moynihan, 1993), 'tsunami of ethnic conflict' (Gurr, 2000: xiii), 'clash of civilizations' (Huntington, 1996), etc. Never since World War II has there been so many conflicts, about 20 classified as high intensity and 100 as ongoing, requiring over 70,000 UN peacekeepers costing more than $4 billion annually to maintain. Refugee flows have reached about 15 million externally and about 25 million internally most associated in one way or the other with ethnic conflicts. In a short time, many peoples uprooted had experienced a radical change of identity and citizenship in a world that seemed at once to be contracting as a site of shared global survival and expanding with a proliferation of identity communities. While ethnic conflicts were both inter-communal as well as between states and minorities, for most the crux revolved around the right to self-determination, claims clearly aimed at re-arranging the borders of the international system. The historic watershed of the progressively rising crescendo of ethnic conflicts whose frequency dramatically accelerated in the 1980s coincided with the end of the Cold War. No one had anticipated that the subsequent 'peace dividend' would be quickly consumed by innumerable and sometimes genocidal conflicts that engulfed the world. Note the Rudolphs: 'As political ideology recedes, the politics of identity and community, of religion, ethnicity, and gender have begun to occupy the space vacated by political ideology' (Rudolph and Rudolph, 1993: 29).

With few exceptions, nearly all states are polyethnic with about 40 percent constituted of five of more ethnonational communities. Less than a third contain ethnic majorities. The cleavages, most prominently race, religion, region, language and values, are multiple and coinciding, creating deep intractable divisions. Worldwide there are about 4000 ethnonational groups enclosed in some 187 sovereign states from which have emerged a proliferation of internal strifes that have often spilled their borders. Ted Gurr who had catalogued these conflicts, which had emerged as a significant event after World War II and steadily increased in frequency culminating with its highest critical mass after the end of the Cold, War argued that they had 'reshaped the political landscape in all world regions' (Gurr, 2000: 3) and 'raised grave doubts about the future of the international system of states and the security of citizens' (Gurr, 2000: xiii). The disintegration of the former USSR into 15 independent states as well as Yugoslavia and Ethiopia into warring ethnopolitical camps added to the apocalyptic scenario. Towards the end of the twentieth century, the peak of the ethnic scourge seemed to have run its course. Gurr reported: 'By mid-1990s, armed conflict within states had abated. There was a pronounced decline in the onset of new ethnic wars and a shift from fighting to negotiations'(Gurr, 2000: xiii). This was only partly reassuring since human society, organised from time immemorial into ethno-cultural settlements, has always engendered inter-communal strife over a full range of issues which remain with us today. Walker Connor called 'for a longer view of history' underscoring the historical cycles of troughs and swells of ethnic conflict, warned 'that a relative lull should not be construed as endless', and offered some cautionary remarks that 'explanations for today's ethnically predicated conflict should not be sought in terms of post-Cold war factors' (Connor, 2004: 27). The ethnic factor, in all its heterogeneity and pluralism, whatever its nature, clearly is a permanent feature of human social organisation, even preceding the emergence of the state (Smith, 1986) and will continue to be a critical part in future crises.

ETHNICITY AND IDENTITY

Ethnicity may be defined as collective group consciousness that imparts a sense of belonging derived from membership in a community, bound putatively by common descent and culture. While an ethno-cultural community may construct its collective consciousness and shared identity on commonalties such as region, religion, race, language and/or values that are fictive and imagined, these claims are the bedrock that confers belonging and serve as the means of mass mobilisation in quest of recognition, resources and influence in the state. Among many other groups in which one may simultaneously share multiple identities, the ethnic group is distinguished as a special sort of community that confers gratification for meaning and belonging. Isaiah Berlin underscored the view that 'just as people need to eat and drink, to have security and freedom of movement, so too they need to belong to a group. Deprived of this, they feel cut off, lonely, diminished, unhappy' (Gardels, 1991: 19). Berlin posited that 'people can't develop unless they belong to a culture' (ibid). The ethnic group is such a cultural community, an intimately interactive society of shared symbols and meanings, and as Walker Connor remarked, 'the largest group that can be aroused, stimulated to action, by appeals to common ancestors and to a blood-bond' (Connor, 2004: 23). It is not important that the underlying bases of solidarity – language, religion, race, home-land, customs, ancestry, etc. regarding their uniqueness, 'purity', and other lofty claims – be factual, only that members believe them to be true as the cement of their solidarity. The base, whether it is language, religion or homeland, even though of relatively recent manufacture, anchors loyalty in a mystic membership of sacrifice. Ethnic identity is not necessarily always evident and may in fact be dormant and seemingly non-existent in normal and peaceful times. It becomes activated usually under conditions of disruptive, systemic change serving then as a security blanket in numbers and a buffer against uncertainty and adversity.

In the literature on ethnicity, a convention has emerged truncating analysts into three perspectival categories: primordial (Geertz, 1963), instrumental (Eller and Coughlin, 1993: 183–202) and constructivist (Young, 1993: 23). It suffices to note here that the primordialists explain the behaviour of ethnic groups by giving explanatory weight to the emotional attachments generated by cultural beliefs, values and symbols derived from an imagined sense of kinship (Isaacs, 1975; Connor, 2004). The constructivists view the ethnic community as an imagined community and not a fixed or historically authentic group (Anderson, 1991). They argue that the behaviour of the ethnic community needs to be understood with reference to the various social processes by which it is constantly created and recreated relative to the circumstances affecting the everyday lives of individuals. In contrast to the primordialists and the constructivists, the instrumentalists theorise that inter-ethnic relations are largely configured by material or economic interests and the competition which these interests engender. None of these approaches is entirely satisfactory. Don Horowitz offers a solution to this dilemma proposing that group affiliations can be conceived as either 'hard' or 'soft' arguing that 'a hard emphasis on the responsiveness of ethnic groups to the deep needs of group members is not at odds with a keen sense of the variability of ethnic phe-nomena' (Horowitz, 1998a: 10). He concluded therefore that 'group members may entertain sentiments so intense that theorists identify them as primordial, even though group identities are socially constructed, recently constructed, founded on relatively little in the way of palpable differences, and mutable as environmental conditions change'(ibid).

There are other significant perspectives on ethnicity which set it apart from patterns of other solidarity units. It has been advanced that the nature of the ethnic bond has less to do with its cultural content and everything to do with the symbolic boundary that differentiates it from other groups (Barth, 1967). The boundary hypothesis works very well in tandem with the social psychology of identity theory affirming the need of the human creature for a distinctive positive social identity in a process of social differentiation and categorisation. To belong at once entails being included in an ethnic community and to be separated and differentiated from another or several. Identity formation and sustenance is relational, often oppositional, and conflictual. Ethnic group members may visibly display their distinctive symbolic boundary markers and physical emblems in contact with others. Evidence of the ethnicity bond does not require a condition of persistent overt tension or strife, for proof abounds of prolonged periods of peaceful inter-ethnic co-existence and accommodation prior to the outbreak of inter-sectional strife. Peaceful co-existence notwithstanding, inter-group differences are usually maintained in subtle and symbolic ways, may be re-invented substantially, suggesting the illusion of boundary erasure. While at times it may be benign relative to 'the other', it can easily, in new circumstances of unusual change, systemic disturbances, and upheaval become conflictual, even turn into a marauding monster. In Bosnia, Lebanon, Rwanda, Burundi, Malaysia, Sri Lanka, Guyana, Fiji, Northern Ireland, India, etc., the testimony from participants in the ethnic struggles abundantly underscores periods of prolonged inter-communal amity marked by intimate friendships and many inter-marriages. Once an inter-ethnic struggle commences, it often becomes intransigent over the smallest of claims and counter-claims aptly expressed as the Freudian 'narcissism of trivial differences' (Ignatieff, 1993).

The comparison hypothesis carries a special set of internal behavioural structures that border on the irrational. Social psychologist Henry Tajfel pointed to the propensity of group loyalty to be sustained intensely and irrationally not for 'greater profit in absolute terms' but in order 'to achieve relatively higher profit for members of their in-group as compared with members of the out group' (Tajfel, 1970). Often occurring in a context where the conflicting groups shared at one time the same territorial state and in which a particular distribution of statuses and resources prevailed, the struggle often pivots around an unwillingness of one party to permit the other profit advantageously by its actions. The comparison factor assumes the logic of its own witnessing and wreaking, as if infused by jealousy, incredible havoc and harm on all parties in a policy of mutual denial (Taylor and Moghaddam, 1994: 83). In part, this explanation addresses some of the Serbian, Rwandan, Sri Lankan, Chechen and other excesses in different parts of the world. When ethnic consciousness suffuses a community, it tends to be comprehensive in scope and requires complete conformity with the edicts of ethnic entrepreneurs and the cultural priesthood, be they secular intellectuals or religious leaders. All intermediate zones of moderation or neutrality perish, and deviation from solidarity is deemed heresy, an act of betrayal calling forth intra-fraternal violence that often exceeds that meted out to external enemies (Lewis, 1992: 49). At the macro-level in protracted ethnic conflict, the general pattern demonstrates that the political costs are extensive including the loss of regime legitimacy, the destruction of democracy, pervasive human rights violations, the fracturing of society into polarised parts and persistent instability.

Once ethnic consciousness becomes the animating force that defines competition for the values and resources of the state, all political institutions – parties, voluntary and civic associations, the electoral system, parliament, the public bureaucracy, judiciary, diplomatic services, and the army and police services – become infected by it.

Analysis of ethnic conflict raises the question of how they are articulated. How can they be usefully measured and categorised? For our purposes, an ethnic conflict occurs either from contentions between ethnic groups, or between ethnic groups and the state. They are typically triggered by differences over identity claims and/or the distribution of power and resources, or all of these in combination. Such differences and contentious rivalry may be analytically expressed in a range of action that can be categorised along a continuum spanning from low levels of malaise to high levels of rebellion as set forth in Table 12.1.

In this schema, ethnic conflicts at its lowest level of articulation can be envisaged as domination of one by another (or by a state) assuming the form of day to day ritualised and stereotypical cultural, social and political practices and discriminatory laws backed up by the threat of coercive state enforcement. Examples include the apartheid system of South Africa and anti-Black discrimination in the pre-Civil Rights era in the United States. The second analytic level points to the break out of the bounds of ritualised institutionalised practices into open and challenging if not threatening forms of complaints and grievances but still expressed through methods sanctioned by the law. This level often includes the organisation of lobbying groups as well as political parties. The third level increases the salience of agitation through protests and demonstrations which are still technically legal but with the hovering menace of insurrection. Finally, at the fourth level, the conflict turns violent often manifested in civil war, guerrilla activities and sabotage embroiling civilian populations as well as international

Table 12.1 Levels of ethnic conflict

Level 1	Level 2	Level 3	Level 4
⇦ Low level of conflict: Inter-ethnic malaise; institutionalised domination expressed in psychological, cultural, ritual and political practices and laws. Challenges are low keyed and infrequent.	Higher level of conflict: Articulated in open complaints, expressions of grievances through conventional and non-violent methods.	Higher and more intense level of conflict: Marked by vigorous but legally structured opposition involving destabilising demonstrations and protests (often with some sporadic violence) but still technically within legal bounds.	Highest level of conflict: ⇨ Open and protracted physical violent conflict expressed is rebellion, warfare, guerila activities, sabotage, etc. The survival of all parties in the conflict at stake.

actors and generating extensive human rights violations and refugees (Brown, 1993: 16). This level of action may be continuous but often is interspersed with some dialogue and ceasefires. The analytic schema has essentially created two categories of ethnic conflict, namely conventional and unconventional, focused around institutional and non-institutional modes of articulating grievances (Gurr, 2000). At any moment, a conflict may involve mixes in the repertoire of tactics, even with each tactic conducted by different factions of the same movement. Most of the ethnopolitical conflicts had antecedent pedigrees in low levels of complaints, demonstrations and protests which progressively deteriorated after being rebuffed and met by repressive action by the state (Gurr, 1993). The reaction and counter-reaction in kind tends to evolve into a spiral of self-reinforcing violence that creates many humanitarian crises with refugee flows and ethnic cleansing in their wake (Mann, 2005).

Among the major controversies found in all of the ethnicity literature regarding the underlying nature of communal conflicts is the contention between the economic–materialist and cultural–symbolic schools. It stands so central to the ethnic conflict discourse that it compels some treatment. Taken together, the materialist perspective, often referred to as the resource allocation or the realist or rational or the instrumental schools theorise that inter-ethnic relations are largely configured by material or economic interests and the competition which these interests engender (Bonacich, 1972: 37, 547–559; Despres, 1975: 87–117; Hechter, 1978: 84, 293–318). Generally, undergirding these economic theories are issues regarding equality and distributive justice involving claims over the equitable distribution of material resources such as public jobs, state projects, budgetary allocations, and subsidies (Despres and Premdas, 2000: 13–28; Despres, 1975; Olzak, 1992). For the economic materialists, the problem of inequality in resource allocation and income distribution is a pivotal and pervasive theme that runs through the structure of practically all the conflicts in ethnically and racially divided states. The assumption that inter-ethnic strife is ultimately grounded on differences over material interests reduces cultural symbols of ethnic affirmation to 'masks of confrontation' and to an epiphenomenon with a calculated strategy aimed at maximising material gains (Vincent, 1974: 375–379). It assumes that through rational discourse around underlying material interests, a formula for equity can be found. Rarely, however, are ethnic conflicts erected on the singular pillar of economic interests, for cultural and symbolic factors autonomously and in conjunction with political and economic interests frequently play a salient role (Smith, 1991). One sphere where the salience of symbols in ethnic conflict and its resolution has been well developed, with a respectable literature and methodology, pertains to the recognition of the symbols of group identity (Taylor, 1992). Recognition of the intrinsic self-definition of a group is as important as and often a prerequisite for equality of access to material resources and political participation. Recognition points to the need for all communities in their rich cultural and religious diversity to be accorded juridical and social equality in the official ceremonies of the state, in the celebration of festivals and holidays and the observance of religious events. This in turn requires sensitivity to group rights in appropriate spheres.

Another critical area of contention that warrants extended treatment refers to a variant of ethnic conflict marked prominently by racio-biological markers of identity and differentiation. Solidarity communities that are manifestly expressed around putative racial and biological diacritica, regardless of the scientific accuracy of the claims, are ethnic groups of a particular type, similar structurally to other ethnic communities with linguistic (ethno-linguistic), regional (ethno-regional) or religious (ethno-religious) salience. Generally, ethno-cultural communities in practically all polyethnic states tend to compose their claims to a distinctive identity by attributing to themselves in their narratives of origin not only cultural and historical differences but racial myths of superiority over rival groups (De Vos and Romanucci-Ross, 1975). The term 'race' is used here to refer to socially constructed categories assigned to putative physical and biological human differences (UNESCO, 1951). Or as Omi and Winant define it: 'a social process of categorisation based on supposed physiological differences' underscoring the view that as a socio-historical process, it establishes structures of inequality and political hegemony (Omi and Winant, 1994: 55). In many cases, racial claims in the construction of cultural identities tend to be quite explicit as in apartheid South Africa but in many others, the racial aspect is less evident, intermixed with other factors, and frequently denied altogether. Some obvious cases include Sudan, Rwanda, Sri Lanka, South Africa, the United States, Fiji, Malaysia, Guyana, Mauritius, Trinidad, Canada (indigenous peoples), etc., where solidarity communities are categorised and ideologised in part by their culturally constructed racio-phenotypical traits. In these instances, racial categorisation has bred regimes marked by racially discriminatory policies and practices that have often triggered protests, demonstrations, even violent resistance and 'deadly riots'. Some communities that are today deemed ethno-racial have been recent inventions as in the case of Rwanda (Mamdani, 2001). Colonial conquest accompanied by European scientific racism in the nineteenth century led to the creation of many 'racial' categories among colonial peoples. In the Rwandan case, the idea that Hutus, Tutsis and Twas were members of separate racial stocks was largely a colonial invention (Gourevitch, 1998; Mamdani, 1996: 3–36). In 1933, the Belgian colonial administrators introduced identity cards that pigeonholed everyone into Hutu, Tutsi and Twa categories creating an elaborate myth that the Tutsis were of the 'Hamitic' race and the Hutus and Twas of the 'Bantu' which became common currency with imaginary phenotypical, economic and cultural traits invented and assigned to these groups. In Haiti, a similar racialisation and categorisation occurred between the mulatto and black population. As a socially and culturally constructed idea, race is learnt and malleable but is often taken as a fossilised fact embedded in inter-group relations. Invented racio-cultural differences create social boundaries that imprison and consign communities to a fated destiny of persistent hostility to each other. When fed into ethno-nationalist political mobilisation through political parties and leaders, the consequences of ethno-racial stereotypes instigate ethnic strife that is destructive to social and political stability.

In many of the industrial states of the West, where migration has created a mosaic of ethno-cultural pluralism drawn from all parts of the globe, racialised ethnic competition and conflict has witnessed the deployment of a vocabulary of cultural signifiers as a surrogate for race in a contest for values in the system Castles, S. and Davidson, A. (2004). In Western Europe, where migration has created veritable plural societies especially in cities, the ethnic conflict bears both a cultural and racialised dimension, and is often pivoted around employment discrimination and cultural recognition Castles, S. (1997). However, this type of ethnic and racial conflict in the West is markedly different from most of those in the plural societies of the non-industrial world where grievances are mainly about group discrimination and repression and claims frequently revolve around territorial autonomy and group rights.

Generally, this discourse on race and racism raises fundamental issues in the general scholarship pertaining to race in relation to culture and biology (Bulmer and Solomos, 2004; Appiah and Gutmann, 1996; Goldberg, 1992: 543–564 Banton, M. 1983; Eriksen, T.H. 1993; Glaser, N. and Moynihan, P. 1975 (eds); Rex, J. and Mason, D. 1986 (eds); Smith, M.G. 1993). It is clear that a strict biologistic definition in which genetic heredity and phenotype are paramount has been displaced by a more culturalist dimension so that many of the more nuanced inter-group conflicts involving migrants for instance should be categorised as ethno-racial to take in both the biological and cultural aspects. Many ethnic conflicts are not focused around racial categorisation but engage more prominently other diacritica such as language and region but still compose their claims and identities in a sub-text that includes belief in some sort of descent element. It has now become customary for many ethnic conflicts especially in the Western industrial states to conceal their arguments against migrants by avoiding an outright racist vocabulary. This is equally true of labelling in intra-migrant antagonisms among migrant themselves. This means, as Bulmer and Solomos argue, that the new landscape of ethno-racial conflicts points to a complex spectrum of racisms, to cultural meanings attached to shades of colour, and differentiated fragmentation of ethno-cultural and ethno-racial self-definitions. All of this suggesting that race as idiomatic expression of culture, is a much more pervasive feature of social relations and constitutes a silent subtext in many conflicts including ethnic strife especially in the industrial countries of the West (Bulmer and Solomos, 2004).

ETHNIC CONFLICT IN PATTERNED CATEGORIES OF OCCURRENCE

There are many ways of examining the universe of ethnic conflict. While no list of categories can be truly exhaustive, we have chosen four clusters under which the highest frequency of ethnic conflicts has tended to occur and to which most scholarship has been devoted. Inevitably, there will be overlaps and examples of ethnic conflicts that do not fit any of these categories. In these categories, a narrative is offered accompanied by the major works and approaches which have come to represent scholarship in these fields.

The state, nationalism, and self-determination in ethnic conflict

Perhaps the greatest frequency of open and violent ethnic conflicts over the past two decades responsible for the most deaths and human dislocations in war has transpired when sub-state ethno-cultural groups sought self-determination from the state (Gurr, 2000: 195). Ethnopolitical or separatist movements refer to sub-state groups in multi-ethnic states set apart by self-ascribed cultural characteristics which are politically mobilised to address collective grievances against the state (Horowitz D., 2002). They generally challenge the very territorial definition of the state seeking independence, or short of that aim, settle for internal autonomy. Hardly any state, with the rare exception of St. Kitts and Nevis in the Caribbean (Premdas, 2000: 447–484), has established a constitutional process for a community existing peacefully preferring instead to confront the separatists. Frequently, separatist struggles are prolonged, punishing and prohibitively costly and are fought with fanatical intensity and uncompromising stubbornness involving high civilian casualties (Bartkus, 1999; Premdas, 1996b; Coppieters and Huyssenune, 2002; Stavenhagen, 1996). The Peace and Conflict Ledger at the University of Maryland has estimated that since the 1950s, some 71 ethnoregional groups have conducted armed struggles for autonomy or independence discounting the former European colonies that sought self-government (Gurr and Marshall, 2005: 19). As early as 2005, some 35 armed self-determination movements were still operating; the most prominent of these include the rebels of Darfur in Southern Sudan and the Chechens in Russia. Some minor cases include the Assamese, Kashmir Muslims, Tripuras, and the Scheduled Castes in India; the Karens and Shan in Myanmar; the Basques in Spain; the Kurds in Turkey; the Ijaw in Nigeria, the Malay-Muslims in Thailand; and the Achenese in Indonesia.

A major argument that seeks to explain the source of these self-determination conflicts traces their locus to the very nature and history of the territorial state raising several critical interrogations: does the concept of the state institutionalised in international law understood as a juridical entity with claims to exclusive territory, undivided sovereignty and unequivocal loyalty, become so ossified and inflexible as to render the claim for ethnonational self-determination into an all or nothing symbolic struggle? Clearly, issues related to nationalism as a cement of state unity as well as the borders and integrity of the state loom large in this explanation.

It is easy to forget that the state as a unit of international organisation is a recent invention with its origins often traced back to the Treaty of Westphalia (Seton-Watson H., 1977) in 1648. Ernest Gellner arguing that both the state and its ethno-collective consciousness expressed in nationalism were not ancient

events concluded that 'the basic characteristic of the modern nation and everything connected with it is its modernity' (Gellner, 1989: 49). Eric Hobsbawm
posited that the modern state was first established around an exclusive territory
and a central political authority in response to the intrinsic needs stemming from
rise of capitalism and the industrial revolution (Hobsbawm, 1990). As it evolved,
the state became centralised and armed with a new doctrine of sovereignty and self-
determination (Cobban, 1944; Burcheit, 1978; Hannum, 1990). The boundaries of
the territorial state were first established before a collective consciousness of
citizens emerged according to this argument. The counter-argument advanced by
Anthony Smith posited that while it was true that the state emerged only recently
and from its inception was constituted of several discrete ethnocultural communities, it was not a sociologically invented organised human settlement. In pre-
dating the state to which they imparted their communal structure, ethnic
communities served historically as a receptacle that embodied and was dominated by a central ethno-cultural core (Smith, 1986). While at its founding, in its
incipient and tentative amorphous form it was not a culturally homogenous and
unified self-conscious artefact, it tended and strove in that direction after the
French Revolution. Thereafter, the congruence of culture and state was set forth
as a principle of state formation triggering over the centuries, bursts of ethnic
cleansing, repression, population expulsions, etc. As the European powers established overseas empires, the state model was engrafted onto the newly acquired
colonies indiscriminatingly incorporating diverse ethno-cultural communities
into their boundaries. This process would in part sow the seeds of most contemporary ethnopolitical autonomist and secessionist movements. In the twentieth
century, this was underscored in the provisions of the Treaty of Versailles as
articulated by President Wilson after World WarI. In this vein, Eric Hobsbawm
has contended that the fall of the USSR spawning a proliferation of ethnonational
self-determination movements was but a delayed reaction in the late twentieth
century to the fissiparous process of state formation that was witnessed at the
earlier part of the century when the Ottoman and Hapsburg Empires collapsed
into nation-state units (Hobsbawm, 1990).

The self-determination principle has become firmly fixed to the nature of the
contemporary state and has been enshrined in Article 1 and 6 of the United
Nations Charter: 'All peoples have the right to self-determination; by virtue of
that right they freely determine their political status and freely pursue their
economic, social, and cultural development'. Any internal cultural minority
however that seeks its own self-determination especially through external assistance runs into Article 6 of the United Nations Charter that seems to license
repression: 'Any attempt aimed at a partial or whole disruption of the national
unity and the territorial integrity of a country is incompatible with the purposes
and principles of the Charter of the United Nations'. In turn, this has triggered a
wide-ranging debate regarding the terms under which a self-determination movement can be justified (Moore, 1998). There seems to be a tentative consensus
even though there are many dissenters that, under a limited set of circumstances

such as genocide and illegal acquisition of the contested territory, the creation of a new sovereign state through secession can be justified (Buchanan, 1998: 14–33). It remains a fact however that before the USSR had dissolved, only three cases of separation movements had succeeded in the twentieth century, namely, Norway, Singapore and Bangladesh. Since then, several new states have been created through self-determination drives from the former USSR, Czechoslovakia and Ethiopia (Brubaker, 1998).

There are, however, many more knocking at the door and while many sub-state ethnopolitical communities seem moribund, they tend to come alive again under the right circumstances bringing into play all the familiar pattern of ethno-cultural conflicts and their consequences. In the contemporary international scene, however, more multi-ethnic states are tolerant of minorities and have accorded recognition for internal ethno-cultural pluralism thereby successfully containing a number of these ethnopolitical movements. This is not to say that ethnopolitical autonomist movements have been eliminated altogether in these cases but rather, in reference to the scheme of increased levels of violence set forth in Table 12.1, that the trajectory of articulated grievances and complaints has shifted more pronouncedly to non-violent measures with a view towards finding accommodation within the state. Scholarship in this area of self-determination and ethnic conflicts have shifted from the dominant role of historians and international lawyers (Cobban, 1944; Burcheit, 1978; Hannum, 1990) to political scientists and philosophers (Buchanan, 1998: 14–33; Margalit and Raz, 1990: 439–463; Horowitz, 1998b: 181–214; Philpott, 1995: 352–385; Premdas, 1990: 12–29; 2000; 447–484; Miller, 1998: 62–78). The critical burning issue underlying much of this discourse interrogates, especially in the light of increased globalisation, the state as the optimal receptacle of organising human association.

Plural societies, the post-colonial successor states, modernisation, and ethnic strife

Through arbitrary boundary drawing and population transfers, colonial rule created most of the multi-ethnic Third World states. Within these new states, there was no commonly shared citizenship, nationalist outlook, or joint political will, with each ethno-cultural community suspicious of the other abetted by colonial tactics of divide and rule. Hence, these multi-ethnic colonially constructed plural societies that eventually became independent states, imparted the impression of makeshift settlements consisting of a collection of culturally unrelated persons forced to co-exist by reason of a larger economic imperial enterprise. Nigeria in Africa with over 200 ethno-linguistic communities, India in Asia with a similar number or more, and Lebanon with over 12 ethno-religious and linguistic communities, among scores of others, are typical examples of colonially created states with a multi-ethnic population marked by deep distrust and division and with practically no overarching unifying national bonds. They were literally at war with themselves marked by endemic inter-communal malaise, domination and persistent instability and inter-group inequality. After independence, they faced the unprecedented problem of designing an appropriate participant political system to accommodate the rival claims of their diverse ethno-national communities. The record in this regard is one replete with the wreckage of post-independence Third World governments which have tended to jettison their imported and imperially inspired democratic institutional structures and instead succumbed to authoritarian military or one-party regimes, communal violence and instability, ethnic domination and repression and instances of genocide and secession. With minor variations, examples of this general pattern are numerous exemplified by the cases of Nigeria, Ghana, Malawi, Uganda, Indonesia, Burma, Suriname, Kenya, Pakistan, etc. In the case of Nigeria, ethno-regional and ethno-religious rivalry witnessed successive military coups and a separatist assertion for autonomy by Biafra involving charges of genocide. In India, on the anvil of ethno-religious divisions and fears between Hindus and Muslims, two new states were violently created. In Indonesia, soon after independence from the Netherlands, the fall of Sukarno through a military coup triggered a genocidal slaughter of ethnic Chinese and repression of other groups including the Papuans on the island of New Guinea. In Suriname, not too long after obtaining its independence in 1975, a military coup oversaw a physical elimination of adversaries. One-party states proliferated everywhere in the name of securing national unity which provided a cover for ethnic repression and discrimination in Kenya, Zambia, Zimbabwe, Pakistan, and numerous other places sowing the seed of further ethnic strife.

The post-independence state typically was also in its totality the foremost repository of jobs, contracts and other policy opportunities. Any communal party that captured it could bring the state to the service of its own particular constituents and interests and simultaneously deprive, punish and peripheralise the others. The main rival political parties, each tending to represent one or the other of the major ethnic groups, recognised the value of capturing the government in its entirety. State power was so overwhelmingly powerful, concentrated and centralised, that it could be used as an instrument for promoting personal ambition as well as collective ethnic domination. This was well articulated by the eminent African political scientist, Claude Ake:

> In statist economies, political competition tends to be a fight until death, notably because of the increasing premium being placed on the control of state power. In Africa, this has become the master key to almost everything. Because of its extraordinary importance, the struggle to control the state becomes very intense-one might say Hobbesian. Since the stakes are so high, the competitors will do anything to win … The tendency is to annihilate political opponents instead of merely defeating them. (Ake, 1976: 11)

Democratic mass politics that followed independence after World War II was undermined by sectional leaders invoking ethnic loyalty as they organised their supporters and jockeyed for power. Fear of ethnic domination through internal colonialism featured as a critical aspect of the post-independence politics. Notable cases include Guyana, Fiji, Papua New Guinea, Zaire, India, Malaysia and Nigeria. Prior to the dismantling of the inherited post-independence democratic institutions, competitive elections brought a magnified fear that the victorious party would re-define the rules of the game permanently instituting ethnic discrimination and repression. Hence, election campaigns were waged intensely by the ethnically based political parties which tended to sustain a spiral of communalised conflict in which victory and control of the state apparatus was thus seen as an instrument of ethnic pre-eminence and preference (Premdas, 1995; Milne, 1982). Some of the classic cases of this pattern include Sri Lanka, Guyana, Malaysia, Burundi, Papua New Guinea, the Solomon Islands, etc. State modernisation programmes in the post-independence era undertaken by the new one-party regimes, most of them with vaunted socialist pretensions, tended to confer advantages and disadvantages for resources and recognition unevenly among traditional ethnies, fomenting the seedbed of communal alienation and ethnopolitical militancy. In Sri Lanka, victory by the Sinhalese-dominated Freedom party led to an exclusionary language policy of 'Sinhala Only' which effectively eliminated access to civil service jobs and university scholarships to the Tamil community. From this discriminatory policy emerged the insurgency by the Tamil Tigers which has led to one of the most protracted violent ethnic conflicts in the world. In Guyana and Fiji, the virtual seizure of power by one ethnic community led to capture of coveted state jobs and the exclusion of the defeated community crippling the state and impoverishing the population as it suffered through rounds of mutual sabotage and non-cooperation.

The above narrative captures the causes and manifestations of Third World ethnic conflict that has derived from the colonial condition which at one point encompassed over 80 percent of the world's population in the nineteenth and twentieth centuries under European imperial rule and from which has emerged after World WarII some one hundred new states. The pervasive ethnic strife in these multi-ethnic states has received the analytic attention from three broad schools of inquiry which we shall designate the plural society, modernisation and the political economy approaches. The plural society model accepts the ontological reality of cultural pluralism as a phenomenon that is not reducible to other factors such as economic relations but must be accepted as a fundamental condition of the social structure of multi-ethnic states (Furnivall, 1948: 304; Rabushka and Shepsle, 1972; Smith, 1969: 6). Many scholars, arguing that that the so-called 'plural societies' were as not thoroughly divided as their proponents claimed, underscoring that every society must have some set of integrative values to survive, condemned the model as a poor description of social reality. Marxists joined the fray condemning the plural society model for encouraging ethno-nationalism.

The political modernisation school, also dubbed the structural-functional, or systems school associated with the work of Samuel Huntington, Gabriel Almond, and Lucian Pye, while acknowledging the environment of cultural pluralism, has tended to see this as a barrier that would be submerged and eradicated as institutionalisation takes root and a new society is born. Derived from the Western experience of development, the modernisation approach gave priority to the establishment of political order and emphasised the need for 'institutionalisation' through evolving new norms and practices. It is critical to note that the integration and assimilationist perspectives built into this approach have tended to neglect or underestimate the arousal of ethnic group formation and the durability of ethnic identities and boundaries. These, as experience showed, were critical variables which tended to subvert the aims of the modernisation project. The ethnic factor was resilient and could not be swept away in the tidal wave of technological, economic, institutional and value change as the modernisation school would have it. In case after case, such as Sri Lanka, Guyana, Nigeria, etc., the costs of the strife undermined national development projects and diverted valuable scarce resources for the maintenance of security and order in the face of persistent sabotage and acts of non-cooperation by the excluded ethnic communities. Table 12.1 in the earlier part of the essay offers the escalator through which conflicts tend to spiral as action by the disgruntled ethnocultural communities are met by state reaction directed by the dominant community incurring massive costs crippling practically all efforts at economic development. In recent years, this dynamic of spiraling ethnic conflict with incalculable costs have been witnessed in the former Yugoslavia as the very state disintegrated spawning ethnic cleansing and humanitarian crises.

In diametrical contention against the plural society and modernisation approaches is the political economy school that includes the dependency and Marxist perspectives, even though these two orientations are not the same. Essentially, while the plural society and modernisation schools tend to stress the role of internal economic and political factors in accounting for the condition of Third World 'backwardness' and the persistence of ethnic conflict, the dependency and Marxist approaches point to the role of external actors in imperialism and monopoly capitalism in manufacturing underdevelopment and in sustaining ethnic divisions. Here, with the emphasis placed on centre–periphery exploitation marked by unequal economic and property relations, ethnicity is reduced to an epiphenomenon, which, it was wrongly predicted, would be superseded once the proletarian socialist revolution occurs. While both the modernisation and political economy schools view ethnicity as a temporary atavistic aspect of development that will be eliminated in a new order, the plural society approach accepts the condition of cultural pluralism as embedded in the Third World state that was created by imperialism and colonialism.

Ethnic conflict and the problem of democratic transition and reform

Democratic transition and reform has featured as a major proposition that accounts for many contemporary ethnic conflicts. It is argued that among the numerous recent authoritarian states, it was in the dynamic of the democratisation process itself, with the opening up of a competitive arena for power and office, that incentives for ethnic entrepreneurs and outbidding among rival politicians, were put in place leading to ethnic tensions and conflict. What does the empirical record show about the link between democratisation and ethnic conflict? The record has been mixed, marked by ambiguity as reported by the Peace and Conflict Ledger which monitored the incidence of ethnic conflict in relation to the democratisation process since 1970. Of the states that made partial or abortive transitions to democracy between 1980 and 1995, an equal number showed a propensity for ethnopolitical protests and violence as did not (Gurr, 2000: 157). The evidence discards the opinion about the pacifying effects of democratic transitions confirming substantial increases in ethnopolitical protests instead but not rebellions and insurgencies (ibid: 152–7).

Over the past 50 years since the end of World War II, worldwide decolonisation in the Third World has witnessed the creation of over a hundred new independent sovereign states. In what has been conceived as 'Three Waves' of tectonic change, most of the new states have since progressed from initial constitutional government, to socialist experiments, to authoritarian one-party and military regimes culminating with a new phase of democratic transition. The Sub-Saharan African experience illustrates aspects of these transformations (Bratton and van de Walle, 1997: 8). Only three of Africa's states, Botswana, Mauritius and Gambia, had survived as democracies since independence (Diamond and Plattner, 1999: x). However, after 1990, the scene was altered dramatically so that within five years, the number of sub-Saharan African countries holding competitive legislative elections more than quadrupled to 38 out of a total of 47 countries (ibid). Much of this change occurred when the major lending international financial institutions such as the International Monetary Fund and the World Bank initiated a new policy identifying governance and democratic political institutions as the key variables for successful change (Bangura, 2001: 1). However, there were special problems of adapting democratic institutions in states that were deeply divided by race, religion and ethnicity lacking in shared societal values.

How to discover and adapt democratic principles and institutions to the multiethnic environments raised many controversies and burning issues epitomised by the arguments between two scholars, Arend Lijphart and Donald Horowitz. Both scholars agreed that systems that create permanent political minorities must be avoided. In part, it suggests the need for more inclusive consensus political systems of powersharing requiring special kinds of institutional arrangements, which deviate from standard Western zero-sum adversarial parliamentary models. For some time, the proposals of Arend Lijphart called consociational democracy with its battery of institutions and practices occupied much intellectual support (Lijphart, 1977). It was based on a power-sharing formula through a grand coalition among communal elites and operated under a system of proportional representation that articulated and recognised ethnic identities in proportionately allocating public service jobs and in decentralising power and space for self-governance. So influential were Lijphart's proposals that they became the guiding force in crafting the interim South African constitution after Nelson Mandela's release from prison paving the way for open democratic elections and majority Black rule. There were other notable cases such as the 1979 Nigerian constitution that incorporated aspects of the Lijphart model. More recently, the Lijphartian consociational prescriptions influenced the composition Bosnian government in accommodating the claims of Muslims, Croats and Serbs. No doubt that this system of power-sharing was as powerful as it was persuasive, but in many ways it was rigid requiring several simultaneous and mutually supportive and complex interlocking conditions and practices which reduced the probability of its successful implementation. Besides, in many cases such as Northern Ireland, South Africa and Nigeria, in a short period of time, the experiment succumbed to sectional disputes and infighting, returning the state to its previously perilous ethnically acrimonious and unstable condition, even to civil war accompanied by ethnic cleansing and genocide. The case of Rwanda is noteworthy in this regard. The successful negotiations in power-sharing between the leaders of the Hutus and Tutsis led Hutu extremists to assassinate the Hutu leader blaming the Tutsis for the act setting in motion the slaughter of the Tutsi population and the collapse of the Rwanda state (Prunier, 1997; Adelman and Suhrke, 1995; Gourevitch, 1998). All of this was followed by a new form of ethnic domination, this time by the minority Tutsis over the majority Hutus, a condition that was bound to bring forth new forms of ethnic resistance and repression (Reyntjens, 2004: 117). In many cases, the proposal for power-sharing and the equitable allocation of government jobs and resources as well as the decentralisation of power to ethnic minorities, although this Lijphartian formula has much rational appeal especially in a conflict has been protracted and bloody, still tends to evoke resistance from the dominant ethnic group which fears that extensive decentralisation may actually encourage outright secession. This has happened in Sri Lanka and Russia in relation to the demands of the Tamils and Chechens, respectively (Taras and Ganguly, 2002; 126–152; 182–207). In some cases, the proposal to extend recognition, citizenship, and access to jobs to previously dominant groups, such as the Russian minorities in the Baltic states, has been met with resistance by the new ethnically dominated regimes in the successor states (Brubaker, 1998). Consociational arrangements are always caught up in sensitively balancing a variety of volatile ethnic and other forces so that the least of provocation triggers a collapse in domino fashion of the entire edifice of negotiated power-sharing arrangement. Clearly, the consociational system has proven its value in the short term in a number of cases but it lacks staying power and can actually confirm the worst fears of ethnic adversaries in the alleged perfidy of their rival communities. It makes reconciliation more difficult for groups that have always harboured fears and prejudices of each other.

A counter-proposal emerged, substantially spearheaded by Donald Horowitz who railed against what appeared as the, compulsory and inflexible nature of the consociational institutions and called instead for a new system of facilitating broadly inclusive democratic governments based on incentives and rewards. For Horowitz, the choice of an electoral system was critical to promoting power-sharing in coalition governments. He staked his position mainly on the alternative voter (AV) electoral system in which, through vote pooling, weight is given to second preferences instead of sole reliance on first preferences for victory to a candidate. This, it was argued, blunted the sharp edges of racial and ethnic outbidding and innuendo during political campaigns by encouraging pre-election swapping of voter preferences, and in turn, provided the basis for moderation and compromise among the competing parties (Horowitz, 2002: 23). For Horowitz, then, the AV voting system bore much promise of deliverance from the excesses to which ethnic and communal conflicts tend in democratic competitive politics. A few facilitating conditions were ideally required to allow the incentives approach through AV to succeed, among them the presence of several ethnic communities none with a majority making for multipolar fluidity and calculated rational choice by voters. Horowitz used several select empirical cases from around the world including Fiji, which under AV in the 1997 constitution, did seem to succeed in moderating the stridency of ethnic partisan politics during the election campaign (Premdas, 2002: 16–36; Stockwell, 2005: 382–393). However, on the more general claim that the AV system after the elections are over, would produce moderate coalition governments and contain ethnic conflicts, the jury is still out (Reilly, 2001). Overall, in evaluating the proposals by Lijphart and Horowitz for ethnic conflict management, both systems seek out cross-ethnic cooperation either at the leadership level in either in pre-election or post-election scenarios to achieve their ends. Both argue for some sort of coalition with each prescription containing its own peculiar complexity of institutions and practices. While consociational democracy seeks to impose a top–down formula for power-sharing, the incentiveship system attempts to forge coalition building from bottom up engaging the calculated self-interest of the rival parties in acts of cooperation. Both are wrong to assume that relatively predictable laboratory conditions will exist for the full operation of their prescriptions without the peculiarities of the cultural context and the disorder and irrationality of collective mass mobilisation making their own claims. Underlying much of this discourse on the role of institutional engineering in harnessing and directing collective ethnic behaviour are rival understandings of the nature of the ethnic phenomenon discussed above related to primordialism, instrumentalism and constructivism. For those who hold the constructivist or instrumentalist views, the ethnic claims if rival communities are opportunistic and malleable and amenable to modification and management. For primordialists, the ethnic marker is deep and intractable, and while amenable to some measure of reconciliation with 'the other', this type of accommodation does not yield to assimilation and permanence.

Globalisation, migrations and ethnic conflict

This cluster touches a series of interlocking events – migration, membership, diasporas, identity, globalization, etc. – which have transformed particularly the industrialised West, where migrant minorities constitute about 5 to 14 percent of the population, into a cauldron of ethno-cultural conflicts (Castles, 1984; Baubock, 1994; Premdas, 1991). Dramatic increases in legal immigrants, refugees and asylum seekers add to the multicultural matrix of these countries which in turn has given rise to right-wing racist anti-immigrant political parties as well as stringent militarised border controls (Castles, 1991; Body-Gendrot and Martiniello, 2000). Something similar occurred in North America where, especially for non-white migrants and minorities, their urban semi-segregated neighbourhoods in inner cities constitute a *cordon sanitaire* separating them from more privileged suburban areas. Identity questions are everywhere with claims for space, attention, resources and rights. It is not that minorities have not existed in the earliest states that were originally formed in Europe or that the poly-ethnic state is an innovation, for cultural heterogeneity within the same jurisdiction has been around as long as the state itself. Rather, unlike the past, as Ernest Gellner aptly described, when most sub-national cultures were 'led to the dust heap of history by industrial civilization without offering any resistance' (Gellner, 1983: 47), in the contemporary world these groups are boisterously vocal and militant, seeking recognition and a survival of their own. These processes of change have had implications for a new mode of ethnic conflict that has been daubed 'identity politics' involving activism and mobilisation by migrant minorities in quest of enfranchisement, equal rights and empowerment, policy concessions for the recognition of the symbols of cultural differences and identity as well as equality of access to economic and political opportunities.

The new inflamed sites of migration and diaspora accompanied by issues of dislocation, exile, and identity formation, underscore the embattled vision under assault of a dissolving sovereignist state system in an unchartered frontier of a globalised de-territorialised emergent order (Clifford, 1997). The cutting edge of the new reality is constituted not only of the easy flow of images, commodities, monies and messages across borders under multiple jurisdictions and new supranational institutions, but from a massive movement of diverse peoples in quest of more favourable destinations (Castles and Miller, 1993; Massey et al., 1998; Portes, 2003: 874–892). This tidal movement forces open old definitions of membership and citizenship and interrogates the very nature of state system as a way of politically organising space (Marshall, 1992). All prior claims and definitions are now interrogated (Hall, 1990; Lister, 2003). Particularly for countries which have vaunted claims and traditions of tolerance and minority rights in a democratic order, the arrival and settlement of large numbers of culturally diverse persons and the presence of historic minorities pose special problems of welcome and participation. In many instances, over time, the presence of migrants and minorities may well challenge the very civilisational foundations of a hegemonic host community. Few remember that the state, which itself is of fairly recent vintage as the unit of international organisation, at its inception was never homogenous, and that for the most part was an imaginary domain (Cesarani and Fullbrook, 1996: 1; Riesenbers, 1992). It has repeatedly altered its criteria of membership from territorial links (*ius soli*) to blood and descent (*ius sanguinis*), to custom, culture and beliefs. While citizenship has been as old as human settlement and different communities have adopted different forms of citizenship, the modern state has tended to redefine its meaning inconsistently and opportunistically in response to the exigencies of population shifts, industrial needs and other factors. It has always been a contingent phenomenon in practice. Yet, in the contemporary scene, a new temper seeks to freeze borders and restrict membership in a xenophobic preoccupation with the 'stranger'. The stringent rhetorical claims of citizenship exclusivity then, riding high on imagined purity of lineage, blood and culture, often encapsulate a reactionary defense in support of privileged fortresses within the state. It often signals a justification for discrimination and injustice against persons of a different colour or culture. Herein reside the contemporary ingredients that feed into the making of new forms of ethnic conflict in the Western democracies. Ethnic and cultural claims undergird the discontent, anger and frustrations that are unleashed on the fortresses of privilege and their civilisational claims. It is primarily in the cities of the world in Paris, London, Moscow, New York, Los Angeles, Lagos, Ibadan, Calcutta, Toronto, Rio de Janeiro, Sydney, etc. where nearly half of the world's population resides that this struggle over citizenship rights, equality, justice is carried on daily (Sassen, 1991).

In all these changes stemming from globalisation and mass migration, a new intellectual scholarly outpouring with an assortment of controversial stands has addressed the Western states' efforts in accommodating the new immigrant-generated cultural pluralism and conflict (Kymlicka, 2003). First on the agenda is the matter of assimilation versus multi-culturalism revolving around several axes of contention: the right of a sub-national cultural community to practice its beliefs versus the claims of a cultural core calling for uniformity in cultural practices; the insistence by some for multi-lingual services versus demands that everything be done in one official national language; the claim by ethnic communities for multi-cultural representation in school curriculum versus the view that proclaims a single dominant source of historical meaning (Parekh, 2000; Glaser, 1997; Premdas, 1996a; Rex, 1995). In this regard, the underlying issue of cultural identity is couched in an inter-related set of explosive interrogations: Should there be a national cultural identity? Is one required and if so what are its components and whose cultural construct should it be? Doesn't the problem of cultural pre-eminence encapsulate and conceal the quest for power? Should the question of identity be a personal and private matter with no public attempt to construct an overarching consensus of values and traditions? Is each ethno-cultural identity equal to any other? Should the foreign policy of the state reflect the cultural preferences of the dominant core? The heart of the issues often turns on the rival policy options: multiculturalism; assimilation; and expulsion, all of which address the manner in which the arrivals and their descendants as well as historic minorities are to be accommodated within the dominant society (Goldberg, 1994; Premdas, 1996). The conflictual nature of these issues periodically breaks the bounds of their social controls and takes to the streets in violence and disorder as attested by the conflagration in France in 2005, and in the massive widespread street demonstrations in the United States in May 2006.

In the United States, identity politics has taken a new turn so that in the contemporary era of mass migration, militant ethnic group assertiveness and competition has been reconfigured by a pluralism of rival cultural communities (Bonilla-Silva, 2001; Winant, 2000; Feagin, 2000; Song, 2003; Roediger, 1991). The current differentiated ethno-cultural identities are now constituted not only of Whites and African-Americans but of Mexican-Americans, Koreans, Japanese, Asian Indians, Native Americans, Philippinos, etc., registering claims in a game of identity political rivalry for recognition, resources and rights. Evidence of the change in ethnic and racial conflict as a consequence of this new pluralism has been well described by Steven Gold who noted that 'the most-volatile and widely publicized incidents of racial/ethnic conflict and violence that have occurred in the United States over the past two decades – the Miami riot of 1980, boycotts of Korean grocers in New York, the Crown Heights riot, the 1992 Los Angeles Riot, disputes between Arabs and Chaldean business owners and black customers in Detroit, and ongoing antagonism over government jobs and political power between blacks and Latinos in many locations-have transpired among non-white immigrant and minority groups' (Gold, 2004: 951–968).

CONCLUSION

Displacing the threat of nuclear war during the Cold War era, the pervasiveness of ethnic conflict culminating with its crescendo in the early 1990s stimulated a varied scholarly response generating an assortment of approaches and explanations. Submitted to a multiplicity of hypotheses encompassing materialist to psychological to philosophical explanations and methodologies, the ethnic phenomenon proved elusive. As much as they contributed creatively and fruitfully to a patchwork of partial truths and insights, no single master variable or paradigm commanded a consensus among scholars and analysts, imparting witness to the multi-faceted, complex and often perplexing nature of ethnic strife wherever it occurred both in developed and undeveloped states alike (Wimmer, 2004: 33–361). At various times, a particular hypothetical position or approach seemed most convincing and popular such as the one based on the inevitable recrudescence of historic ancient hatreds or, less sensationally, on a demystifying materialist or rational choice angle (Hechter, 1986: 268–277). These were offset by the appeals of propositions that focused on the mass psychology of nationalist ardour, or the role of ethnic entrepreneurs in democratic transitions or the cross-border contagious effects of ethnic strife. Many schools of thought emerged as well as influential journals with their stellar scholarly protagonists (Horowitz, 1985), some with more or less access to national and international decisionmakers. With the waning of the ethnic wildfire by the mid-1990s, it seemed that an emphasis on ethnic conflict management techniques in peace and conflict studies had become ascendant (Montville, 1996; Rothschild, 1997; Carnegie Commission, 1997; Sriram and Wermester, 2003; Zartman, 2001; Hampton and Malone, 2002).

With this new slant on an ancient persistent problem, the new tools and techniques of conflict management and multitrack diplomacy etc., sought to tame the ethnic monster into a rational sentiment that needed only to be understood in order to be contained if not eliminated altogether. The deep-rooted attachment of communal identity and passionate and excessive manifestation of ethnic conflict that has gone violent discussed in the first part of the essay are set aside. This virtual ontological denial and banishment of the ethnic sentiment into the comforts and seductive techniques of management were rudely displaced by the trauma of 9/11. With it, however, came not the revival of sober and systematic analysis of the ethnic phenomenon but a focus on the salience of ethno-religious irrationality and fundamentalism which literally swamped every area of social science inquiry including the general area of ethnic conflict studies reducing it to the obsessive preoccupation with terrorism (Connor, 2004: 25; Posen, 1993: 27–47). Systematic ethnic conflict analysis had to survive in a lackluster backseat made by some into an extension and branch of security studies. Contemporary events tend to give shape to the form and focus of ethnic conflict inquiry. Many years after 9/11, with the genocidal events of Darfur in the Sudan and the riots and violence in France over the treatment of migrants, a return to the sober and systematic analysis of ethnic strife has returned in some measure.

In this essay, an attempt was made to chart the varied aspects and dimensions of the ethnic factor in human conflict. Some of the most critical issues besetting the field were surveyed and several clustered patterns of related events were identified and described around which ethnic strife seemed to have been manifested and persisted. This list of issues and patterned clusters does not exhaust the full articulation of ethnic conflict behaviour. Nor does the list express a preferred approach or a related set of issues. What we do know is that with the emergence of new contemporary crises, the malleability and the multifacetedness of ethnic variable is drawn out in the shape of new methodologies generative of new insights and unresolved perplexities and enigmas. Hence, in the contemporary context the accentuated convergence of mass migration, globalisation and the erosion of the traditional features of the state, ethnic studies has taken on systematically issues around identity, membership, migration, multiculturalism and transnationalism engaging different methodological perspectives and interests. Similarly, the decline of ethnopolitical assertions for self-determination, which was at one time the single most potent source of war, and related violence and deaths, has been accompanied by the greater scholarship on the role of peacemaking intervention of international organisations and non-governmental associations towards accommodating minorities. However, the ethnic factor as most analysts now concede cannot be banished from human survival in society and will always be around with the permanence of diversity and the need for human belonging. In all of this continuing analysis and systematisation of inquiry, there is no doubt that some of the perennial contentions around the relative claims of materialists, rational choice theorists, instrumentalists, ancient hate primordialists, cultural symbolists, social identity psychologists, democratic and modernisation transitionists, kin selection sociobiologists, postmodern constructivists, security analysts and others will re-appear to grapple with ethnic strife whatever form it will assume (Brass, 1991; Esman, 1994; Young, 1993; Wimmer, 2004). However, new sites of such strife are appearing on the Internet, in new cross-border exclusivist human associations such as faith-based and humanistic communities around the world, in new forms of recreation and tribal sports, and in numerous twilight zones of mixing, fusion and hybridity that defy easy ethnic categorisation. What it all entails in the end with regard to ethnic strife is the continuing challenge for explanations that are willing to transgress old paradigms and perspectives of analysis as the ethnic phenomenon continues in contemporary life everywhere to manifest its many faces of articulation and configurations in rational and irrational ways.

REFERENCES

Adelman H. and Suhrke A. (eds.) (1995) *The Path to Genocide: The Rwanda Crises from Uganda to Zaire*. London: Transaction Publisher.

Ake, C. (1976) 'Explanatory Notes on the Political Economy of Africa', *Journal of Modern African Studies*, 14 (1): 1–23.

Anderson, Benedict (1991) *Imagined Communities*. London: Verso Publications.

Appiah, K.A. and Gutmann, A. (1996) *Color Conscious: The Political Morality of Race*. Princeton: Princeton University Press.

Bangura, B. (2001) *Ethnic Structure and Governance: Reforming Africa in the 21st Century*. Geneva: United Nations Research Institute for Social Development.

Banton, M. (1983) *Racial and Ethnic Competition*. Cambridge: Cambridge University Press.

Barth, F. (ed.) (1967) *Ethnic Groups and Boundaries*. Boston: Little and Brown.

Bartkus, V.O. (1999) *The Dynamics of Secession*. London: Cambridge University Press.

Baubock, R. (1994) *Transnational Citizenship: Membership and Rights in International Migration*. Aldershot: Edward Elgar.

Body-Gendrot, S. and Martiniello, M. (eds) (2000) *Minorities in European Cities*. Basingstoke: Macmillan.

Bonacich, E. (1972) 'A Theory of Split Labor Market', *American Sociological Review*, 37 (5): 547–559.

Bonilla-Silva, E. (2001) *White Supremacy and racism in the Post Civil Rights Era*. Boulder, Colorado: Lynne Rienner.

Brass, P. (1991) *Ethnicity and Nationalism*. Newbury Park, CA: Sage.

Bratton, M. and van de Walle, N. (1997) *Democratic Experiments in Africa*. Cambridge: Cambridge University Press.

Brown, Michael (1993) "Causes and Implications of Ethnic Conflict" in Michael Brown (ed), *Ethnic Conflict and International Security*. Princeton, New Jersey: Princeton University Press. pp. 3–27

Brubaker, R. (1998) *Nationalism Reframed*. Cambridge: Cambridge University Press.

Buchanan, A. (1998) 'Democracy and Secession' in M. Moore (ed.) *National Self-Determination and Secession*. New York: Oxford University Press. pp. 14–43.

Bulmer, M. and Solomos, J. (eds.) (2004) 'Introduction: Research, Race and Racism' in *Researching Race and Racism*. London: Routledge. pp. 1–24.

Burcheit, L. (1978) *Secession: The Legitimacy of Self-Determination*. New Haven: Yale University Press.

Carnegie Commission (1997) *Preventing Deadly Conflict: Final Report*. Washington DC: Carnegie Commission on Deadly Conflict.

Castles, S. (1984) *Here for Good: Western Europe's New Ethnic Minorities*. London: Pluto Press.

Castles, S. and Davidson, A. (2004) *Citizenship and Migration: Globalization and the Politics of Belonging.* London: Routledge.

Castles, S. (1997) *Ethnicity and Globalization: From Migrant Worker to Transnational Citizen.* London: Sage Publications.

Castles, S. and Miller, M.J. (1993) *The Age of Migration: International Population Movements in the Modern World.* Basingstoke: Macmillan.

Cesarani, D. and Fulbrook, M. (1996) 'Introduction' in D. Cesarani and M. Fulbrook (eds) *Citizenship, Nationality, and Migration in Europe.* London: Routledge. pp. 1–17.

Clifford, J. (1997) 'Diasporas' in J. Rex and M. Guibernau (eds) *The Ethnicity Reader.* Cambridge: Polity Press. pp. 283–290.

Cobban, A. (1944) *National Self-Determination.* London: Oxford University Press.

Connor, W. (1994) *Ethnonationalism: The Quest For Understanding.* Princeton, New Jersey: Princeton University Press.

Connor, W. (2004) 'A Few Cautionary Notes on the History and Future of Ethnonational Conflicts' in A. Wimmer et al. (eds) *Facing Ethnic Conflicts: Toward a New Realism.* New York: Rowland and Littlefield. pp. 23–33.

Coppieters, B. and Huysseune M. (eds) (2002) *Secession, History, and the Social Sciences.* Brussels: Brussels University Press.

Depres, L. (ed.) (1975) *Ethnicity and Resource Competition.* Hague: Houghton.

Depres, L. and Premdas, R. (2000) 'Theories of Ethnic Contestation and Their Relationship to Economic Development' in R. Premdas (ed.) *Identity, Ethnicity and Culture in the Caribbean.* Trnidad: School of Continuing Studies, University of the West Indies.

De Vos, George and Romananucci-Ross (1975), Lola (eds.) *Ethnic Identity: Cultural Communities and Change.* Palo Alto, California: Mayfield.

Diamond, L. and Plattner, M.F. (1999) 'Introduction' in L. Diamond and M. Plattner (eds) *Democratization in Africa.* Baltimore: Johns Hopkins University Press. pp. ix–xxvii.

Eller, J. and Couglin, R. (1993) 'The Poverty of Primordialism: The Demystification of Ethnic Attachments', *Ethnic and Racial Studies*, 16 (2): 183–202.

Eriksen, T.H. (1993) *Ethnicity and Nationalism: Anthropological Perspectives.* London: Pluto Press.

Esman, M. (1994) *Ethnic Politics.* Ithaca, New York: Cornell University Press.

Feagin, J.R. (2000) *Racist America: Roots, Current Realities, and Future Reparations.* London: Routledge.

Furnivall. J.S. (1948) *Colonial Policy and Practice.* London: Cambridge University Press.

Gardels, N. (1991) 'Two Concepts of Nationalism: An Interview with Isaiah Berlin' *New York Review of Books*, 21 November.

Geertz, C. (ed.) (1963) *Old Societies and New States.* Glencoe, IL: The Free Press.

Geertz, C. (1963) 'The Integrative Revolution: Primordial Sentiments and Civil Politics in the New States' in C. Geertz (ed.) *Old Societies and New States.* New York: Free Press. pp. 105–57.

Gellner, E. (1983) *Nations and Nationalism.* Oxford: Blackwell Publishers.

Glaser, N. (1997) *We Are All Multiculturalists Now.* Cambridge, MA: Harvard University Press.

Glaser, N. and Moynihan, P. (eds) (1975) *Ethnicity: Theory and Experience.* Cambridge, MA: Harvard University Press.

Gold, S. (2004) 'From Jim Crow to Racial Hegemony: Evolving Explanations of Racial Hierarchy', *Ethnic and Racial Studies*, 27 (6). pp. 951–968.

Goldberg, D.T. (1992) 'The Semantics of Race', *Ethnic and Racial Studies*, 15 (4). pp. 543–569.

Goldberg, D.T. (1994) *Multiculturalism: A Critical Reader.* Cambridge, MA: Blackwell.

Gourevitch, P. (1998) *We Wish to Inform You That Tomorrow We Will Be Killed with Our Families: Stories from Rwanda.* London: Picador Press.

Gurr, T. (2000) *Peoples versus States: Minorities at Risk in the New Century* Washington DC: United States Institute of Peace.

Gurr, T.R. (1993) *Minorities at Risk: A Global View of Ethnopolitical Conflicts.* Washington DC: United States Institute of Peace.

Gurr, T.R. and Marshall, M.G. (2005) *Peace and Conflict 2005: A Global Survey of Armed Conflicts, Self-Determination Movements, and Democracy.* College Park, Maryland: Center for International Development and Conflict Management.

Hall, S. (1990) 'Cultural Identity and Diasporas' in J. Rutherford (ed.) *Community, Culture, and Difference.* London: Lawrence and Wishart. pp. 223–237.

Hampson, F.O. and Malone, D.M. (eds) (2002) *From Reaction to Conflict Prevention: Opportunities for the UN System.* Boulder, CO: Lynne Riennier.

Hannum, H. (1990) *Autonomy Sovereignty, and Self-Determination.* Philadelphia: University of Pennsylvania Press.

Hechter, M. (1986) 'A Rational Choice Approach to Race and Ethnic Relations' in D. Mason and J. Rex (eds) *Theories of Race and Ethnic Relations.* Cambridge: Cambridge University Press.

Hobsbawm, E. (1990) *Nations and Nationalism since 1780.* Cambridge: Cambridge University Press.

Horowitz, D. (1985) *Ethnic Groups in Conflict.* Berkeley: University of California Press.

Horowitz, D. (1998a) 'Self-Determination: Politics, Philosophy, and Law' in M. Moore (ed.) *National Self-Determination and Secession.* Oxford: Oxford University Press. pp. 345–370.

Horowitz, D. (1998b) 'Structure and Strategy in Ethnic Conflict' Paper prepared for the Annual World Bank Conference on Development Economics, Washington D.C., April 20–21.

Horowitz, D. (2002) *The Deadly Ethnic Riot.* Berkeley: University of California Press.

Horowitz, D. (2002) 'Constitutional Design: Proposals versus Processes' in A. Reynolds (eds) *The Architecture of Democracy: Constitutional Design, Conflict Management and Democracy.* London: Oxford University Press.

Huntington, S. (1996) *The Clash of Civilizations and the Remaking of World Order.* New York: Simon and Schuster.

Ignatieff, M. (1993) *Blood and Belonging: Journeys into the New Nationalism.* New York: Farrar, Straus, and Giroux.

Isaacs, H.R. (1975) *Idols of the Tribe: Group Identity and Political Change.* New York: Harper and Row.

Kymlicka, W. (2003) 'Immigration, Citizenship and Multiculturalism: Exploring Links' in S. Spencer (ed.) *The Politics of Migration.* Oxford: Blackwell. pp. 195–203.

Lewis, B. (1992) 'Muslims, Christians, and Jews: The Dream of Co-existence', *New York Review of Books,* 26 March.

Lijphart, A. (1977) *Democracy in Plural Societies.* New Haven, CT: Yale University Press.

Lister, R. (2003) *Citizenship: Feminist Perspectives.* 2nd edition. New York: New York University Press.

Mamdani, M. (2001) *When Victims Become Killers.* New Jersey: Princeton University Press.

Mamdani, M. (1996) 'From Conquest to Consent as the Bases of State Formation: Reflections on Rwanda', *New Left Review,* 216 (1): 3–36.

Mann, M. (2005) *The Dark Side of Democracy: Explaining Ethnic Cleansing.* Cambridge: Cambridge University Press.

Margalit A. and Raz, J. (1990) 'National Self-Determination', *Journal of Philosophy,* 87 (9): 439–463.

Marshall, J.M. (1992) *Citizenship Minneapolis.* Minnesota: University of Minnesota Press.

Massey, D. et al. (1998) *Worlds in Motion: Understanding International Migration at the End of the Millennium.* Oxford: Oxford University Press.

Miller, D. (1998) 'Secession and the Principle of Nationality' in M. Moore (ed.) *National Self-Determination and Secession.* New York: Oxford University Press. pp. 62–78.

Milne, R.S. (1982) *Politics in Ethnically Bi-Polar States.* University of British Columbia Press, Vancouver.

Montville, J.V. (ed.) (1996) *Conflict and Peace Making in Multi-Ethnic States.* Lexington, MA: D. C. Heath.

Moore, M. (ed.) (1998) *National Self-Determination and Secession.* New York: Oxford University Press.

Moynihan, D. (1993) *Pandemonium: Ethnicity in International Politics.* New York: Oxford University Press.

Olzak, S. (1992) *The Dynamics of Ethnic Competition and Conflict.* Stanford: Stanford University Press.

Omi, M. and Winant, H. (1994) *Racial Formation in the United States.* New York: Routledge.

Parekh, B. (2000) *Re-Thinking Multiculturalism: Cultural Diversity and Political Theory.* London: Macmillan.

Philpott, D. (1995) 'In Defense of Self-Determination', *Ethics,* 105 (2): 352–385.

Portes, A. (2003) 'Conclusion: Theoretical Convergences and Empirical Evidence in the Study of Immigration Transnationalism', *International Migration Review,* Fall: 874–892.

Posen, B. (1993) 'The Security Dilemma and Ethnic Conflict', *Survival,* 35 (1): 27–47.

Premdas, R. (1990) 'Secessionist Movements in Comparative Perspective' in R. Premdas and S.W.R. de Samarasinghe (eds) *Secessionist Movements in Comparative Perspective.* London: Pinter Publishers. pp. 12–29.

Premdas, R. (1991) 'The Internationalization of Ethnic Conflict: Theoretical Perspectives' in R. May and K.M. de Silva (eds) *The Internationalization of Ethnic Conflict.* London: Pinter. pp. 10–25.

Premdas, R. (1995) *Ethnicity and Development: The Case of Guyana.* London: Avebury Press.

Premdas, R. (1996a) *Public Policy and Ethnic Conflict.* Paris: UNESCO. Management of Social Transformation Program, Working paper No.12.

Premdas, R. Anderson, A. and Samarasinghe, S.W.R. (eds.) (1996b) *Secessionist Movements in Comparative Perspective.* London: Pinter.

Premdas, R. (2000) 'Self-Determination and Secession in the Caribbean: The Case of Nevis', in R. Premdas (ed.) *Identity, Ethnicity and Culture in the Caribbean.* Trinidad: School of Continuing Studies, University of the West Indies. pp. 447–484.

Premdas, R. (2002) 'Seizure of Power, Indigenous Rights and Crafting Democratic Governance in Fiji', *Nationalism and Ethnic Politics,* 8 (4). pp. 16–36.

Prunier, G. (1997) *The Rwanda Crisis: History of Genocide.* New York: Columbia University Press.

Rabuska, A. and K.Shepsle. (1972) *Politics in Plural Societies.* Merrill Lynch, Ohio.

Reilly, B. (2001) *Democracy in Divided States: Electoral Engineering for Conflict Management.* Cambridge: Cambridge University Press.

Reyntjens, F. (2004) 'Rwanda, Ten Years on: From Genocide to Dictatorship', *African Affairs,* 103 (2004): 177–210.

Rex, J. (1995) 'Multiculturalism in Europe and America', *Nations and Nationalism,* 1 (2): 243–256.

Rex, J. and Mason, D. (1986) (eds) *Theories of Ethnic and Race Relations.* Cambridge: Cambridge University Press.

Riesenbers, P. (1992) *Citizenship in the Western Tradition.* Durham: University of North Carolina Press.

Roediger, D.R. (1991) *The Wages of Whiteness and the Making of an American Working Class.* London: Verso.

Rothschild, D. (1997) *Managing Ethnic Conflict in Africa.* Washington DC: Brookings Institution.

Rudolph, S. I. and Rudolph, L. I. (1993) 'Modern Hate' *New Republic,* 22 March.

Sassen, S. (1991) *The Global City.* Princeton: Princeton University Press.

Seton-Watson, H. (1977) *Nation and States: An Enquiry into the Origins of Nations and the Politics of Nationalism.* Boulder, CO: Westview Press.

Smith, A.D. (1986) *The Ethnic Origins of Nations.* Oxford: Basil Blackwell.

Smith, M.G. (1969) "Institutional Political Conditions of Pluralism". In Leo.Kuper and Michael G.Smith (eds). *Pluralism in Africa.* Los Angeles: University of California Press. pp. 27–65.

Smith, M.G. (1993) 'Race and Ethnicity' in R. Premdas (ed.) *The Anatomy of Ethnicity: An Analysis of Race and Ethnicity in the Caribbean and the World.* Trinidad: School of Continuing Studies, University of the West Indies.

Song, M. (2003) *Choosing Ethnic Identity.* Malden, MA: Polity Press.

Sriram, C.L. and Wermester, K. (2003) *From Promise to Practice: Strengthening UN Capacities for the Prevention of Violent Conflict.* Boulder, CO: Lynn Rienner.

Stavenhagen, Rodolfo (1996) *Ethnic Conflicts and the Nation-State.* New York: St.Martin's Press.

Stockwell, R.F. (2005) 'An Assessment of the Alternative Voter System in Fiji', *Journal of Commonwealth and Comparative Politics*, 43 (3): 382–393.

Tajfel, H. (1970) 'Experiments in Intergroup Discrimination', *Scientific American*, 223 (5): 96–102.

Taras, R.C. and Ganguly, R. (eds) (2002) *Understanding Ethnic Conflict: The International Dimension.* New York: Longman.

Taylor, C. (1992) *Multiculturalism and the Politics of Recognition.* Princeton, NJ: Princeton University Press.

Taylor, D.M. and Moghaddam, F.M. (1994) *Theories of Inter-Group Relations.* New York: Praegar.

UNESCO (1951) *Race and Science: The Race Question in Modern Science.* New York: Columbia University Press.

Vincent, J. (1974) 'The Structuring of Ethnicity', *Human Organization*, 33: 375–379.

Wimmer, A. (2004) 'Toward a New Realism' in A. Wimmer et al. (eds) *Facing Ethnic Conflicts: Toward a New Realism.* New York: Roman and Littlefield. pp. 23–33.

Winant, H. (2000) 'Racism Today: Continuity and Change in the Post-Civil Rights Era' in Peter Kivisto and G. Rumblad (eds). *Multiculturalism in the United States: Current Issues, Contemporary Voices.* Thousand Oaks, CA: Pine Forge Press. pp. 19–29.

Young, C. (1993) (ed.) 'The Dialectics of Cultural Pluralism: Concept and Reality' in *The Rising Tide of Cultural Pluralism: The Nation-State at Bay?* Madison: University of Wisconsin Press.

Zartman, I.W. (2001) *Preventive Negotiations: Avoiding Conflict Escalation.* Lanham, MD: Rowman and Littlefield.

13

Globalisation, Migration and Citizenship

Liza Schuster

INTRODUCTION[1]

The increasing ease and frequency of migration, together with the ability of migrants to sustain links and engage in circular, shuttle and serial temporary migration, and the challenge all of this presents to traditional views of citizenship, is frequently cited as evidence of globalisation (Castles, 2000; Castles and Davidson, 2000; Balibar, 2004; Scholte, 2005; Bisley, 2007). Migration brings into sharp relief the negative and positive consequences of a world in which the borders of communities, nations, societies and states are simultaneously barriers and bridges. Historically, there have always been controls on the mobility of the less well off as states have worked with capital to hold on to, or move around desirable, productive slaves, subjects or citizens, and expel the unproductive or trouble-makers to colonies where they might contribute to the production of wealth (Baseler, 1998; Noiriel, 2007). Racialisation and racism have been important factors shaping this, largely forced, movement of people over centuries, as states have engaged in the process of constructing the state's people and the state's nation, selecting those who belong and rejecting those who do not (Arendt, 1967), and attributing roles and functions to certain groups within the territory on the basis of certain 'natural' characteristics. However, since the end of World WarII, the autonomous movement of individuals, families and groups of people has presented a particular challenge to the state's capacity to control who enters, resides and settles in its territory. In meeting this challenge, states have developed regimes of control that are still more or less explicitly racialised, favouring the entry of some groups over others, using entry criteria that are implicitly racist or racist in terms of outcomes.[2]

It would therefore seem logical to suppose that since migration and racism are two phenomena that have been intimately linked for some considerable time, so too would be the bodies of literature that address these issues. And yet to varying degrees, they have remained discrete and separate from each other, with some scholars in each field scarcely aware of the work of those in the other. This separation can be explained to a certain extent by the genesis of these fields, which differs across the globe. These differences are explored in the first section of this chapter. The second section discusses some of the different ways/disciplines in which migration can be studied, arguing that no matter how one classifies work on migration, racism is always implicit in the study of migration (and perhaps vice versa). The third section of the chapter looks at the actual phenomena of migration and racism, and the ways in which, in Europe in particular, they are linked. This section leads into an argument for a particular approach to research in the future, before ending with some reflections and questions.

States almost self-evidently discriminate between groups of people when deciding who may or may not enter, and while few would deny the discriminatory nature of migration controls, most states would argue that today these controls are not racist. In this chapter, racism is used to mean 'any argument which suggests that the human species is composed of discrete groups in order to legitimate inequality [or unequal treatment] between those groups of people' (Miles, 1989). These groups may be distinguished (and constructed) not solely on the basis of skin colour, but also culture, nationality, ethnicity and/or migration status, and these differences are then used to legitimate unequal treatment, for example, granting multiple entry visas to people of one nationality, but refusing entry to another, or introducing selection criteria that are clearly more difficult for some groups to meet than others (e.g., income levels, language skills). In the same way that race is socially and *politically* constructed, so too is racism (Solomos, 2003), and the study of migration provides numerous examples of this construction process. As David Goldberg (1994: 91) and others have noted, racism is not singular, fixed and unchanging. The concept of race and the reality of racism both need to be located within specific historical and contemporary social and political contexts (slavery, colonialism, fascism, the end of the Cold War, 9/11, etc.); so we cannot assume that what we see as racism is necessarily seen in the same way in all contexts. As Wieviorka (1992, 1993) has stressed, it is important to comprehend social change as playing a large part in reconfiguring particular forms of racism. While there are those who continue to subscribe to a crude, essentialist 'white races superior/black races inferior' mode of thinking, this is not *usually* how it is expressed today, when in Europe we are more likely to find 'illegals', extraCommunitari, migrants, asylum-seekers, or Sans Papiers as the targets of unequal treatment, that is denied access to certain rights, benefits or privileges by virtue of their membership in one or more of these categories. To note that the majority of those who fall into these categories are also the traditional targets of racism overlooks the construction of these categories by states – more or less explicitly to exclude those who do not belong or bring some benefit with them.

Some have suggested that the hostility directed towards migrants is due not to racism but to *xenophobia* – an irrational fear or hatred of foreigners. While some resentment towards migrants may be linked to concerns about jobs, pressure on local services or fear of the unknown, attributing it to xenophobia rather than racism ignores the obvious fact that hostility is not directed at all foreigners, but primarily those who *appear* visibly different (demonstrating the tenacity of biological racism and problems with difference). Furthermore, such attribution also naturalises and trivialises rather than challenges this fear/hatred. We will return to this theme throughout the chapter.

When discussing migration, class (Anderson, 2006; Van Hear, 2006) and gender (Anderson, 2006, 2003; Kofman et al., 2002) are as important as racism (Anderson, 2006), and certainly my own research in Europe and Morocco underlines the importance of a complex approach to a complex phenomenon. One of the challenges of a recent project in Cyprus has been to try and disentangle the relative weight that should be attached to each of these factors when classifying the root of the hostility and difficulties faced by migrants.[3] To what extent is an individual subject to harassment because of his/her socio-economic vulnerability, gender or perceived race? How much of a state's selective entry requirements are shaped by the impulse to control the entry of the poor and unskilled, and how much will they prevent the entry of those seen as 'other' or inassimilable? How can researchers attribute relative weights to these different factors? Although the focus here is on the link between racism and migration, it is important to note that this is only one of a number of factors shaping the experience of migrants, and that the experience of migrants is gendered and classed as well as racialised.[4]

THE GENESIS OF RACE AND MIGRATION STUDIES

The scholarly literature on race and racism is most established and extensive in the United States, where its primary concern has traditionally been with Black Americans, many of whose ancestors, though not all, were brought to what is now the United States and Caribbean as slaves. Although slavery could be seen as an extreme manifestation of 'forced' migration, generally speaking, migration, forced or otherwise, has been a relatively minor issue in US literature on race and racism. The debt incurred by a nation built on slavery and a crude biological racism that defined particular groups as 'naturally' suited to slavery, coupled with the social, economic and political consequences of slavery that are still felt today by a significant section of the American population focussed the attention of scholars on black/white racism and on the threat to the nation represented by inequality and segregation.

The other major factor shaping studies of 'race' and racism was the American Civil Rights Movements, which was driven by a commitment to equality among Americans, equality under the Constitution and a need to redress a massive and damaging injustice. This was a battle fought by Americans (Black and White) for Black Americans (though of course it fed, and was fed by, similar movements around the world) and American society. However, not all scholars of 'race' and racism ignore migration. Immigration to cities such as Chicago meant that in the 1920s the population was one-third foreign born and relations between the established residents and newcomers attracted the attention of the 'Chicago School', including Robert Park (1950) who developed a four-stage theory of assimilation of migrants. Implicit within the work of Park and others was a belief in the superiority of the host society, in the threat to harmony presented by and the need to manage 'race relations' (Park, 1950: Part II).

Given that in the United States, the predominant self-image is that of an egalitarian, confident nation of immigrants, where many Americans are proud to trace a migrant ancestry, and that the predominant ideology is one of meritocracy, where all that counts is individual effort and talent, it is perhaps understandable that many migration scholars were relatively slow to link racism with migration. Much of the early writing on migration approached it from a simple, economistic cost–benefit analysis, which since it concentrated on migrants as individual units of labour, could not really capture the significance of racism. On the other hand, the role of 'race' and racism in the development and implementation of policy should have been clear in the light of laws introduced in the late nineteenth century to exclude Chinese and other Asian migrants, and in the 1920s to preserve the ethnic mix of migrants through national quotas. Post-1945 the Bracero programme, initially a relatively unproblematic response to labour shortages, suffered a 'nativist' backlash (fuelled in part by economic recession in the early 1950s and the political paranoia of the McCarthy era) which led to 'Operation Wetback'. The Civil Rights movement of the 1960s finally removed the racialised laws that systematically blocked the immigration of Asians, Africans and southern Europeans (and led to the end of the Bracero programme), and the minority populations in the United States began to grow significantly.

The literature on post-1965 migration doesn't really talk about race as a factor either in the development of migration policy or the reception of migrants (Portes and Rumbaut's important work [2006] *A Portrait of Immigrant America* now in its third edition devotes three pages to racial discrimination). However, in a recent IJCS paper, Goldberg and colleagues (2006) surveyed the culture of scholarship on 'race' in the US and noted that in response to the Civil Rights Movement's challenge to the racial and colonial formation of the United States, White intellectuals refashioned the terms of reference, espousing 'racelessness' and embracing the terms 'ethnic' and migrant' (severely critiquing Glazer and Moynihan's *Beyond the Melting Pot* along the way). Their argument is that scholars of 'race' and racism in the United States fall into two schools – assimilationists and cultural pluralists – both sharing a 'statist' view of integration (*pace* Park above), though different in that the latter doesn't claim that all will submerge their identities completely, developing instead a new melted identity, but states that they will recreate ethnicity in a new hyphenated form. Goldberg et al.'s problem with these two schools is that both erase 'the timing of the migration as well as the racial discrimination suffered by immigrants of colour' (2006: 262). They also take a swipe at the 'new economic sociology approach' (as taken by Zolberg, Portes and Sassen among others) alleging that the focus on social capital and social networks overlooks the structural conditions of discriminations faced by Puerto-Ricans, Haitian-Americans and African-Americans, the histories of subordination structuring the racial oppression, residential segregation and exploitation suffered by these groups, and finally the class differences of the individuals in 'micronetworks', which condition their access to resources and capital (2006: 265). Nonetheless, Huntington in *Who Are We? America's Great Debate* (2004) or Brimelow in *Alien Nation: Common Sense about America's Immigration Disaster* (1995) did make the link, albeit perhaps not as thoughtfully as some would have wished.

The situation in Europe, including the United Kingdom, is somewhat different, as scholars in both fields have a certain awareness of each others' work largely because the link between the two phenomena is clearer in Europe. As Europe's nation-states were being constructed, it became particularly important to decide who belonged to the nation and who did not. This issue was further complicated for those states who were colonial Empires, given that colonial citizenship did not coincide with any understanding of nation. In spite of this, there is a clear racialised understanding of what it means to belong to one of Europe's nation-states. This is largely because those who look different are presumed to be 'foreign' in a way that is not possible in large sections/cities of the United States today. Nonetheless, this academic awareness is rather cursory and tends to involve scholars from one field visiting the other to gather useful data to make a point, rather than to engage in any meaningful dialogue. Having said that, it would be a mistake to generalise too much – there are important differences across Europe, that are equally a product of particular national histories or of the processes by which European nations were constructed.

There is a link between migration and racism in every European country, but that link varies as a result of a number of factors: whether or not there is a history of immigration (e.g., Britain, France and Germany) and/or a history of emigration (e.g., Greece, Ireland, Italy, Poland, Portugal and Spain),[5] or a history of colonisation (Britain, France, Spain and Portugal), or of being colonised (Cyprus, Greece, Malta and Ireland). We could also usefully consider the impact of political history (nationalism and nation-building, federalism, fascism, Nazism, military dictatorships, liberalism and democracy) and economic developments (industrialisation, lack of industrialisation, post industrialisation, a welfare state, what kind of welfare state). Each of these factors has explanatory value not solely for individual national histories of migration and racism, but also for the development of scholarship within these fields.

In the traditional *emigration* countries, much of the migration literature focused on the experiences of the national diaspora abroad, including their experiences of racism and discrimination: difficulties finding employment or employment commensurate with their skills and experience, problems with terms and conditions of employment, getting a fair wage etc., difficulties finding accommodation and hostility at an individual and institutional level. Scholars of immigration into these countries, however, have tended until recently to overlook the same patterns of treatment experienced by migrants into their countries, although some have noted views expressed that somehow the racism experienced by European emigrants inoculated those left behind, making it impossible for these societies to be racist (Lentin and McVeigh, 2002; Schuster and Solomos, 2002 Triandafyllidou, 2000). However, the relatively new body of work that explores attitudes to and the treatment of migrants in these 'new' countries of immigration tends to give the lie to this complacent attitude. Lentin and McVeigh (2002) writing on Ireland and Anthias and Lazaridis writing on Southern Europe have argued that migration regimes embody racism and thrive on the idea of an inferior 'other' (1999: 1–11).

If we turn to countries with a history of *immigration*, there is obviously a much greater body of literature available both on indigenous racism and migration, as well as on the two phenomena together. Nonetheless, there are differences. In France, the academic debate is shaped very clearly by the weight of history, most obviously its colonial past, but equally the attachment to the *Republic*, in particular one predicated on the principles of liberty, equality and fraternity. This attachment coupled with a government policy that actively recruited migrants as new citizens of that republic, as in the US, has led to the use of the 'melting pot' metaphor (Noiriel, 1988, 1991). As France has historically welcomed, needed migrants, few scholars have, until very recently, made the connection between migration and racism, this in spite of the racialised political and academic debates detailed by Noiriel in his histories of migration in France (2007, 1991, 1988).[6] Instead, this was overshadowed by a concentration in the academy on colonialism and racism, and on colonialism and migration, not least as a result of the work of Maghrebi scholars (Fanon, 1986; Memmi, 2000; Sayad, 2004). Given the great wound inflicted on French society by the Algerian war, this is perhaps not surprising. There are relatively few French scholars of racism (Balibar, 2001; Taguieff, 2001; Wieviorka, 1992, 1993), though there are a significant number of scholars who write on the (problems of) the second and third generations of 'migrants',[7] the daily experience of young French citizens of non-French origins (Beaud and Masclet, 2006) and the place of Islam in a *putatively* secular society (Roy, 2007). Here, the issues of migration and racism are linked, although it tends to focus on these experiences rather than on policy, and this is true too for the Sans Papiers, where the concern is less with racism, than with their lack of rights and security.

In Germany, Klaus Bade (1986), for example, almost founded the field of migration studies with his historical studies of seasonal workers from Poland in the nineteenth century, a group of migrants to whom Germans remain particularly sensitive. However, the single phenomenon that has shaped the development of migration and racism studies in Germany is inevitably the Nazi period, which in much of the literature is treated separately. Here the two areas of study come together as the Nazi's racial policies are intimately entwined with their policies of forced labour migration.[8] Before the Nazis, studies on migration were completely separate – afterwards, migration studies concentrated on the success or failure of the guestworker system, and on the success or failure of integration. Racism became a taboo concept associated exclusively with the Nazis, inconceivable and unusable in post-Nazi Germany. Instead, when speaking of the negative treatment of migrants, the term 'Ausländerfeindlichkeit' literally Xenophobia, is preferred even when the phenomenon being described, such as the mob attacks on migrants in Hoyerswerda in 1991 or Rostock-Lichtenhagen in 1992, defied such trivialisation. At the moment, there are very few German scholars who are prepared to study migration in relation to racism understood as a contemporary phenomenon, rather than as a historical one (Räthzel, 1990; Thränhardt, 199?; Demirovic and Bojadžijev, 2002), and the subject remains a sensitive one.

I have left Britain until last in this section, because although the analysis presented so far holds true here, there is some literature that does cross the field boundaries, especially work on the politics of immigration (Miles, 1989, 1993; Panayi, 1996, 1999; Schuster and Solomos, 2004). However, the fields of migration and racism in the United Kingdom have been sometimes very close, at other times quite separate, and I believe that more recently, we are seeing a *rapprochement* once more.

As in the United States, scholars of 'race' and racism tend to concentrate on Britain's large and established ethnic minorities – Black–British and British–Asian (especially the Bangladeshi and Pakistani communities). However, unlike the United States, Britain's Black and Asian populations before World War II were relatively small. It is only after Britain actively began to recruit migrant labour from the colonies that these communities began to grow. The situation in Britain was similar to that of France, in that those migrants who came, came with British passports, so that while the individuals might suffer racism, they could not be refused entry, could not be deported, but as in France, this colonial immigration of racialised subjects tended to raise concerns about the entry of 'inferior others' into the body of the nation.

In the post-war years, a cadre of scholars grew up concerned with the racism suffered by Britain's non-white population, the children of those who had come in the 1950s, and the grandchildren (Chamberlain and Goulbourne, 2001; Modood, 1992). The link between racism and migration was clear in particular when one looked at the changes to citizenship laws and migration laws, both of which were designed to exclude black and Brown migrants without mentioning 'race' or colour. Dummett and Nicol's classic study *Subject, Citizen, Alien* (1990) carefully deconstructed the manner in which historically and legally the British

State constructed itself and its citizenry in a racialised manner, while others have done the same from different perspectives (policy studies, political science, sociology, etc.).

In the UK, migration really took off as a separate field in the 1990s, as asylum in particular became a focus of academic attention not least as a response to the intense attention it received in public and political discourse. Those of us working on the new arrivals tended to focus on asylum-seekers (Bloch, 2002; Schuster, 2003) or undocumented workers (Anderson, 1999; Jordan and Düvell, 2002). And for a period, very few treated racism as a central issue. However, over time the logic of what we were seeing persuaded some of us at least that we needed look again at our methodology – that racism was too significant a factor to be ignored, or treated as an aside or an add-on.

So to sum up this section, for those studying these phenomena, there are important distinctions between the approaches taken towards the study of migration and racism in different parts of the world. The primary victims of racism in the United States were not only citizens, they were born in the United States – they were not migrants. In France and Britain, they were both citizens (up to the changes in the citizenship laws) and migrants, whereas in other European states those who came were 'just' migrants and frequently remained migrants through generations – without citizenship and increasingly without papers (Germany, Italy, etc.). Nonetheless, scholars from and of different regions are increasingly obliged to include racialisation and racism as factors shaping the migration experience and migration policy. This will be examined in more detail in the next section.

DIFFERENT APPROACHES TO MIGRATION

The literature on migration can be sliced any number of ways and the analysis that follows is certainly not exhaustive, but captures I hope some of the main strands of migration scholarship, and the ways in which racism and racialisation are always implicated, regardless of which approach one takes. This is inevitable given the extent to which the racialisation of national and migrant populations shapes the experience of migrants at each stage of the migration process. For those contemplating the decision to move, the entry, residence and migrant labour policies of receiving countries may influence where they can apply, whether or not they are forced to use facilitators and the ease or difficulty with which they eventually settle and find work, move on to other destinations or return home.

Economic/labour migration

Much early literature on migration focused on labour migration, especially that from a historical perspective (Bade, 1986; Noiriel, 1984, 1988, 2007). Although the nineteenth until the early twentieth-century migrations to Germany and France respectively were inter-European, both Bade and Noiriel have noted that the dominant academic and public discourse at the time was heavily inflected by racialised arguments. These historical accounts chronicle the steady employment of the concept of threat to the indigenous worker. Journalists and scholars warned of the 'threat that immigration posed to the French race' (Pluyette, 1930, cited in Noiriel, 2007: 332),[9] a threat that was simultaneously both to the body and psyche of the race/nation. Noiriel further notes that the growth of the mass press relied upon, and reinforced, a firm line between 'them' and 'us', using not just stories of criminality and disease, but also ridiculing dangerous and child-like savages especially in relation to Black and Arab colonial subjects resident in France (Noiriel, 2007: 162). For historians then, the links between nation, citizenship, migration and racism are clear.

Economists on the other hand, focused on migration in terms of economic costs and benefits either to the receiving society (Borjas, 1995), or as the basis of a rational calculation informing the decision whether or not to migrate (Borjas, 1987). Others analysed migration as the creation of a reserve army of labour designed to depress wages (Cohen, 1987). As migration studies developed, much of the scholarly work took one of these approaches. As mentioned earlier, however, this emphasis on individuals as calculating units of labour, or on migrants as a tool of the bourgeois state tended to overlook racism as a factor influencing any stage of the migration process.

Two of the most thoughtful, theoretically sophisticated and empirically grounded scholars of migration and racism, Castles and Miles, are located within the latter approach, and each has engaged critically with the work of the other over time. In *Racism After 'Race Relations'* (1993) a critique of Britain's race relations paradigm, Miles notes that 'when British academics began to take an interest in [...] domestic developments [i.e. racist attacks on British subjects of Caribbean origin], they drew on concepts, theories and strategies derived from the United States and South Africa' (1993: 35). Miles noted that Castles and Kosack (1973) in their seminal study *Immigrant Workers and Class Structure* – rightly in his view – rejected the United States and South African frameworks arguing instead that the British experience of post-1945 migration should be analysed in the context of capitalist reconstruction across Europe. However, operating within a conventional Marxist analysis, Castles and Kosack (see also Castles, 2000) argued that the social position of migrants in the 'under-class' was due to the workings of the class system and the demands of the capitalist system, rather than race, since only a minority (2 or 8 million migrants) could be considered 'racially distinct'. Miles problematises both their dismissal of race as an explanatory factor in the social position of migrants, and in their unproblematic, undefined and untheorised use of 'race' as a concept.

Sivanandan, of the Institute of Race Relations has built on the study by Castles and Kosack, but insists that race is as significant as class for analysis, including analysis of the migration labour system, which he argues 'prevents the horizontal conflict of classes through the vertical integration of race – and, in the process, exploits both race and class at once' (1982: 104, cited in Miles, 1993: 37). Miles, while welcoming Sivanandan's extra dimension, once again critiques his acceptance of the category of 'race'.

Living with difference

In later work with Davidson, Castles does analyse racism as a factor in the formation of ethnic minorities arguing that such minorities may be self-defined, but are also often other-defined, that is, communities of people grow up because racism and discrimination force them into close proximity and dependence on each other (Castles, 2000), a position shared with Solomos (2003) and Gilroy (1987). Cohen has noted the impact racists have had on the settlement (or not) of particular groups in certain countries (1997: 109). However, there remains a lacuna in studies focused on integration, where those writing on integration and minorities still tend to focus on the failure of migrants and their children to integrate, on parallel communities and a lack of cohesion, on fundamentalism and a youth that does not fit within the 'host', or its 'own' society, rather than on the racism faced by these groups. Certainly, some of those writing on migrants and migration have discussed the discrimination experienced by migrant groups, but in a curiously 'deracialised' manner (e.g., Soysal, 1994, 2000). Soysal's work approaches migration from the perspective of rights, and is typical of the literature that deals with migration and civil and human rights in giving little or no space to racism (see the discussion on France above).

Increasingly, however, migration scholars are noting societal shifts and changes, so that in the United Kingdom, for example, traditional targets of racism such as Black and Asian British people are now joined by East Europeans, Roma and asylum-seekers, and themselves engage in racist discourses targeted at the newcomers. Vertovec has also flagged up 'emergent forms of racism ... among newcomers themselves and directed against British ethnic minorities' (2006). That the roots of alienation, inequality and marginalisation are located in the racism of the receiving society and its state institutions is still under-researched and overlooked.

The politics of immigration

The politics of immigration, in terms of the role of racist politics and mainstream politics, is perhaps the field in which the link between the two phenomena is most clearly developed. Much of this work looks at the extent to which the migration agenda is shaped by the far right, by racists and racism, and by the exigencies of electoral politics. Less often, scholars explore the extent to which the state shapes racist agendas through its migration policies.

As noted earlier, the history of migration to Europe and the United States is one marked by racialisation as over time different groups have been excluded on the basis of 'race', ethnicity or nationality. The exclusion of Chinese and other

Asian migrants from the United States and Australia has been well documented. Less well known is the extent to which various modern states have excluded Jews, although historians such as Kushner and Goldberg have chronicled in particular the exclusion of Jewish refugees in the 1930s (Kushner and Knox, 1999; Kushner, 2006). Schönwälder has detailed the manner in which the German state[10] 'systematically excluded potential migrants of Asian and African migrants' from the 1950s to the 1970s (2004: 248), including putting pressure on the Portuguese government not to send candidates for employment who were 'of African or Indian skin colour' (2004: 250). While it may be assumed that such crass racist discrimination is no longer a feature of the migration policies of European states in the twenty-first century, in 2001 the British government was found to be admitting white Czechs but refusing entry to Czechs from the Roma community (Kushner, 2006: 188).

Guiraudon suggests cautiously that 'politicians are aware that a not negligible proportion of their electorate are hostile or neutral towards the rights of foreigners' (2000: 158).[11] Right across Europe, this has proved a challenge to parties of the left and the right. For the right, espousing racist positions risks legitimating the far right, such that the electorate may prefer to vote for the original, rather than an opportunistic copy, while the left is torn between universal principles and a presumed natural urge to protect its own constituency – a national workforce.

Favell and Hansen have argued for a return to Borjas's neo-liberal and Castles's labour-market-based approaches, arguing that commentators on 'Fortress Europe's migration policies have missed the point, that racism is not a factor (2002) driving policy in Europe. The narrowness of this approach is revealed by recent work by Anderson et al., who note ways in which 'nationality' is used as a code for race (2006: 76–77) among employers in different sectors of the labour market, although their research also uncovered explicit references to skin colour as a factor in choosing employees.

Forced migration

Forced migration or refugee studies as it is sometimes known really only took off as a sub-field of migration in the 1990s as the total of persons of concern to the United Nations High Commissioner for Refugees rose to 20 million (it has since dropped to approximately 9 million in the last five years). These studies tended to focus on the causes of flight (conflict, human rights abuses, authoritarian regimes, etc.), the three preferred solutions to refugee flows (repatriation, resettlement, local integration), on refugee regimes and more recently on the experiences of particular groups of refugees or asylum-seekers in reception states. Although racism may often be a factor impelling individuals and groups to flee, it is rarely the focus of scholars' attention, and rarely considered when discussing local integration, resettlement or repatriation. Unlike work on other forms of migration, much of the literature on refugees and asylum comes from a rights perspective, unsurprising given that international refugee law, including the 1951 Geneva

Convention relating to the Status of Refugees, which spells out the rights of refugees, is well established and almost 60 years old, whereas the International Convention on the protection of migrant workers and their families has not been ratified by any of the major migrant-receiving countries.

Racism does become a factor, though only to a limited extent when considering particular refugees regimes, but again only in very special cases, and often only historically. British and French historians (Porter, 1979; Noiriel, 1991), in spite of Tony Kushner's criticisms, though largely as a result of his own work (1999, 2006) have done a great deal to unpack the interplay between racism and government refugee policy. A special issue of the journal *Patterns of Prejudice* (2003, 37 (3)) brought together a number of articles exploring the links between racism and asylum in Britain (Kushner, Macklin, Back), Ireland (Lentin) and France (Lloyd), and across Europe more generally (Schuster).

What has become apparent, as I argued in that article, is that the hostility now directed against asylum-seekers is part of the process of racialisation. 'Asylum-seekers' are a group of people singled out by the state as legitimate targets for hostility. They have been constructed, not solely as a legal category – those awaiting a decision on their entirely lawful application for recognition as a refugee – but as something more. 'Asylum-seeker' is now a term that is used unambiguously, and immediately conjures up cheat, liar, criminal, sponger – someone deserving of hostility by virtue not of any misdemeanour, but simply because he or she is an 'asylum-seeker' – a figure that has by now become a caricature, a stereotype, in the way that 'Blacks', 'Jews' and 'Gypsies' have been and still are (Schuster, 2003: 244).

MIGRATION AND RACISM IN EUROPE TODAY

Leaving the more academic reflections to one side, let us turn to the substance of those migration/racism studies and the manner in which migration and racism are interwoven in European societies now. Goldberg has argued that 'race is integral to the emergence, development and transformation (conceptually, philosophically, materially) of the modern nation-state'. He extends the claim, noting that race both marks and orders the process of state formation and the related apparatus and technology employed has 'served to fashion, modify and reify the terms of racial expression as well as racist exclusions and subjugations' (1993: 234). For many of us, especially of us who consider ourselves [l]iberal Europeans, children of the Enlightenment, adherents of Universal values and norms, such a claim can and does provoke resistance, it doesn't mesh with our self-image as citizens of modern, liberal democratic European nation-states.

However, those who make a close study of the experiences of labour migrants, of migrant communities, of migration policies and their implementation are, I would contend, forced to accept Goldberg's assertion. The scale of human mobility today,[12] the challenges to the artifices of national identity, the testing of the visible and invisible boundaries that European (and other) citizens draw around themselves all attest to the significance of racism, racialisation and the idea of 'race'. To return to the beginning, the treatment meted out to 'migrants', especially to those deemed undesirable, can only be legitimated by dehumanising them, by accepting that some people are less worthy of having their rights and dignity respected than others. The evidence of this dehumanisation can be seen in the bureaucratic decisions to, for example, withdraw support from families of asylum-seekers in the UK so as to pressurise them to return 'home', or to detain indefinitely men, women and children of all ages – without having to make the case before a judge. In Germany, internal mobility controls (*residenzpflicht*) are imposed only on asylum-seekers. In France and Italy, potential asylum-seekers find it difficult make a claim. Greece and Italy have both expelled arrivals peremptorily without allowing them to make claims. Spanish and Moroccan police have been involved in shooting dead 12 young men attempting to enter the Spanish–Moroccan enclave of Ceuta. And for three days in the summer of 2007, 27 Africans clung to a tuna net in the Mediterranean, because Malta refused to accept them – they were eventually rescued by the Italian navy.

But less emotively – if we take as an example the experiences of the most recent cohort of arrivals into Britain – the Eastern Europeans, especially Poles, it becomes more difficult to resist the explanatory power of 'race' and racism in relation to the entry and integration of migrants. Far smaller numbers of Asian and Black migrants have occasioned much fiercer resistance than the estimated 450,000 white, Christian, European migrants who have arrived in the last three to four years. While the latter have undoubtedly suffered some hostility and resentment due to increased competition for work, in particular in construction, this has been balanced by the welcome afforded to workers construed as pleasant, polite and hard-working. This is in stark contrast to the political and public reaction to asylum-seekers outlined above (p. 343), a group of people to whom a universal commitment has been given.

There is an important issue that needs consideration, and that is the attack on Universalism that is coming from liberals and the left (Dench et al., 2006; Goodhart). This is manifested, unsurprisingly, differently in different contexts but there are two main strands to it, though they are intimately linked. Perhaps most important is the assumption that there is a threshold of tolerance, beyond which 'the majority population [may become] intolerant about existing immigrants' (Favell, 2001a: 112). This is related to a second, equally pernicious assumption, which is that the majority populations are 'victims' of a liberal elite that protects the interests of minorities or migrants, at the expense of its own electorate. Such concerns often revolve around the welfare state, particularly in north European states.

The attack on Universalism gathered strength in the 1990s across Europe and in Australia and crystallised around the response to increasing numbers of refugees and asylum-seekers. While the 'political Right throughout the world has always and continues to milk the issue of immigration' (Phizacklea, 2003), increasingly the Left are accepting the agenda of control and retreating from principles such as internationalism and solidarity. The attack on the commitment to offer refuge to all those in need was justified through use of 'pragmatic' arguments about the material and psychological resources of receiving populations which obviated the need to articulate more explicit racist concerns about the impact on particular national identities, cultures and values (Schuster, 2003b). This strategy could be found across the political spectrum. The colour, ethnicity, nationality or race of migrants did not have to be alluded to, since the core of these arguments was that there were simply too many in need and it would not be possible to help 'everyone', and that therefore choices would have to be made and universal commitments such as the Geneva Convention on the Status of Refugees would have to be qualified. The case for limiting the numbers was deceptively strong because 'genuine' refugees and asylum-seekers were construed as helpless victims, reduced only to their needs, which seemed limitless, rather than seen as potential contributors to the receiving societies. In this case, even an absolute requirement for protection would not guarantee admittance for migrants in desperate straits even from liberal democratic states. This curtailment of an absolute imperative to grant asylum to those needing it was espoused even by governments of the centre left.

Moving from the international to the national level, and from forced to migrants more generally, the left's traditional prioritising of need over belonging has also been challenged here. In Britain, for example, as in the study of London's East End cited above by Dench et al. (2006), it has been argued that a Labour government that housed those in priority need favoured large Bangladeshi families over smaller 'local' families leading to resentment and feeding racism. In this case, the authors failed to challenge the sincerely held, but ill-informed views of the white population, accepting instead that rights and claims arising out of an earlier, more directly exchange-based welfare state ethic should trump need. In this case, the rights and claims are based on historical sacrifices, especially from World WarII and the Blitz that destroyed much of the East End. There is no acknowledgement of the sacrifices made by the parents and grandparents of the British Bangladeshis during the same conflict. Instead, the migrants are construed as different, not 'part of us', not party to the exchange-based welfare state, although most will be contributing to it directly and indirectly through labour and taxes. Though they may be British, their colour means they continue to be construed as migrants rather than British.

THE STUDY OF MIGRATION AND RACISM TOMORROW

So where do we go from here? And in particular what is the responsibility of sociologists and other researchers in the light of continuing migration, and continuing racism directed at migrants? Related to the last point, there is an imperative to keep things in perspective. Just as those cited above are panicked into siding with the 'majority' – especially in Britain, in Europe there has been a worrying trend to engage in extreme rhetoric, taking very real and worrying developments, some of which have been referred to above, and make untenable comparisons with the Holocaust and Nazi extermination camps. Giorgio Agamben's *Homo Sacer* has become a sacred text, cited widely by academics and activists alike, and has spawned a number of theoretical and abstract articles using the 'figure' of the migrant to comment on the State today. Some of this work is valuable and interesting, but much of it borders on the hysterical and is terminally undermined by a lack of understanding of the legal and material realities of migration and the search for refuge.[13] Between the – admittedly far too numerous – individuals who are subject to individual and structural racism and human rights abuses, and the much smaller – highly mobile, highly successful – transnational elite are many hundreds of thousands of people who move from country to country, more or less successfully, negotiating relationships with state officials, employers, fellow workers and neighbours. There is an urgent need for sobriety, based on the accurate and irresistable gathering of empirical data (especially comparative data), which can illuminate the very real potential and actual dangers associated with government policy and its implementation, and the extent to which they shape and impact on the lives of migrants.

At the other end of the spectrum are those studies financed directly or indirectly by governments that are determinedly policy-relevant and concentrate almost exclusively on the gathering of empirical data (see Castles, 2007 on this issue). In the desperate search for funding and resources, researchers are quick to compete for government research grants, themselves offered in the desperate search for a short-term policy solution (i.e., one that coincides with the electoral cycle). As Castles has pointed out, this makes for bad science 'Ministers and bureaucrats still often see migration as something that can be turned on and off like a tap through laws and polices. By imposing this paradigm on researchers, the policy-makers have done both social scientists and themselves a disservice' (2003: 363). A further difficulty with such studies are again the set of assumptions that underpin the research – that it is possible to have non-racist migration controls, that the interests of national states are justifiably privileged and that governments are not responsible for the deaths of unknown migrants who seek to evade those controls.

CONCLUSION

It has not been my intention in this chapter to suggest that every migrant suffers as a result of prejudice, discrimination or racism. Many migrants, well-off, well-educated, well-travelled professionals, and also semi-skilled and unskilled migrants, successfully negotiate the bureaucracies, find work, learn the language, make friends, settle, marry and found families. And perhaps these are the majority though it's hard to tell. Certainly, many find themselves enjoying, and are grateful for the indifference, if not the welcome, of receiving societies.

Migration as a phenomenon is hugely diverse, and consequently a rich field of research. In this chapter, I have tried to indicate that whatever perspective one takes, one cannot adequately consider migration without examining the role that race, racialisation and racism play in shaping the process, whether from the perspective of the individual making the journey or the structures that shape that journey at every stage. Migrants suffer hostility that is sometimes verbalised and sometimes physically manifested, but in European states is more often tacit, but still damaging. This is not only a problem for those who experience racism directly, but is also a problem for receiving societies. Unless racism and discrimination of every kind are addressed, contested and combated, they will remain a poison within receiving societies, shaping both individual perceptions and interactions, and the institutions that underpin society. Equality, like justice, cannot be graded or diluted. The impact of racism is felt by everyone: racists, its victims and bystanders, though perhaps most by those with the least secure status in any society, those who have limited rights to entry and residence. Nonetheless, whichever aspect of migration or group of migrants is being studied, racism must be included in the analysis.

NOTES

1. All translations in the text are my own.
2. For example, the UK Highly Skilled Migrants Programme specifies recent annual income as a criterion for entry. Clearly, migrants from low-income countries will find it harder meet this threshold, and low-income countries are overwhelmingly African and Asian.
3. Policy and Practice: Racism and Discrimination in Cyprus 2005–2007.
4. See e.g., Balibar and Wallerstein (1991), Wacquant (2008), Andall (ed.) (2003), Anthias and Lazaridis (eds) (1999), Kofman et al. (2000). Anthias F. and Yuval – Davis N. (1992).
5. Although historically most of the cities around the Mediterranean had polyglot populations mixing migrants from considerable distances away (see Braudel, 1972), and most of those states regarded as immigration countries sent significant sections of their populations abroad, for example, Britain and Germany.
6. In the introduction to this work, Noiriel, historian of migration describes his personal journey towards an understanding of the link between migration and racism.
7. Though of course those living in the country in which they have been born, who have not experienced migration themselves, should not be called migrants.
8. Given the breadth and depth of this literature, I won't deal with it here.
9. It was still usual at this time to use the words 'race' and 'nation' interchangeably – see for example Bérillon, 'the flesh of the German is not that of a Frenchman ... I have described the *bromidose fétide* of the German race, that nauseous *sui-generis* smell that that imposes itself on one's olefactory system when one is in contact with the Germans' (cited in Noiriel, 2007: 333). Noiriel in particular has tracked the manner in which the mass press of the time presented the foreigner as the enemy within, a theme common in Britain too (Porter, 1979), largely because of political conflicts.
10. Although there seems to have been differences between the Ministry of the Interior, who wished to exclude darker people, and the Foreign Office who protested at this unconstitutional behaviour (Schönwälder, 2004: 251).

11. Guiraudon uses 'foreigner' as a synonym for 'migrant', but notes that hostility is directed not at the most numerous (Portuguese) or 'geographically distant' (Asians) foreigners [present in France], but towards North Africans, and in particular Algerians, those nationals of France's former colonies, that is, very often French citizens.

12. Although it is considerable, it is important to remember, however, that migration is still a minority activity – in which only about 3% of the global population engage (IOM 2008).

13. As a referee for a number of migration related journals, I see two or three such articles annually and find the number of empirical errors enraging.

REFERENCES

Andall, J. (ed.) (2003) *Gender and ethnicity in contemporary Europe*. Oxford, New York: Berg.

Agamben, G. (1998) *Homo Sacer: Sovereign Power and Bare Life*. Stanford, California : Stanford University Press.

Anderson, B. (1999) 'Overseas Domestic Workers in the European Union: Europe's Invisible Women' in J. Momsen, (ed.) *Gender, Migration and Domestic Service*. London: Routledge.

Anderson, B. (2002) 'Just another job? The Commodification of Domestic Labour' in Ehrenreich, B. & Hochschild. A. *Global Woman: Nannies, Maids and Sex Workers in the New Economy*. New York: Henry Holt, pp.104–114.

Anderson, B., Ruhs, M., Spencer, S. and Rogaly, B. (2006) *Fair Enough? Central and East European Low wage migrants in low wage employment in the UK,* Report written for the Joseph Rowntree Foundation, published as a COMPAS Report available at http://www.compas.ox.ac.uk

Anderson, B. (2006) 'A very private business: migration and domestic work' COMPAS Working Paper WP-28-06 Available at www.compas.ox.ac.uk

Anthias, F. and Lazaridis, G. (eds) (1999) *Into the Margins: Migration and Exclusion in Southern Europe*. Aldershot: Ashgate.

Anthias, F. and Yuval-Davis, N. (1992) *Racialized Boundaries: Race, Nation, Gender, Colour and Class and the Anti-racist Struggle*. London: Routledge.

Arendt, H. (1967) *The Origins of Totalitarianism*. London: George Allen & Unwin.

Back, L. (2003) 'Falling from the Sky', *Patterns of Prejudice*, 37 (3): 341–353.

Bade, K. (ed.) (1986) *Auswanderer – Wanderarbeiter – Gastarbeiter: Bevölkerung, Arbeitsmarkt und Wanderung in Deutschlandseit der Mitte des 19. Jahrhunderts*. Ostfildern Auflag.

Balibar, E. (2001) *Nous, citoyens d'Europe? Les frontiers, l'Etat, le Peuple*. Paris: Editions la Découverte.

Balibar, E. and Wallerstein, I. (1991) *Race, Nation, Class: Ambiguous Identities*. London: Verso.

Baseler, M. (1998) *'Asylum for Mankind' America: 1607–1800*. Ithaca: Cornell University Press.

Beaud, S. and Masclet, O. (2006) 'Des "marcheurs" de 1983 aux "émeutiers" de 2005: Deux générations sociales d'enfants d'immigrés', *Annales*, 4: 809–844.

Bisley, N. (2007) *Rethinking Globalization*. Basingstoke, Palgrave.

Bloch, A. (2002) *The Migration and Settlement of Refugees in Britain*. Basingstoke, Palgrave Macmillan.

Borjas, G. (1995) 'The Economic Benefits From Migration', *Journal of Economic Perspectives*, 9 (2): 3–22.

Borjas, G. (1987) 'Self-Selection and the Earnings of Immigrants', *American Economic Review*, 77: 531–553.

Braudel, F. (1972) *The Mediterranean and the Mediterranean World in the Age of Philip II*. Vols. 1 & 2. New York: Harper & Row.

Brimelow, P. (1996) *Alien Nation: Common Sense about America's Immigration Disaster*. New York, Random House.

Castles, S. (2000) *Ethnicity and Globalization*. London: Sage.

Castles, S. (2007) 'Twenty-First-Century Migration as a Challenge to Sociology', *Journal of Ethnic and Migration Studies*, 33 (3): 351–371.

Castles, S. and Davidson, A. (2000) *Citizenship and Migration: Globalisation and the Politics of Belonging.* London: Routledge.

Castles, S. and Kosack, G. (1973) *Immigrant Workers and Class Structures in Western Europe.* London: Oxford University Press for the Institute of Race Relations.

Chamberlain, M. and Goulbourne, H. (eds) (2001) *Caribbean Families in the Transatlantic World.* Basingstoke: Macmillan.

Cohen, R. (1987) *The New Helots: Migrants in the International Division of Labour.* Aldershot: Avebury.

Demirovic, A. and Bojadžijev, M. (eds) (2002) *Konjunkturen des Rassismus.* Münster: Westfälisches Dampfboot.

Dench, G. Gavron, K. Young, M. (2006) *The New East End: Kinship, Race and Conflict.* London: Profile Books.

Dummett, A. and Nicol, A. (1990) *Subjects, Citizens, Aliens and Others: Nationality and Immigration Law.* London: Weidenfeld and Nicolson.

Fanon, F. (1986) *Black Skin, White Masks.* London: Pluto Press.

Favell, A. & Hansen, R. (2002) 'Markets against politics: migration, EU enlargement and the idea of Europe', *Journal of Ethnic and Migration Studies.* 28:4, 581–601.

Favell, A. (2001a) *Philosophies of Integration: Immigration and the Idea of Citizenship in France and Britain.* Basingstoke: Palgrave/Macmillan.

Favell, A. (2001b) 'Multi-Ethnic Britain: An Exception in Europe?', *Patterns of Prejudice,* 35 (1): 35–57.

Gilroy, P. (1987) *There ain't no black in the Union Jack: the cultural politics of race and nation.* London: Hutchinson Education.

Glazer, N. and Moynihan, D. (1970) *Beyond the Melting Pot: The Negroes, Puerto Ricans, Jews, Italians and Irish of New York City.* 2nd edition. Cambridge: MIT Press.

Goldberg, D. (1993) *Racist Culture: Philosophy and the Politics of Meaning.* Oxford: Blackwell.

Goldberg, D., Grosfoguel, R. and Mielants, E. (2006) 'Field of Dreams: Cultures of Scholarship and Public Policy on Race in the United States', *International Journal of Comparative Sociology,* 47 (3–4): 259–280.

Goodhart, D. (2004) 'Too Diverse?', *Prospect.* February 30-37.

Guiraudon, V. (2000) *Les Politiques d'Immigration en Europe: Allemagne, France, Pays-Bas.* Paris: L'Harmattan.

Huntington, S. (2004) *Who Are We? America's Great Debate.* London: Simon & Schuster.

IOM (2008) *Global Estimates and Trends* available at http://www.iom.int/jahia/Jahia/facts-and-figures/global-estimates-and-trends

Jordan, B. and Düvell, F. (2002) *Irregular Migration: The Dilemmas of Transnational Mobility.* Cheltenham: Edward Elgar.

Kofman, E., Phizacklea, A., Raghuram, P. and Sales, R. (2002) *Gender and International Migration in Europe: Employment, Welfare and Politics.* London: Routledge.

Kushner, T. (2006) *Remembering Refugees: Then and Now.* Manchester: Manchester University Press.

Kushner, T. (2003) 'Meaning Nothing but Good: Ethics, History and Asylum-Seeker Phobia in Britain', *Patterns of Prejudice,* 37 (3): 257–276.

Kushner, T. and Knox, K. (1999) *Refugees in an Age of Genocide: Global, National and Local Responses.* London: Frank Cass.

Lentin, R. (2003) *'Pregnant Silence: (En)gendering Ireland's Asylum Space',* Patterns of Prejudice, 37 (3): 301–322.

Lentin, R. and McVeigh, R. (eds) (2002) *Racism and Anti-Racism in Ireland.* Belfast: BTP Publications Ltd.

Lloyd, C. (2003) 'Anti-Racism, Racism and Asylum-Seekers in France', *Patterns of Prejudice,* 37 (3): 323–339.

Macklin, G. (2003) '"A Quite Natural and Moderate Defensive Feeling"? The 1945 Hampstead "Anti-Alien" petition', *Patterns of Prejudice,* 37 (3): 277–300.

Memmi, A. (2000) *Racism.* Minneapolis: University of Minnesota Press.

Miles, R. (1989) *Racism.* London: Routledge.

Miles, R. (1993) *Racism after 'Race Relations'.* London: Routledge.

Modood, T. (1992) *Not Easy Being British: Colour, Culture and Citizenship.* Runnymede Trust/Trentham Books.

Noiriel, G. (2007) Immigration, antisémitisme et racisme en France, XIXe-XXe siècle : discours publics, humiliations privées. Paris: Fayard.

Noiriel, G. (1991) *La Tyrannie du National: le Droit d'Asile en Europe 1793–1993.* Paris: Calmann-Levy.

Noiriel, G. (1988) *Le Creuset Français: Histoire de l'Immigration, XIXe–XXe siècles.* Paris: Seuil.

Noiriel, G. (1984) *Longwy, Immigrés et Proletaires (1880–1980).* Paris: PUF.

Panayi, P. (1996) *Racial Violence in Britain in the 19th & 20th Centuries.* London: Leicester University Press.

Panayi, P. (1999) *The Impact of Immigration.* Manchester: Manchester University Press.

Park, R. E. (1950) *Race and Culture: Essays in the Sociology of Contemporary Man.* New York: Free Press.

Phizacklea, A. (2003) 'Gendered Actors in Migration' in J. Andall, (ed.) *Gender and Ethnicity in Europe.* Oxford: Berg.

Porter, B. (1979) *The Refugee Question in Mid-Victorian England.* Cambridge: Cambridge University Press. pp. 23–37.

Portes, A. and Rumbaut, R. (2006) *A Portrait: Immigrant America.* University of California Press.

Räthzel, N. (1990) 'Germany: one race, one nation?', *Race and Class.* 32(3): 31–48.

Roy, O. (2007) *Secularism Confronts Islam.* New York: Columbia University Press.

Sayad, A. (2004) *The Suffering of the Immigrant.* Cambridge: Polity Press.

Scholte, J.A. (2005) *Globalization: A Critical Introduction.* 2nd edition. Basingstoke: Palgrave Macmillan.

Schönwälder, K. (2004) 'Why Germany's Guestworkers Were Largely Europeans: The Selective Principles of Post-War Labour Recruitment Policy', *Ethnic and Racial Studies,* 27 (2): 248–265.

Schuster, L. (2003a) *The Use and Abuse of Political Asylum in Britain and Germany.* London: Frank Cass.

Schuster, L. (2003b) 'Common Sense or Racism: The Treatment of Asylum Seekers in Europe', *Patterns of Prejudice,* 37 (3): 233–255.

Schuster, L. and Solomos, J. (2002) 'Rights and wrongs across European borders: Migrants, minorities and citizenship', *Citizenship Studies,* 6 (1): 37–54.

Schuster, L. and Solomos, J. (2004) 'Race, Immigration and Asylum: New Labour's Agenda and Its Consequences' ethnicities 4 (2): 267–300.

Solomos, J. (2003) *Race and Racism in Britain.* 3rd edition. Basingstoke: Macmillan.

Soysal, Y. (2000) 'Citizenship and Identity: Living in Diasporas in Post-War Europe?', *Ethnic and Racial Studies,* 23 (1): 1–15.

Soysal, Y. (1994) *Limits of Citizenship: Migrants and Postnational Membership.* Chicago: University of Chicago.

Taguieff, A. (2001) *The Force of Prejudice: On Racism and Its Doubles.* Minneapolis: University of Minnesota Press.

Thränhardt, D. (1994) 'Europäische Feindbilder – alt und neu', *WeltTrends.* 2:5 (November), pp. 77 – 88.

Triandafyllidou, A. (2000) '"Racists? Us? Are You Joking?" The Discourse of Social Exclusion of Immigrants in Greece and Italy' in R. King, G. Lazaridis and C. Tsardanidis (eds), *Eldorado or Fortress? Migration in southern Europe.* Basingstoke: Macmillan. pp. 186–205.

Van Hear, N. (2006) '"I Went as Far as My Money would Take Me": Conflict, Forced Migration and Class', Compas Working paper WP-04-06 Available at www.compas.ox.ac.uk

Vertovec, S. (2006) 'The Emergence of Super-Diversity in Britain' Compas Working Paper WP-06-25 Oxford, University of Oxford (available at www.compas.ox.ac.uk/publications)

Wacquant, L. (2008) *Urban Outcasts: A Comparative Sociology of Advanced Marginality.* Cambridge: Polity.

Wieviorka, M. (1992) *La France Raciste.* Paris: Seuil.

Wieviorka, M (1993) *The Arena of Racism.* London: Sage.

PART IV

Debates and New Initiatives

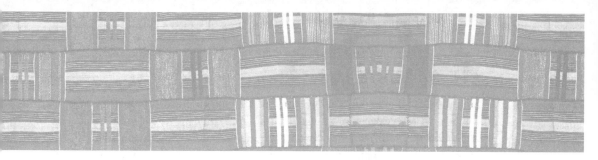

Introduction

In bringing together all the various chapters that form part of this handbook, we have been conscious of the need to give a feel for the questions and research agendas that have shaped this field in the past as well as to reflect on the range of questions that are likely to come to the fore in the future. It is for this reason that in this concluding part of the handbook, the focus shifts to a number of areas of scholarship and research that provide a basis for thinking through issues such as changing research agendas, emerging and future issues in this field, the role of cross-disciplinary scholarship and new arenas of research and policy debate. The six chapters are all suggestive of the need to see the field of race and ethnic studies as evolving and changing, rather than fixed. And perhaps more importantly as a field that can broaden its field of vision to take on board both existing questions and new avenues of investigation.

The first of the contributions to this part of the handbook is by Maxine Baca Zinn and it takes us into a field that has been at the heart of the study of race and ethnicity from the 1930s onwards, namely the role of the family in the context of racialised societies. The question of the family has been a recurrent theme in race and ethnic studies in the United States, although as Zinn points out it has been less a focus in research in this field more generally. Zinn's argument is framed by the need to locate the family as a 'race institution', particularly in societies that have experienced historical patterns of racialisation and forms of racial exclusion and domination. From this starting point, she emphasises the need to develop research on the 'different histories and realities of racial ethnic families as they are situated in multiple systems of domination.'

The next chapter by James Banks and Caryn Park focuses on the role of education, and particularly the school system, as a site for the production and reproduction of racialised social relations and inequalities. Research in both Europe and the United States. has done much to highlight the role of educational inequalities between different communities in shaping racial and ethnic divisions and attitudes. Banks and Park focus their chapter on a critical exploration of a number of analytical paradigms that seek to explain differences in academic achievement, ranging from genetic to cultural accounts. Building on their critical account of these debates, they seek to develop their own account of the role of racial and ethnic stratification in defining disparities in educational outcomes.

The chapter by Cheryl Gilkes provides us with a challenging and vibrant account of the intersections between race and religion in American society. The controversies surrounding this question became evident in the furore that emerged around Barack Obama's affiliation to a black church in Chicago during the presidential campaign of 2008. Gilkes's account focuses particularly on the role of race and religion in the context of US history, from the period of slavery to the aftermath of the Civil Rights movement. She highlights both the importance of this area as a field of scholarly research as well as the relative absence of detailed research on the everyday experiences of the intersections between race and religion.

In the context of current debates about race and ethnicity one of the overarching questions that has come to the fore is the role of social constructions of whiteness in the formation of ideologies and practices about race and colour consciousness. This is the key focus of the chapter by Les Back. Back's account draws on his experiences of research on race and whiteness in the context of British society, and particularly the simmering controversies over the past two decades about the killing of Stephen Lawrence. His critical engagement with the literature on whiteness leads Back to suggest that it is racism rather than whiteness that needs to remain our key analytical and political object of concern. In other words it means that research on the changing meanings of whiteness needs to be linked closely to a deeper understanding of the cultures of racism that shape ideas about race, colour and whiteness in contemporary societies.

The chapter by Michael Hanchard and Mark Q. Sawyer covers an area of the globe, Latin America, where the analysis of race and ethnicity has had a long-standing presence but has been relatively marginal to the study of race and ethnicity in a more global context. Drawing on their detailed knowledge of the development of racial politics and social movements, Hanchard and Sawyer offer an insight into the processes that have impacted on and given new meanings to Afro-Latin community mobilisations. They bring together evidence from Brazil, Ecuador and Colombia to highlight both the growing visibility and forms of social, cultural and political mobilisation among the diverse Afro-Latin communities. In doing so, they also suggest the need for scholars and researchers to broaden their field of vision to look at experiences outside of North America and Europe.

The concluding chapter of the handbook is by Claire Alexander and seeks to situate the analytical frameworks that have sought to capture the preoccupation within contemporary studies of race and ethnicity with issues of globalisation, diasporic identities and hybridisation. Alexander provides us with an overarching look at these debates, and particularly the theoretical frameworks that have emerged since the 1980s in a variety of social science and humanities disciplines. She locates this trend in the increasing social significance of the movement and displacement of peoples and the need to make sense of the complexities of diasporic identities and hybridities. More substantively, she suggests that theories of race and ethnicity need to be open to the need to make sense of the changing meanings of identity formation in a world where difference and disjuncture shape everyday cultural realities as well as social relations.

We shall return to some of the core themes that are covered in this part of the handbook in the concluding chapter, where we shall address them by taking a forward look at wider trends and processes that are likely to shape the study of race and ethnicity over the coming decades.

14

The Family as a Race Institution

Maxine Baca Zinn

A growing body of research and scholarship now makes it possible to identify many strong connections between race and family life. In treating race as a structural force and shaper of family life, this emerging paradigm of race and family studies goes beyond merely acknowledging racial diversity and difference in family outcomes. Although it does not offer a singular theory of race and families, the framework synthesises scholarship that attends to the different histories and realities of racial ethnic families as they are situated in multiple systems of domination. By integrating scholarship on racial inequality, political economy and gender, published largely since 1970, this synthesis offers a unified (but not unitary) view of race and family life in US society. Despite its focus on family life in US settings, this perspective offers much to understandings of race and family in a global context because race is an important feature in the unequal development of a global economy. The collective picture emerging from new research shows that in today's globalising world, race is a social system of inequality, an axis of power, a focus of political struggle and a fundamental force in shaping *families everywhere*, albeit in different ways.

The growth and maturity of scholarship on racial divisions between families have changed the treatment of race from a peripheral concern to one of central importance. Just as the field of family studies has long recognised that 'the family is a class institution' (Barrett and McIntosh, 1998: 220), the ongoing research illustrates that *the family is a race institution as well*. The rich detail of scholarship on race and family defies easy summary. Nevertheless, this chapter aims to trace the emergence of scholarly thinking of the family as a race institution.

The chapter provides a historical context for this new paradigm by comparing and contrasting two core approaches to the study of racial family variations within American social science. First, the chapter reviews a paradigm of cultural determinism that emerged within early twentieth-century social science that formed the framework for American scholarship on race and family. Next, the chapter describes the re-evaluation of cultural determinism by academics and social activists who, beginning in the 1960s, increasingly applied critical ideas about race and other structured inequalities to family life. The emerging structural paradigm fundamentally challenged the cultural paradigm of race and family, yet as current scholarly debates reveal, cultural assumptions have not disappeared. Third, the chapter reviews some tensions, debates, and limits within the now-dominant paradigm of mainstream structural perspectives. This brief review of three controversies that have waxed and waned since the 1970s, illustrates how the study of racial-ethnic families remains ideologically, politically and intellectually contested. Finally, the chapter presents six themes that are currently redirecting the study of race and family life beyond mainstream structural perspectives to view family as in institution patterned by racial conditions in society and the world. By investigating the interconnected effects of race, class and gender in a globalising world, this family as a race institution paradigm not only fosters a more complete view of racial ethnic families, it creates space to reconceptualise *all families* in society as raced institutions.

This is not an exhaustive review of research on race and families. For one, although the chapter aspires to contribute to a global and transnational perspective on race and family, the chapter centres on the US context. The US focus is not meant to view family life from a Western perspective only. While this vantage point has obvious limitations, it is also valuable for understanding family life in a society where race is a pervasive feature of social organisation. Whereas race is central in many other societies, America's long history with race offers one site with a comprehensive body of work and the United States is a central player in the development of race/family scholarship. Although connections between race and family are different everywhere, the US context has relevance for a globalising world in which racial divisions become ever-more pervasive in their effect on the family. For another, while dominant society families are equally influenced by race, the chapter focuses on family formation among people of colour. This should not suggest that only families of colour are affected by racial stratification. Instead, the intent is to counter mainstream approaches in the field of family studies which are based on research involving mostly White middle-class families and treating them as the norm while misrepresenting families of colour as cultural artefacts. Placing families of colour at the centre of inquiry and treating race as a social structure of opportunity and oppression unhinges us from common thought about families and racial difference. This focus uncovers the shaping power of racial inequality on family life by bringing into full view family features that have remained marginal in the field of family studies.

CULTURAL DETERMINISM

Early social thought about family, race and US society

The most pervasive ideas about race and family life can be traced to the origins of the field of family studies itself. In the late nineteenth and early twentieth centuries, the field of family studies emerged out of a belief in the need to document and ameliorate social problems in urban settings (Thomas and Wilcox, 1987: 82). Deteriorating family life was said to be the result of rapid social change, especially in areas where immigrants and other transplants were settling. The influential Chicago school of sociology led scholars to believe that many urban problems were the result of immigration, settlement and poverty. The families of immigrants and other transplants were deeply implicated in social disorganisation because their family lives were different from the family form thought to be 'the building block of society.' (For a discussion of the origins of family sociology in the assorted works of Albion Small, Lester Ward, and especially Ernest Burgess, see Osmond, 1987: 113–114.)

Dominant paradigms of assimilation and modernisation shaped ideas about a standard family form. Prevailing thought assumed that a linear process of modernisation would lead all families along the same path. The family was conceived as a private sphere – distinct and separate from the world at large and especially from work and the marketplace. Family was women's sphere, while men toiled in the workplace. This division of labour was a critical feature of the modern world. All families in society would converge into this uniform family arrangement (Parsons, 1942).

While families in the United States have always been racially diverse, ideas about family uniformity obscured race as a meaningful category of analysis. The many varieties of families in different racial and ethnic groups were thought to be at odds with the social requirements in the new society. Early family scholars may have been liberal or reformist on most social issues, but they were extremely conservative in regard to family (Osmond, 1987: 113). Seemingly pro-family, such scholars did not overtly endorse any one family form but they were preoccupied with an idealised family arrangement that they posited would emerge in the transition from traditional to modern.

Although race was not a formal component of early twentieth-century family studies, it was part of the theoretical *subtext*. The standard family was a social ideal, defined in ways that excluded racialised 'others.' whose family forms and behaviours were thought to inhibit assimilation. Much of the earliest scholarship on racial ethnic families was placed within a bipolar model of opposing family forms: (a) a modern family organised as a self-sufficient nuclear unit, and (b)'*other*' family forms that were shaped by pre-modern traditions and cultural patterns. Immigrants and racial-ethnics were thought to be out of step with the demands of modern society. According to this perspective, racial-ethnic families were encumbrances to be transcended. Once they adopted modern family patterns, they would be assimilated by the dominant society. Implicit in this approach was a model of the 'normal' family against which others were judged. Not only were racial-ethnic families treated as cultural varients, they were viewed as deficient and responsible for group subordination.

Cultural determinism took hold in a field that began as heavily normative, moralistic and mingled with social policy and the social objectives of various action groups (Morgan, 1975: 3). A simplistic modern/traditional dichotomy, with the standard family at one end, and racial variations on the other, *marginalised* family difference rather than treating it as a central feature of family formation.

Structural functionalism, sex roles and cultural stereotypes

By the middle of the twentieth century, a mythical family prototype had become entrenched within structural functionalism, the then dominant social science framework within American sociology. Structural functionalism was a theory of society and sociological refinement of popular ideas about the family. The theory's central image was a society composed of interdependent parts linked together for the good of the whole. Social order was maintained by a high degree of consensus and a division of labour between the various components of society. The most basic component was the family 'organized around a unique and unalterable type of role structure operating for something larger than itself' (Kingsbury and Scanzoni, 1993: 170). Men's instrumental roles linked families with the outside world, while women's expressive roles ensured family solidarity. Structural functionalism made role differentiation an essential feature of families and the larger social order as well. The division of society into public and private components with a corresponding division of men's and women's roles was viewed as a complementary arrangement well suited to advanced, industrial societies. The conjugal family was a haven of consensus in an increasingly competitive public world. Like past family thought, structural functionalism posited one family type (by no means the only family form, even then) and defined it as 'the normal family' (Boss and Thorne, 1989). This glorified a historically specific and a race and class-specific family structure as the benchmark for all families in modern society.

In reality, diverse contexts, including the larger political economy and its racially segregated labour systems produced and required different family adaptations on the part of racial-ethnic people. As a result, their family- and sex-role configurations were often different from those in the dominant society. Nevertheless, structural functionalism made the modern nuclear family with its expressive and instrumental sex roles a falsely universal construct. This went hand in hand with *a social problems framework in which racial-ethnic families were analysed in isolation from larger structural forces.* Common categories of analysis for the study of racial-ethnic families rested on cultural stereotypes of Blacks as matriarchal and disorganised, Mexicans as patriarchal and backward, and Asians as traditional and clannish. Such group-specific family patterns, said to be handed down from generation to generation, were defined as the problem. For example,

Latinos, among whom extended family networks play a strong part in integrating family and community were criticised for being too 'familistic' – their lack of progress blamed on family values that kept them tied to family rather than economic advancement. African American families were criticised as 'matriarchal' because of the strong role women play in extended family networks (Dill et al., 1993). These supposedly opposite family structures and relationships were said to be responsible for each group's status in society.

Within this 'cultural deviance' approach (Allen, 1978), the African American family in particular became equated with family instability and stereotyped as disorganised; in other words, the essence of what families should *not* be. The mistaken idea that slavery weakened kin ties and undermined family values gave way to the matriarchy thesis, arguing that power resided in mother figures, with fathers largely absent from family life. According to this thinking, aberrant sex roles locked families in a 'tangle of pathology.' This was the theme of Daniel Patrick Moynihan's well-known study of Black families – *The Negro Family: The Case for National Action* (1965). The Moynihan report identified the deteriorating family as the main problem facing African Americans.

Similarly, Mexican-origin or Chicano families were stereotyped as disorganised due to their dysfunctional Mexican traditionalism. Like Black families, they failed to follow dominant patterns of masculinity and femininity, clinging instead to a 'backward' Mexican patriarchy. This made them responsible for their subordination. A wave of studies published in the 1960s pronounced the patriarchal Chicano family a stumbling block for future advancement (Heller, 1966; Madsen, 1964; Rubel, 1966).

Structural perspectives

In the late 1960s, scholars began to challenge cultural deficiency approaches for their harmful and inaccurate views of family life among Blacks, Chicanos and Asians in the United States. For example, the Moynihan Report was widely criticised for its theme of Black family disorganisation (Billingsly, 1968; Hill, 1972; Gutman, 1976; Ladner, 1971; Leibow, 1967; Stack, 1974). In the 1970s, scholars working within a 'radical critical' tradition refuted generalisations about family life. Although many fields and specialisations contributed to revisionist thought, two intellectual developments combining social constructionist and structural inequality perspectives were especially important: (1) feminist scholarship, and (2) new scholarship on racial-ethnic families. These specialisations moved on different tracks, with divergent views on many family topics. However, their collective impact on the study of racial-ethnic families was farreaching.

Mainstream feminist challenges and challenges to mainstream feminism

Two themes in early feminist scholarship were profoundly influential in the move away from cultural determinism. First, feminists argued that families are not monolithic universals that exist across time and space. Instead, family forms are *socially* constructed; they develop in the context of broader social and economic realities. An early example of feminist writing that focused on larger social forces and their effects on family life was Juliett Mitchell's conceptualisation of families as composed of several underlying structures including production, reproduction, sexuality and socialisation (Mitchell, 1966). Feminists drew on radical/critical thought, especially Marxism, to explain the relationship between families and the external forces of history, economics and politics. Fredrich Engels's work, *The Origin of the Family, Private Property, and the State* (1942), was especially influential in connecting both the family and women's subordination to the political economy.

Second, feminists posited that the family is responsible for women's oppression. The division of society into seemingly opposing domestic and public spheres of activity, they argued, gives men and women different positions of advantage and disadvantage (Mitchell, 1966; Rubin, 1975; Hartmann, 1976; Bernard, 1973). Women's responsibilities for domestic labour limit their association with highly valued resources. This arrangement separates women and men.

Power relations became a central analytic lens for feminists. Instead of treating the family as a harmony of interests and complementary roles, early feminist scholarship argued that women's and men's roles were, in fact, *power relations closely bound up with broader social systems*. Where functionalism saw the family as a unified system resting on different but complementary sex roles, feminists argued that the patriarchal family constituted a primary site of women's subordination. All women were thought to be separate from men – materially, socially, symbolically and ideologically – through their differential commitments in and outside the home and family. Women's childbearing and childrearing activities were the social structural arrangements limiting women's participation in public sphere activities and allowing men the freedom to participate in and control the public sphere. This universal split between domestic and public spheres was the basic organisational feature that led mainstream feminists to define the family as the universal cause of women's inequality (see Thorne, 1982 and Glenn, 1987 for early reviews of feminism's influence on the field of family studies).

Many studies of minority families were informed by feminist insights, but they developed a different analysis. Whereas mainstream feminists indicted the patriarchal family as the primary site of women's oppression, a substantial body of research on racial-ethnic families that began in the 1970s revealed other realities. For example, some of this research has found that while most families and households are patriarchal, they are also sites of racial and class-based solidarity – places to resist discrimination and exploitation (Caulfield, 1974; Stack, 1974; Baca Zinn, 1975; Kibria, 1994; Pessar, 1995). (See also Theme 5 in the framework below.) Under certain circumstances, gender was found to be less important as families sought to be strong and united in the face of external pressure. Some scholars integrated the 'gender-as-power' insights with questions about racial inequality in their studies of minority families. For example, Evelyn Nakano Glenn's studies of Japanese families (1986), and Patricia Zavella's study of Chicano families (1987) revealed close connections between women's family lives and economic conditions as they were bound up in broader systems of race and class.

By incorporating race and class into the analysis, a powerful lesson took hold: feminist generalisations are not applicable regardless of social context (Collins, 1994: 62). For many scholars of so-called 'minority families,' racial inequality emerged as a primary analytic category. The resulting creative tensions between gender perspectives and those attending to gender *and* race were important in the revisioning of racial-ethnic families in the US. Disputes with mainstream family feminism contained many seeds that would sprout into a new framework on race and family life (see the last section of this chapter).

Challenges from new scholarship on racial-ethnic families

In the 1970s, another body of revisionist scholarship emerged that explicitly challenged functionalist portrayals of racial-ethnic families. A broadly defined structural perspective made it possible for critical scholars to reject the conventional practice of 'culturalising' minority families, that is treating them as products of group-specific behaviours (see, e.g., Billingsly, 1968; Glenn, 1983; Griswold del Castillo, 1984; Gutman, 1976; Hill, 1972; Stack, 1974; Wagner and Schafer, 1980). In taking issue with mainstream depictions of racial-ethnic families, some scholars drew on the emerging tools of Black Studies, Chicano Studies and Asian Studies (see Staples and Mirande, 1988 for a review of changing perspectives in the literature on minority families). In some cases, emergent perspectives were developed primarily by women of colour, African Americans, Latinas, Asian Americans and Native Americans, women whose analyses were shaped by their unique experiences as 'outsiders within' – marginal intellectuals whose social locations provided them a particular perspective on self and society (Collins, 1986). In Britain, too, minority scholars made their voices heard through critiques and new scholarship on family life (Beck and Beck-Gernsheim, 2004: 507). By refuting cultural caricatures and highlighting the social situations and contexts in which families were embedded, study after study made the case that families were not cultural relics. For example, studies of Chinese Americans and Mexican Americans found that family arrangements among these groups were multiple and varied. Instead of being configured along 'ethnic' or 'cultural' lines, each group displayed different family forms in different historical periods and places marked by immigration laws and other economic and political constraints. Furthermore, the historical study of Chinese and Mexican immigrants in other societies revealed family patterns that were different from those in their countries of origin (Glenn, 1983; Sanchez, 1999a).

Where the old approaches reduced family life to culture, revisionist approaches examined the social location of families within a larger social structure where social and economic imbalances shaped their opportunities and options. For example, studies by Sally Andrade (1980) and Maria Luisa Urdaneta (1980) provided evidence that high fertility rates among Mexican American women could not be explained by ethnic-specific or cultural factors. Rather, economic considerations, availability of birth control services, and behaviours towards minority women by medical personnel explained women's restricted fertility control. Research on African Americans also examined structural conditions that produced distinctive family patterns. In his examination of Black families, Robert Hill (1972) found that adaptations such as gender-role flexibility and kinship bonds were strengths developed in response to social and economic marginalisation.

As the study of racial inequality grew and matured in the 1970s and 1980s, not only did family scholars emphasise the structural connections between race and family, they developed a new focus on race as a defining axis of family life. Historical studies of African Americans, Latinos and Asian Americans documented the diverse contexts that led racial-ethnic families along different paths from the idealised family. Racial domination and different labour markets produced different family forms. In other words, structural conditions required different adaptations on the part of industrial workers, slaves and agricultural workers. And far from being maladaptive, variant family arrangements could be a way of coping with poverty and racism (Stack, 1974).

Revisionist approaches to racial minority families *did not* discount the importance of culture in family life. Instead, culture was reconceptualised – no longer treated as something inherited from past generations, but viewed as originating in larger social forces of particular times and particular places. New research revealed that many family patterns, long assumed to be cultural, had more to do with the *social structural locations* in which racial-ethnic groups were forced to live (see Jarrett, 1994 and Segura, 1994 for excellent examples of this new emphasis). And far from being maladaptive, culture often served as an adaptational response to constraints imposed by economic and social structures. Furthermore, these adaptations were not exceptions to the rule; they are produced by the very structures that organise society as a whole. As a result, the idealised modern family was not a luxury shared by all. 'Even though it was a legally, economically, and culturally privileged family form that conferred advantages to those who lived in it' (Coontz, 2001: 83), those advantages were not evenly distributed. Those outside of society's privileged groups share a historical pattern. Their families were devalued, degraded and destroyed.

Throughout the field of family studies, scholars began to emphasise the social situations and contexts in which families were embedded, and to assign responsibility for their place in society to unequal systems rather than cultures. By 2000, the family field in general had developed a greater sensitivity to families of colour in research (Murray et al., 2001). Studies of African American, Latino and Asian American families began to reflect 'a social adaptation perspective, based on themes of family metamorphosis, resilience, flexibility and cohesion in the face of changing social environments and economic circumstances (Berardo, 1991: 6).

STRUCTURAL PERSPECTIVES: SOME TENSIONS, DEBATES AND LIMITS

Structurally grounded perspectives tend to focus on two aspects of family organisation – marriage and kinship. Many new tensions have arisen within these areas. While family scholars now tend to share some broadly defined contextual perspectives, they also differ on many issues. As a result, the study of racial-ethnic families remains ideologically, politically and intellectually contested. Three issues illustrate some ongoing tensions within the scholarship on race and family. While the following controversies have waxed and waned over the past three and a half decades, they reveal that racial-ethnic groups in general (and African Americans in particular), have long been at the centre of society's most contentious family issues (Hill, 2005: 52).

Debates about marriage, family structure and poverty

Instead of cultural explanations of racial-ethnic families, many family scholars now examine both the larger structural conditions within which families are embedded and the family structure itself. The matter of family structure is controversial, leading to debates about the relationship between race, marriage and family well-being.

Ever since E. Franklin Frazier's classic study, *The Negro Family in the United States*, (1939), the issue of the two-parent family has been at the heart of race and family debates. Frazier's theme (later adopted by Moynihan) traced the difference between White and African American family life to marriage patterns. The reasoning was that among African Americans, the long-lasting effects of slavery, absent husbands and high rates of illegitimacy made for an unstable family form. This argument grew stronger as the proportion of Black families headed by two parents declined in the 1960s, 1970s and 1980s. Increased marital breakups, births to unmarried Black women and the household patterns that accompany these changes were said to cause high poverty rates among African Americans.

A large body of scholarship demonstrates that recent changes in marital patterns among racial-ethnics (less marriage, more divorce, more cohabitation and more non-marital childbearing) are rooted in macro-structural developments. William J. Wilson's analysis of the retreat from marriage among African Americans is the exemplar, revealing connections between declining marriage rates and the structural removal of work from the inner city. Examining the relationship between work and marriage, Wilson (1987, 1996) found that men with higher incomes are more likely to be married than men with lower incomes. He proposed that inner-city male joblessness encourages non-marital childbearing. Structural conditions leave Black women disproportionately divorced and solely responsible for their children. Some scholars are critical of Wilson, arguing that his analysis idealises the two-parent family structure and devotes insufficient attention to the economic realities affecting *women's* work. Nevertheless, the explanation of how economic and demographic realities undermine marriage provides a vital structural perspective on marriage as an opportunity structure in decline for African Americans (Baca Zinn, 1989).

Through the 1980s and 1990s, the question 'What difference does family structure make'? was a fruitful research question for many family sociologists and demographers. A significant body of quantitative research revealed an important relationship between the single-parent family, poverty and race. High poverty rates among racial-ethnic children were often attributed to family structure differences. Still, despite the correlations between family structure and family resources, research did not conclude that single-parent households are the 'root cause of poverty' (McLanahan and Sandefur, 1994: 3).

While research did find that family structure was correlated with racial inequality, especially between Black and White children (Lichter and Landale, 1995: 347), many argued that child poverty could not be reduced to family structure for either Blacks or Latinos. As two family sociologists put it, 'If there were no single parents, Black children would still have much higher poverty rates (McLanahan and Sandefur, 1994: 85). More precisely, for African Americans, emulating the White family structure would close only about one-half of the income gap' (Hacker, 1996: 309). If Puerto Rican Children lived in nuclear families, their poverty would be reduced from 42 to 24 percent (in other words, half is due to family structure). But poverty rates would be reduced only slightly if Mexicans and Cubans had the nuclear family structures of non-Latinos (Lichter and Landale, 1996: 347).

Such research brought a much needed corrective to simplifications about family structure and race. Today, most family scholars agree that there is a relationship between poverty and female-headed families with children. Yet, they continue to disagree on whether marriage and racial differences in family structure are the *cause* or the *consequence* of poverty (Lichter and Qain, 2004).

Through the last quarter of the twentieth century, several macro-structural changes in US society have produced a growing Balkanisation of family life along economic and racial lines. While globalisation and economic restructuring affect each racial-ethnic group differently, African American patterns of marriage and family structure are distinctive. They include higher rates of marital dissolution and lower rates of remarriage than other groups. The retreat from marriage among African Americans is explained by economic and demographic factors including men's employment patterns, the gender ratio and other social conditions that provide different opportunities for marriage by race and class (Taylor, 2000).

Culture versus structure debates about kinship patterns

Despite the prevailing structural work on racial-ethnic families, cultural themes remain an ongoing thread in both popular and scholarly thought. In popular thought, a strong culturalising tendency remains. The public in general, and policymakers in particular, still think of family life in terms of 'group-specific' cultural traits. An idealised model of the nuclear family is posited as the norm, whereas the many varieties of families in different regional, economic, racial, and ethnic groups are treated as artefacts of culture. Not only are racial-ethnic families defined as different from the idealised family of the dominant society, but the singular form is viewed as superior and the cultural standard against which others are judged. Although we now have new understandings of the forms families take and the social and economic contexts in which they develop, alarmist views still make racial-ethnic families a scapegoat for social problems (see Theme 4 in the framework below). Similar debates occur in the United Kingdom, where definitions of culture vary according to the group in question. For example, South Asians are generally regarded as culturally 'more different', than Afro-Caribbeans in their languages, religions and patterns of kinship and marriage, stemming from an early academic prejudice that 'Asians have culture, West Indians have problems' (Benson, 1996, cited in Shaw, 2004: 273).

In US family scholarship, new debates about the impact of culture versus structure on the organisation and dynamics of families have arisen. Some family scholars continue to accept culture as a primary analytic focus. In general, they have abandoned static and ideological definitions of culture. No longer based on racial stereotyping, culture is redefined as dynamic, resilient and a primary shaper of family life (Murray et al., 2001). This offers new perspectives on an old debate about culture versus structure in producing racially distinctive family patterns.

Current dimensions of the culture/structure debate focus on extended kinship ties within minority groups, especially when compared to Whites who are said to emphasise ties between married couples and their children. Natalia Sarkisian and Naomi Gerstel review the literature surrounding the debates as they apply to Black and Latino family scholarship (Sarkisian and Gerstel, 2004, 2005). They explain that for Blacks, cultural resiliency arguments explain extended family involvement in terms of traditional African values of extended familism, childrearing and motherhood. For Latinos, cultural resiliency analyses stress historical values and religious differences that reach beyond the nuclear family for support and solidarity. Using national data, Gerstel and Sarkisian analyse extended family support among Blacks, Latinos and Whites. Their findings confirm higher levels of extended family involvement among Blacks and Latinos. However, important differences in the *kinds* of extended family involvement lead these researchers to conclude that structural rather than cultural differences explain distinctive kinship patterns. In short, *class differences* between groups lead to higher levels of kin involvement among racial-ethnics who count on kin for practical needs including child care, household tasks and rides. Lack of economic resources 'increases their need for help form kin and boosts their willingness of help in return' (Gerstel and Sarkisian, 2008: 451).

New research on family relations among ethnic groups in the United States describes complex households and fluid residential patterns that are markedly different from the nuclear family model of biological parents and children (Chavez, 1992; see Schwede et al., 2005 for a collection of new research). According to the studies, neither cultural factors nor structural factors alone explain such family complexity. Instead, the preference for extended family living among US ethnic groups is best explained by *combined* cultural and structural conditions (Schwede et al., 2005).

The limits of mainstream structural perspectives on race

Structural perspectives on family life among racial ethnics serve as an important counter to normative explanations of family difference. They make it clear that family processes are not uniform. They provide insights about many of the underlying sources of family difference in the United States. Still, despite the paradigm shift in family studies, the overarching structural perspective leaves much to be desired in its treatment of race.

To be fair, the field recognises that along with gender and class, race is a key force leading to differentiated family outcomes. Yet, in mainstream family literature, race lacks the analytic primacy of either gender or class. Despite the now widely cited generalisation that inequalities of class and race construct families differently, race is often conflated with class and economic disparities rather than treated as an independent feature of US social structure. Many structural approaches within mainstream family studies turn out to be purely economic. They reduce unequal opportunities of racial-ethnic families to macro-economic conditions or to their place in the social class system. Others document the family patterns that differ from one racial group to another, while others consider representational elements such as racist and misogynist imagery when examining the marginalisation of racial-ethnic families. However, it is one thing to give lip service to the importance of race in family formation and another to analyse the family as a racialised institution (see Dill et al., 1998 for a discussion of the central structural perspectives on family diversity and difference in the United States).

On another trajectory, some family scholars have made race analytically central in their scholarship. In concert with the 'racial formation' framework developed by Michael Omi and Howard Winant, (1994), this line of thought argues that race itself is an institutional system of stratification that produces aggregate differences in the family patterns of different groups. When applied to families of different racial-ethnic groups, this approach uncovers that 'an entire arsenal of social institutions creates paths in which families assigned to one group receive better jobs, housing, healthcare, schooling and recreational facilities, while those relegated to other groups do worse, or do without' (Collins, 1997: 379). Although this analytic perspective is not widely articulated within the family field, it offers the promise of a more comprehensive and accurate understanding of race and family life.

A FRAMEWORK FOR UNDERSTANDING THE FAMILY AS A RACE INSTITUTION

Scholarship on racial-ethnic families has transformed how we think about them. Asking if race matters – or better, asking *how* it matters opens up new topics on families, their form, and operation. As of this writing, the field of family studies lacks a systematic statement on race/family connections. However, several emergent themes challenge the early twentieth-century family paradigm on all dimensions, and reveal complex means through which race and family are woven together.

This chapter identifies important thought about the family as a race institution. It synthesises social constructionist and structural insights on race and family from many scholarly fields including anthropology, sociology, history and economics to bring new perspectives to bear on familiar family matters. Adding the layer of globalisation offers new directions that are vital for family studies. Although the vernacular of globalisation has not yet penetrated mainstream family studies (Karraker, 2008: 11), racial inequalities are embedded in global economic and political systems (Barlow, 2003; Marabel, 2008; Robinson, 2008). As such, the global context is a crucial component for examining the structural relationship between family and race.

Six themes and conclusions offer a preliminary set of analytic premises for understanding how family and race are intertwined. By no means does the framework presented here capture all of the connections between race and family. It does, however, identify some common themes in the growing body of family research. These themes illuminate many connections that will push the field of family studies to reconstitute itself for the twenty-first century. In short form, these themes are as follows.

Racial patterns of family formation are rooted in labour arrangements and their unequal distribution of work, wages, and the social resources that accompany them

How groups are situated in the larger political economy affects the forms families take and the ways in which families operate. Labour relegates families to different social locations with varied opportunities to meet family requirements. From the founding of the United States and throughout its history, race has been a fundamental criterion in determining the kind of work people do, the wages they receive and the kind of legal, economic, political and social supports provided for their families (Dill, 1994; Glenn, 2002). The historical incorpora-tion of racial ethnics in *coercive labor* – principally slavery and contract labour systems – prevented them from receiving the kind of social support provided for other families. Not only did such social locations undermine family life but in some cases, family life was legislatively denied (Hondagneu-Sotelo, 1995: 183).

Looking at family arrangements through the lens of labour reveals how family structure is affected by coercion. For example, slavery defined Black women and men as labourers and made it impossible for them to conform to the family ideal of the dominant society. Alternative forms of partnering, childbearing, parenting and kinship among African Americans emerged out of necessity (Durr and Hill, 2006: 78; Hunter, 2006: 89). Although each group is distinguishable from the others (and from those of White Americans), racism has created similar family histories for African Americans, Latinos and Asians. Composite portraits of each group show them to share some important commonalities. Even groups with very different cultures display similar family patterns when they are located in similar circumstances (Glenn and Yap, 1994). Despite the restrictions imposed on family life by racial-labour systems, families did not break down. Instead, people of colour created a number of family strategies that allowed them to function. These include fluid family boundaries, flexible family roles and numerous patterns of support in extended kinship structures as adaptive responses to the social and economic hardships imposed by racial inequalities.

Research on families of colour reveals longstanding adaptations to the con-straining realities of their placement in prevailing labour hierarchies. From the many family forms of Black families during and after slavery, to the split house-holds of nineteenth and early twentieth century Chinese immigrants (Glenn, 1983), to the new transnational family networks of present day immigrants, the ability of families to take on different appearances within the context of broader social and economic conditions has always been a family adaptative strategy. It turns out that permeable boundaries and family fluidity arise out of particular forms of race and class stratification. Hence, racial conditions both *produce* and *require* distinctive family arrangements (Baca Zinn, 1990 and 1994).

Global capitalism is transforming labour in ways that link race and patterns of family formation. People of colour are among those disproportionately margina-lised from the global economy (Barlow, 2003, Marabel, 2008; Robinson, 2008). They are displaced when jobs are outsourced and dislocated or forced to migrate for employment. The growing globalisation of labour is reorganising families throughout the world. As jobs move across the borders to low-wage economies, workers leave their homelands to find work. Often, they must leave family mem-bers behind in order to provide for them by taking advantage of labour market opportunities in other countries. These changes are creating a new family con-figuration: transnational families with expanded ties stretching across national boundaries. Today's transnational families are an outcome of transnational employment patterns. They are created when one family member crosses national borders for employment, while others remain behind, a common pattern among undocumented migrants to the United States from Mexico, Central America, Puerto Rico, the Dominican Republic, and elsewhere in the Caribbean, and Southeast Asia (Pyke, 2004).

Global labour demands that are racialised (and gendered) are producing new kinds of multiracial societies. A growing number of labour migrants are made illegal aliens and forced into a relationship with host nations on highly racialised and nationally oppressed terms (Barlow, 2003). Migrants also form transnational families in response to the pressure of nativism in receiving societies. Nativist grass-roots organisations aimed at further restrictions and exclusion of immigrants have sprouted throughout the United States and Europe with anti-immigrant senti-ments. Migrating parents leave their children behind so as not to expose them to 'racial tensions and anti-immigrant sentiments fostered by the social and cultural construction of low-wage migrants as undesirable citizens (Parrenas, 2006: 408). For racially marginalised workers without the full range of social services, transnational family life entails extraordinary financial, physical and emotional costs.

Racial hierarchies are intertwined with societal relations of class, gender and other inequalities to place families and their members in particular social locations

Different social locations produce family differences. They determine how fami-lies generate and allocate social and economic resources. They impact labour market status, education, martial relations and other features of family life. At any time, a society will contain a range of family types that vary with race, class, gender and other structural characteristics (such as region of the country and its socioeconomic characteristics). The convergence of multiple inequalities pro-duces group difference in family patterns.

Converging systems of race and class, and what they mean for families in dif-ferent social locations is explicitly recognised in contemporary family research (Lareau, 2003; Gerstel and Sarkisian, 2008; Patillo-McCoy, 1999, Edin and Kefalas, 2005; Uttal, 1999). Although racial groups have distinctive family pro-files, there are many differences that cut across all groups. For example, not only do race, class and gender shape families in different ways, they mean that people of the same race may experience family differently depending on their location in the class structure as unemployed, poor, working class or professional; their location in the gender structure as male or female; and their location in the sexual orientation system as heterosexual, gay, lesbian and bisexual (Baca Zinn and Dill, 1996: 327).

The emergence of transnational families formed through globalised labour illustrate how class, race, nationality and gender are thoroughly intertwined. Women and men of *specific localities* serve as building blocks of the global order. In some settings, downgraded jobs have been redefined as women's jobs and entered the global marketplace filled with immigrants. Jobs in hotels, restaurants, hospitals and convalescent homes are examples. In some cases (janitorial industry and light manufacturing), jobs have been re-gendered and re-racialised so that jobs previously held by US born Black or White men are now held by Asian and Latina women. Family boundaries expand as the demand for immigrant women's labour has increased, and more women have left their families and young children behind to seek employment in the United States and other post-industrial societies (Hondagneu-Sotelo, 2002: 260–261). Family structure is transformed as family relations extend across several countries or even continents.

Different family forms often involve direct interdependencies of racial privilege and racial subordination

Understanding the social relations between dominant and subordinate racial groups illuminates the *relational* character of family variation. The concept of relationality suggests that 'the lives of different groups are interconnected even without face-to-face relations' (Glenn, 2002: 14). Socially structured power relations mean that racial differences in family life do not simply co-exist, but in any given period, they are sustained through interaction across racial and class boundaries. Hierarchical and interdependent family forms are a key element in sustaining privilege and disadvantage.

Bonnie Thornton Dill's historical study of racial ethnic women and their families in the nineteenth century reveals that power relationships between families of the dominant society and families of colour were central in shaping the family arrangements of *each group*. African American, Mexican and Asian American families were directly influenced by race, class and gender hierarchies within the larger political economy. Through each phase of US history, Anglo American upper and middle-class family life rested on the labour and family arrangements of racial-ethnic people. As Leith Mullings states, 'it was the working class and enslaved men and women whose labor created the wealth that allowed the middle class and upper middle class domestic life styles to exist' (Mullings, 1986: 50).

Today, globalisation links contradictory family forms in farreaching parts of the world. The growing demand for paid domestic workers is part of an international division of labour in which women of colour from developing nations leave their families to work in race and class-privileged US families and those of other post-industrial countries. Their work of caring for families in the home – what family scholars call 'reproductive labour' because it reproduces the conditions of daily living – is *racialised*. It represents a racial division of reproductive labour (Glenn, 1992) that interlocks the race and class status of privileged women and private domestic workers. Furthermore, it rests on differentiated family arrangements. The hiring of domestic workers to take over household labor enables women in privileged families to have public lives and professional careers and simultaneously leaves women of colour disenfranchised and living across the world from their own families. A growing body of scholarship establishes the unequal relationship between domestics and their employers, revealing an emergent global relationship between families of dominant and subordinate groups (Hondagneu-Sotelo, 2001; Parrenas, 2001; Eherenreich and Hochschild, 2002). Although the burdens and benefits of global family differentiation are not equally shared, they are *structurally connected*. Privileges and disadvantages of race, class, gender and nation shape families in both sending and receiving societies and contribute to 'growing disparities between families in the Third World and those in the First World' (Karraker, 2008: 99).

Racial representations of families provide justification for existing social arrangements and their hierarchies of race, class and gender

The dominant definition of 'the family' is an ideological code that expresses differences from and superiority over 'other' family forms. Dorothy Smith calls the idealised family image in the US, the Standard North American Family (SNAF), an ideological code that inserts an implicit evaluation of living arrangements (Smith, 1993). Symbolic meanings of family are shaped in opposition to the family forms of racial 'others', whose so-called lifestyles are a code for social problems. Although this foundational assumption that shaped the origins of US family scholarship has largely disappeared from the field of family studies, many strands of popular thought still implicate racial-ethnic families in social disorganisation.

Family pathology serves as a 'controlling image' (Collins, 1991: 71) that contributes to racial subordination. For example,

> Black women are portrayed as creating pathological forms of families as 'single heads of households,' as drawing on public resources, or as breeding too many children who pose physical, social, and economic risks to others. Their mothering is viewed as something quite different ... as a category of activities enacted in such dissimilar ways from the dominant model that they are constructed as confusing, atypical, and dysfunctional. (Richie, 2009: 327)

Rickie Solinger's historical study of reproductive politics uncovers the power of racial ideologies in shaping US social policy. In the mid-twentieth century, birth control was introduced in a thoroughly racialised manner. In the early 1960s, policies sought to limit African American births. Even in the civil rights era, social policies were guided by notions of unrestrained 'breeding' of African American women and other women of colour who were pressed to get birth control, get sterilised, or suffer public policy punishments. For White women, on the other hand, birth control was defined as 'a right, a choice, a symbol of liberation, and a mark of modern womanhood' (Solinger, 2008: 148).

Racialised representations were re-invoked to provide the political justification for the Personal Responsibility and Work Opportunity Act of 1996 that dismantled the US welfare system. The public discourse surrounding welfare reform rested largely on the stereotypes of Black women whose families and reproductive behaviours deviated from family norms of the dominant society (Dill et al., 1998).

More recently, media reports promoted a causal connection between family breakdown and the stark levels of racial impoverishment following Hurricane Katrina. As one commentator stated, 'if people are stripped of the most basic social support – the two parent family – they will be more vulnerable in countless other ways, especially one assumes in moments of crisis like that that has befallen New Orleans' (Lowrey, 2005).

Race often subsumes other sets of social relations, making them 'good' or 'bad,' 'correct' or 'incorrect' (Higginbotham, 1992). Even though Mexican immigrants embody dominant family values in their close-knit and strong families, their family lifestyles are judged as deviant. Anti-immigrant rhetoric recasts strong families as a menace to society. Racist and misogynist family imagery was used in California's 1994 campaign to pass proposition 187. As Pierrette Hondagneu-Sotelo explains,

> The protagonists were poor, pregnant women who were drawn to the U.S. to give birth in publicly financed country hospitals, allowing their children to be born as U.S. citizens and subsequent recipients of taxpayer-supported medical care, public assistance and education. In this scenario, immigrant families constitute a rapidly expanding underclass draining education and medical resources in the United States. (Hondagneu-Sotelo, 1995: 173)

Such developments reveal how the family can become a powerful symbol of 'otherness'. Furthermore, any family form can be deployed to exclude unwanted racial groups.

Family rhetoric is often found in government policy and the legal system. Family ideals function as a principle of social organisation, often used as a metaphor for belonging to various groups including who belongs to the nation and who does not. As one historian notes, 'over the course of U.S. history, citizenship has been constructed on the shifting ground of race, thus defining the boundaries of the American "family"' (Sanchez, 1999b).

In today's world, race occupies an important place in public discussions about family. As workers move across the globe, many receiving nations such as the United States and Australia have developed strong narratives about family values (Edgar, 2004: 8). Race and gender stereotypes are embedded in these narratives which contrast families of the dominant society with those of immigrant families.

Families often serve as sites of resistance against racial domination

Using the family as a defense against racism is a well-documented practice. Not only do people of colour in the United States find ways of building families when social structure denies their opportunities, they *use* their families to cope, survive and even challenge social institutions that impinge on them. The family site itself serves as a means of resisting domination, both directly and indirectly.

Norrece T. Jones's study of slave families reveals many forms of resistance. While the family was the planters, most effective control mechanism, slaves made the family a setting of survival and empowerment. According to Jones, slaves, when in need, could depend on familial relations, both real and fictive. Mothers and fathers instilled in their children self-esteem, a spirit of independence and various techniques of survival and self-preservation (Jones, 1991). This is a prominent line of analysis, emphasising how families subvert racial oppression.

Activism within families takes various forms. One is creating what Minna Caulfield (1974) called a 'culture of resistance', or a cultural response to imperialistic assaults on group life. Cementing family bonds and building networks of mutual support are subtle but important means of sustaining kinship in the face of outside assaults. Scholars often apply the term *family strategies* to the behaviours family members use in responding to structural barriers. In addition to maintaining cultural identity, the literature highlights strategies such as migration, and adapting family and household configurations as circumstances require. Glenn underscores the flexibility of Chinese Americans in devising a range of different family types that have corresponded to prevailing historical conditions. Such strategies testify to the resilience and resourcefulness of Chinese American families in overcoming obstacles (Glenn, 2002). Yet family strategies are complicated because families are not unitary settings. Struggles for cultural resistance may also generate family conflict. As Nazli Kibria demonstrates, for Vietnamese immigrants, using family traditions to build cultural autonomy also produced struggles between women and men (Kibria, 1994).

An important finding of the family resistance scholarship is that racial-ethnic families often engage in direct political activism. Not only do families serve as settings of survival and adaptation, they are often agents of political change. Research finds that activist identities and involvement in political movements may originate in families. Monica White's study of South African and African American women activists details the family experiences that produce paths to anti-racist political activism (White, 2005). Furthermore, the family itself can serve as the organising structure for political struggle. In the Chicano movement of the 1960s, the Mexican/Chicano family was the basis of group solidarity. *Political familism* was not only symbolic, but an organisational means of involving entire families in activist work (Baca Zinn, 1975). Research also documents that racial ethnic women have a long tradition of extending their mothering roles to the realm of politics. Mothers use their maternal roles as a place of racial resistance. For example, many Native American mothers weave tribal traditions with a 'motherist stance' in fighting together for the survival of their children (Udell, 2001). And African Americans and Latinas engage in different kinds of activist mothering for the benefit of the entire community (Pardo, 1990, Naples, 1992).

Similar political actions on behalf of racially defined families are common throughout the world. For example, one study documents the activism of Jewish

Israeli mothers. Their desire to keep their children safe, led to public protest and the eventual development of a West Bank settlement. These women used maternal ethics of care and an ideology of nonviolence to transform conflict through peaceful protest (Budig, 2004: 429).

Families then, may serve as a principle (if undertheorised) form of resistance. When this occurs, they are what Dorothy Roberts calls *oppostional enclaves* (Roberts, 2009), capable of changing racial structures and even the course of history.

The family is a key institution in maintaining racial inequality

Much of this chapter focuses on the ways in which systemic forms of inequality shape the family lives of different racial groups. Yet, the family is a primary mechanism for perpetuating racial divisions. It is important to see how the family as an institution contributes to racial inequalities in the larger society, in other words to see that 'society makes families and families make society' (Glaser, cited in Billingsly, 1992: 78).

How privilege and disadvantage are organised through family units is the subject of several works by Collins (1994, 1997, 1998a, 1998b, 2000). She illustrates how families are major conduits for reproducing race, class and gender inequalities through the intergenerational transfer of wealth. Emphasising wealth introduces 'family organisation into social class analysis in a distinctively new way. Focusing on family as a race, gendered, age-stratified social institution that is central in intergenerational transmission redefines family as a building block of social class formation' (Collins, 1997: 836–837).

Families are central sites for consolidating racial differences and reinforcing racial hierarchy. This occurs in several ways. First, laws barring sex and marriage played an integral role in enforcing racial boundaries, especially for Blacks and Asians in the United States. Rachel Moran's history of anti-miscegenation laws finds that these groups were uniquely affected: for Blacks, the laws defined them as inferior persons, even after they were nominally free. This blocked Black access to the privilege of associating with Whites.

> For Asians, marked as racially distinct and unfit for citizenship by federal immigration laws, state constrains on intermarriage prevented Asian male immigrants from integrating into communities by thwarting their sexuality, hindering them from developing ties to the United States through marriage, and deterring them from having children who would be American citizens by birth. (Moran, 2008: 126)

Second, marriage and family also reproduce actual populations of 'races' (Collins, 2000: 49) by regulating who marries whom. Race continues to be a sorting mechanism for mating, marriage and adoption. Although anti-miscegenation laws were outlawed in 1967, interracial marriages remain rare. Most marriages still occur between socially designated racial groups (American Sociological Association, 2003; Lichter and Qian, 2004; Qian, 2005).

Racial differences in families also play a part in global inequalities and the shifts that accompany them. Scholars have suggested that the multiplicity of household types is one of the chief props of the world economy (Smith et al., 1985). The actual form that families take is crucial. Transnational families in which third-world women workers migrate across the globe to serve as maids or caretakers of families in post industrial societies while their own children remain 'at home' in poor countries brings this point into full view (Hondagneu-Sotelo and Avila, 1997, Parrenas, 2000). The structural ordering required of transnational families serves to buttress race relations on a global scale.

CONCLUSION

US scholarship on families offers important understandings about racial inequality. The question 'What does family life tell us about race'? signifies a refocusing of research and scholarship agendas in the areas of family studies and racial inequality. Not only must we conclude that different family forms often reflect racial inequalities, but we can also point to many ways in which the family as a social institution sustains inequality. If the framework on race and family life outlined here holds out well, it suggests answers to the following questions: What explains longstanding racial differences in family life? Are racial disparities in family well-being inevitable in a racially stratified society? Will racial differences in family form continue to reflect and produce differences in family well-being? Why do some of the most pressing social and political debates of our time have race and family at their centre? These are vital questions to address as we attempt to cope with twenty-first century social realities.

The extent to which US scholarship on family and race is useful for analysing new developments elsewhere remains to be seen. A world increasingly defined by transnational movement has farreaching social, cultural and political implications for families and for the ways in which families are studied. As people move to improve their economic situations and to flee repression, families throughout the world are becoming more dispersed. The future of family studies depends on the field's ability to incorporate insights on racial divisions and worldwide family diversity. Locating families in the structural inequalities of globalisation provides a different frame of analysis from that which prevailed through most of the twentieth century. Race and family scholars now face a dual challenge. First, 'the family' is no longer bound by the nation-state. The rise of transnational families must shift our inquiry away from territorially distinct units and away from the North Atlantic space (Beck and Beck Gernsheim, 2004: 501). Second, the transnational redefinition of family boundaries must direct our attention to global relations of inequality that produce divided and unequal contexts for family life. Taken together, these challenges will stretch our understanding of race and family in different contexts and in an increasingly complex world.

REFERENCES

Allen, W. (1978) 'The Search for Applicable Theories of Black Family life', *Journal of Marriage and the Family*, 40: 117–129.

American Sociological Association. (2003) *The Importance of Collecting Data and Doing Social Scientific Research on Race*. Washington DC: American Sociological Association.

Andrade, S.J. (1980) 'Family Planning Practices of Mexican Americans' in M. Melville, (ed.) *Twice a Minority: Mexican American Women*. St.Louis: C. V. Mosby. pp. 173–190.

Baca Zinn, M. and Dill, B.T. (1996) 'Theorizing Difference from Multiracial Feminism', *Feminist Studies*, 22 (Summer): 321–331.

Baca Zinn, M. (1975) 'Political Familism: Toward Sex Role Equality in Chicano Families', *Azltan*, 6 (1): 13–26.

Baca Zinn, M. (1989) 'Family, Race, and Poverty in the Eighties', *Signs: Journal of Women in Culture and Society*, 14 (4): 856–874.

Baca Zinn, M. (1990) 'Family, Feminism, and Race in America', *Gender & Society*, 4 (1) (March): 68–82.

Baca Zinn, M. (1994) 'Feminist Rethinking from Racial Ethnic Families' in M. Baca Zinn and B.T. Dill, (eds) *Women of Color in U.S. Society*. Philadelphia: Temple University Press. pp. 303–313.

Barlow, A.L. (2003) *Between Fear and Hope: Globalization and Race in the United States*. Lanham, MD.: Rowman and Littlefield.

Barrett, M. and McIntosh, M. (1998) 'The Anti-Social Family' in K.V. Hansen and A.I. Garey, (eds.) *Families in the U.S.: Kinship and Domestic Politics*. Philadelphia: Temple University Press.

Beck, U. and Beck-Gernsheim, E. (2004) 'Families in a Runaway World' in J. Scott, J. Treas, and M. Richards, (eds) *Blackwell Companion to the Sociology of Families*. Blackwell Publishing, Ltd. pp. 499–514.

Bernard, J. (1973) *The Future of Marriage*. New York: Bantam.

Berardo, F.M. (1991) 'Family Research in the 1980s: Recent Trends and Future Directions' in A. Booth (ed.) *Contemporary Families: Looking Forward, Looking Back*. Minneapolis: National Council on Family Relations. pp. 1–11.

Billingsly, A. (1968) *Black Families in White America*. Englewood Cliffs, NJ: Prentice Hall.

Boss, P. and Thorne, B. (1989) 'Family Sociology and Family Therapy: A Feminist Linkage' in M. McGoldrick, C.M. Anderson, and F. Walsh, (eds) *Women in Families*. New York: W.W. Norton. pp. 78–96.

Budig, M. (2004) 'Feminism and the Family' in J. Scott, J. Treas, and M. Richards (eds) *The Blackwell Companion to the Sociology of Families*. Oxford, UK: Blackwell Publishing, Ltd. pp. 416–434.

Caulfield, M.D. (1974) 'Imperialism, the Family, and Cultures of Resistsance', *Socialist Revolution*, 20: 67–85.

Chavez, L.R. (1992) *Shadowed Lives: Undocumented Immigrants in American Society*. Orlando, FL: Harcourt Brace.

Collins, P.H. (1986) 'Learning from the Outsider within: The Sociological Significance of Black Feminist Thought', *Social Problems*, 33 (December): 514–532.

Collins, P.H. (1991) *Black Feminist Thought: Knowledge, Consciousness, and the Politics of Empowerment*. New York: Routledge.

Collins, P.H. (1994) 'Shifting the Center: Race, Class, and Feminist Theorizing about Motherhood' in E.N. Glenn, G. Chang and L. Rennie Forcey, (eds) *Mothering: Ideology, Experience, and Agency*. New York: Routledge. pp. 45–65.

Collins, P.H. (1997) 'African-American Women and Economic Justice: A Preliminary Analysis of Wealth, Family, and African-American Social Class', *University of Cincinnati Law Review*, 65 (3): 825–52.

Collins, P.H. (1998a) 'Intersections of Race, Class, Gender and Nation: Some Implications for Black Family studies', *Journal of Comparative Family Studies*, 29 (1): 27–36.

Collins, P.H. (1998b) 'It's All in the Family: Intersections of Gender, Race, and Nation', *Hypatia*, 13 (3) (Summer): 62–82.

Collins, P.H. (2000) 'Gender, Black Feminism, and Black Political Economy', *The Annals of the American Academy*, 568 (March): 41–53.

Coontz, S. (2001) 'Historical perspectives on family studies' in R. Milardo (ed.) *Understanding Families Into the New Millennium: A Decade in Review*. Minneapolis: The National Council on Family Relations. pp. 80–94.

Dill, B.T., Zinn, M.B. and Patton, S. (1993) 'Feminism, Race, and the Politics of Family Values', *Report from the Institute for Philosophy and Public Policy*. University of Maryland, 13, (Summer): 13–18.

Dill, B.T., Baca Zinn, M. and Patton, S. (1998) 'Race, Family Values, and Welfare Reform', *Sage Race Relations Abstracts*, 23 (Fall): 4–31.

Dill, B.T. (1994) 'Fictive Kin, Paper Sons, and Compadrazgo: Women of Color and the Struggle for Family Survival' in M. Baca Zinn and B.T. Dill, (eds) *Women of Color in U.S. Society*. Philadelphia: Temple University Press. pp.149–169.

Durr, M. and Hill, S.A. (2006) 'The Family-Work Interface in African American Households' in M. Durr and S.A. Hill, (eds) *Race, Work, and Family in the Lives of African American Families*. Lanham, MD: Rowman & Littlefield Publishers. pp. 73–85.

Edgar, D. (2004) 'Globalization and Western Bias in Family Sociology' in J. Scott, J. Treas, and M. Richards (eds) *The Blackwell Companion to the Sociology of Families*. Oxford, UK; Blackwell Publishing, Ltd. pp. 3–16.

Edin, K. and Kefalas, M. (2005) *Promises I Can Keep: Why Poor Women Put Motherhood Before Marriage*. Berkeley: University of Michigan Press.

Ehrenreich, B. and Hochschild, A.R. (2002) 'Introduction' in B. Ehrenreich and A.R. Hochschild, (eds) *Global Women*. New York: Metropolitan Books.

Engels, F. (1942) *The Origin of The Family, Private Property, and the State*. New York: International Publishers. (Original work published 1884).

Frazier, E.F. (1939) *The Negro Family in the United States*. Chicago: University of Chicago Press.

Gerstel, N. and Sarkisian, N. (2008) 'The Color of Family Ties: Race, Gender, and Extended Family Involvement' in S. Coontz, (ed.) *American Families: A Multicultural Reader*. New York: Routledge. pp. 146–152.

Glenn, E.N. (1983) 'Split Household, Small Produces, and Dual Wage Earner: An Analysis of Chinese American Family Strategies', *Journal of Marriage and the Family*, 45 (1): 35–46.

Glenn, E.N. (1986) *Issei, Nesei, War Bride: Three Generations of Japanese American Women in Domestic Service*. Philadelphia: Temple University Press.

Glenn, E.N. (1987) 'Gender and the Family' in B.B. Hess and M. Marx Ferree (eds) *Analyzing Gender*. Newberry Park, CA: Sage Publications. pp. 348–380.

Glenn, E.N. (1992) 'From Servitude to Service Work: Historical Continuities of Women's Paid and Unpaid Reproductive Labor', *Signs: Journal of Women in Culture and Society*, 18 (1): 1–44.

Glenn E.N. with Yap, S.G. (1994) 'Chinese American Families' in R.L. Taylor, (ed.). *Minority Families in the United States: Comparative Perspectives*. Englewood Cliffs, NJ: Prentice Hall. pp. 134–163.

Glenn, E.N. (2002) *Unequal Freedom: How Race and Gender Shaped American Citizenship and Labor*. Cambridge: Harvard University Press.

Griswold del Castillo, R. (1984) *La Familia*. Notre Dame, IN: University of Notre Dame Press.

Gutman, H. (1976) *The Black Family in Slavery and Freedom*. New York: Pantheon.

Hacker, A. (1996) 'The Racial Income Gap' in K.E. Rosenblum and T-M.C. Travis, (eds) *The Meaning of Difference*. New York: McGraw Hill. pp. 308–315.

Hartmann, H. (1976) 'Capitalism, Patriarchy, and Job Segregation by Sex', *Signs: Journal of Women in Culture and Society*, 1 (3), (Spring): 137–170.

Heller, C. (1966) *Mexican American Youth: Forgotten Youth at the Crossroads*. New York: Random House.

Hill, R.B. (1972) *The Strengths of Black Families*. New York: Emerson Hall.

Hill, S.A. (2005) *Black Intimacies: A Gender Perspective on Families and Relationships*. Walnut Creek, CA: Altamira Press.

Higginbotham, E.B. (1992) 'African American Women's History and the Metalanguage of Race', *Signs: Journal of Women in Culture and Society*, 17 (2): 251–274.

Hondagneu-Sotelo, P. (1995) 'Women and Children First: New Directions in Anti-Immigrant Politics', *Socialist Review*, 25 (1): 169–190.

Hondagneu-Sotelo, P. and Avila, E. (1997) '"I'm Here, But I'm There": The Meanings of Latina Transnational motherhood', *Gender & Society*, 11 (October): 548–571.

Hondagneu-Sotelo, P. (2001) *Domestica*. Berkeley: University of California Press.

Hondagneu-Sotelo, P. (2002) 'Families on the Frontier: From Braceros in the Fields to Braceras in the Home' in M.M. Suarez-Orozco and M.M. Paez, (eds) *Latinos: Remaking America*. Berkeley: University of California Press. pp. 259–273.

Hondagneu-Sotelo, P. (2003) 'Gender and Immigration: A Retrospective and Introduction' in P. Hondagneu-Sotelo (ed.) *Gender and U.S. Immigration: Contemporary Trends*. Berkeley: University of California Press. pp. 3–19.

Hunter, A.G. (2006) '(Re)Envisioning Cohabitation: A Commentary on Race, History, and Culture' in M. Durr and S.A. Hill, (eds) *Race, Work, and Family Life in the Lives of African Americans*. Lanham Hills, MD: Rowman & Littlefield Publishers, Inc. pp. 87–96.

Jarrett, R.L. (1994) 'Living Poor: Family Life among Single Parent, African-American Women', *Social Problems*, 41 (1) (February):30–49.

Jones, Jr. N.J. (1991) *Born a Child of Freedom, Yet a Slave: Mechanisms of Control and Strategies of Resistance in Antebellum South Carolina*. Middletown, CT: Wesleyan University Press.

Karraker, M.W. (2008) *Global Families*. Boston: Pearson Education, Inc.

Kingsbury, N. and Scanzoni, J. (1993) 'Structural Functionalism' in W.J. Doherty, P. Boss, R. La Rossa, W.R. Schumm, and S.K. Stienmetz, (eds) *Sourcebook of Family Theories*. New York: Plenum Press. pp. 195–216.

Kibria, N. (1994) 'Migration and Vietnamese Women: Remaking ethnicity' in M. Baca Zinn and B.T. Dill (eds) *Women of Color in U.S. Society*. Philadelphia: Temple University Press.

Ladner, J. (1971) *Tomorrow's Tomorrow: The Black Woman*. New York: Dubleday.

Lareau, A. (2003) *Unequal Childhoods: Class, Race, and Family Life*. Berkeley: University of California Press.

Leibow, E. (1967) *Talley's Corner: A Study of Streetcorner Men*. Boston: Little Brown.

Lichter, D.T. and Landale, N.S. (1995) 'Parental Work, Family Structure, and Poverty among Latino Children', *Journal of Marriage and the Family*, 57 (May): 346–354.

Lichter, D.T. and Qian, Z. (2004) Marriage and Family in a Multiracial Society.

The American People: Census 2000 in Reynolds Farley and John Hage (eds). *The American People: Census 2000*. New York: Russell Sage Foundation and Population Reference Bureau. pp. 169–200.

Lowry, R. (2005) 'The Coming Battle Over New Orleans', *National Review Online*, (Sept. 2): http.www.nationalreview.com/lowry200509021731.asp

McLanahan, S. and Sandefur, G. (1994) *Growing up with a Single Parent*. Cambridge: Harvard University Press.

Madsen, W. (1964) *The Mexican Americans of South Texas*. New York: Holt, Rinehart and Winston.

Marabel, M. (2008) 'Globalization and Racialization' in D. Stanley Eitzen and M. Baca Zinn, (eds) *Globalization: The Transformation of Social Worlds*. Belmont, CA: Wadsworth Cengage Learning. pp. 317–322.

Mitchell, J. (1966) 'Women: The Longest Revolution' *New Left Review*, (November/December) 44.

Morgan, D.H.J. (1975) *Social Theory and the Family*. London: Routledge and Kegan Paul.

Moran, R.F. (2008) 'Excerpt from Interracial Intimacy: The Regulation of Race and Romance, Antimiscegenation Laws And The Enforcement of Racial Boundaries' in S. Coontz, (ed) *American Families: A Multicultural Reader*. New York: Routledge.

Moynihan, D.P. (1965) *The Negro Family: The Case for National Action*. Washington, DC: Office of Policy Planning and Research, US Department of Labor.

Mullings, L. (1986) 'Uneven Development: Class, Race, and Gender in the United States before 1900' in E. Leacock, H.I. Safa, and contributors. *Women's Work*. South Hadley, MA: Bergin & Garvey. pp. 41–57.

Murray-McBride, V., Phillips Smith, E. and Hill, N.E. (2001) 'Race, Ethnicity, and Culture in Studies of Families of Context', *Journal of Marriage and the Family*, 63 (November): 911–914.

Naples, N.A. (1992) 'Activist Mothering: Cross Generational Continuity in the Community Work of Women from Low Income Neighborhoods', *Gender & Society*, (September): 441–463.

Omi, M. and Winant, H. (1994) *Racial Formation in the United States. From the 1960s to the 1990s.* New York: Routledge.

Osmond, M.W. (1987) 'Radical-Critical Theories' in M.B. Sussman and S. Steinmetz (eds) *Handbook of Marriage and the Family.* New York: Plenum. pp. 103–124.

Parrenas, R.S. (2000) 'Migrant Filipina Domestic Workers and the International Division of Reproductive Labor', *Gender & Society*, 14 (August): 560–580.

Parrenas, R.S. (2006) 'Mothering from a Distance: Emotions, Gender, and International Relations in Filipino Transnational Families' in S. Ferguson, (ed.) *Shifting the Center: Understanding Contemporary Families, Third Edition.* Boston: McGraw Hill. pp. 404–415.

Parrenas, R.S. (2001) *Servants of Globalization.* Stanford University Press.

Pardo, M. (1990) 'Mexican American Women Grassroots Community Activists: Mothers of East Los Angeles', *Frontiers: A Journal of Women Studies*, 11 (1): 1–7.

Parsons, T. (1942) 'Age and Sex in the Social Structure of the United States', *American Sociological Review*, 7(5): 604–616.

Patillo-McCoy, M. (1999) *Black Pickett Fences: Privilege and Peril Among the Black Middle Class.* Chicago: University of Chicago Press.

Pessar, P. (1995) 'On the Homefront and in the Workplace: Integrating Immigrant Women into Feminist Discourse', *Anthropological Quarterly*, 66 (January): 278–300.

Pyke, K. (2004) 'Immigrant Families in the U.S.' in J. Scott, J. Treas, and M. Richards (eds) *The Blackwell Companion to the Sociology of Families.* Oxford, UK: Blackwell Publishing, Ltd. pp. 253–269.

Qian, Z. (2005) 'Breaking the Last Taboo: Interracial Marriage in America', *Contexts*, 4 (4): 33–37.

Richie, B.E. (2009) 'The Social Construction of the "Immoral" Black Mother: Social Policy, Community Policing, and Effects on Youth Violence' in E. Higginbotham and M.L. Andersen (eds) *Race and Ethnicity in Society.* Belmont, CA: Thompson Wadsworth. pp. 352–359.

Roberts, D. (2009) 'Child Welfare as a Racial Justice Issue' in E. Higginbotham and M.L. Andersen (eds) *Race and Ethnicity in Society.* Belmont, CA: Thompson Wadsworth. pp. 352–359.

Robinson, W. (2008) 'Globalization and the Struggle for Immigrant Rights in the United States' in D. Stanley Eitzen and M. Baca Zinn (eds) *Globalization: The Transformation of Social Worlds.* Belmont, CA: Wadsworth Cengage Learning. pp. 99–105.

Rubin, G. (1975) 'The Traffic in Women: Notes on the "Political Economy" of Sex' in R.T. Reiter, (ed.), *Toward and Anthropology of Women.* New York: Monthly Review Press.

Rubel, A.J. (1966) *Across the Tracks: Mexican Americans in a Texas City.* Austin: University of Texas Press.

Sanchez, G.J. (1999a) 'Excerpts from Becoming Mexican American: Ethnicity, Culture, Identity in Chicano Los Angeles, 1900–1945' in S. Coontz, (ed.) *American Families: A Multicultural Reader.* New York: Routledge. pp. 128–152.

Sanchez, G.J. (1999b) 'Race, Nation, and Culture in Recent Immigration Studies', *Journal of American Ethnic History*, (Summer) 18 (4): 66–84.

Sarkisian, N. and Gerstel, N. (2004) 'Kin Support among Blacks and Whites: Race and Family Organization', *American Sociological Review*, 69 (6) (December): 812–837.

Sarkisian, N. and Gerstel, N. (2005) Ethnicity and Extended Families: Exploring Differences between Latinos/as and Euro Americans. Unpublished manuscript.

Schwede, L., Blumberg, R.L. and Chan, A.Y. (2005) *Complex Ethnic Households in America.* Lanham, MD: Rowman and Littlefield Publishers, Inc.

Segura, D. (1994) 'Working at Motherhood: Chicana and Mexican Immigrant Mothers and Employment' in E.N. Glenn, G. Change, and L. Rennie Forcey, (eds) *Mothering: Ideology, Experience, and Agency.* New York: Routledge. pp. 221–233

Shaw, A. (2004) 'Immigrant Families in the UK' in J. Scott, J. Treas, and M. Richards (eds) *The Blackwell Companion to the Sociology of Families.* Oxford, UK: Blackwell Publishing. pp. 270–286.

Smith, D.E. (1993) 'The Standard American Family: SNAF as an Ideological Code', *Journal of Family Issues*, 14 (1): 50–65.

Smith, J., Wallerstein, I. and Evers, H.D. (1985) *The Household and the World Economy*. Beverly Hills, CA: Sage.

Solinger, R. (2008) 'Race, Class, and Reproductive Politics in American History' in S. Coontz, (ed.) *American Families: A Multicultural History*. New York: Routledge. pp. 126–185.

Stack, C. (1974) *All Our Kin*. New York: Harper & Row.

Staples, R. and Mirande, A. (1988) 'Racial and Cultural Variations among American Families: A Decennial Review of the Literature on Minority Families', *Journal of Marriage and the Family*, 40(1): 604–616.

Taylor, R.L. (2000) 'Diversity within African American Families' in D.H. Demo, K.R. Allen, and M.A. Fine, (eds) *The Handbook of Family Diversity*. New York: Oxford University Press.

Thomas, D.L. and Wilcox, J.E. (1987) 'The Rise of Family Theory' in M.B. Sussman and S. Steinmetz, (eds) *Handbook of Marriage and the Family*. New York: Plenum. pp. 81–102.

Thorne, B. (1982) 'Feminist Thinking on the Family: An Overview' in B. Thorne and M. Yalom, (eds) *Rethinking the Family: Some Feminist Questions*. New York: Longman. pp. 1–24.

Uttal, L. (1999) 'Using Kin for Child Care; Embedment in the Socioeconomic Networks of Extended Families', *Journal of Marriage and the Family*, 61(4): 845–857.

Udel, L.J. (2001) 'Revision and Resistance: The Politics of Native Women's Motherwork', *Frontiers: A Journal of Women Studies*, 22 (1): 46–62.

Urdaneta, M.L. (1980) 'Chicana Use of Abortion: The Case of Alcala' in M. Melville, (ed.) *Twice a Minority: Mexican American Women*. St. Louis: C. V. Mosby. pp. 35–51.

Wagner, R. and Shaffer, D.M. (1980) 'Social Networks and Survival Strategies: An Exploratory Study of Mexican-American, Black and Anglo Female Family Heads in San Jose, California' in M. Melville, (ed.) *Twice a Minority: Mexican American Women*. St. Louis: C. V Mosby

White, M. (2005) 'Familial Influence in the Autobiographies of Black South African and African American Women Activists', *Michigan Family Review*, 10 (1): 27–44.

Wilson, W.J. (1987) *The Truly Disadvantaged: The Inner City, the Underclass, and Public Policy*. Chicago: University of Chicago Press.

Wilson, W.J. (1996) *When Work Disappears: The World of the New Urban Poor*. New York: Knopf.

Zavella, P. (1987) *Women's Work and Chicano Families*. Ithaca, NY: Cornell University Press.

15

Race, Ethnicity and Education: The Search for Explanations

James A. Banks and Caryn Park

Schools are sites of competition among different values and norms, interests, cultures and worldviews of diverse groups in multicultural nation-states. As one of society's key institutions, the role of schools in the reproduction and perpetuation of the dominant group culture has been well documented in the history of colonial projects in many different nations (Adams, 1995; Banks, 2009; Kincaid; 1988; Luchtenberg, 2004a; Parsons, 1982; Willinsky, 1998). Historically, schools in the United States have 'Americanised' immigrant and ethnic minority students by assimilating them into dominant Anglo-Saxon Protestant middle-class values, norms, and behaviours (Aguirre and Turner, 2001; Graham, 2005; Lieberson, 1980; Lomawaima, 2001; Lomawaima and McCarty, 2006).

In the United States, the United Kingdom, France and other Western societies, many racial, ethnic and language minority groups are marginalised, concentrated in lower-status occupations, experience limited social and economic mobility, are politically alienated, and do not participate fully in the civic community of their societies (Banks, 2009; Benhabib, 2004; Figueroa, 2004; Guinier, 2003; Koopmans et al., 2005; Solomos, 2005). Schools are integral parts of the social, economic and political structures of the societies in which they are embedded, and reinforce the social and economic stratifications within the societies in which they are located. Consequently, the status of racial, ethnic, cultural and language groups within the schools mirror their status in the larger society.

A number of issues and debates surface at the intersection of race, ethnicity and education in the United States and other multicultural nation-states that are grappling with problems related to equal access to economic opportunity and social mobility (Wilson, 1999). During the 1960s and 1970s, ethnic revitalisation movements occurred in the United States as well as in many other nations (Banks, 2006b; Banks and Lynch, 1986). An important goal of these movements was to reform schools so that students from diverse racial, ethnic, cultural and language groups would experience academic success and be able to attain social mobility and structural inclusion into the mainstream society.

In response to the ethnic revitalisation movements, many school reforms were implemented in the United States as well as in nations such as the United Kingdom, Canada, Germany and Australia (Banks, 2009; Banks and Banks, 2004), including affirmative action (Guinier, 1996, 2003), desegregation (Orfield and Lee, 2006), bilingual education (Luchtenberg, 2004b; Moran and Hakuta, 2001; Valdés, 2001), intergroup relations programmes (Stephan and Vogt, 2004) and culturally responsive teaching (Gay, 2000). Many testing and assessment procedures were also reformed and made more culturally sensitive and reflective of the cultures of students from diverse groups (Kornhaber, 2004).

The educational reforms that were implemented in the United States resulted in significant gains for ethnic minorities, including larger percentages graduating from high schools, fewer dropouts and the narrowing of the test-score gap between mainstream students and students from marginalised racial, ethnic and language groups (Gay, 2005). Most of these achievement gains occurred in the 1980s. This progress was slowed during the late 1980s when the commitment to equal educational opportunity waned and an influential neoconservative movement in the United States emerged.

The influence of the neoconservative movement became strongest during the second George W. Bush administration (2000–2008). However, early signs of its influence were manifested with the publication of Arthur R. Jensen's article in the *Harvard Educational Review* in 1969, in which he argued that educational reforms had limited potential to equalise educational opportunity because of the genetic differences between African Americans and Whites. Jensen's argument was enhanced and extended with the publication of *The Bell Curve* by Herrnstein and Murray in 1994.

In the United States and other Western nations such as the United Kingdom and Japan, an emphasis on high-stakes national testing and assessment emerged in the 1990s. The advocates of national testing argue that it is designed to increase educational equality for all students, to create high academic standards, and to hold educators accountable for student achievement. However, the focus on national testing is having mixed results in US schools (Meier and Wood, 2004) as well as in the United Kingdom and Japan (Hirasawa, 2009; Gillborn, 2008; Gillborn and Youdell, 2000; Luchtenberg, 2004b; Tomlinson, 2004, 2008). The critics of high-stakes tests argue that they reinforce the status quo, further marginalise students from low-status groups, and have resulted in school practices that have increased the achievement gap between mainstream White students and most ethnic minority students (Gillborn, 2008). The exceptions in the United States are Asian American students such as Asian Indians, Chinese and Japanese American students. The test scores of some of these groups exceed those of mainstream Whites in the United States. Indian and Chinese students are also the highest achieving students in Britain (Tomlinson, 2004).

THE ACADEMIC ACHIEVEMENT GAP

The academic achievement gap between majority and minority students from diverse racial, ethnic, social-class and language groups is indicative of the struggles to advance educational equity in many different nations (Banks, 2009). By analysing some of the debates that surround this seemingly intractable problem in the United States, we will illuminate some of the controversies that surround issues of educational equity in various nations. Although we focus on the literature, trends and developments of the United States, we incorporate literature and developments in other nations (Banks, 2009; Banks and Banks, 2004; Figueroa, 2004; Gillborn, 2008; Gillborn and Youdell, 2000; Luchtenberg, 2004a; Tomlinson, 2001). Banks' work in different societies over several decades has enabled him to observe significant parallels in educational inequality and interventions in the United States and other nations (Banks, 2009; Banks, 2004a; Banks, 2006a; Banks, 2005). We hope that readers in various nations will be able to use the concepts and analyses we present in this chapter to examine educational inequality and interventions within their own societies.

We examine seven explanations or paradigms that have been constructed by social scientists and educators to explain the academic achievement gap and to conceptualise and devise school reforms to reduce it. We begin by describing the multicultural education movement in the United States, the academic achievement gap, and the No Child Left Behind (NCLB) Act that was enacted by the US Congress in 2001 and signed by President George W. Bush in 2002. We then describe and analyse seven explanations of the achievement gap and discuss the intersection of race, ethnicity and education. We describe the different explanations – or paradigms – not as value-free or neutral, but rather as reflecting the goals, assumptions and interests of their creators, and examine the implications of each paradigm. We conclude that no single explanation adequately explains the problem of the academic achievement gap, stressing the need for a multifactor paradigm as well as the need for further research and theorising on this complex and significant educational problem.

MULTICULTURAL EDUCATION: BRIEF HISTORICAL BACKGROUND

In the aftermath of the *Brown vs. Board of Education* decision of 1954 – which made *de jure* school segregation illegal in the United States – and in response to the Civil Rights Movement, the war on poverty, and the ethnic revitalisation

movements of the 1960s and 1970s, schools, colleges and universities implemented ethnic studies courses and reformed curricula to make them reflect more
accurately the diversity within US society. One of the hopes of educational
researchers and scholars was that ethnic studies content and perspectives in the
school curriculum would enhance the academic achievement of students from
minority groups and help them develop a strong sense of identify and empowerment. These scholars also hoped that ethnic content would help all students –
including White middle-class students – to develop positive racial attitudes and
behaviours.

When the schools implemented ethnic studies courses and units, the academic
achievement of most minority students and low-income students continued to lag
substantially behind that of White middle-class students (Banks and Banks,
2004). Educational scholars and researchers began to realise that curriculum
reform is a necessary but not sufficient condition for school transformation and
change. Consequently, the scope of the ethnic studies movement was broadened
to include a focus on all of the major variables of the school environment, such
as teacher attitudes and expectations, testing and assessment, the languages and
dialects sanctioned by the schools and school norms and values. This broader
movement became known as *multiethnic education* (Banks, 2006a). Later, when
the focus of the school reform movement broadened to include social class,
gender and exceptionality, it became known as *multicultural education* (Banks,
2006a).

The major goal of multicultural education is to actualise equal educational
opportunities for students from all racial, ethnic, language and income groups
so that they will acquire the knowledge, skills and attitudes needed to participate
fully both within their cultural communities and in mainstream society. The
history of multicultural education goes back to scholars and activists such as
W. E. B. DuBois, Carter G. Woodson, Anna Julia Cooper and George Sánchez,
and their hopes and demands for schools to be reformed so that they would
more accurately reflect the histories, cultures, hopes and dreams of the diverse
racial, ethnic and language groups within US society and schools (Banks, 1996).

THE ACADEMIC ACHIEVEMENT GAP AND THE NO CHILD LEFT BEHIND ACT

The theory and research of multicultural education have become increasingly
complex and nuanced since the field's birth in the 1960s and 1970s. However,
multicultural education has not yet been fully implemented in US schools or in
schools in other nations such as the United Kingdom, Canada and Australia
(Banks, 2009; Gay, 2004). The promise of multicultural education has been only
partially realised, educational inequality is intractable, and the achievement gap
is entrenched in many nations. The 'academic achievement gap' is used in the

United States to describe the difference in the standardised test scores of White mainstream students and marginalised minority students on measures such as the National Assessment of Educational Progress (NAEP) (National Center for Education Statistics, 2008) and other standardised measures of academic achievement used in individual states. The achievement gap also refers to the consequences of this gap in high-stakes testing, such as unequal outcomes in school dropout rates, enrollment in classes for gifted students, admission to colleges and graduate and professional programmes, and degree completion rates (Ladson-Billings, 2006; Talbert-Johnson, 2004). The achievement gap between ethnic minority and majority group students also exists in other Western democratic societies, including African Caribbean, Pakistani, and Bangladeshi students in Britain (Figueroa, 2004; Tomlinson, 2004), Turkish students in Germany (Luchtenberg, 2004b), and North African students in France (Lorcerie, 2004). These findings suggest that the achievement gap is a problem in many multicultural nations (Banks, 2009).

Conceptually, an achievement gap can refer either to a gap between subgroups of students, or a discrepancy between a fixed standard and the actual performance of any group of students (Fusarelli, 2004). Perhaps because of the implication that the performance of middle-class White students serves as the standard against which ethnic minority and lower-income families are measured, some scholars have challenged the terminology, opting instead to use terms such as *opportunity gap*, *resource gap* and *service gap*[1] (Washington School Research Center, 2002; Winerman, 2004). Ladson-Billings (2006) uses *education debt* in order to shift the stigmatising and burdensome focus from low-income students and ethnic minority students to the long-term underlying problems stemming from inequality in the US educational system and the larger society.

The academic achievement of different groups of minority students varies and has changed over time. Groups such as African American, Mexican American and Puerto Rican American students made gains on several indices of the NAEP during the 1980s (Gay, 2005). However, the achievement gap has actually increased in the United States since 1988 at all ages and in all subjects tested (Campbell et al., 2000). The achievement scores of some groups of Asian American students – such as Japanese Americans, Chinese Americans and Asian Indians – equal or exceed those of Whites. The scores of other ethnic minority students lag considerably behind that of Whites.

Under the leadership of President George W. Bush, Congress enacted the NCLB in 2001 to address the academic achievement gap between White middle-class students and low-income and minority students. One of the stated goals of the act is to make school districts and states accountable for the academic achievement of students from diverse racial, ethnic and language groups. The act requires states to formulate rigorous standards in reading, mathematics and science and to annually test all students in grades three through eight in these subjects. The act also requires that the results of the assessments be

disaggregated by poverty, race, ethnicity, disability and limited English proficiency (Guthrie, 2003).

The NCLB Act has intensified discussion and debate about the achievement
gap and evoked an acid debate between its supporters and critics. The defenders
of the act argue that by requiring school districts to disaggregate achievement
data by race, ethnicity, disability and limited English proficiency, the act focuses
required attention on the need to improve educational equality for students in
these groups (Hess and Finn, 2004; Peterson and Hess, 2003). Its critics claim
that the act is grossly underfunded and that it has caused teachers to focus on
narrow basic skills and test preparation rather than on the goals of a broad liberal
education needed to prepare students to live and function effectively in a multicultural nation and world. The critics of the act have also described the negative
effects the act is having on ethnic minority and low-income students (Amrein and
Berliner, 2002; Meier and Wood, 2004). The critics argue that these students are
being penalised for not meeting high standards but are not provided the resources
and opportunities needed to meet the standards. Consequently, the NCLB Act is
increasing rather than reducing educational equality.

Despite the accumulating body of research documenting the negative effects
of the NCLB Act (Amrein and Berliner, 2002; Fusarelli, 2004; Meier and
Wood, 2004; Sleeter, 2005), it has given issues related to minority student
achievement and equality high visibility in educational research, practice and
debate in the United States. A member of the Louisiana State Board of Education
stated:

> We will never reach our goals as a state if we don't improve the performance of our poor
> and black students. ... If you don't measure it, then you don't count it. If you don't count it,
> then you don't pay attention. ... And if you don't pay attention to it, then you don't fix it.
> (Mizell, cited in Fusarelli, 2004: 75)

THE SEARCH FOR EXPLANATIONS

While the study of the academic achievement gap between White middle-class
students and ethnic minority students has taken centrestage in current educational debates in the United States, the search for explanations of the achievement gap has been ongoing for several decades, dating back to the war on
poverty during the 1960s and 1970s. A number of different paradigms or theories
of the middle range have been developed to explain the achievement gap. Kuhn
uses *paradigm* to describe the 'entire constellation of beliefs, values, techniques,
and so on by members of a given [scientific] community' (1970: 15). The
laws, principles, explanations and theories of a discipline are also part of its
paradigm.

Paradigm in this chapter describes an interrelated set of facts, concepts, generalisations and theories that attempt to explain human behaviour or social phenomenon and that imply policy and action (Banks, 1984). A paradigm, which is
also a set of explanations, has specific goals, assumptions and values that can be

described. Paradigms compete with one another in theory, research and policy. This is very much the case with the paradigms that influence educational research, policy, and action.

The way in which we conceptualise paradigm in this chapter is similar to the way that Merton (1968) defines *theories of the middle range*. Merton defines theories of the middle range as explanations that – in contrast to grand theories – explain only part of human behaviour or a social phenomenon. He writes, 'Middle-range theories deal with delimited aspects of social phenomenon, as is indicated by their labels' (1968: 39–40). The paradigms that we describe in this chapter are theories of the middle range because each provides a partial rather than a holistic or complete explanation of the achievement gap between low-income students, ethnic minority students and middle-class White students.

Banks (1984, 1986, 2006b, 2009) has used the paradigm concept in previous publications to categorise and examine explanations related to minority student achievement. In this chapter, we build upon and expand on Banks' previous work by describing and analysing seven paradigms that are used to explain the achievement gap between White middle-class students and ethnic minority students such as African Americans, Mexican Americans and American Indians. To some extent, we discuss these paradigms in the historical order in which they were constructed and became influential. Each of the paradigms reflects the positionality, values and cultural experiences of the researchers, social scientists and educators who constructed them. Before describing the paradigms, we will discuss the ways in which knowledge reflects its creators (Code, 1991; Collins, 2000).

Values and the development of educational paradigms

The cultural communities in which individuals are socialised are also epistemological communities that have shared beliefs, perspectives and knowledge. Critical social science scholars such as Code (1991), Collins (2000) and Harding (1991) have developed important critiques of mainstream empirical knowledge and have argued that despite its claims, modern science is not value-free but reflects important human interests and normative assumptions that should be identified, discussed and examined (Banks, 1996).

The localised values and cultural perspectives of mainstream researchers are often considered neutral objective and universal. Many of these value-laden perspectives, paradigms and knowledge systems become institutionalised within mainstream popular culture, the schools and US colleges and universities because they reinforce existing beliefs and practices that are considered objective, universal and neutral. A claim of neutrality enables a researcher to support the status quo without publicly acknowledging that support (Hubbard, cited in Burt and Code, 1995). The neutrality claim also enables the researcher to avoid what Code (1987) calls 'epistemic responsibility'.

Institutionalised concepts, theories and paradigms considered neutral often privilege mainstream students and disadvantage low-income students and ethnic minority students. These knowledge systems and paradigms are often used to justify the educational neglect of marginalised students, to privilege groups who are advantaged and to legitimise and justify discriminatory politics and practices (Banks, 1998; Kana'iaupuni, 2004).

Many of the paradigms that influence the education of ethnic minority and low-income students were constructed by scholars and researchers outside their cultural communities or by scholars within their communities that Banks (1998; 2006c) has described as 'indigenous outsiders'. These are scholars who were socialised within the ethnic community but for a variety of complex reasons have acquired the values, perspectives and goals of the outsiders – usually outsiders within the mainstream community.

The genetic paradigm

Most respected geneticists and social scientists today discredit the genetic paradigm. However, it remains one of the most tenacious and insidious explanations that influences educators in subtle and often unconscious ways. It maintains that there are distinct racial groups that have hereditary biological characteristics such as intellectual and physical abilities, and that some groups are superior to others. The construction of a group as genetically inferior is almost always done by researchers outside the group and almost never by those within it (Banks, 1998; 2006; Gould, 1981). Researchers within a racial or ethnic group usually produce research that contradicts the claim that their group is genetically inferior (Bond, 1934; Sánchez, 1932).

The genetic paradigm legitimises beliefs and stereotypes that many educators have about the intellectual ability of African Americans and other ethnic minorities. It can also adversely affect the behaviour of the groups that it victimises. When beliefs about the inferiority of a group become institutionalised within a society, the victimised group may internalise these beliefs, which can influence their behaviour (Howard and Hammond, 1985; Steele, 2004).

Some early advocates of the genetic paradigm believed that human racial groups had separate origins and that Caucasians were superior to other races (Nott and Gliddon, 1854; see Pettigrew, 1964, for a critique). These scientists used craniometry – the comparative measurement of skulls – to make claims about racial group differences (Gould, 1981). When the work of these scientists was discredited, the goals of scientific racism were pursued through intelligence testing, 'a more 'direct' path to the same invalid goal of ranking groups by mental worth' (Gould, 1981: 108).

The roots of current debates surrounding race and intelligence testing can be traced back to Sir Francis Galton. Galton applied Darwin's ideas of natural selection to human intellect and theorised that White, middle-class English men were the most evolved, while the Irish, the English working-class and the groups that were colonised by the English were genetically inferior (Rust and Golombok, 1999). Since their inception, intelligence tests have justified and reinforced racial and social-class stratification (Kornhaber, 2004).

The genetic paradigm re-emerges almost every decade and acquires a degree of legitimacy. *The Testing of Negro Intelligence* by Audrey M. Shuey gave the genetic paradigm legitimacy and visibility when it was published in 1958. Shuey examined 382 studies that were conducted over a 50-year period, and concluded that the evidence indicated 'the presence of native differences between Negroes and whites as determined by intelligence tests' (1958: 521).

The genetic paradigm was further given legitimacy in 1969 when Jensen published his controversial study of Black–White intelligence in the prestigious *Harvard Educational Review*. At the time of its publication, there had been tremendous momentum within the United States to address educational inequalities. Early childhood education programmes for low-income children such as Head Start and Follow Through had been implemented on a wide scale as part of the nation's war on poverty. When Jensen published his article, the evidence for the effectiveness of compensatory programmes was contested. He argued that compensatory programmes were limited in their ability to improve the academic achievement of African American students because of the strong effects that genetics have on intellectual ability. The genetic paradigm was most recently revived by the publication of *The Bell Curve* by Richard Herrnstein and Charles Murray in 1994, which remained on the *New York Times* best-seller list for 15 weeks and sold a half million copies in the first 18 months after publication.

Omi (2001) states that there is an 'enormous gap between the scientific rejection of race as a concept, and the popular acceptance of it as an important organising principle of individual identity and collective consciousness' (p. 243). Although most social and natural scientists have concluded that race is not a scientific category, rigid and essentialised differences between racial and ethnic groups are often perceived as natural and regarded as 'common sense' (Haney-López, 2003). As Solomos (2003) perceptively states:

> Notwithstanding the long history of debates on [racism] it has long been recognized that races do not exist in any scientifically meaningful sense. Yet it is clear that in many societies people continue to act as if race exists as a fixed objective category, and this belief is reflected in political discourses and at the level of popular ideas (p. 10).

Omi and Winant state that the 'determination of racial categories is an intensely political process' (1994: 3). History demonstrates that racial categories and their meanings will keep changing, and that groups with power will construct race in ways that benefit themselves and disadvantage powerless and marginalised groups (Rodríguez, 2000). The ways in which race and ethnicity are conceptualised influence how all students are educated. Race is a social construct with very real educational, social, economic and political consequences.

The genetic paradigm continually re-emerges to justify the privileges of some racial and social-class groups and to deny educational opportunities to others. We view the genetic paradigm as detrimental to education and lacking in scientific rigour and validity (Gould, 1981; Omi and Winant, 1994). Dismantling the genetic paradigm in education requires educators to closely monitor the progress of ethnic minority students while exposing race as a socially constructed category of power. It is also essential to construct and disseminate alternative explanations for the unequal educational outcomes of historically disenfranchised groups. In the remainder of this chapter, we critically examine six other paradigms that seek to explain the achievement gap between most ethnic minority students, low-income students and White middle-class students.

The cultural deprivation paradigm

Cultural deprivation was one of the first theories to emerge in the United States in the 1960s to explain the academic achievement of low-income students. Cultural deprivation theorists believe that characteristics such as poverty, fatherless homes and social disorganisation cause children from low-income communities to experience 'cultural deprivation' and 'irreversible cognitive deficits' (Bereiter and Engelmann, 1966; Bloom et al., 1965; Riessman, 1962). Unlike the geneticists, these theorists believe that the social environment influences cognition and social behaviours. They think schools not only have a responsibility to help low-income students to learn, but that they have the ability to achieve this goal.

Cultural deprivation theorists assume that the learning problems of low-income students result primarily from the cultures in which they are socialised. They will achieve academically if the school is able to compensate for their deprived cultural environment and enable them to acquire the knowledge, skills and attitudes needed to function effectively in the mainstream society, including the schools. Cultural deprivation theorists see the major problem as the culture of the students rather than the culture of the school.

The cultural deprivation theory was severely criticised during the late 1960s and the 1970s (Ginsburg, 1972; Valentine, 1968). However, it reemerged in the 1990s in a robust way with the publications of books such as *A Framework for Understanding Poverty* by Ruby K. Payne (1996), *Losing the Race: Self-Sabotage in Black America* by John McWhorter (2000); and *No Excuses: Closing the Racial Gap in Learning* by Abigail Thernstrom and Stephen Thernstrom (2003).

Payne's (1996) book is highly influential among US school practitioners. It essentialises people living in poverty and provides lists of characteristics that supposedly typify people living in poverty, the middle class and people who are wealthy. Payne's work perpetuates oversimplified and misleading ideas about social class stratification in the United States. The Thernstroms compare the family and community cultures of Asians, Hispanics and African Americans. They conclude that the families and community of these groups are major factors in their academic achievement and that Black culture is one of the major impediments to high academic achievement by African American students. They write:

> There is a gap that appears very early in the life of black children; *something about the lives of these children is limiting their intellectual development*. Some risk factors have been identified by scholars; low-birth weight; single-parent households, and birth to a very young

mother. There seem to be racial and ethnic differences in parenting practices as well, and the relatively small number of books in black households and the extraordinary amount of time spent watching TV appear related to parenting practices. (2003: 147, emphasis added)

We are sympathetic to the social scientists and educators who constructed the cultural deprivation paradigm in the 1960s (Bereiter and Engelmann, 1966; Bloom et al., 1965; Riessman, 1962). At the time, this paradigm served as an important counter to the belief that low-income students achieved poorly in school because of their genetic characteristics (Jensen, 1969; Shuey, 1958). However, the cultural deprivation paradigm has become outdated in many ways, not only because of the growing body of research which indicates that culturally responsive teaching can increase the academic achievement of low-income students, but also because it conflates cultural difference with the conditions of poverty (Thernstrom and Thernstrom, 2003). Consequently, middle-class Anglo American culture and values are constructed as the standard and norm; low-income students and their families are considered 'lacking' in culture.

Sociologist Bonilla-Silva (2003) has called the cultural deprivation paradigm *cultural racism*. He argues that the fixing of 'cultural' traits such as inappropriate values or family disorganisation to low-income racial groups serves the same purpose as the genetic paradigm, while avoiding the criticism and stigma attached to genetic explanations.

The approach taken by cultural deprivation theorists is inconsistent with the goal of schools in a democratic society. By alienating students from their home and community cultures and showing little respect for these cultures, by blaming their cultures for their academic failures rather than the school and the larger society, cultural deprivation theorists violate the principles of *cultural democracy* (Banks, 2004a; Drachsler, 1920; Ramírez and Castañeda, 1974), *civic equality* and *recognition* (Gutmann, 2004). Ramírez and Castañeda maintain that schools in a democratic society should foster *cultural democracy* as well as political democracy. Gutmann argues that civic equality and recognition require schools to recognise the community cultures and languages of students from diverse groups. Cultural democracy, recognition and equality give culturally and linguistically diverse students the right to maintain important aspects of their community cultures and languages while participating fully in the national civic culture and community (Carmichael and Hamilton, 1967; Sizemore, 1973; Wong Fillmore, 2005), as long as they do not conflict with the shared democratic ideals of the nation-state.

The cultural difference paradigm

Unlike the cultural deprivation paradigm, the cultural difference paradigm rejects the idea that students of colour have cultural deficits. Cultural difference theorists believe that groups such as African Americans, Mexican Americans and American Indians have strong, rich and diverse cultures (Boykin and Allen, 2004; Delpit and Dowdy, 2002; Ladson-Billings, 1994; Moll and González, 2004).

These cultures, they argue, consist of languages, values, behavioural styles and perspectives that can enrich the lives of all students. Schools frequently fail to help ethnic minority and low-income students achieve because they ignore or try to alienate these students from their home and community cultures and languages (Wong Fillmore, 2005). Proponents of cultural difference are critical of the value assumptions underlying deficit thinking and argue that understanding cultural *conflicts* rather than *deficits* are the key to explaining underachievement (Banks and Banks, 2004; Baratz and Baratz, 1970; Delpit, 1995; Gay, 2000; Ladson-Billings, 1994).

Cultural difference theorists believe that the school must change in ways that will allow it to respect and reflect the rich cultural strengths of students from diverse groups and use teaching strategies that are consistent with their cultural characteristics. Banks has called this approach to teaching 'equity pedagogy' (Banks, 2004b). It is also known in the literature as 'culturally relevant' (Ladson-Billings, 1994) and 'culturally responsive' teaching (Gay, 2000).

Cultural difference theorists frequently cite research that shows how the cultures of the school and of ethnic minority and low-income youth differ in values, behaviours (Gay, 2000), languages (Heath, 1983; Lee, 1995; Valdés, 2001), dialects (Delpit and Dowdy, 2002; Smitherman, 2000) and home cultures (Moll and González, 2004). Studies by John (1972) and Heath (1982) are examples of these types of studies. John described the ways in which verbal interactions differ in the school and in the homes of Navajo students. Heath explained how language use differs among White middle-class teachers, the White working-class and the African American working-class.

Some studies provide empirical support for the premise that when teachers use culturally responsive pedagogy, the academic achievement of minority students increases. Au (1980) found that if teachers used participation structures in lessons that were similar to the Hawaiian speech event 'talk story', the reading achievement of Native Hawaiian students increased significantly. Lee's (1995, 2007) research indicates that the achievement of African American students increases when they are taught literary interpretation with lessons that use the African American practice of signifying. Moll et al. (1992) found that when teachers gain an understanding of the 'funds of knowledge' of Mexican American households and community networks – and incorporate this knowledge into their teaching – Mexican American students become more active and engaged learners. A study by Ladson-Billings (1995) indicates that the ability to scaffold student learning by bridging home and community cultures is one of the important characteristics of effective teachers of African American students.

An increasing body of research provides empirical support for the cultural difference paradigm (Banks and Banks, 2004). An important challenge to this body of work is to accurately describe the enormous diversity *within* different ethnic, racial and language groups and to avoid *essentialising* these groups or their experiences. Some of the earliest work within the cultural difference paradigm essentialised racial and ethnic groups by claiming that ethnic groups had specific and static learning and motivational styles (For a review and critique of this research see Irvine and York, 2001; and Tyler et al., 2008).

Some research and theory on learning styles, if misinterpreted, can contribute to the stereotyping of group differences and the acceptance of racial classifications. Lee (2003) has pointed out that a common problem in discussions of cultural difference or diversity is that culture is conceptualised as though it were a fixed trait. Gutierrez and Rogoff (2003) have warned against a simple 'matching strategy' of overlaying or mapping culture onto racial groups, or lapsing into a 'one style per person' mode of thinking, assuming that an individual student's membership in a group automatically tells teachers about his or her preferred ways of learning (p. 19). Gutierrez and Rogoff argue that this overgeneralisation can lead to a kind of cultural tracking, where students receive instruction based on group categorisation. Unfortunately, this strategy does not help educators develop a nuanced understanding of the history of the individual student's participation in her cultural community, nor does it account for within-group variation or change.

Lorber (2001) offers a potential solution to the tension between the pragmatic need to maintain racial categories and the visionary need to reject them. In her work on gender, she recommends that researchers examine similarities and differences between individuals first – then group them into new categories that are more useful and meaningful – rather than try to fit individuals into already existing and problematic categories. Educational researchers and theorists should not essentialise race or culture, but rather should design educational interventions that reflect the complexity of the social, historical and political contexts in which conceptions of race and culture are formed.

Multicultural education – whose major goal is to reform schools so that students from diverse racial, ethnic, language, and social-class groups will experience educational equality – is most consistent with the cultural difference paradigm. This paradigm is a critical response to cultural deficit thinking, that is, the notion that ethnic minority students and low-income students 'lack' culture, and that the solution is to expose these students to the mainstream American culture in order for them to thrive in school and in society.

The cultural ecology paradigm

The anthropologist John Obgu hypothesised that the poor academic achievement of African Americans was due primarily to their opposition to White mainstream culture and the fear of acting White (Fordham and Ogbu, 1986; Ogbu, 2001). Ogbu distinguished two types of racial minorities: *immigrant* or *voluntary* and *castelike* or *involuntary*. Voluntary immigrants came to the United States because they viewed it as a land of opportunity and hope. Castelike minorities are groups that have experienced institutionalised racism and discrimination in the United States. Voluntary immigrants – such as immigrants from China, India and Jamaica – are more academically successful than castelike minorities because they tend to embrace US mainstream values and behaviours that are manifested in the schools.

Castelike minorities such as African Americans and Mexican Americans resist the academic values and behaviours institutionalised in the schools because of fictive kinship, which cause them to reject mainstream institutions and values. As they have been victimised by structural racism and discrimination in US society, castelike minorities have fictive kinship ties and a sense of peoplehood that are oppositional to mainstream American values and cultures. These groups view assimilation into mainstream culture – including high academic achievement – as a violation of their fictive kinship bonds with members of their racial or ethnic group. They also view academic achievement as 'acting White' (Fordham and Ogbu, 1986). Even though most of the barriers to structural integration and inclusion into US society have been eliminated, castelike minorities still believe that these barriers are real and that success within US society is severely limited.

Ogbu (2003) believed that in order for African Americans to experience academic success, significant changes had to be made in Black culture and within the Black community. In other words, to increase the academic achievement of its youth, the Black community must socialise its children in ways that will enable them to value and assimilate mainstream values, especially those related to academic achievement. In his last published study, which was conducted in Shaker Heights, Ohio (a suburb of Cleveland) in a middle-class African American community, Ogbu (2003) concluded that the oppositional behaviour among Black students was consistent across social classes. The middle-class African American students in Shaker Heights – like the low-income Black students described in his earlier studies – were also oppositional to White mainstream culture.

A number of social scientists have described serious limitations in Ogbu's cultural ecology theory and the research that supports it (Carter, 2004; Gobo and Foster, 2004; Tyson et al., 2004). These criticisms have been both empirical and theoretical. Tyson et al. provide a comprehensive review of studies that test Ogbu's acting-White hypothesis. Studies by Ainsworth-Darnell and Downey (1998) and Cook and Ludwig (1998) did not confirm Ogbu's acting White hypothesis nor his oppositional culture hypothesis.

Tyson and colleagues tested Ogbu's hypotheses in a comprehensive study in North Carolina schools. In their review, Tyson et al. did find several studies that supported Ogbu's hypotheses (Bergin and Cooks, 2002; Ford and Harris, 1996; Horvat and Lewis, 2003; Steinberg et al., 1992). In their own study, they found a 'general sentiment against high academic achievement among adolescents in North Carolina, regardless of race' (2004: 2). Peer pressure against academic achievement existed among African American youths at the high school level only when Black students made up a very small percentage of advanced placement and honour classes. They conclude, 'Black under-representation produces the toxic environment that leads to racialized oppositionality. Black students legitimately view those classes as the property of white students; they are overwhelmingly excluded' (2004: 2).

Ogbu (2003) did not compare the attitudes of Black and White students regarding high academic achievement, which was a serious weakness in his research methodology. Ferguson (2002) studied a sample of 34,128 students in fifteen middle- and upper-middle-income school districts. He found that about 90 percent of the students from each of the racial and ethnic groups in his sample indicated that their friends regarded studying hard to get good grades as 'either important or somewhat important to them'. The largest percentage answering '*very* important' was among African Americans (56 percent), while the smallest percentage was among whites (42 percent)' (emphasis in original) (2002: 18). These findings further contradict Ogbu's observation that African American students do not value academic achievement.

Ogbu's (2003) theory explains Black failure but not Black success. Although they are largely invisible in the educational research literature, many African Americans students are academically successful and do not view academic achievement as 'acting White'. Most students, especially adolescents, do not want to be viewed as highly academic by their peers. The research by Ainsworth-Darnell and Downey (1998) and Cook and Ludwig (1998) indicate that this phenomenon is not limited to African American students, as was suggested by Ogbu.

Valenzuela (1999) examined Ogbu's (2001) 'oppositional culture' hypothesis in an ethnographic study of Mexican American and immigrant youth. She found that the students in her study did not equate achievement with 'acting White'. Instead, they made an important distinction between *education* and *schooling*. The students opposed the subtractive assimilation processes of schooling but valued education highly.

The cultural ecology paradigm has received attention and influence that far exceed its theoretical strength and empirical support. We can only surmise that its visibility and influence reflect the fact that it contains a message that is highly consistent with the beliefs, perceptions and attitudes that many mainstream educators have about African American culture and students. Research is now emerging that challenges some of the major tenets of this paradigm (Carter, 2005). Hopefully, this research will lead to significant modifications within the cultural ecology paradigm and reduce its visibility and influence among educators and policymakers. This paradigm became popular in the press and among the general public before it had been carefully reviewed and critiqued by the scientific community. It diverted attention from the ways in which mainstream school culture teaches students to devalue their home cultures and languages and blamed low-income African American students for their academic failures while giving little attention to the structural factors which victimise them.

The protective disidentification paradigm

The psychologist Claude Steele (1992, 2004) uses an experimental approach to demonstrate a process of protective disidentification, which occurs as a response to *stereotype threat*. Steele's theory focuses on students who are particularly confident as well as competent in a domain such as mathematics or language arts, and as a result, identify with that domain. Stereotype threat is a general threat not tied to the psychology of particular stigmatised groups. It can apply to members of any group, such as females, about whom a negative reputation or stereotype exists (e.g., that females are not as good as males in math). When individuals sense the possibility of conforming to the group stereotype or being judged in terms of the stereotype, it becomes threatening to their sense of self. In an attempt to protect their sense of self, students may respond to stereotype threat by disidentifying with the domain and consequently no longer allowing themselves to be vulnerable to the potential threat. Steele describes the detrimental effect that stereotype threat can have on students who are among 'the academic vanguard of their group' (2004: 686).

In a series of experiments with female college students who were high math achievers, Steele (2004) and colleagues confirmed that women performed equal to men when they were told that the difficult math test they were about to take produced no gender differences. Women performed less well than men did when they were told that the test produced gender differences, even though they took the same test.

In another study, Steele and Aronson (1995) conducted two experiments. In the first, Black and White students attending a prestigious university were divided into two groups: one group was told they were taking a test that would diagnose their intellectual ability, and the other was told they were taking a test unrelated to intellectual ability. As predicted by the stereotype threat hypothesis, the Black students greatly underperformed compared to White students in the first condition in which they thought they were being tested on their intellectual ability, while they equaled White students' performance in the test they believed was non-diagnostic of their intellectual ability. In another experiment, subjects were asked to record their race on a demographic questionnaire just prior to taking a test that was described as non-diagnostic. This treatment alone was enough to depress the performance of domain-identified Black students.

Steele (2004) distinguishes stereotype threat from a more general internalisation of racism manifesting itself as self-doubt or self-hatred. He argues that a stereotype is only threatening if one identifies in the specific domain. If one is not already domain identified, then the stereotype is not as threatening. He also states that students who are less identified with the domain may also underperform because they may be less motivated to succeed, thus contributing to the group's overall underperformance in comparison with groups who are not stereotyped in this domain. Disidentification can become a group norm that is 'sustained by normative pressure from the in-group as well as by stereotype threat in the setting' (Steele, 2004: 696, n. 4).

Steele (2004) interprets African American students' high self-esteem despite low school performance as evidence that these students have disidentified with the domain of schooling. The prospects for identification with school seem much less certain for these students than do the prospects for peer-identification. An important difference between the protective disidentification paradigm and the cultural ecology paradigm is that Steele believes that students can be successful and invested in school and still be at risk of dropping out. He observed this phenomenon frequently among Black college students. Even though they often came to the university with more skills and competencies than some White students, they still experienced stereotype threat.

Steele's (2004) protective disidentification paradigm suggests that well-intentioned remedial programmes for minority students are likely to fail because they confirm the very racial stereotypes that cause students to be at risk of failure. Steele recommends reducing stereotype threat for students who are identified with academic subjects by creating an environment that ensures them that their abilities will not be held in question and that expectations for them will be high. For students who do not already identify with academic subjects, he recommends creating a safe environment in which there is a low possibility for failure and the building of students' sense of self-efficacy and competence in the domain. Steele's research points to the importance of climate and teacher support in the academic achievement of minority students.

The structural paradigm

Most of the theories and paradigms that we have discussed focus on school reform as a vehicle to enhance the achievement of minority and low-income students. At least since the 1970s, a group of social scientists and educators have set forth the hypothesis that school reform is insufficient to increase the academic achievement and social adjustment of low-income students and ethnic minority students. These researchers maintain that structural reforms within the US political economy are essential to increase the achievement of ethnic minority students and low-income students (Anyon, 2005; Jencks et al, 1972). This is the case because student academic achievement is highly correlated with social class and because racial and ethnic groups must experience upward social-class mobility in order for their academic achievement to increase.

In a comprehensive study of the effects of family and schooling on social-class mobility, Jencks et al. (1972) found that student social-class status was the strongest variable in predicting educational outcomes and social-class mobility. Coleman et al. (1966), in one of the most comprehensive studies of educational opportunity and student achievement ever undertaken, found that a child's social-class background and the social-class backgrounds of her peers had a larger influence on academic achievement than schooling. Both of these studies were criticised for underestimating the effects of schools on student achievement and for relieving schools of the responsibility for educating low-income students and ethnic minority students. One of the harshest critiques of the Jencks et al. findings was made by Kenneth B. Clark (1973), the eminent African American psychologist:

> Jencks's contribution to the increasing social science litany of immobility and despair for minority-group youngsters is a significantly new and novel one. These children are not only blocked by their culture and their genes, but they are now also being blocked by the inherent meaninglessness of the schools. If education itself is no value then there can be no significance in the struggle to use the schools as instruments for justice and mobility. Jencks has closed the circle. The last possibility of hope for the undereducated and oppressed minorities has been dashed. (p.81)

The Coleman report (Coleman et al., 1966) and the Jencks et al. (1972) report appear to divert both the responsibility and efficacy of schools to influence the realities of social-class inequality. However, ample empirical evidence indicates that schools often reinforce and reproduce the racial, class and gender stratification within the larger society. Researchers who focus on the social structures that form the context of schooling argue that schools are an 'inextricable part of the layering of society into distinct classes' (Knapp and Woolverton, 2004: 658). Critical theorists such as Apple (1995) and McCarthy (1988) challenge the perception that schools are democratic equalisers. In his ethnography that has attained the status of a classic – *Learning to Labor: How Working Class Kids Get Working Class Jobs* – Willis (1977) describes how a school he studied reproduced the social and economic structures of British society.

School racial segregation and funding disparities are structural sources of inequality that have been identified by researchers such as Orfield and Lee (2006) and Darling-Hammond (2004), and by popular writers such as Kozol (2005). Both factors are inextricably tied to the larger social issue of residential segregation. Talbert-Johnson states, 'Many of the schools that our nation's most vulnerable children attend, especially those in economically strapped urban areas, are dilapidated and segregated' (2004: 26). She points out that a third of all African American and Hispanic students attend schools that have minority enrollments of 90 percent or more, and that these schools are often substandard, with under-qualified teachers and high teacher turnover, large class sizes, and poor equipment.

Frankenberg et al. (2003) report that while the nation's minority student enrollment continues to increase – it was 43 percent of all public school enrollment in the United States in 2003 (Dillon, 2006) – White students are the most racially segregated group, attending schools that are on average 80 percent White. Ladson-Billings (2006) asks why 'funding inequities map so neatly and regularly onto the racial and ethnic realities of our schools'. She continues, 'Even if we cannot prove that schools are poorly funded *because* Black and Latina/o students attend them, we can demonstrate that the amount of funding rises with the rise in

White students. This pattern of inequitable funding has occurred over centuries' (p. 6) (italics in original).

Insightful and careful studies in the United States (Oakes, 2005), the United Kingdom (Gillborn, 2008; Gillborn and Youdell, 2000; Tomlinson, 2001, 2008) and other nations (Banks, 2009; Luchtenberg, 2004b) document the widespread inequality that exists *within* schools. Popular accounts such as the one by Kozol (2005) support the findings of empirical studies. Researchers describe how existing social structures are reproduced through differentiated school curricula (Anyon, 1980) and tracking (Oakes, 2005), and the high correlation between track assignment, race and class (Oakes, 2005). Predictably, middle-class White and some Asian students are placed in the higher tracks while low-income, African American and Latino students are disproportionately assigned to lower tracks. Latino students, who have the highest dropout rates, are more segregated than any other minority group and also experience a 'pattern of linguistic segregation' (Frankenberg et al., 2003: 4).

Some structural paradigm theorists focus on the limited influence of schools and argue that changes in the social and economic structure of the larger society are required to close the academic achievement gap (Coleman et al., 1966; Jencks et al., 1972). Despite the acid controversies that this argument has evoked and its limitations, it reveals the significant ways in which schools are integral parts of the social context and political economy of the nation and are limited in the extent to which they can function beyond these institutional structures.

Some scholars focus on the potential of schools and call for a careful analysis of the ways that schools can counter some of the larger social and structural factors. The continuing importance of schools is reflected in this statement by Haveman about the cumulative effects of unequal education on minority students and society:

> The education debt is the foregone schooling resources that we could have (should have) been investing in (primarily) low income kids, which deficit leads to a variety of social programs (e.g., crime, low productivity, low wages, low labor force participation) that require on-going public investment. This required investment sucks away resources that could go to reducing the achievement gap. Without the education gap we could narrow the achievement gap (R. Haveman, quoted in Ladson-Billings, 2006 (p.5)).

Arguments such as Haveman's appear to reopen the circle that Clark (1973) saw being closed by structural arguments. 'The last possibility of hope for the under-educated and oppressed minorities' (p. 81) may still lie partly in the hands of educators, as indicated in the description of the seventh paradigm in the next section of this chapter.

The effective schools paradigm

The effective schools paradigm – which maintains that the cultures of schools have a significant influence on student academic achievement – contradicts the tenets of researchers who maintain that factors such as student social class, school social class and family background are the most important correlates of student academic achievement (Coleman et al., 1966; Jencks et al., 1972). Effective school researchers maintain that schools of the same social-class composition have significantly different effects on student achievement (Brookover et al., 1979; Edmonds, 1986; Levine and Lezotte, 2001; Sizemore, 2008). Some schools in low-income communities – as well as in high-income communities – have cultures that foster high academic achievement. Effective school researchers called these schools 'effective' or 'improving' schools. Other schools in both low- and high-income communities have cultures that do not foster high academic achievement.

Effective school researchers have identified the important characteristics of effective or improving schools. They include a '*safe and orderly environment, a shared faculty commitment to improve achievement, orientation focused on identifying and solving problems, high faculty cohesion, collaboration, and collegiality, high faculty input in decision-making, and schoolwide emphases on recognizing positive performance*' (Levine and Lezotte, 2001: 525–526) (emphasis in original).

Brookover and his colleagues hypothesised that academic achievement is 'partly a function of the social and cultural characteristics of the school social system' (Brookover et al., 1979: 6). They tested this hypothesis in a random sample of 91 elementary schools in Michigan. They found that the school's social class composition and other personnel inputs, the social structure of the school, and the school social climate explained most of the variance between the schools in student academic achievement, self-concept of ability and self-reliance. They conclude:

> Our data indicate that high achieving schools are most likely to be characterized by the students' feeling that they have control, or mastery of their academic work and the school system is not stacked against them. . . Teachers and principals in high achieving schools express the belief that students can master their academic work, and that they expect them to do so, and they are committed to seeing that their students learn to read, and to do mathematics, and other academic work (1979: 143).

As the effective schools paradigm reveals, schools can and do make a difference in the academic and social lives of students. The effective schools paradigm has been criticised for conceptualising the outcomes of school too narrowly, that is, as academic achievement in the basic skills such as reading and mathematics. Basic skills are an essential but not a sufficient outcome of schooling. An important goal of schools should be to help students develop the knowledge, attitudes and competencies needed to function effectively as citizens within a diverse democratic society as well as across national borders (Banks, 2004a, 2005).

The need for a multifactor paradigm

We have described seven paradigms – or theories of the middle range – that attempt to explain why low-income students, ethnic minority students, and language minority students often perform poorly on academic tasks and tests in school.

These paradigms are summarized in Table 15.1. We believe that each of these paradigms, *except for the genetic paradigm*, provides knowledge, insights, research and theoretical perspectives that merit discussion and analysis when attempts are made to reform schools in order to create equal educational opportunities for all students.

Due to the scope of this chapter, we have limited our discussion to seven influential paradigms in educational research, theory and practice. Other significant and helpful paradigms that we did not discuss in this chapter include critical race theory (Gillborn, 2005; Ladson-Billings and Tate, 1995; Solorzano, 1997), critical pedagogy (Dimitriadis and Carlson, 2003; Giroux, 1997; Kincheloe, 2004; McLaren, 1994), the psychologically based school intervention model developed by Comer (2004), the parent involvement approach structured by Epstein (1992) and the *Success for All* programme developed by Slavin and Madden (2001). We also did not discuss any of the other basic skills programmes designed to increase minority achievement that are similar to *Success for All*.

Research and the insights of school practitioners in the major Western nations within the last four decades teach us that the academic achievement problems of low-income students, racial and cultural minority students, and language minority students are too complex to be solved with reforms based on single-factor paradigms and explanations (Banks, 2009; Banks and Lynch, 1986; Gillborn and Youdell, 2001; Luchtenberg, 2004b). Effective school reform interventions must draw upon and incorporate the most helpful insights from different paradigms as well as upon the wisdom of practice gained by experienced school educators.

The persistence of a racial achievement gap— despite D'Souza's (1995) argument about 'the end of racism' – signals a distressing point of contradiction for US society. The NCLB Act appears to locate the source of this contradiction squarely on the shoulders of schools and teachers, and uses a rigid system of rewards and punishments to solve the achievement gap problem. This policy ignores the structural and cultural difference factors that contribute to the gap, as well as much of the other research we have described in this chapter. We describe two examples below of how education researchers have combined approaches using the insights and findings of several paradigms, demonstrating that a complex, multidimensional problem such as the achievement gap requires solutions that are complex and multidimensional.

Since the research by Jencks et al. (1972) and Coleman et al. (1966), some researchers have described the structural factors in society related to school reform but have also conceptualised ways in which school reform, when paired with reform in the economic system, can increase student achievement. The research by Noguera (2003, 2008) and Anyon (1997) epitomises this work. Noguera believes that reforms in the political economy within the inner city are essential for the improvement of urban schools. However, he also thinks that urban schools must be and can be reformed because they are the only hope for children who live in inner-city communities to escape poverty and to become productive members of society. School reform – in Noguera's view – can take

Table 15.1 Major paradigms explaining the inequitable educational outcomes of ethnic minority students

Paradigms	Key premises	Implications for schooling	Examples of theorists
Genetic	Genetic differences account for the test-score gap between White students and students of colour.	Compensatory education will have little effect on the achievement scores of minority and low-income students.	Shuey (1958) Jensen (1969) Herrnstein and Murray (1994)
Cultural deprivation	Characteristics such as poverty, social disorganisation, and 'lack' of culture lead to cognitive deficits in ethnic minority and low-income students.	Schools should target low-income and minority children through compensatory and remedial programmes to make up for the cultural deficits of their homes.	Bereiter and Englemann (1966) Bloom et al. (1965) McWhorter (2000) Riessman (1962) Thernstrom and Thernstrom (2003)
Cultural difference	Cultural *differences*, not deficits, account for the unequal educational outcomes of ethnic minority students.	Schools should change in ways that respect and reflect the rich and diverse home cultures of students and bridge school and home cultures.	Boykin and Allen (2004) Delpit and Dowdy (2002) Ladson-Billings (1994) Lee (1995, 2001) Moll and González (2004)
Cultural ecology	The poor academic achievement of Black students is due primarily to their status as castelike minorities. They develop an oppositional identity and associate school achievement with 'acting White'.	Black communities need to socialise their children to assimilate mainstream values regarding academic achievement.	Fordham and Ogbu (1986) Ogbu (2001)
Protective disidentification	Students who encounter stereotype threat in school subjects/domains will disidentify from those domains in order to protect their sense of self.	Schools need to reexamine remedial programs for minority students, and create safe environments that reduce stereotype threat and help students develop a sense of self-efficacy.	Steele (1992; 2004) Steele and Aronson (1995)
Structural	Without a change in the social and political structure, the effectiveness of school reform will be limited. Social class is a primary variable that predicts school achievement.	The economic and social structure must be considered in designing and implementing school reform.	Anyon (1997) Coleman et al. (1966) Jencks et al. (1972)
Effective schools	The culture of schools significantly influences student academic achievement.	Important factors characteristic of effective schools have been identified and should be implemented in school reform.	Brookover et al (1979) Edmonds (1986) Levine and Lezotte (2001)

Copyright © 2010 by James A. Banks

place simultaneously with reform in the nation's social, economic and political structures. He writes:

> My faith in the possibility that education can serve as a vehicle of individual transformation, and even social change, is rooted in an understanding that human beings have the ability to rise above even the most difficult obstacles, to become more than victims of circumstances. I have seen education open doors for those who lacked opportunity, and open the minds of those who could not imagine alternative ways of being and living. (p. 10)

In another example, Talbert-Johnson (2004) addresses the sobering structural inequities that contribute to the achievement gap, while her proposed solutions centre on schools and teachers. She believes that high-quality teachers who are committed to serving ethnic minority students and low-income students are the critical mediating link between social and economic structures and student achievement. Confirming the relevance of Steele's (2004) protective disidentification paradigm, Talbert-Johnson views highly qualified teachers who use culturally responsive pedagogical practices as the greatest asset for students from diverse cultural and income backgrounds.

CONCLUSION

The US Census (2008) projects that ethnic minorities will increase from 34 percent of the nation's population in 2008 to 50 percent by 2042 (Roberts, 2008). A number of Western European nations as well as Japan are experiencing near zero population growth. Most of the population growth in these nations result from increases in their immigrant populations (Berlin Institute for Population Development, 2008). Some mainstream citizens in Western nation-states such as France, the United Kingdom, Canada, Germany, the Netherlands, and the United States have responded to the growth of ethnic, language and religious diversity within their nations with hostility, fear and intolerance (Banks, 2009; Cesari, 2004; Modood et al., 2006).

In several US states, including Arizona and California, citizen initiatives have made bilingual education illegal (Crawford, 1999), or passed legislation declaring English as the only official language of the state. In France, the wearing of religious symbols in public schools has been prohibited (Bowen, 2008; Scott, 2007). In the current debates over immigration, globalisation, ethnic, and political conflict – and the changing demands of an increasingly technological and highly competitive global economy – multicultural nation-states face pressing and difficult questions related to the educational, social, economic and political gaps between minority and majority groups, the rights of immigrant and minority groups, and how to make multicultural citizenship possible (Banks, 2004a).

Although the growth of diversity in nations around the world presents challenges to nation-states, it also offers opportunities that can enrich Western nation-states with new languages, ideas and ways of viewing and constructing reality. Okihiro (1994) has argued persuasively that groups in the margins have been the conscience of America, have kept it committed to its ideals and have been the main sites for keeping democracy and freedom alive in the United States. Okihiro's observation is consistent with our study of the achievement gap and the challenges it poses for schools and society at large. The achievement gap raises fundamental questions about how to actualise equal educational opportunities in multicultural democratic nation-states. These questions – and the quest for answers to them – are as important for White mainstream students as they are for racial, ethnic and language minority students because the fates of all groups within nations and indeed within our global society are tied together (Appiah, 2006). As Martin Luther King said, 'We will live together as brothers and sisters or die separate and apart as strangers'.

The issue of minority underachievement is still under-theorised and requires more complex and nuanced explanations and theories than those that now exist. Ladson-Billings' (2006) notion of the education debt is an alternative way to conceptualise the achievement gap. It removes the genetic and cultural deprivationist connotations of an *ability gap in students* and focuses attention on the fact that the measured 'gap' is a symptom rather than the problem, which is social and educational inequality. The achievement gap is not the cause of racial and ethnic stratification. Rather, racial and ethnic stratification manifests itself in many forms, including disparities in educational outcomes.

A major premise of effective school reform is that education is broader than schooling. Many problems that ethnic minority students, language minority students and low-income students experience in schools reflect problems in the wider society (Noguera, 2003). When designing reform strategies, we must be keenly sensitive to the limitations of formal schooling. However, we must also be tenacious in our faith that the school can play a limited but decisive role in bringing about equal educational opportunities for all students and can help them develop the cross-cultural knowledge, attitudes and skills needed to function in a democratic and just society.

ACKNOWLEDGEMENTS

We are grateful to Dr. Diem T. Nguyen, a former research assistant in the Center for Multicultural Education, and Professor Geneva Gay, both at the University of Washington, for their incisive comments on an early draft of this chapter which enabled us to strengthen it. The helpful comments of the editors of this volume – Professors Patricia Hill Collins and John Solomos – also enabled us to improve this chapter.

NOTE

1. We are grateful to Professor Michael S. Knapp of the University of Washington for suggesting these alternative ways to conceptualise the academic achievement gap.

REFERENCES

Adams, D.W. (1995) *Education for Extinction: American Indians and the Boarding School Experience, 1875–1928.* Lawrence: University Press of Kansas.

Aguirre, A. Jr. and Turner, J.H. (2001) *American Ethnicity: The Dynamics and Consequences of Discrimination.* 3rd edition. Boston: McGraw Hill.

Ainsworth-Darnell, J.W. and Downey, D.B. (1998) 'Assessing the Oppositional Culture Explanation for Racial/Ethnic Difference in School Performance', *American Sociological Review*, 63 (4): 536–553.

Amrein, A.L. and Berliner, D.C. (2002) 'High-Stakes Testing, Uncertainty, and Student Learning', *Education Policy Analysis Archives*, 10 (8). Retrieved February 14, 2003, from http://eppa.asu.edu/eppa/v10n18/.

Anyon, J. (1980) 'Social Class and the Hidden Curriculum of Work', *Journal of Education*, 162 (1): 67–92.

Anyon, J. (1997) *Ghetto Schooling: A Political Economy of Urban Educational Reform.* New York: Teachers College Press.

Anyon, J. (2005) *Radical Possibilities: Public Policy, Urban Education, and a New Social Movement.* New York: Routledge.

Appiah, K.A. (2006) *Cosmopolitanism: Ethnics in a World of Strangers.* New York: Norton.

Apple, M. (1995) *Education and Power.* 2nd edition. New York: Routledge.

Au, K.H. (1980) 'Participation Structures in a Reading Lesson with Hawaiian Children: Analysis of a Culturally Appropriate Teaching Event', *Anthropology and Education Quarterly*, 11 (2): 91–115.

Banks, J.A. (1984) 'Values, Ethnicity, Social Science Research, and Educational Policy' in B. Ladner (ed.), *The Humanities in Precollegiate Education.* 83rd Yearbook of the National Society for the Study of Education. Chicago: The University of Chicago Press. pp. 91–11.

Banks, J.A. (1986) 'Multicultural Education: Development, Paradigms and Goals' in J.A. Banks and J. Lynch (eds), *Multicultural Education in Western Societies.* London: Holt. pp. 2–28.

Banks, J.A. (ed.) (1996) *Multicultural Education, Transformative Knowledge and Action: Historical and Contemporary Perspectives.* New York: Teachers College Press.

Banks, J.A. (1998) 'The Lives and Values of Researchers: Implications for Educating Citizens in a Multicultural Society', *Educational Researcher*, 27 (7): 4–17. (AERA Presidential Address).

Banks, J.A. (ed.) (2004a) *Diversity and Citizenship Education: Global Perspectives.* San Francisco: Jossey-Bass.

Banks, J.A. (2004b) 'Multicultural Education: Historical Development, Dimensions, and Practice' in J.A. Banks and C.A.M. Banks (eds), *Handbook of Research on Multicultural Education.* 2nd edition. San Francisco: Jossey-Bass. pp. 3–29.

Banks, J.A. (2006a) *Cultural Diversity and Education: Foundations, Curriculum, and Teaching.* 5th edition. Boston: Allyn and Bacon.

Banks, J.A. (2006b) *Race, Culture, and Education: The Selected Works of James A. Banks.* London/New York: Routledge.

Banks, J.A. (2006c) 'Researching Race, Culture, and Difference: Epistemological Challenges and Possibilities' in J.L. Green, G. Camili, and P.B. Elmore, with A. Skukausaité and E. Grace (eds), *Handbook of Complementary Methods in Education Research.* Washington, DC: American Educational Research Association and Mahwah, NJ: Lawrence Erlbaum. pp. 773–793.

Banks, J.A. (ed.) (2009) *The Routledge International Companion to Multicultural Education.* London and New York: Routledge.

Banks, J.A. and Banks, C.A.M. (eds) (2004) *Handbook of Research on Multicultural Education.* 2nd edition. San Francisco: Jossey-Bass.

Banks, J.A. and Lynch, J. (eds) (1986) *Multicultural Education in Western Societies.* London: Holt.

Banks, J.A., Banks, C.A.M., Cortés, C.E., Hahn, C.L., Merryfield, M.M., Moodley, K.A., Murphy-Shigematsu, S., Osler, A., Park, C. and Parker, W.C. (2005) *Democracy and Diversity: Principles and Concepts for Educating Citizens in a Global Age.* Seattle: Center for Multicultural Education, University of Washington.

Baratz, S.S. and Baratz, J.C. (1970) 'Early Childhood Intervention: The Social Science Base of Institutional Racism', *Harvard Educational Review*, 40 (1): 29–50.

Benhabib, S. (2004) *The Rights of Others: Aliens, Residents, and Citizens.* New York: Cambridge University Press.

Bereiter, C. and Engelmann, S. (1966) *Teaching Disadvantaged Children in the Preschool.* Englewood Cliffs, NJ: Prentice-Hall.

Bergin, D. and Cooks, H. (2002) 'High School Students of Color Talk about Accusations of "Acting White"', *The Urban Review*, 34 (2): 113–134.

Berlin Institute for Population Development (2008) *Europe's demographic future: Growing imbalances.* Berlin, Germany: Author. Retrieved September 1, 2008 from http://www.berlin-institut.org/selected-studies/europes-demographicfuture.html

Bond, H.M. (1934) *The Education of the Negro in the American Social Order.* New York: Prentice-Hall.

Bloom, B. S., Davis, A., and Hess, R. (1965) *Compensatory Education for Cultural Deprivation.* New York: Holt.

Bonilla-Silva, E. (2003) *Racism without Racists: Color-Blind Racism and the Persistence of Racial Inequality in the United States.* Lanham, MD: Rowman and Littlefield.

Boykin, A.W. and Allen, B.A. (2004) 'Cultural Integrity and Schooling Outcomes of African American Children from Low-Income Backgrounds' in P.B. Pufall and R.P. Unsworth (eds), *Rethinking childhood.* New Brunswick, NJ: Rutgers University Press. pp. 104–120.

Bowen, J.R. (2008) 'Republican Ironies: Equality and Identities in French Schools' in M. Minow, R.A. Shweder, and H.R. Markus (eds), *Just Schools: Pursuing Equality in Societies of Difference.* New York: Russell Sage Foundation. pp. 204–224.

Brookover, W., Beady, C., Flood, P., Schweitzer, J. and Wisenbaker, J. (1979) *School Social Systems and Student Achievement: Schools Can Make a Difference.* New York: Praeger.

Brown vs. Board of Education, 347 U. S. 483 (1954).

Burt, S.D. and Code, L. (eds) (1995) *Changing Methods: Feminists Transforming Practice.* Orchard Park, NY: Broadview Press.

Campbell, J., Hombo, C.M., and Mazzeo, J. (2000) 'NAEP 1999 Trends in Academic Progress: Three Decades of Student Performance'. *National Assessment of Educational Progress.* Retrieved April 28, 2006, from: http://nces.ed.gov/nationsreportcard/pubs/main1999/2000469.asp

Carmichael, S. and Hamilton, C. (1967) *Black Power: The Politics of Liberation in America.* New York: Vintage.

Carter, P.L. (2004) 'Beyond Ascription: Racial Identity, Culture, Schools, and Academic Achievement', *Du Bois Review: Social Science Research on Race*, 1 (2): 377–388.

Carter, P.L. (2005) *Keepin' It Real: School Success beyond Black and White.* New York: Oxford University Press.

Cesari, J. (2004) *When Islam and Democracy Meet: Muslims in Europe and the United States.* New York: Pelgrave Macmillan.

Clark, K.B. (1973) 'Social Policy, Power, and Social Science Research' in *Perspectives on Inequality: A Reassessment of the Effect of Family and Schooling in America.* Cambridge, MA: Harvard Educational Review Reprint Series, 8. pp. 77–85.

Code, L. (1987) *Epistemic Responsibility.* Hanover, NH: University Press of New England.

Code, L. (1991) *What Can She Know?: Feminist Theory and the Construction of Knowledge.* Ithaca, NY: Cornell University Press.

Coleman, J.S., Campbell, E.Q., Hobson, C.J., McPartland, J., Mood, A.M., Weinfeld, F.D. and York, R.L. (1966) *Equality of Educational Opportunity.* Washington, DC: US Government Printing Office.

Collins, P.H. (2000) *Black Feminist Thought: Knowledge, Consciousness, and the Politics of Empowerment.* 2nd edition. New York: Routledge.

Comer, J.P. (2004) *Leave No Child Behind: Preparing Today's Youth for Tomorrow's World.* New Haven: Yale University Press.

Cook, P.J. and Ludwig, J. (1998) 'The Burden of Acting White: Do Black Adolescents Disparage Academic Achievement?' in C. Jencks and M. Phillips (eds), *The Black-White Test Score Gap*. Washington, DC: The Brookings Institution Press. pp. 375–400.

Crawford, J. (1999) *Bilingual Education: History, Politics, Theory, and Practice*. 4th edition. Los Angeles: Bilingual Education Services.

Darling-Hammond, L. (2004) 'What Happens to a Dream Deferred? The Continuing Quest for Equal Educational Opportunity' in J.A. Banks and C.A.M. Banks (eds), *Handbook of Research on Multicultural Education*. San Francisco, CA: Jossey-Bass. pp. 607–630.

Delpit, L. (1995) *Other People's Children: Cultural Conflict in the Classroom*. New York: The New Press.

Delpit, L. and Dowdy, J.K. (eds) (2002) *The Skin That We Speak: Thoughts on Language and Culture in the Classroom*. New York: The New Press.

Dillon, S. (2006, August 27) 'In Schools across U. S., the Melting Pot Overflows', *The New York Times*, vol. CLV [155] (no. 53,684): pp. A7 and 16.

Dimitriadis, G. and Carlson, D. (2003) *Promises to Keep: Cultural Studies, Democratic Education, and Public Life*. New York: RoutledgeFalmer.

D'Souza, D. (1995) *The End of Racism: Principles for a Multicultural Society*. New York: The Free Press.

Drachsler, J. (1920) *Democracy and Assimilation*. New York: Macmillan.

Edmonds, R. (1986) 'Characteristics of Effective Schools' in U. Neisser (ed.), *The School Achievement of Minority Children: New Perspectives*. Hillsdale, NJ: Lawrence Erlbaum. pp. 93–104.

Epstein, J.L. (1992) 'School and Family Partnerships' in M.C. Alkin (ed.), *Encyclopedia of Educational Research*. 6th edition. New York: Macmillan. pp. 1139–1151.

Ferguson, R.F. (2002, October) 'What Doesn't Meet the Eye: Understanding and Addressing Disparities in High-Achieving Suburban Schools'. Retrieved August 2, 2006 from http://www.ncrel.org./gap/ferg/

Figueroa, P. (2004) 'Multicultural Education in the United Kingdom: Historical Development and Current Status' in J.A. Banks and C.A.M. Banks (eds), *Handbook of Research on Multicultural Education*. 2nd edition.. San Francisco: Jossey-Bass. pp. 997–1026.

Ford, D.Y. and Harris, J.J. (1996) 'Perceptions and Attitudes of Black Students Toward School, Achievement, and Other Educational Variables', *Child Development*, 67 (3): 1141–1152.

Fordham, S. and Ogbu, J.U. (1986) 'Black Students' School Success: Coping with the Burden of "Acting White"', *Urban Review*, 18 (3): 176–206.

Frankenberg, E., Lee, C. and Orfield, G. (2003) 'A Multiracial Society with Segregated Schools: Are We Losing the Dream?' Retrieved May 2, 2006 from http://www.civilrightsproject.harvard.edu/research/reseg03/reseg03_full.php

Fusarelli, L.D. (2004) 'The Potential Impact of the No Child Left Behind Act on Equity and Diversity in American Education', *Educational Policy*, 18 (1): 71–94.

Gay, G. (2000) *Culturally Responsive Teaching: Theory, Research and Practice*. New York: Teachers College Press.

Gay, G. (2004) 'Beyond Brown: Promoting Equality through Multicultural Education', *Journal of Curriculum and Supervision*, 19 (3): 193–216.

Gay, G. (2005) 'Educational Equality for Students of Color' in J.A. Banks and C.A.M. Banks (eds), *Multicultural education: Issues and perspectives*. 5th edition. Hoboken, NJ: Wiley. pp. 211–241.

Gillborn, D. (2005) 'Education Policy as an Act of White Supremacy: Whiteness, Critical Race Theory and Education Reform', *Journal of Education Policy*, 20 (4): 485–505.

Gillborn, D. (2008) *Racism and Education: Coincidence or Conspiracy?* London and New York: Routledge.

Gillborn, D. and Youdell, D. (2000) *Rationing Education: Policy, Practice, Reform, and Equity*. Philadelphia: Open University Press.

Ginsburg, H. (1972) *The Myth of the Deprived Child: Poor Children's Intellect and Education*. Englewood Cliffs, NJ: Prentice-Hall.

Giroux, H.A. (1997) *Pedagogy and the Politics of Hope: Theory, Culture, and Schooling, a Critical Reader.* Boulder, CO: Westview Press.

Gobo, F. and Foster, K. (eds) (2004) 'The Legacy of John Ogbu', *Intercultural Education*, 15 (4) (Special Issue): 349–466.

Gould, S.J. (1981) *The Mismeasure of Man.* New York: Norton.

Graham, P.A. (2005) *Schooling in America: How the Public Schools Meet the Nation's Changing Needs.* New York: Oxford University Press.

Guinier, L. (1996) 'The Future of Affirmative Action: Reclaiming the Innovative Idea', *California Law Review*, 84 (4): 953–1036.

Guinier, L. (2003) 'Social Change and Democratic Values: Reconceptualizing Affirmative Action Policy', *The Western Journal of Black Studies*, 27 (1): 45–50.

Guthrie, J.A. (ed.). (2003) *Encyclopedia of Education: Vol. 8.* 2nd edition. New York: Macmillan Reference USA. pp. 3087–3090.

Gutmann, A. (2004) 'Unity and Diversity in Democratic Multicultural Education: Creative and Destructive Tensions' in J.A. Banks (ed.), *Diversity and Citizenship Education: Global Perspectives.* San Francisco: Jossey-Bass. pp. 71–96.

Gutiérrez, K.D. and Rogoff, B. (2003) 'Cultural Ways of Learning: Individual Traits or Repertoires of Practice', *Educational Researcher*, 32 (5): 19–25.

Haney-López, I.F. (2003) *Racism on Trial: The Chicano Fight for Justice.* Cambridge, MA: The Belknap Press of Harvard University Press.

Harding, S. (1991) *Whose Science? Whose Knowledge?: Thinking From Women's Lives.* Ithaca, NY: Cornell University Press.

Heath, S.B. (1982) 'Questioning at Home and at School: A Comparative Study' in G. Spindler (ed.), *Doing the Ethnography of Schooling: Educational Anthropology in Action.* Prospect Heights, IL: Waveland Press. pp. 102–131.

Heath, S.B. (1983) *Ways with Words: Language, Life, and Work in Communities and Classrooms.* New York: Cambridge University Press.

Herrnstein, R.J. and Murray, C. (1994) *The Bell Curve: Intelligence and Class Structure in American Life.* New York: The Free Press.

Hess, F.M., and Finn, C.E. Jr. (eds) (2004) *Leaving No Child Behind? Options for Kids in Failing Schools.* New York: Palgrave Macmillan.

Hirasawa, Y. (2009) 'Multicultural Education in Japan' in J.A. Banks (eds), *The Routledge International Companion to Multicultural Education.* London and New York: Routledge. pp. 159–169.

Horvat, E.M. and Lewis, K.S. (2003) 'Reassessing the "Burden of 'Acting White": The Importance of Peer Groups in Managing Academic Success', *Sociology of Education*, 76 (3): 265–280.

Howard, J. and Hammond, R. (1985, September 9) 'Rumors of Inferiority: The Hidden Obstacles to Black Success', *The New Republic*, 193: 17–21.

Irvine, J.J. and York, D.E. (2001) 'Learning Styles and Culturally Diverse Students: A Literature Review' in J.A. Banks and C.A.M. Banks (eds), *Handbook of Research on Multicultural Education.* San Francisco: Jossey-Bass. pp. 484–497.

Jencks, C., Smith, M., Acland, H., Bane, M. J., Cohen, D., Gintis, H., Heyns, B. and Michelson, S. (1972) *Inequality: A Reassessment of the Effect of Family and Schooling in America.* New York: Basic Books.

Jensen, A.R. (1969) 'How Much Can We Boost IQ and Scholastic Achievement?', *Harvard Educational Review*, 39 (1): 1–123.

John, V.P. (1972) 'Styles of Learning—Styles of Teaching: Reflections on the Education of Navajo Children' in C.B. Cazden, V.P. John and D. Hymes (eds), *Functions of Language in the Classroom.* New York: Teachers College Press. pp. 331–343.

Kana'iaupuni, S.M. (2004) 'Ka'aka-lai Ku-Kanaka: A call for Strengths-Based Approaches from a Native Hawaiian Perspective', *Educational Researcher*, 33 (9): 26–32.

Kincaid, J. (1988) *A Small Place.* New York: Farrar, Straus, Giroux.

Kincheloe, J.L. (2004) *Critical Pedagogy Primer.* New York: Peter Lang.

Knapp, M.S. and Woolverton, S. (2004) 'Social Class and Schooling' in J.A. Banks and C.A.M. Banks (eds), *Handbook of Research on Multicultural Education.* 2nd edition. San Francisco: Jossey-Bass. pp. 656–681.

Koopmans, R., Statham, P., Giugni, M. and Passy, F. (2005) *Contested Citizenship: Immigration and Cultural Diversity in Europe.* Minneapolis: University of Minnesota Press.

Kornhaber, M.L. (2004) 'Assessment, Standards, and Equity' in J.A. Banks and C.A.M. Banks (eds), *Handbook of research on multicultural education.* 2nd edition. San Francisco: Jossey-Bass. pp. 91–109.

Kozol, J. (2005) *The Shame of the Nation: The Restoration of Apartheid Schooling in America.* New York: Crown.

Kuhn, T.S. (1970) *The Structure of Scientific Revolutions.* 2nd edition enlarged. Chicago: The University of Chicago Press.

Ladson-Billings, G.J. (1994) *The Dreamkeepers: Successful Teachers of African American Children.* San Francisco: Jossey-Bass.

Ladson-Billings, G.J. (1995) 'Toward a Theory of Culturally Relevant Pedagogy', *American Educational Research Journal,* 32 (3): 465–491.

Ladson-Billings, G.J. (2006) 'From the Achievement Gap to the Education Debt: Understanding Achievement in U.S. schools', *Educational Researcher,* 35 (7): 3–12.

Ladson-Billings, G., and Tate, W.F. IV (1995) 'Toward a Critical Race Theory of Education', *Teachers College Record,* 97 (1): 47–68.

Lee, C.D. (1995) 'A Culturally Based Cognitive Apprenticeship: Teaching African American High School Students Skills in Literary Interpretation', *Reading Research Quarterly,* 30 (4): 608–630.

Lee, C.D. (2003) 'Why We Need to Re-think Race and Ethnicity in Educational Research', *Educational Researcher,* 32 (5): 3–5.

Lee, C.D. (2007) *Culture, Literacy, and Learning: Taking Bloom in the Midst of the Whirlwind.* New York: Teachers College Press.

Levine, D.U. and Lezotte, L.W. (2001) 'Effective Schools Research' in J.A. Banks and C.A.M. Banks (eds), *Handbook of Research on Multicultural Education.* San Francisco: Jossey-Bass. pp. 525–547.

Lieberson, S. (1980) *A Piece of the Pie: Blacks and White Immigrants Since 1880.* Berkeley: University of California Press.

Lomawaima, K.T. (2001) 'Educating Native Americans' in J.A. Banks and C.A.M. Banks (eds), *Handbook of Research on Multicultural Education.* San Francisco: Jossey-Bass. pp. 331–347.

Lomawaima, K.T. and McCarty, T.L. (2006) *To Remain an Indian: Lessons in Democracy From a Century of Native American Education.* New York: Teachers College Press.

Lorber, J. (2001) 'The Social Construction of Gender' in P.S. Rothenberg (ed.), *Race, class, and Gender in the United States: An Integrated Study.* 5th edition. New York: St. Martin's. pp. 47–57.

Lorcerie, F. (2004) 'Discovering the Ethnicized School' in S. Luchtenberg (ed.), *Migration, Education and Change.* London and New York: Routledge. pp. 103–126.

Luchtenberg, S. (2004a) 'Ethnic Diversity and Citizenship Education in Germany' in J.A. Banks (ed.), *Diversity and Citizenship Education: Global Perspectives.* San Francisco: Jossey-Bass. pp. 245–271.

Luchtenberg, S. (ed.) (2004b) *Migration, Education and Change.* London: Routledge.

McCarthy, C. (1988) 'Rethinking Liberal and Radical Perspectives on Racial Inequality in Schooling: Making the Case for Nonsynchrony', *Harvard Educational Review,* 58 (2): 265–279.

McLaren, P. (1994) *Life in Schools: An Introduction to Critical Pedagogy in the Foundations of Education.* New York: Longman.

McWhorter, J. (2000) *Losing the Race: Self-Sabotage in Black America.* New York: Free Press.

Meier, D. and Wood, G. (eds) (2004) *Many Children Left Behind: How the No Child Left Behind Act is Damaging Our Children and Our Schools.* Boston: Beacon Press.

Merton, R.K. (1968) *Social Theory and Social Structure.* Enlarged edition. New York: The Free Press.

Modood, T., Triandafyllidou, A. and Zapata-Barrero, R. (eds) (2006) *Multiculturalism, Muslims and Citizenship: A European Approach*. London and New York: Routledge.

Moll, L., Amanti, C., Neff, D. and González, N. (1992) 'Funds of Knowledge for Teaching: Using a Qualitative Approach to Connect Homes and Classrooms', *Theory into Practice*, 31 (2): 132–141.

Moll, L. and González, N. (2004) 'Engaging Life: A Funds-of-Knowledge Approach to Multicultural Education' in J.A. Banks and C.A.M. Banks (eds), *Handbook of Research on Multicultural Education*. 2nd edition. San Francisco: Jossey-Bass. pp. 699–715.

Moran, C.E. and Hakuta, K. (2001) 'Bilingual Education: Broadening Research Perspectives' in J.A. Banks and C.A.M. Banks (eds), *Handbook of Research on Multicultural Education*. San Francisco: Jossey-Bass. pp. 445–462.

National Center for Education Statistics (NCES) (2008) 'Trends in the achievement gaps in reading and mathematics'. Retrieved August 26, 2008, from: http://nces.ed.gov/programs/coe/2008/section2/indicator16.asp

Noguera, P. (2003) *City Schools and the American Dream*. New York: Teachers College Press.

Noguera, P.A. (2008) *The Trouble with Black Boys and Other Reflections on Race, Equity, and the Future of Public Education*. San Francisco: Jossey-Bass.

Nott, J.C. and Gliddon, G.R. (eds) (1854) *Types of Mankind*. Philadelphia, PA: J.B. Lippincott, Grambo & Co.

Oakes, J. (2005) *Keeping Track: How Schools Structure Inequality*. 2nd edition. New Haven, CT: Yale University Press.

Ogbu, J.U. (2001) 'Understanding Cultural Diversity and Learning' in J.A. Banks and C.A.M. Banks (eds), *Handbook of Research on Multicultural Education*. San Francisco: Jossey-Bass. pp. 582–593.

Ogbu, J.U. (2003) *Black American Students in an Affluent Suburb: A Study of Academic Disengagement*. Mahwah, NJ: Lawrence Erlbaum.

Okihiro, G.Y. (1994) *Margins and Mainstreams: Asians in American History*. Seattle: University of Washington Press.

Omi, M. (2001) 'The Changing Meaning of Race' in N.J. Smelser, W.J. Wilson, and F. Mitchell (eds), *America Becoming: Racial Trends and Their Consequences*. Volume I. Washington, DC: National Research Council. pp. 243–263.

Omi, M. and Winant, H. (1994) *Racial Formation in the United States: From the 1960s to the 1990s*. 2nd edition. New York: Routledge and Kegan Paul.

Orfield, G. and Lee, C. (2006) *Racial Transformation and the Changing Nature of Segregation*. Cambridge, MA: The Civil Rights Project at Harvard University.

Parsons, N. (1982) *A New History of South Africa*. London: Macmillan.

Payne, R.K. (1996) *A Framework for Understanding Poverty*. 4th revised edition. Highlands, TX:aha! Process, Inc.

Peterson, P.E. and Hess, F.M. (eds) (2003) *No Child Left Behind? The Politics and Practice of School Accountability*. Washington, DC: Brookings Institution Press.

Pettigrew, T.F. (1964) *A Profile of the Negro American*. Princeton, NJ: Van Nostrand.

Ramírez, M. and Castañeda, A. (1974) *Cultural Democracy, Bicognitive Development, and Education*. New York: Academic Press.

Riessman, F. (1962) *The Culturally Deprived Child*. New York: Harper and Row.

Roberts, S. (2008, August 14) A Generation Away, Minorities May Become the Majority in U.S. *The New York Times*, vol. CLVII [175] (no. 54,402): pp. A1 and A18.

Rodríguez, C. (2000) *Changing Race: Latinos, the Census, and the History of Ethnicity in the United States*. New York: New York University Press.

Rust, J. and Golombok, S. (1999) *Modern Psychometrics: The Science of Psychological Assessment*. 2nd edition. London: Routledge.

Sánchez, G.I. (1932) 'Group Differences and Spanish-Speaking Children – A Critical Review', *Journal of Applied Psychology*, 16 (5): 549–558.

Scott, J.W. (2007) *The Politics of the Veil*. Princeton: Princeton University Press.

Shuey, A.M. (1958) *The Testing of Negro Intelligence*. New York: Social Science Press.

Sizemore, B.A. (1973) 'Shattering the Melting Pot Myth' in J.A. Banks (ed.), *Teaching Ethnic Studies: Concepts and Strategies.* 43rd Yearbook. Washington, DC: National Council for the Social Studies. pp. 72–101.

Sizemore, B.A. (2008) *Walking in Circles: The Black Struggle for School Reform.* Chicago: Third World Press.

Slavin, R.E. and Madden, N.A. (eds) (2001) *One Million Children: Success For All.* Thousand Oaks, CA: Corwin.

Sleeter, C.E. (2005) *Un-standardizing Curriculum: Multicultural Teaching in the Standards-Based Classroom.* New York: Teachers College Press.

Smitherman, G. (2000) *Talking That Talk: Language, Culture, and Education in African America.* London: Routlege.

Solomos, J. (2003) *Race and Racism in Britain.* 3rd edition. New York: Pelgrave Macmillan.

Solorzano, D.G. (1997) 'Images and Words That Wound: Critical Race Theory, Racial Stereotyping, and Teacher Education', *Teacher Education Quarterly,* 24 (3): 5–19.

Steele, C.M. (1992) 'Race and the Schooling of Black Americans', *The Atlantic Monthly,* 269 (4): 68–78.

Steele, C.M. (2004) 'A Threat in the Air: How Stereotypes Shape Intellectual Identity and Performance' in J.A. Banks and C.A.M. Banks (eds), *Handbook of Research on Multicultural Education.* 2nd edition. San Francisco: Jossey-Bass. pp. 692–698.

Steele, C. and Aronson, J. (1995) 'Stereotype Threat and the Intellectual Test Performance of African Americans', *Journal of Personality and Social Psychology,* 69 (5): 797–811.

Stephan, W.G. and Vogt, W.P. (eds) (2004) *Education Programs for Improving Intergroup Relations: Theory, Research, and Practice.* New York: Teachers College Press.

Steinberg, L., Dornbusch, S.M. and Brown, B.B. (1992) 'Ethnic Differences in Adolescent Achievement: An Ecological Perspective', *American Psychologist,* 47 (6): 723–729.

Talbert-Johnson, C. (2004) 'Structural Inequities and the Achievement Gap in Urban Schools', *Education and Urban Society,* 37 (1): 22–36.

Thernstrom, A. and Thernstrom, S. (2003) *No Excuses: Closing the Racial Gap in Learning.* New York: Simon and Schuster.

Tomlinson, S. (2001) *Education in a Post-Welfare Society.* Philadelphia: Open University Press.

Tomlinson, S. (2004) 'The Education of Migrants and Minorities in Britain' in S. Luchtenberg (ed.), *Migration, Education and Change.* London and New York: Routledge. pp. 87–102.

Tomlinson, S. (2008) *Race and Education: Policy and Policies in Britain.* Berkshire, England and New York: Open University Press.

Tyler, K.M. Uqdah, A.L., Dillihunt, M. L., ReShanta B.-H., Conner, T., Gadson, N., Henchy, A., Hughes, T., Mulder, S., Owens, E., Clarissa Roan-Belle, C., Smith, L. and Stevens, R. (2008) 'Cultural Discontinuity: Toward a Quantitative Investigation of a Major Hypothesis', *Educational Researcher,* 37 (5): 280–297.

Tyson, K., Darity, W., Jr., and Castellino, D. (2004) 'Breeding Animosity: The "Burden of Acting White" and Other Problems of Status Group Hierarchies in Schools'. Unpublished manuscript.

US Census Bureau (2008, August 14) *Statistical abstract of the United States.* Retrieved August 20, 2008 from http://www.census.gov/prod/2006pubs/07statab/pop.pdf

Valentine, C.V. (1968) *Culture and Poverty: Critique and Counter-Proposals.* Chicago: The University of Chicago Press.

Valdés, G. (2001) *Learning and Not Learning English: Latino Students in American Schools.* New York: Teachers College Press.

Valenzuela, A. (1999) *Subtractive Schooling: US-Mexican Youth and the Politics of Caring.* Albany: State University of New York Press.

Washington School Research Center. (2002) *Bridging the Opportunity Gap: How Washington Elementary Schools Are Meeting Achievement Standards.* Seattle, WA: Washington School Research Center, Seattle Pacific University.

Willinsky, J. (1998) *Learning to Divide the World: Education at Empire's End.* Minneapolis: University of Minnesota Press.

Willis, P. (1977) *Learning to Labor: How Working Class Kids Get Working Class Jobs.* New York: Columbia University Press.

Wilson, W.J. (1999) *The Bridge over the Racial Divide: Rising Inequality and Coalition Politics.* Berkeley: University of California Press and New York: Russell Sage Foundation.

Winerman, L. (2004) 'Studying the Opportunity Gap', *Monitor on Psychology*, 35 (8): 64.

Wong Fillmore, L. (2005) 'When Learning a Second Language Means Losing the First' in M.M. Suárez-Orozco, C. Suárez-Orozco, and D.B. Qin (eds), *The New Immigration: An Interdisciplinary Reader.* Routledge: New York. pp. 289–307.

16

Still the 'Most Segregated Hour': Religion, Race and the American Experience

Cheryl Townsend Gilkes

Race and religion both matter mightily in America. The United States is defined by a durable and bitter racial history and a complicated and multifaceted religious history. Those histories merge at highly visible and dramatic historical moments in events such as the abolition movement in the late eighteenth and early nineteenth centuries, the rise in 1865 and the reorganisation in 1915 of racist organisations such as the Ku Klux Klan, and the civil rights movement in the 1950s and 1960s. At times, religion and race operate as two interconnected and co-creative social forces contributing to the production and maintenance of both an oppressive racialised society and an organisational basis for challenging and resisting racial oppression. The United States is not the only racialised social order in today's world (Fanon, 1967). Race matters to some extent in nearly every former slave society in the New World as well as in societies in Asia and Africa that are former colonies of Europe and in European societies with immigrants from their former colonies and other nations of the 'Third World'. Indeed South Africa stands out as a comparable social system that can be used to illustrate the intercalation of religion and race (Frederickson, 1981).

This chapter seeks to place these braided historical realities of religion and race in America in the foreground. Examining religious history provides a perspective on religion's role as a powerful force and vital platform for the invention of race, the construction of racism and the imposition of racial oppression.

Religion in a racialised society defines and maintains community boundaries by producing spaces where racial-ethnic groups, especially those in subordinate or marginal positions, construct ideas and strategies that contest and resist domination. At the same time, dominant groups sharing ideologies of dominance and supremacy 'congregate' to segregate others, the segregated and excluded congregate to resist subordination and to assert their humanity.

In order to understand the co-creative roles of religion and race across these relationships of domination and subordination, this chapter first examines the limitations of sociological analysis surrounding religion and race. Historically, race and religion have both mattered in America but their historical realities have been under-theorised in sociologies of race relations and religion. This situation has fostered limitations that include what Stanford Lyman (1972) called a 'failure of perspective' within sociology regarding history, in particular, the meaning of slavery.

Slavery is a key historical component of the cultural and social connection between religion and race. Understanding slavery is key to understanding 'race' in America and slavery was a powerful social force in shaping Christianity in the US, especially American church history. Slavery was not only an economic institution but also a cultural and social force that made it possible for religion to operate both to racialise and to mirror the fundamental, historical racialisation of American society. The segregated society that followed slavery enforced the black–white racial divide in all aspects of social life including religion. Aspects of white religion facilitated the crystallisation and enforcement of white supremacy while aspects of black religion challenged racial oppression generating what Andrew Manis termed 'two civil religions in conflict'.

The chapter then aims to 'bring history back in' by examining the connections and interactions between religion and race in three time periods namely: (i) slavery and the invention of race as a modern concept; (ii) the construction of Jim Crow; and (iii) Jim Crow's destruction by way of the civil rights movement. Across all three periods, I show how religion matters as an agency of racialisation. Religion also matters when it aggregates communities of conflicting interests and values in a context where race and racism serve to define social situations. Furthermore, religious communities are often the sites of contestation about race. Bringing history back in means examining aspects of this interconnected or braided history. I conclude this chapter by taking a closer look at contemporary realities concerning race and religion in the United States. Many issues complicate this braided history of race and religion, giving it a new form.

RELIGION, RACE AND SOCIOLOGY

Understanding the relationships between religion and race, sociologically, is complicated by the limitations of analysis that have developed over time. Most sociologists presumed that 'race' was either an ideological problem or a transient epiphenomenon. The pre-occupation with social class as the fundamental division in modern political economies underdeveloped sociological understanding of racialised societies and racial stratification as a 'durable inequality'. Furthermore, sociologists presumed that modernity was defined by secularisation (Giddens, 1986). Not until the civil rights movement generated the challenges of the 1950s did sociologists begin to ask the kinds of questions about religion that explored relationships among race, ethnicity and religion (Pope, 1957; Gordon, 1964). American society's most segregated moments were also its most sacred moments and these moments both reflected and generated the braided realities of religion, race and community.

C. Wright Mills (1961) observed the importance of social structure, biography/ethnography and history for doing sociology. It took the impact of the civil rights and black power movements and the grass roots emphases on history to motivate sociologists to take seriously the importance of history in their concepts and theories about race relations. Each historical moment in the racialisation process was glossed over by sociologists' emphases on assimilation and their fundamental concern for when and under what circumstances it would occur. Robert E. Park's (1950) race relations cycle, an idea that came to be criticised as ahistorical (Lyman, 1972), dominated the study of race and ethnicity until the crisis of the civil rights movement prompted new critiques of the assimilationist idea (Hughes, 1963).

One of those criticisms revealed multiple *ideologies* of assimilation at the same time religion was actually a prominent factor in understanding how inter-ethnic relations among white people had evolved (Gordon, 1964). Gordon pointed out that the assimilation that sociologists of race and ethnicity presumed was taking place and inevitable in American life was non-existent when one examined religion as a marker of race and ethnicity. Protestants married Protestants, Catholics married Catholics, Jews married Jews and African American Protestants were in a profoundly distinct and segregated location in social life. Religion revealed the active and dynamic dividing lines within American society (Prentiss, 2003).

Until the late 1960s, sociologists pursued studies of race relations primarily through the prism of the assimilation paradigm (Hughes, 1963; Gordon, 1964; Lyman, 1972). Supported primarily through the work of Robert E. Park (1950) and his students, assimilation was posited as the end point of racial and ethnic progress among Americans. The presumption was that what Gordon identified as two distinct types of assimilation, Anglo-conformity and the melting pot, had fostered a unity among Americans that hastened the disappearance of ethnic boundaries. Additionally, many sociologists and anthropologists presumed that black–white relations were in a state of accommodation (Powdermaker, 1966) and, in assessing progress towards assimilation, their research questions asked some form of the question, 'How long'? (Lyman, 1972). The emergence of a 'militant' direct-action civil rights movement was unexpected and unpredicted by sociologists (Hughes, 1963). The urban rebellions of the mid-1960s and the eruption of a black power movement created additional troubling events challenging the hegemony of the assimilationist model.

Gordon's critique of assimilation theories was an important turning point. He described American society as divided between Protestants, Catholics and Jews – the primary religious affiliations of European immigrants and their descendents. Gordon (1964: 159) summarised the reality of ethnic relations as a structural pluralism, shaped primarily in terms of the religious dynamics among Catholics, Protestants and Jews:

> the most salient fact ... is the maintenance of the structurally separate subsocieties of the three major religions and the racial and quasi-racial groups, and even vestiges of the nationality groupings, along with a massive trend toward acculturation of all groups–particularly their native born–to American cultural patterns.

Gordon's analysis of religious relations pointed out that black Protestants represented a separate and segregated religious component and ignored black Catholics entirely.

The separation of social movements analysis from other areas of sociology also limited understanding of religion and race as braided historical realities. The United States generated two major social movements that contested the injustices associated with race: the abolition movement and the civil rights movement. These movements were both carried forward and opposed by religionists and within religious institutions. There was also a tremendous impact on religious institutions. The powerful pro-slavery movement also made its arguments with and within the churches. As a result, the three largest white Protestant denominations, Baptists, Methodists and Presbyterians, split over the issue of slavery. After abolition, several major terrorist movements arose, movements exemplified by the ideas and actions of the Ku Klux Klans, whose religious mission was the maintenance of white supremacy and segregation. During the civil rights movement, white clergy, especially members of the Southern Baptist Convention, opposed the civil rights movement. Such opposition was the catalyst for Martin Luther King's writing of his famous 'Letter from the Birmingham Jail'.

Ideological conflicts among sociologists also hampered thinking about race. They viewed problems between and among 'the races' as aspects of society that masked the real problems of class. Once the problems of race were solved, the society would be better able to cope with the inevitable crises of class inequality that was, as Marx had taught, the principal source of legitimate conflict in society. Such thinking totally ignored the role of race in shaping the US class system.

Pointing to the structural reality of racism, sociologist Eduardo Bonilla-Silva (1997) argues that the United States must be understood as a *racialised society*. Race is thoroughly integrated into the process of class formation. Understanding the racialised society requires a historical framework where not only the political economy is explored but also those aspects of society where culture and consciousness are shaped and expressed. Recent emphases within sociology and other disciplines have highlighted the importance of culture in terms of the processes by which culture is produced, in the sense of collectively shared strategies, toolkits, and meanings is undertod. If 'race' as we know it is a social construction and a cultural production, some of the most important construction sites can be found in religious institutions and organisations.

Sociologists also disputed the usefulness of colonial models. Colonial models or more specifically *internal* colonial models made it possible to take seriously the social worlds of oppressed or submerged minorities. These models were often rejected either from partisan standpoints or from an insistence that African Americans specifically were so thoroughly American that such a perspective was irrelevant. Some historians and sociologists, arguing for the efficacy of internal colonial models, pointed out that the United States was actually the only colonial power that had never granted independence to any of its colonies (Jacobs et al., 1971; Blauner, 1972; Glenn, 2002). Indeed, as Glenn (2002) points out, the United States was one of the very few societies in the world that built a political economy on the coerced labour and political exclusion of African, Asian, Latin American and indigenous peoples.

A focus on colonialism globally and internal colonialism in the United States also involved examining cultural destruction or disruption (Cesaire, 1972). The destructive forces of economic exploitation and political domination require that colonised peoples reorganise in order to survive. Cultural destruction and disruption invite the formation of cultures of resistance (Caulfield, 1974) where the internal resources of family and religion provide the social and cultural capital necessary to mount opposition to oppression. Additionally, a focus on colonialism and racial oppression invited the missing historical analysis and linked that analysis to the thick description of the everyday life of the individual and community, what C. Wright Mills (1959) meant when he pointed to 'biography' as one of the coordinate points of sociology.

For racially oppressed groups, family and religion became the central institutions where oppositional strategies were devised and upon which political networks were built. Religious institutions not only provided a platform for individuals to connect with the larger society, but religious organisations and religiously connected organisations such as fraternal organisations became the place from which an oppressive society was confronted (Skocpol et al., 2006). Colonised minorities who experienced cultural disruptions along with exploitation and exclusion, were not minorities because of their voluntary migration to America but because they had been involuntarily dislocated through enslavement, conquest or annexation (Blauner, 1972). What analysis from a colonial standpoint provided was a view of life as lived by people of colour and the impact of racial oppression not only on their place in the political economy but also on their family, religious and political lives and the agency with which oppressed peoples challenged the larger society.

In the United States, the relationship between race and religion is long, deep and complicated. Understanding the interplay of race and religion requires an examination of the changes in conceptual approaches in the areas of race relations, the new foci in the sociology of religion on congregation and community, the historical specificities of a particular system of racial-ethnic stratification, and the religious groundings of social movements challenging racial discrimination, propagating nationalisms and fighting the so-called 'culture wars'.

Racial-ethnic divisions past and present in the United States have presented formidable challenges to sociological thinking about race. A major transformation of sociological thought about race and ethnicity occurred in response to a religiously generated civil rights movement. American society depends upon the role religion plays in the social construction of reality, the cultural production of worldviews, and the organisation of bounded and ancestrally defined communities in a pluralist context. Indeed the power of religion is sometimes so taken for granted that it is not interrogated. However, religion needs to be placed in the foreground of questions addressed in any description and analysis of a racialised society. In any society characterised by the durable inequality of race, religion matters. How religion matters depends upon the religious history of that society and the importance of religion in organising and enabling the imagining of community for racialised groups. Both racial and religious histories in America are the histories of communities in conflict. Racialised conflicts often shaped and reshaped religious communities. After a brief discussion of the ways that religion and race have mutually reinforced one another – the ways they both matter to one another, I trace the ways that religion and race have cooperated to constitute distinctive historical periods. Slavery was central to the invention of race and religion both shaped and reflected this racial reality. The period from slavery to segregation represented a veritable race war carried forward by terrorist groups imbued with religious myth and symbols. I pay particular attention to the way that white religion constructed Jim Crow, the American nickname for legalised segregation, and the countervailing role of black religion in the destruction of Jim Crow.

RELIGION AND RACE BOTH MATTER HISTORICALLY

America's most segregated hour is a feature of the intertwined histories of race and religion. 'Race' in America fostered the development of highly bounded human communities and like members of human communities everywhere, these racialised peoples engaged in the activities that constituted and constructed religious life. Those who defined and established themselves as white and dominant developed and shared religious ideas that justified their dominance, denigrated blackness and non-European cultures, and magnified the importance of whiteness and white supremacy. People in communities defined as inferior and targets of exploitation and discrimination developed religious ideas that questioned their suffering and fostered their survival. Sometimes their religious ideas fomented and facilitated rebellions, revolts and escapes. Religion as lived by the oppressed generated resistance of all kinds.

Religion is a motive force in the construction of the United States as a racial-ised society. The United States, along with South Africa, developed racialised political economies with elabourately legislated systems of institutional racism, Jim Crow and *apartheid* respectively. In both societies, religious organisations were deeply involved in both the establishment and disestablishment of these systems.[1] During apartheid, the South African Constitution included theological statements supporting the positioning of white over black. Opponents of apart-heid also attacked it using theological means. In the United States, even with its separation of church and state, the political debates over the humanity, and there-fore legal personhood, of Africans and their descendents were fuelled by religious ideas. The religious confrontations embedded in the abolitionist and the civil rights movements in the United States make this particularly apparent. Not only does race still matter, as Cornel West (1993) has so pointedly argued but religion matters as well. Novelist and social critic, James Baldwin (1984) has argued that 'race' in any society, but especially the United States, is a 'moral choice'. If soci-ety is not possible without moral education, and if religion is presumed to play a central role in that process, then a racialised society is also impossible without a racialised process of moral education. Thus the social organisation of race should teach us something about religion and the social organisation of religion will teach us much about race and its meaning in American society.

An examination of race and religion in the United States illuminates the rela-tionship between race and religion in a particular society. The United States is not the only society characterised by racial-ethnic stratification, however, its social origins are rooted in a distinctive history of racial oppression (Blauner, 1972; Glenn, 2002). The interplay of religion and race is so multi-faceted and complicated, it is possible to argue that race and religion have had an inter-creative relationship in the construction of the idea of race and the United States as a 'the racialised society' (Bonilla-Silva, 1997). Due to the United States' par-ticular religious history, the issues of religion and race are tied simultaneously to the central religious upheavals that redefined and reorganised Europe – the Protestant Reformation and the dislocation of Jewish communities – and to the rise of the Atlantic slave trade and the invention of race.

There is a contradiction between the popularly perceived ideals of contempo-rary Christian faiths and the painful facts of conquest, enslavement and oppres-sion in the New World. This contradiction is at the heart of a complicated and intricate, but poorly understood, relationship between religion and race. While religion seems to be as old as human community, race as we know it in the modern world is the product of only the last half-millennium of intercultural contact and conflict throughout the world. 'The available evidence suggests that racialised social orders emerged after the imperialist expansion of Europe to the New World and Africa ...' (Bonilla Silva, 1997: 473). Powerful constituencies used race, racism and racialisation processes to impose boundaries that gener-ated communities that existed under the pressures of what Charles Tilly (1998) terms a 'durable inequality'.

Boundaries are vital to religion: religion imposes, generates and celebrates boundaries (Prentiss, 2003:1). Religion constitutes and constructs communities of people who share a worldview comprised of a story (myth), a normative framework, a system of belief (doctrine), a view of social relations, an expectation of shared experience and ritual – a set of strategies for investing their worldview with the sacred (Smart, 1983). Religion defines and legitimises discrete communities and is, therefore, one of the most critical construction sites for race and racism. Religion is also one of the most important aspects of social organisation for racialised cultures of resistance.

Religion is both an agency of racialisation and a reflection of the racialised social order. In his invitation to rethink racism, Eduardo Bonilla Silva (1997: 469) contends that the appropriate unit of analysis is the racialised society or 'social system': 'societies in which political, economic, social, and ideological levels are partially structured by the placement of actors in racial categories or races'. Not only are people(s) categorised but they are also placed in hierarchies. Racialised societies are pluralistic societies and therefore the relationships between religion and race are complicated because exploitation, conflict and power contests create multiple interests and worldviews. Religious communities are embedded in these hierarchies of exploitation and conflict.

Depending upon the community and its social location, religion can play either an ideological or a utopian role. In its ideological role, religion can reinforce the *status quo* and in its utopian role, religion can challenge the *status quo*. It depends upon whose religion and how that community lives that religion (Hall, 1997). Religion can be a source of tremendous antipathy as racialised communities engage in direct conflict and seek to maintain or overturn the oppressive system in which they are embedded. Sacred space is a situation where people exercise agency and construct their own definitions of a situation.

Within their own sacred spaces, black people in the United States called one another brother and sister and taught their children that, more than any position or status they could achieve in life, each was first and foremost 'a child of God'. These practices generated an ethic of familyhood that imagined and actualised community and reinforced a theological anthropology tied to an emphasis on 'the fatherhood of God and the brotherhood of man' (Paris, 1985).[2] Additionally, black people learned that the hatred to which they were subjected was a sin; repeatedly they were told that claiming to love God while hating one's fellow human being made one 'a liar' – that the truth was not within such a person.[3] Even the least literate among black men and women were able to select those portions of the Bible that affirmed their humanity and commanded love.[4] Black theological perspectives viewed racism and its historic underpinnings as 'the most vicious and evil sin against humanity anywhere' (King, 1969; Cone, 1991).

At the same time, white people throughout slavery, segregation and some, even today, insisted that 'God did not intend the races to mix' (King, 1969: 42). The most extreme forms of white nationalism insisted that God ordained the segregation of the races, if not from Creation, at the very least from the days of Noah. According to such thinking, the biblical curse on Ham, a culturally sustained misreading of the story in Genesis 9 and 'the most popular story in the slaveholder's arsenal', was a curse on black people that stretched throughout history (Wood, 1990: 84). In his comprehensive history that provides a thick description of the complicity of American Christianity in the construction of racist ideology, Wood (1990: 84–96) details the large body of sermons and religious writing that argued that God had created racial difference as a way of punishing most of the peoples of the earth and of creating privilege for the Elect of God, primarily Anglo-Americans, as they settled in America. Conflicts about the nature and meaning of race were often biblical conflicts and the rise of evangelical religion centred in the Bible facilitated the use of the Bible as a source of popular ideology surrounding race and racialised practices (Emerson and Smith, 2000).

The Church of Jesus Christ of Latter-Day Saints (LDS) carried this biblical understanding of a racial curse even further. A relatively new world religion whose scriptures specifically address the history of white settlement in America, Mormons, believe that 'certain people who at one time had been white – Indians and Africans – had had their skins darkened because of past sins against God, and accordingly, were not eligible for full membership in the church'; Mormon scripture 'also condemned interracial sexual contacts' (Wood, 1990: 96). Although Mormons are a distinct minority in American society and heavily concentrated in Utah, their scriptures and religious ideas about race reflected in pristine detail the racial thinking of 1830s-America and went far towards reinforcing America's racialised system. Furthermore, Utah state law utilised hyper-racialised language (for instance, using the terms 'quadroon' and 'octaroon') in distinguishing who was 'coloured' from who was white (Murray, 1951). The LDS Church did not have a 'revelation' that supported admitting black people to full membership until 1978 (Wood, 1990: 97; Wald and Calhoun-Brown, 2007: 308; Bushman and Bushman, 1998). These two diametrically opposed biblical viewpoints – black people as cursed and white racism as sin – reveal the contentious symbiosis between race and religion in America (Hall, 1997).

In contradistinction to white religious nationalism and white hegemony in every other area of institutional and organisational life, the only truly independent cultural platform from which African Americans challenged the system of segregation was their church (Du Bois, 1903, 1903a). Aldon Morris (1984) called the Southern Christian Leadership Conference, an organisation that emerged during the civil rights movement, the decentralised political arm of the Black Church. Beginning in the eighteenth century, black women and men organised congregations and denominational bodies, used their money to build church buildings, and paid their pastors. It was often these independent pastors who emerged as prominent political leaders and the primary foundation of a black leadership class after the Civil War.

Religion, defined most broadly and narrowly, was a constitutive force in the rise of the idea of race and religious ideology was an enabler for racist practices and institutions. Early in US history, religion became an active tool of societal racialisation and community identity in a persistently dynamic process of racial formation. Rather than simply demarcating racial and ethnic minorities, religion was co-creative and inter-creative in the production of race and racism. In addition to religion being a signifier of social location for members of differently racialised groups, religion and race cooperated in the construction and de-construction of race and racism at any given historical moment. The role of religion in support of slavery was decisive in this moment.

RELIGION, SLAVERY AND THE INVENTION OF RACE

Slavery was central to the construction of America as a racialised society. Slavery as a social institution garnered its legitimacy from the social construction of race and religion was a principal construction site that provided the racialised world-view. For European Protestants, equality was central to their religious worldview. Slavery disrupted that worldview challenging some groups to argue that Africans were not only less than human but somehow benefited from the peculiar institu-tion (Feagin, 2000: 10–16). Those arguments about slavery and the humanity of the enslaved constitute a central thread in American church history.

Indeed, religious historian Sydney Ahlstrom (1972: 36) states bluntly, 'American church history begins on October 11, 1492'. Ahlstrom actually meant '*religious* history' and he pointed out that 'Europe's competition for American empire' (p. 53) is central to a holistic understanding of religious history in the New World. That competition brought all of Europe's and much of Africa's reli-gious diversity to the New World. In addition to the Catholicism of Spain, France, and Portugal, European colonists transplanted the various Protestant movements to the Americas. European anti-Judaism also operated as a push factor sending Sephardic Jews from Spain and Portugal, some by way of the Netherlands (Diner, 1999). Members of Spanish and Portuguese ships' crews and enslaved Africans also carried Islam to the New World (Diouf, 1998).

The early linkage between race and religion stems from what Gustavo Gutierrez (1993: 2) calls the 'collision' – 'the encounter … not only between the peoples of the territory today called [the] America[s] and those who lived in Europe, but including Africa as well ..'.. The well-known encounter between the Spanish and the indigenous peoples is at the root of the evolution of a religious mission to the Indians and the rise of African enslavement beginning in 1502. The attempts to enslave indigenous peoples prompted a series of religious questions that led to restrictions on Indian enslavement and the explosion of the African slave trade. The invention of race and the racialisation of societies in the New World and elsewhere, for example, South Africa, also coincided with the largest and most pivotal upheavals of Western Christianity, the Protestant Reformation. These reli-gious upheavals influenced the settlement of the New World and the evolution of ideologies about slavery and the enslaved throughout the Americas.

At the very same time, the invention and construction of race was just as central to the development and growth of slave societies in the New World. Starting in 1502, economic development in the New World depended specifically on the enslavement of Africans and their descendents. The idea and ideology of race was absolutely essential to the growth and expansion of slavery (Gossett, 1963; Smedley, 2007). The birth of modernity was grounded in the growth of racial slavery. Cornel West (1999: 52) famously summarises this process by saying:

> The great paradox of Western modernity is that democracy flourished for Europeans, especially men of property, alongside the flowering of the transatlantic slave trade and New World slavery. Global capitalism and nascent nationalisms were predicated initially on terrors and horrors visited on enslaved Africans on the way to, or in, the New World. This tragic springboard of modernity, in which good and evil are inextricably interlocked, still plagues us. The repercussions of this paradox still confine and circumscribe us – in our fantasies and dreams, our perceptions and practices.

The American racial divide has its roots in this springboard of modernity. Most popular discussions of slavery focus on either black assertions that reparations are due or white assertions that the slave past does not incur responsibility in the present. Scholarly discussions are more often pointed towards using slavery as an explanation for black disadvantage, particularly those cultural deficits surrounding the family and educational achievement. More than any sociologist, Coretta Scott King (1969: 25), civil rights activist and widow of Rev. Dr. Martin Luther King, Jr., identified the importance of slavery in racialising the United States. She wrote:

> the system of slavery and subsequent segregation, as practiced in the United States, is the most vicious and evil sin against humanity anywhere. It created within the white man a false sense of superiority, while instilling in the black man a false sense of inferiority. Racism, as we define it today, is deeply rooted in these inhuman practices.

While slavery was the central fact in the origins of race, racism and racialised social orders in the modern world (Gossett, 1963), the United States, ironically, was the smallest direct beneficiary of the Atlantic trade. Of all the major slave systems, what is now the United States received less than one-half million Africans. Ironically, the success of the rigid categorisations based on ancestry and the powerful enforcement mechanisms protecting slavery meant that the United States was the only New World slave society whose emancipated population was larger than the total number of africans originally imported and enslaved (Raboteau, 1978: 89–92).

As a social and cultural force in American society, slavery was powerful: it created a racialised labour force and occupational structure; slavery had a profound impact on power relations and law; slavery created a dualistic family system with white families legitimated and incorporated into a system of inheritance and what Tilly (1998) identified as opportunity hoarding. At the same time, black people were categorically excluded from this system of opportunity hoarding. Most importantly for this discussion, slavery split several major

Protestant religious movements. The defense of slavery, according to Gossett (1963), was also at the root of an emerging science of race that in turn fed the political, theological and legal arguments insisting on the inferiority of black people and, therefore, their exclusion from civic and social life.

Without positing a long argument about American exceptionalism, the United States' religious history was distinctive in the New World. British North America became a haven for religious groups seeking refuge from conflicts between Protestants and Catholics, from conflicts within Protestant communions, and from the dislocations of anti-Judaism.[5] Alongside economic organisations such as the Dutch West India Company, many of these settlers chose to secure needed labour through the enslavement of Africans. Prior to 1619, labour in British North America was supplied by white indentured servants. The arrival of 'twenty odd' black people in Jamestown and the utilisation of enslaved Africans in New Amsterdam ignited a series of events that led to the creation of slavery as a life-long and heritable legal status. Ironically, New Amsterdam (later New York) was also the place where the first synagogue was organised by Jews who were descended from the Jewish community expelled from Spain in 1492 (Diner, 1999).

Slavery grew rapidly and black people were a significant component of American culture when the Great Awakenings occurred. Beginning in 1739, a series of revivals that emphasised personal religious experience laid the foundations of American evangelicalism. Raboteau (1999a: 17) describes the interracial foundations laid during the Great Awakenings:

> Not only did slaves and free blacks attend revivals, they also took active part in the services, praying, exhorting, and preaching ... All classes of society were welcome to participate actively in prayer meetings and revival services in which the poor, the illiterate, and even the enslaved were permitted to preach and pray in public.

This religious revolution and this North American emphasis on enthusiastic, evangelical religion did not occur elsewhere in the New World. These revival movements helped to establish evangelical Christianity as the dominant religious mode. In the area of race relations, this evangelical dominance became significant and troubling since conflicts between black and white constituencies were carried out within this context (Emerson and Smith, 2000; Tranby and Hartmann, 2008).

In what was to become a predominantly Protestant and evangelical society, the rise of slavery occurred alongside several debates about religion and political freedom. Raboteau (1999a: 17) points out that: 'Slaves quickly pointed out the discrepancy between the colonists struggle for liberty from British oppression and the colonists' oppression of Africans held in slavery. At the start of the Revolution, slaves issued a series of petitions for freedom'. After the American Revolution, debates over slavery continued among Baptists and Methodists. By the end of the eighteenth century, however, black Methodists, in response to discrimination, withdrew from the predominantly white church forming independent denominations. By the 1840s, internal dissension over slavery among white Baptists, white Methodists, and white Presbyterians led to the division of their denominations. Ironically, the organisational consequences of the Great Awakenings were responsible for making American religion the nation's primary form of voluntarism and making the religious congregation a voluntary association, a distinction emphasised by Alexis de Tocqueville in his observations of the United States.

Such debates over the morality of slavery and its compatibility with an ethic of liberty were not embedded in the development of the majority of New World slave societies. With the exception of British colonies, most New World colonies were Catholic. The ideologies and practices surrounding race that emerged in these societies resulted in systems of race relations that emphasised appearance rather than ancestry; while no less 'racist', these societies did not develop religious systems that actively developed ideas and arguments about race or that supported extensive racial segregation and exclusion from civil society by free people of colour. Furthermore, slave labour in the early years of these South American and Caribbean colonies was so overwhelmingly male that family issues were more ideal than real. However the Catholic Church viewed slaves' marriages as valid and slaves' personhood within the Church was accepted. The 'establishment' of the Catholic Church and the civic legitimacy of slave marriages meant that not only were marriages between slaves valid and legal, but also marriages between slaves and free black people and between slaves and free white people were valid. The United States, on the other hand, did not recognise slaves' marriages because the legal personhood of enslaved women and men did not exist. Any religious ceremony was simply symbolic, and unlike church marriages in Catholic societies, had no force under the law. By 1857, the decision in Dred Scott v. Sanford made clear that black people had 'no rights' that white people were 'bound to respect'.

Audrey Smedley (2007: 95) pointedly distinguishes between the arrival of Africans in North America and their subsequent descent into slavery. The linkage between physical differences and social meaning was the result of a protracted process of labour exploitation involving European, Indian (Native American) and African labourers. Due to a number of distinctive circumstances, Africans became identified as those to be servants *in vita durante*. During the period between 1619 and 1660, various North American colonies that utilised indentured labour devised strategies to control these labourers, particularly punishments that added to these servants' terms of service. Increasingly, those punishments were harsher for people of African descent than for Europeans.

In the process of constructing race and racialising the society, slavery also facilitated the evolution of a culture of resistance (Caulfield, 1974). Africans and their descendents carried their religious traditions to the New World. Africans and their descendents also made religious choices that took seriously their problem of slavery. In other parts of the New World, especially Haiti, African traditional religions such as those rooted among the Fon and the Yoruba served as a basis for social organisation and oppositional organizing (Murphy, 1994).

In Haiti, the social organisation of *voudou* provided the ideology and organisation for a successful slave revolution. While the role of Islam as an African survival is not very well examined, African Muslims were sometimes key organisers of violent resistance to slavery (Diouf, 1998).

In the United States, Africans and their descendents were a numerical minority. Furthermore, the radical dependence of the United States on natural increase among slaves led to very different religious outcomes. In addition to the conversions to Christianity that occurred during the Great Awakening, Africans and their descendents experienced what Albert Raboteau (1978: 44–92) described as 'the death of the gods'. West and Central African deities disappeared from active reverence and African American Christianity developed a distinctive emphasis on the Holy Spirit (Murphy, 1994).

In addition to the independent black Methodist denominations that began in the eighteenth-century North, the African Methodist Episcopal Church and the African Methodist Episcopal Zion Church (AME and AMEZ respectively), black southerners – slave and free – became predominantly Baptist, drawn largely to a polity that emphasised democratic participation and congregational autonomy. At the same time, white southerners also became predominantly Baptist and sometimes found themselves caught between their commitments to whiteness and slavery and their commitments to beliefs in democracy and religious autonomy (Sobel, 1979, 1987). The increased separation between black and white Baptists laid the foundation for what Andrew Manis (2002: 150–151) called 'two civil religions in conflict' – white people in the Southern Baptist Convention and black Baptists in their national conventions and civil rights organisations (Smith, 2003).

Struggles for autonomy were waged throughout the African diaspora in the New World. In Catholic settings, Africans and their descendents masked their African-derived religions with a Catholic veneer. In the Protestant United States, African Americans, slave and free – in the North and in the South, waged their struggle against slavery in religious terms. The most significant slave rebellions were fomented by religious leaders. The two most prominent black women abolitionists, Sojourner Truth and Harriet Tubman, defined their activities in religious terms and were supported in their definitions of the situation. Harriet Tubman was dubbed 'Moses'. The themes of the Exodus and other biblical aspects of liberation pervaded the expressive culture of slave communities. The 'Invisible Church' of the slave community devoted itself to praying for freedom and seeking validation for its petitions in biblical terms. The fact that the laws against unsupervised slave worship and against teaching slaves to read were passed in response to the Nat Turner and Denmark Vesey rebellions points to the threat that slaves' religious emphases and their independent biblical inquiries posed to the slavocracy (Webber, 1978; Callahan, 2006). For enslaved women and men, 'good religion' or 'true religion' stood in direct contrast to what they considered to be what Webber (1978) identified as 'slaveholding priestcraft'. Slaves' evaluation of white religion depended upon whether or not its members were 'friendly toward freedom' (Raboteau, 1999a: 19). As a result, in the aftermath of slavery, African American church denominations were independent and auto-nomous of whites. African Americans in predominantly white denominations formed autonomous networks of churches.[6]

A MAD RUSH OF WORSHIPPERS: FROM SLAVERY TO SEGREGATION[7]

One of the most inhuman practices in the racial-ethnic history of the United States was lynching. According to journalist Philip Dray (2002: 17) '[l]ynching was an undeniable part of daily life, as distinctly American as baseball games and church suppers'. One of these ritualised killings proved to be a turning point in the career and consciousness of W. E. B. Du Bois. In April of 1899, a farm worker named Sam Hose was lynched and dismembered, his burned knuckles placed on display in an Atlanta butcher shop. On his way to the *Atlanta Constitution* to deliver a letter to the editor, Du Bois discovered this display and was so appalled and dismayed that he never delivered his letter to the newspaper and changed his approach to his work claiming that he 'could not be a calm, cool, and detached scientist while Negroes were lynched, murdered, and starved' (Lewis, 1993: 226).

The Sam Hose lynching took place on a Sunday afternoon and it was a patently horrible public spectacle that drew almost five thousand people, four thousand of whom arrived by train from Atlanta. According to Dray, the lynching drew such large crowds because '[w]ord of Hose's capture had arrived in the metropolis that Sunday morning just as many Atlantans were leaving church and there was a mad rush of worshippers to the train station seeking the swiftest possible pas-sage' (Dray, 2002: 12–13). As it was Sunday and because the crowd of lynchers was composed of a 'mad rush of worshippers', it is safe to presume that Sam Hose uttered his last words, 'Sweet Jesus' after being tortured and murdered by white Christians. It is also safe to assume that these were white Christians engaged in an act of violent white nationalism.

Segregation or 'Jim Crow' dramatically underscores the role of religion as a platform for racial-ethnic nationalisms. We speak of the Black Church in spite of its multi-denominational reality (Lincoln and Mamiya, 1990; Raboteau, 1999a, 1999b). There are Black Muslims (Lincoln, 1973; Turner, 1997). Catholics are Italian and Irish and Polish and French. Catholicism is so ethnicised in America that there are national parishes to which members of specific ethnic groups are symbolically affiliated. Orthodox Christians are Greek Orthodox, Albanian Orthodox, Russian Orthodox and Syrian Orthodox. There is even an African Orthodox Church begun by Bishop McGuire at the prompting of Marcus Garvey.[8]

While we do not speak of the White Church, American Christianity is an important vehicle for constructing and asserting whiteness. Violent white Christians have carried 'the stars and bars', the Confederate flag with St. Andrew's Cross, during the Civil War. White segregationists who insisted they were

Christians revived that flag to resist desegregation.[9] Violent white Christians define their whiteness and Christian-ness as central to their identity and purpose as members of the Ku Klux Klan (Blee, 1991). Ku Klux Klansmen burned crosses to terrorise black and white transgressors against the system of segregation.

WHITE RELIGION AND THE CONSTRUCTION OF JIM CROW

Two years before troubles with race and religion prompted black presidential candidate, Barack Obama, to address the United States, on June 14, 2006, Condoleezza Rice, the first black woman to serve as the US Secretary of State, addressed the Annual Meeting of the Southern Baptist Convention. While her speech did not receive the notice and media coverage that Obama's speech received, it was an event that underscores the relationship between religion and race and because of that relationship, it represented a revolutionary and revelatory moment. During her speech, Rice (2006: 39–40) pointed to the imperfections of America's racialised past:

> ... [W]e know ourselves to be imperfect, with a long history of failures and false starts that testify to our own fallibility. After all, when our Founding Fathers said 'We the people', they didn't mean me. My ancestors in America's Constitution were three fifths of a man. And it is only in my lifetime that America has guaranteed the right to vote for all its citizens. ... We are striving and we are making progress. Consider this: If I serve to the end of my time as Secretary of State, it will have been 12 years since a white man was Secretary of State of the United States of America.

In the history of religion and race, her speech was a revolutionary moment. She was a black woman who was one of the most powerful people in the world standing before a predominantly white denominational body that had only recently apologised for its role in supporting slavery in the United States. The speech was also revelatory: as a political scientist Rice not only credited the Civil Rights Movement and Affirmative Action for the shape and content of her professional career but also, as she had on several occasions, she openly discussed the roles of race and religion in the educational history of her family. In the words of poet Maya Angelou, Rice represented 'the dream and the hope of the slave'. By other accounts, Rice represented the Founding Fathers' and the Southern Baptist conservatives' worst nightmare.

The Southern Baptist Convention that Rice addressed was one constituency among a population of American evangelicals to whom the Republicans overtly appealed and to whom George W. Bush owed his elections in 2001 and in 2005. Indeed, the Southern Baptist Convention (SBC) had sponsored an 'information' campaign that may have swayed white Christian voters in several key states, especially Ohio. In spite of the SBC's racist history and that of several key persons and organisations, race was not mentioned much during the elections. The issues that were splayed across evangelicals' consciousness were gay marriage and abortion rights and the subliminal role of race was all but ignored in blue

America's outrage over the self-righteous conservatism of red America. One of the outstanding contradictions of the religious conflict overshadowing the 2004 election was the fact that African Americans, in spite of their predominant affiliations with denominations deemed evangelical, voted overwhelmingly for the Democratic candidate, not because they were less homophobic as evangelical Christians but because they believed that the issue of gay marriage was a smokescreen to obscure what they viewed as the more important issues of poverty, unemployment, prisons, education, the Iraq war and a variety of issues related to inequality.

The duality of life along the black and white axis of inequality generated what Andrew Manis (2002: 150–151) called 'two civil religions' in conflict, both claiming divine sanction for their activities. Using black and white Baptists in the South as his primary example, Manis argued that the central axis of civil rights conflict revolved around a confrontation between the two most populous religious groups in the South, black and white Baptists.

Southern Baptists[10] were prominent leaders and organisers of the White Citizens' Councils that formed in response to black activism. These Citizens' Councils utilised their collective white power to threaten black *and white* people's jobs, restrict their credit and otherwise limit their life chances if they publicly supported desegregation. As the civil rights movement progressed, there were famous and not-so-famous incidents of black exclusion from white congregations. Like most Baptists, Southern Baptists supported missions in Africa, providing scholarships for African students attending what were then called Negro Colleges. Ironically, a Southern Baptist congregation in Richmond, Virginia, congregation blocked the entrance of African students from Virginia Union. Unaware of the rules of segregation, these students wished to attend the church service in order to say 'Thank You' for their scholarships; a Mercer University student from Ghana, who sought to attend a Southern Baptist congregation in Macon, Georgia, was blocked by deacons and physically removed in an incident that was widely covered in the national media (Rosenberg, 1993: 168).[11]

White Southern Baptists along with other white Christians were also central to the massive resistance to school desegregation. Although the Southern Baptist Convention passed a resolution supporting *Brown v. Board of Education of Topeka*, congregations and pastors who supported desegregation were harrassed and some chose or were forced to leave the denomination (Rosenberg, 1989, 1993: 149). Not only were there threats of violence against pastors and congregations that did open their doors to black people, but Southern Baptists organised Christian academies to provide an alternative to desegregated public schools.

The resistance to desegregation was grafted on to the negative responses to the Supreme Court's decision banning prayer in public schools and affirming a woman's right to privacy concerning first trimester abortions (Hankins, 2002). The massive white southern defection from the Democratic Party to the Republican Party was grounded in the resistance to civil rights. Political entrepreneurs like Jerry Falwell, himself a former segregationist, utilised alliances with the

Southern Baptist Convention to galvanise the 'New Right'. Claiming to be following the model of the civil rights movement, leaders like Falwell made white evangelical Christians the foundation of a new politics, using the term 'family values' as an anti-black coded reference black family problems (Rosenberg, 1993: 150). Political organising at white churches in the South harped on what one political scientist called the ABC's of New Right politics: abortion, blacks and communism. Recently, Randall Balmer (2007) has argued that the galvanising event for the New Right was the Internal Revenue Service's denial of tax exemption to Bob Jones University because of its policies of racial discrimination.

BLACK RELIGION AND THE DESTRUCTION OF JIM CROW

Black Baptists were prominent leaders and organisers of various 'Christian' movements aimed at desegregation and the destruction of Jim Crow. These various movements organised the Southern Christian Leadership Conference (SCLC) and became what Aldon Morris called the 'decentralized political arm of the Black Church'. Of course, the civil rights movement was not exclusively Baptist but African American Baptists were and are so numerous that observers often conflate black Baptists with 'the Black Church'. Rev. Dr. Martin Luther King, Jr., a Baptist pastor, was the most famous civil rights leader in the United States. The Montgomery Improvement Association emerged out of a network of pastors called together by former Pullman porter, E. D. Nixon. Mrs. Parks, a member of the A. M. E. Church, and was allied with Nixon by way of the Montgomery chapter of National Association for the Advancement of Colored People (NAACP), which they both served as officers: Nixon as president and Parks as secretary. Throughout the South, networks of ministers, activists and black professionals, who were almost uniformly church members, built the civil rights movement.

Even the Student Non-Violent Coordinating Committee (SNCC) had its religious connections. In the aftermath of student-instigated sit-ins, SNCC was organised by Ella Baker who, though not a member of the clergy, was the Executive Director of SCLC and an active member of a Baptist congregation in New York City (Ransby, 2003). Even though SNCC was independent from the ministers who dominated the movement, SNCC worked with local ministers and appointed a clergy liaison (Prathia Hall). Additionally, part of SNCC's cultural toolkit consisted of freedom songs: Negro spirituals and gospel songs that were re-worked with direct reference to the freedom struggle, what theologian Cheryl Kirk-Duggan (1997: xviii) called 'redacted Negro spirituals'. Not only were SNCC workers pioneers in the development of the freedom song, but they formed the Freedom Singers who travelled the country raising money for the civil rights movement at the same time they shared an important African American cultural artefact with audiences unfamiliar with African American religious culture.

The civil rights movement eventually inspired two of the most significant interfaith mobilisations in the history of the United States: the 1963 March on

Washington and the 1965 march from Selma to Montgomery. The Selma to Montgomery march for voting rights drew participants precisely because of a direct appeal by Dr. King. Protestant ministers, Catholic priests and religious women, and rabbis joined SCLC and SNCC in Selma. Some of the religious activists represented important alliances with the civil rights movement; for instance, Rabbi Abraham Joshua Heschel clearly visible marching next to King signified his success in garnering the support of the national Jewish community for the civil rights movement (Branch, 1998: 167).[12]

However, one group of African Americans fundamentally rejected Christianity as a vehicle for social change and viewed it as primarily a white institution that had forced black conversion and was responsible for racial oppression.[13] Popularly known as the Black Muslims, the Lost Found Nation of Islam generated a highly contentious religious dialogue among black Americans. One prominent spokesperson, Malcolm X, became a significant role model and ideologue for young black Americans. After his silencing by Elijah Muhammad and his conversion to mainstream (Sunni) Islam, Malcolm X became the most visible spokesperson for black nationalism. Prior to SNCC precipitating the black power movement, Mary King (1987) pointed out that nearly the entire leadership of the organisation attended Malcolm X's funeral. Inspired by Malcolm X's position insisting that 'institutional racism' should be the focus of analysis, Stokeley Carmichael and Rev. Charles King placed 'institutional racism' and 'white racism' into popular discourse and sociological analysis: Carmichael through his book with Charles Hamilton (Carmichael and Hamilton, 1967) and King (1983) through his work with the Kerner Commission. This 'discovery' of racism and Malcolm X's admonition to whites to address institutional racism was then carried forward by Louis L. Knowles and Kenneth Prewitt as part of the Stanford chapter of the University Christian Movement and the Mid-Peninsula Christian Ministry. The result of their work was *Institutional Racism in America* (Knowles and Prewitt, 1969).

Ultimately, a braided relationship between religion and race was implicated in a critical moment of religious diversity among black Americans. The rise to prominence of Islam, not just the Nation of Islam but also Sunni Islam, is one of the outcomes. The explosion of the black power movement also challenged churches in a new way. White conservatives utilised the rise of the movement to move away from any alliances with civil rights. At the same time, some mainline Protestants took the black power challenge seriously enough to re-unite (Methodists) or to support serious organisational approaches to religion and race (Congregationalists and the National Council of Churches). The black clergy and theologians also responded to black power very deliberatively with black theology, a form of liberation theology that became part of a national and international academic conversation (Hamilton, 1972; Wilmore and Cone, 1980). Inspired by the black power movement, Chicanoes and Native Americans utilised the power model in their approach to change and utilised religiously grounded leaders (e.g., Caesar Chavez and Vine Deloria).

RELIGION AND RACE IN POST-CIVIL RIGHTS AMERICA

The aftermath of the civil rights movement changed the racial, ethnic and religious geography of the United States. Prior to the 1964 Civil Rights Act and the extension of its protections to Puerto Ricans and Mexican Americans, race in the United States was perceived and confronted almost exclusively on a black–white axis. That is not to say that groups we now refer to as Asian Americans and Latinos/Latinas were not the targets of discrimination and did not constitute colonised minorities within the American system. However, the prevailing image of race was black versus white, a function of the totality and specificity of Jim Crow as it targeted the descendents of slaves in the United States. Changes in the United States after 1965 have provided a new opportunity for religion and race to shape a post-civil rights America, enabling some people of colour to assert religious identities that emphasise their social distance from African Americans.

For many, the passage of the 1964 Civil Rights Act and the 1965 Voting Rights Act defined the success of the civil rights movement (Killian, 1968). That success coincided with a fundamental change in the immigration laws in the United States. Prior to 1965, immigration was restricted to Europeans, with northern and western European nations having the largest quotas. Those nations were predominantly Protestant while the southern and eastern European nations were Catholic, Jewish and Eastern Orthodox. Overall, immigration to the United States was overwhelmingly Christian. US immigration changed radically so that the largest numbers of people began to enter from Asia, Latin America and Africa. This change in immigration changed the religious landscape in America; in addition to Christians from the This World, other world religions, for instance Islam, Buddhism and Hinduism became prominent and visible (Eck, 2001; Levitt, 2007).

At the turn of the twenty-first century, the fastest growing religion in the United States was Islam. Although the history of Islam in the New World goes back to the very beginnings of European presence (Diouf, 1998), the contemporary history of Islam in the United States actually begins in twentieth century black communities. African Americans comprise the largest number of Muslims born in the United States. The presence of religions primarily associated with Asia has also grown with Hinduism, Buddhism, Sikhism and Jainism becoming visibly present in communities of professionals who are able to build places of worship (Eck, 2001). The continent of Africa is sending Christians, Muslims and practitioners of African traditional religions. The connections between Latin Americans, for instance Cuban Santeros, and Yoruba religionists from Nigeria, has transformed Yoruba religion into a world religion, if a world religion is defined by a religion that draws people from beyond its ancestral homeland.[14]

The new immigration has also complicated the religious dimension of the racial-ethnic landscape (Levitt, 2007; Warner and Wittner, 1998). Many of the new faiths that have become prominent since the 1960s are practiced by people whom theologian Jon Michael Spencer (1997) indelicately labelled America's 'new coloured people'. They are visibly brown people who, prior to the destruction of Jim Crow, would have had to expend considerable effort to avoid mistreatment by segregationists or they would not have been able to enter the United States as immigrants. Writing in response to his experience in South Africa, Spencer points to the complications created by America's ancestral definition of race ('the one drop rule') in a world where such a rule makes nearly every one 'coloured'.

However, the reality of America as a racialised society built on the confrontation between black and white has not been lost on the new immigrants who are also people of colour. Religious settings are places where immigrants can reproduce and preserve their ethnicity through rituals and social events (Ebaugh and Chafetz, 2000). Additionally, these settings and the preservation of visible religious ethnicity serve to differentiate immigrants and their descendents from African Americans. Some researchers have observed that these new immigrants may be more religious in America than they were in their home nations and suggested that a subtle motivation for this religious behaviour is not simply to reproduce ethnicity but 'to avoid confronting their problematic racial location in this country' and to mediate 'the pain they experienced growing up with "brown skins" in a predominantly white environment'; one Hindu observer put it quite bluntly: 'better Hindu than black' (Kurien, 1998: 62). New immigrants face a tricultural conflict (Warner and Wittner, 1998) that religion serves to mediate. Part of that conflict involves the new dilemmas of a changing racial landscape where religion is an important but unacknowledged component of the dynamics of racialisation. Racialised America continues to be divided by faith and race with new dimensions of racial and religious division. The religious hours in temples, mosques and churches are still the most segregated moments in American life.

THE MOST SEGREGATED HOUR

During his brief tenure as America's most visible black preacher, Dr. Martin Luther King popularised the earlier observations of sociologist Liston Pope that America was at its most racially segregated in its churches. According to Pope (1957: 105):

> It has been said that 'eleven o'clock on Sunday morning is the most segregated hour in the week'. One could qualify that conclusion: eleven o'clock on Saturday night is even more segregated for the country club set, and other purely social clubs are in general more completely uni-racial than are the churches. Its record indicates clearly, however, that the church is the most segregated major institution in American society. It has lagged behind the Supreme Court as the conscience of the nation on questions of race, and it has fallen far behind trade unions, factories, schools, department stores, athletic gatherings, and most other major areas of human association as far as the achievement of integration its own life is concerned.

Liston Pope's now infamous observations and analysis also pointed out that white voluntary associations in general were the 'last strongholds of segregation' and, therefore, most conspicuous in their exclusion of black people (Hamilton 1972; Hankins, 2002). However churches in America are specialised voluntary associations that are also strongholds of racial-ethnic homogeneity. Baptist churches must vote to admit members and other Protestant groups follow similar practices. Membership is voluntary and admittance to membership is dependent upon mechanisms internal to the congregation. In a society where race is central, those congregational mechanisms also reflect the centrality of race.

If it were possible to assign an army of photographers to generate a massive, composite portrait of the contemporary United States in all of its diversity on a Sunday morning between 9:00 am and noon, their photographs would reveal the continuing truth about American religious life: eleven o'clock on Sunday morning is still America's most segregated hour (Gilkes, 2005; Pope, 1957; Obama, 2008). When first discussed by sociologist Liston Pope and popularised by Martin Luther King, Jr., 'the most segregated hour' referred to the social organisation of race and Christianity along the black–white divide.[15] Christians were the overwhelming majority and at mid-twentieth century in the United States, they attended church around 11:00 A.M. Furthermore, the relationship between race and religion was very obvious; black people attended black churches and white people attended white churches. If black people attempted to attend white churches in the South, they were either arrested, attacked or directed to a 'coloured' congregation.

At the beginning of the twenty-first century, race continues to have an effect on religion in the United States. On March 18, 2008, presidential candidate Barack Obama reminded Americans that eleven o'clock on Sunday morning was still 'the most segregated hour in America'. Black and bi-racial, Obama had advanced farther along the path to the White House than any other black politician.[16] His nationally televised speech on race and race relations in America was one that critics numbered among those significant political speeches in American history, comparing it to speeches by Abraham Lincoln, John F. Kennedy, Lyndon Johnson and Martin Luther King. Ironically Obama's speech on race was in response to a crisis precipitated by a dramatic and jarring intersection of religion and race – a crisis created by public perceptions of Obama's pastor and his church. Media depictions of Obama's pastor as anti-white and unpatriotic prompted Obama's opponents to raise questions about Obama's ability to attract white supporters and by implication to govern a majority white society. His pastor's impassioned critiques of social injustice and white supremacy clashed with white American notions of proper religious practice and discourse – the notion of 'proper' being gentle, non-racial and apolitical. As a member of a predominantly black congregation on the south side of Chicago (Trinity United Church of Christ) in an historically white denomination (the United Church of Christ), Obama found himself forced to offer both a response to the distorted media depictions of his pastor and a statement of the role of faith and race in his own life and political philosophy. By the time Obama became the presumptive nominee for the Democratic Party, he and his family had resigned from the Church and severed his ties with his former pastor. This turning point for Obama and the 2008 presidential campaign was simultaneously religious and racial and presented an early-twenty-first century illustration of the complicated relationship between religion and race in the United States.

The media's success in labelling the liberationist preaching of Obama's pastor as divisive, inflammatory, unpatriotic hate-speech pointed to the highly divergent religious experiences of black and white Americans and the fundamental contradiction and confrontation between the religions of the oppressed and the oppressors. This furore generated by the crash of religion and race highlighted a few of the forces at work producing what is 'still the most segregated hour' in America.

At the beginning of the twenty-first century, Christians remain a majority in American society but things have changed drastically. Assigning photographers to capture the most segregated hours of America would involve the entire Sunday. Congregants now gather as early as 6:00 and 7:00 am in churches that sometimes have multiple worship services in order to accommodate competing commitments of their members and, in the case of mega-churches, to accommodate the multitudes who cannot fit in the sanctuary at the same time. The photographers' assignments would be further complicated by the fact that larger minorities than ever are not Christian. The 1965 changes in the immigration laws have resulted in substantial immigration from nations where Christianity is not dominant or even prominent making Islam and Hinduism a prominent and growing part of the American religious landscape (Eck, 2001). Furthermore, not all Christians gather in churches; if they are recent immigrants they may be renting hotel ballrooms, schools and storefronts. Except for the most occupationally powerless who are required to work – people who clean, serve or respond to emergencies and have the least amount of seniority in their workplaces, on Sunday mornings most people are engaged in the activities of their own choice: church services, athletic activities, brunches, hobbies, house hunting or acquiring the Sunday *New York Times* and a bagel, to name a few.

Whether one is Christian, Muslim, Jewish, Hindu, Jain or a member of the wide variety of 'gatherings in Diaspora' (Warner and Wittner, 1998), Sunday morning activities best reflect identities and attachments to specific communities. Not only do Sunday activities reflect the social organisation of race but these activities are also likely to organise class, status and national origins into highly discrete communal moments. Sunday mornings still contain the most segregated hours in America, the time when the tremendous social complexity rooted in the intercreativity of race and religion in the United States is most highly visible.

STILL DIVIDED BY FAITHS DIVIDED BY RACE

This chapter sought to recover and explore the interaction between religion and race in the United States as they operated to enable people to create, maintain and resist an oppressive racialised society. While little attention has been paid to ethnicity, it is important to realise that religion is the central most important element in a community's identity, the kind of identity we usually refer to as ethnic. Religion has now emerged as a central means of reproducing and maintaining ethnicity in twenty-first century America. The religious story and the racial story are both big stories and they are both plural stories. Race and religion can be addressed differently and for different purposes. The religious story is usually tied to an ideology of religious freedom and democracy. The racial story is usually tied to the problems of exclusion and disadvantage.

Race and religion are both significant factors in the national life of the United States (Emerson and Smith, 2000; Tranby and Hartmann, 2008). They are both social forces shaping a racialised, pluralistic and multi-ethnic society. They are both products of culture and social construction. And they are both sites for cultural production and social construction. Within sociology there is neither a comprehensive theory of American religion nor a comprehensive theory of race and racism. In a dynamic conflict-ridden society it is difficult to develop and maintain a comprehensive theory of anything. However, where two areas are the least developed in terms of sociological theory religion and race – each for its own intrinsic reasons, a sociological examination of their mutuality in society becomes difficult terrain.

The United States is a racialised society whose history and character are products of slavery. The ahistorical nature of sociology and sociological exploration of race and ethnicity muted discussion of slavery's role in shaping society and, instead, focused primarily on slavery's role in shaping the disadvantages and slow assimilation of black people. The secular emphasis of sociology elided the role of religion as an agent of cultural production and a site for social construction (Giddens, 1986). The presumptions embedded in models of secularisation and social differentiation focused primarily on the shrinking role of religion, particularly among the American middle class. The ideology of 'the separation of church and state' further diminished the importance of religion in sociological analysis of race, class, gender and social change. Recovering the braided and helical history of religion and race is essential to understanding fully the nature of racialisation and the tremendously complicated role of religion in a racialised society.

Short of observations about the segregated state of American Christianity and specialised attention to the African American religious experience, there is still relatively little analysis of the inter-relationship between race and religion and their roles in constituting a racialised society. After the Civil Rights and Black Power movements, the discussion of race focused less on the segregation of black and white people and more on race as a social construction, the transformation of the black–white binary, institutional racism and the role of whiteness in contemporary society. The sociology of religion also grew tremendously focusing primarily on issues of secularisation, the faith of baby-boomers, the rise of mega-churches, the importance of congregations and religion as a social/cultural production. Sociologists also discovered culture. In spite of this, there has been almost no real attention to the ways in which religion and race have operated to construct and produce the current social reality. Religion is traditionally seen as a demographic reflection of 'race relations' and students of 'race relations' have addressed the problem of religion as a description of the consequences of race relations. Religion and race need to be seen as mutually creative forces in the construction of a racialised society.

Increasingly, people are beginning to raise questions about the 'most segregated hour' in America. The crisis surrounding religion and race during the 2008 presidential race is only one indication of the tremendous distances Americans still must travel across the divides of racial misunderstanding and religious ignorance. This crisis surrounding religion and race is also a challenge to sociologists to develop more nuanced understandings of the role of religion in shaping a society divided by race and the role of race in shaping the religious infrastructure.

NOTES

1. I have purposely borrowed the language of political and religious conflict in England surrounding the disestablishment of the Church.

2. Paris's analysis points out that African American church denominations are unique in their emphasis within their doctrinal and covenantal statements on the biblical text in Acts 10: 34 that states, 'God is no respecter of persons'.

3. This claim was rooted in the biblical verse in I John 4: 19 which states, 'If a man say, I Love God, and hateth his brother, he is a liar ...'

4. Theologian Howard Thurman (1949) recalls reading to his grandmother who refused to allow him to read from the letters of Paul. She claimed that her aversion to this part of the Bible stemmed from her former owner's use of Paul to justify slavery and to admonish her to be a good slave. On occasion she would ask her grandson to read I Corinthians 13, a portion of Paul's writing that explicitly admonished love.

5. A number of scholars use the term 'anti-Judaism' when speaking of the treatment of Jews prior to the twentieth century, especially prior to the rise of Hitler and National Socialism. Some scholars define anti-Semitism as the older anti-Judaism fused with the ideologies and theories of race that arose in concert with the Atlantic slave trade.

6. This statement glosses over the tremendously complex reality of something like 'the Central Jurisdiction' within the Methodist Episcopal Church, North. Here black people developed their own denominational structure (with their own bishops) within a larger white structure.

7. I am grateful to sociologist Shirley Jackson for her description of an episode of the television programme 'The Twilight Zone' where the distinction between 'segregating' and 'congregating' is the central problem. The people being separated because they are different insist that they are being 'segregated' and the powerful people label the separation 'congregated'.

8. While there are no books that explicitly discuss the role of religion in the social construction of whiteness, such a role can be inferred from monographs on specific religious traditions and their histories of origins and settlement in America (Raboteau, 1999; Erickson, 1999; Bushman and Bushman, 1998; Diner, 1999).

9. Most people do not realise that the bars on the 'stars and bars' are a religious symbol, St. Andrew's Cross along with St. George's Cross are found together on the Union Jack (the British flag). St. Andrew's Cross is a symbol of the Church of Scotland. In the United States, St. Andrew's cross became the symbol of Presbyterian and Presbyterian-derived churches. Presbyterians comprised one of the denominations that split over the issue of slavery and presbyterians did not re-unite until the 1980s.

10. The Southern Baptist Convention is a formal organisation of mostly white Baptist churches. As is the case with American Baptists (the heir to the northern segment of Baptists who split off during slavery), there are black congregations that are 'dually aligned', that is, black congregations

hold membership in both a white denomination and a black denomination such as the National Baptist Convention, USA, Inc. Confusion occurs because the majority of African Americans are southerners and the majority of black Baptist congregations are in the South *or were founded by southerners*. There is a tendency on the part of some African Americans to refer to African American styles of worship as 'southern Baptist', referring to the region and not the organisation. In this paper, all references to Southern Baptists are to congregations or persons who are part of the Southern Baptist Convention. Any references to African American styles will be so specified.

11. The Richmond incident has been told in detail by the then president of Virginia Union, the late Rev. Dr. Samuel DeWitt Proctor.

12. As they focus on 'America in the King Years', all three volumes of Taylor Branch's (1988, 1998, 2006) trilogy illustrate the intercalation of religion and race prior to and during the civil rights movement. Branch not only immerses the reader in the religious worlds that were the primary setting for King and his networks, but he also provides insights into the beliefworld of those who opposed civil rights highlighting the sacred nature of the battle lines surrounding race.

13. One particularly important text, *Jesus and the Disinherited*, was written by Howard Thurman (1981[1949]: 15) in response to a challenge posed to him in Ceylon accusing him of being 'a traitor to all the darker peoples of the earth' because of the historical role of Christians in racial oppression and violence in the United States and globally.

14. In one of his many presentations before the Society for the Scientific Study of Religion, sociologist Rodney Stark suggested such a definition; using this definition Stark once suggested that the LDS Church was the most successful new world religion since Islam.

15. My usage of the term 'race' includes ethnicity. As will become clear, the fact that the United States is, in the words of Eduardo Bonilla Silva, a 'racialised society' means that everyone is 'raced' and that ethnicity, in the form of community membership and individual cultural identity, is something specific to every ancestral grouping in that racialised society.

16. I refer to Obama as both black and bi-racial because, although he self-identifies as black and African American, he also tells his story in terms of both his white American mother and his Kenyan father. The dramatic rise of interracial relationships in post-civil rights America has also made the self-identification and the perception of people as 'bi-racial' a salient social category – so much so that Eduardo Bonilla Silva has argued that the United States may be moving away from its binary approach to race towards a more complicated system of perception similar to the systems of Brazil and other Latin American societies.

REFERENCES

Ahlstrom, S.E. (1972) *A Religious History of the American People.* New Haven: Yale University Press.

Ammerman, N.T. (ed.) (1993) *Southern Baptists Observed: Multiple Perspectives on a Changing Denomination.* Knoxville: University of Tennessee Press.

Baldwin, J. (1984) 'On Being White and Other Lies', *Essence*, (April): 90–94.

Balmer, R. (2007) *Thy Kingdom Come: How the Religious Right Distorts the Faith and Threatens America*, New York: Basic Books.

Blauner, R. (1972) *Racial Oppression in America.* New York: Harper and Row Publishers.

Blee, K.M. (1991) *Women of the Klan: Racism and Gender in the 1920s.* Berkeley: University of California Press.

Bonilla-Silva, E. (1997) 'Rethinking Racism: Toward a Structural Interpretation', *American Sociological Review*, 62 (3): 465–480.

Branch, T. (1988) *Parting the Waters: America in the King Years, 1954–63.* New York: Simon and Schuster.

Branch, T. (1998) *Pillar of Fire: America in the King Years, 1963–65.* New York: Simon and Schuster.

Branch T. (2006) *At Canaan's Edge: America in the King Years, 1965–68.* New York: Simon and Schuster.

Bushman, C.L. and Bushman, R.L. (1998) *Mormons in America.* New York: Oxford University Press.

Callahan, A.D. (2006) *The Talking Book: African Americans and the Bible.* New Haven: Yale University Press.

Carmichael, S. and Hamilton, C.V. (1967) *Black Power: The Politics of Liberation in America.* New York: Random House.

Caulfield, M. D. (1974) 'Imperialism, the Family, and Cultures of Resistance', *Socialist Revolution*, 20/ (1974): 67–85.

Cesaire, A. (1972 [1955]) *Discourse on Colonialism.* New York: Monthly Review Press.

Cone, J.H. (1999) *Risks of Faith: The Emergence of a Black Theology of Liberation, 1968–1998.* Boston: Beacon Press.

Diner, H.R. (1999) *Jews in America.* New York: Oxford University Press.

Diouf, S.A. (1998) *Servants of Allah: African Muslims Enslaved in the Americas.* New York: New York University Press.

Dray, P. (2002) *At the Hands of Persons Unknown: The Lynching of Black America.* New York: Random House.

Du Bois, W.E.B. (ed.) (1903) *The Negro Church: Report of a Social Study.* Atlanta: The Atlanta University Press.

Du Bois, W.E.B. (1903a [1961, 1953]) *The Souls of Black Folk.* Greenwich, CN: Fawcett Publications, Inc.

Ebaugh, H. R. F. and Chafetz, J. S. (2000) *Religion and the New Immigrants: Continuities and Adaptations in Immigrant Congregations*, Walnut Creek, CA: AltaMira Press.

Eck, D.L. (2001) *A New Religious America: How a 'Christian Country' Has Become the World's Most Religiously Diverse Nation.* San Francisco: Harper Collins Publishers.

Emerson, M.O. and Smith, C. (2000) *Divided By Faith: Evangelical Religion and the Problem of Race in America.* New York: Oxford University Press.

Erickson, J.H. (1999) *Orthodox Christians in America.* New York: Oxford University Press.

Fanon, F. (1967) 'Racism and Culture' in *Toward the African Revolution* New York: Grove Press, Inc. pp. 31–44.

Feagin, J.R. (2000) *Racist America: Roots, Current Realities, and Future Reparations.* New York: Routledge.

Frederickson, G.M. (1981) *White Supremacy: A Comparative Study in American and South African History* New York: Oxford University Press.

Giddens, A. (1986) *Central Problems in Sociological Theory: Action, Structure, and Contradiction in Social Analysis.* Berkeley: University of California Press.

Gilkes, C.T. (2005) 'Those Segregated and Sacred Hours: New Perspectives on Religion, Race, and Gender in America', *Du Bois Review*, 2 (2): 319–331.

Glenn, E.N. (2002) *Unequal Freedom: How Race and Gender Shaped American Citizenship and Labour.* Cambridge, MA: Harvard University Press.

Gordon, M. (1964) *Assimilation in American Life.* New York: Oxford University Press.

Gossett, T.F. (1963) *Race: The History of an Idea in America.* Dallas: Southern Methodist University Press.

Gutierrez, G. (1993) *Las Casas: In Search of the Poor of Jesus Christ.* Maryknoll, New York: Orbis Books.

Hall, D.D. (ed.) (1997) *Lived Religion in America: Toward a History of Practice.* Princeton: University of Princeton Press.

Hamilton, C. (1972) *The Black Preacher in America.* New York: William Morrow and Company.

Hankins, B. (2002) *Uneasy in Babylon: Southern Baptist Conservatives and American Culture.* Tuscaloosa: University of Alabama Press.

Hughes, E.C. (1963) 'Race Relations and the Sociological Imagination', *American Sociological Review*, 28 (6): 879–890.

Jacobs, P. and Landau, S. with Pell, E. (1971) *To Serve the Devil, Volume One: Natives and Slaves.* New York: Random House.

Jacobs, P. and Landau, S. with Pell, E. (1971) *To Serve the Devil, Volume Two: Colonials and Sojourners.* New York: Random House.

Killian, L.M. (1968) *The Impossible Revolution Phase 2: Black Power and the American Dream.* New York: Random House.

King, C.S. (1969) *My Life With Martin Luther King, Jr.* New York: Henry Holt and Company.

King, M. (1987) *Freedom Song; A Personal Story of the 1960s Civil Rights Movement.* New York: William Morrow and Company.

Kirk-Duggan, C. A. (1997) *Exorcizing Evil: A Womanist Perspective on the Spirituals,* Maryknoll, N.Y.: Orbis Books.

Knowles, L. and Prewitt, K. (eds) (1970) *Institutional Racism in America.* Englewood Cliffs, NJ: Prentice Hall.

Kurien, Prema. (1998) 'Becoming American by Becoming Hindu: Indian Americans Take Their Place at the Multi-Cultural table' in R. S. Warner & J. G. Wittner, (eds.) *Gatherings in Diaspora: Religious Communities and the New Immigration,* Philadelphia: Temple University Press. pp. 37–70.

Levitt, P. (2007) *God Needs No Passport: Immigrants and the Changing American Religious Landscape.* New York: The New Press.

Lewis, D.L. (1993) *W.E.B. Du Bois – Biography of a Race, 1868–1919.* New York: Henry Holt and Company.

Lincoln, C.E. (1973) *The Black Muslims in America.* Boston: The Beacon Press.

Lincoln, C.E. and Mamiya, L.H. (1990) *The Black Church in the African American Experience.* Durham, North Carolina: Duke University Press.

Lyman, S. (1972) *The Negro American in Sociological Thought: A Failure of Perspectives.* New York: Capricorn Books.

Manis, A. (2002) *Southern Civil Religions in Conflict: Civil Rights and the Culture Wars.* Macon, Georgia: Mercer University Press.

Mills, C.W. (1959) *The Sociological Imagination.* New York: Oxford University Press.

Morris, A. (1984) *The Origins of the Civil Rights Movement: Black Communities Organizing for Change.* New York: The Free Press.

Murphy, J.M. (1994) *Working the Spirit: Ceremonies of the African Diaspora.* Boston: Beacon Press.

Murray, P. (1951) *States' Laws on Race and Color.* New York: [Methodist] Women's Division of Christian Service.

Obama, B. H. (2008) A *More Perfect Union,* New York Times March 18, 2008 http://www.nytimes.com/2008/03/18/us/politics/18text-obama.html

Paris, P. (1985) *The Social Teachings of the Black Churches.* Philadelphia: The Fortress Press.

Park, R.E. (1950) *Race and Culture: Essays in the Sociology of Contemporary Man.* New York: The Free Press.

Pope, L. (1957) *The Kingdom Beyond Caste.* New York: The Friendship Press.

Powdermaker, H. (1966) *Stranger and Friend: The Way of the Anthropologist.* New York: W. W. Norton and Company.

Prentiss, C.R. (2003) *Religion and the Creation of Race and Ethnicity.* New York: New York University Press.

Raboteau, A.J. (1978) *Slave Religion: The Invisible Institution in the Antebellum South.* New York: Oxford University Press.

Raboteau, A.J. (1999a) *Canaan Land: A Religious History of African Americans.* New York: Oxford University Press.

Raboteau, A.J. (1999b) *African-American Religion.* New York: Oxford University Press.

Ransby, B. (2003) *Ella Baker and the Black Freedom Movement: A Radical Democratic Vision.* Chapel Hill: University of North Carolina Press.

Rosenberg, E.M. (1989) *The Southern Baptists: A Subculture in Transition.* Knoxville: The University of Tennessee Press.

Rosenberg, E.M. (1993) 'The Southern Baptist Response to the Newest South' in N.T. Ammerman, (ed.) *Southern Baptists Observed: Multiple Perspectives on a Changing Denomination.* Knoxville: University of Tennessee Press. pp. 144–164.

Skocpol, T., Liazos, A. and Ganz, M. (2006) *What a Mighty Power We Can Be: African American Fraternal Groups and the Struggle for Racial Equality.* Princeton: Princeton University Press.

Smart, N. (1983) *Worldviews: Crosscultural Explorations of Human Beliefs.* New York: Charles Scribner's Sons.

Smedley, A. (2007) *Race in North America: Origin and Evolution of a Worldview.* 3rd edition. Boulder, CO: Westview Press.

Sobel, M. (1979) *Trabelin' On: The Slave Journey to an Afro-Baptist Faith.* Westport, CT: Greenwood Press.

Sobel, M. (1987) *The World They Made Together: Black and White Values in Eighteenth-Century Virginia.* Princeton: Princeton University Press.

Spencer, J.M. (1997) *The New Colored People: The Mixed-Race Movement in America.* New York: New York University Press.

Thurman, H. (1981 [1949]) *Jesus and the Disinherited.* Richmond, Indiana: Friends United Press.

Tilly, C. (1998) *Durable Inequality.* Berkeley: University of California Press.

Thurman, H. (1981 [1949]) *Jesus and the Disinherited.* Richmond, IN: Friends United Press.

Tranby, E. and Hartmann, D. (2008) 'Critical Whiteness Theories and the Evangelical "Race Problem": Extending Emerson and Smith's *Divided By Faith*', *Journal for the Scientific Study of Religion*, 47 (3): 341–359.

Turner, R.B. (1997) *Islam in the African-American Experience.* Bloomington: Indiana University Press.

Wald, K. D. and Calhoun-Brown, A. (2007) Religion and Politics in the United States, Lanham, MD: Rowman & Littlefield Publishers.

Warner, R.S. and Wittner, J.G. (eds) (1998) *Gatherings in Diaspora: Religious Communities and the New Immigration.* Philadelphia: Temple University Press.

Webber, T.L. (1978) *Deep Like the Rivers: Education in the Slave Quarter Community, 1831–1865.* New York: W.W. Norton and Company.

West, C. (1993) *Race Matters.* Boston: The Beacon Press.

West, C. (1999) 'The Ignoble Paradox of Modernity' in *The Cornel West Reader.* New York: Basic Civitas Books. pp. 51–4.

Wilmore, G.S. and Cone, J.H. (1980) *Black Theology: A Documentary History, 1966–1979.* Maryknoll, New York: Orbis Books.

Wood, F.G. (1990) *The Arrogance of Faith: Christianity and Race in America from the Colonial Era to the Twentieth Century.* New York: Alfred A. Knopf.

Wright, R. (1995 [1956]) *The Color Curtain.* Jackson: University Press of Mississippi.

17

Whiteness in the Dramaturgy of Racism

Les Back

Writers and intellectuals in the field of critical race studies have viewed the profusion of academic work on whiteness, putatively referred to as 'whiteness studies', as something of a mixed blessing. The initial enthusiasm for the impulse to turn the tables on the usual lines of enquiry and investigate white power rather than minority communities has given way to scepticism about the 'me too' quality of the reflections on white privilege (Ahmed, 2004). Terrance MacMullan comments that the profusion of books and articles on the subject has resulted in 'a veritable cottage industry within the humanities' (MacMullan, 2005: 268). The emergence of this field was signalled by the publication in the early 1990s of key books within feminist historiography and ethnography (Ware, 1992; hooks, 1992; Frankenberg, 1993) and film and media criticism (Dyer, 1988, 1997) and radical history (Roediger, 1991; Lott, 1993). Since then, interest in whiteness has spread to other disciplines. A recent bibliography compiled by members of the Critical Whiteness Study Group at the Centre on Democracy in a Multiracial Society, University of Illinois at Urbana-Champaign listed over a thousand citations in areas ranging from history, literature, philosophy, psychology, sociology and education (Churchill et al., 2006).

More sceptically, critics like Robyn Wiegman have accused whiteness scholars of possessive commitments inventing a novel object of study (i.e., whiteness) while at the same time disavowing universal epistemological power (Wiegman, 1999). The implication in Wiegman's account is that scholars of whiteness are merely making a smart career move in hard times when resources and tenured positions on US campuses are scarce. It is not my aim in what follows to review this emerging literature or to pass judgement on the motives for writing about whiteness. Rather, I want to make some comments on the directions within this area that are to my mind misadventures. From the beginning, I want to argue that the conception of 'whiteness studies', as a distinct area of study, is a distracting premise to think critically from. This is because in my view, it is *racism* rather than whiteness that needs to remain our key analytical and political object of concern. One of the main misadventures I want to suggest is the degree to which 'whiteness studies' has been fixated with the possibility of a sense of white self-hood without white supremacy. At worst, the preoccupation with identity slips into racial vanity albeit one that is worried and self-absorbed. As a consequence, in this chapter, I want to argue that the study of whiteness needs to be more sociable, and prioritise the ways in which white actions, definitions and under-standing are implicated within cultures of racism. Before exploring this argu-ment in the context of everyday life I want to explore how white identity has come to be such a central concern.

BEING WHITE IS DOING WHITENESS

What are 'white identities'? Should those of us who are 'lighter than blue' – to borrow from Curtis Mayfield's phrase – seek to recover, or discover in ourselves, or create anew, a 'white identity' free from racism? Is it possible to think about white identities in a way that is commensurable with other cultural identities? Should another place be set at the table of multiculturalism for such forms of personhood? The short answer, I want to suggest is an emphatic 'No'. Rather, I want to argue that the contribution of the insights contained within the key work in this field (Ware, 1992; Dyer, 1988) is in understanding how all subjects – including the often paranoid majorities – are implicated in societies structured by racial domination and how it may help identify the rhythms and practices of racism as well as its active inactions. The central argument of this chapter is that whiteness as a discourse and practice of power needs to be reckoned with but not recuperated.

These are not just theoretical questions. There is an impulse within the debate about youth and anti-racism in Britain, for example, that argues that young white people need to be offered cultural identities that are in some way equivalent to their black and brown peers. Even to the point that the educational disadvantage of working-class white young people is being thought as an issue of 'identity' which can be fixed through separate educational provision and 'positive role models'. Also, there is a strong current within recent political discourse on the right that asserts that 'whites' are being treated unfairly, that they are not granted equivalent forms of cultural understanding and self-expression. This is happening on both sides of the Atlantic and the common theme is that whites are the new victims of multiculturalism or civil rights. In his book *Paved with Good Intentions* Jared Taylor – the main American exponent of this kind of victimology – asserts that white men have to assert their rights otherwise they will almost face cultural extinction (Taylor, 1992). The main point to make here is that race as a visual regime of power, has regulated and governed social and cultural life. Culture is understood as adhering to already defined racial bodies. To say that whiteness should not be recuperated as 'cultural identity' is to resist the reification race as a way of defining the social subject and equally to policing the boundaries of culture. In short, being white is doing whiteness. The doing of whiteness involved the interplay between visual categorical judgements that are made within the blink of an eye on the stages of social life. In this sense, the abolitionist positions that seek to eliminate whiteness presume that social transformation can be achieved by an act of will. While I sympathise with the call to whites to act differently and be 'race traitors' (Ignatiev and Garvey, 1996) these actions are always taking place on a social stage where identities and judgements are made on the basis of what we look like. Here the materiality of flesh is coded within a gallery of racial types. Societies based on racism think first with their eyes, although as Mark M. Smith has pointed out, race is made through the work power and history does on all of our senses (Smith, 2006). Some commentators like Arun Salandha, in lines with what might be called a 'material turn' within the humanities, have called for a renewed an attention to phenotype within the embodiment of race (Salandha, 2006). Such a move runs contrary to the aspiration to abolish whiteness (Roediger, 1994) and risks giving biological race thinking legitimacy. It would be more productive as I will show in what follows to explore the ways in which the body as a material amongst other materials features within the dramaturgy of racism.

I want to suggest it is a matter of *reckoning* with whiteness, its meaning, history and materiality, rendering it explicit while at the same time seeking its effacement. In this sense I am not arguing for some 'colour blind' return to universal values, although I can see that it might be interpreted that way. Kenan Malik has warned that 'equality can have no meaning in the plural' (Malik, 1998). His argument with multiculturalism is that the language of particularism and difference militates against the realisation of a society of equals. I am in contrast suggesting that whiteness has nowhere to go politically if conceived as an identity, yet at the same time whiteness as a mode of regulating action, thought and understanding is powerful force affecting the choreography of life. Even a cursory look at the discourse of the extreme Right reveals that the language of 'equality', 'fairness' and 'rights' – and I must emphasise IDENTITY – is assimilated into the lexicon of openly racist politics. Part of the confusion of our time is that problematics and tactics associated with anti-racism and movements for civil rights have travelled.

Under the leadership of chairman Nick Griffin, the British National Party (BNP) has attempted to repackage itself as a 'respectable' electoral organisation along the lines of the Front Nationale in France. In many respects the nature of the BNP's political message has shifted. The racial nationalists of today deny that they hate anyone, but rather that they merely love themselves and want to preserve whiteness as an essentialised social identity which they say is under threat. The house publication of the BNP has been re-named as – you guessed it – 'Identity'. Their dominant motif is that whites are now the victims. In a postmodern twist, racial nationalists have also assimilated a kind of brummagem multiculturalism. For example in the BNP's mission statement, it claims to 'embrace and cherish the native cultural diversity within the British Isles.'[1] Yet it claims that white identity is being lost, their cultural rights violated and whites are invoked increasingly as beleaguered.[2]

Yet, it is not only the racial projects of the racist Right that have taken an identitarian turn. Liberals and social democrats have complained that the debate about multiculturalism has ignored the plight of the white working classes in British cities. The Young Foundation's *The New East End* has been influential in this regard and their claim is that white poverty in London has been overlooked (Dench et al., 2006). Also, academic and political discussions of whiteness have been drawn into a concern with how to understand, transform or even rescue white selfhood from such forces (Wray and Newitz, 1998).

Sara Ahmed has questioned whether a whiteness that is anxious and worried about itself is really any better because: 'anti-racism becomes a matter of generating a positive white identity, an identity that makes the white subject feel good about itself. The declaration of such an identity is not in my view anti-racist action' (Ahmed, 2004: 6). For her studies of whiteness are coloured by narcissism in which 'the conditions are not in place that would allow such "saying" to "do" what it "says"' (ibid: 9). The anxious self-centred reflection on racial privilege results in 'unhappy performatives' concerned with political impression management rather than anti-racism. There is much in this challenging critique that is sound. In a sense, this critique alerts us to two very different possibilities or opportunities within the study of whiteness. The first is identified as self-centred and narcissistic in the way that Ahmed characterises it. This anxious and worrisome endeavour has the danger of being too anchored in the self and too little connected concerned with the rhythms of life and the relationship to others. It is true that some of the key empirical studies of whiteness have focussed on interviews and self-narratives rarely situated beyond their subject's telling or placed within the dynamics of a social of cultural arena (see Frankenburg, 1993; Byrne, 2006). There is, however, another move or direction that I would like to argue for.

The second potential within the study of whiteness is precisely concerned with whiteness as a structure and choreography of action. It focussed on the situations and stages in which whiteness as a dance of power unfolds, or for that matter stumbles or misses a step. John Hartigan's study of Detroit is a good example of such that attends to everyday dynamics in process within local contexts (Hartigan,

1999). Within the literature on whiteness, Hartigan's work is exceptional in that he is committed to ethnographic research and to paying close attention to the complex ambiguous forms of white subjectivity. This second move is committed to understanding what I want to refer to as the dramaturgy of racism, that is, the patterns of action, iteration and unfolding within particular contexts that always involve interplay between the local, national or even global levels. It is here that I would like to enlist interactive sociology (Goffman, 1959; 1971) alongside more recent writing about identity, race and performativity (Bell, 1999; Byrne, 2006; Sharma, 2006).

Richard Dyer, one of the most influential writers in the field, observed that whiteness operates like an absent presence or it can be alive within 'white subjects' regardless of whether they are willing or able to admit it (Dyer, 1988, 1997). The problem here is also that whiteness colonises definitions of normality in ways that remain to some implicit and unspoken. There is a difficult navigation to be made between the implicit processes of normalisation and the development of a consciousness of those spectral norms and their transcendence. This is also a matter of developing an adequate language to name recursive forms, that is, patterns of embodied culture that are registered in actions and not necessarily in words. Perhaps a radical politics for 'white people' entails some kind of suture over what Lillian Smith called 'conscience torn from acts', the separation of ethical reflection from living (Smith, 1950: 25). It is here that Ghassan Hage's distinction between and ethics of 'worry' and 'care' might prove useful.

Hage shows in his analysis of the Australian context how the anxious 'white worriers' articulate a narcissistic racism concerned only with the decline of their society and their place within it (Hage, 1998). A culture of worry produces a self-centred siege mentality in which hope for the future is diminished, where insecure attachments and a paranoid nationalism prevail that ultimate result in a defensive society. In contrast, Hage argues for an ethics of care that is reciprocal, sociable, outward looking and farreaching, concerned with the plight of others 'that generates hope among its citizens and induces them to care for it' (Hage, 2003: 3).

Hage's ethics of care offers an alternative way of paying attention to not only how whiteness is lived but also the damage done by racism to social life. Whiteness is not only a way of seeing but also a pattern or choreography of action and inaction. In order to demonstrate exactly what this means, I want to focus on a specific incident of racist violence and its aftermath. It is hard to overstate the impact of the murder of Stephen Lawrence on the night of Thursday 22 April 1993, close to a bus stop on the streets of southeast London, on British political and cultural life. His brutal stabbing by a racist gang cut short a young life and exposed the nature of the racism that wounds British society as a whole. The Metropolitan police's failure to catch and prosecute his killers exposed the colour-coded nature of the British criminal justice system. Fifteen years after the murder, Stephen Lawrence's killers still walk free and this injustice haunts the streets of the city. Whiteness is shaded into these events from the reactions of people at the crime scene to the indifference and failure of the police investigators. Yet, the name Stephen Lawrence has become synonymous with bringing out into the open both violent and respectable racisms, it is carried through time in memorials, art works, dedicated scholarships, educational trusts and in the art galleries and educational buildings that all bear his name. Remembering Stephen Lawrence involves reckoning with those who want to deepen the wound and equally those who want to heal it.

Walter Benjamin wrote that 'Language shows clearly that memory is not an instrument for exploring the past but its theatre. It is the medium of past experience, as the ground is the medium in which dead cities lie interred' (Benjamin, 1997: 314). The narratives, acts of commemoration and desecration reveal the character of whiteness in the theatre of racism. One of the many lessons of this case is that power and violence hide in silence. The past is entombed or concealed in silence. More than this, racism damages the public apprehension of violent crimes of this sort from the way the police officers reacted at the crime scene, to the response of local residents and the way journalists sought to explain the murder. None of this makes sense without an appreciation of the ways in which whiteness comes to feature within their actions.

The remaining parts of the chapter are divided into three sections. First, a brief chronology of events leading up to the murder will be outlined along with a description of the social landscape in which it took place. Here, the emphasis will be on understanding whiteness as a way of seeing. Second, the chapter will focus on the botched investigation and the struggle to expose the whiteness and injustice that stifled the Lawrence family's struggle for justice for their son. The third section focuses on understanding the struggles over the white coding of place in the context of racist haunting and anti-racist reckoning. Finally, I want to end by returning to the issues of identity, whiteness and racism and offer some conclusions on the turn to identity within whiteness studies. Before doing this, I will try and describe the place where the murder took place and its social history by inviting you to take a walk down Well Hall Road.

WHITE LOOKS

On 5 March 1998, it was reported that the plaque that had been set in the pavement to commemorate the place where Stephen Lawrence had died had been defaced. An off-duty police officer had stumbled across the vandalism of the memorial. Someone had tipped a pot of white paint over the plaque on Well Hall Road. I decided that I was going to go over to Eltham and look at the plaque and take some photographs.

It wasn't the first time that this had happened and there is something deeply disturbing about the repeated violation and vandalism that is directed at this place where Stephen Lawrence fell. A memorial plaque was first laid in the pavement on Sunday 23 July 1995.[3] Well Hall Road was sealed off and 200 friends and supporters gathered and the Bishop of Croydon, Reverend Wilfred Wood, led a roadside service. Racist vandals immediately preyed upon the marble memorial. Doreen Lawrence – Stephen's mother – reflected in her memoir:

> The first plaque laid down in Well Hall Road was commissioned by black workers in Greenwich, who collected money for the purpose. It was a small tablet and it was vandalised so badly that you could not recognise Stephen's name. A company decided to replace it, and they paid for something the size of a small paving stone. (Lawrence, 2006: 219–220).

His body had been taken to Jamaica by his parents where it was laid to rest. Stephen's father Neville Lawrence explained:

> We had fears about burying Stephen here [in London] because of the situation surrounding his death and also the fact that it was explained to us that [racists] were going to be able to go and dig his body after he was buried … I did not wish that to happen to my son so the family sat down just before we knew we were going to have his body and came to the conclusion that the best thing to do was to take him home to Jamaica. (The Stephen Lawrence Inquiry, 1999: Appendix 7)

Shortly after the white paint incident in March 1998, I made the short drive from my home to Eltham. It was around 10 am when I parked the car in a small side road in the middle of Well Hall Road, called Downham Road. What was immediately striking about this part of southeast London was the suburban affluence that stood side by side with the working-class public housing. The road that I parked in was expensive and upmarket. I remember looking out of the window of the car as I pulled up to see the mock Tudor frontage of a four- or five-bedroomed house. I didn't realise at that time, but the spot where Stephen Lawrence was killed was just 50 yards from where I had parked the car. Well Hall Road is a very long road that leads from the top of Woolwich Common right down to the bottom of Eltham. It is close to the Prime Meridian in Greenwich, which is the point from which time is measured and from which the cartography of empire was drawn. Greenwich Council boasted on its billboard advertisements that 'The Millenium Starts Here'.

There are a series of bus stops just after the roundabout where the Coronet Cinema is located. At 10.30 pm on 22 April 1993, Stephen Lawrence stood here in the mouth of Dickson Road to see if a bus was coming. He had spent the evening with his friend Duwayne Brooks, who was standing part way between Dickson Road and the roundabout. He saw a group of five or six white youths opposite where Stephen was looking for the next bus. Duwayne Brooks called Stephen Lawrence. He hestitated. One of the white youths called out: 'What, what nigger'? This first set of deadly white looks identified the two black boys as targets. The group crossed the road quickly and engulfed Stephen. The attack probably lasted less than 15–20 seconds. During this time one or more of the attackers stabbed Stephen Lawrence twice. Duwayne Brooks called to Stephen to run and to follow him. Stephen Lawrence managed somehow to run over 250 yards to the point where he fell. Bleeding profusely he lost consciousness. In a panic Duwayne Brooks went into a phone box and called for an ambulance. He called out to a white couple across the street, they looked at him suspiciously. The couple – Conor and Louise Taafe – had just come from a meeting at the local Catholic Church. Their first thought was that Stephen and Duwayne had been in a fight or that they were about to commit a mugging. A second set of white looks albeit more ambivalent and more fearful than hateful.

Sensing that something was wrong, the Taafes went to attend to Stephen who had collapsed on the pavement. The police officers that had arrived did little to attend to him. Lousie Taafe tried to speak to Stephen. Conor Taafe commented at the inquiry into Stephen's death that they feared he was mortally wounded:

> Louise and I both knew that hearing is one of the last things to go, and so, while he was there, she said: 'You are loved. You are loved'. I had some blood on my hands. When I went home ... and washed the blood off my hands with some water in a container, and there is a rose bush in our back garden, a very, very old, huge rose bush – a rose tree is I suppose more appropriate – and I poured the water with his blood in it into the bottom of that rose tree. So in a way I suppose he is kind of living on a bit. (Norton-Taylor 1999: 37)

The care that the Taafe's demonstrated is poignant yet their initial reaction to Duwayne Brooks and Stephen Lawrence was one of suspicion (Cathcart, 1999: 11–12). Whiteness coloured what the Taafe's saw – two young black boys in the street after dark were viewed as an immediate threat. And yet their reaction at the scene is resonant with Ghassan Hage's comments on an ethics of care that reaches out beyond the scripts of race (Hage, 2003).

The police officers' assessment at the crime scene amount to a third set of white looks. Perhaps the most damning finding contained within the Macpherson Report – the result of the public inquiry into the murder – is the account of the racism that the Lawrence family and Duwayne Brooks suffered at the hands of the police. This is best represented in the words of their own statements. First Duwayne Brooks, who said of the attitude of the police at the scene of the crime:

> I was pacing up and down, up and down. I was desperate for the ambulance. It was taking too long. I was frightened by the amount of blood Steve was losing. I saw his life fading away. I didn't know what to do to help him. I was frightened I would do something wrong.
>
> WPC Bethel said, 'How did it start? Did they chase you for nothing?' I said one of them shouted, 'What, what nigger?' She asked me if I had any weapons on me. She was treating me like she was suspicious of me, not like she wanted to help. If she had asked me for more details of the boys' descriptions or what they were wearing I would have told her. Those would have been sensible questions [...]
>
> I was driven to Plumstead police station. I now know that in their statements the police said I broke a window in the front office. I didn't. I wasn't even in the front office. It just shows they were treating me like a criminal and not like a victim. They kept saying, 'Are you sure they said 'What, what nigger?' I said, 'I am telling the truth'. A senior officer said to me, 'You mean you've done nothing wrong to provoke them in any way?' I said, 'No, we were just waiting for a bus' (Norton-Taylor, 1999: 95–96).

What comes through in this testimony is the extent to which the police saw Duwayne and Stephen as in circumstances of their own making. Two black boys being attacked spells – in the eyes of the white Police – 'gang violence', not a racist attack.

Doreen and Neville Lawrence's treatment at the hands of the police showed incredible insensitivity. They were seen to be the puppets of 'political agitators', being manipulated by 'outsiders'. In her evidence to the Inquiry, Doreen Lawrence outlined this:

> Basically, we were seen as gullible simpletons. This is best shown by Detective Chief Superintendent Ilsey's comment that I had obviously been primed to ask questions. Presumably, there is no possibility of me being an intelligent, black woman with thoughts of her own who is able to ask questions for herself. We were patronised and were fobbed off … (The Stephen Lawrence Inquiry, 1999: 11).

And Neville Lawrence: 'It is clear to me that the police come in with the idea that the family of black victims are violent criminals who are not to be trusted' (The Stephen Lawrence Inquiry, 1999: 12).

The white looks coded the victims of racist crime as either 'gang members' or 'simpletons' manipulated by political agitators. Whiteness here is a way, a seeing that leads to a way of acting. In the case of the racist perpetrators, it is the split second glance that black targets of violence identified, attacked and ultimately killed. Equally, the fear and apprehension of the Taafe's, the most sensitive and caring witnesses at the crime scene, is a product of the association conjured by seeing two black boys in distress after dark. Finally, what the police saw was coloured by the damaged filter of white apprehension. Each of these white looks have different outcomes but they share some of the same qualities, that is, they mark out the presence of the two black boys in this neighbourhood either for attack, fear or suspicion. Racism murders, divides and inflicts brutal forms of harm. It also damages the ability of both victim and perpetrator to apprehend, make sense of, and engage, with the social world. Duwayne Brooks later said in his statement to the inquiry that Stephen didn't know how to read the signs, he didn't understand the danger.

There are three bus stops: two on the right-hand side and one on the left. As I walked up the right-hand side of the road, the first bus stop was covered with National Front[4] graffiti – some of it was in black marker pen, but most was actually etched into the paint of the bus stop. One said 'This is the NF bus stop'. Tens of NF emblems were scratched into the lampost, and onto the bus shelter itself – there were a few things written on the seats, there was a NF sign on the rubbish bin, written in black magic marker. I imagined the many hands it must have taken to etch this defacement. Still other hands have tried to scribble over, scratch out and cover the fascist emblems. As I walked past, a black person was standing at the bus stop.

Still further up the road, I saw an orange police placard which referred to the incident where Stephen Lawrence's plaque had been defaced. I walked past the

Figure 17.1   Bus stop Well Hall Road, Eltham (photography by author).

placard – this is about 15 yards before the second bus stop. On the ground a small plaque is set into the paving stones, which had clearly had white paint cleaned off it recently. The stone is a simple square granite tablet and written in gold lettering: 'IN MEMORY OF STEPHEN LAWRENCE – 13.9.1974 – 22.4.1993 MAY HE REST IN PEACE. The sight of the words puts a different inflection on Walter Benjamin's famous ambulant invitation to go 'botanizing on the asphalt' (Benjamin, 1992: 36).

This area had seen murderous racism before: Roland Adams[5] had his life taken by a gang in neighbouring Thamesmead and Rohid Duggal[6] who was killed outside a Kebab shop in Eltham (see Hewitt, 2006: 44–49). Almost immediately after Stephen Lawrence was killed, anti-racist activists and concerned ordinary Londoners laid flowers at the roadside where he collapsed.[7] It is as if the place where he fell has come to symbolise the wound of racism: people come to this place either to heal or deepen it.

'WALL OF SILENCE', SPEAKING AND SHOWING

After the attack, 26 different people from within the area gave evidence implicating the five main suspects: Neil and Jamie Acourt, David Norris, Gary Dobson and Luke Knight. Information was also passed directly to the Lawrence family.

Despite this, the police complained of a 'wall of silence' in the local community (Jeffrey, 1999). Doreen Lawrence commented later: 'Every time we tried to pass this information to the police, they just didn't seem interested. They kept insisting there was a wall of silence but the only wall of silence was around their ears'.[8] The five suspects had a history of violence, a fixation with knives and vituperative racism. The Acourt brothers self-styled gangsters called themselves the 'Eltham Krays'.[9] All except David Norris lived on the Brook Estate off Well Hall Road. David Norris is the son of Clifford Norris, a notorious gunrunner and drug dealer who lived in a desirable peri-urban mansion in nearby Chislehurst, Bromley. Many believe that Norris used his connections with corrupt police officers to sabotage the investigation from the very beginning.[10] It wasn't until 7 May that the police arrested the main suspects and made them appear in an identity parade. The police investigation was a complete mess: an appalling catalogue of mistakes, along with displays of ignorance and bigotry with regard to Stephen's parents, Neville and Doreen Lawrence, and Duwayne Brooks, Stephen's friend.

In April 1995, the family took out a private prosecution. It was heard a year later in the High Court but the case against Neil and Jamie Acourt and

Figure 17.2   The Stephen Lawrence memorial (photography by author).

David Norris was dropped at the committal proceedings. It is here that the family first saw the surveillance tape that the police had recorded covertly at Gary Dobson's flat in Footscray over a three-week period in December 1994. Doreen Lawrence reflected:

> it was clear that somehow the boys sensed that someone had been in the flat. As if they had an idea that someone was listening ... But they did not realise that it was not just an audio recording, that there would also be visual images. Since they were unaware that a camera was watching, their body language was unguarded and all the more shocking. (Lawrence, 2006: 140)

Doctor Stephen Shepherd described in court the way that Stephen Lawrence had been struck with a large knife from above, downward into his chest. The video evidence showed the young men's obsession with knives. Neil Acourt, the elder brother, rehearsed stabbing moves with a foot-long knife including a motion like the arc of a cricket bowler's action. This dance of white violence was repeated over and over again. Stephen Lawrence's murderer used precisely such a motion to strike the fatal blow. Doreen Lawrence described it later as an 'obscene performance ... It was truly impossible to comprehend how these boys' parents could watch that video without showing any sign of shame' (ibid: 145). While the boys were cocky and shameless in the courtroom they did not look at the bereaved family. Their mothers did not try to hide their contempt and from just a few feet away they glared openly and scowled at Doreen Lawrence.

The Lawrence family lodged a formal complaint against the police officers involved. After the inquest verdict, the Lawrence family met with the Shadow Home Secretary, Labour MP, Jack Straw. Straw initially proposed a general investigation into the state of race relations but was dissuaded by Doreen Lawrence who insisted that any inquiry should be into the events surrounding her son's murder. In July, after the May 1997 general election, the new Labour Home Secretary, Jack Straw, announced that a judicial public inquiry was to be set up and chaired by Sir William Macpherson. This was to be started after the Police Complaints Authority report into the investigation conducted by the Kent Constabulary. In December 1997, the report went to the Home Secretary and revealed that the handling of the Lawrence investigation showed: 'significant weaknesses, omissions, and lost opportunities in the conduct of the case' (Norton-Taylor, 1999: 12).

These are the events that lead up to the Stephen Lawrence Inquiry. It was a historic event. It sat for 59 days in Hannibal House in the Elephant and Castle. It called the alleged murderers to answer along with the key figures in the police force that had bungled the investigation. The first part of the investigation focused on 'the matters arising from the death of Stephen Lawrence'. In addition, the Inquiry sat for a further day to 'identify the lessons to be learned for the investigation and prosecution of racially motivated crimes'. Eighty-eight people gave evidence and thousands of pages of transcription were produced. The report described Stephen's parents, Neville and Doreen Lawrence, as the mainsprings of the Inquiry. They attended virtually all the hearings. Eugene McLaughlin and Karim Murji concluded: 'Anyone who attended the inquiry at the Elephant and Castle in London soon realised that something quite extraordinary and unprecedented was happening' (McLaughlin and Murji, 1999: 372).

It was revealing to watch the five suspects and the police being brought to answer before the Inquiry. It was not just the Acourts, Norris, Knight and Dobson who had hidden in silence. It had also been the police officers. Doreen Lawrence said in her statement after the Coroner's inquest: 'The wall of silence was not only in the surrounding area where my son was killed, but with the officers who were supposed to be investigating the crime' (The Stephen Lawrence Inquiry, 1999: 300). The Inquiry was a matter of reckoning with the perpetrators of the injustice suffered by the Lawrence family. This bringing to book was a daily spectacle in the news media.

Pierre Bourdieu once wrote that: 'a whole system of values reappear in gesture and movements of the body ...' (Bourdieu, 1977: 94). Watching the police officers involved in the botched investigation walk into the Inquiry, holding their papers tightly, symbolised the resistance on their part to admit to any wrongdoing. The fact that the Inquiry took place in inner London was significant, because it meant that it was hosted in a profoundly multicultural and ethnically mixed environment. Holding the Inquiry here forced the perpetrators to return to a world they had fled. One of the general patterns in south London is that white working-class communities have moved out of the inner city into the white suburbs like Eltham and Welling. The five suspects fought tooth and nail to avoid appearing. On 29 and 30 June the five suspects appeared and ran the gauntlet of a hostile crowd. Their image of racism was not what our political culture has come to expect, that is, the Nazi, the shaven-headed skinhead with bovver boots. Rather, they were stylishly dressed in suits and wearing Ben Sherman shirts and Armani sunglasses. What was disturbing was how familiar they looked.[11] They swaggered and bowled[12] into the Inquiry, embodying a form of masculine performance that announced readiness, an unrepentant mastery of their bodies as they moved through this hostile space. Only Dobson looked scared. The rest embraced the challenge. Neil Acourt was 'giving it', his hand in front of him, arms at 30 degrees and his fingers twitched in invitation to his adversaries to 'come on'. Inside the inquiry they said nothing, admitted nothing and accepted nothing.

The Macpherson Report commented: 'All five suspects came into the witness box and answered questions under oath or affirmation. To say that they gave evidence would be to dignify their appearance. They all relied upon alleged lack of memory. They showed themselves to be arrogant and dismissive' (The Stephen Lawrence Inquiry, 1999a: 40). In particular, the five were confronted with the video surveillance evidence recorded by the police in December of 1994. The report referred to this material as 'prolonged and appalling words which sully the paper upon which they have been recorded' (ibid). The transcriptions of this material are truly appalling.

The suspects clearly thought they were only being listened to but their body language and facial expressions were also being filmed clearly.[13] They mocked the police with staged commentary on the murder and the investigation. Neil Acourt and David Norris were sneering and contemptuous. In one extract recorded on the evening of 7 December 1994 Acourt teased his invisible eavesdroppers:

> And they ain't got nothing still. We ain't done nothing that's what I mean, there's none of us done fuck all. But the thing that makes me laugh, Dave, they're gonna be doing it for the rest of our lives mate and I am just gonna be laughing all the way to Leeds. (Ibid: 21)

A few moments later Neil Acourt says of the victims: 'I fancy they've had a crack deal me self I fancy'.

Norris replies: 'Probably had a bit of a toot or something or had a bit of crack it's all gone wrong, the coon's got knackered up and all of a sudden four innocent people are getting done for it'.

Neil Acourt says 'Yeah, that's what I fancy has happened'.

Norris continues: 'That's definitely what's happened Neil. Every time it [Stephen's murder] comes on the news – the real people are sitting laughing their nuts off…'

'What real people' says Neil Acourt.

Norris repeats 'Yeah the real people are sitting laughing their nuts off'.

Luke Knight adds 'Think they've got away with it mate, fucking scott free'.

Unable to resist, but unaware that he is looking straight into the surveillance camera, Neil Acourt says laughing: 'Yeah they're definitely doing that'. Doreen Lawrence wrote in her autobiography: 'The look of gloating triumph on his face as he said that will live with me for the rest of my life' (Lawrence, 2006: 150).

The five suspects' apparent 'loss' of memory was revealed in other ways. Paul Connerton has written that memory and history can be 'sedimented in the body', that in walks, gestures and bodily practices are stored an embodied history (Connerton, 1989: 102). This might also apply to the ways in which we might interpret the way Neil Acourt laughed into the face of the police surveillance camera or his body language as he left Hannibal House. As they 'bowled' out of the inquiry to face a hostile crowd their violence and aggression was manifest in every movement. The expression on their contorted faces spoke volumes and left little doubt. Watching the scenes acted out on the walkway to the Inquiry was like watching south London's history of racism unfold in a microcosm.

It was precisely this sense of the preconceptions and values of police officers that the Inquiry sought to name through the notion of institutional racism. Indeed, the Macpherson Inquiry precipitated an unprecedented level of media interest in this issue. It was an opportunity to reckon not only with racism's violent and hateful face but also its more genteel institutional quality. Those silences and active inactions are part of the choreography of whiteness be it the police's deafness to incriminating evidence or the suspect's convenient amnesia and embodied culpability.

LINES OF HATE, COLOURS OF MEMORY

The memorial plaque on Well Hall Road has been defaced repeatedly. Often the vandalism or desecration has coincided with key moments in the struggle to bring his killers to justice. On 5 March 1998 the stone memorial was battered with a hammer, seemingly in an attempt to erase Stephen Lawrence's name from the plaque. This was just eight days before the inquiry into the murder began on 16 March 1998. The police installed hidden surveillance cameras monitoring the plaque. In May 1998 the plaque was attacked with a hammer by Stuart Hollingdale, a known extremist.[14] Hollingdale was prosecuted and jailed. The family's campaign to seek justice was met repeatedly with a defacement of the memorial. On 24 February 24 1999 the memorial was again daubed with paint. The vandalism occurred less than 24 hours after the release of the judicial inquiry into the murder. The bus stop nearby was daubed in white paint and an empty dog food tin that had contained the white paint thrown over the memorial was found near the scene.[15] Neville Lawrence told *The Voice* newspaper: 'We have no proof of who did this but believe those who did the damage had something to do with Stephen's murder and that they are hoping to deflect us from our purpose ... This will not happen. They are feeling the pressure of our campaign for justice'.[16] No one was prosecuted for these acts because the surveillance camera installed by the police had been replaced with a 'dummy camera' that contained no film. It is particularly astonishing and perhaps revealing that the police should put dummy cameras at the scene, given the ineptitude of the Metropolitan Police exposed in the inquiry. The events unfolded at a national level but were reacted to by racists – both politically active and demotic – within the locality through repeated vandalism.

The Guardian – a national broadsheet newspaper – ran the headline: 'White paint splattered over the memorial to Stephen Lawrence. The racist answer to a new beginning for Britain'.[17] A local resident was quoted, 'I just thank God that the boy isn't buried around here ... These people will never let him rest'.[18] Others locals tried to justify the attack: 'What do you expect? White people around here get all the abuse and they see the Lawrences and the blacks getting special treatment. They are angry because they know the treatment wouldn't be same if it was a white kid who died'.[19] On the 18 July, a man was arrested for spitting food and urinating on the memorial.[20] On the 27 July he was committed to jury for racially aggravated criminal damage and on the 11 February 2000 he was found not guilty. On the 10 July 2004 chippings were discovered on the memorial.

The attacks on the small memorial are not simply attempts at erasure or in the case of the paint a literal 'white out'. There is something else going on here that has an uncanny effect. The defacement of the plaque makes visible the recurrence of racism. This is emphasised by the way in which the vandalism of the memorial has run parallel to key events in the Stephen Lawrence Inquiry and then the release of the judicial inquiry. The memorial becomes a site for a struggle over the nature of the wound, remembering and belonging. Should this be a

Figure 17.3   Flowers and paint (photography by author).

compensation of any kind? It might be suggested that this is evidence of a politics of contestation that should be embraced. Or, as one commentator put it: 'Let
them bring their paint and we will bring our flowers'. But, the thing that is haunting is the consequences this has, not for politics in the abstract, but for the felt
consequences of racism in the particular. In some ways this line of argument –
that the defacement produces both the visibility of racism and a political response –
feels right intellectually but *wrong* ethically. Such a view strikes a clever
intellectual position but it is not a good way to make a home. What must it have
meant to the Lawrences themselves? What does it say to them?

In her memoir, Doreen Lawrence writes of how she has visited Well Hall Road
repeatedly. Her visits are acts of remembering like the many vigils that have been
held there.

> Every year I have a small vigil for Stephen on the anniversary of his death. David Cruise, our
> former minister, always remembers the dates of Stephen's birthday and of his death,
> and makes the effort to come with me if I need him. We go to the exact place on Well Hall
> Road where my son died, sometimes just the two of us … Some people driving past
> stop their cars and come onto the pavement; some toot their horns in respect. Others
> are aggressive, jeering at us as we stand there. I bring flowers to lay on the plaque but
> I don't stay very long, because I am conscious of being watched and I don't feel safe there.
> (Lawrence, 2006: 19)

Sometimes she goes alone to the plaque and wonders whether he was calling for
her on that night and whether she talked it into happening by worrying at him to
be careful. Each time this is a defiant and brave act against those who seek to
make this London street a preserve for 'whites only'.

There are other acts to be recorded. I want to return to 4 March 1998 where we
started, when a pot of white paint was emptied on the plaque. Artist Tim Cousins
passed along Well Hall Road on Thursday 5 March as he did every morning on
his way to his studio in Deptford. Incensed by this act of crass effacement he
used his anger to paint. He made twenty-one drawings in twelve hours, working

without stopping. Tim was a schoolteacher in Greenwich before becoming an artist full-time and he taught some of Stephen Lawrence's relatives. The pictures he produced are striking for their strong, bold lines picking out elements of the landscape such as the mock black and white Tutor frontage of the houses on Well Hall Road. Some of the drawings allude to the shape and colour of the bus stop itself. The paintings do not represent or depict anything figuratively and include a large abstract canvas and a series of small drawings. They capture a strong emotion but avoid any complicity with violent imagery or, for that matter, caricature that seeks to evoke compassion or nobility. He has made the work available for show with the understanding that a donation should be made to the Stephen Lawrence Trust.

Racist graffiti uses a thick impasto to make hateful white inscriptions. Tim's paintings take the same materials and put them to different work. Speaking about his work in July 2000 he connected the images to his experience of the impact that the murder had locally:

> What surprised me [at the time] and really upset me was that some of the teachers, quite a few of the support staff, and probably a majority of the cleaning staff seemed to be very antagonistic to the idea of [Stephen's] body being sent back to be buried in Jamaica. Now I had to argue quite continually that ... 'What would you do in that position?' The question was always coming back 'well you're either part of the community or you're not'. And this to me really becomes a problem [...] and it's something I think that even non-racist people do not understand, that in a way you have to look after yourself and you have to *have memories kept safe*. If they can't be kept safe in this country, then they must be kept safe elsewhere.[21]

Was the vandalism of the plaque evidence that Stephen Lawrence's memory wasn't being kept safe? 'That's precisely the point', he continued.

> I think everyone would agree that it's not a glib comment that for the police not to actually hold video tape in a camera close to the plaque is quite mind-boggling and so insensitive to the issue of memory. There's no way that the body could actually rest in this country I suppose.[22]

This is an indictment on the nature of the offence. The balance of forces remaining in favour of those who would deepen the wound despite the political struggle led by the family and intuitive anti-racist and just sentiment inside the communities themselves.

One of the things that struck me very strongly was the degree to which people in south London – on both sides of the line of colour – identified with the Lawrence family and the police injustice. But as time has passed, resentment has started to gather pace where once there was empathy. Since the Stephen Lawrence Inquiry the police have cast themselves as the victims. A police officer with 20-years experience told me: 'Morale is very low in police force – they've taken a real hiding. It's not helped by people with political axes to grind making things worse. I mean, I have a great deal of admiration for the Lawrence family, but they have been manipulated by people who have other agendas'.[23] It is they who have been misunderstood, they claim, making their job impossible. In an

Figure 17.4 Eltham Bus Stop by Tim Cousins, 1998, (reproduced with artist's permission).

extraordinary commentary, Sir Paul Condon, Chief of the Metropolitan Police, referred to the Macpherson Report as a kind of bereavement that the force had to grieve over. He said:

> The grieving process will be influenced by other big things. So the – the catching of the [white supremacist] nail bomber,[24] you know, that was a world class operation. And so as time goes on, hopefully, there will be other dramatic occasions and situations where their [the Metropolitan Police's] confidence and their sense of pride can be restored.[25]

It is not only the police who have cast themselves as victims. Michael Collins in his book *The Likes of Us* represents the suspects as victims. Collins trains his ire on the class conceit of middle-class liberals in the media who sentenced these young men as guilty. He described the atmosphere at the Inquiry as like one found at public executions: 'From the mouths of middle-class professionals in the crowd, and from the pens of journalists and columnists noteworthy for their liberal sensibilities, came the argument that we should hang 'em high, or at least lock 'em up and throw away the key' (Collins, 2004: 6). Collins has absolutely nothing to say about the evidence that incriminates those men in this murder who still walk free. Yet, for Collins, the portraits of racism became an indictment of the whole community: 'It wasn't simply the suspects, their families, that were on trial, but the neighbourhoods in which the tragedy was played out' (ibid).

True, it is easy to demonise 'racist thugs' and organise the problem into exceptional cases of monstrous violence. It wasn't class conceit that put the knife into the hand of Stephen Lawrence's murderer. Collins' attack on middle-class liberals diverts any discussion of violent racism in working-class life and is little more than denial masked in a language of self-exculpating white victimology. Dealing with class prejudice will not lessen the uneven presence of violent actions and vociferous racism in working-class communities in suburban Southeast London and elsewhere. *The Likes of Us* includes not a line about the surveillance video, the knife wielding or the suspects' hateful tirades. On the 11th May, 2001, Neil Acourt and David Norris hired a car to drive through their neighbourhood and went cruising along Well Hall Road. Half a mile from where Stephen Lawrence was killed, they came across a black man who was walking home. He heard shouts of 'nigger' and one of the men in the car threw a beer can at him. The black man was Detective Constable Gareth Reid, an off-duty police officer, who immediately identified his attackers. David Norris denied that he shouted racist abuse and claimed in court that he threw the drink in 'a moment of madness' caused by 'nine years of persecution' following the investigation and inquiry: he claimed he was a victim.[26] They were sentenced to 18 months in jail and served nine.

On the tenth anniversary of Stephen Lawrence's death, Caroline Jones made her way with her partner Linda Bellos and friend Paula Thomas to place a bouquet of flowers at the roadside plaque. A white man shouted from the window of a red van passing along Well Hall Road that the murder was 'the best thing that ever happened'.[27] It seems clear that London is not yet a place where a hospitable memory can be given to the spectre of Stephen Lawrence. This is made materially evident through the repeated defacement and desecration of the memorial stone. The murder haunts the landscape. Also, the landscape haunts the memory of the racist event, it weaves continually back into it adding extra layers of complexity. Sometimes the viciousness of white racist inscription is shown while at other points the unevenness of racism's power is revealed.

In the *Specters of Marx* Jacques Derrida argues that we have to live with ghosts 'to exorcise, not in order to chase away the ghosts, but this time to grant them the right […] to […] a hospitable memory […] out of a concern for justice' (Derrida, 1994: 175). Is the kind of reconciliation that Derrida points to worth yearning for? Is reconciliation itself a fantasy, or indeed as one observer put to me a white fantasy? The bold lines of artists like Tim Cousins or the actions of Conor and Louise Taafe or those inside the community who tried to feed information about the identity of the killers to the police are themselves evidence that anti-racist impulses are also part of the fabric of southeast London. Those attempts to step out of whiteness, to act differently are complex and partial. But reducing particular areas of the city to hellish no-go areas of whiteness and utter racism extinguishes the spark of hope, while they may provide compensating comfort for those who luxuriate in them. Such a monochrome geography flattens the complexity of these neighbourhoods. Indeed, such views simply mirror the map of exclusion that racism attempts to draw.

Avery Gordon in her eloquent book *Ghostly Matters* alludes to this issue when she writes:

> Offer it a hospitable reception we must, but the victorious reckoning with the ghost always requires partiality to the living. Because ultimately haunting is about how to transform a shadow of a life into an undiminished life whose shadows touch softly in the spirit of peaceful reconciliation. In this necessarily collective undertaking, the end, which is not an ending at all, belongs to everyone. (Gordon, 1997: 208)

The murderers did not just extinguish one life. Doreen Lawrence writes about the effect that the aftermath of the murder had on her marriage and her family but that she takes comfort from the fact that Stephen Lawrence's name is synonymous with change: 'It's as though he now belongs to everybody and not just his family. That is something I still have to come to terms with, the loss of my son and myself to the public world' (Lawrence, 2006: 223).

Perhaps, haunting offers another way to think about this relationship. White guilt often folds into narcissism and inertia but I am suggesting in contrast a productive discomfort which opens out against racism. It is close to Ghassan Hage's ethos of care that rejects a paranoid nationalism racked by worry and denial (Hage, 2003). There have been 68 racist murders since Stephen Lawrence (Athwal and Kundnani, 2006). Such a haunting would jolt the listener out of a silent complicity with racism. The sound of racism jars the ear like fingernails scratching the surface of a blackboard. Within a larger context, the amendment to the 1976 Race Relations Act that was passed in 2000, in large part as a response to the Stephen Lawrence inquiry, has made it an obligation for all statutory bodies to produce race-equality policies and plans for action. Remembering Stephen Lawrence is in part about recognising the extent of the wounds that whiteness and racism continue to inflict while strengthening the sutures of hope.

CONCLUSION: BECOMING NOT WHITE

To end I want to return to the central points I want to make about 'white identities' and the importance of understanding whiteness within the dramaturgy of racism. Through the discussion of the Stephen Lawrence case I have emphasised that whiteness colours what is seen and not seen and shapes actions as well as inactions. These white looks see young black victims of violent crime as in circumstances of their own making (i.e., gang violence) or the bereaved family as gullible simpletons (i.e., prone to political manipulation by activists). Jeffrey Nealon argues that countering white supremacy is not simply a matter of disavowing whiteness. Rather, it is a matter of identifying 'what whiteness is, and what it can do' (Nealon, 1998: 160). Nealon focuses on the conditions of emergence that result from a critical interrogation of whiteness. Others like

Howard Winant have also suggested that 'rather than trying to repudiate [whiteness], we shall have to rearticulate it' (Winant, 1997: 48). The question here though is can whiteness as an identity or a practice be reshaped in this way? Certainly the examples of acting white and doing whiteness offered in this chapter like the tightly choreographed silences and the apologists who cast the police now as the victims would suggest not. Sanjay Sharma points out in his study of multicultural education that: 'It may be the case that in a particular pedagogic situation, "becoming-white" has nowhere productive to go, unable to form affective "alliances" which enhance the capacities of others, as well as itself' (Sharma, 2006: 47). This is the rub. For Nealon there is a sense that it is possible to re-direct 'white anger' or 'resentment', make it productive and shift its coordinates. I am not sure if this is possible because I think the register of this identity is in a different key. Here I want to draw on poststructuralist philosophy with regard to the issue of identity and the conception of self as becoming rather than being.

For Deleuze and Guattari, all becoming or the sense of an emergent or mobile subject is 'becoming-otherwise', that is, they are a shift to 'the minor', or what is referred to as minoritarian (Deleuze and Guattari, 1986). For Deleuze and Guattari, negations are always avoided here because they insist on the proliferation of difference or the de-territorialisation of the coordinates of identity. But, I want to suggest that some becomings are major. In many respects, the racist movements of today, and I would include those who seek affirmative or compensatory white identities, have assimilated the performative, they are often ideological hybrids and are, in many ways, quintessential examples of the postmodern condition.

The difference between a major and a minor chord is one note: the flattened third. I want to suggest that there is an equivalent in the conceptualisation of identities and becomings. It is here that I think negation or refusal is crucial. What is needed is a becoming that is also a refusal, that is, 'becoming not white'. It is a kind of becoming that can acknowledge the place from which it has emerged but cuts its root, like a pianist lifting her finger from the major third to make a minor chord. The major third engenders the musical force in the chord's structure, it serves here as a metaphor for the territorialising logic of race that fixes us within the visual lens of racial classification and colonises the correspondence between culture and subjectivity. Therefore, for whites becoming otherwise necessitates a shift to the minor, a negation comparable to the flattening of a third. Like the minor keys this might result in mournful tones. Yet, it must equally pre-empt a slip into a melancholia that licenses hate and as a compensation for this passing. Anton Gramsci once posed the question: 'is "humanity", as a reality and as an idea, a point of departure – or a point of arrival'? (quoted in Berger, 1967: 166). Thinking of humanity as a point of arrival allows for the possibility of thinking about 'becoming human' outside of the circumscriptions of twentieth-century universalisms. Perhaps, letting go of whiteness may enable those who have been governed by its allure to contemplate what the 'arrival lounge' of humanity might be like. As Ruth Frankenberg pointed out whiteness – as a supra sense of human particularity – masquerades as a universal arbiter of judgement and value (Frankenberg, 1993). Acting white inhibits a worldly, or what Paul Gilroy (2000) calls a planetary, conception of humanity.

James Baldwin once scolded a white interlocutor in the midst of an argument: 'As long as you think you are white, there is no hope for you' (Baldwin 1984). He was right. As a consequence it is important to avoid planting new or old 'whitenesses' in the arboretum of identity politics. The challenge is to work against their normative power because as David Roediger suggests: 'It is not merely that whiteness is oppressive and false; it is *nothing but* oppressive and false' (Roediger, 1994: 13). Whiteness is not anchored in the racialised body but in the colour of the imagination: for racism is a regime of power that damages our ability to sense and make sense. Its coded view defines, orders and straight-jackets the infinite human variability of humankind into racial phenotypes and antagonistic oppositions. Of course, racism works on our other sense as well; be it in concerns about the 'smell of immigrant food' or the phobias about the caress of 'inter-racial sex' and 'miscegenation'. Mark Smith has shown in the context of the United States that race is made through the cultivation of a racist sensorium of sight, smell, touch, sound and even taste (Smith, 2006: 139). However, I would maintain that racism – as a historically produced sensory system – *sees* first. The examples discussed in relation to the Stephen Lawrence case support this claim be it the white look of the murders that picked out Stephen Lawrence and Dwayne Brooks as targets or the reactions of the police offers at the scene.

Saying 'I am not white' does not make me 'not white'. The power and force of the categorical judgements that define and give meaning to the materiality of white flesh endure and cannot be simply wished away. Here the undoing of whiteness is a constant effort to break free from it in the knowledge that at another moment white subjects can be drawn back into its brilliant shadow. Conor and Louise Taafe found themselves precisely on this line on 22 April 1993. Confronted with two black boys in distress, their first glance was defined by white suspicion. Yet, they stopped acting white, they found a greater sense of humane care and comforted a young man through his last moments. Stepping out of whiteness is particularly urgent for those of us who are designated 'white' but racism also damages the attention of its victims. In 2006, Duwayne Brooks was asked how his experience had changed him. He told journalist Simon Hattenstone, 'The way others have treated me has made me more understanding, more caring, and I listen more. As a teenager, I don't think I listened enough'.[28] The lesson of this dreadful ordeal, that changed his life forever, made him more attentive, a better listener. My argument is at core very simple: we need to find ways to repair the harm that racism inflicts on our ability to see, hear, feel and understand. Whiteness is as good a short hand as any to describe the nature and dimensions of this damage.

The drift towards establishing 'whiteness studies' as a distinctive field in the humanities and social sciences does seem inevitable. Some of its more trenchant critics would say that the extent of academic outpouring on the topic is something more akin to a torrent of unwanted scholarship. Rather than dispensing with this burgeoning field, I want to suggest that whiteness needs to be situated at the centre of the analysis of racism. This is because the debates on whiteness have opened up for examination the way racism defines racial majorities as normative while making 'the problem of race' seem relevant only to minorities and people of colour. This step is an important one for it offers the possibility of a greater attention to the ways in which white people are implicated within cultures of racism. It also means engaging with the habitual ways in which whiteness positions and defines people in daily life both explicitly and tacitly. I am arguing for an analysis of whiteness that is sociable, outward looking that is neither confined to racial narcissism nor obsessed with the search for 'better kind of white person': for who wants to be white when there is the promise, or the hope, of being human?

NOTES

1. See http://www.bnp.org.uk/2007/12/15/mission-statement/#more-226 viewed 2nd February, 2008.
2. See Nick Griffin (2001) 'A long hot summer', *Identity*, July: 4–5.
3. *The Mercury*, 27th Thursday July, 1995.
4. The National Front (NF)is one of Britain's racist political parties. It had its political height in the 1970s and has been overtaken in terms of size by the British National Party. The NF emblem is however commonly used opportunistically as potent symbols for racists who have nothing to do with the official party.
5. Roland Adams, a 15-year-old black boy, was stabbed fatally at a bus stop on Friday 21 February 1991.
6. Sixteen year old Rohid Duggal was stabbed in the heart by a gang of white youths in June 1992. ibid. p. 50.
7. 'Kick out the BNP', *Eltham and Greenwich Times*, Thursday 29th April, 1993.
8. Helen Weathers, 'Doreen Lawrence: The Murder of My Family', *The Daily Mail*, Saturday June 3rd, 2006. http://www.dailymail.co.uk/pages/live/articles/news/news.html?in_article_id=388902&in_page_id=1770
9. After Ronnie and Reggie Kray the infamous East London gangsters who rose to prominence in London's gangland during the 1950s and 1960s.
10. In July 2006, a journalist Mark Daly's investigation uncovered new evidence that Detective Sergeant John Davidson – a key detective in the initial investigation – received payment from Clifford Norris.
11. Doreen Lawrence commented: 'And though I might have expected to see evil-looking monsters, these seemed such ordinary young men – cocky, self-assured, threatening, certainly, but those were things that could be said of many young men on the street' (Lawrence, 2006: 143).
12. 'The bowl' is a specific form of working-class masculine embodiment. See Garry Robson (2000: 79–81).
13. There is clear evidence in the transcription of the videotape that the accused realised that the flat was under surveillance. With the assistance of the landlord the police had installed surveillance cameras in electrical sockets. See *The Stephen Lawrence Inquiry* (1999b: 19).
14. 'And So It Goes On', *Daily Record*, Friday 26th February, 1999. p. 5.
15. Andrew Buncombe, 'Memorial is Defaced by White Paint', *The Independent*, Friday 26th February, 1999. p. 2. Stuart Millar', Racists deface memorial which was guarded by dummy camera', *The Guardian*, Friday 26th February, 1999. p. 1.
16. Paul Macey, 'Stephen Memorial Desecrated', *The Voice*, 16th March, 1999. p. 5.

17. 'Blunder Follows Blunder' *The Guardian*, Friday 26th February, 1999. p. 1.

18. Stuart Millar', Racists deface memorial which was guarded by dummy camera', *The Guardian*, Friday 26th February, 1999. p. 1.

19. Ibid.

20. 'Lawrence Plaque Spitting Charge', *The Metro*, Monday 19th July, 1999.

21. Interview by author, Deptford, London, 24th July, 2000.

22. Ibid.

23. Interview 30th April, 1999.

24. This is a reference to white supremacist David Copeland who in 1999 subjected London to 13 days of carnage when three nail bombs in Brixton, Brick Lane and Soho killed three and injured 129.

25. Race Against Crime – TX Sunday 7 November 99, Films of Record Ltd.

26. 'Lawrence Suspects Jailed for Race Attack', *The Guardian*, Friday 6th September, 2002. http://www.guardian.co.uk/race/story/0,,787448,00.html

27. 'Plumber "Shouted Lawrence slur,"' 18th November, 2003. Report from the London *Evening Standard* reproduced by The Monitoring Group at http://www.monitoring-group.co.uk/News%20 and%20Campaigns/news-stories/2003/regions/south%20east/plumber_shouted_lawrence_slur.htm

28. Simon Hattenstone, 'Justice at Last', *The Guardian*, Saturday 18th March, 2006. http://www.guardian.co.uk/crime/article/0,,1732542,00.html

REFERENCES

Ahmed, S. (2004) 'Declarations of Whiteness: The Non-Performativity of Anti-Racism', *Borderlands e-journal*, 2 (2): 1–12.

Athwal, H. and Kundnani, A. (2006) Sixty-eight racist murders since Stephen Lawrence. *Institute of Race Relations News*. Retrieved July 25, 2006 from http://www.irr.org.uk/2006/april/ha000031.html

Baldwin, J. (1984) 'On Being "White" and Other Lies', *Essence*, 14 (12): 90–92.

Bell, V. (1999) (ed.) *Performativity and Belonging*. London: Sage.

Benjamin, W. (1992) *Charles Baudelaire: A Lyric Poet in the Era of High Capitalism*. London: Verso.

Benjamin, W. (1997) *One-Way Street*. London: Verso.

Berger, J. (1967) *A Fortunate Man*. New York: Pantheon Books.

Bourdieu, P. (1977) *Outline of a Theory of Practice*. Cambridge: Cambridge University Press.

Byrne, B. (2006) *White Lives: The Interplay of 'Race', Class and Gender in Everyday Life*. London and New York: Routledge.

Cathcart, B. (1999) *The Case of Stephen Lawrence*. London: Viking.

Churchill, W., Engles, T., Thompson, C. P., Praylow, P., and Rodríguez (2006) *Towards A Bibliography of Critical Whiteness Studies*. Urbana-Champaign: University of Illinois at Urbana Champaign.

Collins, M. (2004) *The Likes of Us: A Biography of the White Working Class*. London: Granta Books.

Connerton, P. (1989) *How Societies Remember*. Cambridge: Cambridge University Press.

Deleuze, G. and Guattari, F. (1986) *A Thousand Plateaus: Capitalism and Schizophrenia*. London: Athlone.

Dench, G., Gavron, K. and Young, M. (2006) *The New East End: Kinship, Race and Conflict*. London: Profile Books.

Derrida, J. (1994) *Specters of Marx: The State of the Debt, the Work of Mourning, and the New International*. London: Routledge.

Dyer, R. (1988) 'White', *Screen*, 29 (4): 44–64.

Dyer, R. (1997) *White*. London: Routledge.

Frankenberg, R. (1993) *White Women, Race Matters*. London: Routledge.

Gilroy, P. (2000) *Between Camps: Nations, Cultures and the Allure of Race*. London: Allen Lane and The Penguin Press.

Goffman, E. (1959) *Presentation of Self in Everyday Life*. Harmondsworth: Penguin Books.

Goffman, E. (1971) *Relations in Public: Microstudies of the Public Order*. Harmondsworth: Penguin Books.

Gordon, A.F. (1997) *Ghostly Matters: Haunting and the Sociological Imagination*. Minneapolis and London: University of Minnesota Press.

Hage, G. (1998) *White Nation: Fantasies of White Supremacy in a Multicultural Society*. Annandale, NSW: Pluto Press.

Hage, G. (2003) *Against Paranoid Nationalism: Searching for Hope in a Shrinking Society*. Annandale, NSW: Pluto Press.

Hartigan, J. (1999) *Racial Situations: Class Predicaments of Whiteness in Detroit*. Princeton, NJ: Princeton University Press.

Hewitt, R. (2006) *White Backlash and the Politics of Multiculturalism*. Cambridge: Cambridge University Press.

Hooks, b. (1992) *Black Looks: Race and Representation*. Boston: South End Press.

Ignatiev, N. and Garvey, J. (1996) (eds) *Race Traitor*. New York and London: Routledge.

Jeffrey, N. (1999) 'The Sharp End of Stephen's City', *Soundings*, 12: 26–42.

Lawrence, D. (2006) *And Still I Rise: Seeking Justice for Stephen*. London: Faber and Faber.

Lott, E. (1993) *Love and Heft: Blackface Minstrelsy and the American Working Class*. New York: Oxford University Press.

MacMullan, T. (2005) 'Beyond the Pale: A Pragmatist Approach to Whiteness Studies', *Philosophy and Social Criticism*, 31(3): 265–292.

Maliq, K. (1998) 'Race, pluralism and the meaning of difference', *New Formations*, 33: 125–136.

McLaughlin, E. and Murji, K. (1999) 'After the Stephen Lawrence Report', *Critical Social Policy*, 60: 371–383.

Nealon, J. (1998) *Alterity Politics: Ethics and Performative Subjectivity*. London: Duke University Press.

Norton-Taylor, R. (1999) *The Colour of Justice*. London: Oberon Books.

Robson, G. (2000) *No-One Likes Us We Don't Care: The Myth and Reality of Millwall Fandom*. Oxford: Berg.

Roediger, D. (1994) *Towards the Abolition of Whiteness*. London and New York: Verso.

Saldanha, A. (2006) 'Reontologising Race: The Machinic Geography of Phenotype', *Environment and Planning D: Society and Space*, 24: 9–24.

Sharma, S. (2006) *Multicultural Encounters*. Basingstoke and New York: Palgrave Macmillan.

Smith, L. (1950) *Killers of a Dream*. London: Cresset.

Smith, M. (2006) *How Race Is Made*. Chapel Hill: University of North Carolina Press.

Taylor, J. (1992) *Paved with Good Intentions: The Failure of Race Relations in Contemporary America*. New York: Caroll and Graf.

The Stephen Lawrence Inquiry (1999a) *Report of an Inquiry by Sir William Macpherson of Cluny, Volume 1*. London: The Stationary Office.

The Stephen Lawrence Inquiry (1999b) *Report of an Inquiry by Sir William Macpherson of Cluny, Volume 2 Appendices*. London: The Stationary Office.

Ware, V. (1992) *Beyond the Pale: White Women, Racism and History*. London: Verso.

Wiegman, R. (1999) 'Whiteness Studies and the Paradox of Particularity', *Boundary* 2, 26, 3: 115–150.

Winant, H. (1997) 'Behind Blue Eyes: Whiteness and Contemporary U.S. Racial Politics' in M. Fine, L. Weis, L. C. Powell and L. Mun Wong (eds) *Off White: Readings on Race, Power and Society*. New York and London: Routledge. pp. 3–16.

Wray, M. and Newlitz, A. (1998) *White Trash: Race and Class in America*. New York: Routledge.

18

No Longer Invisible: Afro-Latin Political Mobilisation

Michael G. Hanchard and Mark Q. Sawyer

Afro-Latin movements for civil rights, political and economic equality and cultural recognition have proliferated since 1985 when democratic transitions began to create openings for social movements that significantly expanded the landscape for political and social mobilisation in many countries of the region, and as a consequence, radically changing scholarly interpretations of the role of the race concept, as well as racism itself, as an organising principle and a factor in national politics. For example, demands arose for quotas and recognition in Brazil, and land rights in Colombia.

This degree of mobilisation is noteworthy when one considers the traditional invisibility of Afro-Latin populations. For the most part, in Latin America despite the massive importation of enslaved Africans, countries have sought to render Afro-Latin Americans invisible. Countries pursued ideologies of 'whitening' and have also emphasised racial mixture or *mestizaje* rather than recognizing the existence or contribution of black populations. In response to this, the black have had to emphasise their cultural and racial distinctiveness and unique history by advancing the concept of being Afro-Latino or a hyphenated member of their nation rather than references to colour that are often seen as apolitical and chromatic or allowing national identity to subsume their unique experience of enslavement and racial discrimination. This shift has contributed to growing political mobilisation.

In broad regional and cross-national terms, Afro-Latin political mobilisation in most of the societies where Afro-Latin political actors and organisations can be found in the region share some, if not all, of the four following characteristics.

- Mobilisation for civil rights in the form of full protection under a national constitution recognition as a distinct cultural group with specific contributions to national society.
- Recognition as a distinct group with settlement in specific territories within a national-state unit that require distinct laws for recognition and conservation of those territories and the peoples who inhabit them.
- Anti-discriminatory laws aimed at alleviating ongoing forms of racism and racial discrimination.
- Acknowledgement by the national government of the history of unjust treatment and enslavement of Africans and their descendents (Sawyer, 2006; Telles, 2006; Hanchard, 1994, 2006; Wade, 1997; Andrews, 2004; Gregory, 2006).

The ensuing dynamics between Afro-Latin political mobilisation and national states and economies has thus involved the drafting and adoption of specific amendments to national constitutions, 'consciousness raising' groups and campaigns for the collective identification of those with some traces of perceived 'African' somatic traits, and the identification of discriminatory practices in the economy, society and culture against those defined as either negro, moreno, mulatto, pardo or many other euphemistic characterisations. These chromatic designations based upon skin colour and other traits have frequently been used to divide people of African descent placing them in different categories while studies of race show that these categorical differences have little effect on life chances (Sawyer, 2006; Telles, 2006). Consequently, Afro-Latin political mobilisation has permeated national politics by pressuring national states and societies to acknowledge the existence of Afro-Latin populations and political actors (Wade, 1997; Telles, 2006; Hanchard 2006).

At the same time, sectors of national elites and some national governments have contested, if not outright rejected, claims of Afro-Latin political actors and their organisations. For example, Cuba eliminated black organisations along with other organisations as the revolution triumphed and Brazil like Cuba has, for much of its post-slavery history, presented itself as a society devoid of racism (Sawyer, 2006; Hanchard 1994).

The tensions between these tendencies have generated interesting debates and intense political conflict over the creation of more egalitarian societies, the role of the state in guaranteeing the social welfare of its citizens, (particularly in a neo-liberal era), and issues of 'racial' versus national identification in many Latin American societies that have historically underplayed racial ascription and classification. The stakes in such conflicts range from electoral representation, cultural and territorial recognition, access to educational and occupational opportunities and freedom from violence and discrimination.

Where once, as written by Roberto Gonzalez Echevarria,[1] the category of race in Latin American countries was subsumed under the category and promise of the nation, Afro-Latin mobilisation around the aforementioned issues provide evidence of race being utilised as an organising principle to obtain rights and recognition from the state and national population. The increasing importance and presence of Afro-Latin mobilisation, distinct from other classic forms of collective action (political parties and trade unions) as well as new social movements (indigenous, environmental, feminist, gay rights) also provide greater opportunities for comparison among students of racial and ethnic politics. Like indigenous identification, once referred to as a 'fugitive ethnicity', Afro-Latin and Afro-national identifications have increased the salience of so-called racial and ethnic distinctions as a concept and organising principle in the Americas. The very development of these movements strikes at a social constructivist view of race that itself tends to essentialise identities. Many observers have suggested that black social movements and organisation in Latin America are somehow 'artificial' due to the historical predominance of nation over race, and the multiple and flexible racial categories (Bourdieu and Wacquant, 1999). However, analysing these movements provides a perfect confirmation that racial identities and race is constructed from above and below and can change over time. In contexts where there has been little emphasis on black identity, black social movements may flourish due to changing domestic and international circumstances.

RACE AND NATION IN LATIN AMERICA

Historically, most scholars of Latin America have highlighted the relative absence of a bi-polar model of racial classification – as normally (though also erroneously) associated with Anglophone models in the United States and elsewhere – as an explanatory source of greater cultural flexibility and mutual acknowledgement of shared traditions in many Latin American societies, the melding of indigenous, African and European cultures, as well as peoples (Wade, 1997). Nevertheless, the association of blackness with negative attributes (ugliness, laziness, hypersexuality) has also negatively impacted national populations within the region (Peña et al., 2005; Sawyer, 2006). The absence of census data, in many instances, distinguishing populations by colour or race, has also led to the 'disappearance' of African descent populations in several countries. Conversely, the redesign and reconceptualisation of census categories to allow for self-identification and classification by individuals, has led to the 'reappearance' of African-descent populations in several countries. Recent census data and interpretation of the national population of Argentina, for example, has accounted for the presence of Argentines of African descent, largely ignored in most scholarly and popular accounts of Argentine history, society and culture (Nobles, 2000; Andrews, 1980).

Reconfiguring the correlation between race and nation in Latin America has required at least two critically important steps by Black actors. These are (i) to challenge their invisibility as either a distinct sub-national or supra-national group and (ii) unearth their unequal inclusion in Latin American societies. Hegemonic constructions of 'racial relations' in Latin America have consistently denied both of these premises. It is here that social science has in some ways helped to invigourate social movements. Social scientific analyses that have unmasked the inequality faced by Afro-Latinos in daily life as well as their unequal incorporation into national projects have provided evidence used by movements to move the hegemonic construction of the existence of racial democracy to the 'myth of racial democracy', like in Brazil. These interventions have also tended to use comparison to challenge myths about Latin American racial politics that use the United States as a paradigm for racial oppression and suggest that since there have been differences in modalities of racial regulation in Latin America, there has been little racial oppression. These challenges from below represent a corrective to scholars of race and ethnicity who attack the adoption of such identities as 'artificial' and inherently problematic (Bourdieu and Wacquant, 1999). These scholars ignore indigenous black movements and their transnational ties and suggest that challenges to Latin American racial orders are being imposed by US 'imperialism'. However, the sustained activism within Latin America belies this argument (Telles, 2006; Hanchard, 2006). Second, for scholars of racial politics in areas like France and other nations that seek to erase racial difference by emphasising nation over race, we can see that such ideas may cover over existing racial prejudice and may be met by significant opposition from below (Begag, 2007). Thus, if we are to take a non-essentialist view of identity, we must grant groups and individuals the agency to construct identities that they see as politically salient efficacious.

The dynamics of comparison as well as international actors and exchanges, point to the centrality of internationalism and transnationalism in the development of Afro-Latino social movements. These movements have included the landless movements in Brazil and various movements for social rights, land and cultural recognition throughout Latin America. This is not to say that these are not wholly indigenous movements but that these movements have utilised comparison, as well as strategies, ideologies and tactics from movements elsewhere. Further, international organisations and foundations have provided critical openings and resources to allow these movements to flourish. Events that have brought these movements into dialogue with international organisations and other movements throughout the black world have played a critical role in the evolution of black social movements. In particular, the 2001 World Conference on Racism provided a clear opportunity to transcend national boundaries and move beyond the boundaries of nation that have constrained Afro-Latin critiques of their nations. Thus, while we are interested in movements in Brazil and elsewhere, we do not consider these movements to be in any sense isolated from one another. In fact, we argue that in fact there is a growing transnational black public sphere of exchange among these organisations (Hanchard, 1994, 2006). By transnational black public sphere we mean a group of organisations, meetings, spaces and formal and informal links that allow for a conversation to occur among black people and organisations. This public sphere draws upon a notion of civil society, but one that is designed around marginalised peoples rather than the powerful (Hanchard, 2006). This builds on a literature that marked the existence of black communities in the United States, but we are extending that notion. Both in the past related to anti-colonial struggles but now through the struggle against racism and beyond black social movement actors are meeting and coming together across national lines more than ever to discuss issues that are central to their lives as black people as well as formulating strategies and tactics to challenge governments and international organisations (Dawson, 2003).

Table 18.1 outlines the number of organisations who applied to participate in an international conference of Black non-governmental organisations (NGOs) created by the Inter-American Dialogs. While this is only a small slice of the Black NGOs in the Americas, it outlines the substantial numbers of groups in places where many scholars argue that these kinds of groups either do not or

Table 18.1

By country	Number of organizations applied
Argentina	4
Belize	3
Bolivia	1
Brazil	232
Chile	3
Colombia	56
Costa Rica	6
Cuba	0
Dominican Republic	14
Ecuador	108
El Salvador	0
Guatemala	7
Honduras	31
Mexico	5
Nicaragua	15
Panama	7
Paraguay	2
Peru	31
Puerto Rico	1
Regional	3
Trinidad	1
Uruguay	5
Venezuela	6
Total organizations	541

should not exist. While again this list is not exhaustive, some of the results conform to basic expectations about the existence of Black NGOs. Brazil having the largest black population in the Americas has the largest number of organisations and has been the place of some of the most expansive activism. While countries like the Dominican Republic and Cuba have large populations of African-descended peoples, there is not as much formal activism in these countries. In the Dominican Republic, the driving force is likely the continued denial of blackness among the population and the deflection of blackness on to the Haitian immigrant population. In Cuba, it is a result of the Cuban state not allowing for the development of NGOs based upon race outside of space controlled by the state. Since the Cuban government has not seen fit to form such organisations there consequently are none in Cuba. Other countries vary along these dimensions depending upon population, level of state control and finally the degree to which black identity is salient as a socio-political identity (Sawyer, 2005).

Now that we have documented the existence of social movements, it is important to address specific cases and developments of these movements. For this we take up three cases: Brazil, Colombia and Ecuador. As the largest country on the South American continent as well as the country with the second largest population of African-descended subjects – Nigeria is the first – Brazil allows us to explore the challenge of Black social movements to the thesis of racial democracy. Further, we understand how the movement from authoritarianism to democracy has opened possibilities for contestation by Blacks. In contrast, Colombia has a much smaller Black population but one that is strategically placed both in urban centres as well as in the countryside between spaces of conflict in the long-standing Colombian civil war. Ecuador provides an opportunity to explore how budding racial and ethnic movements interact with a transition to democracy. Each country provides an opportunity to view how black social movements are interacting with different governmental structures, stable democracy, civil war and struggling democracy. Further, there are also different population dynamics in each country. The Brazilian black and brown population represents a majority; the Colombian population is heavily urbanised and blacks in Ecuador are distributed between urban areas and resource-rich rural areas.

The current conjuncture of national debates and regional or local responses to affirmative action policies in Brazil also points to two larger themes and questions which we will outline and which have broader implications for Latin American countries with African-descendent populations: First, how should states treat race and colour-based inequalities in societies that have not historically acknowledged such inequalities or even the existence of populations marginalised due to racial discrimination? Second, what are the most efficient and equitable means to reduce or eradicate race- or colour-based discrimination and inequality in Latin American societies with a host of other inequities and populations which also merit social and material assistance? We believe these two questions can guide readers to consider the specificities of the Brazilian case as well as the more generalisable aspects of Brazil's current landscape of racial politics.

RACE, POLITICS AND SOCIAL MOVEMENTS

In considering the vast array of groups throughout the world that have been engaged in struggles involving racial hierarchy and discrimination, we have chosen to organise our examination of the phenomena of social movements seeking the cessation or lessening of racism and ethno-national exclusion in terms of analytic categorisation of the routes to power, solidarity and/or recognition, rather than by regional or population-specific focus. Moving beyond the now well-worn adage of race as social construction, we treat the practice of racial discrimination and exclusion as a two-component process. The first component is the process of discrimination against minority or subordinate individuals and groups in their interactions with members of a dominant group. The second component consists of the organisation and distribution of resources in accordance with the preferences of dominant group members, elites and their institutions. Both components of the discriminatory process have occurred simultaneously in various types of societies, ranging from the plural (multinational), the multicultural, the presumably bi-polar (white/black, white/indigenous) as well as the multi-polar (chromatically rather than 'racially' distinguished). Consequently, minority or subordinate groups have responded to the general set of circumstances engendered by the two dimensions of discrimination in the following ways; a) seeking recognition of the material, institutional, civic and societal implications of their discrimination; b) seeking to craft networks of solidarity among subordinate groups members as well as among members of the population who are not among the subordinate groups.

Despite the differences in the perspectives of prior generations of scholarship on the origins and root causes of social movements that are steeped in some idea and practice of ethno-national or racial (actually phenotypical) distinction, we believe it is safe to assert that prior scholarship by students of race and ethnicity such as Pierre Van den Berghe, John Rex, Michael Banton, Guy Hunter and Ira Katznelson (Van Den Berghe, 1967; Rex, 1986; Banton, 1998; Hunter, 1985; Katznelson, 1976) overwhelmingly point to the fact that structural factors, namely, the organisation of a society along lines of racial hierarchy and distinction, not only impacts the process and modalities of discrimination, but the ways in which subordinate groups organise and mobilise in response to conditions of inequality. In societies where a set of legal strictures codified discrimination and inequality, members of subordinate groups countered those legal strictures by constructing legal arguments of their own. This is evidenced in post-colonial societies with indigenous populations, as well as in societies with former slave populations that lived under conditions of apartheid after slavery. In societies where there were few constitutionally or otherwise codified strictures but nonetheless longstanding discriminatory practices against a particular subordinate group, law-based subordinate group activism has only emerged after a more protracted period. The presence of liberal ideologies and some accepted norms of the rule of law, ironically, are key variables in influencing how subordinate groups come to address their conditions of inequality. The case of the Roma ('Gypsies') of Eastern Europe, or the anti-racist movement in Brazil is a perfect example of this distinction.

In the latter case, the willingness of a dominant group and its state apparatus to negotiate with members of a subordinate group to lessen or overturn conditions of racial hierarchy, leads to a third possible outlet and forum for the articulation of grievances, international public opinion and forums. The work of Azza Layton, James Meriwether, Penny Von Eschen, Nikhil Singh and Brenda Gayle Plummer, have described the effects of the Cold War and international public opinion on the civil rights struggles in the United States and South Africa. Now with the increasing visibility of international human rights watch groups, the International Court of Justice (ICJ) and other monitors of racial and ethno-national discrimination in various parts of the world, groups and their organisations do not necessarily have to bring their plight to the attention of the national-state first (Layton, 2000; Mariwether, 2001; Von Eschen, 2007; Singh, 2004; Plummer, 1996).

BRAZIL

Much of the scholarship on colour and race in Brazilian society up until the 1950s focused on the chromatic spectrum of the Brazilian population, contrasting Brazil's celebration of its population's multi-hued variation, rather than the bi-polar categorisations of putatively racial distinction in the United States. As noted by Thomas Skidmore, however, the United States, like many former European colonies in the New World, also had the same chromatic variations amongst its population, even though the categorisation was different and more rigid than that of Brazil's. Brazil's celebration of what Nancy Leys Stepan refers to as 'positive miscegenation' was a result of the confluence of two distinct but overlapping trends; Brazilian elites who sought to downplay the harshness of slave society while at the same time justifying the need for African slave labour, and the response of Brazilian intellectuals such as Gilberto Freyre from Recife, who sought to counter the assumption put forth by Brazilian and European adherents to positivism that Brazil's destiny as a second-class nation was foretold due to the high presence of African-descended peoples in its emerging national population. Much of the post World War II scholarship on race in Brazil focused on chromatic distinction, rather than race or even more specifically racism.

For students of racial and ethnic politics, the Brazilian case provides a unique opportunity to examine facets of a singular 'case' in cross-national perspective.

Its external and internal image of a nation free of colour or race-based hatreds, makes the nation unlike the aforementioned societies with their more unambiguous modes of racist enmity. At the same time, Brazil's celebration of the idea of racial democracy which, according to the Brazilian sociologist Antonio Sergio Guimaraes, was first mentioned by Gilberto Freyre, shares some similarities with ideals of race-blending and mixture in the national ideologies of Mexico, Cuba and Venezuela, as well as several Caribbean nations.

The seeming absence of racism or racial discrimination in Brazilian society led many scholars to conclude, as Charles Wagley did, that the principal mode of inequality in Brazil was class- rather than race-based. Despite the occasional incidents, often involving black foreign visitors from the United States or Africa, and in one much discussed incident in the 1990s, the president of Curacao and his bodyguards were involved in an altercation with Brazilian military police who had mistaken them for criminals. Neither ethnicity, in the case of indigenous populations, nor so-called racial distinction, in the case of Afro-Latin populations, were utilised as organising principals for political and social mobilisation, even though indigenous populations often identified themselves by long standing collective and regional identities.

The increasing use of census data, however, beginning in the 1970s, provided scholars and activists with the means to not only identify and distinguish populations by phenotype, but to control for regional variation, class, education, and other status indicators to determine which sectors of Brazilian society were the most disadvantaged in part, due to racial inequality. The vast gaps in income and overall life chances between a small, mostly white elite, and a largely black and brown poor and marginalised population in Brazilian society has been amply documented by Brazilianist scholars, mostly demographers, who have utilised decanal census data over the past thirty years. Scholars such as Carlos Hasenbalg, Nelson do Valle Silva and Paes de Barros provided the empirical evidence and qualitative interpretation for activists of the black movement to point to the existence of racism in Brazil.

In 2002, the then president Fernando Henrique Cardoso declared in a television broadcast to Brazilian citizens that Brazil was indeed a racist society. Cardoso's declaration was not news to many scholars, politicians, activists and a younger generation of Brazilian people who either experienced contemporary forms of everyday discrimination in employment, housing, education and social interactions first-hand, or who had knowledge of Brazil's history of racial slavery. Like many national societies of the Americas, Brazil's economy, society and culture provided ample evidence of the importance of slave labour and the presence of enslaved Africans as central contributors to cuisine, art, commerce, agricultural production, religion and many other aspects of life in Brazil. What made Cardoso's declaration so strikingly unique was its acknowledgement, after years of popular, elite and national-state denial, that Brazilian society suffered from racial discrimination in ways normally associated with societies that had more formal strictures against 'race-mixture' residential segregation, prohibitions against miscegenation and so-called mixed marriages. The significance of Cardoso's declaration, coming in the UN year against racial discrimination and the conference of the same name in Durban, South Africa, was not lost on Brazilians nor on long-time students of this vast country with the largest population of African-descended peoples in the African diaspora, second only to Nigeria in terms of overall African-descended population. Brazil's international reputation as the country of 'racial democracy' emerged after World War II when many commentators on racial and ethnic conflict throughout the world saw Brazil as an anomaly when compared to South Africa, the United States, or even fascist Germany or Italy.

More recently, however, sociologist Edward Telles has suggested that Brazil is an anomaly in another respect: the first national government to institute affirmative-action policies in a society while not having a mass social movement to support the demands of activists and the interests of elites. Cardoso's own experience with racial discrimination as a sociologist and member of the Sao Paulo school of sociology, which conducted path-breaking studies of patterns of social interaction and discrimination in the state of Sao Paulo in the 1950s, convinced Cardoso that despite the absence of Jim Crow laws and other forms of formal apartheid, Brazil had many examples of *de facto* segregation by colour, if not race, in the material aspects of society, an ambiguous celebration of whitening of Brazilian society, and the often demeaning depictions of darker-skinned Brazilians and African-descended peoples more generally. At the same time, Cardoso was helped by increasingly effective media campaigns and marches by black social movement actors that highlighted the inequality faced by blacks and the problems of racism. These campaigns while short of a mass movement were adept at gaining national and international attention. In addition the election of Benedita da Silva a black woman as City Councilor of Rio de Janeiro in 1982 and her expanding political career also gave a national voice to black issues within the political arena (Telles, 2006).

Melissa Nobles' comparison of the role of census categorisation in the United States and Brazil affirms that census categorisation plays a significant role in the maintenance of racial categories, which in turn, help to justify the use of racial categories to obtain information about the extent or degree of segregation, equal access and opportunity by census population category. Such categories do not represent separate and distinct races, but the social, political and economic consequences of racial categorisation, and fundamentally, racial hierarchy and discrimination.[2] The comparative implications are not restricted to comparisons with national societies outside of Latin America. The 'disappearance' of Argentina's Afro-Argentine population during the nineteenth century was a consequence, in part, of the absence of census categories to determine their presence.[3] Nobles notes further that census categories also serve to reify and reinforce racial categorisation, a fact that opponents of affirmative action policies highlight in their rejection of quotas for vacancies in public educational institutions and employment opportunities. Opponents of 'racial quotas' in Brazil argue that racial categorisation in Brazil will only serve to create racial categories and conflicts that do not exist.

Recent controversies in Brazil over the role of the national state in unilaterally administering affirmative action policies, the incorporation of black movement actors into positions of state responsibility and authority, and the responses of various actors in Brazilian society to the implementation of these policies, provides an opportunity to evaluate the dynamic tension between states and social movements, social movements and the general population, and the tensions between state and local implementation of policies designed to eradicate the vast gaps between whites and non-whites in employment and educational opportunities.

All have equal rights in the Democratic Republic a text distributed to federal deputies in Brasilia was composed by opponents of the affirmative action quotas imposed by the federal government in law PL 73, first brought before the national congress in 1999 during Fernando Henrique Cardoso's tenure as president of the Brazilian republic. Though there have been many public pronouncements and declarations supporting as well as denouncing the 'quota law' this statement succinctly documents the key claims and arguments against the imposition of a 20 percent quota minimum of reserved vacancies for black and indigenous Brazilians in federal employment and educational institutions. First, the signatories to this text declare that PL 73 and its companion bill, PL 3.198 (Statute for Racial Equality) threatens to render obsolete the political and juridical equality of all citizens of the Brazilian republic by implanting 'an official racial classification of Brazilian citizens (uma classificacao racial oficial dos cidadaos Brasileiros)' wherein the Brazilian nation would come to define 'the rights of persons based upon skin tone as a way of marking 'race' (os direitos das pessoas com base na tonalidade dua sua pele, pela 'raca'). Consequently, statistical classifications based on phenotype would be transformed into 'identities and individual rights against the precept of equality of all before the law' (direitos individuais contra o preceito da igualdade de todos perante a lei).

Thus, opponents of these two laws seek to distinguish the existence of social inequalities from the creation of 'official races' which, their document explicitly suggests, has only occurred in societies with apartheid regimes. The creation of state-mandated racial and phenotypical categorisation would, according to their argument, merely create categorisations of populations premised upon ideas of racial hierarchy without addressing conditions of social inequality. Interestingly, the document ends with a quote from Martin Luther King's 'I have a dream speech', the oft-cited 'they will not be judged by the colour of their skin but by the content of their character (numa nacao onde as pessoas nao seriam avaliadas pelo cor de sua pele, mas pela forca de seu carater)'.

In the document 'Manifesto Em Favor da lei de Cotas E Do Estatuto Da Igualdade Racial' (Manifesto in favor of the Quota Law and Statute of Racial Equality), proponents of the PL 73 and PL 3.198 legislation note that while the constitution of 1889, which declared Brazil a republic, did formally acknowledge formal equality of all Brazilian citizens, it did not address the exclusions of former slaves from objective access to land, wage labour. While all Brazilians were equal according to the letter of the law, 'various' policies and incentives were adopted that could be identified as affirmative action, to stimulate the immigration of Europeans to Brazil, (varias politicas de incentive e apoio diferenciado, que hoje podem ser lidas como acoes afirmativas, foram aplicadas para estimular a imigracao de europeus para o brasil). 'Thus, proponents of the law and statute argue that white immigrants were beneficiaries of what could be read as an affirmative action policy' by receiving subsidised immigration and relatively easier access to employment and housing opportunities, as documented by historians such as George Reid Andrews and Robert Brent Toplin. The Brazilian government or state, in other words, encouraged and helped administer preferential treatment for whites in Brazilian society, and were not as colourblind in the early days of the republic as the opponents would have it. Citing national and international law, as well as the examples of multicultural and plural societies (India, South Africa, Malaysia, Australia, New Zealand, Colombia and Mexico) with their own histories of laws designed to promote proportional representation of various ethno-national, religious and cultural groups, the signatories of the manifesto assert that the bill and statute would help 'to repair the assemtries created by the First Republic that offered benefits to the Europeans but explicitly denied those benefits to Afro-Brazilians (reparar as assimetrias promovidas pela intervencao do Estado da Primeira Republica com leis que outogaram beneficios especiais aos europeus recem chegados, negando explicitamente os mesmos beneficios a populacao afro-brasileira)'.

The arguments, pro and con, anticipate many of the points raised in the positions of the opposing side.

This debate resonates with many themes of racial and ethnic politics in plural societies, as well as the peculiarities of Brazilian society. One the one hand, the proposed bill and statute at the core of contention would pertain only to federal educational and employment, not the private sector, with an approximately 22.5 percent reserved spaces for a population that even by conservative estimates stands at 45 percent. On the other hand, the Brazilian state is large by contemporary, neo-liberal standards, and is one of the largest employers in the country. Public colleges and universities are generally considered far superior to private secondary and collegiate-level educational institutions, and are sites of socialisation for the bulk of Brazil's middle and elite classes. One of the key contrasts in the Brazilian case is the juxtaposition of seemingly 'universalist' republican values of liberal individualism, wherein rights of individual citizens are protected and guaranteed under the constitution. National constitutions are premised on the idea of sovereignty and self-rule and consequently, are by their very constitution, non-universalist.

The comparative and international implications of this debate and the prospects of transforming legislation into law are also significant. Both proponents and opponents cite international precedent in their argumentation, with opponents incorporating Martin Luther King's pronouncement in ways reminiscent of neo-conservative attacks on affirmative action in the United States in the 1980s, utilising the rhetoric and language of the civil rights movement to argue against the development of policies that seek to redress conditions of racial inequality by utilising so-called racial or chromatic identification as a means to identify populations enmeshed in dynamics of dominance and subordination. At the same time, support for these policies from the Worker's Party (PT) and the growing prominence of official organs organised to fight racial discrimination has absorbed many black activists into the state apparatus and raised ongoing questions about whether, given the successes can the movement sustain its energy and independence while increasingly holding more formal power in the state.

ECUADOR

Ecuador is a country with a significant Black and indigenous population. In contrast to Brazil and like Colombia, Ecuador is a country where black organisations have struggled with isolation and have often followed the strategies and tactics of organizing by indigenous peoples. However, Ecuador has also been characterised by tropes of mestizaje and whitening that have been the hallmarks of other countries in Latin America. Like in other places, there is a positive valuation of whiteness *vis-à-vis* blackness and a denial of the existence of racial inequality. The black population tends to be isolated in coastal communities surrounding mining and oil production in places like the Esmeraldas Province. Eighty percent of the black population of Ecuador resides in the Esmeraldas Province but there is an increasing urban population in the capitol of Quito Ecuador. This provincial split is significant for the development and maintenance of black social movements because it means that the movements have very different aims and goals. The rural social movements have largely focused on questions of land rights and borrowed from the growing indigenous movements in Ecuador. In contrast, the urban movements have focused on anti-discrimination legislation and improving wages and working conditions for Afro-Ecuadorians. Afro-Ecuadorians make these claims in the context of a thin citizenship regime and only recently emergent democratic norms (see Carlos de la Torre, 2005). However, international forums and organisations have provided an opportunity for Afro-Ecuadorian social movements.

International organisations have played a major role in Afro-Ecuadorian organisation. International development organisations have encouraged both Afro-Ecuadorian and indigenous groups to pursue development goals and seek international funds (Halpern and Twine, 2000). They have also encouraged the government to support Afro-Ecuadorian development projects in Esmeraldas. However, these projects have tended to bring the Afro-Ecuadorian movements like the indigenous groups into corporatist arrangements with the government and political parties (see Carlos de la Torre, 2005). The state thus funnels international aid dollars to organisations to channel their demands to meet the interests of the state. This works both in the urban and rural settings where 'development' can take on different meanings. However, these arrangements fall short of articulating a full set of rights since citizenship is such a thinly recognised concept in Ecuador (Halpern and Twine, 2000). Thus, these claims are quite easily captured and channeled through mechanisms of the state. This leaves the organisations at the mercy of state priorities.

Black social movements have also formed bonds with and among indigenous organisations. These movements consolidated around black groups in a process called El Proceso de Comunidades Negras. This movement joined with the Confederation of Indigenous Nationalities of Ecuador (CONAIE) to form a united front to demand land rights based upon ancestral claims to the land. For blacks, this was based in the historical recognition of palenques for blacks. Specifically, blacks worked with groups of indigenous people knowns as the Cachis to form what became known as the Gran Cormarca in Northern Esmeraldas in 1997 (Halpern and Twine, 2000). This organisation resulted in the election and subsequent assassination of Jaime Hurtado Gonzales of the Democratic Movement Party. With the assassination of Gonzales, the movement lost its most prominent spokesperson but won recognition in the 1998 Constitution through Article 85 that guaranteed 'indigenous rights that are applicable' though it did not clearly delineate what rights are applicable to blacks. This ambiguity again speaks to the weak citizenship regime in Ecuador that does not clearly define rights for groups outside of the interests of the state.

In the urban areas, gender has played a major role in Afro-Ecuadorian organising. While women play roles in all organisations, Ecuador has an especially active black women's movement that includes independent organisations around issues that are central to Afro-Ecuadorian women. These organisations focus on questions of children and family, equal pay and a broader human rights agenda that includes education for themselves and their children (Halpern and Twine, 2000). Many seek relief and dignity at work and in domestic labour in urban areas and want their rights respected in all aspects of society in both urban and rural settings. Afro-Ecuadorian movements have enjoyed some success in gaining state recognition, land rights and anti-discrimination legislation. However, at the same time the thin recognition of citizenship rights renders these movements easy prey to the whims and goals of the state or political parties in general. Ecuador demonstrates that 'rights' claims from black groups in Latin America include things like land rights and cultural rights that are frequently thought of as aspects of indigenous movements. Further, the movements demonstrate the relationship between emergent notions of citizenship and mobilisation.

COLOMBIA

The Colombian motto defines a Colombian perspective on race that is not unusual, 'ONE GOD, ONE RACE, ONE TONGUE' (Arocha, 1998). While there was an exception for indigenous peoples called 'savages' in the

Colombia's original constitution, this changed dramatically in 1991 (Arocha, 1998). The constitution ensured that the state became responsible for recognising the ethnic diversity of the nation and to grant specific ownership rights to culturally distinct groups. Following recognition in 1991, Law 70 was passed in 1993. Law 70 recognised the collective land ownership rights of the black populations of the Pacific Coast or the region known as El Choco.

Social movements by African descended people in Colombia have, like in Ecuador, primarily focused on land rights and, secondarily on anti-discrimination. Most important, they have focused on the ongoing civil war and violence in Colombia. In the context of the growing violence in Colombia, the issue of land ownership has been complicated by the ongoing conflicts in areas inhabited by Afro-Colombians (Angel-Ajani, 2005). Afro-Colombian communities are trapped between the leftist FARC and the para-milirary forces in Colombia and have been the targets of extreme violence and human rights abuses. In addition movements have sought to enforce land rights against the interests of multinational corporations and the Colombian government and para-military forces. These struggles have taken on a variety of forms and used a range of strategies and tactics to advance rights claims.

Fuelled by billions of dollars from the US initiative Plan Colombia, Afro-Colombian communities have faced increasing violence and dislocation. As a result, one solution has been to establish what they call 'Peace Communities'. A network of these communities has been formed to secure a modicum of normalcy in the wake of the growing violence. While the official national statistics estimate the Afro-Colombian population at 600,000, other estimates rate the population at 26 percent of Colombia or around 10 million. It has been estimated that 80 percent of the population lives in poverty. The large undercount speaks to the invisibility of Afro-Colombians in many aspects of Colombian life. However, Afro-Colombians are also using a range of activities to resist these conditions.

Afro-Colombian communities have sought to make their situation known to national elites as well as international actors. They have adopted tropes of maroonage, and human rights to make claims against the state and lobby for international support. Afro-Colombian refugees from violence have been active in the United States and other countries challenging the policies of the US government in much the same way that refugees from the US interventions in Central America challenged US support for the Contra Rebels in Nicaragua and the government's counterinsurgency efforts in El Salvador (Perla, 2005). The peace communities in the Pacific region have their origins in the rubric of maroonage and the fight for land rights. Many of the lands are properties long occupied by Afro-Colombians that were claimed by the government in the 1950s to be sold or leased to transnational corporations for various forms of exploitation including mining and oil exploration.

This movement has also broken into Colombian popular culture. Traditional salsa artists like Joe Arroyo have taken up the themes of Afro-Colombian resistance as well as an emerging hip hop movement that utilises the themes of the movements including maroonage and anti-violence in the lyrics of their music

(Sawyer, 2005b). Thus, the struggle for Afro-Colombians has been to not only overcome invisibility but also to make their situation known from frequently isolated communities to the world. Colombia is also a case where thin notions of citizenship as well as the prevalence of indigenous movements and the protracted civil war have caused Black movements in Colombia to focus on issues of land rights and basic security.

CONCLUSION

The above examples from various parts of Latin America all resonate with more generalisable themes and questions for the study of racial and ethnic politics. These cases raise several general questions. First, how does one determine who is most deserving of social assistance by a state or government in a society with divergent and overlapping inequalities? A second question is, does 'race talk' in Latin America exacerbate or diminish the state and society's capacity to redress inequality in the region? Third, do Afro-Latin movements for group rights and recognition (in the form of land rights and cultural recognition by the state) complicate liberal understandings of individual rights?

These questions, among many others, motivate scholars who examine the correlation between ethno-national and cultural diversity and democracy in other parts of the globe. We raise these questions and issues to suggest that Afro-Latin political movements in all their diversity can generate as many complex arguments and examples for students of power and equality as any other region on earth. In the case of Latin America, we have a moving target. The recent emergence of these movements was spurred by forces we identified nationally and internationally. But the full implications of these movements remain to be seen yet, the questions for scholars and observers articulated above are not unique to Latin America. These questions are particularly important as nations as diverse as France, Spain and Russia confront anti-black racism and immigration. Further, the logic of colourblindness that is coming to dominate racial discussion in the US can be understood by examining its legacy in Latin America. Many pundits in places like France and the United States use Latin America as some form of 'example'. The challenges and questions faced by black social movements in these areas are central questions for racial social movements throughout the world and in a variety of circumstances, in particular the growing recognition of racial diversity.

NOTES

1. Roberto Gonzalez Echevarria *The Voice of the Masters* Austin: University of Texas Press
2. France, for example, has never organised its national population by race or ethnicity, which demographers have increasingly challenged in order to determine who actually constitutes the French population

3. See George Reid Andrews The Afro-Argentines of Buenos Aires Patricio Downes, Clarin.com, 2/4/05.

REFERENCES

Andrews, G.R. (1980) *The Afro-Argentines of Buenos Aires, 1800–1900.* Madison: University of Wisconsin Press.

Angel-Ajani, A. (2005) 'Out of Chaos: Afro-Colombian Peace Communities and the Realities of War', *Souls*, 6 (2): 10–19.

Arocha, J. (1998) 'Inclusion of Afro-Colombians: Unreachable National Goal?', *Latin American Perspectives*, 25 (3): 70–89.

Banton, M. (1998) *Racial Theories.* 2nd edition. Cambridge: Cambridge University Press.

Barbary, O., Ramirez, H.F. and Urrea, F. (2002) 'Identidad y ciudadanía afrocolombiana en la Región Pacífica y Cali: elementos estadísticos y sociológicos para el debate de la "cuestión negra" en Colombia', *Estudos Afro-Asiaticos*, 24 (3): 75–121.

Barbary, O. and Rabenoro, M. (2002) 'Measurement and Practices of Social and Racial Segmentation in Cali: A Survey of African Colombian Households', *Population*, 57 (4): 765–792.

Begag, Azouz (2007) *Ethnicity and Equality: France in the Balance.* Translated with Introduction by Alec G. Hargreaves. Lincoln Nebraska: University of Nebraska Press.

Bourdieu, P. and Wacquant, L. (1999) 'On the Cunning of Imperialist Reason', *Theory Culture & Society*, 16 (1): 41–58.

Dawson, M.C. (2003) *Black Visions: The Roots of Contemporary African-American Political Ideologies.* Chicago: University of Chicago Press.

Gregory S. (2006) *The Devil behind the Mirror: Globalization and Politics in the Dominican Republic.* Berkeley: University of California Press.

Hanchard, M. G. (1994). *Orpheus and Power: The Movimiento Negro of Rio de Janeiro and Sao Paulo Brazil, 1945–1988.* Princeton, N.J.: Princeton University Press.

Hanchard, M. G. (2006). *Party/Politics: Horizons in Black Political Thought.* New York: Oxford University Press.

Halpern, A. and Twine, F.W. (2000) 'Antiracist Activism in Ecuador: Black-Indian Community Alliances', *Race & Class*, 42 (2): 19–31.

Katznelson, I. (1976) *Black Men, White Cities: Race, Politics and Migration in the United States 1900–1930 and Britain 1948–1968.* Chicago: University of Chicago Press.

Layton, A.S. (2000) *International Politics and Civil Rights Policies in the United States, 1941–1960.* Cambridge: Cambridge University Press.

Meriwether, J.H. (2001) *Proudly We Can Be Africans: Black Americans and Africa, 1935–1961.* Chapel Hill: University of North Carolina Press.

Nobles, M. (2000) *Shades of Citizenship: Race and the Census in Modern Politics.* Stanford: Stanford University Press.

Peña, Y., J. Sidanius, et al. (2004). "Racial Democracy in the Americas: A Latin and U.S. Comparison." *Journal of Cross-Cultural Psychology.* 35 (6): 749–762.

Perla, H. (2005) *Revolutionary Deterrence: Lessons Toward a Theory of Asymetric Conflict.* Dissertation, UCLA Department of Political Science.

Plummer, B.G. (1996) *Rising Wind: Black Americans and U.S. Foreign Affairs, 1935–1960.* Chapel Hill: University of North Carolina Press.

Rex, J. (1986) *Race and Ethnicity.* Buckingham: Open University Press.

Sawyer, M.Q. (2005a) *Racial Politics in Post-Revolutionary Cuba.* Cambridge: Cambridge University Press.

Sawyer, M.Q. (2005b) 'Du Bois' double consciousness versus Latin American exceptionalism: Joe Arroyo, salsa and negritude', *Souls*, 7 (3–4): 88–98.

Sawyer, Mark Q. (2006). *Racial Politics in Post Revolutionary Cuba.* New York: Cambridge University Press.

Singh, N.P. (2004) *Black is a Country: Race and the Unfinished Struggle for Democracy.* Cambridge, MA: Harvard University Press.

Telles, E. Edward. (2006). *Race in Another America: The Significance of Skin Color in Brazil.* Princeton, N.J.: Princeton University Press.

Van Den Berghe, P. (1967) *Race and Racism a Comparative Perspective.* New York: John Wiley & Sons.

Viveros V.M. (2002) 'Dionysian Blacks: Sexuality, Body, and Racial Order in Colombia', *Latin American Perspectives,* 29 (2): 60–78.

Von Eschen, P.M. (1997) *Race against Empire: Black Americans and Anticolonialism 1937–1957.* Ithaca: Cornell University Press.

Wade, P. (1997) *Race and Ethnicity in Latin America.* New York: Pluto Press.

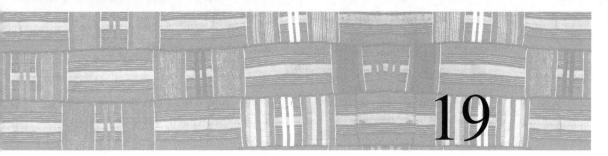

19

Diaspora and Hybridity

Claire Alexander

*The diaspora experience as I intend it here, is defined, not by essence or purity, but by rec-
ognition of a necessary heterogeneity and diversity; by a conception of 'identity' which lives
with and through, not despite, difference; by hybridity*

(Stuart Hall, 1990)

INTRODUCTION

In 1903, W. E. B DuBois famously prophesied that 'The problem of the twentieth
century is the problem of the color line' (1995[1903]: 41). While the subsequent
hundred years have proved DuBois's words terribly, bloodily true, it is also
the case that the past century has been challenged by the transformation and
transgression of this line as well as by its (re)inscription. The twentieth century
is characterised as much by the movement and displacement of peoples as by
their separation, by their encounters as much as by their divisions, by difference
and disjuncture as much as by categorisation and control. While the history of
modernity is the history of movement and (often violent) interaction between
peoples and cultures, 'travellers and merchants, pilgrims and conquerors'
(Appadurai, 2003: 26), the past 100 years have seen dramatic upheavals that have
transformed the racial and ethnic landscape globally, and in the small, local and
intimate spaces of everyday lives. In the wake of two world wars, decolonisation
and mass labour migration from the 1940s, ongoing smaller-scale conflicts and
the displacement of millions of people as refugees and asylum seekers, the scale
and scope of movement have been unprecedented. Avtar Brah thus notes (1996)
that in 1992 an estimated 100 million people could be designated as 'migrants'
(of whom 20 million were refugees and asylum-seekers). In addition, in the last
30 years particularly, the development of communication technologies and mass

transportation, the opportunities for relocation, short-term travel and tourism for large numbers of people have become at once possible and unremarkable. Such developments have transformed both the ways in which we imagine the world and our immediate surroundings: Arjun Appadurai, for example, thus writes of the changing *ethnoscapes* that migration and travel generate, challenging and translating the former certainties of nation, neighbourhood, community, family, friendship, work and so on, 'the warp of these stabilities is everywhere shot through with the woof of human motion' (2003: 32). Rather than boundaries and borders (or lines), he asserts, we should now think in terms of deterritorialisation, imagination, disjunctures, scapes and flows.

A number of sometimes overlapping, sometimes competing, theoretical frameworks have emerged, particularly since the 1980s, that seek to capture and unravel the complexities of contemporary migration and movement – for example, globalisation (particularly in its more cultural formulations), transnationalism, postcolonial theory, border theory, migration theory, trends within race and ethnic studies (particularly 'new ethnicities') and so on. What these different frameworks share is a recognition of the unfinished and multi-faceted nature of migration and settlement, particularly of the role of culture and identity in creating and contesting notions of home, nation and belonging. These ideas challenge the often reductionist economistic focus on migration as the movement of labour, along with its assumption of the 'once-and-for-all' break made between the 'sending' and 'receiving' countries, to insist on the multiple trajectories, two (or more) way traffic in financial, cultural, political and social resources, and the historical, social and political contexts and specificities of migration and settlement. Theorisations of diaspora and hybridity have emerged alongside, and in dialogue with, these frameworks, focusing particularly on the changing cultural practices and identities that the historical and contemporary movement and mingling of peoples has generated. More particularly, they have explored the encounters and intersections of peoples, defined through racial and ethnic difference, in new Imperial and post-Imperial spaces and across Du Bois's colour line. As with postcolonial theory, border theory and 'new ethnicities', with which they intersect, contemporary notions of diaspora and hybridity form part of a broader post-structurally inspired move to locate, unpack and dismantle racial meanings and identities, and to emphasise fluidity, contestation and ambiguity in the ways that race and ethnicity are 'made', practised and lived (Alexander and Knowles, 2005). Such theorisations have been crucial too in shifting the focal point away from the ascriptions and presumptions of the Imperial centre to the experience of the colonised periphery, the salience of marginalised knowledges and the unsettling, 'anxious' encounters of the colonial subject within the heart of the metropolis (Jacobs, 1996) – what Stuart Hall has termed the presence of 'The Rest in the West' (1992).

Alongside these contemporary forms of movement, theorisations of diaspora and hybridity have also been important in challenging the ways in which the boundaries of the nation-state are imagined and enforced, and the ways in which racial and ethnic identities are defined and legislated within these constructed and defended borders. Where recent years have seen the resurgence of exclusionary territorial notions of nationhood, citizenship and belonging, often linked to narrowly ascribed ethnic identities or imagined historical, linguistic, religious or cultural traditions – for example, in the construction of 'Fortress Europe' or the policing of the US-Mexican borderlands – diaspora and hybridity assert the impossibility of absolute boundaries, and insist on the imbrications of global histories and transnational affiliations. Diaspora and hybridity focus crucially then on movement across borders/boundaries and on processes of translation and cultural fusion which transcend and transgress the nation, and disrupt the ascription of neat, bounded and homogeneous cultural/minority identities. The focus of both concepts is very much on the creation of identity 'from below', and this often more people-centred, subjective and occasionally 'messy' approach provides a crucial, and salutary, alternative to other, more abstracted and mechanistic perspectives.

It is perhaps for this reason that black, postcolonial and minority scholars have been at the forefront of developing and using these frameworks. In Britain, for example, the concepts have developed as part of the broader analysis of racial and ethnic studies, exploring the arrival and settlement of post-war migration from the former Empire, and in opening up space for black and minority ethnic communities, cultures and identities within the discourse of British nationhood and citizenship. In the pioneering work of scholars such as Homi Bhabha on hybridity and Paul Gilroy and Stuart Hall on diaspora, reified notions of 'Britishness', rooted in a narrative of Imperial nostalgia, have been challenged and displaced through the insistence on the ambiguous intimacies of Empire at the heart of Britishness – 'the sugar you stir' (Hall, 1978) – and the global trajectories of contemporary black cultures (Gilroy, 2004).

However, both diaspora and hybridity – like ethnicity – are reclamations of older terms, and the contemporary reformulations carry with them the traces of these earlier histories and meanings (Goldberg, 1993). By contrast with the British debates, for example, as Brent Hayes Edwards has argued (2001), diaspora in the United States is linked to a specific history of African American struggle, rooted in an American-centred Pan Africanism, while 'hybridity' maintains its closer, and more troubled, association with the prohibitions of interracial sex and miscegenation. This gives these concepts a very ambivalent status, in which both can be seen to re-inscribe and champion essentialised notions of racial and ethnic difference, as well as contest and fracture them. Some theorists have thus argued that this legacy renders these terms at least problematic and at most almost irredeemable (Anthias, 1998; Cohen, 1999; Gilroy, 1994; Young, 1995), while others have argued that the often celebratory and uncritical use of diaspora and hybridity in their more contemporary poststructuralist garb have stripped them of the political content and context necessary to confront the issues of racial violence and terror in the twenty-first century (Bhatt, 2005; Cohen, 1999; Kalra et al., 2005).

It should be noted that although diaspora and hybridity are linked concepts, they are not fully interchangeable. Kalra et al. (2005) have argued that diaspora can be conceptualised as a way of thinking about movement and the creation or recreation of boundaries/identities in new settings, where hybridity is what happens at the borders of these imagined groups – where cultures meet and mix. However, this distinction is not always sustained, and some theorists see the notion of diaspora cultures (or Brah's (1996) 'diaspora spaces') as the space of hybridity – what Homi Bhabha has called 'the third space' (1990). In these formulations, diaspora is itself a hybrid formation, while hybridity is the inevitable result of diaspora encounters; and, as the opening epigram from Stuart Hall makes clear, both arise from the confrontation and negotiation of racial and ethnic difference.

DIASPORA

Diaspora, as Paul Gilroy notes, 'is an ancient word' (1994: 207). First found in the *Septuagint*[1] in the third century BCE (Braziel and Mannur, 2003), the term is drawn from the Greek *diasperien*, combining *dia*, 'through' or 'across', and *sperien,* 'to sow or scatter seeds', and was used specifically to describe the Jews living in exile from Palestine. However, in recent years, the notion of diaspora has become, as Phil Cohen has argued, 'one of the buzzwords of the postmodern age' (1999: 3), a shorthand for the proliferating contemporary experiences of migration, exile and settlement. Khachig Tölölyan thus writes 'Diasporas are the exemplary communities of the transnational moment' (1991: 4). Indeed, the explosion of the term in academic, cultural and political arenas since the late 1980s (Anthias, 1998; Brubaker, 2005; Cohen, 1999; Kalra et al., 2005), and its increasingly profligate application to diverse groups and identities, has led some to speak of 'a "diaspora" diaspora' (Brubaker 2005: 1), and to question both the remit and utility of the term (Cohen, 1999; Edwards, 2001; Kalra et al., 2005). Others, however, have argued for the significance of diaspora theory in providing 'critical spaces for thinking about the discordant movements of modernity, the massive migrations that have defined this century' (Braziel and Mannur 2003: 3), while cautioning against 'the uncritical, unreflexive application of the term "diaspora" to any and all contexts of global displacement and movement' (ibid).

While accepting the need for caution, and for attention to the historical and political specificities of the term (Brah, 1996), how one quite draws the boundaries of diaspora is less clear.[2] Can all groups who have experienced migration and resettlement be seen as diasporic? Can we talk of diasporas of privilege ('the white diaspora')?[3] Do we need to maintain the notion of common origin or homeland to define a diasporic identity (or can we speak of global religious 'diasporas')? Or, as is increasingly argued, can we use the term to encapsulate global identities where movement is not a requirement (e.g., in terms of 'queer diaspora' or 'the digital diaspora') and where the term diaspora serves as a semantic substitute for identities of all kinds? (Brubaker, 2005).[4] On the other hand, should 'diaspora' be reserved for particular groups and movements bound inescapably with a history of trauma and violence (as with the Jewish or Black diasporas)? How does such a conception confront the diversity within these histories, successive movements and sojourns and the tapestry of their encounters in new places? Can we avoid the attribution of diasporic identity as simply a re-inscription of a racialised minority status – as being always outside the nation (what Clifford describes as being '"not here" to stay' (1997)) or is this, indeed, precisely the identity we are claiming, whether to proclaim our cosmopolitan outlook or contest local inequalities and discriminations? Are we all diasporic, or – if we take the arguments for historical specificity seriously – are none of us?

While answering these questions is beyond the scope of the current chapter, they are significant in underlining the need for a critical engagement with the concept, particularly in the light of the increasingly ubiquitous appearance of the term in the past 20 years, across disciplines, in journals, and outside the academy – in the media and on the Internet, for example, where it overlaps with the idea of 'community' (Brubaker, 2005; Cohen, 1999; Kalra et al., 2005). More than this, this expansion points to the fact that the concept of diaspora can be used to understand and make claims for diametrically opposed views – one which privileges essentialised notions of blood and being, nation and tradition (Safran, 1991; Tölölyan, 1996), and one which claims it as the antithesis of these very notions (Gilroy, 1993a, 1997). Floya Anthias (1998) characterises this division as between the idea of diaspora as a descriptive *typological* tool, and that of a *social condition* or *process* (see also Kalra et al., 2005), while Rogers Brubaker similarly sees the difference as between diaspora as an 'entity' and a 'stance' (2005). Others place the division as a teleological transformation, with '*earlier* notions of diaspora as grounded in the fixed or metaphysical' (Braziel and Mannur, 2003: 6, my emphasis) giving way to a more contemporary and critical theoretical engagement with difference. However, it is usually the case that most theorisations of diaspora find the mixing of the essentialist and transgressive, old and new, diasporas inescapable (Anthias, 1997; Cohen, 1997; Cohen, 1999; Kalra et al., 2005), and it is this encounter – the inability to erase the classical foundations of diaspora – that both generates and constrains its more contemporary formulations.

DEFINING DIASPORA: THE CLASSICAL MODEL

As with its companion 'hybridity', diaspora carries an integral sense of the organic, living nature of culture and identity, with a dual emphasis on dispersal and transplantation, or germination in unfamiliar soil. The gardening trope, with its etymological links to seeds and sperm, points to the centrality of notions of cultural reproduction (and a masculinist bias (Anthias, 1998)), at the heart of the concept (Kalra et al., 2005). In his important article on diaspora, William Safran

(1991: 83–84) identifies diasporas as 'expatriate minority communities' which share six key features:[5]

1) They are dispersed from an originary centre to at least two 'peripheral' places.
2) They maintain a 'memory, vision or myth about their original homeland'.
3) They 'believe that they are not – and perhaps cannot be – fully accepted by their host country'.
4) The ancestral home is seen as a place of return.
5) They are committed to the maintenance or restoration of this homeland.
6) They share a consciousness and solidarity as a group through a continuing relationship with the homeland.

An additional defining characteristic of classic diaspora is the notion of involuntary or forced dispersal. Paul Gilroy (1997: 328) thus defines diaspora as:

> A network of people, scattered in a process of non-voluntary displacement, usually created by violence or under threat of violence or death. Diaspora consciousness highlights the tensions between common bonds created by shared origins and other ties arising from the process of dispersal and the obligation to remember a life prior to flight or kidnap.

Classic notions of diaspora, then, are focused on a collective identity derived from a history of forced movement, permanent exile and a sense of loss and longing for the homeland. The archetypal diaspora, as the origin of the term itself suggests, is usually held to be the Jewish experience, which Safran describes as the 'ideal type', although it has been also applied, in this classic form, to Greek, Armenian and especially African/Black diasporas.[6] However, as Clifford has argued (1997), even the Jewish diaspora does not fully conform to the model set out by Safran (see also Boyarin and Boyarin, 2003). This is particularly true of the last three criteria – the desire to return to the homeland, a commitment to its maintenance and a sense of collective identity. Clifford states that, historically, the Jewish diaspora was more of a 'sprawling social world ... linked through cultural forms, kinship relations, business circuits and travel trajectories' (1997: 248) with links to different religious centres, national and city spaces than a coherent consciousness. Similarly, Daniel and Jonathan Boyarin note (2003) that many Jewish communities had lived voluntarily for centuries outside of Palestine before the fall of Judea, and that the desire for a homeland articulated within the Zionist vision has been experienced as problematic for many Jewish communities within and outside Israel. Indeed, they argue that it is the maintenance of cultural identity *without* recourse to a homeland, ideologically, politically or geographically, that marks out the primary conceptual contribution of the Jewish diaspora. Clifford thus writes: 'We should be able to recognise the strong entailment of Jewish history on the language of diaspora without making that history a definitive model. Jewish ... diasporas can be taken as non-normative starting points for a discourse that is travelling and hybridizing' (1997: 249). Certainly, recent work on diaspora communities has taken Clifford at his word, and many of the elements of Safran's definition have undergone transformation, or become part of a diasporic pick and mix. Brubaker (2005) has thus noted the expansion of the concept to include 'long distance nationalists', who retain a continued involvement with homeland politics (e.g., Hindu Nationalists, Kurds, Irish, Kashmiri, Albanians), and the inclusion of labour migrant communities who may maintain links with home countries (as with Bangladeshi, Italian, Indian, Mexican, Turkish, Polish, Vietnamese diasporas). The term can be used where there is no homeland, no forced expulsion, no break, no myth of return, and where groups are relatively assimilated in their new surroundings (Irish and Italian, or indeed, Jewish communities) and to describe groups separated by national borders (Mexicans in the United States). As Robin Cohen notes (1999: 3) '"Diaspora" proposes itself as a master trope of migration and settlement'.

Brubaker (2005) has argued that this expanded use of diaspora has three core elements – dispersion (or division), homeland orientation and boundary maintenance. The latter element for Brubaker, and others, points to the crucial role of diaspora as signalling difference, and in enabling the notion of diasporic 'communities'. This suggests distinction from others, internal solidarity or homogeneity, and continuity across time and space. Diaspora here becomes a form of categorisation or social description, rather than a mode of analysis, and runs the risk of creating self-fulfilling typologies that emphasise coherence and objectivist measurement (Anthias, 1998; Brubaker, 2005). An example of this approach can be found in Cohen's *Global Diasporas* (1997), in which he defines a typology of diaspora forms – victim (African), labour (Indian), trade (Chinese), Imperial (British), cultural (Caribbean). Brubaker similarly points to Gabriel Sheffer's construction of diasporas as 'bona fide actual entities' (Sheffer, 2003: 245, cited in Brubaker, 2005: 10), which can be quantified and counted.[7]

This raises a number of questions: how does one count membership of a diaspora? Should one count members who, fully assimilated into their host society, do not feel any sense of lateral or historical connection, or do not define themselves as part of a diaspora? Does it make sense to conflate under one heading what might be a multiplicity of historical movements, sojourns and settlements, with differing motivations and consequences? If we take 'the Indian [labour] diaspora' (all 9 million of us, by Sheffer's reckoning), for example, does this label capture the different histories and experiences of indentured labour, the Imperial relocations of migrants to the buffer zones in Africa and their later expulsions (the 'twice migrants'), displacement after partition, the migrations to Europe of the 1950s and 1960s and the more recent high-tech migrations to the United States? How can it account for the dramatic reconstruction of 'India' itself in the years after Independence/Partition? How does it explain the very different national, economic and political ties between 'communities' and this homeland,[8] or position Indian groups whose originary links are almost forgotten (as for Indians in Guyana or Fiji)? How do different state structures impact on transnational connections, and what are the local processes of settlement and accommodation? How do gender, class, religion, sexuality and age cut across this supposedly coherent and quantifiable identity? (Brah, 1996; Kalra et al.,

2005). As Brubaker notes (2005), the foundational characteristic of these diasporic entities – its ur-identity – is an attributed 'ancestry', but this recourse to primordiality seems to predetermine what begs to be explored and erase the very textures of the experience it claims as its purview. Clifford thus argues (1997) that it is important to avoid the slippage between the use of diaspora as a theoretical concept, diasporic discourses and distinct historical experiences of diaspora.

CONTESTING DIASPORA: IDENTITY AND DIFFERENCE

The notion of diaspora as a bounded, transhistorical and homogeneous entity has been challenged by a number of theorists working particularly in race and ethnic studies and postcolonial theory, who have sought to reclaim and redefine the term to capture the fluid and unbounded flows, mixings and transgressions of both historically located and contemporary migrant and minority identities. In his seminal article on 'Cultural identity and diaspora' (1990), Stuart Hall thus draws a distinction between a view of diasporic identity as 'a sort of collective "one true self" … which people with a shared history and ancestry hold in common' (p. 223), and one which places identity as constituted as much by difference and rupture as similarity. He writes:

> Cultural identities come from somewhere, have histories. But like everything which is historical, they undergo constant transformation … Far from being grounded in a mere 'recovery' of the past, which is waiting to be found, and which, when found, will secure our sense of ourselves into eternity, identities are the names we give to the different ways we are positioned by, and position ourselves within, the narratives of the past. (1990: 225)

Avtar Brah (1996) similarly places the coherence of an entity such as 'the South Asian diaspora' as constituted through narrative, memory and performance rather than any predetermined reality: 'The identity of the diasporic imagined community is far from fixed or pre-given. It is constituted within the crucible of the materiality of everyday life; in the everyday stories we tell ourselves individually and collectively' (1996: 183). Hall is keen to maintain the tension between similarity and difference, history, culture and representation, but much of the contemporary work on diasporic identities has tended to focus on difference at the expense of identity and continuity. In this framework, influenced by the poststructural/postmodern (Cohen, 1999) and deconstructive turn in cultural theory, the emphasis shifts from borders/boundaries to border/boundary crossings, from continuity to disjuncture and from the idealisation of a 'homeland' to the multiplicities of 'homing' (Brah, 1996) in local, national and global spaces. Diaspora here becomes a *position* or *process* through which difference is both marked and contested, an active and relational category that is used to engage with issues of inequality, discrimination and marginalisation rather than an assertion of absolute social, cultural and political distinction or destiny (what

Cohen refers to as 'the diasporic condition' (1999: 9)). Brubaker thus argues: 'We should think of diaspora in the first instance as a category of practice … used to make claims, to articulate projects, to formulate expectations, to mobilise energies, to appeal to loyalties … It does not so much describe the world as seek to remake it' (2005: 12).

From this perspective, diaspora poses a set of challenges to ways of thinking about racial, ethnic and national identity, defining itself against fixity and claims to natural belonging. Paul Gilroy thus argues that diaspora provides 'an alternative to the metaphysics of "race", nation and bonded culture coded into the body' (1997: 328), placing instead the 'emphasis on contingency, indeterminacy and conflict' (ibid: 334). For ethnic minority communities in the West (where most of these scholars are located, and where the discourse is primarily directed), this version of diaspora is crucial in challenging the reification of the nation and its links to ethnicity and citizenship (Brah, 1996; Gilroy, 1993b), asserting the significance of ties that transcend national borders, and contesting the demands for assimilation into the host society. At the same time, this stance sets itself equally against the claims to belonging, authenticity and 'groupism' (Brubaker, 2005) that defines the more classic notions of diaspora discussed above, privileging movement over origin, translation over tradition, and 'routes' over 'roots'. As Gilroy (1993b) pithily captures it, 'It ain't where you're from, it's where you're at'.

Gilroy's epigram conveys strongly the present- and future-oriented aspect of this version of diaspora as process, in which the key focus is the encounter between the diasporic community and its place of settlement, rather than the 'homeland'. The stress is placed on heterogeneity of experience, and on tropes of exile and liminality as the expression of freedom and creativity rather than of displacement and loss (Cohen, 1999). Diaspora becomes a way of rethinking racial and ethnic identities as socially, historically and politically constructed rather than given, as subject to unequal relationships of power, and open to the 'play' (Hall, 1990) of individual and collective agency. As Hall writes, 'The diaspora experience … is defined, not by essence or purity, but by the recognition of a necessary heterogeneity and diversity … Diaspora identities are those which are constantly producing and reproducing themselves anew, through transformation and difference' (1990: 235). Such an approach throws into question whether, and how, diaspora communities can return 'home', even in their imagination (see e.g., Rey Chow (1993) on Chinese American or Lisa Lowe (2003) on 'Asian American' identity), and explores the way in which diaspora consciousness is used as a way of making claims in the place of settlement – using a global discourse in very local settings (as, e.g., with the use of the 'umma' for British Muslims (Kalra et al., 2005)). Clifford thus suggests that diasporas think globally but live locally, creating 'alternate public spheres, forms of community consciousness and solidarity that maintain identifications outside the national time/ space in order to live inside, with a difference' (1997: 251).[9] Brah (1996: 208) similarly argues for the idea of 'diaspora spaces' in which borders, diasporas and dis/location intersect 'as a point of confluence of economic, political, cultural, and psychic processes'. Diaspora spaces, according to Brah, bring together and transpose 'diasporian' and 'native', as well as different diasporas, in relations of power and in intersection with axes of gender, class, sexuality and so on.

The notion of diaspora space lies at the heart of Paul Gilroy's influential text *The Black Atlan*tic (1993a). Gilroy's analysis of black/African diaspora cultural forms and identities points to difference, to transformation and to change, to the process of movement through slavery, settlement, migration, resettlement and to the different histories of emancipation, colonisation, segregation, decolonisation and anti-racist struggle. Like Hall, Gilroy is concerned to hold in tension processes of continuity and memory, and translation and change – what he terms (*pace* Leroi Jones) 'the changing same' – and to assert the significance of both 'roots' and 'routes'. Rather than looking back to an idealised homeland, Gilroy argues for the complex circulation of ideas and expressive cultures across the Black Atlantic, between Africa, the Americas, the Caribbean and Europe, as creating a space of political intervention:

> I have settled on the image of ships in motion across the spaces between Europe, America, Africa and the Caribbean as a central organising symbol … Ships immediately focus attention on the Middle Passage, on the various projects for redemptive return to an African homeland, on the circulation of ideas and activists as well as the movement of key cultural and political artefacts: tracts, books, gramophone records, and choirs. (1993a: 4)

For Gilroy, diaspora identities inhabit 'contested "contact zones" between cultures and histories' (ibid: 6), which challenge both Euro-American categorisations and borders and the 'ethnic absolutism' of some forms of black cultural politics. Gilroy's interest is particularly in music as transgressing boundaries and creating new syncretic, hybrid cultural forms (see also Sharma et al., 1996), and the focus on cultural practices such as music, literature, film and photography has been predominant in work on diaspora (Kalra et al., 2005). However, this focus on cultural production has led some theorists to criticise diaspora theory as too celebratory, and too bound up with processes of commodification, and argue that this has stripped it of its political potential and intent (Cohen, 1999; Kalra et al., 2005; Sharma et al., 1996), or erased the specificities of particular diasporic histories (Edwards, 2001). Gilroy himself is critical of absolutist and hyper-masculine versions of some black musical cultures – particularly around issues of homophobia and misogyny – although he too has come under fire for underplaying the gendered and sexualised dimensions of diaspora in his own work (Anthias, 1998). These concerns should alert us to some of the dangers of this version of diaspora theory – as in its more classic forms, this diaspora may be reactionary in its politics, exclusive in its scope and may ignore or subsume internal differences or ambiguities around class, gender, sexuality, disability, etc. In addition, it has been argued that even a fragmented notion of diaspora relies on a previous inscription of a fixed identity, centred on ethnicity and origin as a basis for belonging (Anthias, 1999).

HYBRIDITY

The notion of identity as a stance or process, formed in interaction and contestation with both old and new homelands and forged in the 'turbulence of migration' (Papastergiadis, 2000), is where the concepts of diaspora and hybridity meet and intersect. As argued earlier, hybridity is often conceptualised as what happens at the border of diaspora; where the diaspora meets and interacts with the 'host society', or indeed with other diasporic cultures and identities, and where new cultural forms and identities emerge (Kalra et al., 2005). Hybridity can be conceptualised as the culture of the borderland, of the in-between, of what Avtar Brah calls 'diasporic space' (1996) or Homi Bhabha has termed 'the third space' (1990) – it is, to quote Bhabha, 'how newness enters the world' (1994: 227). Ashcroft et al. note 'hybridity commonly refers to the creation of new transcultural forms within the contact zone produced by colonisation' (1998: 118). If we can think of diaspora as the human face of globalisation, then hybridity stands as the cultural consequences of these global encounters (Papastergiadis, 2000; Pieterse, 2004); an assertion of complexity and (con)fusion that challenges notions of 'pure' cultural or national origins and ontologies – Jan Pieterse thus argues 'hybridity is the antidote to essentialist notions of identity and ethnicity' (2004: 71). Like diaspora, then, hybridity is concerned 'with the meaning of cultural difference in identity' (Papastergiadis, 2000: 14), and it similarly defies any attempt at resolution or closure: Pieterse describes hybridity as 'a journey into the riddles of recognition' (2004: 86).

As with diaspora, the popularity of hybridity as a way of conceptualising new forms of identity has emerged since the late 1980s, and forms part of the same deconstructive gesture. While forms of mixing – social, economic, institutional, political and cultural – are not new phenomena (indeed, as Anthias (2001) notes, hybridity is a feature of *all* cultural and social forms),[10] contemporary theorisations of hybridity are primarily focused on the subversive and transgressive forms and potentialities of cultural exchange between racialised and ethnicised collectivities and individuals. Brah and Coombes note, 'Much contemporary criticism has focused on hybridity as the productive emergence of new cultural forms which have derived from apparently mutual 'borrowings', exchanges and intersections across ethnic boundaries' (2000: 9). The term thus becomes synonymous with forms of cultural melding captured in notions such as creolisation, melange, metizaje/metissage, orientalisation, interculture, syncretism, fusion, cosmopolitanism (Pieterse, 2004), 'cut and mix' (Chambers, 1996), cyborg identities (Werbner, 1997; Kalra et al., 2005), morphing (Papastergiadis, 2000), the polyglot (Braidotti, 1994) and heteroglossia (Bakhtin, 1981). Hybridity here is reclaimed and celebrated as an almost inherently progressive political challenge to all forms of exclusion and boundary building, representing the voice of the marginalised, the impure, the nomadic, the in-betweens (Van Der Veer, 1997). Papastergiadis comments, 'In the last decade there has barely been a debate on cultural theory or postmodern subjectivity that does not acknowledge the productive side of hybridity and describe identity as being in some form of hybrid state' (2000: 169).

More recently, hybridity, like diaspora, has been subject to conceptual inflation and is increasingly postulated as *the* definitive condition of late modern identities and societies (Young, 1995).[11] Hybridity has 'acquired the status of a common-sense term, not only in academia, but also in the culture more generally' (Brah and Coombes, 2000: 1), referring to everything from fusion food, fashion and dual fuel cars to the commodified complacencies of multicultural 'Cool Britannia' (Back, 2002). As with 'diaspora', the expansion of the term has, some theorists argue, stripped it of its critical and transgressive potential (Hutnyk, 2000), leading one of hybridity's foremost spokespeople, cultural critic Kobena Mercer to note, 'the subversive potential once invested in notions of hybridity has been subjected to pre-millennial downsizing. Indeed, hybridity has spun through the fashion cycle so rapidly that it has come out the other end looking wet and soggy' (2000: 235).

Others have argued, however, that the problems with hybridity lie closer to its conceptual heart. Pnina Werbner (1997), for example, has astutely observed that there is a paradox in seeing hybridity as a transgressive and interruptive force, and as something that is commonplace and part of everyday cultural practices (Back, 2002). If everyone and everything is hybrid, then no-one and nothing is distinctively so, and its critical analytical power disappears (Anthias, 2001, Kalra et al., 2005). Furthermore, Werbner asks, 'What if cultural mixings and cross-overs become routine in the context of globalising trends? Does that obviate the hybrid's transgressive power' (1997: 1)? Others have argued that the notion of hybridity is inescapably tainted by its historical roots, in particular its association with notions of racial classification and the fears of mixing (Young, 1995) – what Papastergiadis refers to as 'the dark past of hybridity' (2000: 169). Hybridity thus inevitably conjures notions of 'anterior purity' (Young, 1995; Gilroy, 2000; Kalra et al., 2005), though theorists are divided on the extent to which this renders the term unusable. I will return to this point later, but for now it may be worth using Pieterse's (2004: 87) distinction (*pace* Hall, 1990) between 'old' and 'new' hybridity, in which the latter engages with, but is not fully constrained by, the former.

A SHORT AND BIZARRE HISTORY OF HYBRIDITY

As Robert Young (1995) has noted, the term 'hybridity', of Latin derivation, emerged into popular discourse in English in the nineteenth century. Like 'diaspora', hybridity has botanical and biological underpinnings, used originally to refer to the cross-fertilisation of plants (Pieterse, 2004), and of animals.[12] Nevertheless, as Papastergiadis has commented, 'A quick glance at the history of hybridity reveals a bizarre array of ideas' (2000: 169). The use of the term can be traced in a variety of domains, and academic disciplines, from the mythological combinations of animals, or animals and humans, to the melding of human and machine in cyborg technology, and, in anthropology, to describe forms of religious and cultural syncretism (Pieterse, 2004; Kalra et al., 2005). Pieterse (2004) refers to the use of the concept to describe art, institutional, organisational and economic forms, scientific interdisciplinarity, food and consumer choices. However, the contemporary use of hybridity as cultural fusion has its conceptual roots in two linked legacies – the 'dark past' of nineteenth-century racial science and linguistic creolisation.

Young asserts, '"Hybrid" is the nineteenth century's word' (1995: 6), not only because its popular usage expanded throughout the 1800s but because its meaning emerged alongside, and integral to, the explosion of discourses around race and racial difference that characterised this period. By the mid-1800s, hybridity was commonly used to refer to forms of human intermixture and Young notes that by 1890 it was used to refer to racial and linguistic fusion, the overlapping of the biological and cultural notions of hybridity that linger on today.[13] While the period of the Enlightenment had seen the obsession with classifying and typifying the natural and human world, and given rise to the taxonomies of race we still recognise (Brah and Coombes, 2000; Solomos and Back, 1996), the nineteenth century fused these religiously inspired classifications with the new found certainties of scientific and evolutionary racism. As Young has demonstrated in rich detail in his provocative text *Colonial Desire: Hybridity in Theory, Culture and Race* (1995), these theories of 'race' were inextricable from theories of sex (and sexual desire), and in particular the fears of interracial sex and its mixed-race offspring. Young argues that the figure of the human hybrid was central to the furious debate over the origin of racial difference, as to whether different racial types came from a single origin (monogenesist) or were, in fact, different species (polygenesist) – the more popular nineteenth-century view. He writes, 'the claim that humans were one or several species (and thus equal or unequal, same or different) stood or fell over the question of hybridity, that is, intra-racial fertility' (1995: 9). Drawing explicit parallels with the animal world, polygenesists argued that while different 'races' could interbreed (as the proliferating numbers of mixed-race people in the colonies attested), these offspring, as the product of different species, were themselves likely to be infertile (the equation most usually drawn was with mules – the offspring of a horse and ass – from which the term 'mulatto' is derived). With the prevailing insistence on racial purity, and the mapping of pure 'races' onto a hierarchy of biological and cultural superiority and inferiority, hybridity was viewed, for the most part, as a form of degradation and pollution,[14] while hybrid people were reviled as confused, rootless, pathological and threatening (Papastergiadis, 2000; Ifekwenigwe, 2004).[15] These views lasted well into the twentieth century, translating into eugenicist movements across Europe and North America (Papastergiadis, 2000), and the attempted regulation of inter-racial sexual contact – as, for example, in the miscegenation laws of the United States or apartheid South Africa (Goldberg, 1997).

As Werbner has commented (1997: 2), the sense of fear and threat is strongly associated with liminal or in-between spaces, at the edge of categories or the crossing of boundaries. However, more than this, the existence of hybrids stood as a challenge to the very existence of 'race'. Young writes:

> Paradoxically, these 'raceless masses' which attain no new species through hybridisation threaten to erase the discrimination of difference: the naming of human mixture as 'degeneracy' both asserts the norm and subverts it, undoing its terms of distinction, and opening up the prospect of the evanescence of 'race' as such. (1995: 19)

While many contemporary theorists celebrate the power of hybridity to undo 'race' in this way, Young warns that this paradox means that, on the one hand, hybridity can work to erase issues of racial injustice and oppression, and on the other, that it acts as part of a dialectic through which the idea of 'race' asserts and defines itself.

It is important to recognise, in addition, that these ideologies of 'race' and hybridity were also played out in colonial spaces with social, cultural and material consequences, often in intersection with ideologies of gender performed through the violation of the bodies of colonised women. Papastergiadis has commented that 'emerging theories of hybridity were for the most part normative prohibitions' (2000: 170), and the increased rigidity of racial ideologies during this period was underscored through the regulation and scrutiny of the minutiae of everyday interaction and intimacy in the colonies (Caplan, 2001; Stoler, 2002). While 'hispanicisation' was encouraged in parts of Latin America, in most places racial mixing was seen as a threat to colonial control and mixed-race people were viewed as either potential fifth columnists, traitors to the 'race' (Brah and Coombes, 2000; Papastergiadis, 2000; Stoler, 2002) or caricatures of their colonial masters (what V.S. Naipaul termed 'mimic men'(1967)).

The ambiguity of hybrid forms that Young points to is also apparent in linguistic models of hybridity, and in particular in the focus on creole or pidgeon languages emerging through the forced cultural encounters of slavery and colonialism. Although language development had been previously used to underpin diffusionist and evolutionary models of cultural contact, linked to the ancient migration of peoples, linguistic hybridity is concerned not only with fusion and adaptation, but also with struggle, conflict and contestation: it involves, as Kalra et al. have remarked 'one language's vocabulary *imposed on* the grammar of another' (2005: 75, my emphasis) and testifies to the historical, social and political context of language mixing. Although language research itself often overlooked this broader context, the linguistic model of hybridity has proved a fruitful one for theorists of cultural hybridity, drawing particularly on Mikhail Bakhtin's (1981) work (Young, 1995; Werbner, 1997; Papastergiadis, 2000). Bakhtin's work on heteroglossia and polyphony has been taken up by some contemporary cultural theorists as a way of celebrating multiplicity and the carnivalesque in identity construction and performance[16] (Ashcroft et al., 1998; Werbner, 1997) and has been criticised for ignoring or erasing the relationships of power in which cultural translation and innovation takes shape (Kalra et al., 2005; Sharma et al., 1996). However, Bakhtin's version of hybridity is centrally concerned with the ambiguity of language, the disruption and transgression of meaning that is internal to the layering of forms – its 'double voice' (Young, 1995: 20). Young quotes Bakhtin:

> What is a hybridisation? It is a mixture of two social languages within the limits of a single utterance, an encounter, within the arena of an utterance, between two different linguistic consciousnesses, separated from one another by an epoch, by social differentiation or by some other factor. (1995: 20)

Hybridity here is not the seamless fusion of language or culture but an encounter that generates uncertainty – what Young terms 'an undecidable oscillation' (ibid). More than this, however, different meanings within the encounter serve to unsettle and disrupt each other, and may be ultimately contradictory, divisive and conflictual (Papastergiadis, 2000). Bakhtin here makes an important distinction between organic, unconscious or unintentional hybridity – by which languages (or, by extension, cultures) mix and evolve historically[17] – and intentional, conscious hybridity, which is deliberately contestatory, dialogic and politicised (Young, 1995; Werbner, 1997).

CULTURAL HYBRIDITIES: 'THE THIRD SPACE' AND THE POLITICS OF HYBRIDITY

Bakhtin's linguistic model, in both its intentional and unintentional forms, has been translated into the sphere of cultural expression by recent theorists of hybridity. While for some, the focus is on what Les Back terms 'the fact of hybridity' (2002: 450), the ordinary and everyday forms of cultural fusion that emerge within urban multicultural or diasporic spaces (Back, 1996), others have been concerned with the way hybridity offers up space for radical political intervention through a conscious critique of essentialised cultural, ethno-racial or national boundaries. This latter work highlights the uneven, provisional and contestatory dimensions of cultural encounter and exchange, and draws on themes from poststructural and psychoanalytic theory to insist on the unfinished and fragmented nature of cultural identities.

Perhaps the most influential account of hybridity can be found in the work of Homi Bhabha, who translates Bakhtin's notion of the double-voice and the inherent instability of meaning into the historical setting of colonial discourse and practice (Young, 1995) and later into a discussion of multicultural and postcolonial metropolitan spaces (Bhabha, 1990; Papastergiadis, 2000). Where Young's work demonstrates the ambivalences internal to colonial discourses around race and race-mixing, Bhabha's concern is with the ways in which this ambivalence enters into the very structures of colonial management and authority. Bhabha thus asserts the interdependence and mutuality of constructions of the coloniser and his colonised subjects, in which the coloniser is unable to simply read himself from a wholly subjugated (or absent) 'Other' (as Said's

Orientalism (1978) had suggested), and finds instead a self-refracted and fragmented through the encounter with 'other'/'othered' selves. He thus defines hybridity as 'a problematic of colonial representation and individuation that reverses the effects of the colonialist disavowal, so that other "denied" knowledges enter upon the dominant discourse and estrange the basis of its authority' (1994: 114). Hybridity works here not as fusion or exchange, but as imperfect translation and dislocation. This inherent instability necessitates the repeated performance of colonial authority to create and mark out difference (and erase hybridity) while simultaneously attesting to its incompleteness and impossibility (Bhabha, 1994; Childs and Williams, 1997; Young, 1995). In a connected concept, Bhabha invokes, and subverts, Naipaul's notion of mimicry in which the native acts as a distorted reflection of, and challenge to, the figure of the coloniser – 'a difference that is almost the same, but not quite' (1994: 86) – undermining the claims to absolute distinction and authenticity upon which authority rests. Hybridity here then 'terrorises authority with the ruse of recognition, its mimicry, its mockery' (1994: 115), and it is in the process of repetition and disruption that the place of resistance – what Bhabha terms 'the third space' – arises, to 'produce new forms of knowledge, new modes of differentiation, new sites of power' (1994: 120).

Bhabha's notion of 'the third space' or of the 'in-between' has also been taken up as a way of understanding the generative space of contemporary post-colonial cultural production in the metropolitan centres, and here his work finds common ground with Gilroy's notion of diasporisation and Hall's notions of 'new ethnicities'. Hybridity provides a model for understanding both cultural syncretism and cultural difference, and emphasis is placed on the partial and contested forms of identity construction, or 'identification' (Bhabha, 1990). Young comments, 'Though here the inflection is more partial and more locally conceived, hybridity once again works simultaneously in two ways: 'organically', hegemonising, creating new spaces, structures, scenes, and 'intentionally' diasporising, intervening as a form of subversion, translation, transformation' (1995: 25). For Bhabha, 'The process of cultural hybridity gives rise to something different, something new and unrecognisable, a new area of negotiation of meaning and representation' (1990: 211), an area that is produced as much through contradiction, conflict and 'incommensurability' as through synthesis.

A good contemporary example here might be the recent controversies in Britain, and across mainland Europe, about the status of the Muslim veil/headscarf/hijab, and in particular the niqab (the full length dress with the face covering), which has been represented in the dominant discourse as outside of, and a threat to, national cultures and ideologies of 'European civilisation'. Former Foreign Secretary Jack Straw sparked major controversy in the UK in October 2006 by suggesting that this 'visible statement of separation and difference' marked Muslim young women as outside of wider British society, while the Dutch parliament proposed in the run up to the General Election that year that they would ban the wearing of the veil in public places (*The Guardian* 6/10/06).

In contrast, some young Muslim women see the hijab as a way of participating in the public sphere as equals, and use it as a way of both negotiating the cultural and religious traditions of their parents and asserting a more pluralistic (or anti-racist) version of national identity. The veil here becomes suffused with meanings that are inseparable from dominant discourses of alienness (and alien-ation), culture clash and tradition, and form more localised demotic struggles for recognition in a multicultural landscape within a contemporary globalised context, but in ways that resist either exclusion or incorporation.

It can be argued, however, that Bhabha's commitment to difficulty and incom-mensurability has been diluted in the more celebratory accounts of hybridity which have tended to privilege processes of cultural crossover and fusion as inherently progressive and transgressive. Pieterse comments: 'In cultural studies, hybridity denotes a wide register of multiple identity, crossover, cut'n'mix, expe-riences and styles, matching a world of growing migration and diaspora lives, intensive intercultural communication, everyday multiculturalism and erosion of boundaries' (2004: 87).

These versions of hybridity are closely linked to diaspora and contemporary cultural forms of globalisation, and are intertwined with processes of commodi-fication and consumption which some commentators have argued militates against any political agenda. As Kalra et al. note:

> The dynamic of exchange and mixture in the work of contemporary 'hybridity theorists' is intended as a critique of the negative complex of assimilation and integration that is so prevalent in dominant popular culture ... The questions that should be put here has not to do with the evaluation of this diversity, but with the ways its advent leads either to new possibilities in a diasporicised polity or, as seems just as likely, to the increasing incorporation of the mobile-phoned youth into the 'host society', the culture industry, and more generally into a hybridised mode of capitalism. (2005: 82)

As the above quote makes clear, one of the primary sites for the celebration of hybrid cultural production is youth culture, and particularly the arena of musical expression (see Pieterse, 2004). In Britain, for example, the history of migration of Caribbean and South Asian peoples has generated a range of musical fusions from ska to jungle, hip-hop to ragga, Brit-Soul to post-Bhangra (Gilroy, 1993b; Sharma et al., 1996; Dudrah 2007), along with all the borrowings and crossings these labels belie. On one level, these expressions testify to 'the fact of hybridity' (Back, 2002) linked to the transnational and transcultural experiences of second-generation migrants in the multicultural metropolis (Gillespie, 1995; Back, 1996). Rajinder Dudrah's (2007) recent study of Bhangra music, for example, points to the genesis of the genre in the fusion of folk Punjabi musical traditions of first-generation migrants with the youth cultures of urban Britain in the 1980s and the stylings of contemporary Bollywood cinema. Dudrah traces the subsequent travel of the form from the Soho Road in Handsworth, Birmingham back to the Punjab as well as through Europe and the United States, where it has been again translated in the sampling of African American hip-hop.

However, it would be misleading to read these expressions either as inherently progressive or as necessarily generating radical political or social change. As Back (2002) notes, even hybrid forms can generate claims to purity and exclusivity (Werbner 1997)[18] and can incorporate (and obscure) divisions around ethnicity, gender or sexuality. Similarly, a recognition of hybrid cultural expressions can erase the forms of power inequality, commodification and exploitation that underpin both their production and consumption, while offering up illusory cultural solutions (or placebos) to structural social, political and economic patterns of racialised and ethnicised exclusion and violence (Sharma et al., 1996; Kalra et al., 2005).[19] This is even more the case where the assertion of hybridity works to undermine claims to collective action and rights, through the privileging of individualised or privatised forms of self-identification (Pieterse, 2004; Gilroy, 2004), something that has been argued in response to the 'mixed-race' movement in the United States, (e.g., Ifekwenigwe, 2004). Indeed, as the ongoing wrangling over 'mixed race' makes very clear, the notion of hybridity has yet to escape its historical implications of racial and ethnic absolutism: Gilroy thus comments: 'Who the fuck wants purity? ... the idea of hybridity, of intermixture, presupposes two anterior purities ... I think there isn't any purity ... that's why I try not to use the word hybrid ... Cultural production is not like mixing cocktails' (1994: 54–5).

CONCLUDING COMMENTS

Gilroy's rejection of 'hybridity' as a term reflects a broader ambivalence about the provenance of the concept and the ways in which contemporary re-theorisations can (or cannot) effectively reclaim it (Young, 1995; Hall, 1996). As argued above, similar concerns have been voiced about the use of 'diaspora' in conjuring up idealised notions of absolute origins. Indeed, both 'diaspora' and 'hybridity' have been criticised on very similar grounds – for being dependent on (and evoking) notions of absolute boundaries; for privileging the individual and the subjective over the collective, change over continuity and the textual over the lived; for erasing inequalities of power and continued material discrimination and racial violence; for overlooking historical and cultural specificity; and for mis-taking cultural expressions for structural solutions.

Most recently, a number of scholars and writers have expressed their misgivings about the valency of these terms in explaining current social, cultural and political formations and conditions, most particularly in the post 9/11 context and the ongoing war on terror in which the triumph of ethnic and racial absolutes (of all kinds and on all sides) are writ large, and the overwhelming mood is not to live with difference, but eradicate it (Bhatt, 2004; Kalra et al., 2005). However, in this context, and where multiculturalism is increasingly understood as the practice and consequence of living separately rather than the process of living together, diaspora and hybridity are positioned as an alternative to these imagined 'parallel lives' (Home Office, 2001)[20] containing the possibility of their transgression or dismantling. If the optimism that underpinned the emergence of 'diaspora' and 'hybridity' as theoretical tools through the 1990s has waned, nevertheless it is precisely in this post-Millennial context that both the 'fact' of hybridity and diaspora, and their critical potential in opening up new spaces for engagement – for thinking and living differently – assume even more significance.

NOTES

1. The Septuagint is the Greek translation of the Hebrew Scriptures intended for the Hellenic Jewish communities in Alexandria (Braziel and Mannur, 2003).

2. Phil Cohen has argued that diaspora has become 'a portmanteau word, one that may mean almost all things to all people' (1998: 7).

3. See Caroline Knowles (2004) for a discussion of this issue.

4. Brubaker (2005) thus notes that 'diaspora' increasingly overlaps with other meanings such as immigrant, refugee, expatriate, guestworker, exile, ethnic group and so on. (see also Kalra et al., 2005; Tölölyan, 1991).

5. See Clifford (1997) for a fuller discussion of these criteria.

6. Phil Cohen notes in his survey of the use of 'diaspora' in the academy that work on the Black/African diaspora has increased exponentially since the mid-1980s, while work on the Jewish diaspora has declined during this period (1999).

7. Sheffer claims that the 'real numbers' of historical diasporas include Chinese (35 million), Indian (9 million), Jewish and Gypsy (8 million each). 'Modern' diasporas include African American (25 million), Kurdish (14 million), Black Atlantic (1.5 million) (see Brubaker, 2005: 11).

8. Clifford (1997) thus points to the essentialisation and idealisation of 'the nation' in perpetuating conservative and reactionary diasporic political formations, for example, the support of Hindu nationalist groups in the UK and North America for right wing Hindutva movements in India and the persecution of non-Hindu Indians (Bhatt, 1997).

9. Clifford argues further that diaspora consciousness is formed through two processes – 1) a negative experience of exclusion and discrimination by the majority community and 2) the positive embracing of alternative histories, cultures and experiences (however imagined these may be) to position oneself 'wherever one has settled, differently' (1997: 256–257).

10. Aijaz Ahmed similarly writes, 'cross-fertilisation of cultures has been endemic to all movements of people ... and all such movements in history have involved the travel, contact, transmutation, hybridisation of ideas, values and behavioural norms' (1995, cited in Werbner ,1997: 5).

11. Papastergiadis notes 'In the rush to find an alternative to aggressive and chauvinistic forms of identity, the concept of hybridity has frequently been promoted to the position of a new form of global identity' (2000: 15).

12. Young notes that 'in Latin it meant the offspring of a tame sow and a wild boar' (1995: 6), and that in Webster's Dictionary of 1828 the term was defined as 'a mongrel or mule; an animal or plant, produced from the mixture of two species' (ibid).

13. Young cites the 1890 OED 'The Aryan languages present such indications of hybridity as would correspond with ... racial intermixture' (1995:6).

14. Although as Brah and Coombes note (2000) in parts of Latin America, racial mixing was advocated as a way of lifting the indigenous Indians from degeneracy through a process of 'hispanicization'.

15. John Hutnyk (2005) has also argued that early anthropology viewed cultural syncretism as a form of loss, giving rise to traditions of 'salvage anthropology'.

16. See for example work on linguistic performativity and identity such as Roger Hewitt *White Talk, Black Talk* (1986) and Roxy Harris' *New Ethnicities and Language Use* (2006).

17. Young cites Bakhtin 'such unconscious hybrids have been ... Profoundly productive historically: they are pregnant with potential for new world views' (1995: 21).

18. It is interesting to trace, for example, the reclamation of hybrid or mongrel identities in mixed-race studies, such as in Gloria Anzaldua's claims that 'At the confluence of two or more

genetic streams ... this mixture of races, rather than resulting in an inferior being, provides hybrid progeny, a mutable, more malleable species with a rich gene pool' (cited in Parker and Song, 2001: 9).

19. Pieterse thus notes Friedman's criticism 'Hybridity is not parity' (2004: 108).

20. In the aftermath of the urban unrest across the north of England in the summer of 2001, the Home Office Report headed by John Denham argued that the tension between South Asian and White communities arose from 'Parallel Lives' 'the fragmentation and polarisation of communities – on economic, geographical, racial and cultural lines – on a scale which amounts to segregation, albeit to an extent by choice' (2001: 12).

REFERENCES

Alexander, C. and Knowles, C. (eds) (2005) *Making Race Matter: Bodies, Space and Identity.* Basingstoke: Palgrave.

Anthias, F. (1998) 'Evaluating "Diaspora": Beyond Ethnicity?', *Sociology,* 32 (3): 557–580.

Anthias, F. (2001) 'New Hybridities, Old Concepts: The Limits of "Culture"', *Ethnic and Racial Studies,* 24 (4): 619–641.

Appadurai, A (2003) 'Disjuncture and Difference in the Global Cultural Economy' in J.A. Braziel and A. Mannur (eds) *Theorizing Diaspora.* Oxford: Blackwell.

Ashcroft, B., Griffiths, G. and Tiffin, H. (1998) *Postcolonial Studies: The Key Concepts.* London: Routledge.

Bakhtin, M. (1981) *The Dialogic Imagination: Four Essays.* (trans. C. Emerson and M. Holquist). Austin: University of Texas Press.

Back, L. (1996) *New Ethnicities and Urban Culture.* London: UCL Press.

Back, L. (2002) 'The Fact of Hybridity: Youth, Ethnicity and Racism' in D.T. Goldberg and J. Solomos (eds) *A Companion to Racial and Ethnic Studies.* Oxford: Blackwell.

Bhabha, H. (1990) 'The Third Space' in J. Rutherford (ed.) *Identity: Community, Culture, Difference.* London: Lawrence and Wishart.

Bhabha, H. (1994) *The Location of Culture.* London: Routledge.

Bhatt, C. (1997) *Liberation and Purity: Race, New Religious Movements and the Ethics of Postmodernity.* London: UCL Press.

Bhatt, C. (2004) 'Contemporary Geopolitics and "Alterity" Research' in M. Bulmer and J. Solomos (eds) *Researching Race and Racism.* London: Routledge.

Boyarin, D. and Boyarin, J. (2003) 'Diaspora: Generation and the Ground of Jewish Diaspora' in J.A. Braziel and A. Mannur (eds) *Theorizing Diaspora.* Oxford: Blackwell.

Brah, A. (1996) *Cartographies of Diaspora: Contesting Identities.* London: Routledge.

Brah, A and Coombes, A. (eds) (2000) *Hybridity and Its Discontents: Politics, Science, Culture.* London: Routledge.

Braidotti, R. (1994) *Nomadic Subjects.* New York: Columbia University Press.

Braziel, J.A. and Mannur, A. (eds) (2003) *Theorizing Diaspora.* Oxford: Blackwell.

Brubaker, R (2005) 'The "Diaspora" Diaspora', *Ethnic and Racial Studies,* 28 (1): 1–19.

Caplan, L. (2001) *Children of Colonialism: Anglo-Indians in a Postcolonial World.* Oxford: Berg.

Chambers, I. (1996) 'Signs of Silence, Lines of Listening' in I. Chambers and L. Curti (eds) *The Postcolonial Question.* London: Routledge.

Childs, P. and Williams, P. (1997) *An Introduction to Postcolonial Theory.* Harlow: Pearson Education.

Chow, R. (1993) *Writing Diaspora: Tactics of Intervention in Contemporary Cultural Studies.* Bloomington, IN: Indiana University Press.

Clifford, J. (1997) *Routes: Travel and Translation in the Late Twentieth Century.* Cambridge, MA: Harvard University Press.

Cohen, P. (1999) 'Rethinking the Diasporama', *Patterns of Prejudice,* 33 (1): 3–22.

Cohen, R. (1997) *Global Diasporas: An Introduction.* London: UCL.

DuBois, W.E.B. ([1903]1995) *The Souls of Black Folk.* New York: Signet Books.

Dudrah, R. (2007) *Bhangra: Birmingham and Beyond*. Birmingham: Birmingham City Council.

Edwards, B.H. (2001) 'The Uses of Diaspora', *Social Text*, 19 (1): 45–73.

Gillespie, M. (1995) *Television, Ethnicity and Cultural Change*. London: Routledge.

Gilroy, P. (1993a) *The Black Atlantic: Modernity and Double Consciousness*. New York: Verso.

Gilroy, P. (1993b) *Small Acts: Thoughts on the Politics of Black Cultures*. London: Serpent's Tail.

Gilroy, P. (1994) 'Black Cultural Politics: An Interview with Paul Gilroy by Tommy Lott', *Found Object*, 4: 46–81.

Gilroy, P (1997) 'Diaspora and the Detours of Identity' in K. Woodward (ed.) *Identity and Difference*. London: Sage.

Gilroy, P. (2004) *After Empire: Melancholia or Convivial Culture?* London: Routledge.

Goldberg, D.T. (1993) *Racist Culture: Philosophy and the Politics of Meaning*. Oxford: Blackwell.

Goldberg, D.T. (1997) *Racial Subjects: Writing on Race in America*. London: Routledge.

Hall, S. (1978) 'Racism and Reaction' in *Five Views of Multi-Racial Britain*. Commission for Racial Equality, London.

Hall, S. (1990) 'Cultural Identity and Diaspora', in J. Rutherford (ed) *Identity: Community, Culture, Difference*. London: Lawrence and Wishart.

Hall, S. (1992) 'The West and the Rest: Discourse and Power' in S. Hall and B. Gieben (eds) *Formations of Modernity*. Cambridge: Polity Press.

Hall, S. (1996) 'When Was "the Postcolonial"? Thinking at the Limit' in I. Chambers and L. Curti (eds) *The Postcolonial Question*. London: Routledge.

Harris, R. (2006) *New Ethnicities and Language Use*. Basingstoke: Palgrave Macmillan.

Hewitt, R. (1986) *White Talk, Black Talk*. Cambridge: CUP.

Home Office (2001) *Building Cohesive Communities*. London: HMSO.

Hutnyk, J. (2000) *Critique of Exotica: Music, Politics and the Culture Industry*. London: Pluto Press.

Ifekwenigwe, J. (ed.) (2004) *Mixed Race Studies: A Reader*. London: Routledge.

Jacobs, J.M. (1996) *Edge of Empire: Postcolonialism and the City*. London: Routledge.

Kalra, V.S., Kaur, R. and Hutnyk, J. (2005) *Diaspora and Hybridity*. London: Sage.

Knowles, C. (2004) *Race and Social Analysis*. London: Sage.

Lowe, L. (2003) 'Heterogeneity, Hybridity, Multiplicity: Marking Asian-American Differences' in J.A. Braziel and A. Mannur (eds) *Theorizing Diaspora*. Oxford: Blackwell.

Mercer, K. (2000) 'A Sociography of Diaspora' in P. Gilroy, L. Grossberg and A. McRobbie (eds) *Without Guarantees: In Honour of Stuart Hall*. London: Verso.

Naipaul, V.S. (1967) *The Mimic Men*. London: Penguin.

Papastergiadis, N. (2000) *The Turbulence of Migration*. Cambridge: Polity Press.

Parker, D. and Song, M. (eds) (2001) *Rethinking 'Mixed Race'*. London: Pluto Press.

Pieterse, J.N. (2004) *Globalization and Culture: Global Melange*. New York: Rowman and Littlefield.

Safran, W. (1991) 'Diasporas in Modern Societies: Myths of Homeland and Return', *Diaspora*, 1 (1): 83–99.

Said, E. (1978) *Orientalism*. London: Penguin.

Sharma, S., Hutnyk, J. and Sharma, A. (eds) (1996) *Dis-Orienting Rhythms: The Politics of the New Asian Dance Music*. London: Zed Press.

Solomos, J. and Back, L. (1996) *Racism and Society*. Basingstoke: Macmillan.

Stoler, A.L. (2002) *Carnal Knowledge and Imperial Power: Race and the Intimate in Colonial Rule*. Berkeley: University of California Press.

The Guardian, 'Veiled Issue' (6/10/06)

Tölölyan K (1991) 'The Nation State and Its Others: In Lieu of a Preface', *Diaspora*, 1 (1): 3–7.

Van Der Veer, P. (1997) '"The Enigma of Arrival": Hybridity and Authenticity in the Global Space' in P. Werbner and T. Modood (eds) *Debating Cultural Hybridity: Multi-Cultural Identities and the Politics of Anti-Racism*. London: Zed Press.

Werbner, P. (1997) 'Introduction: the Dialectics of Cultural Hybridity' in P. Werbner and T. Modood (eds) *Debating Cultural Hybridity: Multi-Cultural Identities and the Politics of Anti-Racism*. London: Zed Press.

20

Issues for the Twenty-first Century

Patricia Hill Collins and John Solomos

In this concluding chapter of the *Handbook of Race and Ethnic Studies*, we focus on two objectives. First, we aim to provide an overview of some of the key themes raised within the 18 substantive chapters. A recurrent concern in the various chapters has been the critical analysis of the changing terms of analysis in various sub-fields of race and ethnic studies as well as the emergence of new analytical perspectives and the articulation between academic and policy debates, and therefore we focus on these themes in this chapter. Second, an important element of this concluding chapter will be to identify some especially promising trends and developments that seem likely to shape the study of racial and ethnic relations in the coming decades. This forward-looking focus enables us to discuss emerging research questions and potential policy responses to the challenges that face a wide range of societies at the beginning of the twenty-first century.

TAKING STOCK: THE FIELD OF RACE AND ETHNIC STUDIES

The last two decades of the twentieth century and the beginning of the twenty-first century have been characterised by a dramatic growth in the field of race and ethnic studies. In part, this growth reflects the field's efforts to respond to the greatly changing terrain of global social relations where race and ethnicity seem to be undergoing substantial transformation across heterogeneous societies (Winant, 2001). Issues of race and ethnicity now pose important challenges to societies where these constructs were not historically central to their internal dynamics. This is the case, for example, in Germany, France, the United Kingdom, Spain and similar multiethnic Western European societies where immigration has changed the fabric of domestic national identity, or with postcolonial nation-states in Asia and Africa confronted with issues of ethnic conflict. Democratic societies that have long struggled with questions of race and ethnicity, most notably the United States, also face social issues such as job creation, educational equity, and healthcare that require new understandings of race and ethnicity (Fredrickson, 2002).

The growth in the field of race and ethnic studies also reflects the emerging academic interest in interdisciplinary research and its accompanying expansion of intellectual approaches to many themes, in this case, the study of race and ethnicity.[8] Interdisciplinary initiatives have enabled scholars of race and ethnicity to draw upon knowledge bases and theoretical traditions both from pre-existing academic disciplines such as sociology, political science, history and anthropology, as well as from interdisciplinary areas such as women's studies, cultural studies, postcolonial studies, queer theory and similar areas of inquiry. This changing intellectual context has infused a new vitality into the field. One sees fresh approaches to longstanding questions within the field, such as critical race theory's use of literary criticism in legal scholarship (see Mutua, Chapter 11), or using ideas of performativity gleaned from poststructuralist social theory to analyse racial violence (see Back, Chapter 17).

In this changing social, political and intellectual context, we see two issues that have implications for the study of race and ethnicity in the twenty-first century, one external to the field, the other internal. The first issue concerns the changing contours of racial and ethnic organisation in a global context, as well as the significance of these changes for racial/ethnic meanings and practices. We ask, how effectively might the field of race and ethnic studies engage the new social and political realities of the twenty-first century? The empirical bent of much contemporary work in race and ethnic studies remains linked to the field's longstanding impetus to understand observable racial and ethnic phenomena. In a context of rapid social change that is bringing new social and political realities, maintaining this empirical focus is a significant dimension of the field. Simply keeping track of the social changes brought about by reconfigured labour markets, the racial/ethnic distribution of poverty, discrimination in housing, jobs, schooling or public access, and seemingly massive immigration, has enabled researchers of race and ethnicity to develop a substantial corpus of empirical work on issues that concern policymakers, employers and ordinary people. Another question is, which significant social trends might emerge as important areas of inquiry for the field of race and ethnic studies? Important social problems remain intertwined with the study of race and ethnicity and addressing these increasingly complex social problems will require equally rigorous analyses of race and ethnicity.

A second significant issue framing the study of race and ethnicity in the twenty-first century concerns developments within the field itself. In what specific ways, if any, might a field that emerged in response to one specific set of historical and social phenomena better prepare itself to address the concerns of contemporary global social realities? Current phenomena such as debates over the meaning of racial and ethnic terminology, the field's emphasis on selected social institutions and its relative neglect of others, its emphasis on Western societies and similar preoccupations of the field, reflect its origins in nineteenth and twentieth-century racial formations of slavery, colonialism and imperialism. This history has shaped the questions, content, paradigms, theories and methodologies of the field.[2] Yet, the massive changes in global social institutions in the twenty-first century lead us to query whether these historical frameworks will remain adequate for understanding the types of phenomena that the field is likely to encounter in coming decades. We ask how the field of race and ethnic studies might move beyond much-needed internal critique in order to craft new questions, areas of investigation, paradigms, theories and methodologies that are adequate to the twenty-first century. Thus, this process of understanding its own contributions and limitations constitutes a key area of analysis for the field (see Feagin and O'Brien, Chapter 3; Bhatt, Chapter 5).

In the following sections, we explore issues that we anticipate having significant implications for race and ethnicity in the twenty-first century. We do so by mapping important new directions in the field of race and ethnic studies, specifically, how the field of race and ethnic studies will need to sustain a dual focus both on the external social and political context in which it is situated as well as its own internal practices. When joined recursively, this dual focus on actual social and political phenomena and sustained internal development should catalyse a dynamic field of inquiry for the twenty-first century. The following sections take up these two focal points.

SOCIAL AND POLITICAL REALITIES OF RACE AND ETHNICITY IN THE TWENTY-FIRST CENTURY

The questions that typically preoccupy scholars of race and ethnicity usually do not emerge solely or even primarily from scholarly literature. Rather, the political and social aspects of race and ethnicity across specific local, regional, national and increasingly global contexts catalyse much work in contemporary race and ethnic studies. The many issues raised by authors in this volume, for example, the racial gap in educational achievement (see Banks and Park, Chapter 15), citizenship debates and questions of national belonging (see Anthias, Chapter 9; Schuster, Chapter 13), the significance of family to sustaining and resisting racial and ethnic inequalities (see Zinn, Chapter 14) and how religion can be annexed by systems of racial rule (see Gilkes, Chapter 16), illustrate how issues of race and ethnicity are central to contemporary debates and public policies. When it comes to the study of race and ethnicity, it is impossible for the field to extract itself from the subject of its study, nor, some would say, should it.[3] As a result, work in this field stands in a particular relationship to contemporary social and political realities.

Politics flow from structures of racism and ethnic engagement, and as Caroline Knowles (Chapter 2) suggests, there is no need to analyze race in the absence of racism. There seems little doubt that one of the key questions we shall have to confront in the future is how to understand and tackle the social and political impact of racism, both as a set of ideas and as a form of political mobilisation. In broad terms, we shall need to be able to explain both the roots of contemporary racist ideas, practices, organisational forms and social movements as well as the source of their current appeal. We have compelling historical arguments that document the lineage of racism (see Feagin and O'Brien, Chapter 3; Bhatt, in Chapter 10). Yet it is precisely on the issue of their contemporary appeal that current research seems to be least enlightening. Researchers have not, by and large, had much to say about the reasons why we have seen the persistence of racist ideas and practices in recent times. We shall also need to consider what kinds of counter-strategies can be adopted to challenge new types of racist mobilisation. Again, research on the historical trajectories of anti-racist mobilisation is enlightening, yet as we discuss later on in this chapter, the theme of studying resistance remains underemphasised in the field.

Looking ahead to the twenty-first century means that the field would not shy away from tough questions concerning racism – it would examine how inequalities of race and ethnicity are being reconfigured and resisted within new global social realities. Our authors have provided us with a wealth of sites for this reconfiguration and resistance – education, citizenship, gender relations, multicultural social policies, family organization and relations, law and religion all constitute sites where race and ethnicity are being reconfigured. Looking ahead would continue to analyse these sites, yet would also ask how race and ethnicity persist as *explanatory* factors in global reorganisation as well as seemingly unraced social phenomena.

In the remainder of this section, we sketch out three significant sites that we think signal important issues for the twenty-first century where race and ethnicity may play a central, albeit often under-recognized role.[4] All three sites are currently central to racial/ethnic reconfiguration and anti-racist mobilisation in a global context. They are (1) global poverty as a racial/ethnic formation; (2); communications technologies, mass media and racial/ethnic phenomena; and (3) politicised ethnicity and politicised religion. For each of these areas, we sketch out some emerging political and social trends where race, ethnicity and/or racism might be made a more central component of analysis.

Global racial/ethnic formations: the case of poverty

Continuing to study race, ethnicity and racism primarily within the framework of national traditions – a reasonable approach given that much social policy until now has focused on the nation-state for redress of racial/ethnic inequalities. Yet, a parallel and often overlooked question concerns how race, ethnicity and racism may be part of new transnational processes of globalisation. The specifics of national contexts certainly shape particular constellations and remedies of racial/ethnic social issues. Yet, analysing racism and ethnic domination primarily within the contexts of specific national traditions or comparatively across a few hand-picked national case studies may miss the significance of race and ethnicity to broader global phenomena (Winant, 2001).

Poverty constitutes one important social problem that takes specific racial/ethnic forms within particular nation-states, yet whose persistence may also reflect transnational, global phenomena. The deeply entrenched nature of poverty seemingly has been exacerbated by neo-liberal, nation-state policies of the late twentieth century, yet racial/ethnic analyzes of poverty need not be contained within state policies. By whatever measures, a sizable proportion of the globe's population remains poor. This seems obvious, yet an equally obvious and less often acknowledged phenomenon is visible but less often discussed. Whether across nation-states in Africa, the Middle East, and Latin America with majority non-white populations or within Western, industrialised nations where racial/ethnic minorities are over-represented within a nation-state's poverty population, people of colour constitute the majority of the world's poor.

Analysing poverty within a global context or a world systems framework suggests that one can only make sufficient sense of one nation's poverty by placing it in relationship to other nations. In this way, poverty can only be comprehensively understood in a global context. Moreover, conceptualising poverty 'profoundly raced' within national settings also provides a compelling argument for exploring/analysing racial formations within a global context. This is a line of analysis that has been suggested by Balibar and Wallerstein, although it has remained relatively underdeveloped in the literature on the global world system. (Balibar and Wallerstein, 1991).

More analyses of how contemporary global capitalism in works with transnational racial/ethnic systems of power might better illuminate the causes of poverty as well as its remedies in the twenty-first century. As nation-states not only provide citizenship rights to individuals but also serve as the primary site for addressing social issues, in this case, racial redress and poverty, nation-states have garnered considerable attention in the literature of race, ethnicity and poverty (Newman et al., 2006; Platt, 2007). Such analyses must guard against logic that uses racial and ethnic concepts as analytical categories to explain racism and anti-racist initiatives within particular nation-states, yet abandons this analytical framework in favour of using racial and ethnic concepts as descriptive categories to depict people who are living in poverty in a global context.

These concerns raise several provocative areas for investigation. First, more robust empirical descriptions of global racial formations, a conceptual map of the racial and ethnic face of global poverty in the twenty-first century, might give a clearer picture of the race and poverty. This kind of empirical documentation would go far in spurring analysis of important economic questions, such as the racial/ethnic dimensions of global labour markets, the racial/ethnic segmentation of consumer markets and how ideas about race and/or ethnicity shape corporate decisionmaking about topics as diverse as where to open and close factories and where to dump industrial waste. This approach might also counteract the tendency to see economic disparities primarily in class terms, without fully understanding how race and ethnicity might persist as vital dimensions of economic inequality in the twenty-first century. These types of analyses should be of special interest to policymakers because, without solid empirical research that analyses the relationships among racial/ethnic patterns of stasis and change and economic development, confronting global poverty is likely to remain elusive.

Second, the field of race and ethnic studies might place greater emphasis on comparative analyses of racial/ethnic groups in order to more aggressively track and analyse the racial/ethnic dimensions of these emerging patterns of wealth and poverty. As racial/ethnic migration across national borders has generated such an expansive literature, this phenomenon might serve as an important anchor for such an investigation. As immigration alters the parameters of national populations, mapping the parallel economic contours of the shifting mosaic of global immigration raises important questions. For example, how have migration patterns affected poverty among racial/ethnic groups in sending and receiving nation-states? What effect, if any, has migration had on indigenous populations as well as long-term racial/ethnic subjugated minority populations? What are the racial/ethnic contours of who has escaped poverty, who is newly poor, and who has remained poor for generations? Racial/ethnic comparisons remain one important vehicle for mapping these shifting patterns of global poverty.

Third, more studies on the extremely wealthy individuals and families, a new global elite, might produce important descriptive racial/ethnic profiles of this population as well as catalyse increased analytical work on its significance. If this global elite is no longer white, Western, and/or male, what implications, if any, might this have for current debates about poverty and strategies for addressing it? The emergence of a wealthy, global elite of colour could be seen as evidence that the saliency of race and ethnicity are diminishing. Yet debates about colourblind racism suggest that racism without whiteness at the centre, or at least biological understandings of whiteness, might remain significant in framing economic outcomes. Poverty is a relational construct that only makes sense in contrast to gradations of wealth. If poverty is raced, what role, if any might elites groups who are not exclusively white, Western and male play in justifying its existence if not deriving economic benefits from non-poor people? A discussion of a global elite that is not exclusively white (resembling a global poverty population that is not exclusively people of colour) might raise interesting questions about the material factors that underpin racial/ethnic domination.

Communications technologies, mass media and racial/ethnic phenomena

Together, rapidly changing communications technologies and greatly expanded mass media content constitute another important issue where race and ethnicity promise to play a central role in the twenty-first century. How are the rapid expansion of the Internet, cell phones, wireless protocols and similar communications technologies as well as satellite and cable television, DVDs , MP3 devices, and similar global mass media reformulating social relations of race and ethnicity as well as racial/ethnic discourse? Here we identify selected issues for how race, ethnicity and/or racism might be a central component of analysis within the rapidly changing contours of new communications technologies and mass media content.

One crucial issue concerns basic access to new communications technologies. The phrase the *digital divide* references differential access to communications technologies – equipment such as computers, cell phones, MP3 players, satellite television, and the electricity and battery power to run them, as well as the information communicated via this equipment, for example, the Internet, e-mail and social networking sites. In this environment, those who enjoy the tools of the information society fare far better than those who do not. Moreover, because basic access to technology reflects race, class and ethnicity, new communications technologies may become important mechanisms both in reproducing racial and ethnic inequalities and in challenging racial/ethnic hierarchies. The question of basic access to the Internet and new communications technologies might emerge as a civil rights issue in the twenty-first century.

Another important issue for the twenty-first century concerns how these new communications technologies are changing social relations of all sorts, including those of race and ethnicity. This is a broad area of investigation that has several provocative possibilities for race and ethnic studies. The Internet, in particular, enables people to gain information about other ways of life that were historically difficult to obtain or managed by social institutions. The replacement of news reporting within newspapers, print media and television by so-called citizen journalists armed with video camera cell phones promises to change the landscape of racial/ethnic news. Similarly, social networking sites and cell phones enable people to form new social groups that transcend historical boundaries of geography and/or family. The outcomes of these communications technologies are not predetermined. Such technologies can be used to forge entirely new racial and ethnic identities, to strengthen existing ones or to argue that such identities constitute artefacts of the twentieth century.

When it comes to changing patterns of racial/ethnic social relations in the twenty-first century, a related idea concerns how new communications technologies may constitute important new areas for social control, in particular the use of new technologies for relations of surveillance. In essence, the visual nature of race and ethnicity where people can be racialised because they can be seen as being different from the so-called norm, works well with the growing significance of seeing and surveillance as part of new media technologies. From the voluntary postings on YouTube, to the operations of surveillance cameras in high crime neighbourhoods, to the growth of mass media spectacle in manufacturing new racial/ethnic ideologies, the visual nature of race and ethnicity takes on immediacy in an era of public surveillance.[5]

New communications technologies promise to shape the content of racial/ethnic discourse and belief systems. Thus, another important issue for the field of race and ethnic studies in the twenty-first century concerns how the explosion of a global mass media that is anchored within new communications technologies influences racial/ethnic representations and/or ideologies. Media has long been central for manufacturing racial and ethnic meanings. Yet as the textbooks, greeting cards, and other print media of prior eras gives way to the electronic media of DVDs, Internet downloading of movies and YouTube, we might ask how race and ethnicity are situated within and reproduced by these new media?

Much is at stake here, because discourses of race/ethnicity do not simply reflect racial/ethnic relations but also construct those relations. The field of racial and ethnic studies has effectively examined how representations have contributed to historical relations of domination and subordination. In the current context of changing patterns of globalisation, the effects of mass media transcend issues of political control yet may also be essential to the global economy. Commodity culture and consumerism, and the marketing of racial and ethnic representations might be essential in creating consumer demand and even more segmented consumer markets. Such markets require race and ethnic differentiation, thus emerging as yet another site of racialisation (Collins, 2006).

A final important area for the twenty-first century concerns how these emerging connections among new communications technologies, new social relations of race and ethnicity, and changing mass media patterns of racial/ethnic representation might catalyse new forms of political organising. Cell phones and the Internet in particular have enabled people form groups that express diverse goals and political agendas and that may be racially/ethnically homogenous or heterogeneous. For example, the Internet and new communications technologies have catalysed events as diverse as new forms of anti-racist organising; the reemergence of social identities that are hard to sustain within nation-state borders but that take on life when new technologies go across national borders (e.g., native peoples and LGBT communities; the resurgence of a global white supremacist discourse that links hate groups across national locations; and a vibrant, global hip-hop youth culture.

Politicised ethnicity, politicised religion

As religion promises to shape the political landscape of the twenty-first century in a number of ways, it constitutes an area of great significance for the field of race and ethnic studies. As noted across numerous chapters in this handbook, race and ethnicity remain significant phenomena across diverse societies. Whether race and ethnicity are becoming more visible or whether they are increasing in significance remains a matter of debate, yet most agree that race and ethnicity are likely to constitute important topics of debate in the twenty-first century. Similarly, religion seems to be following a related path of being more visible and increasingly identified as an important dimension across diverse societies.

These two trajectories raise important questions for investigating the connections between race, ethnicity and religion in the twenty-first century. One question concerns the connections, if any, between the increasing visibility of religion across heterogeneous societies and the seeming persistence of racial and ethnic phenomena in similar contexts. Are these parallel yet distinct phenomena whose seemingly simultaneous saliency constitutes happenstance? If not, in what ways are these two trajectories shaping one another?

The field of race and ethnic studies might examine several important issues for the twenty-first century that are related to these questions. One concerns how subordinated groups increasingly craft a politicised ethnicity using religion as a tool for political organising. Christianity, Islam, Judaism and similar religious traditions can be crafted to serve diverse and often antithetical social agendas ends. In some cases, religion can serve as a powerful catalyst for oppressed groups to craft political claims within ethical frameworks. For example, traditions of liberation theology enable the poor to advance social justice agendas (Rowland, 2007). In other cases, religion can uphold conservative political agendas. For example, the growth of religious fundamentalism across a range of religious traditions can suppress women, sexual minorities and other subjugated groups (Ayoob, 2008; Howland, 1999). The diversity of Muslim populations both within Western democracies and across non-Western states (e.g., Turkey, Indonesia and Nigeria) illustrates how one belief system can serve multiple political purposes for heterogeneous racial/ethnic groups. Religion itself is not at fault – rather, the political ends to which religion is put remain increasingly visible and contested.

Another significant issue concerns how racial/ethnic groups use religion as a vehicle for making claims on the modern nation-state. Within the vast array of claims, such as requests for anti-discrimination protection for religious minorities and state-support for religious schools, acts of terrorism that have been justified by using religious ideologies have garnered the most attention. Juergensmeyer (2008) examines why militant uprisings are occurring in the early twenty-first century, throughout the world and in virtually every religious tradition. He concludes that incidents of religious violence are not really about religion in that all but rather that religious faiths can be used to promote political causes and justify violent acts. Instead, radical religious ideologies may have become the vehicles for a variety of rebellions against secular authority that are linked with non-religious issues, a myriad of social, cultural and political grievances. For this reason religious activists involved in radical assaults on the symbols of secular society and national authority may constitute expressions of a widespread cultural and political rejection of the twentieth-century Western vision of an international order based on a network of discrete national societies in a secular nation-state world.

Thus, migration patterns that have brought formerly colonised peoples into the Western states as well as patterns of upward social mobility by racial/ethnic minorities have fuelled new debates that question the necessity of secularism for liberal democracies. The truism that the modern, democratic nation-state constitutes the next logical stage of development for all populations, in part, due to secularisation, is generating new questions about the centrality of secularisation for political empowerment. Religion not only provides a voice for the dispossessed, in many cases it also serves as the basis for a fundamental critique of the modern nation-state. In doing so, it challenges the legitimacy of secular institutions and national identity.

KEY INTERNAL CONCERNS FOR THE FIELD OF RACE AND ETHNIC STUDIES

The corpus of scholarship of the field of race and ethnic studies is broad and heterogeneous. On the one hand, this heterogeneity reflects a vibrancy that accrues to any field of study that addresses issues that people from diverse settings deem to be important. The field has both a longstanding historical trajectory as a field of study and a newfound relevance in the contemporary global context. On the other hand, this same heterogeneity and dynamic vibrancy raises crucial epistemological questions about what lies at the core of the field as well as the boundaries that distinguish it from other intellectual endeavours.

Recall that the internal workings of the field of racial and ethnic studies is increasingly shaped by two broad factors: (1) the shifting academic terrain that is bridging traditional academic disciplines where race and ethnic studies has been housed, namely, history, sociology, political science and literature; and (2) the emergence of entirely new interdisciplinary fields of study such as women's studies, cultural studies, postcolonial studies and queer theory. The field of race and ethnic studies participates in both sets of relationships – it both draws upon its history as a series of specialisations within traditional academic disciplines and is also positioned as an interdisciplinary field in its own right. This dynamic situation has catalysed multiple sets of porous boundaries both *within* the field of race and ethnic studies as well as *between* the field and similar areas of inquiry. As a result, the epistemological concerns of the field of race and ethnic studies are complex.

All this leads to a set of broad questions that will face the field in the twenty-first century. Exactly what counts as race and ethnic studies? Do all studies that incorporate race and/or ethnicity in some fashion fit within the purview of the field? Does field require specific theoretical frameworks, conceptual paradigms and/or methodological tools to distinguish it from other areas of inquiry? If not, why not? If so, what are they and how were they determined? These are not idle questions for a terrain of study where so much may be at stake in the twenty-first century. It will be crucial for the field to tell the difference between a conceptual confusion that might limit its prospects and a healthy ambiguity that generates the kinds of questions that moves an area of study forward.

Take, for example, the issue of how various conceptualisations of race, ethnicity and racism remain fluid. By now, it should be apparent that authors in this handbook adhere to no standard definition of race, or ethnicity, or racism. When it comes to the epistemological contours of the field, our authors raise more questions than they answer. Is race a subset of ethnicity or vice versa? How might we theoretically link race and ethnicity? What relationship do these terms have to racism? Is racism an ideology or a set of institutional practices? Are race and/or ethnicity identity categories that can be harnessed by systems of racism? These are tough questions that show how the very definition of race, ethnicity and racism are far from settled and remain issues of debate. If the terminology is a subject of epistemological debate, disentangling thorny questions of theoretical frameworks, conceptual paradigms and/or methodological tools promise to be even more daunting.

In the previous section, we discussed selected social phenomena outside the field of race and ethnic studies in order to identify suggestive areas of investigation for the field in the twenty-first century. In the following sections, we look inward in order to identify core areas of theory and practice that might also affect future directions for the field. They are (1) colourblind racism and modern science; (2) intersectionality and the theoretical development of the field; (3) incorporating non-Western issues; and (4) placing more emphasis on anti-racist theory and practice.

Colourblind racism and modern science

One area of exploration for the field of race and ethnic studies concerns how changing understandings of race within the biological sciences and medicine might articulate with new racial formations. In the nineteenth and twentieth centuries, scientific truths about race, in particular, biological analyses of genetic inferiority, helped legitimise racial inequalities. Such knowledges also served as the axes around which the health and vitality of a population could be managed by political organisations, and the disciplining of bodies could be achieved. Scientific racism helped explain and therefore reinforced systems of racial domination by masking the unequal racial power relations of global capitalism and by attributing racial and ethnic inequality to 'the nature of things', to 'science' (Winant, 2001, 94). Moreover, as a core element of the enlightenment, Western science itself was a distinguishing feature of modernity. Scientific racism was hegemonic and linked to hegemonic social, economic and political practices, for example, colonialism, slavery and racial discrimination after emancipation.

Historically, the field of race and ethnic studies has exerted considerable effort to refute scientific racism by contesting the narratives and social practices of Western natural and social sciences. Within this quest, showing the ways in which Western science upheld racial projects but also itself depended on racial thinking constituted a core feature of critical race projects. These projects were largely successful in that it is now widely recognised that race and ethnicity are socially constructed categories having no grounding in biology or nature. Eliminating this foundational principle by showing the fiction of race as a biological entity suggests that racism itself is a socially constructed system.

The accomplishments of traditional and contemporary critical race scholarship in unpacking the workings of scientific racism have been hard-fought and, since the mid-twentieth century, increasingly effective. Challenging the notion that human capacities for intelligence, sexuality and violence can be categorised such that some groups or 'races' show differential abilities that can be explained solely or predominantly by biology and not as a consequence of socioeconomic and political inequalities has been a repeated objective of critical race scholarship (Brown et al., 2003).[6] The goal has been to eliminate racism by rejecting its fundamental premise of race. Yet, the erasure of race may have ushered in a new set of problems, namely, the emergence of racism without race, or a seemingly colourblind racism (Bonilla-Silva, 2003).

One important question that confronts the field of race and ethnic studies in the twenty-first century concerns how colourblind racism might operate in the most unlikely places, in this case, within natural sciences that have seemingly abandoned nineteenth and twentieth-century racial categories. Patterns of participation of contemporary science in shaping racial formations may not be readily obvious, especially in a period of seeming colourblindness where biological underpinnings of race as a category have been discredited. When it comes to questions of race and contemporary science, its own object of study may inadvertently influence the field, namely, an assumption that because race has seemingly been discredited within science (ironically by the very tools of science), that science itself is now colorblind. One might ask how effectively the field of race and ethnic studies grapples with the centrality of science to twentyfirst-century racial formations? Do its assumptions about a discredited scientific racism foster a myopia concerning the possibilities of a twentyfirst-century scientific racism?

In his 2005 ASA Presidential Address, Troy Duster outlined how these challenges play out in sociology in ways that are especially germane to the field of race and ethnic studies (Duster, 2006). Duster argued that sociology faces the challenge of contesting the increasing authority of a reductionist science, the hallmark of racial thinking that reduces complex social phenomena to simplistic racial or ethnic arguments. Duster argues that it is insufficient to simply assert the arbitrariness of the social construction of scientific claims, in this case, the arbitrariness of race and ethnicity. Instead, the processes of the social construction of race and ethnicity in science and medicine must be demonstrated, a particularly important task in the context of growing consensus that, because race was a construct of the past, racism too is passé. Duster advised sociologists to emulate an earlier generation of researchers and turn greater attention to an analysis of data collection at the site of reductionist knowledge production. Within reductionist science, partial evidence upholds superficial explanations for wide-ranging problems. Until the field of race and ethnic studies comes into closer alignment with critical science studies, the competing explanations of race advanced by a reductionist science will have far greater significance on public policy than desired.

Intersectionality and the theoretical development of the field

Scholars within the field of race and ethnic studies have had to be mindful of continuing to create the conditions to ensure the integrity of the field. As noted earlier, the study of race and ethnicity currently reflects the theoretical frameworks and practices of traditional disciplines as well as insights gained from interdisciplinary scholarship. This distinctive social location of the field creates benefits and challenges. On the one hand, this diversity catalyses new ideas and approaches to traditional topics and introduces new ones. On the other hand, this same placement includes pressures to subsume the study of race and ethnicity under other categories (ironically a tendency also illustrated by the tendency within the field to subsume race under ethnicity or vice versa).

These tensions are especially visible in the theoretical frameworks that guide empirical work in the field. In this regard, the field of race and ethnic studies participates in a set of broader debates shaping social theory overall. The shift from the institutional perspectives that accompanied the influence of Marxist social theory to the poststructuralist perspectives that characterised later twentieth-century academic circles raises important theoretical debates for many areas of inquiry, including this one. Prior to the 1980s, the traditional theoretical frameworks that loosely marked the boundaries of the field of race and ethnic studies were grounded in institutional analyses drawn from the political and social sciences. As a result, the field did reflect the social issues and social policy concerns that stemmed from processes of desegregation and decolonisation (for a review of these debates, see Virdee, Chapter 6). In contrast, following the groundbreaking work of philosopher Michel Foucault, the so-called cultural turn that was marked by the growth of poststructuralist social theoretical frameworks in the 1980s raised entirely new questions about the relationship between power, knowledge and culture (Foucault, 1980).

Two features of the cultural turn within contemporary social theory have been especially important for the field of race and ethnicity. For one, poststructuralist analyses highlight language/discourse/and representation as central to relations of racial/ethnic domination/subordination. In the handbook, for example, Mutua's tracing of critical race theory (CRT) using the discourse of law in Chapter 11 and Alexander's discussion of hybridity and diaspora in Chapter 19 both illustrate the kind of theoretical archaeology grounded in racial discourse analysis. For another, poststructuralist frameworks emphasise the significance of identities and culture for analyses of race, ethnicity and power (Morley and Chen, 1996). Take, for example, how dynamic categories of racial/ethnic identities, such as the emergence of biracial and multiracial identities in the United States, and the increased visibility of black identities in Brazil, constitute important sites for studying racial and ethnic dynamics.

This move to develop the theoretical foundations of the field of race and ethnic studies by incorporating both institutional analyses as well as poststructuralist frameworks constitutes an overarching challenge for the twenty-first century. In this regard, one promising direction for the theoretical development of the field of race and ethnic studies lies in conceptualising race, ethnicity and racism through intersectional frameworks. Part II of the *Handbook* asked authors to consider intersections of race with similar systems of power, specifically, with class (Virdee, Chapter 6), gender (Andersen, Chapter 7), sexualities (Nagel, Chapter 8) and nation (Anthias, Chapter 9). The variability of how authors approached this common task across these four chapters illustrates the breadth of emerging efforts to reconceptualise race, ethnicity and racism through the lens of intersectionality. Moreover, in reviewing other handbook chapters, we find additional authors who also explicitly or implicitly acknowledged emerging paradigms of intersectionality in approaching their specific topics. For example, Mutua's Chapter 11 examines how race constituted a starting point for CRT that evolved into the intersectional area of Lat/Crit Studies.

From the vast array of themes that might guide intersectional analyses within the field, topics that have preoccupied traditional disciplines might be an especially fruitful starting point for intersectional analyses of race, ethnicity and racism. Take, for example, the important issue of developing a materialist analysis of contemporary racism that draws upon intersectional paradigms. The groundwork for such an analysis exists within the field and tends to be situated in one of two locations.

On the one hand, the most comprehensive and longstanding approaches examine questions of political economy through intersections of race and class, especially using Marxist social theory (see Virdee, Chapter 6). Materialist analyses grounded in political economy approaches also emphasise the centrality of state-power in producing racially and ethnically unequal outcomes (see Feagin and O'Brien, Chapter 3). On the other hand, while they are not typically recognised as such, theories of the body advanced within poststructuralist social thought and subsequently within feminist and queer theory constitute a second location for developing a materialist analysis of race, ethnicity and racism. This work argues that bodies do not contain sexuality or gender, but rather, that sexuality and gender are socially constructed categories inscribed upon the materiality of the body.[7] Rather than social institutions of work and the state forming core sites of material analysis, the body itself constitutes the basis of material social analysis (see Nagel, Chapter 8; Back, Chapter 17).

When combined, institutional, political economy frameworks and poststructuralist analyses of the body provide rich avenues for developing materialist analyses of race and ethnic studies that might contribute to the theoretical advancement of the field. French feminist sociologist Colette Guillaumin provides a provocative project to bridge this dichotomy between actual material conditions (political economy) and theories of the bodies (the female and black bodies as captive bodies) (Guillaumin, 1995). Guillaumin argues that a materialist analysis should not start with the theft of labour from the body, the starting point of Marxist social theory, but rather with the appropriation of the body itself. By focusing on the appropriation of women's bodies by men, Guillaumin develops a provocative analysis of the material foundations of gender oppression, not primarily through the appropriation of women's labour (although this certainly is a factor), but also through the more basic premise of bodily ownership. This analysis enables Guillaumin to see parallels between the appropriation of women's bodies and those of black people. While Guillaumin does not make this argument, her approach suggests a materialist analysis of intersections of class and gender, or class and race, or more recently, of class, gender and race that is centrally situated in both a political economy framework and poststructuralist analyses.

The construct of intersectionality constitutes an especially fruitful area of investigation for the field of race and ethnic studies in the twenty-first century that should preoccupy scholars over the coming decades. As it becomes increasingly impossible to think about race and ethnicity as mono-constructs unaffected by gender, age, sexuality, ability, citizenship status and economic status, achieving a more comprehensive understanding of topics within the field of race and ethnic studies, the case with abbreviated materialist analysis of racism presented above, suggests that intersectional paradigms may become an increasingly significant part of the field in the twenty-first century. In this regard, we ask how might we envision racial politics (the many topics described earlier) and racial theory (e.g., questions of theories of racism) through a lens of intersectionality.

Incorporating non-Western issues[8]

Despite the significance of taking on reductionist science as an important issue for the field, or the possibilities of developing intersectional paradigms to further the theoretical development of the field, we wonder whether these and similar topics that permeate the handbook would be identified as top priorities by racial/ethnic populations who form the object of study of the field. Would thinkers from African, Latin American, Asian and Middle-Eastern regions as well as racial/ethnic populations living within the contours of Western societies identify themes such as these as most crucial for their lived experiences as for a field that aims to study them? For the twenty-first century, if one were to ground the study of race, ethnicity and racism in non-Western cultures as well as in the racial/ethnic dimensions of global phenomena (such as poverty), in what ways, if any, might the epistemological concerns of the field of race and ethnic studies be altered?

For one, incorporating non-Western issues might identify themes that are currently neglected or overemphasised within the field. For example, indigenous peoples are far less concerned with issues of paid labour, a core premise of Western scholars immersed in industrial societies, than with issues of land rights and environmental concerns. Incorporating an indigenous focus on land and the environment suggests new angles of vision on global capitalism that might prove to be immensely helpful in the twenty-first century. Similarly, questions of racial/

ethnic identity constitute a current preoccupation of scholars of race and ethnicity. This issue is vitally important to Western subjects who are guaranteed the individual protections of citizenship rights. In the United States, for example, questions of individual identity can appear to be more salient than group-based experiences – whites, blacks, Asians, Latinos and indigenous populations all grapple with issues of racial and/or ethnic identity. In these contexts, the racial and ethnic identities of the person remain secondary characteristics that can be debated within the framing assumptions of Western citizenship. Yet might different understandings of identity emerge within non-Western settings where race and ethnicity may also saturate social relations, but in a different way?

A similar case can be made for developing a more robust understanding of race, ethnicity, space and place that goes beyond the field's disproportionate emphasis on migration. Quite simply, legions of ordinary people do not move and, while they are certainly affected by migration, their needs and concerns differ substantially from the policy preoccupations within the field. Analyses of migration have been framed in response to the perceived needs and concerns of Western nation-states, often government policymakers. Yet, for a variety of reasons such as age, family status, lack of resources, lack of desire to leave home communities, etc., the vast majority of people in racial/ethnic populations do not migrate. What tools of analysis might the field of race and ethnic studies bring to the lives of these populations, especially in an increasingly interdependent global context? The emphasis placed on movement and migration overshadows issues that concern people who are stuck in ghettos, barrios and nation-states with little future.

Incorporating non-Western issues into the field of race and ethnicity might catalyse new debates about how effectively the field's terminology travels outside of its contexts of origin. The relationships among terms may become reconfigured in light of the kinds of questions that emerge from within non-Western settings. Take, for example, the widespread use of the terms *postcolonial* and *postcolonialism* to describe the contemporary era. In an era where the prefix post- is applied to a series of Western constructs – postmodernism and the aforementioned poststructuralist social theory – this simple prefix suggests that the social relations of prior eras are past. On a basic level, this practice continues to privilege Western interpretive frameworks. Western scholars often use the term postcolonial uncritically, a descriptive phrase applied to the period following formal colonisation. Yet, when it comes to contemporary racial/ethnic power relations, uncritical use of such terminology may misread current social conditions. Formal colonialism may be over, yet a more pernicious *neocolonialism* may have emerged to take its place. Members of seemingly postcolonial societies might take issue with this depiction of their social and political realities (Alexander and Mohanty, 1997).

Incorporating non-Western issues might also create possibilities to develop more robust theoretical analyzes of racism for the twenty-first century. Doing so might shed light on racism as a system of power that transcends guiding assumptions of the field. One such guiding assumption is that racism operates through a race relations paradigm of white dominance and non-white subordination. The paradigm itself may be less of a problem than the more narrow arenas to which it is applied. As this paradigm reflects the experiences of dominant white racial groups in Western nation-states with minority populations, particularities of this history shape the assumption's application. For example, commonsense understandings of racism focus on social interaction among individuals, an emphasis that views racially heterogeneous situations as social locations where racism is most likely to occur and racially homogeneous settings as somehow standing outside racial analysis. Broadening the scope of racial analysis beyond this application of the concept of race relations might generate new avenues of investigation for the field in the twenty-first century.

Work on continental Africa might be especially useful in providing a series of opportunities to unpack the race relations and similar framing assumptions about racism. One might easily assume that analyses of racism through traditional race relations paradigms are less applicable to continental African societies, simply because such societies not only have formal white rule, but also many societies have few whites in their populations. Rooted in assumptions of postcolonialism, this assumption sees the emergence of independent nation-states as evidence that racism is thing of the past in continental Africa. Thus, diverse patterns of continental African experiences within emerging global racial formations, experiences that might be more adequately examined through neocolonial frameworks, may simply be neglected or relegated to marginal treatment in the field. Whereas continental Africa may experience less 'racism' understood as occurring through traditional lenses of race relations within one nation-state, yet ironically, continental Africa may provide a provocative set of opportunities to examine the workings of a colourblind racism that affects Africa as a continent where racial processes (e.g., selecting racial/ethnic labour and the exploitation of natural resources) are no longer seen as raced events, yet may be crucial for emerging structures of global, seemingly colourblind racism.

As the black/white binary has been so prominent in shaping the race relations paradigm, continental Africa has been of interest to scholars studying racism. In contrast, non-Western settings where racism has historically been analytically unimportant provide new opportunities in the twenty-first century for developing more robust analyses of racism. For example, the interconnections of race, ethnicity and racism in nation-states in Asia and the Middle East where racism is seen as a recently imported phenomenon from the West provide provocative opportunities to analyse racism. Societies where race has seemingly been absent (suggesting that racism was also absent), where ethnicity constitutes primary category of analysis (often refracted through discourse of religion) and that seemingly have traditions of indigenous 'ethnic' discrimination constitute promising avenues of investigation for conceptualising racism. These settings highlight the interconnection of race and ethnicity as interlinking categories as well as the varieties of racism during different historical eras.

The types of changes that might be needed within the field of racial and ethnic studies to incorporate non-Western issues may be more complicated than adding neglected themes, casting a critical eye on existing terminology or striving for more complex analyses of racism. The current contours of the field reflect its origins in nineteenth and twentieth-century racial formations, especially within US and European societies. The historical and emerging demographics of the field also tap this issue of incorporating non-Western issues. Historically, white male scholars who studied non-white populations, primarily through the lens of their own preoccupations, have predominated. Scholars may have incorporated indigenous knowledges and social and political issues that concerned non-white populations, yet non-Western concerns generally entered the Western canon refracted through the interests of dominant scholars. In essence, the questions, theories and methodologies of the field have often said more about the preoccupations of Western scholars and their views of non-white populations, for example, the inordinate attention paid to the sexual practices of indigenous peoples, or the moral laxity of primitive peoples as evidenced by predilection to violence; or explanations for such cultural differences that lay in assumptions of intellectual inferiority.

Whereas this preoccupation of Western scholars was dominant at the founding of the field, the field also incorporated scholars who advanced a minority albeit less visible position that was dedicated to refuting dominant claims. Thus, the field of race and ethnic studies has reflected an uneasy tension between two competing and typically unstated assumptions, the field's involvement in producing knowledges that justified and helped structure slavery, colonialism, imperialism and similar forms of racial rule, and a longstanding critical perspective advanced by scholars within the field, initially overwhelmingly white and Western, but increasingly scholars of colour, who rejected this dominant view (see Feagin and O'Brien, Chapter 3).

Only recently has this balance of power been altered by the inclusion of more scholars of colour as well as a broader constituency of scholars of race and ethnicity who are not themselves people of colour. Including more scholars of colour is certainly an encouraging development that suggests that a broader range of ideas will permeate the field of race and ethnic studies in the twenty-first century. Yet the changing demographics of the field provides no epistemological guarantees that the kinds of concerns identified here as non-Western will be included in the twenty-first century racial/ethnic canon. As scholars of colour themselves reflect heterogeneous experiences and perspectives, the approach that they might take to new issues will be diverse. Still, nineteenth and twentieth-century practices of overwhelmingly white and Western groups of scholars of race and ethnicity studying non-white, non-Western populations in relation to concerns of the West seem passé. What remains to be seen is how the twenty-first century contours of the field will reflect the changing demographics of scholars who constitute the field.

Placing greater emphasis on anti-racist theory and practice

As stated earlier, the field of race and ethnic studies would not exist were it not for the realities of racism. As the chapters in the handbook depict, the field casts a wide net over a range of issues, using diverse theoretical and methodological approaches to study racism. Yet because the field has emphasised the preoccupations of Western scholars, issues that concern non-Western people may have been neglected. Specifically, non-Western populations who bear the brunt of racism might encourage the field to place greater emphasis on questions of anti-racist resistance. Thus, another important issue for the field in the twenty-first century might be to place greater emphasis on anti-racist theory and practice.

Simplistic and monolithic accounts of racism will, in the final analysis, do little to enlighten us as to why it is that in particular social and political contexts people respond to the images, promises and hopes which are at the heart of mass racist movements. Additionally, they tell us little about the possibilities and limits of political strategies and policies that aim to challenge institutionalised racial inequalities. Practitioners within the field of race and ethnic studies often focus on specific mechanisms by which racism is reproduced. As a result, we have wonderful theories of domination – but know far less about racism as a system of power that reflects human agency on both sides of racial domination.

As the field of race and ethnic studies occupies the political space that encourages the empirical study of important social issues as well as policy solutions to social problems, the field's empirical work should have continued significance for public policy. Clearly this has been important for developing more effective social policies and in shedding light on social problems that have accompanied the trajectory of racism itself. As illustrated throughout the chapters of this handbook, the scope of work within the field of racial and ethnic studies can make potentially significant contributions to important social phenomena (e.g., Premdas's analysis of ethnic conflict in Chapter 12 or Kivisto's discussion of racial democracy in Chapter 10).

When it comes to public policy, what worked in the twentieth century may not be adequate for the realities of the twenty-first century, and what works in one national setting may not travel smoothly to another. One important direction for the field lies in revisiting anti-racist strategies within public policies in order to assess what works and what doesn't. This can be difficult because public policy can become so politicised and critiqued on ideological grounds, the case of affirmative action or positive action for example, that careful analysis of the efficacy of these public policy initiatives remains difficult to root out. Ideological debates aside, we might ask whether poverty rates decreased for targeted populations and, if they did, how much can be attributed to public policies such as affirmative action, no matter how unpopular they may be. Reparation movements, reconciliation commissions and similar policy remedies as anti-racist practice also merit further review.

As a number of our contributors have tried to show in previous chapters, one of the limitations of anti-racist politics as it has developed is precisely the pattern of reifying minority communities as static and unchanging cultural and political collectivities. There is a need to confront the reality that in the present environment we have, in one way or another, to move beyond the certainties both of racism and simplistic multiculturalism and anti-racism. The preoccupation in much of the recent literature in this field with issues of identity, and the assertion of the relevance and importance of understanding the role of Stuart Hall's notion of 'new ethnicities', has not resolved the fundamental question of how to balance the quest for ever-more specific identities with the need to allow for broader and less fixed cultural identities.

This focus on anti-racist practice might be guided by greater attention to developing robust theories of anti-racism that would be part and parcel of earlier discussions of developing more complex theories of racism. Thus, another theme for the twenty-first century might be to examine coalition-building efforts among social justice organisations who might draw upon intersectional paradigms to craft anti-racist theory and practice (Dill and Zambrana, 2009). If the field of race and ethnic studies begins increasingly to recognise and analyse intersecting identities, it makes sense that anti-racist theory and practice (especially 'practice') will necessarily need to become central to social justice initiatives in areas of class, sexuality, gender, age and immigrant status. So, for example, LGBT and feminist groups might perceive it to be more important to be explicitly anti-racist in their political activities. Similarly, African American political organisations might develop a greater predilection to develop anti-racist strategies that took gender and sexuality into account (Collins, 2004).

In placing more emphasis on anti-racist theory and practice in the field of race and ethnic studies, it is important not to conflate the necessary attention to public policy with broader questions of multiple expressions of resistance. We can safely assume that effectively addressing the myriad social problems associated with racism, for example, will require a comparable multi-pronged activist agenda, one of which would be public policy prescriptions by the state. Examining the anti-racist ideas and actions of those who are harmed by racism constitutes one pivotal issue that the field might address in the twenty-first century, especially if nations decrease their commitment to state-based solutions to social problems. If a field assumes that individuals and groups who are harmed by racism have no active resistance traditions, then that field is not likely to search for something that it cannot imagine to be possible.

Take, for example, Hanchard and Sawyer's discussion in Chapter 18 of emerging patterns of Afro-Latin political mobilisation. The authors explain that black activism remained invisible to scholars and policymakers who routinely assumed that racial identity generally, and blackness in particular, was less salient than identities of nation or class. Yet when researchers looked for this seemingly invisible mobilisation, they realized that it may have been invisible to them, but that questions of anti-racist political activism that incorporated a racial analysis were especially salient for Afro-Latin populations across several national settings. Examples such as these suggest that racially/ethnically subjugated populations might desire new questions, content and practices from the field of race and ethnic studies itself that simultaneously acknowledges their experiences from their points of view and that is responsive to their expressed needs for anti-racist scholarship.

CONCLUSION

We think the field of race and ethnic studies is poised to become a broadly defined, theoretically robust and empirically rigorous field of inquiry in the twenty-first century. The types of issues that were raised in the eighteen substantive chapters, in the introductory chapter as well as in this concluding chapter provide a broad framework that reflects the wide range of concerns and perspectives of practitioners within this field of inquiry. As our authors are situated within different disciplines, they approach questions from different vantage points. Similarly, the places where authors ground their arguments (e.g., race, or ethnicity or both, materialist or symbolic or both, micro-, macro- or mid-level analysis) also shed light on the exciting possibilities that characterise the field of racial and ethnic studies

By presenting an overview of the field of race and ethnic studies as well as the ways it has evolved and been transformed in recent decades, this handbook covers the history of this field of scholarship and research. It also offers insights into the changing concepts and methods that have been utilised in studies of specific historical situations or aspects of the social relations on which racial and ethnic divisions are based. The field illustrates how race and ethnicity are increasingly recognised as significant dimensions of contemporary social realities, as well as how multiple disciplines that engage questions of race and ethnicity in some form.

NOTES

1. For examples of interdisciplinary research, see, for example, (Essed, 1991).
2. For a discussion of this issue, see (McKee, 1993; Bash, 1979) among others.
3. In other fields of study, approaches taken in the field may be more distant from the object of study.
4. We remind readers that, in this volume, we could only present a small sample of the heterogeneous and far-reaching work in the field of race and ethnic studies. For this section, we emphasise trends that have not been extensively discussed by our contributors.
5. The field of sports studies constitutes one location where these ideas about a materialist analysis of social institutions and bodies are more fully developed. For work in this field, see Carrington (1998).
6. Increased attention to whiteness studies (Andersen, 2003; Lewis, 2004), the social construction of race in everyday life (Myers, 2005; Bonilla-Silva, 2003), cross-cultural analyses of racialisation, the centrality of race to the research process (Zuberi, 2001; Twine and Warren, 2000), the centrality of race and racism to Western notions of modernity (Goldberg, 1993), the study of social policy as racial discourse (Van Dijk, 1993), and similar themes have given critical race scholarship a new vitality.

7. Judith Butler's discussion of performativity reintroduces and updates social constructionist approaches to sexuality and gender (Butler, 1990). Building on Butler's theoretical approach, scholars of race and ethnicity drew upon these categories to de-centre race as a biological category in order to unpack its social construction.

8. We use the phrase *non-Western issues*, recognising its imperfections in continuing to privilege the West. By this term, we mean issues that would be of greater interest to heterogeneous populations that have been historically excluded from the field as scholars. For example, the field may have a long history of studying black people, suggesting that the issues of black people as non-whites are well represented in the field. Instead, we wish to access patterns of exclusion that are more difficult to root out, namely, the absence of issues that would be more prominent if the perspectives and concerns of black people and other subordinated populations shaped the field. We are also aware of similar limitations of the phrase *non-white*, yet using it highlights the central preoccupations of the field with the world's populations that is considered to be, from the vantage point of the field, not white. We want to emphasise that we do not frame these issues as the property of non-Western peoples, but rather suggest that some issues may be more prominent among excluded populations.

REFERENCES

Alexander, M.J. and Mohanty, C.T. (1997) 'Introduction: Genealogies, Legacies, Movements in M.J. Alexander and CT. Mohanty (eds) *Feminist Genealogies, Colonial Legacies, Democratic Futures.* New York: Routledge. pp. xiii–xlii.

Andersen, M.L. (2003) 'Whitewashing Race: A Critical Review on "Whiteness"' in A. Doane and E. Bonilla-Silva (eds) *Whiteout: The Continuing Significance of Racism.* New York: Routledge. pp. 21–34

Ayoob, M. (2008) *The Many Faces of Political Islam: Religion and Politics in the Muslim World.* Ann Arbor: University of Michigan Press.

Balibar, E. and Wallerstein, I. (1991) *Race, Nation, Class: Ambiguous Identities.* New York: Verso.

Bash, H. (1979) *Sociology, Race, and Ethnicity: A Critique of Ideological Intrusions upon Sociological Theory.* New York: Gordon & Breach.

Bonilla-Silva, E. (2003) *Racism without Racists: Color-Blind Racism and the Persistence of Racial Inequality in the United States.* Lanham, MD: Rowman & Littlefield.

Brown, M.I., Carnoy, M., Currie, E., Duster, T., Oppenheimer, D.B., Schultz, M.M. and Wellman, D. (2003) *Whitewashing Race: The Myth of a Color-Blind Society.* Berkeley: University of California Press.

Butler, J. (1990) *Gender Trouble: Feminism and the Subversion of Identity.* New York: Routledge.

Carrington, B. (1998) 'Sport, Masculinity, and Black Cultural Resistance', *Journal of Sport & Social Issues,* 22 (3): 275–298.

Collins, P.H. (2004) *Black Sexual Politics: African Americans, Gender, and the New Racism.* New York: Routledge.

Collins, P.H. (2006) 'New Commodities, New Consumers: Selling Blackness in the Global Marketplace', *Ethnicities,* 6 (3): 297–317.

Dill, B.T. and Zambrana, R. (2009) *Emerging Intersections: Race, Class, and Gender in Theory, Policy, and Practice.* New Brunswick, NJ: Rutgers University Press.

Duster, T. (2006) 'Comparative Perspectives and Competing Explanations: Taking on the Newly Configured Reductionist Challenge to Sociology', *American Sociological Review,* 71(1): 1–15.

Essed, P. (1991) *Understanding Everyday Racism: An Interdisciplinary Theory.* Newbury Park: Sage.

Foucault, M. (1980) Power/Knowledge: Selected Interviews and Other Writings, 1972–1977. (ed.) Colin Gordon. New York: Pantheon.

Fredrickson, G.M. (2002) *Racism: A Short History.* Princeton: Princeton University Press.

Goldberg, D.T. (1993) *Racist Culture: Philosophy and the Politics of Meaning.* Cambridge, MA: Blackwell.

Guillaumin, C. (1995) *Racism, Sexism, Power and Ideology*. New York: Routledge.

Howland, C.W. (ed.) (1999) *Religious Fundamentalisms and the Human Rights of Women*. New York: St. Martin's Press.

Juergensmeyer, M. (2008) *Global Rebellions: Religious Challenges to the Secular State, From Christian Militias to Al Qaeda*. Berkeley: University of California Press.

Lewis, A.E. (2004) '"What Group?" Studying Whites and Whiteness in the Era of "Color-Blindness', *Sociological Theory*, 22 (4): 623–646.

McKee, J.B. (1993) *Sociology and the Race Problem: The Failure of a Perspective*. Urbana: University of Illinois Press.

Morley, D. and Chen, K-H. (eds) (1996) *Stuart Hall: Critical Dialogues in Cultural Studies*. New York: Routledge.

Myers, K. (2005) *Racetalk: Racism Hiding in Plain Sight*. Lanham, Maryland: Rowman & Littlefield.

Newman, K.S., Massengill, R.P. (2006) 'The Texture of Hardship: Qualitative sociology of poverty, 1995–2005', *Annual Review of Sociology*, 32: 423–446.

Platt, L. (2007) *Poverty and Ethnicity in the UK*. York: Joseph Rowntree Foundation.

Rowland, C. (ed.) (2007) *The Cambridge Companion to Liberation Theology* 2nd Edition Cambridge: Cambridge University Press.

Twine, F.W. and Warren, J.W. (eds) (2000) *Racing Research, Researching Race: Methodological Dilemmas in Critical Race Studies*. New York: New York University Press.

Van Dijk, T.A. (1993) *Elite Discourse and Racism*. Newbury Park: Sage.

Winant, H. (2001) *The World Is a Ghetto: Race and Democracy since World War II*. New York: Basic Books.

Zuberi, T. (2001) *Thicker Than Blood: How Racial Statistics Lie*. Minneapolis: University of Minnesota Press.

Index